German Immigrants

Lists of Passengers Bound from Bremen to New York, 1868–1871

GERMAN IMMIGRANTS

Lists of Passengers Bound from Bremen to New York, 1868–1871

With Places of Origin

Compiled by

Marion Wolfert

CLEARFIELD

Reprinted for
Clearfield Company, Inc. by
Genealogical Publishing Co., Inc.
Baltimore, Maryland
2006

Library of Congress Catalogue Card Number 92-74385
International Standard Book Number 0-8063-1368-4
Made in the United States of America

In Fond Memory of
GARY ZIMMERMAN

Explanation of the Text

The destruction of the Bremen passenger lists has been a great hindrance to the historical and demographic study of German immigration to America. In many cases the Bremen lists were the sole source of information concerning the place of origin of an immigrant family. The importance of Bremen as a port of departure makes this loss even more lamentable.

As far as can be ascertained by German archivists, lists of emigrants sailing from Bremen were kept beginning in 1832. These lists were used to compile statistical reports for the government and port authorities. Owing to a lack of space, the lists from 1832 to 1872 were destroyed in 1874. Thereafter the lists were shredded every two years. From 1907 the original lists were again kept on a permanent basis, but with the destruction of the Statistical Land Office on October 6, 1944, all remaining lists perished. Transcripts of some twentieth-century lists (1907, 1908, 1913, 1914) were recently discovered at the German State Archives in Koblenz—the product of a college study—but no nineteenth-century transcripts have as yet been uncovered.

This partial reconstruction of Bremen passenger lists, 1868–1871, is based on American sources, specifically, *Passenger Lists of Vessels Arriving at New York* (National Archives Microfilm Publication M237), and is a continuation of three earlier volumes covering 1847–1854, 1855–1862, and 1863–1867 respectively. Not all Bremen passengers of the 1868–1871 period are included in this work, however; only those for whom a specific place of origin in Germany is given. Of the total number of passenger arrival records, roughly 21% provide such information; the other 79% give only "Germany" as the place of origin. The benefit of having these 32,000 passenger arrivals indexed is that it provides immediate access to place of origin information, which the voluminous nature of the New York arrival lists heretofore prevented. Future volumes in this series will cover Bremen arrivals at other major U. S. ports.

Imperfections and peculiarities in the original lists, as well as difficulties encountered in the computerization process, make it imperative that all entries found herein be compared against the original manifests. It is apparent from the lists themselves that the information had been supplied verbally by the passengers, since obvious name and place-name misspellings occur frequently. Therefore, all possible spelling variations must be searched for. A good example is the surname MEYER, which is found in the lists under eight different spellings: Meyer, Meier, Mayer, Meir, Mayr, Myar, Myer and even Mjar. The majority of spellings may vary only slightly, but because of the alphabetical arrangement of this work these variants are often separated.

In the original lists many given names and surnames were partially or completely anglicized. More often than not given names were carried over into their English equivalents; and on rare occasions a surname was translated. The name SCHMIDT, for example, might be listed as SMITH; BRAUN as BROWN, etc. When this occurs, as with other questionable spellings, an entry is added under what is assumed to be the original German spelling, to facilitate the researcher.

Misspelled place names have been corrected on a limited basis. Place names with spellings grossly in error were examined, and an accurate spelling sought. Sometimes a correct spelling could not be established, and the spelling as found in the original was retained. The corrected spellings sometimes represent the compilers' opinion of the way the original should read; but since there is the risk that an incorrect judgment was made, all entries should be compared with the original.

Some names may be difficult to locate because of peculiarities in the German language. German surnames that carry an "umlaut," i.e. a modified vowel (Ä, Ö, Ü), have been changed to their English equivalents; thus Ä = AE, Ö = OE, Ü = UE, and are so indexed. Some surnames that should have had modified vowels were left unmodified in the originals. The name MÜLLER is found as both MUELLER and MULLER in the text, as well as the anglicized form MILLER. Surnames composed of two or more distinct words have been alphabetized under the final word. Thus von WEGNER is found as WEGNER, v.; de GREVE as GREVE, de; and AUF DEM KAMP as KAMP, auf dem. French names like D'ARTENAY are not separated.

The majority of the records contain abbreviations that vary from list to list. Many are standard German abbreviations, but some given-name abbreviations are odd, and are therefore difficult to recognize. A table of the most frequently used abbreviations is included in this work. Names that have been abbreviated often make it difficult to tell the sex of the passenger. In many cases, therefore, the sex of the passenger is noted in parenthesis. Several lists were composed entirely of initials, and several others employed the use of German nicknames, which may be unfamiliar to researchers. Some of the more commonly used nicknames and their equivalents are listed below:

Bernhard = Bernd	Johann = Hans
Catharina = Trina	Magdalena = Lena
Elisabeth = Beta, Louise, Elise	Margaretha = Greta
Friedrich = Fritz	Matthias = Theiss
Friederike = Rika	Valentin = Veit
Georg = Joerg	Wilhelmine = Minna
Helena = Lena	

German regional dialects account for a great deal of inconsistency in surname and place name spellings. Certain consonants can be pronounced alike, allowing for a variety of spelling possibilities. The following table of equivalent consonants will assist in determining alternative spellings:

B = P	as Ebstein = Epstein	TZ = Z	as Dietz = Diez = Tietz
F = V	as Focke = Vocke	C = K = G	as Cunkel = Kunkel
D = T	as Dentel = Tendel		= Gungel
S = Z	as Seidler = Zeidler	I = J = Y	as Ide = Jede = Yde

German dipthongs also allow for a great deal of variety in spelling. Some combinations of vowels produce exactly the same sound, which make them interchangeable. Some examples of these are:

AE = E = EE as Faendrich = Fendrich = Feendrich
AI = AY = EI = EY as Kaiser = Kayser = Keiser = Keyser
OI = EU = AU = AEU as Broihahn = Breuhahn = Bräuhahn
= Braeuhahn
I = IE = IH as Bilke = Bielke = Bihlke = Biehlke
E = EE = EH as Frese = Freese = Frehse
Also sometimes I = UE as Gingerich = Guengerich = Juengerich

Use of the German unasperated "H" occurs frequently in these manifests. Not having a sound, this letter can be placed in several locations without affecting the pronunciation. The process of alphabetization will make such spellings widely separate, however, such as WOLLEBEN = WOHLLEBEN, WALTER = WALTHER, OELSNER = OEHLSNER. The doubling of letters is also frequently found, as in the names HERMANN = HERRMANN and ULMANN = ULLMANN. All possibilities should be sought, although duplicate entries have been added under the more common spellings of some surnames.

The computerization process has necessitated the abbreviating of place names. Most of these are suffixes and prefixes, and have been abbreviated as follows:

Unt.	= Unter	---fd.	= ---feld
Ob.	= Ober	--hsn.	= --hausen
Gr.	= Gross	--bch.	= ---bach
Kl.	= Klein	---bg.	= ---berg or ---burg
Ndr.	= Nieder	---df.	= ---dorf

Increasing numbers of Poles and Czechs appear in the manifests, many of whose names are grossly misspelled. The ships' captains who made these lists often transposed these names into German phonetic spellings, such as KUTSCHERA for KUČERA, NÜRSCHAN for NÝŘANY, etc. Additional problems were encountered in trying to read the captains' handwriting. Easily mistaken were the letters "u" for "n", "o" for "a", "t" for "f" and "l". A good example of this is the name HAUSCHILDT, which was several times mistaken for HANSCHILDT. With the more common names these problems were corrected, but undoubtedly some errors are still to be found. With any questionable spelling, great care has been taken to preserve the manifest's original version.

When more than one person of a particular surname travelled together (as in a family), they have been grouped under the name of the first family member appearing on the list. Thus the wife and children of a passenger will follow on the line just below that of the head of household. The integrity of the family was in this way retained, but it is necessary to scan all entries of a particular surname in case the individual sought is listed under another family member.

The reference numbers are composed of two parts. The first part is the year of arrival, the second the number of the passenger list for that year. Within each year all the lists are numbered. The table of references included in this volume provides the name of the arriving vessel, the date of its arrival in New York, and the call number of the National Archives' microfilm (series 237). A sample entry follows:

BEIERLEIB, Johann 60 Lustberg 61-1640

This entry states that the 60-year-old Johann Beierleib arrived in New York in 1861 (61 = 1861) and appears on list 1640 for that year. The table of references, under 61-1640, gives

Norma 10 Nov 1861 107

This indicates that Johann Beierleib was on the ship *Norma* which arrived in New York on November 10, 1861. The original list can be found on microfilm roll 107.

Questions regarding the transcription of the names and places which appear in this volume can be directed to Marion Wolfert, 2541 Campus Drive, Salt Lake City, Utah 84121.

Marion Wolfert

TABLE OF ABBREVIATIONS

Places

A., Aus.	Austria
B., Ba.	Baden, Bavaria
Bad., Bd.	Baden
Bav., Bv.	Bavaria
Br.	Braunschweig
C.H., Curh.	Kurhessen
H.	Hessen, Hannover
Ha., Hann.	Hannover
He., Hess.	Hessen
KH., KHe., Kurh.	Kurhessen
Na., Nass.	Nassau
N.Y.	New York
O., Old.	Oldenburg
Oest.	Austria
P., Pr., Prss.	Prussia
S., Sa., Sachs., Sax.	Saxony
W.	Wuerttemberg, Waldeck
Wa., Wald.	Waldeck
Wu., Wue., Wuert., Wrt.	Wuerttemberg

Ages (infants)

bob	born on board ship
by	baby
d	days old
m	months old
w	weeks old

Given Names

A.	Anna
Ad.	Adam, Adolph, Adalbert
Alb.	Albert, Albin, Albrecht
Andr.	Andreas

Ant.	Anton
Aug.	August, Augusta
Balt.	Balthasar
Bar., Barb.	Barbara
Bern., Bernh.	Bernhard
Carol., Carole.	Caroline
Cas., Casp.	Caspar
Cat., Cath.	Catharine
Charl.	Charles, Charlotte
Chr., Christ.	Christian, Christoph
Chr'tne	Christine, Christiane
Clem.	Clement, Clementine
Con., Conr.	Conrad
Dan.	Daniel
Diedr.	Diedrich
Dom.	Dominicus
Dor.	Dorothea, Dorette, Doris
Eberh.	Eberhard
Ed., Edw.	Eduard
El., Els.	Elisabeth
Em.	Emil, Emanuel, Emma, Emilie
Eman.	Emanuel
Eng.	Engel
Ern.	Ernst, Ernestine
Ferd.	Ferdinand
Fr.	Friedrich, Franz
Fr'd, Friedr.	Friedrich
Fr'ke	Friederike
Fr'z	Franz
Geo.	Georg
Gert.	Gertrude
Gottfr.	Gottfried
Gotth.	Gotthard
Gottl.	Gottlieb
Gust.	Gustav
Heinr., Hr., Hch.	Heinrich
Hen., Henr., Hen'tte	Henriette
Her., Herm.	Hermann, Hermine
Ign.	Ignatz
J.	Johann
Jac.	Jacob
Jas.	James
Joh., Johs.	Johannes
Jos.	Joseph
Jul., Juls.	Julius, Julie
Kath.	Katharine

Lor., Lor'z	Lorenz
Lud., Ludw.	Ludwig, Ludolph
M., Mar.	Maria
Magd.	Magdalena
Marg.	Margaretha
Mart.	Martin
Matth.	Matthias, Mathilde
Max.	Maximilian
Mic., Mich.	Michael
Nic., Nicol.	Nicolaus
Pet.	Peter
Ph., Phil.	Philipp
Reg.	Regina
Rob.	Robert
Ros.	Rosine, Rosalie
Rud.	Rudolph
Sal., Sol.	Salomon
Seb.	Sebastian
Sim.	Simon
Soph.	Sophia
Th.	Theodor, Thomas, Theophilus
Theo., Theod.	Theodor, Theophilus
Ther.	Therese
Traug.	Traugott
Val., Valen.	Valentine
Vic., Vict.	Victor, Victoria
Vin., Vinc.	Vincent
Wilh., Wm.	Wilhelm, Wilhelmine
Wilh'mne	Wilhelmine
Wolfg.	Wolfgang

Table of References

YR–LIST	SHIP	DATE OF ARRIVAL			FILM #
68-0014	Bremen	6	Jan	1868	290
68-0314	Weser	20	Apr	1868	293
68-0419	Tuisko	12	May	1868	294
68-0456	Hansa	18	May	1868	294
68-0534	America	1	Jun	1868	295
68-0566	Weser	6	Jun	1868	296
68-0610	Hermann	15	Jun	1868	296
68-0625	Union	20	Jun	1868	297
68-0647	New York	25	Jun	1868	297
68-0661	Deutschland	27	Jun	1868	297
68-0707	Hansa	6	Jul	1868	297
68-0753	Niagara	17	Jul	1868	298
68-0760	America	18	Jul	1868	298
68-0770	Johannes	21	Jul	1868	298
68-0786	Weser	25	Jul	1868	298
68-0820	Hermann	1	Aug	1868	299
68-0852	Union	10	Aug	1868	299
68-0865	America	13	Aug	1868	299
68-0872	Therese	14	Aug	1868	299
68-0884	New York	17	Aug	1868	300
68-0907	Deutschland	22	Aug	1868	300
68-0939	Hansa	31	Aug	1868	300
68-0957	America	7	Sep	1868	300
68-0982	Weser	12	Sep	1868	301
68-1002	Schmidt	18	Sep	1868	301
68-1006	Hermann	19	Sep	1868	301
68-1027	Union	25	Sep	1868	301
68-1049	Harzburg	2	Oct	1868	302
68-1085	Deutschland	10	Oct	1868	302
68-1111	Rhine	17	Oct	1868	302
68-1129	Hansa	24	Oct	1868	302
68-1153	America	2	Nov	1868	303

YR-LIST	SHIP	DATE OF ARRIVAL			FILM #
68-1174	Weser	9	Nov	1868	303
68-1190	Hermann	16	Nov	1868	303
68-1213	Union	21	Nov	1868	304
68-1246	Schmidt	2	Dec	1868	304
68-1258	Rhein	7	Dec	1868	304
68-1298	America	22	Dec	1868	305
68-1319	Weser	29	Dec	1868	305
69-0015	Hermann	6	Jan	1869	305
69-0029	Union	11	Jan	1869	305
69-0049	Adolphine	18	Jan	1869	305
69-0050	New York	18	Jan	1869	305
69-0067	Deutschland	25	Jan	1869	306
69-0079	Donau	1	Feb	1869	306
69-0100	America	8	Feb	1869	306
69-0169	Weser	1	Mar	1869	306
69-0182	Schmidt	6	Mar	1869	307
69-0208	Hermann	15	Mar	1869	307
69-0229	Union	22	Mar	1869	307
69-0292	Hansa	3	Apr	1869	308
69-0321	Main	10	Apr	1869	308
69-0338	America	16	Apr	1869	308
69-0389	Donau	26	Apr	1869	309
69-0429	Hermann	3	May	1869	309
69-0438	Union	8	May	1869	310
69-0490	New York	13	May	1869	310
69-0542	Hansa	24	May	1869	311
69-0547	Everhard Delius	26	May	1869	311
69-0560	America	28	May	1869	311
69-0572	Main	31	May	1869	311
69-0576	Ceder	1	Jun	1869	312
69-0592	Weser	5	Jun	1869	312
69-0659	America	16	Jun	1869	313
69-0672	Hermann	19	Jun	1869	313
69-0771	Hansa	7	Jul	1869	314
69-0784	Weser	10	Jul	1869	314
69-0798	Deutschland	13	Jul	1869	314
69-0842	America	22	Jul	1869	315
69-0848	Donau	23	Jul	1869	315
69-0923	Union	7	Aug	1869	316
69-0968	Deutschland	21	Aug	1869	316
69-1004	Hansa	30	Aug	1869	317
69-1011	America	1	Sep	1869	317

YR–LIST	SHIP	DATE OF ARRIVAL			FILM #
69-1059	Donau	11	Sep	1869	318
69-1076	Hermann	11	Sep	1869	318
69-1086	Weser	18	Sep	1869	318
69-1212	Rhein	22	Oct	1869	320
69-1309	Union	22	Nov	1869	321
69-1363	Hansa	6	Dec	1869	321
69-1377	Rhein	20	Dec	1869	322
69-1421	America	29	Dec	1869	322
70-0006	Helene	5	Jan	1870	322
70-0031	Weser	17	Jan	1870	323
70-0052	Hansa	24	Jan	1870	323
70-0076	Deutschland	31	Jan	1870	323
70-0089	Rhein	8	Feb	1870	323
70-0100	Donau	15	Feb	1870	323
70-0135	Union	26	Feb	1870	324
70-0148	Weser	5	Mar	1870	324
70-0170	America	14	Mar	1870	324
70-0178	Hansa	16	Mar	1870	324
70-0184	Deutschland	19	Mar	1870	324
70-0204	Rhein	28	Mar	1870	324
70-0223	Donau	2	Apr	1870	325
70-0259	Hermann	13	Apr	1870	325
70-0272	Union	16	Apr	1870	325
70-0308	America	25	Apr	1870	326
70-0329	Deutschland	2	May	1870	326
70-0355	Rhein	7	May	1870	327
70-0378	Donau	13	May	1870	327
70-0384	Hansa	14	May	1870	327
70-0443	Hermann	26	May	1870	328
70-0452	Union	28	May	1870	328
70-0508	America	9	Jun	1870	329
70-0523	Deutschland	13	Jun	1870	330
70-0569	Hansa	23	Jun	1870	330
70-0583	Donau	25	Jun	1870	330
70-0682	Weser	16	Jul	1870	332
70-0683	Frankfurt	16	Jul	1870	332
70-0728	Union	30	Jul	1870	332
70-0816	America	26	Aug	1870	333
70-1003	Rhein	22	Oct	1870	335
70-1023	Deutschland	2	Nov	1870	335
70-1035	Donau	7	Nov	1870	335
70-1055	Hermann	14	Nov	1870	335

YR–LIST	SHIP	DATE OF ARRIVAL			FILM #
70-1066	Main	17	Nov	1870	337
70-1142	Hansa	19	Dec	1870	338
70-1161	Rhein	23	Dec	1870	338
71-0143	America	23	Feb	1871	339
71-0167	Hansa	3	Mar	1871	339
71-0172	Rhein	6	Mar	1871	339
71-0226	Hermann	27	Mar	1871	340
71-0300	Hansa	20	Apr	1871	341
71-0363	Hermann	8	May	1871	342
71-0393	Main	13	May	1871	342
71-0444	Gessner	28	May	1871	343
71-0456	Rhein	27	May	1871	343
71-0479	Hansa	2	Jun	1871	343
71-0492	Deutschland	5	Jun	1871	343
71-0521	Donau	10	Jun	1871	344
71-0581	Koeln	24	Jun	1871	344
71-0582	Main	24	Jun	1871	344
71-0643	Rhein	8	Jul	1871	345
71-0684	Frankfurt	17	Jul	1871	345
71-0712	Deutschland	24	Jul	1871	346
71-0727	Harzburg	26	Jul	1871	346
71-0733	Bremen	28	Jul	1871	346
71-0736	Donau	29	Jul	1871	346
71-0789	Main	12	Aug	1871	346
71-0792	Hannover	12	Aug	1871	346
71-0815	Koeln	18	Aug	1871	346
71-0821	Weser	19	Aug	1871	347
71-1046	America	16	Oct	1871	349

German Immigrants

Lists of Passengers Bound from Bremen to New York, 1868–1871

NAME	AGE	RESIDENCE	YR-LIST
AAL, Abraham	16	Crailsheim	71-0521
AALBERS, Johann	36	Muenster	68-0786
Johanna 31, Gerrit 23			
AASMANN, Adelheid	33	Altendorf	68-0566
ABBELSTIEL, Philippine	9	Weimar	69-1319
ABEL, August	11	Zittlen-Pommern	70-0006
ABEL, Elisab.	30	Schaffhausen	71-0581
ABELE, Heinrich	24	Sersheim	68-0907
ABELER, Hermann	54	Wuetentrebelits	71-0456
ABELES, David	16	Weintentrebetis	69-0490
ABELING, FR. W.	41	Lessum	70-0683
Christine 25, Herm. 9, Louise 11 months			
ABELING, Julius	47	Lausitz	69-0559
Auguste 46, Hermann 20, Wilhelm 19, Otto 15, Carl 13, Martha 7			
ABELS, Johann	39	Middelsfoehr	69-0229
Anke 34, Thecla 12, Bertha 8			
ABEN, Christian	17	Lengsfeld	68-0661
ABEND, Martin	18	Wehingen	70-1003
ABENDROTH, Friedrich	50	Coeln	68-0661
Louise 54, Louise 21, Friedrich 17, Simon 16, Heinrich 7, Lidia 6			
ABENDROTH, Otto	27	Dresden	68-0753
ABENDSCHEIN, Bab.	14	Neiderstetten	71-0581
ABENS, Susanne	48	Heiligkrug	68-1027
Sophie 25, Anna 22, Helene 17, Gertrud 16, Peter 9			
ABERLE, Johann	24	Pflegelberg	68-0852
ABRAHAM, Albert	26	Nasebund	69-0208
ABRAHAM, Fanny	22	Coblenz	70-0052
ABRAHAM, Gottlieb	38	Guntergott	71-0393
Betke J. 23			
ACHARD, Louis	29	Homburg	69-1212
ACHELIS, Fritz	25	New York	69-0457
ACHLEY, Alfred	26	Braunschweig	69-0583
ACHMANN, Marie	20	Hambuch	71-0681
ACKER, Adam	23	Orb	68-0852
ACKERMANN, Ed.	15	Aurich	71-0821
Anna 18			
ACKERMANN, Henry	49	Miehlen	70-0508
Cath. 42, Johanne 14, William 7			
ACKERMANN, Hermann	29	Muensterberg	71-0736
ACKERMANN, Peter	29	Coeln	68-0707
ACKERSBERG, Peter	23	Coeln	69-1004
ACKMANN, Justine	15	Obernkirchen	68-0647
ACKULACIUS, Georg	31	Schotten	69-0542
ADAM, Emil	18	Loffenau	71-0789
ADAM, Magdalena	30	Asch	68-0884
Marg. 5, Ernst 5, Baby 9 months			
ADAM, Rebecca	48	Lyck	68-0707
Therese 20, Hedwig 17			
ADAMS, Henry	17	Darmstadt	70-0308
ADAMS, Peter	28	R.B.Coblenz	68-1006
ADAMS, Peter	25	Rheingau	68-1027
ADAMSON, W.	16	Bremerhaven	71-0582
ADDICHS, Anna	23	Rothweil	70-0329
ADELMEIER, Gottfried	60	Loeve	70-1023
ADELSMANN, Anna	26	Millrichstadt	70-1003
ADELUNG, Herm.	14	Hannover	69-1086

NAME	AGE	RESIDENCE	YR-LIST
ADELUNG, Jacob	18	Fuerth	71-0172
ADEN, Habbe	51	Holtrup	69-0208
Toebke 45, Margarethe 9, Trientje 7, Ehme 4, Baby-boy 6 months			
ADICKS, Theodor	16	Dorum	71-0521
Anna 19			
ADLER, Anna	26	Wallerfangen	68-0939
ADLER, Johanne	19	Frankfurt a/M	70-1003
ADLER, Marie		Coburg	69-0572
ADLER, Martin	52	Koenigsberg	71-0681
Marg. 56, Heinr. 16, Anna 14			
ADLER, Simon	17	Hessbach	71-0643
ADLER, Sophie	14	Kallin	70-1023
ADOLPH, Christ.	17	Borgholzhausen	71-0393
ADRIAN, Phil.	22	Hoerdt	68-0982
AEHLE, Bertha	36	Osnabrueck	68-1006
Ida 9, Baby daughter 9 months			
AGATTE, Maria	23	Neutrengstedt	69-0229
AHLBRAND, Anna Marg.	20	Offenbach	68-1049
AHLERS, Annchen	17	Oldenburg	70-0384
AHLERS, Diedrich	23	Hassel	68-0566
AHLERS, Friedr.	41	Schierndorf	71-0821
Marie 43, Dorothea 9, Margarethe 8			
AHLERS, Margreth	23	Ringner	71-0456
AHLERS, Maria	16	Holtrup	69-0572
AHLERS, Mettje	26	Ostfriesland	70-0329
AHLERS, Sophie	26	Ardinghausen	71-0581
Meta 17			
AHLERS, Wilh.	17	Twelbaeke	68-0884
AHLERT, Hermann	26	Hannover	70-0148
AHLFELD, Heinrich	69	Letzlingen	69-0672
AHLHORN, Sophie	30	Hannover	69-1212
AHLRICHS, Hermann	30	Lastrup	70-0682
Heinrich 26			
AHRENDT, Gust.	25	Lauterberg	68-1002
Johanna 29, Dora 2, Johanna 6 months			
AHRENHOLZ, Johann	17	Eitzendorf	71-0429
AHRENS, Anna	40	Bremen	69-0208
AHRENS, Anna	24	Hannover	69-1004
AHRENS, Bernhard	27	Wilmington	69-1086
AHRENS, Carl	42	Braunschweig	70-1003
Carl 10, Gustav 6			
AHRENS, Caroline	43	Dorste	69-1059
AHRENS, Christian	18	Cenin	68-0939
AHRENS, Fritz	24	Lichtenfeld	69-0583
AHRENS, Georg	29	Columbus	70-0184
AHRENS, Gertine	36	Oldenburg	69-0338
Mary 9, John 7, Ad. 3, Emil 2			
AHRENS, Heinr.	27	Hannover	70-0443
Marie 21			
AHRENS, Jacob	17	Koehlen	68-0852
AHRENS, Johann	42	Osterholz	68-0625
Meta 15			
AHRENS, Johann	26	Esterweyen	68-0907
AHRENS, Luehr	17	Hannover	70-0204
AHRENS, Mary	26	Hoya	68-0957
AHRENS, Nicolas	30	Brooklyn	70-1003
AHRENS, Wilheline	9	Peine	71-0456
AHRENTIANS, Florentine	18	Detmold	70-0308

NAME	AGE	RESIDENCE	YR-LIST
AHRNSMEIER, Friedrich	19	Minden	68-0419
AICHMANN, Ludwig	23	Nueslingen	68-0647
AICKMANN, Heinrich	19	Pfullingen	70-1142
AILINGER, Josef	26	Goesslingen	70-0355
AILINGER, Marie	17	Gaerlingen	71-0456
AIMMER, Marga.	62	Schluechtern	71-0821
Hinr. 26, Friedr. 15			
AIPLE, Cha.	18	Rottweil	70-0170
AKKERMANN, Regine	27	Stein	71-0643
Ida 9, Emma 8			
ALBACH, Jacob	17	Nassau	69-0560
ALBER, Conrad	19	Gebersheim	69-1363
ALBER, Fried.	25	Bessighei	70-0508
ALBERDING, Gerhard	28	Wildeshausen	68-0786
Gesine 23, Catharine 11 months			
ALBERS, Carl	22	Hannover	68-0939
ALBERS, Eduard	27	Hutterwerfehn	68-0907
ALBERS, Emma	25	Hannover	69-1059
Louise 3			
ALBERS, Friedr.	29	Nordlohe	68-0884
ALBERS, Georg	16	Bremen	70-1003
ALBERS, Gerhard	23	Oldenburg	69-0268
ALBERS, Heinr.	17	Bremervoerde	71-0581
ALBERS, Joh.	33	Hannover	70-100
ALBERS, John	24	Altenlingen	68-0957
ALBERS, Nanke	70	Wiesens	69-1004
ALBERS, Sophia	18	Oldenburg	69-0559
ALBERS, Wilh.	16	Hannover	69-1363
ALBERS, Wilhelmine	21	Vesterwannen	68-0770
ALBERT, Franzisca	49	Essen	69-0572
Franz 15, Marie 8, Francisca 7			
ALBERT, Leonhard	22	Burgebach	68-0939
ALBERT, Louise	48	Iserlohn	71-0492
ALBERT, Marie	34	Gerabronn	69-1309
Ida 9			
ALBERT, Theod.	18	Frankenthal	71-0300
ALBERT, Wilhelm	31	Schwelentrup	68-0456
Florentine 28, Caroline 6, Diedrich 2, Fike 9 months			
ALBERTS, Bernhardine	28	Esens	68-0939
ALBERTUS, Elisabeth	21	Berka	69-1011
ALBIETZ, Barth.	30	Kuernberg	68-1002
Anna Cath. 26, Marie 11 months			
ALBOLDT, Heinr. Fr.	39	Hopfgarten	68-0661
Marie 36, Carl Emil 7			
ALBRECHT, Adolf	35	Oldenburg	69-0162
ALBRECHT, Alois	21	Heilig Kreuz	71-0479
ALBRECHT, Caroline	28	Darmstadt	68-0707
Wilhelmine 6			
ALBRECHT, Frd.	20	Boitzenburg	71-0393
ALBRECHT, Friedrich	25	Berlin	69-0208
Friederike 15, Reinhold 2, Max 3 months			
ALBRECHT, Fritz	29	Sondershausen	71-0172
ALBRECHT, Heinr.	22	Freiburg	71-0681
ALBRECHT, Jacob	23	Zuerich	70-0508
ALBRECHT, Maria	14	Lobbach	68-0456
ALBRECHT, Marie	24	Friedland	71-0736
Carl August 22			
ALBRECHT, Martin	17	Bamberg	71-0712
ALBRECHT, Peter	18	Neudrossenfeld	69-0848
ALBRECHT, Rosina	50	Immendingen	68-0534
Mary 17			
ALBRECHT, Rudolph	24	Bremen	70-1003
ALBRECHT, Samuel	25	Bremen	70-0569
ALBRECHT, Wilhelm	16	Ulm	69-0848
ALBRESCH, Eugen	31	Neustadt	71-0712
ALBUS, Mar.	32	Cobach	68-0753
Friedrich 5, Louis 3			
ALDAG, Elise	23	Bremen	70-0259
ALDEN, J. B.	43	Boston	70-1035
ALDERMANN, Carl	28	Rothoorwald	68-0661
ALERS, Ferdinand	16	Nofelden	69-0015
Dorothea 22, Carl 11 months			
ALEXANDER, August	34	Eberdorf/Prussi	69-0547
Caroline 29, Therese 11 months			
ALF, Josepha	44	Zimmern	70-0308
Anton 9, Johannes 1			
ALFEI, Ernst	41	Hildesheim	70-0204
ALFING, Phil.	25	Wester Casch.	71-0300
Cath. 27, Elise 1			
ALFRED, Martini	22	Hudermoor	69-0321
ALIAS, Bruno	30	Posen	68-0786
ALJETS, Jelde	17	Ostfriesland	69-0672
Anna 16			
ALLEINHOFF, C.	28	Gilgenburg	70-0184
ALLEMANN, M.	18	Carlsruhe	71-0712
ALLENDORF, Johannes	23	Mecklar	69-0321
Elisabeth 23, Elisabeth 9 months			
ALLENSTEIN, Caroline	42	Bitow	69-0547
ALLERICH, H.	18	Hannover	69-0583
ALLERS, Joh.	30	Schiffdorf	68-0610
ALLERSHAUSEN, Ad.	14	Braunschweig	71-0363
ALLERT, Oskar	14	Stolp	71-0643
ALLMANN, Johann	19	Danzig	68-0770
ALLMERS, Adele	20	Oldenburg	68-0566
ALLSTADT, female	24	Ottendorf	71-0363
ALMENDINGER, Gg.	19	Dettingen	68-0610
ALMENDINGER, Marie	23	Deggingens	70-1035
ALPERS, Henr.	17	Hesslingen	71-0479
ALS, Adam	17	Niederhorberg	69-0798
ALSENZER, Catharina	38	Hannover	68-0456
Wilhelm 7			
ALSLEBEN, Theo.	40	Ballenstedt	69-1421
Louise 42			
ALSTER, Sophie	30	Oberkaufungen	70-0329
ALT, Caroline	22	Friedelhausen	69-1319
ALT, Jacob	34	Offenbach	70-0452
ALT, Johann	37	Frankfurt	69-0798
Marie 35, Louise 13			
ALT, Maria	15	Bernsburg	68-0786
ALT, Peter	43	Coblenz	68-0884
Anna 36, Peter 11, Johannes 8, Heinrich 7, Matthias 5, Caroline -			
ALT, Therese	18	Schimmersdorf	71-0581
ALTENBEREND, Wilhelm	34	Detmold	69-0457
Louise 35, Wilhelm 9, Louise 1			
ALTENBURG, Elisabeth	50	Creuzburg	68-0566
ALTENHENNE, Friederike	48	Waldeck	68-0566

NAME	AGE	RESIDENCE	YR-LIST
ALTENHOFF, M.	4	Gilgenburg	70-0184
Helene 11 months			
ALTER, Anna	27	Niederhausen	71-1046
ALTER, Marie	32	Hagenau	71-0581
Baby-girl 8 months			
ALTHARDT, Georg	53	Dorheim	71-0581
Anna 30, Johann 9, Anna 4, Gertrude 10 months, Konrad 48, Anna 18, Georg 16,			
ALTHEIMER, Franziska	24	Darmstadt	70-0508
ALTHEN, Casp.	20	Coblenz	68-0884
ALTHER, Jacob	19	St. Gallen	69-1004
ALTHOEFER, August	16	Hannover	71-0821
ALTHOEFER, Louise	23	Hannover	71-0821
ALTHOEFER, Wilhelmine	22	Heustdorf	69-0968
ALTHOFF, Heinr.	59	Dissen	70-1035
ALTMANN, Therese	24	Neuenburg	71-0681
ALTMANNSBERGER, G.	30	Homburg	71-0821
ALTSTADT, Clara	27	Kreuznach	68-0456
ALZERT, Wilh.	24	Fulda	71-0684
Lisette 27			
AMAN, Julie	22	Brombach	70-0204
AMANN, Elisa	29	Vorarlberg	69-0560
AMANN, Minna	16	Carlsruhe	71-0815
AMBACH, Eduard	42	Greiz	69-0968
Christine 38, Julius 15, Hermann 9, Eduard 8, Heinrich 2			
AMBACH, Heinrich	59	Pittsfeld	69-0968
Caroline 57, Helene 16			
AMBACH, Wilhelm	24	Greiz	68-1006
AMBROZ, Johann	56	Boehmen	70-1142
Karoline 33, Franz 15, Adalb. 9, Barbara 8, Josef 7, Anastasia 3, Aloys 4 months			
AMBRUNN, Fr.	17	Meiningen	69-0560
AMELANG, Franz	27	Coethen	70-1003
AMELSBERG, Johann	19	Ockenhausen	68-0939
Maria 24			
AMELUNG, Friedrich	30	Halle	71-0492
AMENA, Cathrine	62	Steinau	70-0355
AMENT, Conrad	19	Forchheim	71-0712
Johann 17			
AMERT, Mary	29	Kerstenhausen	68-0957
AMMAN, Bertha	15	Suhl	70-0355
Friedrich 7			
AMMANN, Marie	18	Laubheim	69-0079
AMME, Christine	32	Allstedt	68-0534
Therese 9 months			
AMMON, Adolph	57	Suhl	71-0363
Johanne 53, Friedrich 16, Emil 9			
AMT, G.	18	Neerlage	71-0429
ANBEL, Diedr.	22	Baumbach	68-0884
ANBELANG, Moritz	25	Nordhausen	69-1396
ANDERS, Gottl.	48	Oberwitz	71-0521
ANDERS, Metta	18	Kirchtimeke	69-0338
ANDERSON, Olaf	12	Copenhagen	68-1027
ANDERSON, William	34	Chemnitz	68-0907
August 6			
ANDERSSON, Peter	30	Kalmar	68-0647
ANDING, Anna	21	Strang	69-0490
ANDRES, Caroline	20	Coburg	69-0672
ANDRES, Franz	32	Muenster	69-1309

NAME	AGE	RESIDENCE	YR-LIST
Anna 59			
ANDRIST, Walburga	25	Boehringen	70-0223
ANELLA, Conrad	28	Spangenberg	68-0661
Anna 27, Christine 5, Elise 3, Heinrich 11 months			
ANGE, Dorothea	24	Beuren	68-0707
ANGELBECK, Christine	24	Lohe	68-0907
ANGERMUELLER, Anna	20	Coburg-Gotha	69-1212
ANGERMUELLER, Elise	24	M. Hildburghen	69-0015
Caroline 9 months			
ANGERMUELLER, Mart.	37	Lindenau	68-1002
ANGERSTEIN, Philipp	16	Quernheim	68-0907
ANGSTENBERGER, Eug.	18	Buedderlaun	69-1004
ANGSTMANN, Ferdinand	26	Eberbach	68-0770
ANINGER, Georg	34	Muenchen	69-0592
Marga. 32, Barbara 3			
ANK, Robert	49	Frankenberg	68-0760
ANKENER, Ernst	21	Carlsruhe	68-0852
ANKLANG, Ludwig	25	Czarnikau	68-0753
ANSBACHER, Issac	21	Dottenheim	68-0939
ANSELM, R.	20	Altdorf	71-0712
ANSORGE, Gottfr.	57	Rainbach	68-0753
ANTHES, Cath.	23	Breidenheim	69-1319
Cath. 11 months			
ANTHES, Catharina	19	Arberlingen	71-0456
Christine 14, Anna 9			
ANTHOLZ, Heinr.	21	Graul	71-0821
ANTHONI, Joh.	32	Kuttenberg	71-0821
ANTHONY, Anna	58	Hadamar	68-0957
Franz 14			
ANTHONY, Joseph	52	Nassau	69-0560
Marie 17			
ANTON, Albert	38	Berlin	68-1002
APEL, Anna	22	Riedebach	68-0534
APEL, Cath.	19	Hollstein	71-0789
APEL, Jacob	27	Altenburg	68-0610
APEL, Johanna	44	Muehlberg	68-0852
Friederike 9, Heinrich 8, August 6, Augusta 4, Fritz 1			
APEL, Kunigunde	18	Kreisdorf	69-0429
Anna 16			
APEL, Kunigunde	58	Steinbach	68-0534
APEL, Maria	27	Naumburg	71-0492
APELD, Gesine	20	Heede	68-0939
APENHINK, Wm.	25	Brake	70-0308
APFELBACH, Friedricke	33	Mirtingen	68-0647
APPEL, Adam	18	Altheim	71-0821
APPEL, Adam	42	Darmstadt	71-0712
APPEL, Cath.	44	Kreisdorf	71-0393
Georg 6, Cath. 8, Elisabeth 4			
APPEL, Dorothea	24	Ober Franken	69-1086
APPEL, Georg	13	Kraisdorf	69-0429
APPEL, Gust.	20	Cassel	69-0050
APPEL, Heinr.	19	Heinbach	71-0733
APPEL, Heinrich	7	Darmstadt	71-0393
APPEL, Lassar	21	Borken	68-1002
Fanny 28			
APPEL, Louise	20	Hannover	70-1142
APPEL, Sophie	53	Altheim	71-0821

NAME	AGE	RESIDENCE	YR-LIST
APPELT, Auguste	21	Berlin	68-1002
APPELT, Caroline	54	Leipzig	70-0683
Lena 19, Paul 16, Marie 15, Carl 9			
APPENZELLER, Carl	17	Zuffenhausen	68-0982
APPMANN, Friedrich	27	Bremen	70-0184
ARBITTER, Anton	63	Fregefeld	71-0712
Barbara 61			
ARCHUT, Friedrich	40	Bitow	69-0547
Marie 35, Heinrich 6, Albert 3, Wilhelm 40			
ARDEMANN, Henriette	30	Hungen	68-0939
AREND, Adolph	22	Lippramsdorf	71-0712
ARENDS, Anne	40	Walle	68-0884
ARENDS, Tonjes	34	Boen-Boln	69-0672
Lina 23, Hamke 58			
ARENDT, Adelaide	22	Hannover	70-0135
ARENHOLTZ, Hinderk	26	Oltmansfehn	69-0429
Luebbert 16			
ARENHOLZ, August	17	Mellbergen	68-1027
ARENS, Adam	44	Rode	70-0272
Josepha 39, Anton 9 months			
ARENS, Anna	25	Herschbruch	71-0429
ARENS, Georg	19	Wotiez	70-1023
ARENS, Gesche	19	Hopert	68-0982
ARENS, Jans	24	Wieboldsbur	69-0229
ARENTZMEYER, Herm.	19	Luebeke	69-0576
ARFMANN, Bertha	35	Brooklyn	70-1003
ARINZ, Johann	18	Holle	68-0707
ARMBACHER, Michael	20	Nobera	69-1212
ARMBRECHT, Caroline	23	Bremen	70-0355
ARMBRUSTER, Adolph	19	Gruenthal	69-1212
ARMBRUSTER, Sophie	30	Coeln	68-0647
ARMBRUSTER, W.	19	Oensbach	71-0226
ARNCKE, Christ.	71	Hajen	71-0167
ARNDT, Andreas	27	Lutonambaum	68-0770
Josepha 22			
ARNDT, Georg	14	Rotenburg	71-0363
ARNDT, Jacob	19	Oetisheim	69-0672
ARNDT, Marie	34	Gelnow-Prussia	70-0006
Hedwig 15, Emma 9, Martha 7, August 5, Hulda 3, Anna 2, Emil 2 months			
ARNHOELTER, Diedr.	27	Gahlfelde	68-1027
Louise 24			
ARNHOLTER, Louise	53	Melbergen	69-1059
Carl 16, Heinrich 13			
ARNIM, Herm.	29	Berlin	68-0957
ARNOLD, Anna	17	Zittmannsdorf	71-0643
ARNOLD, August	31	Bremen	69-0029
ARNOLD, Charles	28	Aalin	69-1004
ARNOLD, Chr.	27	Gedern	69-0490
ARNOLD, Christ.	21	Greiz	71-0167
ARNOLD, Fanny	17	Ueberlingen	71-0643
Emilie 22			
ARNOLD, Franz	16	Gmuenden	69-0457
ARNOLD, Georg	62	Erlangen	71-0821
ARNOLD, Kunigunde	23	Kaubenheim	69-0592
Elisabeth 21, Apollonia 17, Michael 30			
ARNOLD, Laura	18	Hirzenheim	71-0792
ARNOLD, Lorenz	26	Kanbenheim	68-0884
Barb. 32			
ARNOLD, Maria	38	Camenz	68-0786
ARNOLD, Wilhelm	59	Melbergen	69-1059
ARNOLD, Wilhelm	22	Duschroth	68-1027
ARNOLDI, Wilhelm	39	Traben	69-0162
ARNS, Joseph	16	Borgentreich	68-0770
ARNSAH, Conr.	40	Friedland	70-0135
ARNSBERG, Catharina	48	Vegesack	71-0681
ARNSTEIN, Johanna	21	Wodiau	69-0572
ARSMANN, Catharine	23	Scharmbeck	69-1059
ARTMANN, E.	44	Gotha	69-0050
ARUMMA, Sophie	29	Paddington	69-1086
ASCH, Adolph	34	Berlin	70-0452
ASCH, H.	50	Breslau	68-0820
ASCH, Heinrich	21	Goettingen	71-0736
ASCHAUER, Franz	26	Udorf	68-0661
ASCHE, Bernhard	26	Doehlen	69-0268
ASCHENBRENNER, A.	22	Muenchen	68-0661
ASCHER, Emil	23	Obergrund	71-0581
ASCHER, Julius	16	Schloppe	71-0815
Ernestine 22			
ASCHLENA, Fanny		Wertach	69-0182
ASCHNER, Jeanette	42	Kattowitz	71-0643
Emmanuel 8, Bruno 6, Nathan 2, Isidor 9, Hermann 14			
ASCHOFF, Johann	30	Cassel	70-0682
ASEL, Theob.	21	Julbach	71-0815
ASENDORF, Nanni	31	Artlenburg	68-0852
ASH, Barbara	56	Contwiz	68-1298
ASMANN, Georg	19	Dreckenburg	69-0547
Wilhelm 19			
ASMUS, George	39	New York	69-0572
ASMUS, Pauline	15	Smazin	71-0479
ASSENHEIMER, Christ.	19	Beilstein	68-0786
ASSMUS, Carl	25	Meiningen	69-1076
ASSMUS, Doris	27	Bremen	71-0643
ASSMUS, Franz	30	Paducak	69-1076
Anna 28			
ASSUNIS, Carl	25	Meiningen	69-1076
ASTRICH, Bruno	9	Pleschen	68-0820
AUBEL, Joh.	66	Graefenhausen	71-0684
AUER, Catharine	22	Speerdingen	68-0852
AUER, Heinr.	33	Fuerth	71-0684
Clara 20			
AUF DEM ORTE, Dina	17	Thorst	69-1059
AUFENHANGER, Marie	18	Beveringen	69-0771
AUGERSTEIN, Philipp	16	Quernheim	68-0907
AUGGARTH, Georg	18	Ziegenhain	68-0456
AUGSBURG, Heinrich	32	Oetzen	68-0707
Trina 30, Charles 11 months			
AUGUSTIN, Anna	27	Meppen	70-1003
Bernhard 9, Marie 7, Josef 5, Adolf 4			
AUGUSTIN, Emil	18	Dresden	70-0272
AUGUSTIN, Josef	36	Boehmen	70-1161
Marie 29, Marie 2			
AUGUSTIN, Theodor	40	Rinkerode	69-0547
Anna 39, Theodor 7, Bernhard 6, Heinrich 10 months			
AUK, Georg F.	42	Hohenstein	69-0848
AUKAMP, Anna	27	Achine	71-0492

NAME	AGE	RESIDENCE	YR-LIST
AUKENER, Ernst	21	Carlsruhe	68-0852
AULENBACH, Ant.	23	Buerrstadt	70-1055
AULL, Lina	23	Mainz	69-0560
AUSRIKER, Wilh.	15	Nittelstaedt	69-0583
AUSTERMANN, Joseph	27	Muenchen	70-0523
AWEILER, Elise	23	Darmstadt	69-0490
AYASTE, Joh.	19	Pfiffingen	69-1363
AYKENS, Ayka	21	Emden	69-1076
Ahnen, Aug.	38	Adeleben	70-0308
Wilhelmine 39, Dora 6, Hermine 3, Louis 5			
BAACH, Jacob	53	Hochdorf	68-0610
Barbara 58			
BAADE, Friedr.	28	Kunz	68-0566
BAAS, Elise	43	Darmstadt	69-1086
BAAS, Maria	25	Worms	69-1212
Anna 6			
BAAS, Marie	26	Worms	71-0492
Casper 30			
BABEL, Elis.	25	Freinsheim	71-0581
BABKA, Anna	15	Tyrol	70-0308
BACH, Julia	23	Niederhorn	69-0576
BACH, Peter	26	Plankstadt	69-1059
BACHBERGER, Wolfgang	42	Fuerth	71-0429
Franciska 42, Marie 9, Francisca 7, Barbara 4, Wolfgang 1			
BACHENAUER, Gustav	18	Kuernbach	68-1027
BACHENHEIMER, Hirsch	16	Rauschholzhause	69-0208
BACHMANN, Adolf	14	Bremervoerde	71-0643
BACHMANN, Christ.	38	Ruderitz	68-0907
Christine 37, Hermine 15, Christine 13, Heinrich 7, Gustav 6, Bertha 2, Christ			
BACHMANN, Ferd. Jac.	19	Oberkaufungen	68-0647
BACHMANN, Georg	38	Nussloch	69-0429
Gertrude 31, Mathias 8, Heinrich 6, Jacob 3, Wilhelm 2			
BACHMANN, Gottlieb	24	Eisenach	69-0560
BACHMANN, Heinrich	18	Gleichen	68-0647
BACHMANN, J. C.	30	New York	70-0170
BACHMANN, Kath.	25	Trunstadt	71-0821
BACHMEIER, Herm.	34	Darmstadt	69-0841
Barbara 22, Susanne 4, Georg 2			
BACHMEYER, Elise	23	Bueren	68-0939
Marie 17, Sophie 15, Joseph 9, Johann 8			
BACHRACH, Julie	18	Paderborn	69-1076
BACK, Franz	38	Altenburg	69-0542
Henriette 36, Otto 12, Carl 7			
BACKER, Valentin	20	Baden	70-0148
August 17			
BACKHAUS, Ernst	29	Wisba	71-0581
Caroline 31, Carl 4			
BACKHAUS, Johanne	17	Delligsen	69-0592
BACKHAUS, Maria	18	Hellwege	71-0712
BACKINGER, Wend.	38	Gallingen	71-0789
Ernst 19			
BACKUS, Friedrich	44	Detroit	69-1212
BADBERGER, Ludwig	25	Buchlohe	68-0865
BADE, Dr. C.	29	Saginan	69-1076
BADE, Friedrich	34	Erfurt	68-1027
BADE, Herm	18	Stolzenau	71-0821
BADEN, Georg	21	Muenchen	70-0569

NAME	AGE	RESIDENCE	YR-LIST
BADEN, Peter	50	Schwalingen	68-0820
Marie 48, Chr. W. 9, Heinrich 9 months			
BADENHOP, H.	29	Ottersberg	69-0560
Louise 2, Baby 4 months			
BADER, Anton	23	Pfaffenhofen	69-1421
BADER, Barbara	47	Oberhausen	69-1076
Anna 16, Gottlieb 9			
BADER, Frdr.	30	Rendern	68-0610
BADER, Gustav	33	Harthausen	69-1363
BADER, Marie	17	Oberfranken	70-0384
BADER, Math.	57	Hohenstaufen	69-0592
BADERS, Martin	29	Zimmern	70-0223
BADERSCHNEIDER, C.	19	Doebra	71-0681
Adam 15			
BADERSCHNEIDER, S.	41	Helmbrechts	71-0643
Ludwig 9			
BADMER, Johann	25	Enslingen	69-0542
BAEBIG, Marie	6	Vegesack	69-1004
BAECKE, Hinrich	41	Oldenburg	69-0542
Habke 44			
BAECKENDORF, Heinr.	24	Osnabrueck	68-1027
Louis 20			
BAECKER, Elisabeth	21	Brechingen	69-0592
Cath. 17			
BAECKER, Emil	23	Forst	69-0457
BAEDEKER, Anna	36	Delmenhorst	70-0443
Joh. F. 15, Joh. Heinr. 5, Anna Sophie 2			
BAEHRE, Emilie	20	Hildesheim	68-0566
Anna 9 months			
BAEHREN, Carl	25	Neuss	69-0490
BAEKE, Josef	30	Obergrund	71-0581
Josefa 24			
BAENDER, Carl	20	Bitzfeld	70-0076
BAENERLEIN, Margareth	25	Oberfranken	69-0321
Margareth 4			
BAER, Adam	36	Oberfranken	70-0384
BAER, Aloys	44	Enskirchen	68-0957
BAER, August	26	Wien	71-0581
BAER, Bernhard	25	Neckarbischofsh	69-1059
BAER, Eduard	18	Schierbach	69-1309
BAER, Elise	46	Siemiki	68-0820
Daniel 18, Wilhelm 9, Gustav A. 6, Julius 4, Hulda 11 months			
BAER, Isaac	17	Neckarbischofsh	69-1059
BAER, Pauline	27	Kanzig	68-0770
BAERN, Edwin S.	27	Friedensburg	70-1142
BAESEL, Daniel	33	Bialken	71-0521
BAESSLER, Mart.	19	Budesheim	71-0300
BAETZ, Louise	27	Rotenburg	68-0982
BAEUERLE, Jac.	19	Langenbrand	69-0338
BAEUMEL, Andr.	24	Meeringen	68-0753
Anna 20			
BAEUMEL, Marie	24	Weisnach	68-0625
BAEUSLE, Wilhelmine	25	Pfaffenhofen	68-0760
BAGEL, Heinrich	25	Bedingen	68-0014
BAHENBURG, Heinrich	16	Otterstadt	68-0982
BAHENSTY, Jos.	29	Duby	68-0566
Marie 27, Anna 6, Wenzel 2			
BAHLING, Marg.	16	Borchel	69-1004
BAHLMANN, Anna	22	Schinkel	68-0907

NAME	AGE	RESIDENCE	YR-LIST
BAHMANN, Richard	25	Ilmenau	70-1003
BAHN, Carl	40	Menzingen	71-0736
BAHNEMANN, Friedrich	53	Henkenhagen	71-0456
Emilie 33, Bertha 9, Hermann 4, Emma 6			
BAHR, P.	16	Aschwarden	69-1076
BAHRMANN, Amalie	20	Meissen	69-1004
BAICHERSHOFF, Agnes	22	Oldenburg	69-0798
BAIER, Anna	21	Oberschulz	69-0771
BAIER, Caspar	26	Austria	70-0170
BAIER, Catharine	53	Tangenroth	71-0429
Friedrich 14			
BAIER, Heinrich	17	Horbach	69-0672
BAIER, Josef	19	Rottweil	69-1363
BAIER, Robert	35	Breslau	68-0760
BAIERLE, Elisabeth		Havre	70-0259
BAILER, Pauline	19	Revingen	69-0576
BAISER, John	26	Mantel	69-0338
BAISINGER, Rosa	27	Hechingen	70-0443
Henry 3			
BAISSIER, Fritz	26	Duesseldorf	70-0569
Herm. 24			
BAIST, Ida	21	Roedelheim	69-1309
BAKE, Ernst	18	Hannover	69-0798
Albertine 15			
BAKEMEYER, Christ.	32	Adrianopel	68-0647
Louise 32, Maria 7, Friedr. 25			
BAKER, Clemens	19	Dahlhausen	69-1363
BALDES, Josefa	22	Ditlefrod	69-0457
Anna 3 months			
BALEER, Friedrich	58	Vegesack	70-0148
BALKE, Heinrich	54	Natho	68-0647
Henriette 50			
BALKE, Jos.	22	Loitz	68-0884
BALKE, Sophie	24	Bremen	69-0542
BALLER, Maria A.	18	Hohenthal	68-0884
BALLHOEST, Aug.	26	Steinfeld	71-0300
BALLIN, Charles	30	Dannerville Cit	69-1309
BALLIN, Charlotte	17	Berlin	71-0736
BALLNEY, Marie	24	Steinferel	69-0292
BALMER, Johann	20	Hebsack	68-0786
BALS, Eleonore	25	Hannover	68-0852
BALSER, Margarethe	53	Obersenne	69-0015
BALTEMEIER, Catharine	22	Visbeck	69-0457
BALTZER, Theodor	29	Bruessow	69-1396
BALTZER, Wilhelm	51	Darmstadt	69-0923
BALZ, Adam	63	Flonheim	71-0643
Elise 53, Cathrine 16			
BALZ, Barbara	54	Hessen	70-0508
Elisabeth 22, Henry 19			
BALZ, Friedr.	20	Nuestlingen	69-1004
BALZ, Jacob	45	Zizischhausen	68-0786
BALZ, Jacob	18	Bibelnheim	71-0429
Anna 18			
BALZER, Anna	22	Muskau	68-0786
BALZER, Heinrich	16	Wolfersrode	68-0647
BAM, Gustav	19	Barmen	70-0148
BAMANN, Franz	16	Henitzendorf	68-0707
BAMBEI, Kath.	27	Duerkheim	71-0393
BAMBERGER, Helene	31	Emden	69-0547
BAMESBERGER, Ferd.	17	Lanberg	71-0167
BANA, Josefine	28	Oldenburg	71-0681
BANDENDISTEL, Heinr.	19	Renchen	71-0821
BANDER, Wilhelm	19	Mannheim	70-0223
BANDERMANN, Wilhelm	23	Nordkirchen	68-0852
Louise 17			
BANDLOW, Maria	59	Mecklenburg	70-1055
August 17			
BANDVOGEL, Mathilde	18	Schoenlanke	71-0821
BANER, Caroline	24	Brachenheim	68-0957
BANGER, Gertrud	22	Darmstadt	69-1086
Franciska 20			
BANGERT, Fr.	24	Waldeck	68-0753
Catharine 26, Heinrich 11 months			
BANGERT, Martin	23	Dallau	69-0848
BANGHOFF, Catharina	25	Thalheim	71-0733
BANGRATZ, Joseph	22	Gruen	68-0957
Margareth 21			
BANHARD, Anna	56	Geggingen	70-0204
BANK, Hermann	23	Blankenstein	69-0542
BANNENSCHUR, Georg	23	Stellichte	69-0572
BANNINGER,Anna	34	Embrach	68-1027
BANNSICH, Johann	50	Fischbach	69-0429
Marie 42, Marie 7, Johann 5			
BANRATH, Georg	47	Oberschonau	69-0672
Catharine 46, Marie 18, Emil 9			
BANSTEDT, Alb.	24	Danzig	68-0884
BANSTERT, Fried.	17	Clausthal	71-0300
BANTE, Bernhard	36	Ohme	69-0572
BAPP, Heinr.	46	Darmstadt	70-1142
Cath. 36, Marie 3, Heinrich 1			
BAPSILBER, Conrad	21	Bernburg	71-0821
BARABAS, Hermine	44	Graudenz	69-0182
Gustav 15			
BARBACH, Johanette	22	R.B.Coblenz	68-0647
BARBIER, Joh.	25	Grunstadt	71-0167
BARBRAKE, Joh. Fr.	30	Kuhlenkamp	68-0610
BAREMLE, Caroline	21	Goettelfingen	68-0456
BARENBURG, Meta	22	Lehe	68-0820
BARESS, Marie	19	Zarawic	71-0479
BARGER, V. Helene	17	Ottersburg	68-0982
BARGFREDE, Peter	17	Ottersberg	68-0820
Sophie 24, Anna 22			
BARGHAUER, Ph.	25	Wetzlar	69-1011
BARGMANN, Mich.	26	Otternsen	70-0052
BARHORST, H.	28	Steinfeld	71-0736
Lisette 16			
BARKART, Georg	18	Hagenbach	68-0647
Carl 27			
BARKEMA, Trientje	20	Ditzum	68-0534
BARKLAGE, Fried.	16	Westersheps	71-0300
Sophie 26			
BARLING, Wilhelm	26	Luedde	68-1027
BARNEWALD, Ulrich	47	Walle	68-0566
Marie 30, Albert 5, Joh. 2			
BARNFELD, male	42	Villars Esperna	68-1006
BARNING, Christ.	15	Sonderbreitenmo	71-0521
Johann 14			
BARNSDORF, Emilie	40	Braunschweig	69-0182
Conradine 11 months			

NAME	AGE	RESIDENCE	YR-LIST
BARNSTORF, Antoni	15	Braunschweig	69-0182
Alwine 9, Louise 6			
BARRENDAMM, Marie	60	Bremen	71-0172
BARSCH, Franz	32	Naumburg	71-0363
BARSCHIG, Helene	21	Berlin	70-0308
BARSTEDT, Alb.	24	Danzig	68-0884
BARTELS, Becca	15	Eissel	68-0610
BARTELS, Caroline	20	Bueckeburg	69-0292
BARTELS, Diedrich	40	Tuschendorf	68-0907
Anna 44, Heinrich 7, Friedrich 6, Doris 5			
BARTELS, Gottfried	21	Halle	69-1076
Wilhelmine 18			
BARTELS, Heinr.	56	Horsten	71-0363
Maria 53, Hans 23, August 14			
BARTELS, Heinrich	17	Cassel	69-0576
Conrad 15			
BARTELS, Heinrich	50	Wechold	68-0907
Adelheid 48, Adelheid 21, Margaretha 15, Catharina 7			
BARTELS, Hermann	18	Achim	68-0760
BARTELS, Philip	17	Bremen	69-0572
BARTH, Fried.	36	Tuebingen	70-1142
Ludwig 8, Carl 6, Wilh. 3			
BARTH, Johann	18	Oetisheim	69-0672
BARTH, John	19	Muehlen	71-0456
BARTH, John W.	44	Wanna	68-0534
Wilhelmine 37, Peter 12			
BARTH, Josef	18	Floehingen	69-0162
BARTH, Lorenz	29	Esslingen	71-0492
BARTH, Louise	27	Berlin	71-0300
Louise 7, Paul 5, Georg 3, Martha 9 months			
BARTH, Margreth	24	Hasforth	69-1059
BARTH, Marie	20	Jeggen	68-0647
BARTHELMUSS, Barb.	26	Altenstein	68-0957
Dorothea 2			
BARTHOLD, Johannes	49	Ramrod	68-0625
Heinrich 7, Catharina 4, August 17			
BARTHOLDI, Anna	18	Cassel	71-0821
BARTHOLOMAE, Georg	19	Heidelberg	70-0683
BARTLING, Alexander	19	Siesen/Seesen	69-1076
BARTLING, Carl	36	Schaumburg	68-0753
BARTLING, Catharina	33	Buer	68-0884
Marg. 3			
BARTLING, Wilh.	60	Eggeberg	68-0884
Elisabeth 28, Catharina 17			
BARTZ, Wilhelm	20	Hecklingen	68-0707
BARTZEN, Peter	32	Krainel	71-0521
BARUCH, Malchen	17	Landau	70-1003
BARWISCH, Heinr.	23	Schadwalde	69-1011
BARZ, Carl	35	Pommern	69-0559
Caroline 28, Hermann 5, Carl 3, August 4 months			
BARZ, Hermann	23	Neustettin	68-0625
BASCH, Georg	18	Oberiflingen	68-0534
BASCH, Joh.	16	Budweis	71-0581
BASCHNAGEL, Alois	40	Herdern	68-0820
BASE, Reike	17	Crailsheim	71-0643
BASEDOW, Adolph	20	Berlin	69-0547
BASS, Charlotte	26	Nossow-Rossow	71-0712
BASSE, Franz	28	Steinbach	71-0492
BASSENHORST, Diedr.	40	Steimke	68-0957
Dorothea 40, Mary 15			
BASSLER, Anton	22	Tersenbach	69-1421
Terfenbach			
BASSLER, Carl	17	Carnstadt	69-0292
BASSNER, Adelhaide	19	Wien	70-0329
Constantina 18			
BASSOW, Adalbert	23	Sitzenroda	70-0184
BASTIA, Francisca	60	Bonn	69-1212
BASTIAN, Conrad	52	Kuppenheim	71-0363
Louise 24			
BASTIAN, Wilhelm	11	Oldenburg	71-0363
BASTIANI, Franz	19	Offenburg	69-1421
BATSCH, Josef	22	Moehringen	69-0798
BATSCHE, Maria	20	Wolsten	69-0968
BATTENFELD, Ernst	19	Rennertshausen	68-0760
Johann 20			
BATTER, Hubert	60	Derkweiler	70-0308
BATTERMANN, Heinrich	20	Schaumburg	68-0872
BATZINGER, Helene	28	Leppach	71-0429
BAU, Christ.	57	Leupoldsgruen	70-0443
Elisabeth 37, Johann 18, Anna 11, Georg 6, Margareth 3			
BAU, Johann	43	Leupoldsgruen	70-0443
BAUCHMEYER, Jos.	28	Munich	69-1421
BAUDER, Joh.	26	Heubach	69-1319
BAUER, Andrea	32	Wuerzburg	69-0542
BAUER, Andreas	43	Herda	68-1002
Anna 39, Anna 8, Heinrich 6, Adam 4, baby boy 8 months			
BAUER, Anna	20	Fuerth	68-0820
BAUER, Anton	19	Hohenstadt	68-0456
BAUER, Aug.	18	Unterensingen	71-0789
BAUER, Balth.	36	Hausen	71-0815
BAUER, Barb.	28	Rauschenst.	70-0378
BAUER, Barbara	52	Diessenhofen	69-1421
BAUER, Bernardine	23	Duschhausen	68-0957
Sebastian 18			
BAUER, Betty	18	Hanau	69-0542
BAUER, Carl	23	Hochel	69-0572
BAUER, Carl	37	Brehmen	68-1027
BAUER, Carl	16	Reutlingen	71-0492
BAUER, Cath.	64	Cusel	69-1363
BAUER, Catharina	28	Hafersiohen	68-0707
Sophia 11 months			
BAUER, Christine	26	Langenburg	68-0753
BAUER, Creszentine	58	Oberingingen	71-0681
BAUER, Elise	17	Bayreuth	68-0939
BAUER, Emil	16	Schwarzenberg	68-0647
BAUER, Engelberth	23	Esgeltingen	69-0672
BAUER, Ernst	25	Freiburg	69-0050
BAUER, Ernst	19	Hanau	71-0363
BAUER, Franz	18	Laiterschbach	68-1006
BAUER, Fred.	29	Letzlingen	69-1421
BAUER, Friederike	31	Heutenbach	68-0939
BAUER, Friedr.	26	Alfeld	71-0792
BAUER, Friedrich	14	Merzbach	69-1363
BAUER, Georg	25	Edelfingen	70-0052

NAME	AGE	RESIDENCE	YR-LIST
BAUER, Gerh.	16	Norelsen	69-1004
BAUER, Gottl. A.	17	Uebbingen	69-0321
Peter Jacob 19			
BAUER, Herm.	19	Peine	68-0534
BAUER, Jan.	31	Schluechtern	70-0308
BAUER, Johann	20	Reinsberg	70-0031
BAUER, Johann	65	Eglasheim	69-0848
BAUER, Johann	27	Bambach	71-0521
BAUER, John G.	21	Reinsbronn	68-0760
BAUER, Karl	24	Kupferberg	68-0872
BAUER, Katharina	19	Tegernau	71-0363
BAUER, Louis	25	Ravis	71-0492
BAUER, Marcus	18	Schotten	68-0456
BAUER, Marie	26	Untergimpern	68-0610
BAUER, Mary	44	Lauterbach	69-1011
BAUER, Mathias	19	Erlangen	71-0429
BAUER, Michael	54	Mittelfranken	70-1142
Elisab. 58, Kunig. 18, Therese 16			
BAUER, Nicolaus	28	Ringschneit	70-1055
BAUER, Peter	15	Peffingen	70-1003
BAUER, Philipp	22	Bedwitz	69-0592
BAUER, Robert	16	Dessau	69-0923
BAUER, Rudolph	17	Wiesbaden	69-1396
BAUER, Simon	30	Nendes	69-1076
BAUER, Wm. A.	22	Abstatt	68-0610
BAUERLE, Anna M.	17	Untermusbach	68-0820
BAUERLE, Caroline	21	Mittelbach	71-0479
BAUERLEIN, Margaretha	56	Oberfranken	69-0968
Barbara 28			
BAUERSACHS, Johann	46	Gotha	68-0939
BAUKNECHT, Barbara	20	Neckarhausen	69-0229
BAUM, Catharina	28	Haferslohen	68-0707
Sophia 11 months			
BAUM, David	14	Merzhausen	68-0760
BAUM, Eduard	21	Weitentrebetisc	71-0456
BAUM, Georg	33	Fischbach	69-0079
BAUMANN, Aus.	33	Rust	71-0492
BAUMANN, Barthold	23	Endingen	69-0457
BAUMANN, Fred.	33	Weimar	68-1298
BAUMANN, Friedrich	31	Fistel	69-0784
BAUMANN, Helene	22	Rhodts	68-0661
BAUMANN, Henry	22	Grombach	68-0534
BAUMANN, Johann	18	Mitstedt	68-0456
Sophie 18			
BAUMANN, Jos.	22	Goetzingen	68-0314
Heinrich 19			
BAUMANN, Louise	30	Tuebingen	69-0429
Carl 3, Wilhelm 3 months			
BAUMANN, Philipp	19	Niederauerbach	71-0492
BAUMANN, Wilhelm	19	Hannover	71-0821
BAUMBACH, Heinrich	16	Gehaus	68-0939
BAUMEISTER, Friedrich	20	Balingen	69-0848
BAUMEISTER, Max	23	Neiderstein	68-0647
BAUMER, Josef	27	Ensdorf	68-0625
BAUMFALK, Joh. Ludw.	40	Leer	68-1049
BAUMGAERTNER, Elise	26	Klein Sachsenhe	69-0100
Christ. 21			
BAUMGARTEN, Bernh.	28	Altmannshofen	68-0786

NAME	AGE	RESIDENCE	YR-LIST
BAUMGARTEN, Ernst	30	Schoeppenstedt	69-0029
BAUMGARTEN, Friederike	46	Braunschweig	69-0429
Louise 16, Minna 9, Helene 7, Emil 11 months			
BAUMGARTEN, Jans	23	Westerhausen	69-0576
BAUMGARTER, Dorothea	26	Koenigsberg	69-0559
Andreas 3, Margaretha 1			
BAUMHOEFER, A.	16	Minden	70-0184
BAURATH, Georg	47	Oberschonau	69-0672
Catharine 46, Marie 18, Emil 9			
BAURIEDEL, Xaver	42	Gundelfingen	69-0848
BAUSAK, Th.	30	Potulin	71-0226
BAUSCH, Elise	52	Darmstadt	68-0707
Nathalie 9			
BAUSCH, Franziska	31	Loeffingen	71-0300
BAUSCHKA, Johann	31	Boehmen	70-0384
Marie 26, Adelb. 8, Anna 6, Marie 4, Catharine 11 months, Josef 19			
BAUSCHMANN, Joseph	53	Boehmen	70-0728
Anton 19, Wenzel 16, Antonia 35, Johann 11 months Joseph 28			
BAUST, Andreas	19	Heidelberg	71-0821
Anna 9			
BAUTZ, Carl	22	Carlsruhe	69-0572
BAXMANN, Lina	15	Jeinsen	69-0592
BAYARD, Chr.	40	Bislan	70-0178
Mary 30			
BAYER, Adrian	27	Schloitzingen	70-0184
BAYER, Caspar	18	Duermane	68-0456
Margarethe 15			
BAYER, Franz	12	Darmstadt	69-0841
BAYER, Georg	28	Zell	68-1002
Ursula 17			
BAYER, Lisette	30	Memmingen	68-0566
BAYER, Magdalene	27	Zell	69-0208
BAYERLEIN, Leonh.	36	Burghaig	71-0363
BAYKEN, H.	23	Hannover	69-1004
BEAUZAINE, Helene	31	Wiesenfeld	71-0821
BEBHAN, Caroline	19	Coburg	70-0170
BEBION, Cathar.	17	Beinstein	68-0957
BECHER, Bernhard	18	Noerlenbach	68-0707
BECHER, Friedrich	27	Solz	68-0625
Catharina 24, Anna 3 months			
BECHER, Georg	17	Herford	68-0939
BECHER, Jacobine	29	Albisheim	68-0707
BECHHOF, Samuel	20	Zierenberg	70-0148
BECHLER, Rudolf	20	Ehingen	70-0443
BECHSTEIN, Carl	26	Hessen	69-0559
Friederike 25, Maria Catharine 1, Johannes Lorenz 3 months			
BECHT, Schrist.	14	Kurla	71-0581
BECHTEL, Magdalena	38	Mainz	68-0982
BECHTOLD, August	17	Ramrod	68-0625
Johannes 49, Heinrich 7, Catharina 4			
BECHTOLD, Jac.	17	St. Martin	71-0479
BECK, Carl Wilhelm	36	Aurich	68-0419
BECK, Cath.	22	Doetlingen	68-0884
BECK, Charles	22	Cassel	68-0534
BECK, Christine	19	Weilheim	71-0643
BECK, Christine	20	Greibel	71-0581

NAME	AGE	RESIDENCE	YR-LIST
BECK, Conrad	17	Herford	71-0479
BECK, Friedr.	19	Wadgassen	71-0581
BECK, Ignitz	24	Patleschtin	71-0479
Marie 18			
BECK, Johann	27	Tuebingen	69-0229
Friedrich 32, Marie 1, Christoph 25, Michael 18, Johannes 24			
BECK, Johannes	58	Weuch	69-0292
Marie 51, Marie 20, Christine 13, Christian 19			
BECK, Joseph	32	Baden Baden	68-0872
BECK, Julius	23	Weimar	70-0178
BECK, L.	24	Gotha	69-1309
BECK, Magd.	27	Maulbach	70-1161
BECK, Rosine	19	Reghof	68-0939
BECK, Samuel	19	Neustadt	71-0479
BECK, Sophie	22	Ebreuth	69-0542
BECK, Theodor	27	Cottenstedt	68-0707
BECK, Theresa	21	Waexbenhausen	69-0963
BECKEFELDT, Friedr.	29	Wietzen	71-0736
Diedr. 32, Louise 26, Heinrich 3, Diedrich 3 months			
BECKEL, Ludwig	22	Wengershausen	69-0321
BECKER, Anna	26	Mimmelage	68-0566
BECKER, Anna	13	Orb	68-0852
BECKER, Anna	20	Bebra	71-0363
BECKER, Anton	32	Kurtscheid	70-0135
BECKER, Auguste	18	Wien	70-0728
BECKER, Carl	36	Stadthagen	70-1161
Sophie 26, Frida 2, Amenda 7 months			
BECKER, Carl	23	Suelbeck	68-0534
BECKER, Caroline	36	Kl. Slawochin	69-0672
Auguste 11			
BECKER, Caroline	23	Oldenburg	70-1003
BECKER, Cath.	18	Oberhofen	69-0592
BECKER, Catharine	17	Norderweidentha	71-0429
BECKER, Christine	29	Eich	68-0982
Christine 4, Catharine 9 months			
BECKER, Clara	27	Ebersheim	68-0982
BECKER, Claus	17	Neuenballstedt	68-0625
BECKER, Cornel	20	Leer	68-0753
BECKER, Eleonore	35	Cincinaty	69-1076
Fritz 29			
BECKER, Elise	24	Hessen Darmstad	70-0076
BECKER, Franz	52	Weingarten	68-0647
M. Eva 19, Joseph 14, Christiane 6, A. Gebh. 6			
BECKER, Friedr.	23	Hannover	70-0089
BECKER, Friedrike	27	Burgdamm	70-0443
Louis 6			
BECKER, Georg	15	Hannover	70-1003
BECKER, Georg	15	Obermillrich	69-0576
BECKER, Gottfried	26	Sinslau	69-0547
BECKER, Heinrich	48	Oldenburg	69-0672
Gesche 34, Heinrich 8, Gerhard 6, Ernst 11 months			
BECKER, Heinrich	33	Altenburg	69-0542
BECKER, Heinrich	39	Hildesheim	68-1027
BECKER, Ida	20	Borham	69-0848
BECKER, Jacob	16	Birkenfeld	69-0079
BECKER, Jacob	23	Eschmann/Eichma	69-1059
BECKER, Joh.	26	Richelkirchen	71-0521
Marg. 26, Heinrich 2			
BECKER, Johann	19	Liese	68-1027
BECKER, John	27	Niederweiler	70-0355
BECKER, Josef	33	Osnabrueck	69-0583
BECKER, Julie	25	Bimroth	69-1076
BECKER, Julius	24	Barmen	68-0760
BECKER, Katharina	20	Breitenbach	71-0363
BECKER, Lenchen	22	Basel	71-0363
BECKER, Leo	24	Eisenbach	69-0162
BECKER, Louise	17	Bremen	68-0907
BECKER, Margarethe	23	Oldenburg	69-0268
BECKER, Margarethe	32	Wura	69-0547
Catharina 7, Elisabeth 6, Heinrich 4, Anna 10 months			
BECKER, Maria	26	Morzhied	69-0672
BECKER, Maria	10	Kirrweiler	71-0521
BECKER, Marie	21	Kirtorf	68-0625
BECKER, Martha	25	Blankenheim	69-0229
BECKER, Martin	25	Ludwigshoehn	70-0378
BECKER, Mary	46	Warden	69-0338
Henry 8, Rinele 6, Catharina 4			
BECKER, Mathias	28	Cochen	69-1212
BECKER, Otto	25	Obberwiddershei	68-0647
BECKER, Peter	58	Dittersweiler	68-0820
Catharina 46, Wilhelmine 17, Elise 13, Marie 8, Christian 9			
BECKER, Peter	34	Schaffhausen	71-0643
Marie 27, Marie 5, Nicolaus 3, Johann 10 months			
BECKER, Sophie	22	Giessen	69-1396
Balthasar 17			
BECKER, Valentin	30	Guntersleben	70-0148
Marie 21			
BECKER, Valentin	27	Erbenhausen	68-0456
BECKER, Wilh.	31	Elberfeld	68-1002
BECKER, Wilh.	36	Suestedt	69-0162
BECKER, Wilhelm	40	Bonn	70-0583
BECKER, Wilhelm	19	Stadthagen	71-0456
BECKERLE, John	49	Grauersheim	68-0534
Anna 44, Anna 8, Henry 6			
BECKERMANN, Leopold	28	Westerwinner	68-1006
Wilhelmine 14, Wilhelmine 10 months			
BECKERT, Anna	19	Sachsen	70-1161
BECKHAUSEN, Bertha	17	Brake	69-0162
BECKHUSEN, Her. Hinr.	15	Neuenlande	68-0770
BECKMANN, Anna	20	Westerwangen	69-0542
BECKMANN, Auguste	22	Detmold	70-0384
BECKMANN, Charles	27	Oelde	70-0170
BECKMANN, Heinrich	17	Moys	68-0884
BECKMANN, Mina	16	Hardegsen	70-0384
BECKMANN, Theodor	21	Weddewarden	69-1309
BECKMANN, Wa.	45	Barnhausen	68-0957
Catharina 36, Catharina 8, Wilhelm 3			
BECKMEIER, Fr.	16	Hannover	70-1055
BEDNARIK, Elisabeth	9	Boehmen	69-1363
BEDOW, Carl	23	Erkener	68-0610
BEE, Helene	26	Winzeln	68-0982

NAME	AGE	RESIDENCE	YR-LIST
BEER, Fr. Aug.	30	Altenburg	69-0572
BEER, Friedr.	27	Eisfeld	70-0089
BEER, Georg	30	Koenigswart	68-0566
Elisa 22, Antonia 3			
BEER, Johann	30	Bern	68-0753
Ursula 30, Elisabeth 5, Barbara 4, Maria 2, Johannes 8 months			
BEERMANN, Anna	17	Wanna	70-0052
BEERMANN, Josef	23	Berlin	71-0681
BEERMANN, Margrethe	21	Hammingen	69-0798
BEFFERT, Margreth	51	Buskenbronn	69-1059
BEHLING, Marie	24	Wehe	68-0884
BEHLING, Wilhelm	15	Steinhude	68-0534
BEHLMER, Heinrich	19	Eupershausen	69-0798
BEHM, Christine	18	Koenigsberg	71-0681
BEHM, Herm. H.	15	Otterndorf	68-0647
Marie C. 17			
BEHMANN, Marie	25	Detern	71-0712
BEHMER, Frd.	25	Wittlage	71-0789
BEHNKE, Hr.	14	Otterndorf	69-0338
BEHNKE, Martin	28	Hannover	68-0456
BEHNKEN, Wilh.	15	Bremen	68-1002
BEHR, Christian	24	Buehle	68-0661
BEHR, Wilhelmine	22	Landau	71-0643
BEHRENDS, Friedr.	25	Velgau	68-0884
BEHRENDT, Ida	21	Neufahrwasser	70-1161
Baby 11 months			
BEHRENS, Catharine	19	Ostemburg	71-0736
BEHRENS, Edmund	17	Braunschweig	68-0707
BEHRENS, Fritz	37	Diepholz	70-0031
Anna 13			
BEHRENS, Gesine	22	Bremen	71-0521
BEHRENS, Gretchen	17	Moorsum	69-1309
BEHRENS, Julius	45	Gladebeck	68-1002
Sophie 45, Minna 22, Caroline 15, August 18, Julius 9, Heinrich 8, Emilie 6, Augusta 2, Marie 2			
BEHRENS, Sophie	26	Grupenbuehren	70-1003
Gesine 26, Baby 10 months			
BEHRENS, Sophie	21	Gilten	68-0456
BEHRENS, Wilh.	32	Stolham	68-0534
BEHRENS, Wilhelm	16	Sudwege	68-0456
BEHRENS, Wilhelm	15	Soltau	71-0456
BEHRENSMEYER, Ernst	27	Rehme	69-1004
BEHRINK, Marie	30	Aachen	69-0100
BEHRMANN, Balths.	30	Roethemeyer	71-0815
BEICH, S. J.	34	New York	69-0321
Bianca 22, Albert 13, Bianca 3, Jacobine 2, Minna 9 months			
BEIER, Paul	23	Dresden	71-0363
BEIERSDORF, Elisa	18	Meiningen	70-0170
BEIERSDORFER, F.	28	Birkenfeld	68-0014
Catharine 30			
BEIHOFER, Joseph	26	Ersingen	68-1027
BEIL, Friedr.	53	Katzenelnbogen	68-0982
Wilhelmine 13			
BEILER, Magdalena	57	Boodenmeiss	68-0770
Marcus 27, Catharina 21, Michael 17			
BEILSTEIN, Elise	55	Nassau	69-0672

NAME	AGE	RESIDENCE	YR-LIST
BEINE, Henry	19	Luetjeneda	71-0456
BEINHAUER, Heinrich	24	Melungen	68-0865
Katharina Elisabeth			
BEINKAEMPER, Frdke	13	Lingen	69-0968
Wilhelm 11			
BEINSEN, Aug.	25	Wenzen	68-0610
BEIRAU, Gust.	25	Friedland	71-0479
BEISCHLAG, Emilie	30	Noerdlingen	68-0852
BEISEL, Gottfried	62	Rohrbacherhof	68-1006
Louise 62, Barbara 32, baby born on board 13 days old			
BEISICH, Franziska	18	Oestreich	70-0728
Alois 16			
BEISINGER, Peter	22	Reichenbach	69-0015
BEISMANN, Franz Ant.	26	Ubstadt	68-1006
Adam 24			
BEISMANN, Veronica	30	Bruchsal	68-0760
BEISSWENGER, Christ.	21	Niederndorf	70-1055
BEITJER, Focke	35	Stichhausen	69-0547
Francolina 30, Geboalina 30			
BEKEL, Wilhelm	17	Dittelsheim	71-0681
BEKOFSKY, Georg	27	Osnabrueck	69-0050
BELEKAMP, Jacob	33	Wersen	71-0821
Catharine 41, Friedr. 3			
BELEKAMP, Lisette	16	Wersen	71-0821
Christine 9			
BELING, Louise	34	Bothmer	69-1076
BELKO, Xaver	20	Gr. Rautzig	71-0492
BELL, August	32	Neuenburg	69-0542
Henriette 35, Anna 6, Emma 4, Reinhold 11 months			
BELLA, Anton	48	Zamarta/Polen	69-0576
Anna 33, Paulina 12, Aleander 6, Johanne 6 months			
BELLAGE, Heinrich		Borgentruck	70-0443
BELLEME, Caroline	32	Darmstadt	68-0456
BELLERMANN, Emil	29	Dresden	69-1004
Elise 36			
BELLERS, Dorothee	48	Bremen	69-0338
Fred. 8, Minna 4, U. 3			
BELLINGER, Josefa	25	Ramsthal	69-1319
Christine 19			
BELLOF, Rosine	23	Darmstadt	70-1003
BELMONTE, Marcus	19	Alzey	69-0457
BELOW, Caroline	20	Cassen	71-0821
BELTEDIN, Ludwig	34	Waltershofen	69-0784
BELZ, Johann	28	Marbonn	69-1319
BELZNER, Rob.	20	Baden	70-0170
BENDEL, Marga.	22	Burrweiler	69-1086
BENDER, Anna	17	Darmstadt	69-1004
BENDER, Conrad	30	Hesse Darmstadt	70-0329
Elisabeth 28, Anna 6 months			
BENDER, Hermann	24	Malsch	71-0456
BENDER, Joh.	26	Etchelbach	69-1086
Helene 35			
BENDER, John	22	Wieseck	68-0760
BENDER, Marie	17	Boehmen	69-0490
BENDER, Theord.	21	Kirchen	70-0378
BENDICK, Jacob	23	Hanau	69-0268
BENDIX, Benjamin	32	Borgholte	69-0079

NAME	AGE	RESIDENCE	YR-LIST
BENDORF, Ed.	26	Teuchern	69-1421
BENDY, Theresia	19	Budweis	71-0581
BENEKE, Louise	46	Stoecken	68-1027
Dorothea 21, Wilhelm 16, Heinrich 11, Otto 8, Sophie 6, August 3			
BENEMANN, Julius	30	Berlin	68-1027
BENGAL, Ludwig	19	Groffelbach	71-0581
Carl 23			
BENGEL, Marie	30	Trunstadt	71-0821
BENGELE, Adolph	30	Rotenburg	68-0786
BENGMANN, Adolf	35	Oldenburg	69-0162
Anna 35,, Georg 6, Diedrich 5			
BENICKE, Joh.	15	Bremen	70-0569
BENISCH, Louise	25	Berlin	68-0939
Emma 11 months			
BENJAMIN, Max	16	Luetzelsachsen	69-0592
BENJAMIN, Wilh.	48	Hannover	68-0610
BENJES, Dorothea	23	Uentzen	68-0610
BENK, Eva	23	Wornstadt	69-0457
BENKELBERG, Louis	23	Leopoldsthal	68-0534
BENKEN, Wilh.	16	Walle	68-0566
BENKMANN, Wilh.	16	Hannover	69-0583
BENN, Wilhelm	42	Krojanke	71-0792
Justine 34, Emilie 13, Carl 9, Mathilde 8, Auguste 2, Bernhard 5, Wilhelmine 3			
BENNERT, Gottlieb	55	Sablonowo	69-0457
Ernestine 55, Carl 17			
BENNICK, Carl	26	Mecklenburg	69-0067
Wilhelmine 24, Wilhelm 10 months			
BENNING, Anton	17	Friesaythe	69-1004
BENRACK, Rudolph	21	Elberfeld	69-1076
BENSICK, Jobst	25	Eberdissen	68-0939
Hanna 19			
BENTE, Louise	23	Preussen	68-0456
BENTE, Marie	17	Hildesheim	69-0771
BENTER, Ad.	40	Offenbach	68-0753
Barbara 32, Christiane 14, Adam 5, Anna Maria 10, Johann 11 months			
BENTER, Hildegart	20	Dettlingen	69-0208
BENTER, Johannes	17	Wremen	70-0523
BENTING, Albert	47	Luenten	68-0820
BENTLER, Chr.	42	Palswitz	69-0208
BENTZ, Adam	34	Wendelsheim	71-0429
BENZ, Anna	34	Rohrdorf	69-0208
BENZ, Philip	29	Belheim	69-0457
BERAHER, Leopold	27	Oberehringen	68-0939
BERAN, Franz	49	Boehmen	69-0559
Barbara 49, Franz 16, Adolph B. 8, Emanuel 10			
BERBOHM, Louise	30	Bremen	70-0452
Joh. 8			
BERCHLAND, Charlotte	36	Gerbstadt	70-0355
Anna 6			
BERCKE, Lina	31	Ihlienworth	68-1298
Elisa 5, Ferdinand 4, William 2			
BERE, Kunigunde	27	Leimburg	68-0957
Johann 11 months			
BERECK, Claus	15	Doehren	71-0581
BERENDT, C.A.	35	Schweidnitz	69-0672
BEREROW, Albert	26	Bublitz	68-0786

NAME	AGE	RESIDENCE	YR-LIST
BERG, Anna	20	Colden	71-0456
BERG, August	44	Klein Freden	63-0244
Henriette 31, Fritz 9, Charles 3, Caroline 5, Mary 6 months			
BERG, Gottfried	44	Posen	70-1161
Ernestine 34, August 9, Wilhelm 7, Ottilie 4, Gustav 2			
BERG, Hirsch	31	Oberhausen	71-0821
Beta 31			
BERG, Johann	24	Ueberau	69-0848
BERG, Leonh.	18	Warburg	71-0581
BERGDORFF, Dorothea	33	Wiesbaden	69-0268
Auguste 4			
BERGE, Gottl.	35	Braunschweig	69-0542
Ernestine 37, Louise 7, Franz 5, Emma 10 months			
BERGENER, Heinrich	56	Osterode	69-0572
Wilhelmine 52, Wilhelm 28, Louise 19			
BERGER, Ad.	34	Leipzig	68-0707
BERGER, Adrian	27	Schloitzingen	70-0184
BERGER, Anna M.	30	Eikum	70-0443
BERGER, Bernh.	21	Geithain	68-0957
BERGER, Bernhard	19	Detmold	68-314
BERGER, Carl	35	Radolfszell	71-0684
BERGER, Caspar	14	Zempelburg	68-0707
BERGER, E. A.	22	Waldberg	70-0135
BERGER, Friedr.	41	Burgstaedt	70-0384
BERGER, Friedr.	18	Huellhorst	68-314
BERGER, Henry	23	Bayreuth	68-0760
Emilie 20			
BERGER, Herm.	39	Nordhausen	68-0982
Hermann 17			
BERGER, Johann	19	Erfurt	71-0736
Wilhelmine 26			
BERGER, Louise	32	Altenburg	68-0939
BERGER, Marie	30	Waldshut	68-0314
BERGER, Theresia	18	Steinau	71-0363
BERGERHAUSEN, Joh.	40	Ohio	69-0321
BERGEWISCH, Johann	20	Quakenbrueck	69-0208
BERGFELD, Helene	41	Lastrup	69-0968
Lisette 11 months			
BERGFELD, Margarethe	47	Harnstrup	69-0968
BERGFREDE, Christian	15	Ottersberg	69-0848
BERGHAEUSER, Elisa	59	Wetzlar	70-0308
Conrad 23, Christine 21,			
BERGHAUER, Peter	34	Hessen	69-0672
Anna 34, Jacob 7, Catharine 4, Elise 10 months			
BERGHOLZ, Johanne	36	Triebsee	71-0226
BERGHORN, Heinr.	16	Trestorf	68-0610
Caroline 19			
BERGHORN, Wilhelmine	15	Hannover	70-0178
BERGMANN, August	20	Ulbstadt	69-0798
BERGMANN, Carl	17	Essdorf	68-0661
BERGMANN, Caroline	51	Darmstadt	69-0592
BERGMANN, Dorothea	25	Westerholz	68-0456
BERGMANN, Fanni	15	Gundelfingen	68-0625
BERGMANN, Fredericke	17	Willmars	68-0534
BERGMANN, Heinrich	41	Oldenburg	70-0683

NAME	AGE	RESIDENCE	YR-LIST
Agnes 30, Diana 9, Heinrich 8, Elisabeth 7, Agnes 5, Lina 3, Marie 9 months			
BERGMANN, Heinrich	45	Lueben	68-0707
Wilhelmine 45, Henriette 11			
BERGMANN, Johann	44	Werdau	68-0625
BERGMANN, Lina	20	Andreasberg	69-0338
BERGMANN, Margreth	20	Mergentheim	71-0456
BERGMANN, Wilhelm	25	Herford	69-0771
BERGMANN, William	26	Bielefeld	68-0534
BERGMEIER, Gertrud	22	Laehr	69-1086
BERGNER, Bertha	18	Coburg	69-1086
BERGOLD, Ludwig	25	Greiz	70-0443
BERGSTIDE, Carl	23	Oldenburg	69-0292
BERINGER, Friedrich	18	Plochingen	69-0229
BERKEMEYER, Adolph	45	Voxtrup	68-0907
Caroline 43, Sophie 20, Gertrud 18, Caspar 15, Marianne 13, Dorothea 7, Elisab			
BERKEN, Johan	24	Hannover	70-0308
BERKENHOF, August	36	Westfalen	69-0672
Heinrich 30			
BERKENSTEDT, Bernh.	15	Damme	71-0789
BERKMANN, Heinrich	20	Hannover	69-0784
Anna 16			
BERKOB, Johann	64	Pinnow	71-0733
Henriette 64			
BERLET, Emma	34	Eisenach	68-0820
Clara 9, Bertha 4			
BERLET, Johannes	15	Niederaula	68-0939
BERLI, Metha	20	Bremen	68-0661
BERLICH, Bertha	27	Barmen	70-1003
BERLIN, Caroline	42	Wenzen	68-0625
August 19			
BERLINER, Julius	50	Neuwied	71-0363
Jacob 30			
BERMANN, Amalie	46	Bremen	69-1212
BERMANN, Hermann	14	Sandfleth	69-0542
BERMANN, Louise	19	Werden	68-0820
Wilhelmine 20			
BERNARD, Bertha	23	Berlin	70-0378
BERNAUER, Cathrine	28	Weilheim	71-0643
BERNAUER, Fanny	27	Chicago	69-0572
BERNAUER, Fanny	40	Zuerich	71-0456
BERNELB, Ludwig	42	Dabernkau	69-0321
Sophie 39, Marie 16, Johann 13, Carl 9, Albert 8, August 9 months			
BERNER, Gottfried	23	Hildrizhausen	69-0672
BERNER, Heinr.	22	Meiningen	71-0479
BERNHARD, Eduard	21	Carlsruhe	68-0982
BERNHARD, Fried.	23	Laufen	69-0560
Julia 7 months			
BERNHARD, Georg	65	Horschbach	70-0308
BERNHARD, Louise	18	Freudenstadt	71-0792
BERNHARDI, Ludwig	39	Berlin	68-1027
BERNHARDT, Hartmann	27	Hermannshoeh	69-1076
BERNHARDT, Joh.	17	Itzeburg	68-0566
BERNING, Carl	38	Gillespie	68-0957
BERNSCH, Gustav	24	Wundschuetz	69-0457
BERNSTIEL, Carl	19	Gera	69-0559
Albert 17, Lina 13, Auguste 10, Aline 7			

NAME	AGE	RESIDENCE	YR-LIST
BEROSCH, Andreas	30	Dernbach	69-0572
BERSCH, Ernst	21	Hanau	71-0736
BERSTELMANN, Carl	47	Rotenburg	70-0272
BERTELSOACKER, Wilh.	18	Leonberg	70-0135
BERTHLEIN, Kilian	20	Gebrand	71-0643
BERTHOLD, Johann	25	Gundhelm	68-0566
BERTRAM, A.E.	30	New York	69-0572
E.G. 4			
BERTRAM, Anna	59	Rheinprovinz	69-1363
Marie 5, Johann 3			
BERTRAM, Christian	57	Welscherau	68-0707
Maria 55			
BERTRAM, Heinrich	42	Nordheim	71-0736
Caroline 30			
BERTRAM, Hermann	32	Braunschweig	68-0661
BERTRAM, Pauline	22	Nikosken	68-0786
BERTSCH, Joh.	20	Wachbach	70-0089
BERTSCH, Josef	22	Moehringen	69-0798
BERTSCH, Maria	20	Dormettingen	69-1076
BERTSCH, Stephan	22	Unterhausen	69-1076
BERTTE, Conr.	14	Ehlen	71-0479
BERTZEL, Cath.	18	Berghausen	71-0681
BESCH, Carl Friedr.	18	Munchinger	69-0576
BESEN, Died.	17	Hannover	70-1066
BESSERER, Friederike	15	Riedlingen	68-0625
BESSERT, Carl	28	Neustettin	68-0707
BESSMER, Jacob	16	Nabern	68-0760
BEST, Elisabeth	37	New York	70-0031
Elisabeth 8, Franz 4			
BEST, Joh.	19	Pfalzdorf	68-0566
BESTER, Wilhelm	27	Olfen	69-0798
BESZE, Cath.	18	Affoldern	69-0592
BETKE, J.	23	Guntergott	71-0393
BETTENHAUSEN, Bernh.	20	Konigswald	70-1142
BETTENHAUSEN, Elisa	21	Koenigswalde	69-1086
BETTHAUS, Therese	22	Coeln	68-0884
BETTMANN, Fritz	17	Nuernberg	68-0786
BETZ, Adelheid	18	Ebnet	69-1309
BETZ, B.	14	Salmuenster	69-0560
BETZ, Barbara	20	Leitschmuehle	70-0223
BETZ, Conrad	18	Oberfranken	69-1004
BETZ, Rosine	18	Tuebingen	69-0162
BETZLER, Bernhard	45	Wittenbach	70-0443
Marianne 43, Emilie 9, Georg 7, Otto 3, Josephine 11 months			
BETZNEARTSCH, Ther.	24	Mies	68-0939
BEUNING, Heinr.	27	Horstmar	68-0610
BEUNNECKE, Friedrich	24	Kurhessen	69-0672
BEUTEL, Heinr. Ferd.	16	Barchfeld	68-1002
BEUTER, Matheus	23	Bietenhausen	69-0457
Susanne 22			
BEUTLER, Julius	23	Gotha	70-0170
BEUTLER, Leopold	16	Gotha	69-0798
BEUTLER, Michael	25	Putzig-Hauland	69-0547
Henriette 18			
BEVENSTEIN, Abrah.	31	Siedenburg	71-0393
Adelh. 28, Clar. 6 m., Isidor 6 m.			
BEVERFERDEN, August	43	Bramsche	68-0770
Heinrich 15			

NAME	AGE	RESIDENCE	YR-LIST
BEVERMANN, Joh. Fr.	50	Schwagstorff	68-0647
Joh. H. 16			
BEVERSTEN, Wilhelm	16	Wehdel	68-0647
BEWIG, Dina	21	Hannover	68-0865
BEYDERBECK, Henry	34	Bremen	71-0456
Friedrike 37, Carl 11 months			
BEYER, Anna	30	Raulenhausen	69-1363
BEYER, Carl	29	Weichersheim	69-1396
BEYER, Carl	16	Apolda	70-0682
Emilie 14			
BEYER, Catharina	19	Gramentin	68-0456
BEYER, Christian	55	Geyer	68-0014
BEYER, Eduard	34	Rauenstein	68-1002
Caroline 23			
BEYER, Friederike	24	Damerow	68-0625
BEYER, Jacob	29	Roppenhausen	71-0479
Anna 23, Justus 5, Cath. 6 months			
BEYER, John	34	Grombach	68-0534
BEYER, Joseph	27	Chrosie	68-0770
Elisabeth 23			
BEYER, Maria	18	Ringsheim	69-0229
BEYERLE, Henny	19	Maubag	68-0957
BEYERSDORF, Charles	27	New York	69-1086
BEYFUSS, male	47	Wien	68-1006
BEYREISS, Louis	14	Cassel	68-0939
BEZDEKOVSKY, Adalbert	47	Boehmen	70-1161
Kathrine 45, Anna 12, Wenzel 19, Adalbert 3,			
BIALLIS, Emilie	19	Dratzig/Boehmen	69-0321
BIANKA, August	24	Thurn	70-0135
Lepinska 26			
BICK, Christine	21	Schoeningen	69-1212
BICK, Clara	18	Hannover	70-0184
BICK, Julius	35	Solingen	69-0429
BICKEL, Amalia	22	Thengen	68-1002
Maria 21, Johann 18			
BICKELMANN, Georg	18	Bueckeburg	71-0643
BICKLER, John	36	Coblenz	68-0760
Sabine 46, Heinrich 8, Catharina 5			
BICKMANN, Christian	15	Westerwanna	71-0429
BICKMEYER, Louise	22	Dettmold	69-0542
BICKNAESE, Caroline	21	Landesbergen	69-0490
BICKNUEFE, Grete	27	Quendorf	68-0566
BIDLEK, Michael	23	Lupkau	69-0457
Johann 25			
BIEBINGER, George	31	Glatz	68-0939
Christiane 26, Charlotte 11 months			
BIEDEBACH, Just.	31	Rumershausen	69-0338
BIEDELMANN, Johann	15	Brinkum-Rettent	69-0672
Gerhard 14			
BIEDENBACH, Louise	36	Carlsruhe	71-0429
BIEDENSTEIN, Cath.	26	Laer	71-0429
Caroline 20			
BIEDERMANN, Caroline	20	Hildburghausen	70-1003
BIEDERMANN, Franz	23	Bugzell	69-1059
BIEDERMANN, Josefine	19	Bachzimmer	71-0429
BIEDERMANN, Marta	18	Bachzimmern	71-0429
BIEGE, Joh.	26	St. Goar	70-0204
Elisabeth 23, Heinrich 8, Friedrich 7, Karl 23			
BIEGELER, Auguste	40	Elbing	71-0492

NAME	AGE	RESIDENCE	YR-LIST
BIEHL, Caroline	19	Heinbeck	71-0643
BIEHL, Friedrich	34	Hirschfeld	68-0419
BIEKEN, Anton	37	Wittmund	69-1011
BIEL, Marga	34	Wollmar	71-0821
Elisabeth 9, Marga. 7			
BIEL, Peter	32	Trier	69-0229
BIELEFELD, Anton	26	Warndorf	68-0760
BIELEFELD, Diedrich	28	Rieste	66-0734
BIELER, Anna	34	Anselfingen	68-0786
BIELER, Engelbert	32	Coeln	68-0760
Elisabeth 34, Margareth 5, Christine 2			
BIELER, X.	29	Osnabrueck	69-0050
BIELING, Albert	20	Oldenburg	69-0292
BIELITZ, Hubert	33	Bergen	69-1319
BIEN, Therese	23	Mies	69-0848
Johanna 2			
BIENDER, Louise	20	Wieklas	71-0479
BIENE, August	24	Detmold	70-0308
BIERAEUGEL, Joh.	32	Weimar	68-0786
Henriette 30, Richard 8, Martin 5, Emilie 3, Selma 11 months			
BIERBAUM, Therese	20	Laer	68-0852
BIERITZ, Georg	32	Arendshausen	68-0625
Caroline 31, Hermine 4, Hermann 3, Georg 10 months			
BIERKUESSE, Charles	25	Muenster	69-1004
BIERMANN, Eduard	28	Gera Bronn	70-0682
BIERMANN, Erich	32	Melle	68-1002
Bertha 30, Betha 30, Oswald 4, Johanna 3			
BIERMANN, Gottfried	70	Magdeburg	68-0610
BIERMANN, Heinrich	15	Gilten	71-0492
BIERMANN, Johann	21	Hummingen	69-0798
BIESE, Aug.	24	Detmold	70-0308
BIESINGER, Peter	22	Reichenbach	69-0015
BIESTER, Elise	30	Duesseldorf	71-0226
Oswald 11 months			
BIETHMANN, Anna	15	Osterndorf	68-1027
BIETON, Helene	22	Westernohe	68-0760
BIGALKE, Johann	40	Bromberg	68-0625
Anna 36, Caroline 9, Bertha 6, Julius 9 months			
BIHLER, Magd.	22	Unterkieneck	68-0884
BIHR, Vitus	26	Holzleiten	69-0229
BIKEL, Georg Wilhelm	22	Oberschonau	68-0661
Sawina Barb. 24			
BIKLI, Reinhard	27	Wangen	69-0208
BILANG, Christian	31	Untendorf	68-0661
Rudolph 19			
BILANSKA, Marie	34	Bianhawa	71-0479
Cath. 9, Josef 7, Vinzent 6			
BILDHAEUSER, Marg.	41	Laubach	68-0760
BILECKY, Hyronimus	16	Mrasteczko	71-0429
BILGERI, Johannes	36	Krumbach	69-0229
BILGERS, Peter	33	Rievensberg	71-0393
Magdalene 24			
BILHARZ, Franz	19	Kenzingen	68-1027
BILLE, Ferd.	39	Mannheim	70-1066
BILLHARDT, Friedrich	28	Langensalza	68-0786
BILLHORN, Jos.	31	Ottweiler	68-0753
Sophie 2, Georg 7			

NAME	AGE	RESIDENCE	YR-LIST
BILSE, Adolph	18	Barmen	68-0939
BINDER, Jacob	18	Goeppingen	69-1319
BINDER, Johann	28	Imnau	69-0457
BINDER, Johann	32	Truchtelfingen	68-0566
BINDER, Joseph	30	Schaffera	69-0542
BINDFUSS, Barbara	22	Ingenheim	70-0728
BINGER, Wilhelm	27	Dietz	69-0229
BINNER, Charlotte	48	Egichenberg	68-0456
Philipp 36			
BINNEWIES, Aug.	26	Greene	68-0534
BINSCH, Carl	24	Pollnow	69-1319
BINWEILER, Catharine	16	Dallau/Dallan	69-1309
BINZ, Pauline	27	Voerenbach	68-0707
BIRBAUM, Bernh.	25	Ochtrup	68-0610
BIRKENFELD, Carl	24	Elbersfeld	69-0798
BIRKENFELD, Therese	30	Nieheim	71-0643
Johanne 6, Auguste 4			
BIRKENHAUER, Heinrich	17	Alzeg	69-0672
BIRKHEIM, Joh.	27	Ottersheim	71-0300
BIRKHOLZ, Richard	17	Bahn	68-0566
Henriette 9			
BIRKNER, Gustav	20	Aaran	71-0733
BIRN, William	18	Ulrichstein	68-0957
BIRNBAUM, Abraham	15	Crakau	68-0647
BIRR, August	35	Wollin	69-0672
BISCHER, Doris	33	Bremerhaven	70-1142
BISCHER, Georg	38	Schlittis	68-0760
BISCHOF, Jacob	50	Rudolstadt	69-0547
Anna 40, Jacob 16, Anna 13, Emilie 5, Theodor 9 months			
BISCHOFF, Anna	21	Geger-Geyer	70-0135
Baby 6 months			
BISCHOFF, Ferdinand	42	Politz/Tolitz	70-0523
BISCHOFF, Heinr.	20	Darmstadt	69-1004
BISCHOFF, Johann	14	Brinkum	68-0661
BISCHWALL, Anna	21	Gauelgisheim	70-1161
BISSELBERG, Heinrich	35	Steinhude	68-0534
Sophie 33, Doretta 8, Heinrich 5, Sophia 3, baby-daughter 6 months			
BISSKA, Matthilde	21	Neuzelle	71-0733
BISTAU, Carl	28	Stajonitz	71-0429
BITSCH, Elisabeth	21	Sassbach	71-0226
BITTER, Heinrich	27	Altenstedt	69-0229
BITTNER, Heinrich	25	Hessen	69-1086
BITZ, Conrad	21	Weisenheim	71-0712
Jacob 51			
BITZ, Friedrich	25	Steinbach	69-0208
BITZER, Johanne	28	Darmstadt	68-0456
BLACKWEDEI, Carl	16	Broshdorf	69-1059
BLAICH, Johannes	22	Oberfranken	68-0852
BLAICHER, Cath.	16	Burladingen	69-1086
BLANCKEN, Dan.	18	Glinstedt	69-0560
BLANDERNA, Rebecca	20	Scharmbeck	71-0521
BLANE, Joseph	30	Bruchsal	70-0728
Anton 25			
BLANK, Arend	14	Tiekelwarf	71-0456
BLANK, Barbara	19	Bischofsheim	71-0712
BLANK, Friedr.	31	Kunz	68-0566

NAME	AGE	RESIDENCE	YR-LIST
BLANKE, Bernhard	26	Brochterbeck	69-0429
BLANKE, Heinrich	16	Wiste	69-1076
BLANKEN, Marie	20	Hannover	69-1004
BLANKENBACH, Louise	19	Guetersloh	68-0939
Wilhelm 22			
BLANKENBERGER, Franz	26	Ebersheim	69-0672
BLANKENBURG, Louise	24	Greiz	69-0968
Richard 5, Alfred 3			
BLANKENHORN, Eva	22	Dettingen	68-0760
BLANKENHORN, Joh.	19	Dedingen	71-0521
BLANSTOCK, Rud.	28	Osnabrueck	69-0050
BLAS, Anna	26	Rothelmeyer	71-0821
BLASCHA, Barbara	18	Boehmen	69-0321
BLASE, Geo.	45	Schottinghausen	70-0308
Clara 68, Elisabeth 24, Charlotte 19, Franz 9, Heiner 7			
BLASE, Johanna	50	Gandelsheim	69-0292
Jacob 25, Catharine 14, Carl 10, Louise 9			
BLASE, John	27	Offelten	69-1011
Anna 27, Fred. 47, Anna 9 months			
BLASINGER, Jean	26	Mainz	69-0542
BLASS, Eduard	36	Buerten	68-0770
Elisabeth 28			
BLASS, Friedrich	26	Langensalza	68-0786
Marie 28			
BLASTER, Adam	28	Walzhausen	71-0736
BLAUDING, F. L.	30	Providence	69-1076
BLAUFENS, Cath.	41	Nassenerfurth	71-0581
Cath. 15, Marie 6, Marie Elise 5			
BLAUM, Peter Jos.	21	Darmstadt	69-0583
BLAUTH, Heinrich	19	Lambrecht	69-1212
BLAZEK, Franz	27	Schirakowitz	70-0329
BLAZIL, Joseph	36	Zahori	68-0770
Anna 32, Johann 11, Rosalia 10, Anton 8, Wojteck 3 months(died on ship)			
BLECHEN, Chr. Friedr.	16	Lesum	71-0226
BLECKWEDEL, Carl	16	Broshdorf	69-1059
BLEI, Jacob	38	Unterhausen	69-1076
BLEICHER, Johanne	21	Oestreich	70-0728
BLEICHERODE, A. M.	50	Berlin	68-0647
Adeline 46, Augustina 15, Julia 8, Therese 7, Jenny 5			
BLEIER, Augusta	40	Pilsen	68-0982
BLEIER, Caroline	21	Kalup	71-0479
BLEIER, Sigmund	15	Dohlau	68-0760
BLEIN, Marin	21	Grossengrim	69-0771
BLENDERMANN, Georg	25	Oldenburg	70-0308
BLENDERMANN, Johann	34	New Orleans	69-0429
Johanne 9			
BLENDSTATLER, Johann	27	Schaffhausen	71-0643
BLENK, Friederike	20	Niederstochstad	68-0647
BLESS, Franz	28	Goetzingen	68-0314
BLESSING, Catharina	19	Wangen	71-0492
BLESSING, Theo.	30	Weil	71-0681
Marie 29, Pauline 7, Emma 6			
BLEY, Barbara	15	Flonheim	71-0643
BLEYMUELLER, Steph.	22	Meiningen	68-0753
BLIM, Walburga	31	Elberfeld	69-1011
BLOCH, Manuel	31	Hertzviller	71-0581

NAME	AGE	RESIDENCE	YR-LIST
BLOCH, Salomon	16	Hochheim	71-0581
BLOCHBERGER, Pauline	23	Graefendorf	71-0643
August 28			
BLOCK, Abraham	24	Mutterholz	71-0643
BLOCK, Carl	24	Nakel	69-0542
Ernestin 24			
BLOCK, Catharina	18	Guetersloh	68-0661
BLOCK, Clara	20	Leer	68-0982
BLOCK, Clara	24	Norden	68-1027
Adelheid 22			
BLOCK, Edw.	32	Bremen	69-0050
BLOCK, Ferd.	19	Ulm	68-1002
BLOCK, Jann	16	Ackelsberg	69-0208
BLOCK, Johann	16	Braunschweig	71-0521
BLOCK, Max	19	Floss	70-1003
BLOCK, Rachel	20	Dieppigheim	71-0581
BLOCK, Theodor	18	Boehmen	69-1396
BLOECHER, John	27	Biedenbach	68-0760
BLOECHLE, Christine	21	Untermusbach	71-0226
BLOESE, Christian	40	Zeven	68-0625
Henriette 48, Heinrich 6, Marie 6 months			
BLOESER, Juliane	20	Sichenhausen	70-1035
BLOHM, Hein.	18	Bruchweiler	71-0733
BLOHME, Doris	24	Intschede	68-0707
BLOME, Johann	25	Scharme	69-0229
BLOME, Louis	17	Essen	69-0208
BLOME, Wilhelm	18	Hannover	69-0592
BLOMEYER, Charlotte	30	Bremen	69-0429
BLOTENBERG, Louise	18	Lenzinghausen	68-0939
BLUCH, Auguste	17	Vacha	69-0182
BLUECHER, Ferd.	23	Salzgitter	71-0815
Auguste 14			
BLUEMKE, Andreas	41	Michorwice	69-0542
Rosine 36, August 7, Pauline 6 months			
BLUM, Adam	52	Geindheim	69-0229
Barbara 22, Peter 16			
BLUM, And.	16	Ahlenbach	71-0393
BLUM, Caroline	26	Guntersleben	70-0148
BLUM, Catharine	18	Herndsbach	69-1004
BLUM, Cathrine	16	Grossenmoor	69-1059
BLUM, Franz	26	St. Catharinen	68-0610
BLUM, Georg	17	Gersheim	69-0067
BLUM, Simon	30	Hochfelden	71-0581
BLUM, Walburga	31	Elberfeld	69-1011
BLUME, Cath.	59	Duerkheim	71-1046
John 16			
BLUME, Jacob	26	Hille	69-1076
Friederike 26, Carl 9 months			
BLUMENAUER, Marie	30	Zweibruecken	71-0821
BLUMENFELD, Fanny	21	Bueckingen	71-0643
BLUMENSTEIN, Minna	22	Hongenhausen	68-1006
BLUMENSTEIN, Peter	24	Darmstadt	70-0384
Catharine 18, Eva 21			
BLUMENTHAL, Jacob	18	Berkburg	70-0184
BLUMENTHAL, Schei	23	Fordan	69-0229
BLUMLEIN, Henriette	20	Hammelburg	68-0625
BLUST, Anna	22	Deisslingen	68-0647
BLUTBACHER, Marie	22	Bodelshausen	71-0393

NAME	AGE	RESIDENCE	YR-LIST
BOAS, Minna	29	Berlin	69-0490
Pauline 8, Franz 4			
BOAS, Theodor	18	Paderborn	68-1002
BOCH, Leo	25	Altsimonswalde	68-0786
BOCHASKA, Maria	25	Liebentig	66-0576
BOCHMANN, Babette	19	Leoville	70-1023
BOCK, Adam	64	Heilmes	69-0572
Elisabeth 63			
BOCK, Amalia	30	Muenchen	70-0378
Leo 9, Emilie 8, Christilde 7, Theresia 6			
BOCK, Carl	23	Rattay	69-0162
BOCK, Catharine	17	Otterndorf	69-0229
BOCK, Charles	40	Boeckenheim	70-0272
Therese 28			
BOCK, Eva	9	Bienack	70-0031
BOCK, Ferdinand	16	Kehrzell	69-0592
Juliane 18			
BOCK, Friedrich	17	Halle	69-0672
BOCK, Friedrike	27	Goettingen	70-0728
Gustav 5			
BOCK, Ignatz	24	Patleschtin	71-0479
Marie 18			
BOCK, John	23	Nordstetten	71-0456
Catharine 25, Regine 21			
BOCK, Lev.	40	Munich	69-1421
BOCK, Philipp	18	Waldmoemingen	69-0672
BOCK, Rosalie	20	Boehmen	70-0728
BOCK, Theodor	17	Gruenstadt	70-0452
BOCK, Wilhelm	23	Romerskirchen	68-0707
Jacob 20			
BOCKELMANN, Fritz	32	Visselhoevede	69-0208
BOCKER, Catharina	14	Langenschwarz	70-0378
BOCKER, Johann	22	Haubern	69-0798
BOCKER, Johann	42	Ostrau	68-1027
BOCKERLE, Johanne	19	Einseltham	69-0968
BOCKERMANN, Gottfried	17	Hueffen	71-0821
BOCKHOFF, Gesine	19	Ostfriesland	69-1059
BOCKINS, Philipp	25	Offenheim	69-0100
BOCKMANN, Ernst	25	Hannover	70-0378
BODE, Dina	17	Adersheim	69-0968
BODE, Elisabeth	15	Breitenbach	69-0229
BODE, Ernst	38	Herborn	68-0982
Pauline 18			
BODE, Friedrich	52	Detmold	69-0572
Franciska 53, Charlotte 14, Franz 10, Wilhelmine 10			
BODE, Georg	44	Aerzen	71-0492
Wilhelm 16, Pauline 19			
BODE, Heinr.	18	Wenzen	68-0610
BODE, Heinr.	23	Salzgitter	71-0684
BODE, Henry	15	Nienburg	69-0572
BODE, Henry	16	Stotel	71-0456
BODE, Hermann	17	Hoxter	70-0728
BODE, Ida	25	Friedland	71-0521
BODE, Lina	40	Lingen	69-1212
Charlotte 14			
BODE, Met.	29	Roennebeck	68-0566
Fritz 18			
BODE, Ottilie	20	Andreasberg	69-1086

NAME	AGE	RESIDENCE	YR-LIST
BODE, Wilhelmine	28	Auenstein	70-0308
Caroline 29			
BODE, Willy	30	Bruchhausen	71-0456
BODEKOR, Chr.	48	Heisshagen	69-0338
BODENMUELLER, male	25	Neudorf	68-1298
BODENSCHNEIDER, Joh.	19	Dalbrael	69-0542
BODENSTEIN, Jacob	16	Nesselroeden	68-0770
BODES, Heinr.	18	Bueckeburg	71-0479
BOEBBING, Louise	21	Barmen	69-1212
Laura 18			
BOECHLER, Johanne	18	Engenhausen	71-0393
BOECKEL, Magd.	26	Weisenheim	68-1002
BOECKELMANN, Bernhd.	25	Bersenbrueck	68-1002
BOECKER, Heinrich	22	Schnithen	68-0907
BOECKHORST, Carl	26	Mecklenburg	69-0067
Johann 18			
BOECKLING, Friedrich	35	Binde	70-0031
Dorothea 35, Friedrike 4, Dorothea 7, Friedrich 3, Wilhelm 1			
BOECKMANN, Heinrich	17	Treckenhorst	69-0429
BOEDDEKER, Gust.	60	Cincinatti	70-100
BOEDDEKER, Gust.	33	Hoerde	70-100
BOEDEKER, Aje	20	Wybelsum	69-0208
BOEDEKER, Augusta	21	Bramsche	68-0852
BOEDEKER, Christian	16	Bremen	69-0067
BOEFER, Henry	21	Bremen	70-0031
BOEGER, Fr. Ernst	27	Hannover	69-0572
BOEGER, Joh.	56	Schaumburg	71-0479
BOEGER, Sophie	22	Niederasphe	71-0821
BOEHLAND, Johann	14	Koenigsberg	69-0559
BOEHLER, Agathe	24	Vorarlberg	69-0560
BOEHLING, Friedrich	42	Schwalingen	68-0820
Catharina 45, Friedrich 17, Heinrich 9, Sophie 13, Wilhelm 7			
BOEHM, August	26	Bruchstein	71-0712
BOEHM, Friedr.	25	Neuenstein	69-1363
Rosa 19			
BOEHM, Frietz	25	Unterfranken	69-0321
BOEHM, Leo	28	Gersfeld	69-1363
BOEHM, Margareth	70	S. Meiningen	70-1003
BOEHME, August	22	Chemnitz	69-0848
BOEHME, Rudolph	23	Berlin	69-0079
BOEHMER, Ch.	26	Bremen	71-1046
BOEHMER, Johanna	40	Wetzlar	68-0625
Lina 14			
BOEHMLER, Christ.	28	Flacht	71-0581
BOEHNE, Juliane	21	Grunfier/Prussi	69-0547
BOEHRINGER, Friedrich	28	Waiblingen	69-0672
BOEHRINGER, Georg	16	Buhlbach	71-0582
BOEHRINGER, Jacob	28	Laubach	68-1002
BOEHRINGER, Wilhelm	22	Waiblingen	69-0015
BOEKER, Gustav	24	Remscheid	68-1027
BOELING, Joh.	26	Echternach	69-1363
BOELKE, Carl	30	Schoenhagen	68-0625
BOELLING, Louise	21	Barmen	69-1212
Laura 18			
BOELLING, Lucas	16	Holdorf	68-1002
BOELSTER, Georg	57	Boehmenkirch	71-0479
Barb. 56			

NAME	AGE	RESIDENCE	YR-LIST
BOEMING, Kunig.	29	Gerach	70-0178
Elise 6, Georg 2, Friedr. 18 months, Franz 4 months			
BOENHOF, Anna Cath.	19	Posthausen	68-0770
BOENIG, Mary	21	Oberndorf	68-0957
BOENING, Aug.	18	Bueckeburg	71-0479
BOENING, Emma	26	Henkenhagen	71-0456
BOENING, Peter	39	Hollenbach	69-0592
Anna 34, Adam 9, Anna 8, Leonhard 5			
BOENING, Soph.	30	Hunfeld	70-1066
BOENKEN, Carl	27	Stockhausen	68-0566
Friedrich 24			
BOENNER, Barbara	22	Rotorf	71-0643
BOENNING, Elisabeth	55	Canum	69-0457
Helene 14, Siemon 12			
BOENZELMANN, Ludwig	28	Clueversborstel	69-0560
BOERKEL, Jacob	60	Alzey	69-0457
Elisabeth 52, Marie 14, Catharine 9			
BOERKENHAGEN, Carl	48	Owiatzeck	69-0547
Juliane 31, Caroline 28, Auguste 7, Adolph 5, Gustav 3, Hermann 3 months			
BOERMANN, Antoinette	26	Handorf	68-1006
BOERNER, Dorothea	32	Frankfurt	69-1309
BOERNER, Gesine	18	Hatten	68-0884
BOERNSTEIN, Saul	10	Herstelle	68-0939
BOERTZEL, Friedr.	20	Obrigheim	71-0521
BOES, Gesche	16	Lintig	71-0581
BOES, Heinrich	26	Saalmuenster	68-0786
BOES, Joh.	19	Thalsimmen	71-0581
BOESCH, Anna	30	Hannover	68-0456
BOESCH, Catharine	40	Riedlingen	70-0443
BOESCH, Ernst	28	Anderten	69-0321
BOESCHEN, Claus	26	Wormdorf	69-0672
BOESCHEN, Heinrich	19	Ringstedt	71-0429
BOESCHEN, M.	9	Bremerhaven	70-1142
BOESE, Anna	24	Staffhorst	69-0583
BOESE, Friederike	8	Bremen	68-0534
BOESE, H.	40	Mickelsen	69-0560
Sophia 35, Heinz 6, John 4, Baby 11 months			
BOESE, Hermann	26	Westerburg	69-1004
BOESE, Joh.	34	Greffen	68-314
BOESE, Joh. Diedr.	16	Eckstoever	68-0770
BOESE, Joh. Hr.	27	Stellenfelde	68-0610
BOESE, Justus	15	Wietzen	71-0736
BOESING, Andreas	30	Gerach	69-0771
BOESSELMANN, Diedrich	38	Meckelstedt	69-0560
BOESSIG, Carl	48	Alfeld	69-1086
BOETJER, Meta	26	Bormreid	68-0534
Adelheid 21, Catharine 23			
BOETTCHER, Adolf	41	Limbach	69-0592
BOETTCHER, Frdr.	26	Friedrichshorst	68-0610
Caroline 20			
BOETTCHER, Friedrich	19	Drena	69-0547
BOETTCHER, Friedrich	36	Limbach	68-0707
BOETTCHER, Johanna	43	Calbe	68-0314
Carl 20, Caroline 17, Wilhelm 15			
BOETTCHER, Wilhelm		Seifersbach	69-0771
BOETTGER, Minna	27	Erfurt	68-1002

NAME	AGE	RESIDENCE	YR-LIST
Louise 3, Friedke. 10 months			
BOETTINGER, Carl	18	Darmstadt	68-0456
BOETTJER, Adolf	33	Stettin	69-0182
Caroline 30, Alwin 12, Hermine 3			
BOETTJER, Claus	19	Sudweyhe	68-0610
BOETTJER, Gesine	18	Meyenburg	71-0429
BOETTJER, Herm.	16	Osterholz	69-1212
BOETTLER, Lotte	36	Rothenburg	71-0456
Anna 8, Sophia 7			
BOGEMANN, Johann	19	Ehln	68-0939
BOHDE, Friedrich	16	Sievern	71-0492
BOHL, Johanna	26	Dettum	68-0566
Marie 4, Carl 11 months			
BOHLE, Marie	22	Wiensdorf	68-0456
BOHLEN, Anne	18	Bollen	69-1086
BOHLEN, John.	33	Hannover	70-0308
BOHLENDER, Nicolaus	26	Schluechtern	69-0592
BOHLING, Conrad	19	Bullstedt	68-0982
BOHLKEN, G. H.	21	Reepsholt	70-0308
BOHLMANN, Marg.	18	Moorsum	69-1309
BOHMANN, Anna	20	Friedrichsthal	70-1035
Franziska 14			
BOHMER, Gustav	27	Lowissa/Boehmen	69-0576
BOHN, Andreas	42	Thalau	69-0848
BOHNACK, Anna	27	Hannover	69-1212
BOHNE, Heinrich	21	Metze	68-0647
Marie 19			
BOHNE, Johanne	29	Bremen	70-1055
Anna 7			
BOHNE, Metha	28	Bremen	70-1003
Dora 6, Friedrich 4, Bab. 6 months			
BOHNENBERGER, John	30	Wuterrerchenbac	70-1035
Martin 19			
BOHNET, David	21	Hochdorf	70-1003
BOHNKE, Marie	18	Cekzin	71-0479
BOHR, Georg	21	Trier	68-1027
BOHR, Wilhelm	27	Gotha	68-0939
BOHREL, Carl	58	Auma	71-0479
Ernestine 57			
BOHRENBURG, Diedrich	18	Zeven	68-0625
BOKELMANN, Charlotte	20	Hannover	69-0457
BOKELOH, Theodore	21	Hannover	70-0329
BOLD, Chr.	18	Muntershausen	68-0820
BOLDT, Herm.	24	Mellwin	71-0521
BOLECK, Anna	21	Skrekow	68-0770
BOLEKE, Eduard	18	Bremervoerde	71-0456
BOLENDER, Nic.	75	Hanau	71-0521
Friedr. 36			
BOLGE, Heinr.	29	Vilber	69-0292
Minna 24			
BOLL, Aug.	25	Merzhausen	68-0566
Victor 18			
BOLL, Georg	29	Ay	70-0184
Xaver 23			
BOLL, Louise	19	Ay	70-0329
BOLL, Otto	15	Lorsch	71-0167
BOLL, Rosina	20	Neuenhaus	68-0957
BOLLENBACH, Friedrich	14	Duschroth	68-1027
BOLLER, Ed.	18	Hohenthengen	68-0820

NAME	AGE	RESIDENCE	YR-LIST
BOLLING, Peter	52	Barmen	71-0521
Wilhelmine 52, Fritz 18, Maria 13, Ida 11			
BOLLINGER, Maria	20	Haichelheim	68-0852
BOLLMANN, Herm.	17	Wietzen	71-0736
BOLLMEYER, Friedrich	18	Isenstaedt	68-0907
BOLLMEYER, Hermann	19	Schwelentrap	69-1309
BOLLRATH, Heinrich	26	Hannover	70-0452
BOLT, Ernst	43	Doelen	71-0521
BOLTE, Adelh.	21	Wedelhorn	69-0771
BOLTE, Christ.	26	Lichtenfeld	69-0583
BOLTE, Friedrich	50	Neustadt	69-0429
Marie 49, Sophie 22, Friedrich 15, Elizabeth 13, Heinrich 9, Christian 6			
BOLTE, Louise	19	Tuschendorf	68-0907
BOLTE, Louise	19	Tuschendorf	68-0907
BOLTER, Johann	68	Heselsbronn	68-0852
Catharine 47, Louise 22, Friederike 16, Louise 1			
BOLTMER, Julie	24	Omiezek	71-0479
BOLTS, Friedrich	25	Scharrel	68-0939
Margaretha 26, Catharina 4, Johann 3, Anna 9 months			
BOLZ, Oscar	21	Stuttgart	68-0610
BOLZ, Wilh.	23	Ammendorf	68-0957
BOMANN, John	18	Neumark	68-0957
BOMGARDEN, Gretje G.	19	Uttum	71-0226
BOMMEL, Henriette	32	Frankfurt	69-0560
Rudolph 8			
BOMMURT,Marie	26	Sontheim	71-0479
David 8, Magd. 6			
BON, J. S.	44	Paris	69-1212
Anna 42, H. S. 7,			
BONCH, Johann	26	Ceiszmirochow	69-0547
Marianne 24, Stanislawa 6 months			
BONIN, Friedrich	41	Salesch	68-0786
Caroline 36			
BONING, Carl	40	Oldenburg	71-0643
Helene 38, Helene 9, Johanne 8, Johanne 11 months			
BONISCH, Johann	24	Zose	68-0770
BONITZ, Carl	28	Greiz	69-0968
BONNE, Wilhelm	19	Reda	69-0208
BONNEMAUER, Jette	16	Bischberg	68-0852
BONNEMEYER, August	27	Detmold	69-0457
BONTZ, Elise	36	Quirnheim	71-0789
Philippine 43			
BONTZ, male	44	Clarence	71-0789
Caroline 30, Philipp 11 months			
BOOMS, Caroline	27	Rhede	70-0355
BOOS, Christ.	23	Peine	68-0314
BOOS, Heinrich	16	Dorum	71-0521
BOOSE, Adolf	26	Volmarstein	69-0229
BOPP, Elise	31	Landau	69-1309
BOPP, Heinrich	26	Landau	68-0534
BOPP, Therese	21	Laibach	71-0521
BOPPIN, Char.	21	Wiesenfeldt	69-0490
BOPPIN, Jacob	18	Wiesenfeld	69-0490
BORCHARD, Friedrich	27	Nesselroden	69-0229
BORCHERS, Claus	15	Hassel	68-0625
BORCHERS, Friedrich	21	Leer	68-0419

NAME	AGE	RESIDENCE	YR-LIST
BORCHMANN, Aug.	31	Geiglitz	69-0542
Carl 15, Caroline 30, Georg 9 months			
BORCKERT, Mary	22	Loewenbruecken	69-1011
Fred 3, Mary 11 months			
BORENBERGER, J.	24	Friederichsburg	70-0728
BORENNENTHER, Joh.	24	Obernsees	70-0135
BORG, Friedrich	51	Alfeld	69-0229
BORGER, Anna	19	Trottenheim	68-0014
BORGERDING, Joh.	25	Oldenburg	70-1023
BORGMAN, Elisa	25	Brengeldanz	69-1212
BORGMANN, J.	40	Oldenburg	71-1046
female 42			
BORGMANN, Sophie	16	Bremervoerde	71-0429
BORGMEYER, Heinr.	59	Laer	69-1086
BORK, Wilh.	30	Hurbach	71-0821
BORKE, Christian	17	Braunschweig	71-0643
BORKE, Ernst	18	Hannover	69-0798
Albertine 15			
BORMANN, Anna	18	Wittlage	71-1046
BORMANN, August	16	Alsum	69-1059
BORMANN, Conrad	44	Hoya	68-0820
Marie 16, Doris 17			
BORMANN, Fritz	39	New York	70-1003
BORMANN, Joh.	25	Alsum	68-0786
BORMANN, Lisette	20	Buttel	69-1086
BORMANN, Minna	21	Horsum	70-1003
BORMGARTEN, Jans	23	Westerhausen	69-0576
BORN, Eugen	19	Wuerzburg	71-0456
BORN, Henry	26	Rennertshausen	68-0760
BORN, Louise	48	Muehlhausen	69-1059
BORNEFELD, Robert	20	Duesseldorf	70-0378
BORNEMANN, August	32	Wethen	69-0429
Heinrich 21			
BORNEMANN, Carl	41	Allstedt	68-0786
Wilhelmine 40, Carl 15			
BORNEMANN, Catharina	26	Hohewart	68-0707
BORNEMANN, Catharine	43	Bueckeburg	68-0456
BORNEMANN, Fr.	17	Rinteln	71-1046
BORNEMANN, Minna	15	Ilfeld	68-0982
BORNGRAESSER, Marie	55	Menis	69-0079
BORNHEIM, Marie	60	Wiesbaden	71-0456
BORNSCHEID, Louise	20	Birghausen	70-0728
BORNTRAEGER, Georg	46	Darmstadt	70-0378
BORRIES, J.	33	Hannover	71-0393
BORST, August	30	Muehldorf	68-0770
BORTFELD, Marie	22	Zeserlingen	70-0355
BOSCH, Friederike	20	Colima	70-0452
BOSCH, Meta	22	Hannover	69-1086
Meta 9 months			
BOSCHEN, Carl	27	Naumburg	68-0982
BOSCHEN, Christian	26	Bremen	68-0770
BOSCHEN, Marga.	24	Otterstedt	68-0982
BOSCHERT, K.	17	Oensbach	71-0226
BOSINGER, Martha	41	Muenchen	71-0792
BOSKOWITZ, Moritz	17	Floss	70-1003
BOSS, Aug.	17	Kirdorf	71-0821
BOSSE, Carl	31	Heerte	69-0162
BOSSELMANN, Heinrich	50	Mursum	68-0770
Sophia 26, Claus 15, Catharina 7, Hinrich 1			
BOSSENT, Paul	21	Dusslingen	69-0229
BOSSERT, Wilhelmine	28	Cannstadt	68-0852
BOSSO, Fred.	25	New York	69-1421
BOTE, Aug	49	Laurenhagen	71-0479
BOTH, Hermine	23	Goettingen	69-0572
BOTHE, Henry	18	Osterwiek	69-0338
BOTT, Alexander	18	Kaemmerzell	68-1002
BOTT, Catharine	31	Unterwaldbehrun	71-0456
Julie 6, Leo 2			
BOTTE, Louise	17	Hannover	69-1011
BOTTLER, Georg	32	Schillingsfuers	68-0786
BOURGIGNON, Hel.	30	Hirzenstain	69-0490
BOXHORN, Carl	14	Fischerdorf	68-0456
BOYER, Johann	15	Bremen	71-0429
BRAATZ, William	25	Nimischhof	68-0957
BRABANT, Cathrine	18	Ludingwerth	69-1059
BRACH, Henriette	27	Zalkenhagen	69-0292
BRACHER, Elise	30	Meinigsheim	71-0479
BRACK, Albert	40	Bitow	69-0547
Albertine 33, Otto 6, Martha 4, Hermann 10 months			
BRACK, Cath.	21	Darmstadt	70-1142
BRACKE, Franz	37	Bensen	68-1002
BRACKMANN, Fred.	54	Hannover	70-0170
Caroline 51, Charles 23, August 14, John 9			
BRADA, Martin	20	Radowitz	69-0050
BRADAC, Johann	40	Deditz	70-0329
Katharina 44, Wenzel 7			
BRADER, Carl	19	Neuzerecka	68-0770
BRAEMLICH, Marie	16	Weida	68-0456
BRAEUNINGER, Christine	23	Neuenstein	71-0492
BRAEUNLICH, Eduard	18	Waltersdorf	71-0479
BRAEUNLING, H.	22	Glotzdorf	69-0560
BRAEUTIGAM, Christian	19	Obernsees	70-0135
BRAEUTIGAM, Elias	28	Eisfeld	69-0923
Maria 25, Ernst 9, Catharine 7, Johannes 4			
BRAEUTIGAM, Jette	19	Tann	71-0479
BRAEUTIGAM, Johs.	15	Hadamar	68-1002
BRAEUTIGAM, Joseph	24	Wiesentheid	69-1309
BRAHM, Charles	42	New York	69-1396
BRAHM, Elisabeth	22	Villmar	71-0226
BRAHM, Johs. B.	18	Sevelten	68-1006
BRAKFELD, Lisette	18	Minden	68-0786
BRAMBERGER, Adolph	30	Coeln	69-0321
Henriette 33, Ernst 7, Hugo 3, B.Paula 5, Rudolph 11 months			
BRAMLAGE, Julie	19	Oldenburg	69-0798
BRAMMER, Carsten	26	Manhorn	68-0760
BRAMSTEDT, Auguste	26	Buecken	71-0456
BRAND, Adam	63	Ersrode	68-0534
Anna 60, Catharine 14			
BRAND, Albertine	21	Lischkowo	71-0456
BRAND, Aug.	24	Lippe Detmold	70-0355
BRAND, Carl	28	Cantzan	71-0479
Friederike 29, Wilhelmine 3, Auguste 4 months			
BRAND, Catharina	18	Orb	69-1309

NAME	AGE	RESIDENCE	YR-LIST
BRAND, Elisabeth	30	Aulenbach	69-0100
BRAND, Friederike	23	Spork	68-0907
BRAND, Friedrich	21	Biebelnheim	69-0229
BRAND, Georg	22	Herzogenrach	69-0229
BRAND, Heinrich	21	Obrel	68-1027
BRAND, Hugo	23	Waldeck	69-1059
BRAND, Sophie	16	Walsrode	69-1086
BRANDAU, Adam	17	Solz	70-0355
BRANDAU, Anna	22	Armershausen	68-0625
BRANDAU, Louis	17	Herzberg	68-0534
BRANDENBURGER, Jos.	25	Gailingen	71-0521
BRANDENHUZER, Aug.	39	Nassau	70-0308
Wilhelmine 35, Emma 9, Bertha 7, Siegfried 4, Clemens 9 months			
BRANDES, August	37	Braunschweig	70-0329
Henriette 28, Caroline 7, Henriette 5, Minna 9 months			
BRANDES, Auguste	18	Schwarzbg.Sonde	70-1023
BRANDES, Dorothea	21	Dorum	71-0521
Heinrich 16			
BRANDES, H.	17	Braunschweig	69-0560
BRANDES, Heinrich	68	Bremke	68-0566
BRANDES, Johanna	18	Hannover	70-1003
BRANDES, Sophie	39	Bremen	71-0429
Wilhelmine 9			
BRANDES, Wilhelm	17	Erichhagen	68-0939
Diedrich 19			
BRANDHORST, Hermann	24	Hannover	69-0798
Catharina 18			
BRANDHORST, Hermann	55	Minden	68-0939
Christine 53			
BRANDLE, Jacob	48	Bietigheim	68-0661
Johanna 43, Maria 17, Wilhelm 13			
BRANDNER, Friedr.	29	Genzenhausen	68-0647
BRANDT, Adelheid	57	Okel	71-0521
Heinrich 16			
BRANDT, Anna	29	Moorberg	68-0982
BRANDT, Anna	15	Brinkum	71-0521
BRANDT, Carl	25	Muenster	70-0052
BRANDT, Carl	23	Magdeburg	68-0707
Dora 18			
BRANDT, Cath.	24	Birkenried	68-0314
BRANDT, Diederich	14	Weyhe	68-0760
BRANDT, Ernst	30	Schaumburg	68-0852
Wilhelmine 29, Lina 4, Heinrich 1			
BRANDT, Friedrich	35	Walsrode	69-0490
BRANDT, Friedrich	29	Brakelsiek	68-0314
Dorothea 26			
BRANDT, Heinrich	43	Odenheim	69-0572
Babette 42, Bertha 16, Hannchen 15, Henriette 13, Jacob 8, Ernestine 2			
BRANDT, Ilse	19	Langhausen	71-0479
BRANDT, Jac.	21	Hannover	70-0443
BRANDT, Joh.	27	Tennever	69-1004
BRANDT, Johann Fr.	39	Rudolstadt	68-0760
Augusta 33, Sophia 8, Hermine 6, Bertha 4, Theresea 9 months			
BRANDT, Louise	28	Walsrode	70-0508
Mary 6, John 8			
BRANDT, Marg.	29	Eissel	68-0610

NAME	AGE	RESIDENCE	YR-LIST
BRANDT, Wilhelm	13	Hamburg	69-0208
BRANNER, Christine	35	Weisshosen	69-0798
BRASS, Julius	25	Coeln	68-0865
BRASS, Mart.	21	Wiesville	70-0569
BRASSLER, Marga.	20	Duttweiler	71-0429
BRASTER, Johann	26	Bissingen	68-0820
BRATSCH, Andreas	13	Rattelsdorf	69-0321
BRAU, Louise	23	Schwanewede	69-1363
BRAUER, Wilhelm	16	Bremen	71-0736
BRAUMERTH, Johanna	59	Carlsruhe	68-0707
Sophia 25			
BRAUN, Adolph	26	Nierenstein	70-0204
BRAUN, Anna	59	Hahnheim	71-0167
Appollonia 20, Barb. 5			
BRAUN, Antonia	22	Neustadt	68-0753
BRAUN, Carl	26	Klonowo	68-0610
Dorothea 60, Pauline 2			
BRAUN, Carline	19	Kurhessen	70-0443
BRAUN, Charles	18	Brakenheim	68-1298
BRAUN, Christ.	20	Heiningen	69-1363
BRAUN, Christine	22	Woenersberg	68-0820
BRAUN, Elisabeth	23	Leusel	68-1002
BRAUN, Ernst	18	Plochingen	69-0457
BRAUN, Eva	24	Zempelburg	68-0707
BRAUN, Franz	34	Augsburg	68-0610
BRAUN, Friedr.	22	Manchenheim	70-0378
Jac. 17			
BRAUN, Friedrich	28	Theisbergstegen	70-0378
BRAUN, Georg	57	Hammelburg	69-1363
BRAUN, George	30	Weidenhausen	69-1212
BRAUN, Gottfried	15	Wittlensweiler	69-0848
Anna 20			
BRAUN, Gustav	40	Hoffdamar	68-0770
BRAUN, Hans	20	Gotha	69-1212
BRAUN, Isaac	63	Lemgo	68-0707
Caroline 51, Frida 26			
BRAUN, Jacob Fr.	34	Enzkloesterle	68-0610
Anna M. 35, Elise 9, Wilhelmine 6			
BRAUN, Johann	34	Augsburg	70-0031
BRAUN, Johann	30	Haf	69-0542
BRAUN, Josef	32	Messkirch	70-0170
BRAUN, Joseph	32	Coblenz	68-0865
BRAUN, Julius	24	Oberthalhausen	69-0457
BRAUN, Lorenz	36	Klonowo	68-0610
Eva 34, Heinr. 3			
BRAUN, Louisa	16	Butzbach	71-0492
BRAUN, Magd.	20	Speyer	69-1011
BRAUN, Martin	15	Wittendorf	71-0456
BRAUN, Theod.	24	Stein	71-0363
BRAUN, Therese	33	Frankfurt	71-0456
BRAUN, Victor	21	Herrenalb	70-0378
BRAUN, Wilhelm	17	Hoeringen	69-1059
Cathrine 19			
BRAUNHOEFER, Barbara	57	Haimfurt	69-0923
Sara 19			
BRAUNLING, Cath.	27	Bayreuth	70-1142
Anna 4			
BRAUNSCHWEIG, E.	39	Peckelsheim	71-0815

NAME	AGE	RESIDENCE	YR-LIST
Bertha 36, Hermann 5, Emil 3, Johanna 11 months			
BRAUNSCHWEIG, Frdr.	45	Braunschweig	69-1004
Caroline 43, Alwine 2, Robert 15			
BRAUNSCHWEIGER, G.	32	Braunschweig	70-0052
BRAUSCHEID, Marie	40	Wermelskirchen	69-0968
John 75			
BRAXMAVER, Elise	17	Ganalgesheimer	69-0321
BRECHT, August	26	Albershausen	69-1011
BRECKEL, Julius	17	Lautern	69-0771
BRECKSCHMIDT, Joh.	30	Osnabrueck	68-1027
BREDE, Friedrich	27	Bremen	69-0572
BREDEHOEFT, Joachim	47	Hannover	68-0456
Margarethe 49, Christine 13, Joachim 9, Johann 8			
BREDEHOEFT, Peter	45	Hannover	68-0456
Christiane 36, Luetje 9, Catharina 8, Marie 7, Metta 3			
BREDEMEYER, Marie	19	Bueckeburg	71-0429
BREDEN, August	19	Engerte	71-0643
BREDEN, male	19	Myhle	71-0393
Heinr. 16, Meta 21			
BREDENDIEK, Wilhelm	14	Hausfelde	69-1309
BREDLOW, August	35	Falkenberg	69-0547
Emilie 31, Emilie 4, Franz 1, Dorothea 64			
BREHM, Amalie	22	Sullixgen	71-0300
BREHM, Ludwig	27	Mannheim	69-0798
BREHMER, Auguste	34	Noerenberg	69-1319
Ottilie 4, Louise 11 months			
BREI, Franziska	16	Neumark	68-0957
BREITAG, Sigismund	53	Margonin	71-0736
Justine 44			
BREITENBACH, Anna	46	Sandenbach	71-0363
BREITENBACH, Aug	18	Heligenstedt	70-0728
Oscar 9, Carl 7			
BREITENBUERGER, M.	14	Roedinghausen	68-1002
Alwine 8			
BREITENFELD, Anna	25	Schnathorst	68-0957
BREITENKAMP, Heinrich	17	Zeven	68-0625
BREITENMUELLER, J.	28	Oberhofen	71-0733
BREITER, Carl	25	Cassel	71-0821
BREITHAUER, August	16	Markoldendorf	68-0566
BREITNER, Franz	24	Muhlhausen	68-0939
BREITSPRECHER, W.	26	St. Petersburg	68-0852
BREITTING, Caroline	24	Esslingen	71-0581
BREITUNG, Henriette	22	Rudolstadt	69-0547
BREITUNG, Otto	18	Fladingen	69-0798
BREITWEG, Alois	21	Simisweiler	68-0534
BREITWIESER, Jac.	23	Gruenstadt	68-0957
BREIVOGEL, Johann	27	Preussen	66-0221
BREM, Maria Agathe	22	Lienheim	68-0661
BREMEIS, Wilh.	13	Nuestenbach	71-0581
BREMEN, Bernh.	16	Bremen	71-0681
BREMEN, V. John	15	Bramke	68-0957
BREMER, Aug.	17	Hopfgarten	71-0681
BREMER, Carl	26	Bruesken	71-0736
BREMER, Dorothea	18	Borstel	69-0229
BREMER, Gottlieb	22	Oberschwandorf	69-1396
BREMER, Henriette	34	Noerenberg	69-1319

NAME	AGE	RESIDENCE	YR-LIST
Auguste 9, Marie 8, Wilhelm 7, Emilie 11 months			
BREMER, Johann	25	Bremerhaven	70-0031
BREMER, John	42	Charleston	69-1059
Elise 32			
BREMER, Marie	23	Hiddingen	71-0363
BREMERICH, Peter	23	Stockum	69-1086
BREMERLOH, Gottfried	15	Meyenburg	69-0572
BREMERMANN, Heinr.	30	Petershagen	69-1212
BREMIS, Marie	18	Tauberbischofsh	71-0456
BREMSER, Georg	46	Bremen	69-0050
BRENDEL, Peter	28	Quidersbach	69-0672
BRENDEL, Peter	26	Zahlbach	70-0384
BRENDEL, Philipp	25	Offenheim	69-0100
BRENN, August	25	Herges Vogtei	68-0907
Margaretha 31			
BRENNECKE, Theod.	18	Braunschweig	71-0821
David 15			
BRENNEIS, Joh.	19	Niestenbach	68-0753
BRENNEKE, Henriette	26	Spandem/Prussia	69-0547
Reinhold 7			
BRENNEKE, Pauline	37	Spandau	69-0560
BRENNER, Carl	27	Baden	70-0148
Adam 17			
BRENNER, Ferdinand	42	Groebning	68-0907
BRENNER, Johann	28	Egenhausen	68-1027
BRENNER, Louise	26	Mannheim	68-0534
BRENNICKE, Rud.	34	Berlin	69-1363
BRENNING, Charles	30	Wuerzburg	69-1421
BRENNINGER, Caroline	47	Trockenheim	71-0521
Marie 16, Emanuel 9, Carl 8, Hermann 6			
BRENZEL, Friederike	66	Follstein	68-0820
Emil 9			
BRESKA, Joh.	24	Krojanke	71-0581
BRESSEL, Elise	19	Duerkheim	70-0170
BRESSMER, Gottlob	22	Uhingen	68-0014
Johanna 19			
BRESSNER, C.	32	Schwiebendingen	70-0170
BRETTNER, Richard	24	Gleine	69-0490
BRETTSCHNEIDER, R.	28	Drachhausen	71-0429
Auguste 32, Otto 3			
BRETZ, Rosalie	20	Allendorf	71-0581
BREUER, Carl	21	Solingen	71-0521
BREUKER, Marie W.	58	Cochem	68-0647
BREWES, Carl	59	Hannover	71-0821
BREWES, Hermann	30	Hannover	69-0923
BREYMANN, J.	21	Paderborn	69-1004
BRICKWEDEL, Corad	15	Hannover	70-1003
BRICKWEDEL, Matha	17	Koehlen	68-0852
BRIEHL, John	28	Darmstadt	70-0308
BRILL, Catharine	25	Staufenbach	71-0521
BRILL, Elisabeth	16	Hueffler	71-0712
BRILL, P.	19	Steppach	71-0582
BRIMJES, Anna	30	Ritterhude	71-0456
Hermann 6, Sophie 3			
BRIMMELMEIER, Ernst	17	Wehringdorf	68-0760
BRINKER, Wilh.	30	Bremen	71-0521
Johanna 30			

NAME	AGE	RESIDENCE	YR-LIST
BRINKMANN, Amalia	32	Detmold	69-0457
BRINKMANN, Anna	29	Oldenburg	71-0456
BRINKMANN, Auguste	20	Detmold	69-1076
BRINKMANN, Carl	38	Hannover	70-0076
BRINKMANN, Diedr.	59	Backhoof	69-1004
Mary 51, Heinr. 16, Mary 19, Wilh. 12			
BRINKMANN, F.	34	Weitfel	70-0272
Johanne 29, Paul 6, Ferdinand 5, Margarethe 3			
BRINKMANN, Frdr.	56	Vorra	71-0300
BRINKMANN, Friedrich	16	Rheda	70-0329
BRINKMANN, Heinr.	16	Barchel	71-0300
BRINKMANN, Johann	22	Hannover	68-1006
BRINKMANN, Maria	44	Recklinghausen	68-0647
Maria 17, Wilhelm 15			
BRINKMANN, Therese	19	Dossel	70-1035
BRINKMANN, Wilhelm	25	Brinkum	69-1212
BRINKMAYER, Friederike	21	Rodinghausen	69-1011
Anna 11 months			
BRINKMEYER, Fr.	45	Roedinghausen	69-1011
Anna 45, Juergen 60, William 18, Lina 7, Henry 7			
BRINKMEYER, Louise	22	Isenstaedt	68-0907
BRINTEMANN, Georg	16	Rodenberg	71-0479
BROCHMER, Carl	26	Reinthal	68-0456
Bertha 32, Albin 6			
BROCK, Christine F.	16	Christes	68-0610
BROCK, Hannchen	60	Osnabrueck	70-0452
BROCKELMANN, Conrad	34	Nedderavebergen	68-0566
BROCKENHAMME, Wilh.	26	Stettin	68-0566
Maria 51			
BROCKMANN, Dorothea	43	Bremen	68-0314
BROCKMANN, Frdke.	17	Bremervoerde	71-0456
BROCKMANN, Gottlieb	23	Barmen	68-0939
BROCKMANN, Heinr.	14	Otterndorf	71-0429
BROCKMANN, Rebecca	24	Bremen	68-0982
BROCKMEYER, Franziska	20	Luegde	68-1027
BROCKSCHMIDT, Cath.	28	Vaxtrup	69-0542
BROCKSCHMIDT, Fritz	30	Sudheide	68-1006
Hanna 32			
BRODEMANN, Hermann	29	Gilten	68-0456
BRODESSER, Wilhelm	36	Coeln	68-0625
BRODLER, Johanne	31	Grotschonau	68-0625
BROECK, Henry	16	Hannover	70-0355
BROECKER, Robert	18	Detmold	70-0384
BROECKING, Heinr.	53	Heimsem	71-0300
Sophie 48, Friederike 15, Aug. 17, Friederike 15, Wilhelmine 12, Caroline 3, E			
BROEHM, Lisette	29	Eberbach	68-0534
BROEKER, Anna	18	Huellhorst	68-0566
BROEKER, Franz	16	Lintorf	68-0852
BROEKING, Ernst	34	Frille	68-0625
Christine 34, Christian 14, Christine 8, Sophie 6, Frierich 4, Eleonore 11 mon			
BROERS, Felde	25	Oldendorf	68-0707
BROETZLER, Friederike	17	Pfitz....	70-0223
BROICH, Adam	24	Coeln	68-0760
BROKAMP, Henry	24	Drummerslohh.	69-0338
BROKENHOFF, Anna	52	Creefeld	71-0815

NAME	AGE	RESIDENCE	YR-LIST
BROKOPP, Michael	48	Posen	69-0559
Anna 31, Julius 10, Wilhelm 7, Imke 6			
BROKOPS, Carl	28	Pinnow	71-0733
Wilhelmine 34, Alwine 9, Johan 5, Carl 4, Minna 4			
BROKSCHMIDT, Johann	49	Venedig	68-0852
Anna 43, Gustav 9, Wilhelm 6, Eduard 3, Johann 38			
BROMBERGER, Otto	23	Muenchen	68-1298
BROSCHEID, Joh.	60	Niederwennersch	68-314
BROSE, Augusta	26	Kolmar	68-1002
BROSE, Fritz	35	New York	70-1003
BROSE, Mary	27	New York	70-0089
Fritz 9			
BROSING, Johanne	47	Oestreich	70-0728
BROSS, Friedrich	14	Darmstadt	68-0314
BROTSCHLER, Alb.	28	Neftenbach	70-1066
BROZ, Anton	29	Boehmen	70-1161
Marie 22, Johann 11 months Peter 57, Josefa 25			
BRUBACHER, Fred.	24	Trossingen	68-0957
BRUCH, Jacob	20	Leetz	69-1212
BRUCK, Therese	21	Offenburg	69-0672
BRUCK, W.	30	Werdau	68-0610
Carl 9			
BRUCKMUELLER, C.	41	Oberdorf	68-0566
Maria 9			
BRUDER, Dorothea	20	Einthal	71-0736
BRUDERLI, Daniel	47	Schweiz	70-0329
BRUEBACH, Elias	24	Umysterode	69-0542
BRUECHLER, Philomena	23	Tiris	69-1059
BRUECK, Balthasar	43	Holler Wustig	70-0204
BRUECK, Rosine	16	Oberroth	70-0355
BRUECKNER, C. F.	24	Kleinwelsbach	69-1011
Mary 22, Julius 3 months, Johanne 55			
BRUECKNER, Franz	28	Darmstadt	70-1142
BRUECKNER, Franz	28	Darmstadt	70-1142
BRUECKNER, Marg.	20	Antenhausen	68-0957
BRUEGGEMANN, Anna	26	Guetersloh	68-0957
BRUEGGEMANN, Claus	17	Hellwege	69-1004
BRUEGGEMANN, H.	33	Essen	69-0923
BRUEGGEMANN, Henry	17	Herwege	71-0456
BRUEHE, Thomas	17	Mannheim	69-0592
BRUEHN, Henrietta	21	Adorf	68-0884
BRUEMMER, Anna	24	Bawinkel	69-0968
BRUEMMER, Gerhard	16	Plankorth	69-0968
BRUENGE, Elise	24	Scharmbeck	71-0821
Elise 11 months, Anna 11 months			
BRUENING, Adam	45	Neuenkirchen	68-0661
BRUENING, H.H.	28	Charleston	69-1076
BRUENING, Hein.	18	Nordleda	68-0982
BRUENING, Joh.	32	Teupe	69-1004
BRUENING, Johann	15	Westerwanna	71-0429
BRUENING, Marie	19	Holzhausen	70-1161
BRUENING, Wilhelm	16	Johannesroth	70-0378
BRUENINGS, Henry	19	Lilienthal	71-0456
BRUENJES, Anna	20	Bremen	69-0592
BRUENS, Mar.	18	Mickelstedt	69-0560
BRUETT, Catharina	18	Cadenberge	69-0560

NAME	AGE	RESIDENCE	YR-LIST
John 18, Anna 14			
BRUGGEMANN, Anna	27	Zuerschenalm	70-0355
BRUGGEMANN, Friedrich	23	Oldenburg	70-0355
BRUGGER, Anton	25	Weihungszell	69-0672
BRUGGER, Xaver	33	Dettnau	71-0456
BRUGMANN, Louise	34	Bischoffszell	68-0625
BRUMMER, Heinr.	15	Hannover	70-0443
BRUMMERLOH, Helene	16	Aschwarden	68-0852
BRUNCKHORST, Gache	18	Schlessel	70-0508
BRUNE, Anna	32	thimen	68-0907
Marie 28			
BRUNE, Charles	22	Lierne	68-0534
BRUNE, Wilhelm	59	Theine	68-0907
BRUNEN, John	27	Wiesedermoor	69-0338
BRUNING, Lorette	9	Braunschweig	69-0100
Pauline 8			
BRUNKE, John	26	Hildesheim	71-0456
BRUNKE, Marie	26	Doehren	68-0786
BRUNKHORST, John	25	Windeswohl	68-0884
BRUNKHORST, Juergen	18	Hannover	70-0508
BRUNN, Lorenz	26	Zell	71-0479
BRUNNER, Rosine	22	Wuerenlos	68-0982
Franz 43			
BRUNS, A. D.	26	Oldenburg	69-1212
BRUNS, Antje	59	Weenen	69-0490
Annette 16			
BRUNS, Franz	28	Bersenbrueck	68-1002
BRUNS, Fritz	31	Hannover	68-0456
BRUNS, Georg	16	Niedorf	71-0492
BRUNS, HAnke	16	Langen	69-1059
BRUNS, Heinr.	15	Rodenkirchen	71-0581
BRUNS, Heinr.	16	Barchel	71-0300
BRUNS, J.C.	25	Hannover	71-0521
BRUNS, Joachim	15	Hannover	70-0170
BRUNS, Johann	32	Hannover	71-0792
BRUNS, Nauke	9	Wiesens	69-1004
Jacob 7, Gerd 5, Albert 2, Hinr. 10 months, Wilke 55			
BRUNS, Petrus	45	Rysum	68-0852
Ida 33, Detert 7, Tytje 5, Johann 3, Enno 7 months			
BRUNS, Ulke	34	Wieseno	69-1004
Trientje 29			
BRUNS, W.	20	Vegesack	69-0490
BRUNSIECK, Heinrich	35	Lippe Detmold	70-0384
Charlotte 28, Louise 6, Charlotte 3 months			
BRUNSWILLER, Charlotte	17	Wehden	71-0821
BRUNWINKEL, Johanna	22	Brinkum	68-0786
BRUSIUS, Elisa	22	Niederweimar	68-0534
BRUSSLER, Nicol.	28	Zanchreten	70-0728
BRUST, Marie	19	Ottersweiler	68-0884
BRUST, Peter	34	Nagold	68-0982
Cath. 35, Agatha 9, Jacob 6			
BRUST, Theodor	25	Neustadt	71-0456
BRUTT, Joh.	17	Zeven	71-0479
BRZCZINSKY, Wilhelmine	30	Krzurouke	71-0300
BRZUCHALSKY, Felix	26	Flatow	68-0647
BUBERLE, Joseph	25	Reidnitz	69-0182

NAME	AGE	RESIDENCE	YR-LIST
BUBOLZ, Wilhelmine	25	Sossnow	68-0852
BUCH, Catharina	26	Wuestenberg	71-0792
BUCH, Marie	16	Kirchenarmenbac	68-0753
BUCH, Peter Stephan	23	Uelferskirchen	71-0226
BUCHDESCHAL, J.	22	Gruenstein	71-0684
BUCHENAUER, Jacob	30	Eichelsachsen	68-0939
Louise 24, Carl 2, Wilhelm 4 months			
BUCHER, Bernhard	52	Wellendingen	69-0592
Walburga 49, Augustine 18, Bernhard 15, Xaver 13, Johann 9			
BUCHER, Ludw.	25	Derdingen	70-0089
BUCHER, Marie	17	Worrstadt	69-0848
BUCHERT, Fr.	26	Steinferel	69-0292
BUCHERT, Hermann	24	Thueringen	69-1396
Erdmann 22			
BUCHHOLZ, Carl	16	Oldenburg	70-0583
BUCHHOLZ, Dorothea	50	Hannover	69-1212
BUCHLER, Phil.	15	Lorch	69-0542
BUCHMANN, Aug.	55	Sangershausen	70-0683
Friederike 36, August 9, Ottomar 9, Marie 5			
BUCHMEYER, Georg	30	Deckbergen	69-0015
BUCHOLT, Anton	29	Oberbergdorf	70-0443
BUCHRODER, Elise	24	Buer	69-0542
BUCHTENKIRCHEN, Carl	20	Stoteler Wald	69-0572
BUCK, Gottfried	16	Reuss	69-1004
BUCK, Joh.	21	Hannover	70-0443
Behrend 19			
BUCK, John	32	Mickelsen	69-0560
Anna 33, Hein. 3, Baby 11 months			
BUCK, Julius	35	Solingen	69-0429
BUCK, Wilh.	58	Kirchdorf	71-0581
Johanne 57, August 29			
BUCKERT, Georg	27	Lindenberg	68-0456
BUDDE, Anna	19	Zeven	68-0625
BUDDE, Caspar	60	Klosterbauersch	68-0982
Anna 46, Heinrich 17, Anna 7			
BUDDE, Herm.	40	Varelgraben	71-0167
BUDDE, Joh. Hr.	19	Hannover	68-1006
BUDDE, Johann	23	Steinau	71-0363
BUDDE, Louise	19	Sonneborn	68-0456
Friedrich 17			
BUDDEMEYER, Anna	15	Steinshorn	69-0583
BUDELMANN, Julie	30	Hagen	71-0456
Dorette 25			
BUDWEISER, Carl	30	Schwarzenbach	69-0050
BUDWEISER, Carl	35	Hasselbach	71-0681
BUEBLER, Marie	44	Rottenburg	69-1059
Cathrine 19, Barbara 11, Andreas 7, Magdalene 9 months			
BUECHE, Lorenz	72	Ewattingen	71-0815
Agathe 60			
BUECHLE, Barbara	21	Dettensen	71-0456
BUECHLER, Alois	63	Chicago	69-0572
BUECHLER, Peter	23	Bernersberg	69-0968
BUECHNER, Eduard	25	Hildburghausen	70-0135
BUECHNER, Joh.	26	Oberriedenberg	68-0314
Theresia 24			
BUECHS, Augusta	30	Fladingen	68-0647
Rosina 8, Andreas 6, Hermine 2			
BUECKER, Anna	30	Hannover	71-0821

NAME	AGE	RESIDENCE	YR-LIST
BUECKING, Heinrich		Motzfeld	69-0798
BUECKLEIN, Jacob	27	Lambsheim	68-1298
BUEDDEMANN, Wilhelm	42	Elberfeld	70-0223
Ida 36, Emil 5, Antonie 4, Helene 11 months			
BUEDENICK, Marianne	39	Mecklenburg	70-0728
Joseph 2, Franz 9 months			
BUEGGE, Marie	14	Wittorf	69-0429
BUEGGELN, Meta	17	Uthleda	68-0852
BUEGMANN, Elise	18	Linz	71-0712
BUEHLER, Cathr.	65	Weiler	69-1421
William 25			
BUEHLER, Franziska	76	Philadelphia	69-1363
BUEHLER, Friedrike	60	Metzingen	69-0592
BUEHLER, Heinrich	22	Hessenhorst	69-1309
BUEHLER, Leonh.	19	Sulpach	69-0560
BUEHLER, Leopold	23	Gaerlingen	71-0456
BUEHLER, Max	18	Carlsruhe	71-0363
BUEHLER, Xaver	20	Ruhberghausen	69-1059
BUEHN, Catharina	17	Oberrobisheim	69-0429
BUEHN, Johann	54	Gondelsheim	69-0457
Wilhelmine 26, Jacob 24, Lisette 19, Carl 17, Louise 15, Gustav 13, Frieda 9,			
BUEHR, George	17	Heilbronn	68-0760
BUEHRING, Rudolf	24	Schwerin	68-0314
BUEHRLE, Rosine	23	Cappel	71-0456
BUEHRMANN, Johanne	15	Gittelde	70-0378
BUEKLER, John	17	Hallenhofen	71-0456
BUEKNER, Ernst	22	Schweinfurt	70-0052
BUELCKEN, Julius	25	Charleston	70-1161
Anne 35			
BUELOW, Friedrich	27	Neustettin	68-0625
BUELOW, Johann	45	Jenkebelich	70-1055
Sophie 47, Carl 16, Marie 22, Caroline 19, Wilhelmine 15,Marie 19			
BUELTER, Ernst	49	Sinslau	69-0547
Caroline 53, Wilhelmine 22, Carl 21, August 18, Caroline 16, Friedrich 12, Hel			
BUENGER, Nicolaus	27	Nordleda	68-0661
BUENJES, Meta	24	Ohlenstedt	69-0592
BUERCHER, Adelrich	21	Zuerich	71-0521
BUERGER, Johann	54	Urmersbach	69-0547
Margarethe 53, Anna 26, Joseph 24, Catharine 20			
BUERGER, Johanna	32	Barigau	68-1027
BUERGERHOFS, Heinr.	16	Wedel	69-0592
BUERHAUS, August	23	Muenster	69-0798
BUERK, Erh.	19	Schwemingen	68-0884
BUERKLA, Max	19	Hausach	70-0223
BUERKLE, Gottlob	38	Steinenberg	68-0661
Catharina 35			
BUERKLE, Josefa	31	Usen	70-0508
Marianne 2, Albert 3 months			
BUERMELE, Jacob	22	Ilshofen	69-0229
BUESCH, Anna	35	Lehe	71-0521
Heinrich 15, Anna 9			
BUESCHEL, Anna	25	Vorarlberg	69-0560
BUESCHER, Anna	18	Hannover	70-0728
BUESE, Sophie	22	Bruchhausen	68-0907
BUESING, Elise	37	Hildesheim	68-0647
BUESS, Mathias	26	Wimpsheim	68-0661
BUESSENSCHUETT, Hel.	18	Wulmsdorff	69-1011
BUESSENSCHUITT, H.	15	Bremerhaven	69-0542
BUEST, August	26	Jeetze	69-1212
Friederike 26			
BUETELING, Joh.	14	Ehlen	71-0479
BUETEPOGE, Heinrich	48	Hohenborstel	68-0760
BUETOW, William	34	Berlin	68-0534
BUETTEL, Elisabeth	24	Pfingstadt	69-1076
BUETTER, Heinr.	15	Brinkum	71-0821
Christine 18			
BUETTLER, Catharine	22	Gundheim	69-0229
BUETTNER, Antonette	20	Bremerhaven	68-0884
BUETTNER, Carl	51	Stettin	68-0884
Johann 41			
BUETTNER, Clara	30	Orb	69-0560
John 8, Anna 6			
BUETTNER, Ernst	35	Eddingen	68-0707
BUETTNER, Heinrich	40	Orb	68-0852
BUETTNER, Herm.	35	Berlin	71-0684
BUETTNER, Joh.	49	Pollychen	68-0647
Florentine 40, Franz 19, Robert 17, Alwine 13, Anna 11, Emil 8, Gustav 6, Erns			
BUETTNER, Magd.	40	Frankfurt	69-1421
BUETTNER, Margarethe	57	Gustenfelsen	68-0647
BUETTNER, Martin	30	Eichenberg	71-0821
Barbara 36, Philippine 8			
BUETTNER, Pauline	30	Falkenberg	68-0661
Paul 6			
BUETTNER, Peter	19	Somoczyn	71-0643
BUETTNER, Regina	40	Meines	69-0338
BUETTNER, Wilh.	44	Berlin	68-1002
BUETZER, Aug.	63	Crefeld	70-0728
BUGGE, Wilhelm	27	Uthlede	70-0384
BUHL, Joh. Mart.	21	Neustadt	68-1006
BUHLERT, Ernst	18	Hannover	69-1309
Wilhelm 16			
BUHLMAN, John	29	Nassau	70-0308
Wilhelmine 25, baby daughter 6			
BUHLMANN, Caroline	56	Niederwoehren	68-0456
BUHNER, Marie	21	Wolzheim	69-0268
BUHR, Dorothea	19	Hannover	69-0841
BUHRE, Carl	18	Noerten	70-1003
BUHRKE, Julius	28	Silkorn	70-0308
BUING, Heinr.	27	Bork	68-0610
BUKAWITZ, Johann	17	Krain	70-0384
BUKLEIN, Georg	27	Lambsheim	71-0643
BUKNER, Ernst	22	Schweinfurt	70-0052
BULAND, Georg	29	Schwarzenbach	69-0050
BULKERT, Friedrich	22	Niederstad	69-0182
BULLINGER, Maria	20	Haichelheim	68-0852
BULLWINKEL, Geo.	15	Scharnbeck	69-0583
BULLWINKEL, Kath.	34	Hannover	70-1142
BULLWINKEL, Martin	21	Hannover	69-1363
BULLWINKEL, Meta	22	Hannover	69-1004
BULMANN, Carl	25	Minden	68-0786
BULTENSCHMIDT, J.	55	Nauenburg	70-0308
Mary 54, Margreth 19, Fred 17			
BULTMANN, Anna	17	Writzen	68-0707

NAME	AGE	RESIDENCE	YR-LIST
BULZ, Ernst	19	Offenburg	69-1363
BUMMELING, Anna	19	Hollich	69-0208
BUMUELLER, Hugo	27	Schekingen	69-0592
BUNDER, Johann	18	Neustadt	68-0770
BUNGENAAR, Jan	25	Groothusen	68-0760
BUNNEMANN, Heinrich	28	Oldenburg	70-0452
BUNS, Thida	22	St. Sost	70-0452
BUNTE, Mathilde	27	Bremke	68-0566
Mathilde 3, Marie 6 months			
BUNTE, Theod.	27	Lemgo	71-0736
BUOB, Carl	20	Altenstaig	69-1059
BURAN, Friederike	24	Dessau	68-0760
BURAND, Marie	34	Stolzenberg	68-0610
Adolph 1			
BURCHHARDT, Georg	28	Oberfranken	68-0786
BURCKSCHNEIDER, V.	26	Alsfeld	71-0393
BURDIEK, Agnes	21	Damme	69-0923
BURESCH, Anna	51	Kallin	70-1023
Josef 17			
BURESEL, Anna	51	Kallin	70-1023
Josef 17			
BURFEIND, Diedrich	27	Bremervoerde	71-0643
BURFEIND, Hans	19	Otterndorf	68-0534
BURFEINOL, Anna	26	Hannover	70-0443
BURG, Peter	24	Lell	71-0733
BURGAUER, Aron	19	Jehenhausen	70-0728
BURGAUER, Jeanette	22	Frankfurt	70-0728
BURGDORFF, Wilhelm	34	Hannover	68-0820
Carl 9			
BURGE, August	34	Sneconesheff	68-0456
Angelica 23, Wilhelm 8, Bartha 4, Friedrich 2, Heinrich 3 months, Caroline 23			
BURGER, Andreas	21	Schoenberg	71-0456
BURGER, Barbara	20	Wien	71-0363
BURGER, Caroline	20	Einoed	71-0821
Marie 23			
BURGER, Elisabeth	18	Stebin	69-0542
BURGER, John	31	Glashuetten	68-0957
BURGER, Leopold	21	Prag	68-0625
BURGER, Lisette	35	Gerlachsheim	68-0707
Carl 4, Ernst 10 months			
BURGER, Michael	31	Ebendorf	71-1046
Mar. 26			
BURGFREDE, Doris	21	Ottersberg	71-0521
BURGGRAF, Albert	49	St. Paul	70-0355
BURGHARD, H.	27	Hoboken	69-0572
BURGHOLD, Philippina	22	Bieberich	69-1319
BURGTORF, Adolf	17	Hannover	70-0523
BURK, Ernst	14	Reuss Schleiz	69-0583
BURK, Joh.	20	Greiz	71-0789
BURK, Johann	22	Reuss Schleiz	69-0583
BURKAMP, Minna	19	Osterode	71-0681
BURKARD, Andreas	60	Cos	69-1396
BURKARDT, Caroline	39	Reichenbach	69-0457
Eugenie 4			
BURKART, Ant.	14	Rottweil	71-0581
BURKHAIDE, Marg.	57	Oberrichheim	68-0647
BURKHARD, Cathar.	17	Stuttgart	68-0534
BURKHARD, Wilhelm	25	Bernbach	70-0308

NAME	AGE	RESIDENCE	YR-LIST
BURLAGE, Max	45	Radolin	69-1319
Bertha 23			
BURMEISTER, Friedrich	24	Hille	69-1076
BURMEISTER, Heinrich	15	Minden	68-0907
BURRICHTER, Theresia	19	Mettingen	69-0592
BURTAN, Marcus	25	Hochberg	71-0479
BUSCH, August	26	Jeetze	69-1212
Friederike 26			
BUSCH, August	21	Chemnitz	71-0712
BUSCH, Barbara	25	Lehrberg	69-0229
BUSCH, Conrad	31	Osnabrueck	69-0583
BUSCH, Elise	27	Duesseldorf	70-0170
BUSCH, Eliza	28	Hildesheim	68-0661
BUSCH, Ferd.	24	Kartjunke	71-0792
BUSCH, Francisca	21	Unternenbrunn	68-1027
BUSCH, Friderike	22	Quakenbrueck	69-0208
BUSCH, Friedr. Aug.	23	Solingen	71-0226
BUSCH, Gesche	17	Nordstade	68-0566
BUSCH, Julius	16	Leipzig	70-1142
BUSCH, Marg.	25	Lastrup	71-0521
BUSCH, Martha	48	Hollon	69-0429
Gesine 22, Stephan 20, Wilhelm 16, Eilert 14, Gertrud 12			
BUSCH, Stephan	50	Kunheiten	69-0162
BUSCHBAUM, Anton	20	Peine	68-0314
BUSCHBORN, Hermann	24	Winsen	68-0456
BUSCHE, Wilh.	18	Reeda	69-1363
Joh. 21			
BUSCHE, Wilhelm	15	Nienstedt	68-0534
BUSCHELLE, Georg	32	New York	69-0572
Anna 28			
BUSCHHAUPT, Herm.	38	Barmen	68-0957
BUSCHING, August		Diethe	69-0429
BUSCHKE, Christian	42	Miaskowo	69-0457
BUSCHKOWSKY, H.	24	Mersin	68-0820
BUSCHMANN, Gesine	20	Brinkum	68-0786
BUSCHMANN, Johann	17	Nuertlingen	68-0939
Catharina 19, Amalia 11 months			
BUSCHMANN, Lud.	68	Sachsenhagen	68-0957
Friederike 19			
BUSCHMOEHLE, Heinr.	20	Asslage	68-0610
BUSCHNER, Carl	34	Rasberg	68-0014
BUSEMANN, Hinr.	34	Hannover	70-1142
BUSER, Johannes	25	Bremen	69-0968
BUSGEN, Caspar	25	R.B. Coeln	68-0610
BUSJAEGER, Georg	21	Bremen	71-0456
BUSKOHL, Gretje	20	Warsingfehn	68-1027
BUSOLD, Mary	20	Eiterfeld	71-0300
BUSS, August	30	Gross Benz	69-0771
Wilhelmine 26, Wilhelm 16,			
BUSS, Johann	33	Oldenburg	70-0452
BUSS, Maria	33	Schirum	69-0229
Johanne 5, Heinrich 1			
BUSS, Marie	22	Hannover	70-0178
BUSS, Roolf	68	Strackholt	68-0884
Wuebke 66, Wuebke 22, Voelke 30			
BUSSE, Anna	17	Schnathorst	68-0957
BUSSE, Carl	17	Patzig	71-0479
BUSSE, Christian	38	Hessen	70-0523

NAME	AGE	RESIDENCE	YR-LIST
Maria 40, Wilhelm 15, Maria 6, Minna 4, Christian 6 months, Maria 73			
BUSSE, Johann	59	Nisbeck	70-0031
BUSSE, Richard	29	Rogosen	69-0542
Carl 24			
BUSSE, Wilhme.	21	Vechta	71-0581
BUSSHORN, Franz	27	Oldenburg	70-0355
BUSSMANN, Anna	28	Neukannitz	68-314
BUSWEILER, Wilh.	23	Weinaehr/Weinac	68-0957
BUTE, Aug.	26	Schieda	68-314
Ernst 16			
BUTELER, Magd.	25	Albersweiler	70-1066
Cathar. 9 months			
BUTERSTEIN, Marg.	20	Mossingen	70-0443
Heinr. 9 months			
BUTNER, Julius	27	Stolzenau	71-0821
BUTT, Martha	54	Lendorf	69-1319
BUTTEL, Maria	17	Urphar	71-0581
BUTTERFASS, Lisette	29	Gruenstadt	69-1076
Ludwig 6			
BUTTINGER, Wilhelm	59	Cannstadt	68-0456
BUTTLER, Gebhard	16	Riechelsdorf	69-0572
BUTTNER, Rich.	22	Wildflecken	71-0479
BUTZ, Wilh.	25	Kock	71-0167
BUTZEL, Cath.	18	Berghausen	71-0681
BUZICKA, Mathias	43	Boehmen	70-1003
Venzemia 9, Pauline 7, Baby 10 months			
BYRAM, Helene	30	Bremen	69-1363
CACCIA,Arnold	17	Twiste	68-0884
CAEMMANN, William	31	Lewe	69-0848
CAESAR, Sophie	23	Delmenhorst	69-1086
CAEVEMEYER, Heinr.	17	Necktelsen	68-0884
Doris 14			
CAHN, Maier	26	Alsfeld	69-0923
CAKARIUS. C.	29	Friedrichsroda	70-1035
CALLENBACH, Christ.	23	Feinbreitenbach	69-1363
CAMMANN, George	40	S. Francisco	69-0923
Charlotte 24, Georgine 6, Charles 4			
CAMPE, Theodor	34	New York	69-0321
CAMPEN, Hedwig	26	Hannover	69-0559
Friederike 21			
CAMPHAUSEN, Marie		Coeln	68-1002
Daughter			
CANITZEL, Herm.	30	Berlin	69-0771
CANTURIER, Charles	24	Hamburg	68-1298
CANTUS, Werner	15	Frankenberg	71-0456
CAPELLE, Heinrich	26	Detmold	69-0229
CAPLAN, Robert	48	Danzig	69-0547
Amalia 37, Heinrich 15			
CAPPEL, Margarethe	23	Rammelsbach	69-0572
Caroline 18, Catharina 14			
CARLE, Herm.	46	Oldenburg	70-100
CARLS, Bertha	30	Oldenburg	70-0378
Annchen 22, Wilhelm 13, Tomi 11, Hermine 4, Baby 6 months, Helene 18			
CARLS, Otto	22	Crefeld	69-0841
Anna 20			
CARLSRUTE, Regine	36	Gelshausen	68-0566
Abraham 9			
CARLSSON, Nils Peter	21	Kalmar	68-0647
Carl Victor 19			
CARN, Johanne	18	Geestemuende	71-0479
CAROSELLI, Laura Himela	22	Elberfeld	71-0363
CARSTEMS, Johann	57	Osterhesslingen	68-0456
Engel 31, Marie 16			
CARSTENDIEK, Gerh.	16	Hastedt	68-0647
CARSTENS, Henry	29	Ebstorf	69-0338
Catharina 23, Henry 3, Mary 11 months			
CARTAP, Bernh.	30	Peitz	71-0684
CARTIER, Caroline	32	New York	69-0572
CASIUS, Margareth	22	Schweinfurt	69-0572
CASPAR, Nicolas	14	Zell	68-1027
CASPARI, Louise	38	Hannover	70-0089
Conrad 9			
CASPER, Agnete	23	Carlsruhe	69-0592
Louise 3			
CASSAU, Henriette	22	Lueneburg	70-0569
CASSEBAUM, Joh.	14	Minden	71-0581
CASSEBORTH, Johann	70	Hannover	68-0647
CASSEL, Leopold	22	Mainz	68-0456
CASWALL, R. Henry	59	Franklin-Pa.	70-0089
Mary 62, Robert 31			
CATHEREN, Chr.	27	Eltmanshausen	69-0560
CAUFORD, Charlotte	35	New York	69-0923
Ludwig 3, August 1, Elisabeth 9 months, Catharina 24			
CAVET, Maria	34	Berlin	70-0683
CEHLAR, Johann	23	Sohn	70-0329
CENTS, Caroline	19	Elsins	69-1076
CEPICKA, Anna	65	Repin	68-0770
Maria 36, Anna 2, Anton 1 (died on ship)			
CERBST, male	28	Braunschweig	69-0100
CERMAK, Josefa	5	Boehmen	69-1363
CERNY, Leonore	18	St. Catharina	71-0363
CEVENKA, Josef	26	Doubrava	70-0329
CHALUPA, Franz	23	Boehmen	68-0456
CHARFUER, Louise	59	Braunschweig	69-0542
CHARTRON, Christine	36	Bremen	68-0534
Friedrich 4			
CHARUSO, Ferd.	18	Santau	69-0542
CHARVATZ, Joh.	40	Lhota	71-0521
CHAUTEM, Jean	27	Friburg	68-0014
Elise 21			
CHEDORN, Heinr.	28	Otterberg	68-0982
Barbara 25, Richard 1, Magda. 2 months			
CHILDGER, Conrad	16	Stockheim	63-1218
Marie 23			
CHLADEK, Aloys	20	Sadska	68-0314
CHRIST, Heinrich	23	Worrstadt	69-0848
CHRIST, Joh.	14	Rosenthal	70-0452
CHRIST, Johanne	44	Gibichenstein	69-1076
Hermann 17, Louise 15			
CHRIST, Margarethe	16	Wura	69-0547
CHRIST, Marie	18	Frankenhausen	71-0681
CHRIST, Wilhelmine	41	Chur	69-0592
Emil 9, Caroline 8			
CHRISTEL, Georg	39	Schindelsee	71-0643
CHRISTIAN, Georg	19	Wendlingen	70-0728

NAME	AGE	RESIDENCE	YR-LIST
CHRISTIANE, Wilhelm	19	Lingen	70-0204
CHRISTIANZ, John	36	Huettengesaess	68-0760
Catharine 39, Henrika 8, Mary 6			
CHRISTMANN, Carl	20	Pfalzgrafenw.	68-0820
CHRISTMANN, Marg.	25	Rustweiler	70-0308
CHRISTOFFERS, Hinr.	28	Brill/Brell	69-1004
CIASSEN, Joh. Peter	14	Meinberg	69-0572
CILLIS, Hubert	24	Coeln	69-0100
CIZLER, Jacob	39	Hochwarth,Austr	69-0547
Dorothea 26, Georg 45, Anna 27, Bartholomaeus 39, Anna 27			
CLAAS, Christ.	31	Rehe	68-0314
Emilie 36, Emilie 6 months			
CLAS, Peter	21	Hueffler	71-0712
CLASHAGEN, Meta	22	Blumenthal	69-0100
CLASSEN, Janssen	25	Twixlum	69-0208
CLASSEN, Joh. Peter	14	Meinberg	69-0572
CLATT, Claus Dan.	19	Lamstedt	68-0610
CLAUS, Adam	27	Amushausen	69-1363
Anna 20, Anna 9 months			
CLAUS, Lebrecht	25	Dresden	71-0429
CLAUS, Paulina	38	Marburg	70-0569
CLAUS, Sophie	17	Kurhessen	69-1086
CLAUSSEN, Conrad	17	Hannover	70-0204
CLAUSSEN, Joh. W.	25	Bremen	69-0583
CLAUSSEN, John	16	Schoenemoor	70-1003
Beda 18			
CLAUSSEN, John C.	38	Charleston	69-1059
Marie 32			
CLAUSSEN, Wilhelm	25	Walle	68-1027
CLEMENS, Meta	21	Aumund	68-0982
CLEMENT, Johann	26	Landskrone	68-0770
CLEMME, H.	55	Detmold	70-0308
CLOSE, Marie	20	Elbing	71-0492
CLOVER, Carl	40	Bruchsal	68-0957
CLUEVER, Heinrich	41	Weehold	68-0625
Wilhelmine 39, Johann 9, Doris 8, Diedrich 7, August 5, Margaret 3, Diedrich 1			
COELLEN, Joh.	26	R.B. Coeln	68-0610
COERLIN, Joseph	31	Sagemuehl	69-0559
COESTER, Hermann	26	Rosenthal	68-0456
COETZMANN, Ludwika	46	Offenburg	68-0534
COHEN, Friederike	40	Hannover	69-1011
Philipp 15, Louis 8, Hannette 6, Filly 4			
COHEN, Jacob	17	Adelsdorf	69-1004
COHEN, Moritz	40	Duesseldorf	69-1363
COHN, Clara	38	San Francisco	69-1212
Emma 7, Allies 5, Constanze 3, William 17, Rosa 18			
COHN, Henry B.	26	Wixburg	69-0067
COHN, Louis	27	Schwerin	68-0661
COHN, Marie	22	Berlin	71-0736
COHN, Michael	24	Luedge	68-0456
COHN, Simon	16	Braunschweig	69-0067
COHN, Simon	64	Lichtenfels	68-0625
Bertha 60			
COHN, Therese	19	Liebeschitz	71-0581
Julie 15			
COHNE, Chr.	18	Offelten	69-1011

NAME	AGE	RESIDENCE	YR-LIST
COHNEN, J.L.	29	Eschweiler	69-0338
COLLARD, Herbert	20	Jeverton	70-0148
COLLET, Mathias	26	Sien	69-0784
COLMANN, Reiner	39	Hannover	69-0559
Anna Margaretha 31, Antje Helena 2, Maria Adeline 9 months			
COMMLUTZ, George	21	Volkach	68-0534
CONCENTHER, Hirsch	69	Altencunstadt	69-1004
Babette 63			
CONNELL, Margarethe	30	New York	69-0321
CONRAD, Adelheid	26	Wollin	68-0314
CONRAD, Anna	24	Hannover	69-0672
CONRAD, August	22	Ramrod	68-0625
CONRAD, Carl	45	Rodels	69-0572
CONRAD, Charlotte	17	Riedelberg	71-0821
CONRAD, Claus	27	Obergrenzbach	69-0542
Anna 25, Heinrich 15, Elise 3 months			
CONRAD, Elise	26	Frankfurt a/O	68-1002
CONRAD, Fried.	18	Chur	69-0572
Elise 19, Ursula 16, Johanna 14			
CONRAD, Henriette	33	Potsdam	68-0314
CONRAD, Johann	19	Wuerzburg	71-0684
CONRAD, Ludw.	36	Darmstadt	71-0167
Anna 26, Elisabeth 6			
CONRAD, Margarethe	22	Rheinprovince	69-1076
CONRAD, Philippine	22	Regalchamin	69-0672
CONRAD, Rich.	18	Gruncin	71-0581
CONRAD, Wilhelm	51	Elberfeld	69-0338
Ottilie 23			
CONRADI, Conrad	38	Windheim	69-0923
Charlotte 38, Conrad 9, Charlotte 7, Sophie 5, Friedrich 11 months			
CONRADI, Georg	16	Michelbach	68-1027
Philipp 15			
CONRADI, Leopold	27	Neuertingen	68-1006
COOPS, Ludwig	31	Hollen	68-0661
Elisabeth 26			
COORDES, C.	40	Hannover	70-0308
Gesine 30, Ludwig 7, Mary 6			
CORA, Joseph	24	Assiago	68-0760
CORDES, Adelheid	21	Kampe	69-1086
CORDES, Aug.	25	Braunschweig	71-0521
Bruno 16			
CORDES, Berend	52	Adolfhausen	69-0229
CORDES, Bertha	17	Willstedt	71-0521
Adelheid 19			
CORDES, Catharina	21	Jever	69-1212
CORDES, Catharina	18	Thedinghausen	68-0760
CORDES, Heinrich	24	Bremerhaven	69-0784
CORDES, Henry	16	Lottrum	70-0378
CORDES, Meta	16	Hannover	71-0712
CORDICK, Joseph	40	Rottenbaum	68-0770
Catharina 42, Joseph 10, Anton 7, Johann 5, Carl 2, Franz 9 months			
CORDIER, Jacob	37	Einoed	71-0821
CORDLER, Fritz	25	Lueneburg	70-0683
CORDMANN, Friedrich	60	Brunswick	69-0542
CORELL, Elise	20	Ziegenhain	70-1035
CORNELSEN, John	26	Fiegenhof	71-0456
Helene 26, Emilie 3 months			

NAME	AGE	RESIDENCE	YR-LIST
CORNELSSEN, Gustav	15	Jongwarden	70-0523
CORNETT, Catharine	18	Edenkoben	71-0733
CORSSEN, Johanna	28	Fedderwarden	68-0534
CORTJOHANN, Caroline	21	Wilmington	69-1059
COURT, Goetze	34	Zeithain	68-0707
Therese 34, Eduard 7, Alma 6 months, Anna 6			
CRAICHHEIMER, Mathias	16	Rheinbischofshe	71-0712
Sophia 17			
CRAICI, Joseph	34	Rebnitz	70-0006
Marie 30			
CRAMER, Carl	28	Schweinfurt	70-0204
Anna 19			
CRAMER, Gretchen	30	Oldenburg	71-1046
CRAMER, Telsche	24	Langholt	68-0610
CRENZINGER, Emanuel	18	Harovitz	70-0329
CRIDNER, Wilhelm	28	Ochtershausen	68-0707
CRON, Gustav	34	Schlawe	68-1006
CRONEBOLD, Elise	24	Darmstadt	69-1212
CRUEGER, Hermann	21	Schneidemuehle	68-0907
CULLMANN, Carl	27	Niederworresbac	69-1319
CULMANN, Wilh.	35	Breitenkamp	68-0610
Wife 38			
CUNI, Magdalene	55	Schweighafen	69-1363
Barb. 28, Marie 21, Heinrich 17			
CUNZBERGER, Bernh.	38	Berlin	71-0300
CURTINS, Hugo	28	Zuellschau	69-0583
CYEWWSKY, Joseph	26	Rekau	69-0457
CZAPEK, Barbara	40	Kuttentag	70-0329
CZASTKA, Carl	20	Wien	69-0592
CZERNITZKY, Michael	50	Danzig	69-0547
Anna 45, Justine 25, Laura 20, Ottilie 7, Johanne 6, Georg 4			
CZISCHOCK, Franz	45	Leipzig	70-0184
Cornelius, Carl	15	Dorum	69-1059
Cyriacks, Beta	26	Etelsen	68-0661
Trina 23, Gesche 16			
DAAK, Georg	25	Osterode	68-1006
DAAK, Wilh.	17	Hessen	69-1086
DACHSE, Paulus	36	Africa	70-0089
DAEHLKE, Cath.	34	Tuchel	71-0581
Johann 8, Catharina 3, August 2, Franz 9 months			
DAFFERNER, Elise	58	Zeuthen	69-0429
DAFUSS, Joh.	29	Martoffelern	70-1142
Anna 34			
DAGEL, Marie	38	Bruchsal	70-1142
Marie 4			
DAHL, Heinrich	23	Mainz	70-0816
DAHLE, Mrs.	60	Coblenz	69-0100
DAHLMANN, Anton	39	Saerbeck	69-0429
DAHM, Albert	20	Remscheid	69-1309
DAHM, August	27	Pommern	69-0672
DAHMANN, Eleonore	15	Hannover	69-0923
DAHNKEN, Meta	23	Bollen	71-0429
DAHONS, Albert	25	Hintersee	68-0566
DAIG, Adolph	50	Rochester	69-1076
DAITZ, Christiane	61	Oberurbach	68-0786
DAKE, Christoph	24	Schaumburg	69-0542
DALBERG, Albert	23	Coesfeld	68-0982
DALDER, Carl F.	22	Bremen	68-0661
DALLB, Jacob	33	Herchweiler	69-0015
DALLINGER, Jeanette	25	Mittelfranken	68-0786
DALLMANN, Johann	28	Saagen	68-0770
Friederika 26, Alheit 1, Carl 2 months			
DALLMEYER, Rudolf	14	Diesen	71-0821
DALLMEYER, Wilhelm	41	Jefferson City	71-0821
Louise 31, Ferd. 10, Pauline 9, August 2, Randolf 2			
DALUEGE, August	34	Moschuetz	71-0521
Auguste 31, Auguste 9 months			
DALWIG, Catharina	37	Freysa	71-0492
Wilhelmine 8, Arthur 3			
DAMAAGER, Franz	24	Muenchen	69-0923
DAMBACHER, Cresenzia	22	Oberiflingen	68-0534
Wallburga 23			
DAMBACHER, Elias	37	Buhl	71-0363
DAMBROWSKIE, Jacob	39	Marienau	70-0006
Marie 40, Jacob 7, Peter 7, Martin 5, Paul 6 months			
DAMEKE, Ferd.	20	Hannover	70-0170
DAMHAUSEN, Max	15	Berlin	69-0923
DAMM, Caroline	19	Crailsheim	71-0521
DAMM, Catharina	23	Reiskirchen	68-0907
DAMM, Eduard	28	Norden	70-0135
Anna 22			
DAMM, Johann	22	Forchheim	71-0684
DAMM, Michel	40	H. Darmstadt	70-1003
Henry 20			
DAMMANN, Claus	17	Mursum	68-0770
DAMMANN, Margaretha	15	Hannover	68-0456
DAMMANN, Peter	17	Fahrendahl	71-0226
DAMMASCH, Louis	16	Bremerhaven	70-1161
DAMMASCH, Marie	19	Gustendorf	69-1212
DAMMER, Cath.	21	Freckenhorst	71-0821
DAMMER, Meta	42	Quakenbrueck	69-0923
Marie 16			
DAMMEYER, Heinrich	46	Salzgitter	71-0429
Carl 14			
DAMMEYER, Louisa	16	Salzgitter	70-0184
DAMPINSKY, Josef	46	Poun	69-0771
Josefa 27, Marianne 13, Emilie 9, Johanne 7			
DANE, Albertine	40	Hamburg	69-1076
DANEGGER, Sabine	23	Biesendorf	68-0786
DANGEL, Michael	18	Oberleimingen	71-0521
DANGER, Jacob	19	Weidenbach	71-0429
DANIEL, Caroline		Niederaula	68-1002
DANIEL, Ida	22	Hersfeld	71-0456
DANIEL, Josepha	19	Rheingau	68-1027
DANIEL, Theodor	17	Schleusingen	68-0647
DANKENBRUECK, Friedr.	39	Sabbenhausen	68-1027
DANKER, Joh.	16	Bremen	68-0786
DANNEBERG, Aug.	29	Hannover	70-100
DANNEBERG, Johann Fr.	29	Jueterbrog	69-0321
DANNENBROCK, Joh.	60	Wersen	71-0821
Bernh. 38, Marie 36, Christine 4, Heinrich 10			
DANNHAUSEN, Max	15	Berlin	69-0923

NAME	AGE	RESIDENCE	YR-LIST
DANNIES, Friedr.	53	Sichau	71-0681
Elisabeth 37, Friedr. 9, Adolf 8, Friedr. 6, Louise 6			
DANSEE, Robert	21	Tilsit	71-0712
DANTZIG, Wilhelmine	25	Oldenburg	70-0384
DANZ, Carl W.	28	Gunsdorf	69-0572
DANZER, Andreas	53	Truskowitz	68-0770
Anna 23, Maria 21, Mathias 17, Veronica 15, Anton 11, Franz 12, Margaretha 8,			
DARE, Edmund	26	Herford	70-0329
Sarah 24			
DARIGEL, Franz	39	Minden	71-0789
Carl 7, Aug. 10 months			
DARRENKAMP, Lisette	28	Oldenburg	69-1004
DASGE, Heinr.	24	Vechta	71-0821
DASSLER, Heinrich	38	Greiz	68-1006
DATECK, Joh.	17	Niederasphen	71-0821
Gertrude 21, Peter 21, Gertrude 16			
DATZ, Wilhelm	16	Darmstadt	69-0923
DAU, Margatethe	52	Carlshafen	70-0384
Lenore 18			
DAUB, Joh.	16	Nottingen	71-0479
Barb. 19			
DAUBE, August	26	Frankenthal	71-0456
DAUBER, Friedrich	64	Belheim	69-0457
DAUBER, Heinrich	16	Battberg	69-0429
DAUBERT, Ernestine	20	Offenbach	68-0610
DAUBLE, Anna	47	Holzhausen	69-1396
DAUER, August	27	Braunschweig	69-0229
DAUKE, Peter	41	Tyrol	69-0798
DAULSBERG, Diedr.	28	Hannover	68-0647
DAUM, Edward	24	Darmstadt	69-1011
DAUM, Nicolaus	29	Caldern	69-0268
DAUM, Peter	31	Tyrol	71-0167
DAUN, Paul	31	Danzig	69-1309
DAUR, Clodwige	18	Ueberlingen	68-0610
DAUT, Friedrich	22	Mainz	68-0647
DAUT, Kunigunde	25	Strickendorf	71-0792
Elisabeth 8, Margaretha 11 months			
DAUTH, Elisabeth	18	Westhofen	69-0229
DAVID, Carl	16	Rehweiler	70-0223
DAVID, Ephraim	22	Eberheim	68-0456
DAVID, Friedr.	27	Tarnowske	71-0792
DAVID, Mechold	31	Malsch	71-0456
DAVID, Philippine	17	Rehweiler	68-0610
DAVIDSON, Minna	30	Appenrode	69-0321
DAWO, Jacob	30	Omersheim	71-0429
DE BAER, Anoni	28	Dillerwehn	70-0569
DE BARBER, Boer	50	Neermoor	68-0760
DE BERGER, Hugo Jack	21	Wittlich	68-0770
DE DROSTE, Constantin	35	Wuerzburg	69-1086
DE JUNG, Wibka	33	Bunde	68-0770
Michael 11, Joh. Hermann 9, Margaretha 5, Johann 1			
DE KROM, Peter	42	Bargcyk	68-1027
DE WALL, Claas	31	Ostfriesland	70-0452
DE WITT, Ernst	22	Amsterdam	69-0162
DE YUNG, Wibka	33	Bunde	68-0770

NAME	AGE	RESIDENCE	YR-LIST
Michael 11, Joh. Hermann 9, Margaretha 5, Johann 1			
DEADMAN, James	40	Baden	68-0456
DEAM, Gg.	17	Urphar	71-0581
DEBBE, Henriette	17	Hannover	71-0821
Lina 14			
DEBNER, Diedrich	48	Hannover	70-0443
Louise 41, Heinrich 16, Caroline 15, Sophie 9, Marie 8			
DEBRING, Henriette	19	Cloppenburg	69-1076
DEBUS, Wilh.	17	Battenberg	71-0821
DECHLER, Sebastian	34	Herchenheim	68-0982
DECKEN, Carl	17	Markoldendorf	71-0581
DECKER, Be.	20	Sievern	70-0728
DECKER, Elisabeth	15	Gottelhausen	71-0363
DECKER, Heinrich	19	Naumburg	70-0259
DECKER, Henny	17	Arenhain	69-1011
DECKER, Jacob	17	Eidlingen	71-0792
DECKER, Josef	31	Sachsbachwalden	71-0456
DECKER, Wilhelmine	16	Tecklenburg	68-0753
DECKERT, Ernestine	21	Heckengereutz	68-0707
DECKERT, Gottl.	31	Hildburghausen	69-0572
DEDERE, A.	28	Bargstedt	71-0792
Maria 10 months			
DEDERN, Eduard	24	Aachen	71-0821
DEEG, Christian	17	Esslingen	69-0848
Cathrine 16			
DEEPKE, Rudolph	42	Siedenbruenzau	69-0321
Alwine 26, Bertha 3, Rudolph 2			
DEESTEN, Anna	20	Nordleda	70-1055
DEETJEN, Carl	40	Matanzas	69-1309
DEETJEW, Meta	36	Bremen	69-0067
DEFAER, Philipp	27	Lambsheim	71-0643
DEFTECKER, Christine	25	Breitenholz	70-0089
DEGE, Herm.	30	Oldenburg	69-0292
DEGEL, Carl	24	Liebengruen	69-0457
DEGEL, Georg	21	Neudorf	71-0643
DEGENCALL, Christ. Alb.	28	Gassfenreuth	68-0647
DEGENER, Charlotte	16	Minden	69-1076
DEGENER, Martin	27	Baehringen	69-1363
Christine 4			
DEGENER, Wilhelm	31	Dreussen	68-0707
DEGENHARDT, Fr.	16	Schwarnse	69-1011
Anna 6			
DEGENHARDT, Joseph	48	Dingelstadt	71-0712
Elisabeth 46, Anna Maria 20, Anton 18, Anna 16, Josepha 12, Genofeva 8			
DEGENKOLB, Agnes	14	Schleiz	68-0625
DEGUENTHER, Ludwig	46	Trettenheim	68-0014
Gertrude 48, Friedrich 20, Therese 18, Peter 13, Anton 12, Elisabeth 6			
DEGUNTHER, Ad. Frd.	18	Worms	68-0820
DEHLING, Louise	14	Stettin	70-0308
Louise 9, Julius 5			
DEHM, Fedelius	40	Wuerzburg	69-1086
DEHNHOF, Heinrich	25	Buchenberg	71-0712
DEIBER, Margarethe	20	Ebingen	68-314
Traugott 17			
DEICHER, Martha	27	Licherode	71-0681

NAME	AGE	RESIDENCE	YR-LIST
DEICHGRAEBER, J. W.	32	Oldenburg	69-0079
DEICHMANN, J. H.	34	Bremen	71-1046
DEIMEL, Franz	22	Brilon	68-0534
DEIPENTRACK, Bernh.	19	Einerswinkel	71-0821
DEITEMEYER, Anna	20	Haltern	71-0479
DEITERS, Henry	18	Leschede	68-0957
DEITZ, Christiane	61	Oberurbach	68-0786
DEITZ, Marie	16	Gauersheim	71-0643
DELERET, Charles	32	Paris	69-0848
Victor 30			
DELGER, Helene	26	Godenholt	68-1002
Anna 5, Sophie 2, Emil 11 months			
DELHOEG, Caroline	25	Coeln	69-1212
Caroline 11 months			
DELIES, J.B.	58	Wittmund	69-1011
Mary 57, Johann 29, Mary 7			
DELIKAT, Heinrich	53	Wedelhorn	69-0771
DELIUS, Carl	23	Aachen	70-0052
DELIUS, Louis	29	Berlin	68-0907
DELL, Johannes	20	Weinheim	68-1027
DELLVIG, Auguste	20	Goslar	69-0079
DELTHEIM, Simon	20	Mutterstadt	71-0736
DELVENTHAL, Cathrine	18	Buchholz	71-0643
Anna 12, Henry 25			
DELVINDAHL, Heinrich	15	Rodenburg	70-0204
DEMBROWSKY, Joseph	31	Goblenowo	69-0547
DEMBROWSKY, Joseph	25	Neulongwitz	69-0547
DEMLER, Eduard	21	Nuernberg	70-0355
DEMMELMEYER, Emilie	25	Ingolstadt	68-0610
DEMMERICH, Anna	25	Geroda	.68-0647
Carl 27			
DEMUTH, Michael	35	Dingelstedt	68-0314
Clara 36, Catharine 2			
DEMUTH, Zacharias	56	Rimbach	68-0566
DENCHLER, Friedrich	25	Unteriwissheim	68-1006
DENHEIMER, Joh.	18	Spiesheim	70-0308
DENLENDORF, W.	24	Hohenhausen	68-0610
DENNHEIMER, Anna	20	Gr. Heuen	69-0015
DENNINGER, F.	30	Oelenbach	71-0789
DENTZ, Rosalie	16	Truskowitz	68-0770
DENZEL, Michael	24	Kreuznach	68-0456
DEPMANN, Hermann	28	St. Clair	69-0968
Anna 20			
DEPPE, Carl	17	Herstelle	71-1046
DEPPE, Carl	17	Herstelle	71-0712
DEPPE, Catharina	28	Bremen	68-0456
Dora 9			
DEPPERT, Franz	52	Bensheim	71-0300
Agnes 28, Georg 20, Catharina 15, Franz 13			
DEPPERT, Marg.	25	Island	68-0820
DEPPING, Friedr.	35	Detmold	69-0583
Henriette 22, Friederike 9 months			
DEPPING, Heinrich	38	Detmold	69-0583
DEPRUIN, Wilh.	47	Barmen	68-0753
Hermann 18, Laura 16			
DERASZINSKI, male	27	Riegelokoty	71-0815
DERINGER, Heinrich	19	Funkersdorf	69-0968
DERN, Helene	19	Langons	68-0625
Christine 28			
DERN, Nicolaus	28	Altenbamberg	71-0736
DERNDINGER, Arn.	30	New York	69-0490
DERSCH, Elisabeth	35	Warzenbach	71-0821
DERSICH, Maria	15	Borkenkringhaus	69-0583
DESENIS, Engel	22	Hohnhorst	69-1396
DESKAMP, Anna Marie	59	Elsass	71-0736
Marie 22			
DESSLER, Christian	50	Muehlhausen	69-0798
DETERMANN, Heinrich	18	Koenigsberg	69-0672
DETERMANN, Heinrich	23	Lengerich	68-0939
DETERS, Tamme	28	Buende	68-0534
Rumberta 20			
DETERT, Friedr.	43	Brunswick	69-0542
DETMERS, Elise	23	Altfunnixsiel	68-0314
DETTEL, Moritz	44	Clusfenitz	70-0384
DETTINGER, Gottl.	46	Dettingen	68-0760
Catharina 40, Gottlieb 12, Wilhelm 6, Barbara 4, Christian 6 months, Wilhelm 16			
DETTINGER, Jacob	46	Hochdorf	68-0610
Barbara 46, Jacob 17, Christine 13, Sophie 4			
DETTINGER, Johannes	20	Dettingen	68-0610
DETTKE, Marie	35	Greifswald	69-0784
DETTLING, Eva	59	Knibis	71-0792
Catharina 30			
DETTMER, Anna	17	Lockhausen	71-0456
DETTMER, August	32	Berlin	69-0798
Ferdinand 6			
DETTMER, Gottfr.	28	Mahnen-Mahuen	69-0049
DETTMER, Jan	48	Ostfriesland	69-1004
Antje 45, Frerich 27, Ida 16, Engel 16, Antje 12, Geesche 9, Baye 6, Johanne 4			
DEUBERT, Johann	18	Neubissingen	69-0457
DEUCHERT, Johannes	57	Eichenrod	71-0521
DEUERLEIN, Georg	17	Bieberbach	71-0363
DEUERLING, Geo.	22	Muehlendorf	70-0308
DEUGLER, Herrmann	21	Carlsruhe	69-0542
DEUKER, Johann	17	Verden	69-1396
DEUSCH, Emilie	25	Hollanderdorf	71-0393
Rich. 6 months			
DEUSCHLE, Marie	19	Unterweisbach	69-0848
DEUTSCH, Franz	59	Duby	68-0566
Anna 55, Wenzel 22, Franz 19, Anna 14			
DEUTSCH, Marcus	25	Bonghad	68-0760
DEUTZ, Carl	9	Coeln	68-0566
Hermann 6			
DEUTZ, Katharina	46	Coeln	68-0566
DEVERS, Joh.	15	Hannover	68-0753
DEWER, Rosa	18	Hamburg	70-1142
DEXHEIMER, Peter	73	Biebelheim	69-0672
Philipp 24, Eva 22			
DICK, Maria	30	Wilsenroth	68-0534
Catharine 9, Margaretha 7, Peter 6, Maria 11 months			
DICK, Wilhelm	60	Niedermendig	68-314
DICK, Wilhelm	16	Osterwanna	71-0429
DICKEL, Conrad	16	Hessen	69-1086
DICKEL, Friedrich	30	Berleburg	68-0939
DICKEL, Wilhelm	28	Petersgrund	69-0542
DICKEN, Heye	29	Hannover	70-0204

NAME	AGE	RESIDENCE	YR-LIST
Altje 27			
DICKERT, Anna	21	Niederaula	71-0456
DICKMANN, Heinr.	16	Lehe	68-0982
DICKMANN, Heinrich	25	Hamburg	68-0625
DICKOPF, Pet.	26	Herschbach	68-0610
Cathar. 19			
DIEBEL, Heinrich	31	Hirschfeld	68-0419
Anna 29, Heinrich 5, Valentin 3, Johann Heinrich 21, Jacob 15, Anna Gela 54			
DIEBMANN, Fanny	17	Crailsheim	71-0521
DIEBOLD, Cris.	24	Schweiz	70-1142
DIEBOLD, Johann	26	Mainleus	69-0848
DIEBOLD, Paul	20	Irslingen	69-0490
DIEBROCK, August	30	Herford	71-0492
DIECK, Charles	34	Bremen	68-0534
DIECKMANN, Caroline	16	Loxstedt	71-0492
DIECKMANN, Carsten	21	Stenz	69-0968
DIECKMANN, Henriette	60	Bremen	69-0542
Helene 23			
DIECKMANN, Johann	27	Sachsen Meining	69-0798
DIECKMANN, Louis	17	Hannover	68-0456
DIECKMANN, Marie	59	Hahlen	71-0789
Aug. 17			
DIEDERICH, Louis	20	Hannover	68-0939
DIEDRICH, (male)	38	Leinbach	70-0272
DIEDRICH, Catharina	19	Oberhochstadt	71-0492
DIEDRICH, Catharine	19	Wiehdorf	68-0314
DIEDRICH, Fritz	20	Selsingen	69-0338
DIEDRICH, Mathilde	26	Bremen	69-0050
DIEDRICHS, Charles	34	Ratzeburg	68-0534
DIEFENBACH, Carl	46	Eberstadt	69-0771
DIEFENBACH, Georg	45	Nassau	70-0384
DIEHEN, Mathias	24	Dornbirn	71-0643
DIEHL, Anna	17	Langgoens	69-0229
DIEHL, Christina	16	Richelkirchen	71-0521
DIEHL, Elise	22	Wiesbaden	70-1035
DIEHL, Henriette	24	Lehmberg	70-0031
DIEHLENMUELLER, C.	23	Bollbronn	71-0712
DIEHM, Cathrine	20	Gaisberg	71-0456
DIEK, Wilhelm	60	Niedermendig	68-314
DIEKEL, Caroline	25	Louisenburg	69-0968
DIEKHAUT, Joh.	51	Schrecksbach	69-0841
C. 51			
DIEKMANN, Anna	47	Senner	69-0572
Meta 14, Friedrich 5			
DIEKMANN, Heinr.	16	Lehe	68-0982
DIEKMANN, W.	27	Detmold	70-1066
DIELIGEN, Fr.	58	Hannover	69-1004
Engel 43, Fritz 17, Herm. 14, Elisabeth 20, Heinr. 9, Marie 6			
DIEMANA, Alouis	32	Benhau	70-0204
Franz 17, Caroline 19			
DIEMER, Michael	51	Palmira	70-100
DIENER, Conrad	25	Pirmasens	69-0784
DIENER, Johann	26	Mainhus	68-0707
DIENER, Margreth	14	Mainbeus	69-0848
DIENER, Wilhelm	34	Heffingen	71-0643
DIENST, Edw.	16	Coeln am Rhein	69-0050
DIENST, Friedrich	28	Hohelage	69-0542
DIEPENBECKER, Johann	15	Bargcyk	68-1027
DIEPHOLD, Carl	18	Hornberg	71-0363
DIERHACKE, Adolf	51	Lengerich	71-0821
Cath. 50, Friedr. 16, Wilhelmine 13			
DIERKER, Heinr.	18	Bersenbrueck	68-1002
DIERKING, D.	31	Creefeld	71-0815
DIERKS, Female	19	Emden	68-1006
DIERKS, Friederike	16	Wittmund	69-1011
DIERKS, Heinrich	35	Friedeburg	71-0492
Anna 34, Heinrich 9 months, Anna 50			
DIERKS, Henry	14	Bremerhaven	69-0672
DIERKS, Hermann	16	Marx	71-0492
DIERKS, Johann	19	Hannover	70-0308
DIERKS, Johann	16	Rachtenfleth	71-0492
DIERKS, Wilhelm	25	Hannover	68-0647
DIERKSEN, Johann	36	New York	69-0672
DIERSMANN, Anna	50	Warsingfehn	68-0884
Thekla 10			
DIESDORF, Margarethe	25	Hochstetten	71-0712
DIESEL, Elise	30	Peine	68-0314
DIESEM, Antonie	29	Wissgoldingen	69-0208
DIESSEL, Otto	18	Gr. Elbe	70-0204
DIESTELHORST, Auguste	30	Magdeburg	70-0523
Ernst 7, Louise 5, Ida 3, Julius 11 months			
DIETENMEIER, Rosine	19	Oberiflingen	68-0534
DIETER, Catharina	15	Wilmandingen	68-0566
Joh. 13			
DIETER, Fritz	57	Arheilger	71-0456
Friedrich 24, Sophie 19			
DIETER, Johann	36	Dusslingen	68-0566
Barbara 33			
DIETER, Michael	29	Zwingenberg	69-0229
Elisabeth 28, Georg 4, Emilie 1			
DIETERICH, Wilhelm	26	Ersingen	70-1003
DIETERLE, Eduard	22	Waldmoeningen	69-0672
DIETERLE, Johann	24	Hallnengen	69-0429
Barbara 18			
DIETMANN, Carl	29	Neuss	69-1086
DIETRICH, Anna	58	Hamweiler	71-0684
DIETRICH, August	18	Muehringen	71-0736
DIETRICH, Carl	29	Marburg	69-0182
DIETRICH, Eleonore	22	Wiesbaden	68-0982
DIETRICH, Friedrich	19	Goettingen	68-0753
DIETRICH, Johann	78	Michelbrock	68-0939
DIETRICH, Michael	20	Obermuehle	69-1086
DIETRICH, Wilhelmine	63	Frauen Zimmern	69-0229
Wilhelmine 22, Louise 9, Marie 8, Jacob 1			
DIETSCH, Maria	20	Wuerzburg	68-0625
DIETSCHE, Andr.	30	Todtnauberg	68-0566
DIETZ, Anna	25	Zeulenroda	70-0184
Ida 22			
DIETZ, Aug.	30	Erlau	68-0314
DIETZ, Bernhard	28	Ulm	69-0429
DIETZ, Christian	28	Knittlingen	69-0182
DIETZ, Dorothea	13	Gauersheim	71-0581
Philipp 9, Ludwig 7, Philipp 7			
DIETZ, Georg	16	Arenhain	69-1011
DIETZ, Georg	36	Kitzingen	71-0815

NAME	AGE	RESIDENCE	YR-LIST
DIETZ, Henriette	60	Zeulenroda	71-0429
Pauline 26, Alwine 19			
DIETZ, Henry	20	Romsthal	71-0143
DIETZ, Jacob	15	Spielberg	68-0852
Gottlieb 9			
DIETZ, Joh.	16	Sicke	71-0581
DIETZ, Johann	25	Arburgheim	69-0798
DIETZ, Julius	19	Schoenlanke	68-0786
DIETZ, Marg.	20	Gauersheim	68-0610
DIETZEL, Heinr.		Reuss	71-0393
W. 28, Frz. 3, Wilh. 4 months			
DIETZEN, Catharine	18	Tarfirst	71-0643
DIETZINGER, Ronald	45	Esslingen	71-0681
Rosine 54			
DIGERSEN, Ludwig	23	Elberdissen	69-0490
DIGESSER, Martin	27	Baehringen	69-1363
Christine 4			
DILL, Marie	23	Burghausungen	69-1059
DILLENBERG, Johann	32	Orenberg	69-0292
DILLMANN, Bernh.	30	Dinklage	68-1002
Josephine 30, Heinr. 9, Joseph 1			
DINGEN, Carl	27	Lauscha	69-0162
DINGER, Barbara	18	Petersheim	68-0610
DINGES, Jacob	24	Oberhoechstadt	68-1298
DINKEL, Paul	22	Uetzing	71-0300
DINKEL, Valentin	14	Neu Ulm	71-0643
DINNISSON, Elise	24	Cassel	69-1086
DINNORICH, Vincent	28	Wuerzburg	69-1086
DINTER, Eugen	16	Bittendorf	71-0681
DIONYIUS, Louise	21	Hannover	69-1076
DIRKS, Anna	22	Elsfleth	70-0384
DIRKS, Gerhard	26	Cleverus	69-0490
DIRKS, Gesine	16	Fettens	69-0457
Maria 19			
DIRKS, Johann	41	Nedderavebergen	68-0566
DIRKSEN, Gesine	9	Elsfleth	68-0625
DIRKSEN, Jantje	29	Jennelt	68-1027
Elisabeth 4 months			
DIRNA, Aug.	27	Nakel	70-100
DISCH, John	44	Paris	69-0208
DISCHER, Johann	19	Ins	68-0314
Rosine 17			
DISCHINGER, John	39	Pfaffenweiler	69-0583
Justine 37, Albert 14, Pauline 7, Friedrich 2			
DISTRUH, Friedrich	40	Laufen	69-0560
Eva 33, Charles 4, Therese 4 months			
DITTEICH, Emilie	34	Waldheim	70-0443
DITTMANN, Carl	36	Bochum	70-0089
DITTMAR, Richard	28	Floh	68-0760
DITTMARSCH, E.	19	Wallhugen	70-0184
DITTMER, Anna	20	Ehingen	70-0443
DITTUS, Marie	26	Ebhausen	69-1363
DITTWEILER, Elisab.	39	Sulzbach	71-0521
Marie 8, Abraham 7, Heinrich 6, Christina 5, Heinrich 6, Christina 5, Christia			
DITZ, Franz	25	Schweighafen	69-1363
DITZEL, Elise	17	Alfeld	68-0939
DITZEL, Wilhelmine	22	Meiningen	71-0736
DITZERHOLD, Albert	18	Zeitz	71-0456

NAME	AGE	RESIDENCE	YR-LIST
Amalie 16			
DITZINGER, Crescenzia	23	Dortmeckinger	68-0534
DIVISER, Carl	18	Ramstein	71-0429
DIX, Clara	19	Zeulenrode	71-0429
DJURPLEIOSKY, Franz	28	Zarmarta/Polen	69-0576
Antonia 24, Johann 6 months			
DLONKY, Anna	25	Boehmen	70-0508
DOBBERSTEIN, Pauline	21	Rosenfelde	71-0736
DOBERENZ, Anna	23	Bernbruck	68-0707
DOBIAS, Cath.	19	Boehmen	70-1035
DOBLER, Christine	24	Unterreningen	69-0672
Marie 4, Wilhelm 3			
DOBMEIER, Wilhelm	36	Gleisenberg	68-1027
DOBROWSKY, Ferd.	50	Pinnow	71-0733
DOCTOR, Louis	15	Walldorf	69-0784
DODT, Albert	21	Herstelle	68-0939
DOEBELE, Carl	17	Ulm	70-0089
DOEBELY, Bertha	30	Muhhausen	71-0363
DOEBLER, Traugott	30	Deutsch Luppa	68-0820
DOECHLER, Josefine	34	Marburg	71-0167
DOECK, Margaret	16	Steinau	68-0625
DOEFFNER, Margarethe	25	Nuernberg	68-0865
DOEGE, Pauline	26	Lubs	68-0786
DOEHLE, Joseph	24	Kirtorp	68-0456
DOEHRMANN, Cord Hch.	49	Warmsen	68-1002
Adolph 15			
DOEJAR, Jacob	24	Lakowo	71-0815
Cath. 27			
DOELFEL, Friedrich	48	Pruehl	70-0728
DOELKER, Johann	19	Hallnengen	69-0429
DOELLBOR, Franz	22	Leinenbach	68-0625
DOELMKE, Elise	20	Hagen	71-0479
DOELP, Jac.	21	Hessen	70-0204
DOEPKE, Herm	15	Hastede	68-0647
DOEPP, Dorothea	18	Lehe	69-0490
DOERAM, Charles	20	Ninstadt	70-0508
DOERFER, Catharine	22	Baiern	70-0384
DOERFFLER, Apolonia	22	Neudorf	68-1298
DOERFLINGER, Ad.	17	Mannheim	68-0647
DOERGELOH, Georg	18	Weyhe	68-0760
DOERGER, Amalie	24	Cassel	69-1363
DOERING, Alfred	37	Jena	70-0569
DOERING, Elisabeth	28	Guxhagen	68-0566
Elisabeth 6 months			
DOERING, Marie	21	Hoergenau	68-0770
DOERINKEL, Aug. Chr.	16	Willingshausen	70-0204
DOERNIG, Conrad	40	Birkungen	68-1002
Sabine 18, Anton 8			
DOERR, Johann	18	Mergentheim	69-0798
DOERR, John	28	Grombach	68-0534
DOERR, Valentin	36	Quincy	69-1212
DOERSCHER, Herm.	25	Widdern	68-0534
DOERTING, Minette	18	Oldendorf	68-0707
DOES, John	30	Einselthum	68-0760
DOESCHER, Becka	24	Meckelstedt	69-0560
John 5			
DOESCHER, Christian	26	Rodersdorf	68-0760

NAME	AGE	RESIDENCE	YR-LIST
Johanna 28, Ernest 3			
DOESCHER, Doris	17	Dorum	69-1363
DOESCHER, Doris	26	Midlam	70-1003
DOESCHER, ELis.	16	Lintig	71-0581
DOESCHER, Eibe	31	Hannover	70-1003
DOESCHER, Johann	16	Ringstedt	70-1023
DOESCHER, Johann	15	Ankelohe	68-1006
DOESCHER, Mart.	17	Freisdorf	70-0308
DOESCHER, Mathilde	17	Hepstedt	71-0429
DOESCHER, Sophie	18	Koehlen	71-0429
DOETSCHEL, Ferd.	48	Coburg	70-0170
Dorothea 49, Mary 14			
DOFFERNER, Josef	26	Odenheim	71-0456
DOHMEN, Wilhelm	26	Bonn	69-0457
DOHMEYER, Elise	21	Oberschulz	69-0771
Bartholomaeus 18			
DOHRMANN, Fritz	16	Osterholz	68-1298
DOHRMANN, Georg	15	Bueren	69-1319
DOHRMANN, Henry	29	Hoboken	69-0229
Anna 21			
DOHRMANN, Sophie	67	Jessum	69-0229
DOHRMANN, Wilhelm	16	Clueversborstel	69-0560
DOLCH, Charlotte	18	Thalheim	68-0534
DOLD, Elise	24	Sasbach	71-0789
DOLGE, Alfred	25	Neuhaven	68-0625
DOLL, Julie	22	Pfalz	71-1046
Clara 20, Wilhelm 9, Philipp 8			
DOLL, Nicolaus	19	Sasbachwelden	71-0821
DOLLDORF, Rud.	26	Hannover	69-0583
DOLLJCH, Katharina	20	Boehmen	70-0728
DOMANN, Bertha	41	Pforzheim	69-0079
Mina 8			
DOMBROWSKY, Mary	36	Jaurig	70-0308
Eugen 9, Clara 8, Margareth 3, Pauline 9 months			
DOMEYER, Georg	16	Bayreuth	69-0208
DOMINSKY, Carl	44	Albrechtshof	69-0049
Caroline 50, August 18			
DOMMENGEL, Victoria	13	Worms	71-0492
Carl 9			
DOMMERICH, Ab.	45	Hanau	70-0452
DOMMING, Eduard	45	Witzieschken	68-0939
Gustav 18			
DON, Heinrich	17	Carlshafen	69-0321
DONBATSCH, Jean	25	Metz	71-0456
DONNATH, Catharina	19	Bernroth	70-0184
DONNER, H.	22	Wittmund	71-0712
DONNER, Wilh.	22	Berlin	68-0982
DONNERMUTH, Cath.	17	Villmar	68-0625
DONNERMUTH, Joseph	23	Dousenau	68-0661
DOORMANN, Anrovie	34	Amsterdamm	69-0923
Anna 12, Willem 7			
DOPFING, Carl	18	Hoexter	70-0569
DOPMANN, Becka	15	Altenbruch	69-1309
DOR, Maria	21	Bergen	68-0760
DORDT, Wilhelm	18	Gr. Busek	68-0534
DORFFLINGER, Madlene	45	Colmar	71-0363
DORFMUELLER, Emilie	16	Solingen	68-0647
DORN, Kunigunde	17	Gasseldorf	71-0479
DORN, Marie	23	Niederzell	71-0393
DORNBECK, Augusta	8	Barmen	68-0760
DORNENBURG, Gottfried	25	Duesseldorf	69-0208
DORR, Alois	34	Rievensberg	71-0393
DORR, Aug.	38	Augusta	69-1086
DORSCH, Jos.	21	Bayreuth	69-1011
DORSCHT, Johann	46	Mittelstren	71-0521
Margarethe 45, Margarethe 16, Gustav 9, Otto 7			
DORSEBUSCH, Pauline	34	Berlin	69-0771
DORTTINGER, Wilhelm	30	Gandelsheim	69-0292
DORUFF, Simon	17	Villmar	68-0625
DORZOPP, Christine	22	Beltheim	68-0707
DOSCKING, Wilhelm	13	Geestendorf	70-0329
DOTEZAL, Josef	60	Kallin	70-1023
Helene 58, Franz 24, Helene 30, Marie 3, Georg 27, Minna 19, Wenzel 9 months			
DOTTEL, Abraham	30	Kletzko	68-0456
Cacilie 34, Marie 5, Leopold 4, Hannchen 11 months			
DOTTERER, Emilie	24	Speyer	69-1011
DOTTERES, Margarethe	16	Kirchardt	71-0736
DOTZERT, Johann	25	Grebenau	68-0647
DOWER, Henriette	21	Hof	70-1142
DRABER, Wilh.	51	Kandel	71-0684
DRACHLER, Caroline	16	Neckarsulm	68-0625
DRAESSAR, Hugo	36	Ahrweiler	68-0957
DRAGORIUS, Gustav	25	Berlin	68-0610
Marie 22			
DRAHLIM, Mich.	43	Tarnowske	71-0792
Friedrich 17			
DRALLE, Anna	15	Berlin	71-0300
DRALLE, Wilhelm	40	Wiedenbrueck	68-1002
Christine 35, Wilhelm 9, Wilhelmine 5, Heinrich 3, Gustav 29			
DRAND, Cath.	19	Aue	71-0821
Louise 17, Anna 15			
DRASIDE, Elise	21	Fritzlar	69-1004
DRAUDE, Elise	21	Fritzlar	69-1004
DRAWE, Christian	30	Lippe Detmold	69-0268
DREBES, F.	43	Waldeck	70-1066
DRECHSLER, Carl Hugo	25	Schedewitz	68-0610
DRECHSLER, Hermann	27	Wogau	69-1059
DRECKE, Adelheid	23	Holln	71-0643
Baby-girl 9 months			
DREES, Caroline	8	Melle	68-0957
William 6, William 9 months			
DREES, Henry	42	Surburg	68-0957
Caroline 39			
DREGEN, Henriette	28	Strelitz	69-0848
Emilie 11 months			
DREHES, Friederike	35	Bringhausen	71-0521
Marie 9, Friedrike 7, Louis 3, Carl 9 months			
DREHFORTH, Friedrich	15	Linden	69-0321
Heinz 13, Wilhelm 9			
DREIER, Wilhelmine	16	Vorl	71-0300
DREIFUSS, Wolf	15	Richelsdorf	68-1027
DREIKORN, Friederike	21	Ludwigstadt	68-0566

NAME	AGE	RESIDENCE	YR-LIST
DREILING, Adam	8	Spiesheim	70-0308
DREINHOFF, Bernhard	33	Rekum	68-0939
DREISCH, Andr.	29	Bischofsheim	71-0479
Eva 24, Fried 2, Carl 4 months			
DREISEKEN, Hermann	26	Senden	70-0523
DREISMANN, Johannes	27	Berlin	69-0292
DREME, Joh.	26	Tyrol	71-0167
DRENTH, Heinrich	22	Wetzburg	68-0014
DRESCH, Christian	21	Dietlingen	69-1309
DRESCHER, Franz	25	Altenburg	71-0792
DRESCHER, Johann	25	Benhau	70-0204
DRESCHER, Johanne	16	Hanninghausen	71-0479
DRESCHER, Robert	16	Grosshausitz	68-0760
DRESEKLER, Eggidius	24	Sorgenzahl	70-0006
DRESNAK, Andr.	19	Krojanke	71-0581
Stephan 44			
DRESSEL, Georg	24	Meiningen	69-0592
DRESSLER, Johann	62	Muehlhausen	70-0329
DRESSLER, Wilhelm	39	New York	70-100
DRESSLER Betty	20	St. Mag.	71-0681
DRESTE, Josef	19	Hofheim	69-1319
DREUEL, Wilh.	28	Haffeld	69-0292
Henriette 24, Carl 11 months			
DREWES, Emilie	19	Haberstadt	69-1212
Julie 17			
DREWES, Henriette	21	Hannover	71-0821
Adele 17			
DREWES, Johann	43	Barkfeld	68-0770
Friederike 43, Wilhelmine 7, August 6, Fritzel 2, Johanna 6 months			
DREWES, Johanne	19	Barth	70-1003
Bab. 3 months			
DREXEL, Josef	24	Dornbirn	71-0643
DREY, Max	19	Fuerth	69-0672
DREYER, Carl	14	Vahle	71-0643
DREYER, Elise	53	Markoldendorf	68-0566
DREYER, Joseph	36	Glatz	68-0939
DREYER, Marie	31	Verden	69-0771
Sophie 9, Hinrich 6, Willy 6, Molly 2, Anna 5 months			
DREYER, Marie	15	Oldendorf	69-0968
DREYFUSS, John	15	Mannheim	68-0534
DRIEHAUS, H.	19	Peine	68-0884
DRIESEN, Gertr.	29	Haldern	68-0820
DRIFTMANN, Carl	45	Lippe Detmold	70-0355
Wilhelmine 44, Friederike 17			
DRIFTMEYER, Anna	22	Melle	71-0479
DRISHAUS, Rud.	24	Peine	68-0534
DRIVER, Alex	24	Soningen	71-0521
DROCK, Friedrich	27	Altenbruch	69-1086
DROEGE, Anna	16	Floegeln	69-0457
DROEGE, August	16	Essens	69-1076
DROEGE, Carsten	21	Lehe	68-1298
DROEGE, John	20	Floepeln	71-0456
DROESSEL, Carl	20	Moehringen	70-0204
DROESSEL, Marie	24	Weimar	70-0384
DROHOTA, Rud.	25	Greiz	69-1363
DRONENBITTER, C.	29	Dettingen	71-0456
DROOP, Gottlieb	15	Esslingen	68-0786
DROOP, Julius	30	Osnabrueck	70-0135
DROSSELMEIER, Herman	20	Buer	68-1027
DROSSELMEYER, Hr.	26	Luveke	68-0753
DROSTE, Herm.	14	Heishoefen	68-0957
DROUVE, Gerhard	18	Vlotho	69-0848
DROZ, J.	18	Vienaden	69-1421
DRUEBBER, Charlotte	22	Bremen	69-0457
DRUECKER, Hy.	24	Guetersloh	68-0957
DRUECKLER, Elisa	36	Osterrieden	68-0314
Carl 14, Melchior 9, Therese 4			
DRUECKLER, Gottlieb	50	Osterrieden	68-0314
Caroline 49, Amalie 18, Wilhelmine 10			
DRUEDING, Johann	22	Cloppenburg	68-0661
DRUEMMER, Richard	22	Luebeck	68-0707
DRUMM, Daniel	36	Selchenbach	69-0572
DRUPKE, Helene	39	Pirsitz	71-0479
Pauline 13, Beate 11, Caroline 6			
DRURKEN, Heinrich	40	Mollbergen	69-0208
DRYER, Gesine	21	Cassel	69-0576
DUBOIS, Mich. Wilh.	20	Bingen	69-1212
DUCKWITZ, Aug.	22	Bremen	69-0162
DUDEN, Hermann	21	Schirnen	69-0208
DUEBBER, Elise	16	Engter	68-0647
DUEBBER, H.H.R.	13	Rieste	68-0647
DUEFFELMEYER, Clamor	15	Essen	71-0456
DUEKER, Friedrike	20	Minden	68-0786
Wilhelmne 18, Louise 16, Justine 9, Heinrich 7			
DUENGEL, Friedrich	52	Pommern	69-0672
Caroline 43, August 7, Friedrich 15, Anna 3			
DUENSING, Sophie	22	Jeversen	68-0456
DUENWALD, Emilie	32	Reusrath	70-1161
Elise 8, Arnold 11 months			
DUERINGEN, Joh.	27	Barmen	68-0820
DUERKEMANN, Emanuel	17	Mittelberg	71-0736
DUERR, Carl	30	Cleveland	69-0583
Julia 70			
DUERR, Georg	49	Wildberg	68-0907
Caroline 48, Adolph 7, Pauline 17, Caroline 14, Friedrich 5			
DUERR, Johann	42	Sulzbach	69-0784
Marie 33			
DUERR, John	48	Langenfeld	69-0338
Susanna 48, John 19, Michael 13, David 8, Christoph 6, Magdalena 17, Susanne 3			
DUERR, Louis	20	Langenburg	68-1027
DUERR, Marg.	18	Rentweinsdorf	69-1011
DUERR, Marie	23	Schwabach	69-1309
DUERR, Marie	28	Sulzfeld	71-0456
DUERRBECK, Sophie	38	Buehl	71-0492
DUESCH, Franz	19	Thun	71-0492
DUESSNER, Carl	44	Loge	68-0907
Henriette 50, Carl 22, Hedwig 17, Heinrich 7			
DUFAHL, Marcel	16	Monkawarsk	68-0770
DUFENTHALER, Therese	21	Alzeg	69-0672
DUHN, Margarethe	18	Hellwege	71-0712
DUKAR, Salomon	17	Sulzburg	71-0492
DULCH, Wilhelm	29	Kaltenwesten	69-0162
DULFER, Conrad	29	Schaffhausen	69-0268

NAME	AGE	RESIDENCE	YR-LIST
DULT, Martha	18	Wellen	71-0429
DULTGEN, Max	20	Wald	68-0661
DUMBERT, Georg	22	Niendorf	69-1363
DUMKE, Adolf	18	Selaw	70-0052
DUMPAT, Carl	16	Koenigsberg	71-0681
DUMPF, Heinrich	37	Altenbruch	68-0625
Catharina 40, Wilhelm 7			
DUMSER, Eduard	19	Bremen	71-0736
Alexander 17			
DUNCKER, Louis	22	Bremen	68-0907
DUNKA, Gertrud	31	Laer	70-1142
DUNKEL, Geo.	32	Eupen	70-0308
Mary 26, Baby daughter 11 months			
DUNKEL, Joseph	29	Huellstedt	69-0321
DUNKEL, Joseph	38	Wichdorf	68-0707
Mathias 28, Albert 8			
DUNTEMANN, August	47	Bollenzen	71-0643
Hermann 16			
DUNTEMANN, Carl	18	Bollenz	71-0643
DUNZEL, Caroline	28	Rodeck	70-1035
DURCHSCHLAG, Chr.	41	Neustadt	69-0338
DURING, Ferdinand	66	Brunswick	69-0542
Dorette 59			
DURLACHER, Hanna	30	Meinzeschein	70-1035
DURLACHER, Sarah	23	Meinzeschein	70-1035
(Brooklyn)			
DUTTER, Conrad	20	Deisslingen	68-0982
DWORACK, Johann	43	Radaun	68-0770
Marie 40, Anna 19, Joseph 15, Elisabeth 8, Maria 3, Joseph 4 months			
DZIERNOWSKI, Franziska	31	Nakel	70-1035
Wlada 5, Therese 11 months			
DeBLOIS, Bertha	25	Coblenz	68-0884
EB, Hugo	25	Kronenberg	70-0076
EBBERS, Meinolph	27	Wewelsburg	68-1002
EBEL, John	29	Landau	71-0172
EBEL, Marie	27	Hermannsrode	70-0204
EBEL, Mary	78	Schlienstadt	69-1363
Eva 10 months			
EBELING, Heinrich	41	Braunschweig	70-1035
Henriette 33, Carl 9, Albert 6			
EBELING, Heinrich	31	Bodenwerder	68-0647
EBELING, Henrich	21	Bueckeburg	69-0292
EBELING, Ida	57	Hessisch Oldend	69-0968
EBELING, Wiebel	27	Hannover	68-0707
EBEN, Resi	18	Weitentrebelisc	69-0490
EBER, Abraham	30	Coeln	69-0079
EBER, Heinrich	26	Oberfranken	70-0443
EBERANTZ, Katharina	26	Lasbach	71-0733
EBERDING, Helene	52	Witzenhausen	68-0753
Maria 19, Friedrich 14, Heinrich 17			
EBERG, Catharina	21	Marienthal	71-0792
EBERHARD, Sophie	23	Rehburg	68-0884
EBERHARD, Stephan	20	Erbach	69-0208
EBERHARDT, Ernst	26	Sandershausen	71-0167
EBERHARDT, Marie	28	Embrach	68-1027
EBERHARDT, Sinon	24	Rothenburg	69-1059
EBERHEIM, Heinr.	41	Schotten	68-0456
Sophie 35, Heinrich 9			
EBERLE, Eduard	38	Huetterheim	69-0672
Ursula 30, Aloys 9, Victoria 9, Ulrich 7			
EBERLE, Heinrich	25	Selzheim	68-0852
EBERLE, Marianne	21	Unterroth	68-0014
EBERLE, Michael	24	Burrweiler	69-1086
Peter 12			
EBERLEIN, Fred.	18	Rodenberg	68-0957
EBERLEIN, Herm.	15	Coburg	68-0610
EBERLEIN, Johann	25	Stubig	71-0492
EBERLY, Barbara	36	Wattenheim	71-0363
EBERS, Minna	6	Farge	70-1055
Child male, baby female			
EBERSALD, Heinrich	27	Trier	69-0229
EBERSON, Julius	23	Emmerich	68-1027
EBERT, Friedr.	21	Frankfurt	70-0728
EBERT, Friedr. Wilhelm	50	Britzig	69-0576
Christine 47, Christine 19, Fr. Wilhelm 18, Regine 10, Marie 8, Anna Marie 7			
EBERT, Heinr. Ferd.	37	Barchfeld	68-1002
EBERT, Heinrich	29	Lippe Detmold	71-0821
EBERT, Hermann	24	Waldberg	70-0135
EBERT, Louis	19	Doettingen	68-1027
EBINGER, August	15	Engweiler	68-0661
EBKEN, Fr.	23	Hollwege	69-1011
EBLING, Barbara	46	Nierstein	70-1003
Friedrich 9			
EBLING, Fr.	26	Nierstein	70-0204
EBLINGER, Caroline	19	Daetern	68-0820
EBSENBERGER, Am.	22	Sullixgen	71-0300
EBURG, Marie	22	Grossdingen	68-1006
ECHS, Lina	21	Blumenthal	69-1076
ECKARD, Philippine	24	Niederorschel	71-0643
ECKART, Lena	18	Hannover	70-0384
ECKEL, Elisabeth	16	Willersdorf	69-0321
ECKEL, Heinrich	21	Brightwater	69-0583
ECKELKAMP, Joseph	27	Westerwiede	68-0852
Catharine 20			
ECKER, Heinr.	54	Hannover	70-0052
ECKERMANN, Franz	18	Breitenberg	71-0581
Christine 20			
ECKERMANN, J. L.	29	Breitenberg	68-1002
ECKERT, Andreas	41	Sachsen Meining	69-0321
ECKERT, August	41	Altenau	66-0577
Auguste 36, Friederike 18, Louis 15, Louise 10			
ECKERT, Eva Marg.	24	Darmstadt	69-1212
ECKERT, Friedrich	20	Weissach	70-0148
ECKERT, Marg.	25	Bodenstein	68-1298
ECKHARD, Carl	40	Niederorschel	71-0581
Clara 24			
ECKHARD, Georg	15	Obermoellrich	71-0521
ECKHARDT, Anna Marg.	25	Germbach	69-0576
ECKHARDT, Caroline	35	Feuerbach	69-1059
ECKHARDT, Cath. Elisab.	22	Seifertshausen	68-0770
ECKHARDT, Heinrich	26	Hermannsstein	71-0643
ECKHARDT, Wilhelmine	18	Dobel	68-0884
ECKHOFF, Johann	17	Zesen	71-0712
ECKLER, Stephan	22	Mannheim	68-0982
ECKS, Dorette	20	Verden	69-1309

NAME	AGE	RESIDENCE	YR-LIST
ECKSTEIN, Barbara	19	Meiningen	68-0786
ECKSTEIN, W.	31	Muenchen	71-0582
EDEBOHLS, Heinrich	16	Sievern	69-0672
EDEL, Emilie	25	Leipzig	70-0683
EDEL, Joseph	35	Weihungszell	69-0672
Therese 40, Mathias 13, Joseph 3, Clara 2			
EDELMANN, Jacob	9	Rothenburg	71-0456
Ludwig 8			
EDELMEIER, Joseph	34	Mueltzau	68-0770
Anna 32			
EDEN, Albert	27	Oldenburg	68-0314
EDEN, Ellen	30	Aurich	68-0884
Anke 23, Dirk 2, baby 8 months			
EDER, Elisabeth	16	Wallerheim	70-100
EDINGER, Anton	55	Hypolz	71-0815
Maria 32, Anton 21, Franz 13, Engelina 4, Maria 9, Rosa 8, Adolf 9 months			
EDINGER, Jacob	17	Breitenbach	68-0786
EDLER, Catharine	33	Morristown	69-0848
Emilie 7, Heinrich 9			
EDLER, Ernst	27	Muehlhausen	69-0771
EFFINGER, Johann	20	Zimmern	69-0798
EFFINGER, Johann	34	Aixheim	69-0923
Ottilie 43, Therese 6, Agathe 4, Johannes 2			
EFFINGER, John	27	Aischheim	71-0456
Willy 18, Adolph 18			
EFFINGER, Josef	20	Aixheim	69-0968
EFFINGER, Leutgarde	23	Aixheim	69-0592
EFFINGER, Marianne	25	Lauffen	68-1006
EGARIUS, Cath.	29	Edenkoben	70-1055
EGARNIS, Marie	23	Eschingen	71-0733
EGBERT, Friedrich	43	Hannover	69-1059
Sophie 32, Minna 8, Ludwig 9 months			
EGDER, Fritz	15	Linden	71-0300
EGELI, Johann	28	Nordheim	68-0939
EGENBERGER, Joh.	25	Wallhausen	71-0792
EGERLAND, Gottfried	42	Debles	68-0760
Elisabeth 38, Sophia 16, Antonia 6, Wilhelmine 15, Ernestine 15, Friederike 12			
EGERTER, Bernhard	23	Pittsburg	70-0031
EGGENS, Otto	30	New York	71-1046
Wilhelmine 18			
EGGER, John	30	Schwendberg	69-0338
EGGERLING, Heinrich	24	Bremervoerde	68-0939
EGGERMANN, Gottlieb	32	Schweitz	69-1076
Agnes 28			
EGGERS, Ahrens	19	Brockzetel	69-1004
EGGERS, Elisabeth	17	Locktansen	68-0647
EGGERS, Henriette	50	Buffalo	69-1076
Johanne 14			
EGGERS, Joh.	17	Bollen	69-1086
EGGERS, Joh.	47	Graul	71-0821
Anna 47, Sophie 16, Dorothea 13, Carsten 9, Margarethe 6, Friedrich 4			
EGGERS, Ludwig	26	Wenzen	68-0625
EGGERS, Wilh.	35	Hannover	69-1004
EGGERS, Wilhelm	17	Lehrte	70-0329
EGGERT, Christoph	38	Oldendorf	69-0968
Marie 40, Carl 9, Ernst 8, Francisca 5, Caroline 69			
EGGERT, Wilhelm	26	Zewelinen	68-0770
EGGERT, Wilhelmine	18	Dissen	68-0957
EGGERT, Wilhelmine	25	Stettin	69-1086
EGGSTEIN, Bennedick	20	Volleringenstad	71-0492
EGINK, Th. Heinr.	32	Coesfeld	68-1002
EGLER, Julie	24	Sickenhausen	69-0798
EGLI, Anna	26	Kutlig	68-0661
EGLI, Minna	21	Schweitz	68-0456
EGNER, Henry	14	Niederhall	69-1396
Christiane 13			
EH, Hugo	25	Kronenberg	70-0076
EHEL, Hermann	16	Rinteln	68-0314
EHLEBRACHT, Heinrich	30	Asmissen	68-0456
EHLENBECK, Anna	64	Solingen	70-0272
EHLENS, Carl	23	Ehlendshoff	71-0792
EHLERS, Aug.	53	Bukau	71-0300
Louise 58, Emilie 18, Gustav 15			
EHLERS, Carolina	25	Hannover	70-0184
EHLERS, Carsten	48	Suedbostel	68-1002
Eleonore 42, Catharine 17, Fritz 7, Georg 3			
EHLERS, Elise	29	Wildeshausen	71-0643
Marie 19			
EHLERS, Friederike	30	Bremervoerde	69-1076
EHLERS, Friedrich	59	Hannover	70-1003
EHLERS, Hermann	63	Grossendorf	68-0982
Christine 59			
EHLERS, John	31	Brooklyn	69-1011
Adelheid 26, Anna 3, Elise 4 months			
EHLERS, Marie	28	Ohlendorf	69-1363
EHLERS, Wilhelmine	17	Oldenburg	71-0429
EHMANN, Barbara	18	Hallnengen	69-0429
EHMANN, Ernst	31	Waiblingen	70-0135
EHMANN, Frd.	27	Plochingen	71-0789
EHMANN, Nicol	27	Oppenheim	68-0534
EHMERT, Anna	18	Schrozberg	68-1027
EHNI, Philip	39	Bissingen	68-0534
Barbara 31			
EHNMANN, Nicol	27	Oppenheim	68-0534
EHRENBECK, Dorete	24	Bremen	70-0523
EHRENSTAMM, Salomon	18	Darmstadt	68-0982
EHRENSTEIN, Eugenie	25	Hammerstadt	70-0443
Max 4, Ernst 3, Victor 11 months			
EHRENSTRAUSS, Joh.	37	Doenningstadt	71-0581
EHRHARD, Anna M.	32	Meiningen	68-1049
EHRHARDT, Christ.	30	Sievern	68-0566
EHRHARDT, Galln.	30	Wuerzburg	69-1086
EHRICHS, Heinrich	15	Osterholz	68-0419
EHRLE, Babette	28	Constanz	71-1046
EHRLICH, Friedrich	19	Santra	69-1004
EHRLICHER, Anna	16	Bessungen	70-1055
EHRMANN, Moses	51	Mainz	69-0050
EHRT, Paul	30	Bremen	69-1086
Emma 23			
EIBEL, Jos.	28	Burkardtberg	71-0581
EIBERGEN, Johann	34	Tembach	69-0542
EICH, Joh. Jac.	46	Neuenweg	70-0443
EICH, Mathias	50	Chicago	70-0135
EICHEL, Carl	43	Priepest	68-1002

NAME	AGE	RESIDENCE	YR-LIST
EICHEL, Jacob	16	Steinbach	71-0479
EICHENAUER, Franz	16	Salmuenster	71-0456
EICHENBERGER, John.	22	Gramichen	71-0521
Rudolf 24			
EICHENHORST, G. F.	24	Gnernheim	68-0647
EICHENTLER, Aug.	22	Darmstadt	70-0170
EICHHORN, Aug.	45	Adorf	70-0272
EICHHORN, Marie	50	Cassel	70-1003
Martin 17			
EICHHORN, Mary	17	Heidelbach	68-0957
EICHHORN, Minna	24	Heilbronn	70-0052
EICHHORST Fr.	24	Ludwikems	69-1011
EICHKAMMER, Joh.	19	Zweibruecken	71-0821
EICHLER, Bertha	43	Dramburg	68-0314
Marie 5, Franz 4, Emma 2			
EICHLER, Georg	56	Vacha	71-0712
EICHLER, Wilhelm	25	Schoenebeck	69-1396
EICHMANN, H.	23	Granzow	68-0820
EICHMANN, Marie	16	Sottrum	70-0728
EICHMUELLER, Jac.	25	Hessen	70-0204
EICHSTEDT, Elisabeth	27	Feideldorn	70-0728
Emil 3, Hulda 9 months			
EICKE, Albert	19	Neusem	71-0429
EICKEMEYER, Carl	21	Einbeck	68-0610
EICKERT, Carl	47	Chemnitz	69-1059
EICKHOFF, Felix	26	Holtinau	69-0572
EICKHOFF, Friedr.	25	Breitenkamp	68-0884
EICKHOFF, Heinr.	39	Eversberg	71-0300
EICKHOFF, Heinrich	34	Herford	70-0378
Anna 21			
EICKMEYER, Carl	18	Lemgo	68-1006
EIDANN, Barbara	24	Holzheim	68-0852
EIFERT, Elisabeth	18	Katzenbach	68-0760
EIGENBROTH, Elisa	26	Ebersheim	68-0982
Cath. 19			
EIKELMANN, Hermine	38	Minden	68-0907
Friedrich 14, Minna 7, Mathilde 4, Julie 6			
EIKENHORST, G. F.	24	Gnernheim	68-0647
EILERS, Anna	21	Remels	68-0661
EILERS, August	16	Neustadt	69-0429
EILERS, Cath.	21	Hannover	70-1142
EILERS, Diedrich	24	Oldenburg	68-0707
EILERS, Gerd	27	Bockhorn	69-1059
EILERS, Gerhard	26	Varel	68-0419
EILERS, Heinrich	26	Westerholz	68-0456
EILSEN, Joh.	25	Cuxhafen	71-0479
EINERT, Catharina	18	Niedorf	69-0429
EINGAERTNER, Joseph	26	Dingelfingen	68-0786
EINHAEUSER, Ferd.	25	Austria	70-0170
EINHAUS, Bernhard	20	Listrup	68-0939
EINHOLZ, Lud.	34	Werda	68-0753
Ottilie 24, Otto 1, Carl 1 months			
EINHOLZER, Agatha	22	Kluefien	68-1027
EINIG, Jacob	28	Coblenz	68-0661
EINSIEDEL, Philippine	15	Lichtenberg	71-0479
EINWAECHTER, Johann	15	Kurhessen	70-0443
EINZEL, Heinrich	37	Unterleinitz	68-1006
EISEBACH, Eduard	28	Holler Wustig	70-0204
EISELE, H.		Neuningen	69-0229
EISELE, Isidor	30	Revingen	69-0576
Johanna 25, Scholaska 3			
EISELE, Wilhelmine	29	Engertingen	70-0223
EISELER, Rosine	21	Ihlingen	71-0456
EISEMACHER, B.	24	Braunschweig	69-0583
EISEN, Ludwig	23	Olsen	69-0049
EISENBEIS, Julius	29	Stuttgart	68-0647
EISENBERG, Catharine	19	Meiningen	68-0907
EISENER, Fritz	17	Giessen	68-0760
EISENGART, Anna	19	Berka	68-0760
EISENHAUER, Cath.	22	Wattmichelbach	71-0681
EISENHAUER, Heinrich	30	Plaggenburg	69-0547
Johanne 31, Johann 7, Marie 5, Hilke 3, Peter 8 months			
EISENHAUER, Hermann	18	Hessen	70-0204
EISENLOHR, Louis	29	Carlsruhe	70-0135
Franz 19			
EISENMANN, Catharina	22	Nordensteinenbg	68-0661
EISENMANN, Georg	16	Herrenthierbach	71-0521
EISENMANN, Moses	19	Hainstadt	71-0363
EISENMEYER, Fr.	51	Leoville	70-1023
John 44			
EISENMEYER, Maria	47	Leoville	70-1023
EISENTRAUT, Wilhelm	18	Altstadt	68-0661
EISFELD, Elise	27	Wandershausen	69-0542
EISKAMP, Friedrich	16	Hannover	69-0559
EISLER, Anna	20	Marthlos	68-314
EISMANN, Betty	21	Meppen	69-0576
EISTMANN, Anton	52	Sulzbach	71-0492
Caroline 53, Joseph 9, Rosa 8			
EITEL, Bertha	23	Goeppingen	71-0456
EITH, Adolf	20	Tuebingen	69-1319
EITZERT, Andreas	17	Vacha	71-0736
ELBERDING, Hermann	22	Elberfeld	70-0355
ELBERT, Bernh.	28	Laufach	71-0479
ELBRECHT, Heinrich	26	Luer	70-0683
ELFERS, Anna	19	Achim	68-0566
ELFLEIN, Andreas	23	Ebern	63-0244
Elisa 25			
ELFLEIN, Susanne	20	Reuteremsdorf	71-0479
ELFRING, Hermann	27	Hundenich	68-0820
ELFS, Carl	25	Stressow	69-0338
ELIAS, NATHAN	22	Rothenburg	70-100
ELIEL, Herman	16	Rinteln	68-0314
ELL, Friedrich	19	Oensbach	71-0226
ELLENBERGER, Fr.	30	Northeim	71-0521
Marie 29, Lena 3, Maria 2			
ELLERBROCK, Ferdinand	31	Burlington	69-0229
Caroline 27			
ELLERHOF, Mary	25	Nettelstedt	68-0957
ELLERING, Gerhard	57	Esse	68-0907
Maria 44, Anton 15, Heinrich 7, Bernhard 6, Joseph 4, Georg 4, Clemens 11 mont			
ELLERMANN, August	18	Engerte	71-0643
ELLERMANN, Barb.	23	Zimmerode	70-1011
ELLINGER, Co.	16	Cassel	68-1002
ELLINGHAUSEN, Wilhelm	17	Oldenburg	70-0204
ELLMAN, Charles	28	New York	69-1421

NAME	AGE	RESIDENCE	YR-LIST
ELMEN, Albert	58	Aurich	69-1004
ELNIS, Mich.	19	Oberweiler	71-0479
ELSAETTER, Sophie	17	Beerfelden	69-1319
ELSASSER, M.	24	Nuernberg	71-0815
ELSCHE, Christian	24	Braunsdorf	71-0429
Pauline 22, Hermann 11 months			
ELSTE, Louise	28	Wiehe	68-0610
Clemens 3, Caroline 11 months			
ELZ, Wendel	39	Mainz	71-1046
ELZE, Mina	17	Meimerhausen	68-0314
EMANUEL, Elisabeth	22	Merzalpin	71-0581
EMANUEL, Sal.	23	Coeln	69-1421
EMDE, Caroline	32	Nitze	68-0625
Auguste 14			
EMDEN, Veis	18	Wauerbruelingen	69-1363
EMER, Johann	36	Edemuehle	69-0542
Therese 29, Barbara 2, Therese 3 months			
EMERICH, Jacob	52	Wippenbach	70-0355
EMET, Louise	27	Frost	71-0643
EMHORN, Carl	31	Berlin	71-0733
Louise 28			
EMICH, John	22	Durnweiler	71-0456
EMME, Wilhelmine	23	Ilvese	69-0457
EMMEL, Cath.	21	Gelnhausen	70-0452
EMMELMANN, Charlotte	38	Armstadt	69-0672
Pauline 12, Antonie 9 months			
EMMERICH, Joh.	20	Abenthauer	69-0583
EMMERICH, Nicol	23	Ruedesheim	69-1004
EMMINGER, John	20	Deisslingen	70-1161
EMMINGER, Vincenz	18	Deislingen	68-0534
EMRICH, Jacob	32	Hopstaedt	69-0457
EMSHOFF, August	16	Stolzenau	71-0492
ENDERS, Caroline	27	Oehringen	69-0457
ENDERS, Conrad	31	Stumpterod	69-0672
Meta 19, Nicolaus 16			
ENDERS, Conrad	31	Stumpterod	69-0672
Meta 19, Nicolaus 16			
ENDERS, Elisabeth	42	Wallenrod	69-0542
Elisabeth 2			
ENDERS, Franz	27	Hachenheim	68-0610
ENDERS, Otto	20	Freyburg	68-1002
ENDLER, Pauline	17	Hannover	69-1212
ENDLICH, Emma	19	Stuttgart	68-0939
ENDRESS, Johann	26	Bonn	69-0162
ENDRESS, Marie	19	Ehringen	68-0566
ENDRESS, Sophie	26	Oberfranken	68-0456
ENDRICHS, Franz	29	Solingen	70-0308
ENGEL, Carl	19	Herford	71-0492
ENGEL, Cathrine	30	Cincinnati	70-1161
ENGEL, Heinrich	49	Orb	68-0852
Margaret 19, Anton 16, Jacob 25, Rosine 28			
ENGEL, Jacob	30	Baierfeld	69-0321
ENGEL, Levi	19	Muenzenberg	69-0429
ENGEL, Theresia	24	Marienwerder	68-0786
ENGELBRECHT, Herm.	15	Nied Nels	69-0542
ENGELBRECHT, Hermine	20	Goettingen	69-0848
ENGELBRECHT, Mich.	18	Neumersdorf	69-0560
ENGELCKE, C.	24	Frankfurt a\ O	70-0272
Bertha 23			

NAME	AGE	RESIDENCE	YR-LIST
ENGELER, Christoph	45	Rosefeld	70-1003
Friederike 45, Pauline 18, Franz 17, Friederike 9, Friedrich 8, Carl 6			
ENGELHARD, Alois	29	Kirchheim	68-0534
ENGELHARD, Wilhelm	26	Bremen	69-0182
Josephine 26			
ENGELHARDT, Johanna	18	Butzbach	71-0581
Cath. 16			
ENGELHARDT, Marg.	16	Wanzleben	68-0661
ENGELHARDT, Marg.	50	Schwaben	71-0226
Anna 21, Sophie 22, Marie 20, Johann 17, Christine 14			
ENGELHARDT, Oscar	18	Grossbreitenbac	71-0429
ENGELHARDT, Robert	27	Frankfurt a/M	69-0079
ENGELHART, Thusnelda	19	Cassel	68-0852
ENGELKE, Anna	24	Hueddingen	68-0566
ENGELKE, Joh.	25	Bruehl	71-1046
ENGELKING, Anna	52	Bremen	70-0378
Johanna 20, Louise 16			
ENGELKING, Heinr.	16	Hannover	71-0479
ENGELKING, Sophie	20	Hannover	70-0443
ENGELMANN, Georg	61	St. Louis	69-1212
Dorothea 53			
ENGELMANN, Johann	17	Hannover	69-1059
ENGELMANN, Justine	20	Margoninsdorf	69-0229
Marie 3			
ENGELN, Josefine	20	Lingen	69-0490
ENGELS, Bernhard	26	Epe	71-0712
ENGELS, Rosa	40	Danzig	68-0610
Johannes 7			
ENGEMANN, H.	32	Warburg	66-0413
Mathilde 31			
ENGEMANN, Joseph	27	Westfalen	70-0728
ENGERSSER, Johann	16	Deisslingen	70-0308
ENGERT, Carl Aug	21	Nordhausen	69-0542
ENGESSER, Susanne	38	Mauch	71-0456
Cathrine 14, Rosine 9			
ENGLER, Carl	37	Beck	71-0736
Wilhelmine 34, Gustav 9, Bertha 7, Albert 10 months			
ENGLERT, Catharine	22	Ruebesheim	69-0672
ENGLISCH, Catharina	49	Wien	68-0647
Leupolda 8, Adam 6, Julius 5			
ENGSTES, Mary	50	Rochester	69-1011
Lina 8, Louise 6			
ENGTER, Wilhelm	47	Hinsdorf	69-0923
Wilhelmine 48, Carl 17, Minna 15, Emilie 6			
ENNEKING, Herm.	24	Drummerslohhaus	69-0338
ENSLIN, Ludwig	22	Bopfingen	71-0429
ENSNER, Georg Leonhd.	43	Schelbert	68-1002
Catharine 40, Leonhard 8, Lorenz 5, Paulus 4, Martin 11 months			
ENTELMANN, Adelheid	19	Osterode	68-0707
ENTRESS, Albert	21	Rothenburg	68-0707
ENZ, Theresia	24	Wagenstadt	68-0957
ENZIAN, Fried.	17	Ohlendorf	71-0479
ENZTER, Wilhelm	47	Hinsdorf	69-0923
Wilhelmine 48, Carl 17, Minna 15, Emilie 6			
EPHIMOFF, Louise	25	Petersburg/Russ	69-1086
Louise 10 months			
EPPELSHEIM, Bernhard	18	Mainz	68-0852

NAME	AGE	RESIDENCE	YR-LIST
EPPENBACH, Christine	26	Grotzingen	71-0226
EPPLE, Pauline	23	Bettnang	71-0789
EPPLER, Albert	32	Zimmelhausen	68-314
EPPSTEIN, Carl	15	Kalup	71-0479
EPSTEIN, Ma.	40	Schuesselburg	71-0521
ERB, Georg	17	Nieder Ohmen	68-1002
ERB, Marie	22	Rueddinghausen	68-0820
ERB, Philipp	25	Bremen	71-0684
ERBSLOEH, Julius	48	Barmen	69-1076
ERBST, Louise	23	Langenholzhause	68-0647
Baby 11 months, Caroline 17			
ERDBRUEGGER, Caspar	58	Buende	68-0534
ERDER, Wilhelm	18	Carlshafen	71-0429
ERDMANN, Emilie	12	Neu Subeza	71-0521
ERDMANN, Ferdinand	18	Friedland	68-0786
ERDRICH, Josef	35	Altenheim	71-0456
ERHARDT, Wilhelm	32	Lahr	69-1319
ERLENBACH, Otto	17	Wiesbaden	69-0229
ERLULER, Caroline	17	Sandersweiler	69-0848
ERMANN, Johann	28	Mainz	69-0162
ERNI, Eva	19	Trins	71-0226
ERNO, Carl	23	Stuttgart	69-0162
ERNSKING, Johann	17	Oldenburg	70-1023
ERNST, Augusta	19	Huelzum	68-0647
ERNST, Carl	28	Tennstaedt	68-0786
ERNST, Erhard	25	Rodesgrun	68-0939
Margaretha 21, Andreas 11 months			
ERNST, Frd.	18	Sasbach	71-0789
ERNST, Gust.	16	Wolfenbuettel	68-0534
ERNST, Joh.	23	Muenchen	70-0052
ERNST, Joh.	40	Lengsfeld	71-0681
ERNST, Louise	27	Frost	71-0643
ERNST, Mary El.	27	Georgenzell	68-0957
August 4			
ERNST, Mathias	15	Bottendorf	71-0456
ERNST, Philipp	25	Effenbach	69-0542
ERNSTING, Frank.	60	Mecklenburg	70-1023
Christine 53, Sophie 22			
ERNSTING, Ludw.	19	Nienburg	70-0170
ERSATZ, Wilhelm	34	Bielefeld	70-0184
ERWIN, Carl	19	Schwemmingen	69-0229
ERZLER, Florian	25	Obergrund	71-0581
Caroline 24, Caroline 6 months			
ESBACH, Carl	16	Buchholz	68-0820
ESCHENBACHER, Franz	23	Darlanden	69-0672
ESCHENBERG, Ludw.	17	Bremen	71-0821
ESCHENSCHEID, C.	27	Bornheim	71-0492
ESCHER, Gertrude	27	Herschbruch	71-0429
ESCHHOFEN, Heinr.	15	Dotzheim	71-0167
ESCHMANN, Clemens	16	Bueckeburg	70-0569
ESCHRICH, August	21	Gschwenda	70-0508
ESENWEIN, Gust.	19	Niederbriegen	71-0736
ESKUCHE, Heinrich	17	Cassel	68-0647
ESPITALIER, Gustav	40	Frankreich	68-0456
Marie 23			
ESSDORN, Heinrich	28	Syke	68-0760
ESSER, Wilhelm	35	Coblenz	70-0816
Anna Catharina 3			
ESSIG, Pauline	18	Flacht	69-0592
ESSIG, Wilhelm	18	Leonberg	70-0135
ETERLIDE, Auguste	26	Pusigke	69-0672
ETTEL, Therese	37	Ob. Dischingen	70-1003
ETTELMANN, Con.	22	Sausenheim	70-1055
ETTERSBERGER, B.	32	Wuerzburg	69-1086
ETTI, Franciska	20	Unterwald	69-1309
ETZ, Caroline	23	Sonnenberg	69-0429
ETZEL, Ludwig	16	Hochdorf	68-0610
EUCHENBACH, Thomas	29	Walderssen	71-0643
EUCHENHOFER, Carl	29	Dettingen	71-0226
EUCHNER, Frdke.	40	Hochdorf	68-0610
Rosine 9			
EUFINGER, Jacob	38	Oberbrechen	71-0226
EUK, Georg	17	Ampferbach	71-0643
EUKER, Diedrich	40	Marburg	70-1003
EUKLER, Henry	32	Landusky	71-0456
EUMREL, Louis	27	Argenthal	69-0672
Elise 20			
EUNEN, Maria	18	Friedeburg	71-0492
EURICH, Dorothea	28	Finsterroth	71-0643
Carl 3			
EURICH, Rosine	63	Finsterroth	71-0643
EUSSLEIN, Joh. G.	28	Bopfingen	68-1006
EUVENMANN, Anna	19	Leismathousen	69-0292
EVERMANN, Catharine	15	Rahe	69-0429
EVERS, Cord	16	Leeste	68-0939
EVERS, Gerhard	42	Diepholz	69-0560
Friederike 36, Johanna 7, Sofia 4			
EVERS, Justine	22	Walle	68-0566
EVERS, M. F.	39	Lueneburg	68-0884
Marie 33			
EVERS, Meta	23	Hobaken	70-0052
EVERS, Theodor	44	Borgenstreich	68-0884
EVERS, Wilhelm	51	Visgnard	69-0429
Hancke 51, Jan 9, Auguste 6			
EVERS, Wilhelm	20	Nichtern	68-0820
Bernhard 61, Margarethe 61, Johanna 26			
EVERSMEIER, Sophie	23	Wersen	71-0821
EVERSZ, Ferd.	29	Rotterdam	68-1006
EVERTBUSCH, Jac. O.	18	Kronenberg	70-0223
EVERTZ, Albert	36	Michelshaus	69-0457
EVOY, Pajetan	27	Wuerzburg	69-1086
EWALD, Elisabeth	18	Reichensachsen	71-0684
EWALD, Friedrich	17	Pfeddersheim	69-0572
EWALD, Philipp	41	Ernsthausen	71-0429
Eva 39, Conrad 14, Johannes 3			
EWERT, Hans	24	Draussnitz	68-1002
EYLERS, Johan	22	Bockhorn	69-1059
EYRING, Lisette	22	Gempertshausen	68-0566
Elitt, Cathrine		Koenigsthal	69-1059
FABER, Charlotte	17	Stuttgart	68-1027
FABER, Friedr.	31	Ludwigsburg	71-0681
Anna 25			
FABER, Isaac	18	Kitzingen	68-0852
FABER, Jacob	30	Muenster	68-0456
FABERSKA, Cath.	33	Posen	68-0884
Eva 2			

NAME	AGE	RESIDENCE	YR-LIST
FABIAN, Johann	17	Ternilin	70-0329
FABRICIUS, Friedr.	17	Weilburg	71-0363
Carl 9			
FABY, John	38	Bremen	69-1396
FACHINER, Joh.	13	Frankenberg	70-0452
FACKER, Minna	20	Wallhofen	69-1363
FACKING, Fr.	29	Wildeshausen	71-0581
FAEBER, Amalie	23	Wallhoefen	69-1363
FAEBER, Mina	20	Wallhofen	69-1363
FAECHSEL, Ernst	35	Fuerstenfeld	69-0798
FAEHR, Gust.	30	Bremen	69-0050
FAEHRIDERS, Claassen	58	Hannover	70-0384
Catharine 55, Claas 29, Jan 16, Folkert 15, Heinrich 9			
FAELINGER, Caroline	33	Leipzig	70-0508
FAERBER, Andreas	30	Sandhorst	68-0939
FAERBER, Carl	17	Oberndorf	69-0672
FAERBER, Gretchen	20	Alzei	70-0355
FAHLBUSCH, D.	16	Oldenbuettel	71-0521
FAHLE, Sophie	22	Zeittingen	71-0792
FAHRENBACH, Therese	22	Buchholz	69-0542
FAIST, Georg Ulr.	47	Rock	68-0647
Jacob B. 24, Michael 18			
FALBER, Joseph	23	Himkirchen	70-0223
Eva 21, Thomas 11 months, Xaver 2 months			
FALCH, Otto	20	Esslingen	68-0014
FALK, Anton	20	Ubstadt	68-1006
FALK, Friedrich	20	Bibersfeld	71-0643
FALK, Louise	19	Gr. Garde	68-0566
Dora 17			
FALK, Louise	20	Gnesen	71-0300
FALK, Marie	34	Tuebingen	69-1059
FALK, Wilhelmine	22	Adelshofen	69-1421
FALKENHEIM, Johanna	30	Voersten	68-0939
FALKENSTEIN, Marg.	22	Dettingen	71-0521
FALLER, Pauline	22	Zunsweiler	71-0792
FALLERT, Christian	26	Sasbachwelden	71-0821
FANDEL, Friedrich	19	Echternach	69-0841
Anna 16			
FANDREI, Albertine	14	Wollin	69-0771
FANGEMANN, Brune	15	Morsum	68-0647
FANITZSCH, Franz	22	Busdorf	70-0329
FANNER, Julka	40	Emden	69-0572
Georg 5, Siebold 3, Gerhard 11 months			
FARGUHA, Amalia	17	Aachen	68-0939
FARK, Maria	24	Haltern	71-0479
FARKE, Dorothea	27	Hegersdorf	69-0968
FARMER, Helene	40	New York	69-0923
Bertha 6, Abraham 4			
FARMER, Jacob	25	Ischeim	71-0821
FARR, Jacob	18	Gettenbach	71-0581
FASEL, Aug.	18	Emmendingen	68-0760
FASEL, Johann	26	Rheinfereussen	69-0771
FASELER, Dirk	60	Aurich	68-0884
FASS, Elisabeth	21	Eitzendorf	68-0566
FASSE, Heinr.	32	Aplern	71-0479
Caroline 29, Heinr. 6, Friedr. 4, Caroline 9 months			
FASSEN, Cathr.	50	Fassen	70-0170

NAME	AGE	RESIDENCE	YR-LIST
FASSMAN, Carl	18	Bremervoerde	71-0643
FASSUNG, Jacob	20	Omersheim	71-0429
FAST, Johann	34	Nuernberg	69-0841
FASTAG, Hermann	41	Berlin	69-0771
FASTEHARD, Johann	50	Paaberg	69-0798
Henrich 17, Johann 15			
FATH, Friedrich	24	Eichenberg	68-0647
FAUBEL, Elise	60	Osthofen	70-0683
FAUHLHABER, Andr.	37	Wuerzburg	68-0753
FAULHABER, John	23	Mertzhausen	71-0643
FAULHABER, Lina	26	Greisdorf	69-0560
FAULHUBER, Georg	28	Buerkheim	68-0456
FAUSEL, Wilhelmine	23	Pforzheim	70-0135
FAUST, Anna	28	Schifferstadt	71-0393
FAUST, Heinrich	46	Grossenmoor	70-0204
FAUST, Lorenz	16	Darmstadt	71-0456
FAUTH, Catharina	32	Friedewald	69-1212
FAY, Catharine	39	Siegen	68-0314
Amalie 16, Lina 14, Lisette 9, Robert 8, Heinrich 3 months			
FAY, Jac.	54	Bissersheim	69-1086
FAYEL, Jacob	24	Villmar	68-0625
FEBOHM, Sigmund	42	Waldkirch	70-0052
FECHHEIMER, SAmuel	33	Bayreuth	71-0492
FECHT, Rud.	35	Wiesens	69-1004
FEDDEN, Adolph	15	Hannover	69-0429
FEDDEN, Julius	25	Hagen	69-0923
Hilwine 23			
FEDDERMANN, Johann	17	Schweindorf	69-0457
FEDER, Joh.	20	Hagenbuch	71-0479
FEDERLIN, Jacob	35	Darmstadt	71-0492
FEDERMANN, Joseph	49	Stubschad-Bohem	70-0006
Marie 40, Rosalie 16, Aloise 13, Adolph 10, Francisca 7, Friederich 4, Therese			
FEGBLE, Jacob	28	Einsiedel	69-0572
Louise 21			
FEGEL, Louis	14	Minden	68-0907
FEGEL, Marie	45	Hille	71-0581
Marie 16, Christ. 9, Friedr. 7, Carl 5			
FEGMEIER, Doris	18	Argenstein	68-0534
FEHLBETER, J.	37	Bremen	70-1066
FEHLING, Theodor	15	Lamspringe	69-0208
FEHLIS, Louise	18	Rothenburg	68-0939
FEHN, Franz	13	Kehlbach	69-1059
Kunigunde 20			
FEHR, Elisabeth	25	Wurgasch	68-0625
FEHRMANN, Heinrich	30	Marssel	68-0760
FEI, Elisabeth	26	Marburg	71-0521
FEICK, Cathr.	20	Hessen	70-1066
FEIK, Adam	28	Rienbach	69-0208
FEIL, Adolph	29	Calwe	68-0760
Minna 35, Margarethe 7			
FEILER, Adam	30	Asch	68-0939
FEILSMANN, Minna	19	Neustadt a/R	69-0572
FEIN, Bath.	37	Nassau	71-0581
Anna 35, Anna 70, Anna 6, Johann 4, Infant			
FEIND, Charles	25	Nieheim	68-0957
FEINE, Fredr.	36	Allstedt	68-0534

NAME	AGE	RESIDENCE	YR-LIST
FEINTHEL, Heinrich	28	Landstedt	68-0939
FEIST, Marie	70	Waldeck	69-0592
Semi 9			
FEITNER, Barbara	15	Ebersheim	68-0770
FELD, Christoph	30	Vollmers	71-0736
Margaretha 30, Heinrich 11 months			
FELDEN, Nicolaus	32	Bilsseken	71-0821
FELDHAUS, Ernst	19	Barmen	69-1004
FELDHAUS, Stephan	59	Bassen	69-1086
Engelika 53, Joh. 27, Adelheid 24, Elisa 20			
FELDHUSEN, Adelheid	66	Ritterhuede	69-1212
FELDHUSEN, Catharine	21	Ritterhude	68-0770
FELDKAMP, Gerd	60	Ostfriesland	69-1059
Gesine 55, Antje 23, Baby 8 months			
FELDKAMP, John	38	Schale	69-0338
Anna 44, Hermann 8, Gerhard 5, Lambert 4			
FELDMANN, Al.	20	Aspel	71-0363
FELDMANN, Anna	15	Twistringen	69-1004
FELDMANN, Died.	48	Celle	69-1363
FELDMANN, Dorothea	23	Visselhoevede	68-0566
FELDMANN, Heinrich	12	Hauluenne	70-0204
FELDMANN, Jobst	20	Ennigloh	68-1002
FELDMANN, Sophie	50	Isenstaedt	68-0907
FELDMANN, Wilh.	52	Mohlberg	69-0576
Caroline 29, Carl 5			
FELDPUSCH, Anna	34	Hessen	69-0771
FELDSCHER, Heinrich	56	Hartenfeld	68-0456
FELDSCHER, Heinrich	22	Wien	68-0456
FELDTMANN, Margarethe	15	Altenbruch	68-0661
FELGENHAUER, Edmund	24	Wien	69-0559
Antonie 23, Edmund 11 months			
FELKE, August	44	Koenigsdorf	68-0707
Elise 44, August 17, Johann 6, Joseph 5, Robert 46, Johanna 46, Johann 7, Juli			
FELL, Nicolaus	50	Kreimerad	68-0770
Nicolaus 28, Maria 25			
FELLHAUER, Elisabeth	19	Mardich	70-0683
FELLHEIMER, Carl	16	Wengsfeld	71-0521
FELLKOETTER, Anna	19	Glaudorf	69-0429
FEMER, Elise	21	Siegermuehle	71-0492
FENDRICH, Adam	22	Birkenau	71-0643
FENSLAFF, Auguste	21	Stettin	69-0572
FENSPOLDE, Johann	61	Crosewick	68-0884
Marie 60, Johann 22, Marie 19, Gertrud 18, Dina 16, Johannes 16			
FENZL, Maria	29	Boehmen	70-1066
FERCHER, Henriette	46	Bremen	71-0226
FERCHLAND, Ernst	36	Gerbstadt	70-0259
FERDREDING, Cathrine	62	Thorst	69-1059
Cathrine 20			
FERGEN, John	19	Coblenz	70-0508
FERGUSON, John	65	Stamford	69-0784
Henry 65, Helen 28, Emmy 18			
FERICHS, Hermann	25	Oldenburg	70-0308
FERKEL, Theodor	23	Schwarzenbach	68-0707
FERLING, Gesine	16	Brinkum	69-0672
FERNEDING, Cathrine	62	Thorst	69-1059
Cathrine 20			
FERNERDING, B.	19	Dinklage	69-0208

NAME	AGE	RESIDENCE	YR-LIST
FERNSCHILD, Wilhelm	31	Muehlhausen	68-0314
FERRE, Michael	24	Wadgassen	71-0581
FESCHLER, G.	29	Schubin	70-0052
FESENFELD, Joh.	17	Upheisen	69-1086
Hermann 16			
FESSMANN, Carl	27	Nordlingen	68-0939
FESTER, Marie	35	Schweiz	71-0581
Johann 9, Agnes 8, Felix 6, Chist. 4			
FETTE, Marie	56	Salzgitter	71-0429
FETTEN, Robert	17	Dehlen	68-0820
FETTENAU, Fritz	19	Doeverden	71-0643
FETZ, John	45	Lampertheim	69-0338
Charlotte 40, Jacob 16, Fred 13, Adam 8, Charlotte 7, Martin 4, Catharina 5, M			
FETZNER, Reinhard	25	Untergronebach	68-0852
Rosalie 23			
FEUCHT, Marie Agnes	19	Dottinger	71-0226
FEUCHTINGER, Josef	22	Donauwerth	71-0643
FEUERBACH, Friedrich	26	Coblenz	68-0456
FEUERHENN, Bertha	28	Repplin	68-0314
FEUERPFUL, Ernst	32	Meiningen	69-0583
Thekla 22			
FEUERSTEIN, Friedrich	18	Warthausen	69-0672
FEULING, Leonh.	18	Darmstadt	69-0841
FEULNER, Andreas	15	Unterbrumberg	68-0661
Friedrich 14			
FEULNER, Margareth	19	Buttendorf	71-0643
FEURING, Carl	17	Laaspe	68-0625
FEUSEL, Friedrich	43	Meiningen	71-0429
Auguste 41, Melanie 13, Colthilde 9			
FEUSKE, Emil	25	Offenbach	69-0784
FEUSTEL, Ernst	28	Plauen	70-1003
FEUTNER, Marg.	17	Unterlangenstad	69-1011
FEXTOR, Elisabeth	20	Weyher	68-0907
FEY, Johann	30	Pottberg	70-0178
Pauline 28, Franz 3, Herm. 2, Max 3 months			
FEY, Just.	20	Alsfeld	71-0393
FEYERABEND, Ludwig	19	Wimpfen	68-0939
FIALA, Josef	34	Boehmen	69-0321
Barb. 29, Wenzel 9, Josef 5, Anna 11 months			
FICHEISSEN, Aug.	23	Ulmet	70-0204
FICHN, Peter	49	Schoenebeck	70-0508
FICHTEL, Friederike	60	Pottberg	70-0178
Auguste 18			
FICHTEN, Helene	20	Sievern	68-0566
FICHTER, Margarethe	42	Soetern	68-0786
Catharine 16			
FICK, Caroline	24	Breitenbach	71-0733
FICK, Gesine	17	Zeven	68-0625
Sophie 17			
FICK, Johann	35	Rhade	68-0625
Anna 37, Anna 9, Sophie 11 months			
FICK, Johann	40	Tarmstedt	68-0760
Gesine 38, Johann 15, Heinrich 8, Cord 36			
FICK, Johanna	24	Debstedt	68-0534
FICK, Johanne	30	New York	69-1086
Johanne 11 months			
FICKE, Diedr.	32	Meienburg	70-0052
FICKE, Mathilde	25	Hannover	70-1142

NAME	AGE	RESIDENCE	YR-LIST
Catharine 27			
FICKE, Nicolaus	16	Bremen	69-0182
FICKEL, Anna	40	Dresden	68-0625
FICKEL, Phil.	17	Heppenheim	69-1086
FICKEN, Anna	20	Seedorf	68-0982
FICKEN, Anna	19	Zeven	71-0479
FICKEN, Engelb.	32	Schoeppingen	71-0479
FICKEN, Marg.	16	Wellen	70-1035
FICKER, August	34	Ehln	68-0939
FICKERT, Alb.	18	Sandstedt	71-0363
FICKLEN, Ludwig	18	Brest	68-0534
FIEBIG, Minna Louise 5	33	Paderborn	71-0643
FIEDEL, Friederike Minna 24, Emma 21, Ludwig 17, Minna 6 months	55	Raguhn	69-0672
FIEDLER, Amalie Georg 3, Emma 2, Martha 3 months	28	Graudenz	70-0569
FIEH, Caroline	24	Breitenbach	71-0733
FIEHN, Marie	21	R.B. Potsdam	68-0820
FIEHN, Peter	49	Schoenebeck	70-0508
FIEKEN, Henry	16	Scharmbeck	71-0456
FIGEL, Rosine	20	Kemnath	68-0760
FILLHAUER, Baptist	17	Heppenheim	71-0167
FINCK, Anton	22	Waldeck	70-0135
FINCK, Henry	15	Bernsburg	69-1011
FINGER, Johann	26	Jemgum	69-0848
FINGLER, Wilhelmine	21	Schweihausen	71-0736
FINK, Andreas	19	Neustadt	71-0456
FINK, Anselm	30	Leibhardt	68-0566
FINK, Christ.	15	Meienburg	70-0052
FINK, Edmund	30	New York	69-1086
FINK, Friedr. Catharine 27, Marie 4, Magdalene 11m.	30	Runkel	71-0226
FINK, Magdalena	16	Kaichen	68-0566
FINK, Pauline	16	Cassel	69-0923
FINKBEINER, John Louise 9	18	Freudenstadt	68-0534
FINKE, August	26	Porlage	71-0456
FINKE, Cath.	25	Iprum	71-0167
FINKE, Christoph	45	Hannover	68-0939
FINKE, Claus Catharina 15	34	Ceestmuende	68-0456
FINKE, Fritz	16	Schweringen	71-0684
FINKE, Heinr. Aug. 21	27	Schwafoerden	68-0884
FINKE, Henry	32	Wilmington	70-1003
FINKE, Ludw. Dorothea 25, Wilhelmine 4, Sophia 2	33	Vellage	68-0610
FINKE, Maria	20	Kassenbruch	71-0821
FINKE, Meta	22	Hashagen	68-0884
FINKE, Peter	15	Bremervoerde	71-0521
FINKE, Wilhelmine Richard 11 months	26	Berlin	69-1059
FINKE, Wilhelmine	24	Brosen	71-0226
FINKEL, Elisabeth	19	Bretzenheim	70-0308
FINKELNBURG, Wm.	35	St. Louis	69-1421
FINKHEIM, Friedrich	18	Freudenstadt	71-0643
FINKMANN, Philipp	24	Niederhellersch	69-1059
FINTEISEN, Gabriel Guenthrina 29	25	Arnstadt	68-0852
FIPPMEYER, Margareth Catharina 3, Margarethe 11 months	29	New York	69-0321
FIRCHBAUER, Friedrich Catharine 20	28	Heselbronn	70-0443
FISCH, Moses	23	Walicka	71-0712
FISCHBEINER, Friedrich Catharine 20	28	Heselbronn	70-0443
FISCHBEINER, Joh.	16	Iberberg	71-0479
FISCHEL, William	19	San Francisco	69-1212
FISCHER, Adeline	18	Leipzig	68-1298
FISCHER, Adolf	33	Reichenbach	68-0852
FISCHER, Alwine Richard 11 months	24	Leipzig	68-0566
FISCHER, Amand	19	Steinenstadt	68-0610
FISCHER, Anton Therese 29, Anton 4, Josef 2	38	Wargemied	71-0429
FISCHER, August	37	Preussen	68-0456
FISCHER, Augusta Ernst 15, Henry 6, William 3, Dotette 8	32	Heslingen	68-0957
FISCHER, Barbara Babette 16, Ulrich 8	45	Neudrossenfeld	69-0848
FISCHER, Carl	27	Breslau	69-1059
FISCHER, Carl	23	Wommen	70-0204
FISCHER, Carl	20	Barmen	68-0625
FISCHER, Caroline	20	Geisslingen	70-0682
FISCHER, Christ.	33	Lesse	69-0162
FISCHER, Clara	17	Duerckheim	69-1076
FISCHER, Clara	18	Minden	68-0647
FISCHER, Dora	30	Hannover	69-1059
FISCHER, Dorothea	20	Thueringen	71-0821
FISCHER, Elisabeth	21	Guenthers	68-0939
FISCHER, Eva	28	Heldberg	70-0272
FISCHER, Eva Elise	33	Rensburg	68-0753
FISCHER, Ferd.	29	Weimar	69-1004
FISCHER, Franziska Markus 9	50	Boehmen	70-0728
FISCHER, Friedr. Barb. 25	19	Holzwarden	71-0581
FISCHER, Friedr. Henriette 14, Johanne 8, Otto 4	35	Markoldendorf	71-0300
FISCHER, Georg Therese 37	30	Winzingen	69-0208
FISCHER, Georg	19	Eissen	68-0957
FISCHER, Georg Christine 32, Marie 4	35	Ober Finkenbach	68-0661
FISCHER, Gg. Fr. L. 32, Ferd. 7, Caroline 6, Marie 4, Carl 2, Franz 9 months	37	Hoffenheim	71-0684
FISCHER, Gust.	25	Prag	71-0582
FISCHER, Gustav	26	Etrau	71-0492
FISCHER, Heinrich	52	Schwelm	69-0490
FISCHER, Heinrich	16	Bremen	68-0820
FISCHER, Jacob Barbara 30, Catharina 4, John 6 m.	36	Goennheim	71-0712
FISCHER, Jan	20	Ostfriesland	69-1004
FISCHER, Jette	42	Gotha	68-0939
FISCHER, Joh.	30	Rosefeld	71-0393

NAME	AGE	RESIDENCE	YR-LIST
FISCHER, Johann	27	Hallnengen	69-0429
FISCHER, Johann	17	Rust	71-0492
FISCHER, John	31	Saxonia	70-0508
Auguste 31, Auguste 9, Louis 6, John 6 months			
FISCHER, Josef	27	Stackesried	71-0429
Anna 25, P. 6 months			
FISCHER, Joseph	53	Borndorf	69-1212
Therese 50, Franz 18, Johann 13, Joseph 7,			
FISCHER, Joseph	19	Donaustetten	69-1076
FISCHER, Joseph	18	Neufra	68-0852
FISCHER, Lambert	21	Anhalt	69-1363
FISCHER, Laura	25	Asch	69-0457
FISCHER, Magd.	24	Schauerstein	69-0542
FISCHER, Marga	18	Altenbruch	71-0821
FISCHER, Maria	20	Otterndorf	70-0329
FISCHER, Maria	36	Vacha	68-0661
George 14, Elise 7, Bertha 6, Friedrich 5, Ernst 3, Carl 3, Andreas 5 months			
FISCHER, Matthaus	30	Meiningen	71-0456
FISCHER, Matthias	44	Schonberg	68-0753
FISCHER, Nicolaus	69	Eyben	68-0707
FISCHER, Pauline	17	Grafenthal	68-0707
FISCHER, Ph. Conr.	37	Mariette	68-0647
FISCHER, Rob.	31	St. Paul	69-0490
FISCHER, Rosa	23	Baikensahl	71-0492
FISCHER, Sophie	38	Heilbronn	68-1027
FISCHER, Susanna	44	Nordhausen	68-0770
Waldemar 12			
FISCHER, Wilhelm	32	Chicago	71-0643
Marie 32, Franz 9, Marie 10 months			
FISCHHOEFER, Louise	29	Wulferode	69-1396
Bab. 9 months			
FISCHHOFER, Joh.	29	Osnabrueck	69-0050
FISCHLER, Gottlieb	26	Zeithain	68-0707
FISCHMANN, Emanuel	32	Sell	68-1027
FISLER, Franz	22	Zwikowetz	68-0707
FISTER, Eberhard	19	Neudrossenfelde	68-0707
FITTER, Friedrich	17	Sievern	69-0490
FITTERL, Fritz W.	16	Sievern	71-0492
FITTLER, Conrad	23	Niedermoellrich	68-1002
FIXEN, Marie	18	Wersabe	71-0479
FLAAKE, Friederike	32	Schoenemark	68-0957
Fred. 7			
FLAAKE, Mary	54	New York	70-1003
FLACH, Sophie	24	Wenigs	71-0479
FLACHMANN, August	29	Suedheide	68-1006
Hanna 27, Florentine 58, Henriette 24, Caroline 19, August 9 months			
FLACHMEIER, Louise	17	Bankau	70-0443
FLAD, Gottfried	48	Dettingen	71-0521
FLAIG, Catharine	21	Villingen	68-0534
FLAKE, Adolf	36	Galveston	70-1003
Minna 30			
FLAKE, Wilhelm	17	Hannover	69-0429
FLAMM, Gottlieb	20	Riederich	68-0625
Marie 22			
FLANDER, Herm.	19	Hall	71-0363
FLAPST, Gertrude	44	Prim	71-0581

NAME	AGE	RESIDENCE	YR-LIST
Peter 9, Georg 6			
FLATAU, Berhardina	39	Great Falls	70-0308
Rebeca 18, Cerline 9, Hatti 8			
FLATTEN, Andreas	50	Oberdreis	70-0355
FLECK, Adam	44	Eschenbach	68-1002
Eva 35, Marg. 9, Peter 4, Magdalene 10 months			
FLECK, Martina	20	Streufa	68-0907
FLECKENSTEIN, Johann	22	Habischthal	68-0625
FLEGE, Caroline	22	Heimbeck	70-0523
FLEGE, Johann	15	Himsbeck	69-0572
FLEGEL, Sophie	20	Lemgo	68-0707
FLEGLER, Marg.	19	Urphar	71-0581
FLEISCHER, Cathrine	19	Gauelgisheim	70-1161
FLEISCHER, Helene	20	Rastadt	71-0429
FLEISCHER, L.	19	Goeppingen	71-0521
FLEISCHER, Maria	21	Dabernkau	69-0321
FLEISCHER, Moritz	15	Boehmen	68-0456
FLEISCHHAKER, Hugo	23	Niederaula	71-0681
FLEISCHHAUER, Marg.	22	Oberndorf	70-0308
FLEISCHMANN, Andr.	25	Oberrodach	71-0521
FLEISCHMANN, Anna	28	Stangard	68-0314
FLEISCHMANN, Conrad	32	Culenbach	68-0770
FLEISCHMANN, Elisabeth	21	Empfertshs.	68-0939
FLEISCHMANN, Fritz	42	Hannover	70-0076
FLEISCHMANN, Henry	22	Greitz	71-0456
FLEISCHMANN, Herm.	29	Boehmen	69-0572
FLEISCHMANN, Jacob	19	Gr. Bottwar	68-1027
FLEISCHMANN, Johanne	18	Zillbach	69-0592
FLEISCHMANN, Laura	30	Coburg	68-0957
Johanna 8			
FLEISCHMANN, Marg.	18	Gruensfeldhs.	68-0707
FLEISCHMANN, Rudolph	22	Weissenburg	68-0707
FLEISELBAUER, Heinrich	39	Wacher	71-0712
Catharina 37, Hermann 3, Anna 67, Elisabeth 9 months			
FLEISSA, Henriette	22	Greiz	69-0560
FLEISSNER, Aug.	23	Oldenburg	70-0452
Wife 21, baby son 6 months, Louise 20			
FLEMMING, Wilhelm	32	Labes	68-1027
Mathilde 29, Herman 7, Ida 5			
FLENTJEN, Louis	17	Apelern	68-0610
FLESSHER, E.	44	Ludwigsdorf	69-1011
Barbara 36, Anna 11, Mary 8, Ekke 7, Engel 6, Hartje 5, Andreas 3, Baby boy 8,			
FLETHENMEYER, Hein.	21	Lienen	71-0492
FLICK, Karl	28	Bitow	69-0547
FLICKINGER, Clara	22	Zweibruecken	69-1086
FLIER, Joh. Mich.	28	Neundettelsau	70-1055
FLINK, Helena	20	Ubstadt	68-1006
FLINTJER, Diedde	56	Rhauderfehn	70-0204
Grethe 45, Arnold 11, Marg. 9, Everh. 6, Anton 3			
FLOERKE, Adam	37	Djablonowow/Pru	69-0547
Rosalie 47, Ottilie 15, Amalie 7, Auguste 5			
FLOERSCH, Johann	26	Guntersheim	69-0672
FLOESSLER, Anton	34	Bremen	71-0226
FLOH, Diebold	54	Ottenheim	71-0363
FLOHR, Charlotte	21	Luebbecke	68-0647

NAME	AGE	RESIDENCE	YR-LIST
FLOMER, Sophia	14	Hille	69-1076
FLORSCHUTZ, Caspar	24	Weissenbrunn	70-0259
FLOTO, Regine	23	Cassel	69-0457
FLUEGEL, Carl	59	Neuenburg	69-1076
Regine 59			
FLUEGGE, Johann	21	Haast	68-1027
FOCHE, Carl	26	Bremen	71-0789
FOCHS, Maria	46	Celle	71-0492
Elise 9, Caroline 8, Georg 6, Maria 4, Dora 4, Theodor 11 months			
FOCKE, Heinrich	25	Hannover	70-1055
Herm. 14			
FOCKE, Jacob	32	Lennverder	70-0378
FOCKE, Wilhelmine	23	Weningerode	70-0355
FOCKEN, Folkert	55	Holtgast	71-0429
Clara 48, Johannes 27, Clara 14, Gesine 9, Friedricke 7, Heye 11 months			
FOCKEN, male	28	Hannover	70-1066
Gretje 30,			
FODDER, Marie	50	Towolla/Polen	69-0576
FOEKE, Georg	14	Frankenberg	71-0456
FOELL, Friedrich	25	Hanau	68-0820
FOERDRUNZ, Anna	23	Freiburg	68-0534
FOERKEN, Georg	15	Wattens	71-0363
FOERSTER, A.	48	Conitz	68-0610
Henriette 41, Antonia 17, Carl 15, Franz 13, Emma 9, Anna 8, Paul 7, Hedwig 6,			
FOERSTER, Everhard	19	Kasendorf/Bayer	69-0547
Catharina 27			
FOERSTER, Joh.	24	Zeil	68-0566
FOERSTER, Jul.	30	Vienaden	69-1421
FOERSTER, Magdalene	37	Worms	71-0492
FOERSTER, Rosina	16	Ottelsmanshaus	69-0457
FOERSTERLING, H.	56	Hamburg	70-0089
FOERSTERMANN, C.	18	Luethorst	69-0968
FOERTNER, Chr.	25	Wemberg	69-0208
FOGERT, Jacob	17	Schellweiler	70-0135
FOHLENRIEDE, Betty	25	Buecken	71-0456
FOHN, Carl	28	St. Bernhardt	69-0268
FOLKERS, Wuebke	56	Ostfriesland	68-1049
Johanna 15			
FOLKERTS, Falk	26	Wiesede	69-0672
Taalke 28, Falk 1 months			
FOLTHORSTER, Heinrich	19	Herstelle	68-0939
FOOST, Tonjes	42	Koehlen	69-1076
L. 25, Helene 9			
FORDUNG, Louis	43	Buettendorf	69-0968
Wilhelmine 15, Friedrich 9, Marie 5			
FORMER, Herm.	22	Reuss	69-1004
FORQUIGNON, Heinrich	25	Bremen	68-1027
FORST, Tonjes	42	Koehlen	69-1076
L. 25, Helene 9			
FORSTER, Aug.	23	Hinternah	71-0815
FORSTER, Rudolph	27	Olpe	68-0982
FORTLAGE, Heinrich	21	Brockhausen	66-0668
Carl 19			
FORTMANN, Joseph	34	Ehrendorf	69-0050
Josephine 24, baby girl 6 months			
FOSSEK, Carl	25	Moehren	71-0821
FOTLER, Johann	31	Everswinkel	71-0492

NAME	AGE	RESIDENCE	YR-LIST
Catharine 31			
FOTSCH, Wilhelm	21	Schaffhausen	69-0268
FOURBIER, Louise	37	R.B. Potsdam	68-0820
August 12, Carl 11, Marie 7, Louise 4			
FRAMBURG, Carl	26	Berlin	71-0821
FRANK, Adolf	14	Esslingen	71-0456
FRANK, August	26	Armwalde	69-0672
FRANK, August	19	Alzenrod	69-0490
Marie 23			
FRANK, Barbara	16	Weisweiler	70-0378
FRANK, Catharina	19	Laubach	68-0760
FRANK, Christian	17	Unterkessach	68-1006
FRANK, Eduard	25	Coslin	70-0076
FRANK, Elisa	23	Niederohmen	68-0957
FRANK, Elisabeth	16	Thalmessing	71-0792
FRANK, Ernestine	24	Mittwitz	68-0534
FRANK, Fr.	26	Rudolstadt	71-0363
Friedrika 26			
FRANK, Franz	33	Kornbach	69-0208
Agnes 17, P. 20			
FRANK, Friederike	25	Neuendorf	69-0784
Anna 9, Anton 12, Aloys 8, Catharina 7, Wilhelm 3			
FRANK, Herm.	13	Gera	69-0050
Elise 11, Catharine 9, Maria 7			
FRANK, Jacob	17	Muehlhausen	69-0321
FRANK, Joh.	18	Paschungruen	71-0681
FRANK, John	18	Zimmern	70-0355
FRANK, Josef	48	Buringen	71-0479
FRANK, Josef	30	Weingarten	71-0226
FRANK, L.	18	Fuerth	68-0014
FRANK, Lipp	49	Gleidingen	68-0456
Franziska 48, Adele 19, Julius 16, Anna 9, Moses 7			
FRANK, Ludwig	34	Schillingstadt	71-0521
Marie 30, Ludwig 9, Albina 7, Bertha 3, Friederike 9 months			
FRANK, Magdalena	27	Wetterdingen	68-0534
Friedrich 27, Ferdinand 18			
FRANK, Marga.	40	Schwarzbeck	69-0592
Barbara 19			
FRANK, Minna	25	Buchen	71-0479
Simon 16			
FRANK, Moritz	18	Herford	68-0419
FRANK, Philipp	27	Deisslingen	70-0308
FRANK, Richard	17	Weimar	71-0429
FRANK, Roeschen	45	Grossendorf	66-0734
Betha 9, Emma 6, Henriette 4			
FRANK, Rosine	25	Moschuetz	71-0521
FRANK, Rudolph	19	Sangershausen	69-1212
FRANK, Sam.	32	Nieder Ohassen	68-0957
Bertha 21			
FRANK, Schoenchen	37	Grossendorf	66-0734
FRANK, Thekla	33	Varnhalt	68-0014
FRANK, Theodor	23	Obernstunsen	69-0208
FRANK, Theodor	36	Giessen	69-1319
FRANK, Wilhelm	43	Wolschow	69-0547
Louise 41, Friederike 15			
FRANKE, Amalie	20	Wirsitz	69-0429

NAME	AGE	RESIDENCE	YR-LIST
FRANKE, Ludwig	29	Spiessinghall	69-0429
Max 25			
FRANKE, Theodor	28	Gunsdorf	69-0572
FRANKEL, Daniel	17	Meisenheim	68-0939
FRANKEN, Max	19	Stuttgart	70-0170
FRANKENBERG, Teo	27	Idstein	70-0031
FRANKENFELD, Alfred	17	Osnabrueck	69-0457
FRANKLE, Friedrich	32	Hausenheim	71-0492
FRANKLIN, Marie	21	Braunschweig	69-1396
FRANKMUELLER, Gertrud	26	Muenster	68-0314
FRANKSEN, Hermann	38	Wien	68-1006
FRANKSEN, Peter	28	Oldenburg	71-0581
FRANSSEN, Helene	20	Emden	69-0560
FRANSSEN, Marie	45	Emden	69-0592
Marie 16			
FRANTZ, Julius	20	Stettin	69-1011
FRANTZ, Martin	50	Ohlspech	71-0643
FRANTZ, Wilhelmine	15	Unterhausen	69-1076
FRANTZEL, Albert	26	Spottau	68-0566
FRANTZEN, Peter	16	Wittmund	68-0982
FRANTZKE, Wilhelmine	28	Berlin	69-0050
FRANZ, Carol.	51	Reuss	70-1066
Er. 14			
FRANZ, David	29	Steglitz	69-1212
Marie 25, Marie 6 months			
FRANZ, Eduard	36	Tribes	68-0852
Sophie 40, Gustav 9, Otto 8, Oswald 6, Alwine 10 months			
FRANZ, Ferdinand	33	Weimar	69-1076
Therese 20			
FRANZ, Magd.	21	Orbis	69-0457
FRANZ, Magdalena	19	Eberbach	68-0852
FRANZEN, Anna	28	Coeln	68-0760
FRANZEN, Eilert	26	Ochtersum	69-0547
FRANZEN, Joseph	49	Coeln	71-0226
FRARI, Jacob	27	Schweiz	70-1161
FRAUE, William	26	Bonn	69-0208
Anna 18, Gertrude 58, Mary 29			
FRAUENDINER, Joh.	34	Hannbersbron	70-0728
FRAUSSEN, Carol.	9	Emden	69-0592
FRECH, Marie	23	Oppan	68-0647
FREDRICH, Dorothea	19	Mecklenburg	70-0443
FREESE, Adolf	19	Friolyheim	69-1363
FREESE, Diedrich	18	Seppenhausen	69-0547
FREESE, Georg	52	Hannover	69-1212
FREESE, Johann	16	Schoettlingen	71-0363
FREESE, Ludwig	33	Rhoden	71-0736
FREESE, Mary	16	Bremen	69-0338
FREIBER, Richard	26	Teichel	69-0572
FREIBERG, J.	27	Schlawe	70-1142
Lina 2, Ida 4			
FREICHLINGEN, David	17	Boehmen	69-1396
FREIDL, Rud.	28	Berlin	69-0923
Gust. 26			
FREIGANG, Auguste	18	Fackenheim	71-0733
FREIHARDT, Joseph	36	Reimersheim	68-0770
Catharina 36			
FREIHEIT, Emilie	22	Gr. Lubs	71-0733
FREILING, Jac.	55	Wollmar	71-0821
Louise 48, Joh. 16, Louise 9			
FREILING, Johann	16	Schlagasitze	69-0457
FREILING, Thomas	50	Peoria	71-0815
Elisabeth 50			
FREILING, Volpert	23	Wollmar	71-0821
Elisabeth 15, Johannes 24			
FREIMANN, Johann	70	Lienzingen	68-0852
Johann 30, Johanna 32, Johann 8, Paul 4, Louise 11 months			
FREIMANN, Leopold	7	Zeiten	68-0456
FREISE, Ernst	28	Braunschweig	69-0848
FREISSLICH, Armin	27	Meiningen	69-1086
FREITAG, Anton	19	Muenster	68-0625
FREITAG, Daniel	60	Heuchelheim	68-0786
Catharine 60, Heinrich 15			
FREITAG, Friedrich	55	Coeslin	70-0452
Henriette 49, Franz 9, Johann 13			
FREITAG, Fritz	27	Dorow	69-0429
FREITAG, Georg	38	Pegan	68-0566
Rebecca 32, Louisa 25			
FREITAG, Ignatz	48	Posen	68-0852
FREITAG, Philip	21	H. Darmstadt	70-1003
FRENZEL, Heinrich	26	Taubenhain	68-0707
FRERICH, Joh.	17	Hannover	70-100
FRERICHS, Gesche	19	Lippe Detmold	69-0268
FRERICHS, Heinrich	23	Warden	69-0490
FRERICHS, Hermann	25	Mauburg	70-0178
FRERICHT, Friedr.	25	Oldenburg	69-0162
FRERIKS, Gerd	37	Lossen	68-0534
FRESE, Wilh.	34	Hannover	70-1055
Louise 34, Anna 8, Heinr. 7, Lina 2			
FREU, Marg.	26	Offelten	69-1011
Cunigunde 5			
FREUCHTLINGER, Fanni	34	Haimfurt	69-0923
Therese 8			
FREUDE, John	46	Ibbenbrihsen	70-0170
FREUDEKAMP, Bernhard	27	Holtmar	69-0572
FREUDEMANN, Fried.	42	Bremen	69-1011
FREUDENBERG, Louise	26	Umysterode	69-0542
FREUDENBERGER, C.	23	Rappenau	71-0821
FREUDENSTEIN, Georg	31	Dissen	71-0429
FREUND, Adolph	15	Odenheim	69-0572
FREUND, Amalie	19	Spannyeht	69-1059
FREUND, Ang.	17	Lengsfeld	71-0521
FREUND, Anna	16	Fuerth	71-0479
Lorenz 9			
FREUND, August	49	Sandershausen	70-0569
Wilhelmine 30, Robert 16, Oscar 9, Auguste 7, Frierich 3			
FREUND, Catharina	30	Winnweiler	69-0672
Charlotte 7, Friedrich 5, August 3			
FREUND, Rosalie	16	Solingen	69-0457
Wilhelmine 18			
FREUND, Theodor	36	New York	69-1086
FREVERT, Johann	31	Goldbeck	68-0852
FREY, August	24	Winham	68-0786
Augusta 25			
FREY, Barbara	23	Steinsdorf	68-1006
FREY, Cath.	71	Stetten	68-0982

NAME	AGE	RESIDENCE	YR-LIST
FREY, Georg	19	Groembach	68-0456
FREY, Heinrich	15	Roeth	71-0712
FREY, Jac. Fr.	26	Pfalzgrafenw.	68-0820
FREY, Jacob	25	Sulzheim	70-0443
FREY, John	18	Taurendau	71-0456
FREY, Josephine	26	Hochmossingen	68-0566
Magdalene 23			
FREY, Maria	22	Coblenz	69-0560
FREY, Marie	22	Erfurtshausen	69-0592
FREY, Otto	25	Kurhessen	69-1076
FREY, Rosine	51	Wilkan	69-0490
Louise 14			
FREY, Wallburga	32	Westheim	69-1076
Wallburga 10 months			
FREYMARK, W.	29	Prawomysh	69-0338
Ernestine 22, Ottilie 9 months			
FREYTAG, Richard	18	Weichselberg	69-0572
Edw. 15			
FRICK, Angela	45	Louisville	69-1076
FRICK, Geo. F.	15	Niederhausen	71-1046
FRICK, Heinr.	38	Lieblos	71-0581
Cath. 45, Elise 22, Carl 19			
FRICK, Helene	19	Neuss Urvarden	70-0272
FRICK, Reinhilde	24	Neuenburg	71-0681
Gust. 4			
FRICKE, Auguste	23	Hannover	69-1421
FRICKE, Conrad	59	Hannover	69-1212
Dorothea 50, Wilhelmine 17, Caroline 7, Friedrich 5			
FRICKE, Friederike	17	Diepholz	71-0479
FRICKE, Friedrich	19	Wahnebergen	69-0672
FRICKE, Fritz	17	Verden	71-0226
FRICKE, Georg	16	Hagen	70-0170
FRICKE, Heinrich	16	Rodenburg	70-0204
FRICKE, Helene	16	Oldenburg	70-1066
FRICKE, Johann	20	Schwanewede	70-0523
FRICKE, Johanne	20	Schwanewede	70-0523
FRICKE, Simon	40	Hazelbeck	69-0560
Carolina 29			
FRICKE, Sophie	65	Waldrow	71-0712
Friederiecke 23			
FRICKEN, Betty	21	Westheim	71-0684
FRICKER, Joh.	17	Hannover	71-0821
FRICKINGEN, Anna	23	Muenchen	69-0798
Joseph 2, Caroline 11 months			
FRICKNER, Anna	19	Tormueth	69-0592
FRIEBE, Ferdinand	32	Lippe/Lippe	69-0576
FRIED, David	24	Prag	71-0733
FRIED, Regine	22	Doerrbach	70-1003
FRIEDE, Georg	31	Trebnitz	69-0592
FRIEDEBERG, Christian	25	Osnabrueck	68-0707
Joseph 19, Marie 21			
FRIEDEHORN, Wme.	16	Minden	70-0355
FRIEDEL, Henriette	38	Reichenbach	68-0566
Therese 14, Emilie 8			
FRIEDEL, Joh.	31	Sittmensgruen	68-0647
FRIEDEL, Joseph	26	Langenfeld	70-1055
FRIEDERICHS, Friederike	17	Etzel	71-0492
FRIEDGEN, George	45	Bebra	71-0363
Elsa 45, Anna 20, Martha 9, Katharina 7, Georg 4			
FRIEDHOFF, Johann	15	Westerwanna	71-0429
FRIEDHOFF, Wilh.	52	Otterndorf	68-0566
FRIEDLAENDER, Israel	60	Zempelburg	69-0572
FRIEDLAENDER, Jacob	38	Cassel	69-1309
FRIEDMANN, Christ.	25	Brakenheim	68-1298
FRIEDRICH, Adam	28	Birkenau	69-0182
FRIEDRICH, Clem. A.	27	Glauchau	70-0443
FRIEDRICH, Conrad	29	Heubsch	68-0707
FRIEDRICH, Gust.	23	Tscheinitz	71-0815
Marie 20, Anna 21			
FRIEDRICH, Heinrich	22	Preuss.Schlinz	69-0229
FRIEDRICH, Johann	20	Zemel	68-0770
FRIEDRICH, Johann	60	Boehmen	69-1309
FRIEDRICH, Kunigunde	20	Weisslenreuth	68-0982
FRIEDRICH, Leonh.	23	Kurhessen	71-0521
FRIEDRICH, Louis	16	Werdau	68-0939
FRIEDRICH, Louise	24	Bremen	68-0534
FRIEDRICH, Marie	17	Weimar	70-0569
FRIEDRICH, Mart.	15	Hessen	70-0204
FRIEDRICH, Theo.	30	Polin	68-0760
FRIEDRICH, Wilhelm	23	Doertel	68-0852
FRIEDRICHS, Elise	20	Osterholz	68-1027
FRIEDRICHS, Hermann	24	Oldenburg	70-0683
FRIEDRICHS, Hugo	23	Gotha	68-1006
FRIEDRICHS, Peter	45	Sandhorst	69-0182
FRIEDRICHS, Sophie	21	Lemgo	71-0172
FRIEDRICHS, Th.	47	Sandhorst	70-1035
Johanna 19, Johann 15, Erta 12, Marie 9, Entje 7			
FRIEDRICHSOHR, Peter	19	Hannover	69-0208
FRIES, Gustav	22	Darmstadt	69-0321
FRIES, Wilhelmine		Caan	69-0798
FRIESCH, Peter	49	Madenmuehle	69-0457
FRIESE, Marie	23	Stede	69-1004
FRIESEL, Thom	22	Goldscheuer	69-1421
FRIESELER, Ernst	19	Wehringdorf	68-0760
FRIK, Max	17	Altheim	71-0226
FRINGER, Anna	15	Aldingen	68-0957
FRION, Christ.	25	Carlsruhe	71-0363
FRION, Martin	17	Aldingen	71-0492
FRIRITA, Wenzel	35	Hlizoo	70-0329
FRISSE, Friedrich	18	Anroechte	68-0314
FRITSCH, Chls.	15	Aschaffenburg	68-0957
FRITSCHE, August	46	Posen	68-0625
FRITSCHE, Bertha	16	Leopoldsgruen	71-0300
FRITSCHE, Paul	26	Leipzig	71-0821
FRITZ, Adolphine	29	Haegelsheim	71-0492
FRITZ, Albert	30	Bremerhaven	68-0820
FRITZ, Carl	27	Jeziovken/Pruss	69-0547
FRITZ, Caroline	25	Hattenhofen	69-0542
FRITZ, Christine	46	Baden	70-0148
Marie 38, David 15			
FRITZ, Fred.	24	Reulried	68-0760
FRITZ, Georg	36	Nuernberg	69-0841
FRITZ, Michael	27	Klehow/Polen	69-1076

NAME	AGE	RESIDENCE	YR-LIST
Christian 17			
FRITZ, Peter	22	Oberzenzheim	69-1086
FRITZ, Wilhelm Heinrich 22	25	Portsmover	69-0547
FRITZE, Julia	22	Meiningen	68-0707
FRITZLAR, Wm.	29	Holperath	68-314
FROBOESE, Louise	22	Bremen	69-1212
FROEBIG, Bernhard	23	Emmershausen	69-0968
FROECHTENIGHT, Theo	42	Celle	71-0581
FROEHLICH, Aug.	42	Sheboygan	69-1421
FROEHLICH, Christ.	26	Wahlen	71-0815
FROEHLICH, Chrs. Susanna 61	21	Kl. Jena	69-1421
FROEHLICH, Elisabeth	17	Heringen	68-0884
FROEHLICH, Gerson	21	Ullrichstein	68-0957
FROEHLICH, Juh. Ernestine 20	28	Neuwedel	68-0760
FROEHLICH, Wilh.	33	Neuwedel	69-0338
FROEHLICH, Wilhelmine	14	Ellhofen	69-1363
FROEHLIG, Carl	24	Stuttgart	68-0610
FROEHLIG, Ed.	36	Amelith	69-1086
FROEHLIG, Heinr. Theodor 17	39	Werlte	69-0229
FROEHLING, Trientje	24	Weener	69-0268
FROELICH, Marie Wilh. 14	49	Rudolfheim	71-0479
FROELKE, Josef	36	Remsede	71-0429
FROELKE, Wilhelmine	60	Niewerder	71-0479
FROEMMELT, Henriette Clemens 18, Eduard 16, Ehrgott 9, Hermann 7	42	Meerane	68-0014
FROEMMER, Ernst	17	Cassel	69-1086
FROHMUELLER, F.	19	Calw	69-0182
FROHMUELLER, Richard	16	Carlsruhe	68-0456
FROMDLE, Theodor Maria 18	20	Ay	70-0184
FROMMELT, Florian	32	Meeraue	69-0429
FROMMERHAUSEN, G. Henriette 47, Friederike 15, Catharine 6	46	Coblenz	68-0456
FROSCH, Margaretha	20	Ludwigstadt	68-0707
FROSPER, Jac.	16	Bechtheim	71-0393
FROST, Wenzel	29	Hochwarth,Austr	69-0547
FRUCHS, Ernst Johan 15	17	Walderhaus	69-0542
FRUDHOFF, Heinr. Anna 38, Anna 7, Heinr. 5	38	Bremen	71-0681
FRUEHAUF, Ad.	23	Nordhausen	69-0162
FRUEHNING, Johann	17	Rotenburg	71-0712
FRUELING, Henriette	18	Laisa	71-0821
FRUEMBACH, Heinr. Pauline 37, Richard 9, O. 7, Adolph 9 months	37	Altenburg	71-0736
FRUENEL, Ernst	17	Werste	68-0852
FRUND, August Wilhelmine 30, Robert 16, Oscar 9, Auguste 7, Frierich 3	49	Sandershausen	70-0569
FRUNGE, Alb.	19	Hannover	70-0308
FUCHS, Anna Jacob 14, Cathrine 12, Elise 10, Philipp 8	36	Neukirchen	71-0456

NAME	AGE	RESIDENCE	YR-LIST
FUCHS, Carl	18	Alzey	71-0429
FUCHS, Christine	23	Duerkheim	68-0852
FUCHS, Christoph	18	Eger/Austria	69-0547
FUCHS, Ernstine	20	Altenburg	69-0583
FUCHS, Georg	16	Koenigsbronn	71-0363
FUCHS, Gustav	16	Frankfurt	69-1059
FUCHS, Jacob Johann 21, Kath. 9	58	Thalfing	71-0815
FUCHS, Joh.	18	Baechlerbaum	69-1004
FUCHS, Margaretha	21	Friedewald	69-1212
FUCHS, Nic. Carline 15	17	Lengsfeld	71-0521
FUCHS, Trinette Elise 3	27	Schwarzenbach	68-0707
FUCHSLOCHER, Carl Caroline 28	32	Esslingen	70-0089
FUCKSIUS, Friedrich	32	Coeln	68-0647
FUDE, Caroline	27	Hugowo	68-0786
FUEHRER, Adam	18	Heufa	68-0852
FUEHRER, Adam	24	Oberaula	68-0852
FUEHRING, Ernst	16	Neisse	68-1298
FUEHRING, H.	18	Bueckeburg	70-0308
FUELLER, Rosamunde	21	Schmalnau	69-0968
FUELLING, Anna Henriette 21, Louise 18, Ludwig 16, Julie 13, Ernst 9, Wilh. 4	48	Hannover	70-1055
FUENDELING, Bertha Wilhelm 3	25	Hannover	71-0456
FUERCHTENICHT, Herm.	17	Voelkersen	69-0592
FUERCHTENICHT, John	15	Hannover	70-1161
FUERK, Georg Anna 63, Elisab. 31	67	Weimar	70-0569
FUERST, Caroline	20	Dermbach	68-0760
FUERST, Mathilde Ernst 13	17	Oberfladungen	68-0760
FUERSTENAU, Friedrich	27	Weizen	69-1309
FUERSTENBERG, David	19	Stolp	69-0560
FUESTE, Carl	19	Plochingen	69-0229
FUHR, Friedrich	33	S. C. Gotha	69-0848
FUHR, Peter Elisabeth 21	28	Monzingen	68-0661
FUHR, Wilhelm	28	Bieberich	69-1319
FUHRMANN, Cath.	25	Coblenz	68-1002
FUHRMANN, Margaret	16	Zillbach	68-0625
FUHRMANN, Rosalie Hulda 6 months	26	Bromberg	68-0419
FUHRMANN, Wilhelm	22	Petersburg	69-0923
FUHRMEISTER, Louise August 21	15	Frankenhausen/P	69-0547
FULLER, Mich. Franz X. 18	19	Westernheim	68-0610
FUNCK, Henry	24	Praest	68-0957
FUNCKE, Johann	18	Boehmen	68-0456
FUNK, Conrad	28	Sellenrod	68-0534
FUNK, Friedrich	22	Hildesheim	69-0592
FUNK, Julius Emma 25, Hermann 7	29	Magdeburg	68-0753
FUNKE, Ernst Heinrich 9	58	Braunschweig	69-1076

NAME	AGE	RESIDENCE	YR-LIST
FUNKE, Fritz	33	Buenten	68-1006
Hanna 30, Wilhelm 6 months			
FUNKE, Herm.	14	Goettingen	71-0736
FUNKE, Louise	33	Gera	68-0566
Louise 9, Marie 8			
FUNKE, Simon	39	Werl	68-1006
Wilhelmine 35, Louise 9, Charlotte 4			
FUNKE, Wilhelmine	42	Goettingen	71-0736
Therese 8			
FUSELMANN, Juergen	33	Oldendorf	69-0968
FUSS, Barbara	20	Hallnengen	69-0429
FUSS, Johann	20	Bellings	71-0479
FUSS, Paul	30	Obergrimpen	69-0229
FUTELHA, Elise	27	Leiberstung	71-0492
GABALKA, Franz	27	Boehmen	70-0728
Franziska 26, Joseph 11 months			
GABEL, Franz	19	Ebersheim	69-0672
GABEL, Friedr.	34	Solingen	70-0272
GABELIN, Martin	16	Stebin	69-0542
GABELMANN, Lisette	16	Ruppau	68-0786
GABIELLI, Antoni	33	Tyrol	69-1059
GABRIEL, Elisabeth	18	Linz	71-0712
GACHRY, Louis	27	Weissenburg	71-0681
GACK, Julius	27	Rotenburg	69-1319
GADELMANN, Diedrich	14	Ostfriesland	69-1059
GADEN, Caroline	24	Isernhagen	71-0456
GADEZINSKY, And.	27	Arolsen	68-0753
GAEBEL, Louis	18	Hausheim	70-0308
GAEHNER, Johann	42	Westerenge	68-0939
Christine 40			
GAEHRING, Friedrich	54	Leipzig	70-0329
GAERLITZ, Christ.	45	Doedelsheim	71-0167
GAERTNER, Bertha	40	Berlin	69-1059
Agnes 22, Hedwig 20, Hermann 18, Karl 14l, Friedrich 12, Bertha 9, Oscar 8, Al			
GAERTNER, Bonifaz		Ahl	69-0429
GAERTNER, Georg	25	Bremen	68-0419
GAERTNER, Heinr.	22	Hastedt	69-1212
GAERTNER, Heinrich	20	Hansteinbeck	70-0204
Henriette 23			
GAERTNER, Johannes	16	Osterode	68-0661
GAERTNER, Wilh.	22	Philippsthal	69-0321
GAETJEN, Albert	25	Kuehrstedt	68-1002
GAETJEN, Fabian	25	Albershausen	69-1011
GAETJEN, Heinrich	25	Bremen	69-1212
GAETJEN, Johann	47	Hammersbeck	68-0770
GAETZKE, August	25	Neustadt a/R	69-0572
GAFFKE, Joseph	20	Luebkan	69-0457
GAGSTELLE, Catharina	68	Crailstein	68-0939
GAHN, Niclas	22	Langheim	71-0172
GAIER, Michael	58	Bruesken	71-0736
Catharine 54, Jacob 16, Philipp 9			
GAILS, Bernhard	41	Hudermoor	69-0321
Helena 42, Johann 9, Gesina 6			
GAILS, Elisabeth Adele	22	Vielstedt	69-0321
GAIRSFELD, Ad.	28	Wien	68-0884
GAISELMANN, Johann	17	Wellendingen	70-0223
GAISS, Valentin	36	Trebelsdorf	71-0456

NAME	AGE	RESIDENCE	YR-LIST
Caroline 36, Georg 11, Barbara 9, Henry 5, Eva 3, Philipp 10 months			
GAISSERT, Gottfr.	19	Hoefingen	68-1002
GALL, Caroline	23	Wolfsolden	69-0490
GALLEE, Anton	30	Rosna	70-0443
GALLIEN, Friedr.	25	Jahmo	68-1002
GALLNE, Abraham	57	Berlin	71-0736
Esther 43, Moritz 18, Jacob 6			
GALLWITZER, Lorenza	23	Leuchtenburg	68-0939
GALTS, Johann C.	27	Marx	71-0492
GANDER, Christian	22	Mutterholz	71-0643
GANG, Christian	10	Dallau/Dallan	69-1309
GANGWISCH, Marie	50	Westhofen	71-0736
Bernhardine 14			
GANS, Samuel	15	Neustadt	71-0581
GANTERT, Krescentia	49	Uehlingen	71-0733
Josephe 21, Leopolt 15			
GANTHER, Rosina	20	Weingarten	68-0647
GANZEMUELLER, Carl	17	Sinsheim	69-0592
GANZLOSEN, Carl	20	Geggingen	70-0204
GAPP, Friedrich	18	Nassau	69-0672
GARAIS, Franz	25	Thein	70-0329
GARB, Josephine	33	Rotenburg	68-0786
GARBADE, Luder	16	Bramsche	70-0452
GARBADE, Meta	36	Bremerhaven	71-0521
Hanni 9, Johanne 6, Heinrich 5			
GARBERDING, Heinrich	29	Hannover	69-0784
Marie 25, Marie 10 months			
GARDNER, Ellen	13	Paddington	69-1086
Ch. 11, Bu. 10, Ahnry 8, Fred. 6			
GARLOW, August	22	Gursen	68-0770
GARNER, Philippine	20	Graben	71-0456
GARNIER, Paul	22	Cette	68-0014
GARNKAEUFER, Louise	30	Voerden	68-0647
GAROLD, Nic.	18	Hamweiler	71-0684
Christine 26			
GARREL, Marie	11	St. Louis	69-0784
Caroline 12			
GARRELS, Cassen	21	Saatholt	68-0939
GARS, Heinrich	27	Hatmann	69-0208
GARTEMANN, Juergen	45	Ostfriesland	69-0672
Tantje 40, Weertz 16, Juergen 9, Ewert 5, Brechtjedina 7			
GARTH, Otto	24	Darmstadt	70-0170
GARTKE, Marg.	20	Lamstedt	69-0457
GARTUNG, Georg	30	Braunschweig	69-1363
GARVES, Wilh.	13	Schwalingen	68-0820
GASPEDAR, Peter	17	Flatow	71-0300
GASSEN, August	43	Berlin	69-1309
GASSMANN, Catharine	18	Hessen	70-0178
Anna 9			
GASSMANN, Friedrike	62	Heilbronn	71-0429
Marga. 27			
GASSMANN, Thilo	24	Kl. Wenthe	68-0957
GASSMUS, Eduard	20	Hilbersdorf	68-0456
GAST, Joh.	36	Erfurt	68-0753
GATHMANN, Michael	43	Hannover	68-0647
Marg. 33, Anna 8, Metta 7, Johann 5, Adelheid 26			

NAME	AGE	RESIDENCE	YR-LIST
GATJEN, Marie	30	Bremen	70-0329
Therese 8			
GATZ, Mathias	23	Kamnitz	69-0576
GAUCH, Charles A.	42	New York	70-1055
GAUGER, Julius	28	Treptow	68-0419
GAUL, Friedrich	29	Zemmen	69-0576
GAULKE, Ferdinand	28	Treptow	68-0566
Albertine 24			
GAUS, Agnes	20	Hohenzollern	69-0208
Johann 24			
GAUSCH, Peter	18	Monzernheim	69-0672
GAUSKE, Wilh.	30	Sabbenhausen	68-0884
GAUSS, Christine	22	Rothenberg	71-0643
GAUSS, Ma.	25	Bierlingen	71-0643
GAUSS, Marie	19	Grebenhain	68-0982
GAUTER, Engelb.	20	Lenzkirch	71-0363
GAUTHIER, Emma	40	New York	69-1076
GAVENS, Eugene	15	Rolla	71-0581
GAY, Wilh.	25	Untermutschl	69-1004
Eva 22, Wilh. 9 months			
GEBEL, Marg.	19	Westhofen	69-0583
GEBELEIM, George	22	Reimlass	69-0049
GEBER, H.	37	Bremen	71-0792
GEBERT, Bernh.	53	Oldenburg	70-0089
GEBHARD, Wilh.	23	Schwehn	69-0572
GEBHARDT, Ad.	36	Nordhausen	71-0167
Conradine 24			
GEBHARDT, Anna	26	Freishoestaedt	71-0643
GEBHARDT, B.	52	Horsten	68-1006
Heike H. 20			
GEBHARDT, Gottlieb	29	Halle	70-0031
GEBHARDT, John	31	Tettenhausen	70-1003
GEBHARDT, Magdalene	27	Gangsweiler	68-0786
GEBHARDT, Walter	23	Gena	71-0581
Reinhold 16			
GEBHORST, Louise	23	Rula	71-0479
GEBMAR, Karoline	21	Breisach	71-0492
GEBSERT, Reinhard	9	Lippstadt	69-0457
GEBUHR, Elisabeth	21	Heringen	68-0661
GEDEITZKA, Julius	21	Bockwa	68-0907
GEDIAN, Auguste	23	Rickingen	71-0681
Minna 20			
GEERD, Gg.	16	Uentzen	68-0610
GEERDTS, Geerd	17	Lehe	69-0229
GEERKEN, Anna	26	Loxstedt	68-0534
Henry 16			
GEERKEN, Anna	18	Etelsen	68-0661
GEERKEN, Friedericke	19	Triefrete	69-0457
GEERKEN, Friedr.	12	Friedrichsdorf	68-0982
GEERKEN, Gesine	19	Langenhausen	69-0672
GEERKEN, Heinrich	16	Wedderwarden	69-1076
GEERKEN, Joh.	47	Friedrichsdorf	68-0982
Marga. 42, Diedrich 15, Joh. 73, Adelheid 67			
GEERKEN, Mary	18	Selsingen	68-0957
GEERS, Gerhard	41	Bawinkel	69-0968
Marie 29, Anna 8, Adelheid 5, Anna 9 months, Johann 35			
GEESING, Elisabeth	23	Hollwick	69-0268

NAME	AGE	RESIDENCE	YR-LIST
GEESING, Hermann	27	Wuellen	69-0268
GEEVE, Ernst	24	Rensburg	69-0067
GEFFEL, Carl	22	Stolp	71-0581
GEFFGA, Joh.	27	Reissenberg	71-0681
Marg. 29, Johann 3, Carl 10 m.			
GEFFKEN, Dierk	26	Lilienthal	71-0456
GEHLE, Ernst	24	Hohenhausen	70-0308
GEHLE, Simon	26	Lippe Detmold	70-0148
GEHLINGER, Marie	33	Nuernberg	70-0569
Michl. 8			
GEHLKEN, Cord	27	Westertimke	68-0760
GEHRE, Christ.	24	Frankfurt	71-0300
GEHRHEN, Corel	29	Mulsum	69-0542
GEHRING, Anton	30	Wuerzburg	69-1086
GEHRING, Ernst	34	Clausthal	70-0170
GEHRING, Hermann	32	Naumburg	69-0338
GEHRING, Roderich	23	Ottowind	68-0786
GEHRING, Wilh.	19	Detmold	68-0982
GEHRKE, Heinrich	58	Dransfeld	69-0547
Ludwig 20, Friedrich 18, Wilhelm 12, Hermann 7			
GEHRKE, Henriette	19	Wonzow	71-0581
GEIB, Carl	21	Neustadt	69-1076
GEIB, Carl	18	Seelen	71-0643
GEIBEL, Ludwig	20	Hahn	69-1319
GEIBERTZ, August	24	Osnabrueck	70-0355
GEIBOYKEISKA, Jadwiga	16	Wita Slavia/Pru	69-0547
GEIER, Adolph	23	Eisenberg	68-0610
GEIER, Christine	19	Lindenau	70-1035
GEIER, Isidor	25	Hirnkirchen	70-0223
GEIER, Margar.	18	Schneweissach	69-0542
GEIER, Marie	15	Baden	70-0148
GEIGAND, Joseph	25	Regensburg	68-0820
GEIGER, Cathinka	24	Wangen	68-0566
Pauline 6 months			
GEIGER, Friedericke	24	Lienen	71-0492
GEIGER, Georg	7	Aschaffenburg	71-0789
GEIGER, Johann	25	Neigenmuenden	66-0734
GEIGER, Maria	62	Dorfnerskirchen	69-0672
Hedwig 9			
GEIGER, Paul	19	Friedlingen	71-0681
GEIGER, Peter	48	Leipzig	69-1319
Caroline 29, Emilie 9, Carl 2			
GEIL, Catharine	18	Wollmar	71-0821
GEIL, Jacob	23	Duschroth	68-1027
GEIL, Louise	56	Sonderhausen	70-1066
GEILER, Alex	27	Altenburg	68-0661
GEILS, Cathrine	19	Ritterhude	71-0456
GEILS, Wilhelm	18	Nordholz	68-0625
GEIPEL, Margreth	18	Boehmen	69-0848
GEIS, Bernhard	47	Hockenheim	71-0521
Dorothea 44, Catharina 19, Abraham 17, Juliane 9, Michael 7, Johann 3			
GEIS, Regina	19	Sandberg	68-0770
GEIS, William	43	Neustadt	68-1006
Vincenz 14			
GEISEL, Ernst	18	Darmstadt	71-0712
GEISELBRECHT, Louise	42	Bremen	70-0272

NAME	AGE	RESIDENCE	YR-LIST
GEISELBRECHT, Wilhelm	57	Marienwerder	69-1309
GEISER, August	21	Westfalen	70-0728
GEISLER, Ferd.	38	Mellwin	71-0521
Wilhelmine 35, Carl 9, Otto 11 months			
GEISLER, Jos.	15	Berlichingen	68-0884
GEISS, Georg	58	St. Langsfeld	71-0681
Friederike 60			
GEISSE, Rudolph	18	Goeppingen	71-0736
GEISSE, Wilhelmine	28	Marburg	69-1011
Charles 9			
GEISSEL, Gottlibine	28	Stuttgart	70-0569
Marie 6 months			
GEISSLER, Ferdinand	34	Neubrandenburg	68-0770
Maria 36, Carl 6, August 3, Louise 9 months			
GEISSLER, Georg	24	Tyrol	70-100
GEISSLER, Math.	30	Austria	70-0170
GEISSLER, Mich.	21	Tyrol	71-0167
GEISSLER, Pet.	26	Wolfshausen	70-0378
GEIST, Friedrich	39	Pittsburg	69-0784
Charles 9			
GEIST, Johanna	26	Volleringenstad	71-0492
GELBRICH, Louis	23	Heiningen	68-0982
Laura 23			
GELHAUS, Wilhelm	24	Detmold	69-0457
GELLER, Marie	27	Graach	68-1027
GEMANN, John H.	32	New York	68-1006
GEMERDINGER, Wilhelm	20	Unterjesingen	70-0089
Auguste 45			
GEMICKE, Louis	15	Wreschen	68-0939
GEMKE, Johann	31	Bremen	70-0006
GEMMELS, Christ.	31	Peine	68-0314
Louise 30, Anna 4, Marie 2			
GENNERICH, Georg	13	Scharnbeck	68-0820
GENNERICH, Heinrich	20	Bremervoerde	68-0820
GENNERLICH, Adelheid	30	Breslau	69-0321
GENNEROTH, Martha	22	Spangenberg	69-0457
GENOVEFA, Maria	32	Sultz	68-0566
GENRICH, Franz	36	Liebers	71-0643
Anna 56			
GENSLER, Andr.	26	Stolberg	68-1002
Christine 19			
GENTNER, Carl	36	Eggelstetten	71-0492
Therese 24			
GENTNER, Creszentia	34	Egelstetten	68-0314
GENTNER, Friedrich	19	Leonberg	70-0135
GENTNER, Johann	23	Leonberg	69-0848
GENTSCH, Carl	26	Gossnitz	69-0229
GENTZ, Johann	32	Mecklenburg	69-0542
Johanne 28, Friedrich 10 months, Johann 61, Marie 58, Wilhelm 34			
GENZEL, Gottfr.	25	Albersiede	70-0308
GENZEL, Minna	19	Magdeburg	69-0672
GEORG, Carl	31	Elberfeld	68-0456
Henriette 28, Robert 4, Emma 11 months			
GEORG, Gertrude	22	Doerrebach	69-0841
GEORGAS, Carl	42	Horla	68-1002
GEORGE, Carl	28	Ronneburg	68-0770
Friederike 49, Hermann 13			
GEORGE, Catharine	20	Hansen	71-0681
GEORGE, Conrad	15	Steindorf	68-0770

NAME	AGE	RESIDENCE	YR-LIST
GEORGE, Eleonore	52	Iba	68-0625
GEORGENS, Ludw.	20	Bildensheim	71-0300
GEORGI, Lobegott	29	Rothenkirchen	68-0707
Anna 24, Lilie 10 months			
GEORGI, Simon	49	Hirschfeld	68-0419
Elisabeth 54, Christine 21, Anna Elise 19, Anton 17, Veronica 14, Elisabeth 12			
GEORKEN, Heinrich	16	Wedderwarden	69-1076
GEPFERT, Julius	37	Berlin	68-0907
GEPPERT, Cath.	67	Gengenbach	69-1319
GEPPNER, Adam	46	Baiern	69-0559
GERACH, Gen.	29	Hammermuehe	71-0681
Therese 23			
GERACK, Moritz	39	Wien	69-0457
GERARD, Marie	47	Bueren	68-0939
GERATEWOLE, Sieg.	19	Mainz	69-0672
GERAZ, Friederike	24	Munchhofen	71-0479
GERAZ, Sophie	26	Munchhofen	71-0479
GERBER, Ludwig	36	St. Joseph	68-0661
GERBER, Michel	19	Bettenhausen	71-0643
GERBER, Ottilie	25	Nagelberg	69-0162
Maria 11 months			
GERBER, Wilhelm	27	Gotha	68-1027
GERBITZ, Friedrich	18	Neudrossenfelde	68-0707
Franz 19			
GERBRACHT, Marie	23	Mengshausen	71-0456
GERDELMANN, Caroline	27	Mettingen	69-0592
GERDES, Centre	22	Ochtersum	69-0547
GERDES, Christian	22	Ringstedt	71-0429
GERDES, Gerd	24	Aurich	69-1004
Tietje 19			
GERDES, Gerd.	24	Felde	69-1004
GERDES, Heinrich	50	Elmlohe	69-0490
GERDES, Herman	31	Osnabrueck	70-0135
GERDES, Hermann	53	Holtrup	69-0208
Gesche 42, Ahltje 16, Heinrich 83, Heinrich 9			
GERDES, Jann	59	Wiesederfehn	68-0907
Maria 49, Gerd 19, Friedrich 17, Toalke 7, Johann G. 5			
GERDES, Johann	18	Bilkau	70-0148
GERDES, Lena	19	Esens	68-0661
GERDES, Luecke	24	Utarp	68-314
GERDES, Magdalene	19	Bremen	70-0816
GERDES, Marie	20	Zeven	71-0479
Herm. 21			
GERDES, Mathilde	20	Oldenburg	70-0682
GERDES, Nicolaus	17	Elmeloh	68-0939
GERDES, Wilhelm	30	Bockhorst	68-1027
Franziska 20			
GERDING, Carl	29	Haaren	68-0786
GERDING, Fr. Wilh.	28	New Haven	69-0572
GERDS, Albertina	16	Vossberg	68-0884
GERFEN, Carl	19	Huelsen	68-0566
GERHARD, Carl	19	Dressebach	69-0841
GERHARD, Caspar	25	Bingen	69-0162
GERHARDT, Anna	59	Langel	69-0923
GERHARDT, Margarethe	32	Wetzlar	68-0820
Marie 9, Phil. 7, Elise 5			

NAME	AGE	RESIDENCE	YR-LIST
GERHARDT, Maria	16	Neu Freistadt	71-0712
GERHAUER, Josefine	34	Landsberg	71-0456
Anna 9, Cilli 5, Ludwig 2, John 11 months			
GERHAUER, Marie	25	Obermikelbach	71-0456
GERHEIM, Gust.	18	Zeitz	70-0355
GERHOLD, Anna	19	Kurhessen	70-1142
GERK, John	25	Utersen	68-0957
GERKE, Anna	25	Niedorf	69-0429
GERKE, Heinrich	35	Oldenburg	69-0542
GERKEN, Anna Bab.	22	Sievern	68-0610
GERKEN, H. Jos.	24	Oldenburg	69-0583
Rosalie 20			
GERKEN, Heinr.	16	Lesum	71-0736
GERKEN, Heinrich	16	Hannover	70-1035
GERKEN, Trina	19	Huettendorf	68-0907
GERLACH, Anna	28	Berlin	69-0560
GERLACH, Anna	20	Carden	71-0429
GERLACH, August	17	Alzey	71-0492
GERLACH, Christine	20	Marfeld	69-1086
GERLACH, Wilhelm	16	Iba	70-0355
GERLAND, Marie	19	Warburg	70-1003
GERLICH, Herm.	25	Kespergerde	70-0452
GERLING, Bernhard	18	Bersenbrueck	68-1002
GERLING, Friedr.	25	Minden	68-0786
GERLING, Heinrich	26	Minden	68-0907
GERLING, Johann	24	Stockum	69-0208
GERLING, Michael	32	Steinfeld	71-0712
Leonhard 27			
GERLITZ, Catharina	24	Duedelsheim	68-1006
GERMANN, Pauline	23	Hellenhausen	70-0569
GERNBACH, Franz	24	Erpertshausen	69-0560
GERNER, Carl	27	Richelkirchen	71-0521
GERNER, Friedrich	54	Betteville	69-0208
GERNER, Marie	53	Adelheim	68-0610
Elise 9			
GERNHARD, Martin	17	Bebra	68-0770
GERNRECK, Augusta	25	Celle	68-0625
Carl 8 months			
GERRMANN, Johannes	37	Eisenbeck	68-0770
Elisabeth 30, Johannes 5, Marie 3, Anna 2, Peter 8 months			
GERSTENBERG, Johann	40	Ronneburg	69-0848
GERSTER, Anna	25	Schwenninger	68-1002
Anna 6 months			
GERSTMEYER, Lorchen	25	Menningen	71-0821
GERSTNER, Eduard	25	Weimar	69-1076
GERTS, Franz	16	Offenbach	70-0308
GERWECK, Anton	19	Heilbronn	69-0572
GESAUER, Adam	45	Celfeld	71-0492
Louise 35, Magdalene 9, Catharine 7			
GESELL, Franziska	21	Delitsch	68-0820
GESINICK, Florian	40	Obergrund	71-0581
Therese 27, Vio. 2			
GESKE, Christian	32	Braunschweig	69-0542
Louise 32, Carl 7, Louise 6, August 11 months			
GESKE, Friedr.	25	Brunswick	69-0542
Wilhelmine 22			
GESKEN, Johann	24	Schwemmingen	69-0229
GESNING, Ernestine	29	Medewitz	69-0542
Carl 7, Eglouis 3			
GESSLER, Joh.	36	Diesendorf	69-0050
GESSWEIN, Albert	18	Leonberg	70-0135
GESSWEIN, Elisabeth	25	Obersterfeld	68-0786
GEST, Carl	63	Mecklenburg	70-1023
Caroline 64, Wilhelmine 35, Johanne 25			
GESTMER, Fr.	22	Rogassen	70-1023
GETTENBACH, Friederike	20	Alttenhofen	69-0968
GETTMANN, Jacob	23	Oldenburg	69-0560
Catharine 27, Mary 4			
GEUSS, Johann	20	Heubach	70-0076
GEVERS, Joh.	35	Bremen	70-0089
GEYER, Catharine	18	Keferod	68-0852
GEYER, Christine	21	Neu Leidinden	69-1363
GEYER, Heinr.	23	Reuss Schleiz	69-0583
GEYER, Heinrich	59	Breitenbach	69-0542
Barbara 58			
GIBBONS, James	58	New York	69-1421
GIEBE, Aug.	38	Detmold	68-0314
Wilhelmine 29			
GIEBEL, Ferd.	35	Pyrmont	71-0815
Minna 32			
GIEBISCH, Franz	17	Bischofsteinitz	68-0610
GIEGERICH, Barnabas	27	Eisenbach	68-1002
GIEL, Wilh.	15	Worms	71-0821
GIERSA, Joseph	34	Petersburg	68-0872
GIERSDORF, Joseph	20	Steinau	71-0363
GIES, Conrad	64	Detroit	69-0848
GIESCHAUN, Fritz	48	Muenden	70-0452
GIESCHEL, Conrad	17	Stadtlengsfeld	68-0707
GIESCHEN, Heinrich	17	Carlhofen	68-0625
GIESCHEN, Johann	16	Porthausen	69-1309
Posthausen			
GIESE, Anna Rosina	64	Wieseck	68-0770
GIESE, Aug. Frd.	30	Buchholz	68-0820
Henriette 27, August 8, Augusta 9 months			
GIESE, Friederich	25	Nossow-Rossow	71-0712
Albertine 26, Auguste 9 months, Emilie 19, Ferdinand 16			
GIESE, Georg Gottlieb	32	Gallis-Pommern	70-0006
GIESE, Wilhelm	26	Buchholz	68-1006
GIESECKE, Adolph	24	Braunschweig	71-0363
GIESEDKE, Herm.	25	Braunschweig	71-0363
Otto 15			
GIESER, Reinhard	24	Wieflingen	70-0135
GIESER, Reinhard	24	Wieflingen	70-0135
Johann 42, Agnes 46, Paul 3			
GIESIN, Carl	19	Emmendingen	69-1309
GIESIN, Wilh.	19	Mundingen	68-0884
GIESING, Therese	47	Kirchschlag	70-0355
Franz 17, Marie 19, Ferdinand 9			
GIESMANN, Philipp	16	Philippsthal	70-0523
GIESS, Betty	23	Fuerth	70-0170
Baby girl 6 months			
GIESS, Jean	30	Fuerth	70-0135
GIESSLER, Carl Fr.	25	Freiburg	70-0259
GILBERT, Kunigunde	56	Einartshausen	69-0592

NAME	AGE	RESIDENCE	YR-LIST
Johannes 26, Cath. 22			
GILCH, Johann	22	Uhingen	68-0014
GILDEHAUS, Wilhelm	36	Hilter	68-0907
Louise 27, Diana 7, Fritz 6, Heinrich 4			
GILG, Jos.	28	Schoenberg	69-0100
GILKER, Gottlieb	19	Destel/Distel	69-1076
GILL, Ruppert	21	Attenhofen	69-1086
GILLARDEN, Wilhelm	17	Bretten	70-0378
GILLE, Werner	22	Birkenfeld	69-0968
GILLING, Caspar	65	Woerstadt	69-0592
GILLSDORF, Carl	23	Ebersheim	69-0672
GILSHAUSER, Christiane	18	Sachsen Meining	69-0559
GIMBEL, Catharine	23	Marbach	69-1396
GIMBEL, Justus	28	S. Franzisco	69-1396
Cathrine 28, Emma 11 months (Marbach)			
GIMSCHEN, Riklefs	28	Rodenkirchen	68-0534
Sophie 25			
GINGERICH, Julius	25	Kirchheim	68-0707
GIPP, Friederike	59	Kraatz	68-0770
Wilhelmine 26, Emilie 25, Wilhelmine 5			
GIRSCHEN, John	39	San Francisco	69-0560
Dorothea 32, Lewis 8, Baby daughter 1			
GISSAU, Max	46	Philadelphia	69-1363
Therese 39, Marie 9, Franziska 6			
GISSLER, Johann	18	Holzelfingen	69-1076
GITZINGER, Peter	24	Fata	68-0852
GLAAR, Albert	27	Loenach	69-0079
GLACKEMEIER, August	25	Dramfeld	68-0647
GLADISCHOFSKY, Otto	18	Berlin	69-0583
GLAHN, Herm.	16	Hannover	68-0456
GLAMEYER, August	14	Westerwanna	71-0429
GLAMSER, Marie	23	Schlatz	69-0321
GLANDER, Anna	24	Oldenburg	70-0452
Elise Johanne 16			
GLANNER, Caroline	18	Freudenstadt	71-0792
GLASCHER, Frdr.	20	Destel	68-0610
Ludwig 17			
GLASEL, Eleonore	20	Arzberg	71-0821
GLASER, Abraham	33	Kusel	71-0727
Abraham 42			
GLASER, Barbara	47	Kaiserslautern	69-0457
August 14			
GLASER, Carl	24	Neustadt	68-0982
Elisabeth 26			
GLASER, Cath.	28	Gammersbach	71-0363
Marie 11 months			
GLASER, Magdalene	18	Elsass	68-0610
Marie 19			
GLASER, Michael	17	Diesterfeld	71-0712
GLASISCHEFSKY, Herm.	23	Berlin	70-0728
GLASS, Rud.	19	Ulm	69-1004
GLATTFELD, Otto	25	Pyrmont	68-0456
GLAUBER, Helene	17	Birkenfeld	70-1142
GLEBER, Henry	31	Kirspenhausen	71-0456
GLEIM, Martha	22	Kurhessen	69-1086
GLEISTEIN, Hermann	29	New York	69-1086
Mary 23			
GLEITEMANN, Fr.	36	Altenburg	71-0736
GLESSNER, Caroline	21	Preussen	68-0456

NAME	AGE	RESIDENCE	YR-LIST
GLEUE, Heinrich	34	Nienhagen	69-0321
GLIED, Marie	20	Hardenstetten	68-0852
GLIENTZ, Maria	58	Hosenpferrena	68-0770
Johann Georg 18			
GLISS, Peter	22	Leitgettern	69-1319
GLOCK, David	27	Birnstein	69-0229
GLOCK, Georg		Weisbach	70-0259
GLOCK, Georg	29	Altnindorf	71-0789
GLOCK, Johann	24	Gundhelm	68-0566
Peter 19			
GLOCKEMEIER, August	25	Dramfeld	68-0647
GLOCKER, Julie	22	Stuttgart	71-0429
GLOCKMANN, Gustav	19	Pochersleben	71-0456
GLOECKNER, Elisabeth	19	Ramstadt	68-0786
GLOECKNER, Heinrich	64	Lieh	70-0184
GLOVANNA, Albert	28	Scharcowitz/Boe	69-0576
GLOVER, Balthasar	34	Weisweil	71-0456
GLUECKERT, Francisca	20	Hohenkirchen	71-0429
GLUECKHAUS, Ernst	23	Remscheid	69-1059
GLUECKSTEIN, Elisabeth	24	Creen	68-0707
GLUTH, Julius	27	Naseband	69-0338
Caroline 23, Frederic 9 months			
GNADE, Caroline	22	Iburg	68-0456
GNADE, Wilhelmine	22	Rischenau	68-0610
GOCKE, Friedrich	34	Blomberg	69-0798
GOCKER, Johann	26	Paderborn	68-0456
GODDRAUS, Ad. Georg	9	Holler Wustig	70-0204
Jan 39			
GODE, August	24	Wangezin	69-0672
GODE, Johann	52	Oldenburg	69-0268
Catharine 45, Heinrich 9, Johann 8, Claus 6, Friedrich 1			
GODJE, Heinrich	55	Wildeshausen	69-0798
Catharina 53, Catharina 20, Heinrich 16, Bernhard 6, Friedrich 5			
GODSTEIN, Minna	22	Oldenburg	71-1046
Emilie 6			
GOEBBER, Friedr.	17	Grauel	71-0821
GOEBBER, Heinrich	19	Wietzen	71-0736
GOEBEL, Anton	28	Lichtenau	69-0848
GOEBEL, Carl	24	Gudenberg	71-0821
GOEBEL, Dorothea	16	Schemmer	69-0672
Barbara 14			
GOEBEL, John	21	Wollmar	71-0821
GOEBEL, Ludwig	20	Bremen	69-0968
GOEBELS, Martin	18	Wollmar	68-0852
GOECKING, Carl	16	Holsen	68-0566
GOECKLER, Carl	29	Tiefenbronn	70-0031
GOEFTLING, Caroline	15	Strassburg	68-0566
GOEHN, Anna	20	Emden	70-0384
GOEHR, Michael	29	Altdorf	69-0162
GOEHRING, Adolf	14	Ueberlingen	69-0923
GOEHRING, Christine	22	Pfaeffingen	70-0089
GOEHRING, Friedr.	16	Leonberg	71-0581
GOEHRING, Jacob	19	Darmstadt	70-0378
GOEHRING, Louise	22	Untermerzbach	71-0479
GOEKE, Friedrich	34	Blomberg	69-0798
GOEKE, Wilhelmus	21	Brosen	69-0968

NAME	AGE	RESIDENCE	YR-LIST
GOELLER, Carl Cath. 23	26	Bromberg	71-0581
GOELLER, Christine	21	Roppenreuth	68-0852
GOELZKE, Christian	59	Gieskow	70-0523
GOENICKE, Albert	36	Soest	69-0923
GOENNER, Franz	24	Weilersbach	71-0492
GOENS, Andr.	28	Spabruecken	71-0581
GOEPEL, Anna	19	Stuttgart	69-1212
GOEPPNER, Andreas	31	Wartenfels	71-0300
GOEPPNER, Maria	42	Oberfranken	70-0523
GOERBACH, Jacob Elise 24, Christian 2	24	Etmansweiler	68-0852
GOERGER, Therese	62	Rudolfzell	71-0456
GOERING, Jul.	22	Menterode	71-0479
GOERING, Wilhelm	43	Grabsleben	68-0456
GOERINGER, Marie Frdr. 25	20	Grottkau	68-0610
GOERKE, Caroline Auguste 7	40	Memel	70-0443
GOERKE, Mathilde Rosalie 9	41	Danzig	69-1421
GOERL, Brigitte	19	Erlangen	71-0429
GOERLITZ, Carl	17	Kleinkarlbach	70-1055
GOERLITZ, Philipp Juliane 52, Ludwig 23, Christine 9, Philipp 7, Juliane 16	52	Nahbuellenbach	68-0786
GOERNER, Hugo	19	Stuttgart	70-0170
GOESER, Alberti	27	Neuningen	69-0672
GOESER, Otto	20	Neuningen	69-0229
GOETEL, Marie Louise 4	28	Sachsenhausen	71-0479
GOETH, Andreas	17	Oppenheim	68-0534
GOETHE, Carl	30	Burkau	68-1027
GOETSCH, Marie	22	Nuernberg	68-0566
GOETTE, Friedr.	26	Berndorf	68-0982
GOETTEL, Carl	25	Schoeneberg	69-0542
GOETTEL, Theodor Emilie 27	30	Frumstadt	70-0329
GOETTINGER, Philipp	31	Reidesbach	71-0521
GOETTNER, Johann	19	Westerenge	68-0939
GOETZ, Andreas Kunigunde 51, Jacob 18, Elisabeth 15, Kunigunde 13	48	Dettendorf	69-1004
GOETZ, Aug.	17	Hopfingen	71-0393
GOETZ, Catharina Johanne 18	13	Schweenfurt	69-0572
GOETZ, Christina Margaretha 2	25	Friedewald	69-1212
GOETZ, Elisabeth Georg 9	6	Worms	70-0308
GOETZ, Franz Rosina 18	20	Darmstadt	70-0728
GOETZ, Franz Antonie 19	22	Severne	71-0643
GOETZ, Heinrich Margarethe 23	23	Baiern	69-0559
GOETZ, Josef	26	Stadtamhof	69-1059
GOETZ, Marg.	23	Hessen	70-0204
GOETZ, Marg. Kunig. 22	25	Immermannstadt	71-0815

NAME	AGE	RESIDENCE	YR-LIST
GOETZ, Regina	23	Oberschuetz	68-0939
GOETZ, Susanne Peter 14	19	Hersa	71-0521
GOETZE, Babette	49	Jolsch	69-1363
GOETZER, Nic. Meta 34, Hermann 7, Eduard 5, Baby son 10 months, Baby 10 months	37	Hannover	70-0378
GOETZMANN, Julius	23	Frankfurt a/M	70-0272
GOHDE, Ludwig	16	Rechtenfletherm	69-1059
GOHL, Elise	9	Stuttgart	69-1059
GOHL, Joh.		Havre	70-0259
GOHL, Marie	22	Buergstadt	69-0592
GOLDACKER, Friederike Carl 17, Emil 16, Albert 9, Pauline 14	43	Berlin	68-0770
GOLDBACH, Albert	26	Wolferts	68-0610
GOLDBACH, Bonifazius	24	Marbach	68-0661
GOLDBACH, Franz	25	Ebersberg	71-0479
GOLDBECK, Friederike	17	Cassel	71-0521
GOLDBERG, Alexander	34	Preussen	68-0456
GOLDBERG, Caroline	24	Wormsdorf	71-0733
GOLDE, Julie Oscar 3	29	Coburg	69-0067
GOLDE, Louis Wilhelmine 50, Bertha 9, Amalie 8	43	Tenchern	68-0610
GOLDERNSTEIN, Jan.	16	Westochtersum	69-0457
GOLDFUSS, Johann Kunigunde 17	19	Wuerzburg	68-0852
GOLDHORN, Charlotte	29	Trarbach	68-0852
GOLDMEIER, Georg	17	Leive	69-1212
GOLDNIG, J. Herda 2	9	Bickelsberg	71-0521
GOLDORF, Cath. Auguste 18	20	Ritzebuettel	69-1212
GOLDSACH, Gertrud Johannes 3, Therese 2	25	Lindern	71-0684
GOLDSCHMIDT, Bertha	17	Enzen	71-0643
GOLDSCHMIDT, Caroline	21	Langenselbald	71-0643
GOLDSCHMIDT, Celina	21	Nordhausen	70-0135
GOLDSCHMIDT, Hanche	60	Erdmannsrod	70-0523
GOLDSCHMIDT, Jette	25	Heubach	71-0643
GOLDSCHMIDT, Louis	21	Abterrode	71-0429
GOLDSCHMIDT, Thilo	16	Nordhausen	70-0135
GOLDSCHNEIDER, Clara Mathilde 11 months	26	Boehmen	70-0728
GOLITZ, Ludwig Marie 27	25	Traumburg	68-0753
GOLK, Golk H. Frauke 25, Hilke 9, Harm 7, Heinr. 4, Heinr. 25	30	Coldinne	68-1002
GOLKARDT, Georg Lisette 18	46	Gotha	71-0479
GOLL, Elisabeth	20	Brettin/Baden	69-0049
GOLL, Margareth	21	Bissingen	68-0534
GOLLISCHON, Adolf	28	Frankfurt	69-1059
GOLLMER, Catharine	24	Unterlenningen	69-0208
GOLM, Friedrich	20	Diedelsheim	68-0647
GOLTNITZ, Richard	20	BEERWALDE	70-1035
GOLZWARDEN, Helene	20	Brake	70-1003
GOMBERT, Martha	17	Homberg	70-1003

NAME	AGE	RESIDENCE	YR-LIST
GONTJES, Gesche	36	Ostfriesland	69-1011
Berend 8, Jan 7, Imkens 4, Eiltje 10 months			
GOODMANN, Emanuel	19	Niederstein	69-1086
GOOS, Anton	19	Sassbeck	71-0456
GOOS, H. A.	25	Otterndorf	71-0521
GOOSCH, Friedr.	36	Armenhof	68-0314
GOOSEN, Marg.	22	Estorf	71-0581
GOOSMANN, Habbe	24	Strackholt	69-0457
Dirk 20			
GORDES, Louise	17	Untermutschl	69-1004
GORDES, Victor	43	Brenham	69-1004
GORETZKY, Franz	14	Tuchel	71-0581
GORSCHEN, Adelheid	23	Pfaffenweiler	69-0583
GOSEWISCH, Wilhelm	18	Neustadt	68-0534
GOSKAR, Meta	20	Detmold	69-0572
GOSKER, Regina	22	Aachen	68-0939
GOSLAR, Erhard	39	Romersreck	68-0939
GOSLAR, Gustav	14	Neustadt	68-0534
GOSSKER, Bertha	13	Botnang	68-0982
GOTTE, Marie	22	Westfalen	70-0728
GOTTHARD, Ernst	36	Fuerstenwalde	69-1059
GOTTHARDT, Anton	37	Mittelhofen	69-0162
GOTTHARDT, Ernst	28	Essingen	69-0457
Anna 22			
GOTTHARDT, Heinrich	24	Reinheim	71-0492
Friderike 24			
GOTTHELF, Henri	19	Beckum	71-0479
GOTTHILF, Fr.	25	Reval-Rival	70-1161
GOTTLAND, Franz	26	Neuland	71-0492
GOTTLIEB, Carl	40	Glauchau	68-0456
GOTTLIEB, Samuel	24	Holzmuenden	68-0566
GOTTSCHALCK, Friedr.	25	Maroldsweisach	68-1002
GOTTSCHALDT, Friedr.	25	Maroldsweisach	68-1002
GOTTSCHALDT, Joh.	20	Maroldsweisach	68-1002
GOTTSCHALK, Abraham		Stolpe	69-0559
Caecilia 23 (came originally in August of 1856 to Ohio)			
GOTTSCHALK, Caroline	22	Wimpfen	71-0479
Babette 15			
GOTTSCHALK, Ernst	54	Stolberg	68-0786
Lina 57, Henriette 15			
GOTTSCHALK, Herz	23	Nimheim	69-0542
GOTTSCHALK, Maria	43	Muehlhausen	68-0456
Sophia 21, Friederike 19, Rosa 18, Clara 9, Ida 8, Emil 5			
GOTTSCHALK, Rosina	21	Sachsen Meining	69-0321
GOTTSCHALK, Simon	17	Mainz	71-0456
GOTTSCHALK, Wilh.	32	Delmenhorst	69-0583
Sophie 31			
GOTTSTEIN, Anna	38	Boehmen	70-0728
Vincenz 9, Emm. 9 months			
GOTTSTRODER, Franz	44	Brokhorst	68-0907
Wilhelmine 44, Wilhelm 7, Heinrich 6, Catharine 4			
GRAALBERG, Karoline	22	Breisach	71-0492
GRAALMANN, Neske	24	Tietnin	70-0523
GRAB, Carl	24	Eschelbronn	68-1006
GRAB, Catharina	19	Villingen	68-0884
GRAB, Gottlieb	20	Flohafen	69-0798

NAME	AGE	RESIDENCE	YR-LIST
GRABAU, Claus	14	Stokenborstel	69-0672
GRABE, Karl	34	Celle	71-0712
GRABERT, Heinrich	18	Heilbron	70-0523
GRABHORN, Albertine	24	Bremen	71-0643
GRADE, Wm.	37	New York	70-1035
Mary 26, Aug. 6			
GRAEBER, Johann	50	Ahrweiler	68-0770
Anna Maria 20			
GRAEBING, Carl	20	Kleinem	68-0566
GRAEBNER, Auguste	18	Rodinghausen	69-0923
GRAEF, Daniel	18	Pfingstedt	69-1076
GRAEF, Wendelin	19	Rothwehl	71-0727
GRAEFENSTEIN, Cath.	22	Mertelsheim	69-0162
GRAEFER, Bernhard	18	Lorstedt	71-0492
GRAEFINGER, C.	30	Malsch	71-0456
GRAEFRER, Alb. Fr.	22	Varel	69-0079
GRAEHNER, Hanchen	22	Westerengen	68-0939
Marie 20			
GRAESSER, Thomas	28	Malsch	71-0456
GRAETER, Friedr.	32	Bechlingen	71-0521
GRAETH, Carl	24	Thiemersdorf	68-0707
GRAETZER, Maria	19	Mainz	68-0661
GRAEUER, Caspar	25	Muenchen	69-0923
GRAEVER, John H.	41	Charleston	69-1059
GRAF,	22	Babenhausen	69-1212
GRAF, Anton	26	Muenchen	70-0272
GRAF, August	29	Neu Dambach	68-0456
GRAF, Bernhard	30	Barmen	70-0329
GRAF, Carl	41	Freysing	69-0015
GRAF, Carl	26	Berndorf	68-0982
GRAF, Caroline	21	Oldenburg	69-1004
GRAF, Friedrich	16	Dornduerkenhm.	71-0821
GRAF, Friedrich	24	Luzern	71-0821
Anna 22			
GRAF, Georg	44	Villingen	68-0884
GRAF, Herm.	21	Braunschweig	71-0684
GRAF, Hermann	18	Padesen	69-0429
GRAF, Jos.	17	Dummingen	68-0566
GRAF, Josefine	25	Altendorn	68-0534
GRAF, Ludwig	44	Wolfsgrube	71-0226
GRAF, Pauline	17	Ruhl	68-0707
GRAF, Regine	26	Meinzeschein	70-1035
GRAFE, Theodor	28	Hannover	70-0329
GRAFFSTEDT, H.H.	25	New York	69-0572
GRAGEL, Peter	23	Hesse Darmstadt	70-0329
GRAHN, Otto	26	Muenster	70-0204
GRAJEWSKY, Stanislaus	50	Sabathof/Polen	69-0576
Marianne 50, Johann 19, Stanislaus 8			
GRAMANN, Bernhard	19	Steinfelde	69-0798
GRAMBERG, Rosa	20	Oldenburg	69-0490
GRAMBO, Eduard	18	Hostenbach	71-0581
GRAMBO, Franz	23	Horstenbach	71-0581
GRAMLICH, Carl	19	Wallhausen	71-0792
GRAMLICH, Christian	24	Boedigheim	68-1002
Caroline 22			
GRAMM, Anton	24	Frankfurt a/M	69-1396
GRAMM, Friedr.	72	Neustaedt	68-1027

NAME	AGE	RESIDENCE	YR-LIST
GRAMMANN, Minna	41	Berlin	70-1035
GRANDEMANN, Adele	16	Oldenburg	69-1086
GRANDWEG, J. F.	24	Eningerloh	71-0521
GRANEWINKEL, Fritz Louise 23	30	Dettmold	69-0542
GRANITZ, Therese Mathilde 17, Louise 15	56	Sachsen	69-1059
GRANKE, Carl	25	Scherandorf	71-0479
GRAP, Friedr.	49	Koenigsberg	71-0733
GRAPENSTEIN, Wme.	23	Prenzlau	71-0479
GRAPPERHAUS, Bernh.	30	Quakenbrueck	71-0681
GRAPPERHAUS, Jos.	20	Ahrhausen	69-0050
GRAS, Gertrude	17	Caminchen	69-0321
GRASCH, Carl	22	Woerrstadt	69-0672
GRASCH, Therese	17	Schleussingen	69-1004
GRASS, Wilhelm	19	Hall	69-1004
GRASSEL, John	35	Zausville	68-0852
GRASSMAN, Charles	9	Redenberg	69-0771
GRATWOHL, Marie	16	Markdorf	68-1027
GRATZER, Anton Josephine 9	45	Philadelphia	69-1076
GRAU, Caroline	24	Kaisersbach	69-0429
GRAU, Herm.	16	Crispendorf	68-0820
GRAU, Reinhard	22	Chrispentorf	68-0852
GRAUL, Eduard	55	New York	69-0490
GRAUL, Franz	23	Naundorf	68-0982
GRAUL, Henriette	17	Kelbra	68-0566
GRAUL, Julius	31	Muehlheim	70-0682
GRAUL, Phil.	18	Soden	71-1046
GRAUMUELLER, Herm.	26	Braunichwald	68-0647
GRAUMUELLER, Julius Ernestine 32, Emma 6, Franz 4, Robert 11 months	38	Altenburg	69-0542
GRAUNE, Dorothea David 9, Rosine 8, Gustav 7	42	Botnang	68-0982
GRAUPNER, Traugott	27	Lugan	69-0560
GRAUTERSTUECK, Wm.	26	Kleinenberg	69-0429
GRAVELMANN, Heinrich	19	Arendshausen	68-0625
GRAWE, Ant.	28	Lippstadt	68-0753
GREBE, Catharine	16	Adorf	68-0456
GREBE, Elise	28	Rothenburg	68-0707
GREBE, Heinrich	22	Langenselbad	69-0848
GREBE, Ludwig	32	Darmstadt	71-0226
GREBENSTEIN, Friedr.	16	Niederhorn	69-0576
GREBNER, Kunigunde	29	Bamberg	71-0429
GREDE, Joh.	18	Altenstedt	68-0884
GREEF, Bernhard	30	Barmen	70-0329
GREENEBAUM, Auguste	27	Wuerzburg	68-0982
GREEWE, Dorchen	22	Bielefeld	68-1027
GREHL, Valentin	21	Hoerdt	68-0982
GREIF, Andr.	36	Hessen	69-1011
GREILING, Bernhard	65	Hoppenton	68-0456
GREINER, Albin	15	Weimar	71-0429
GREINER, Alma	19	SSchwarzb. Rude	69-0672
GREINER, Cath.	18	Wien	68-1002
GREINER, Gotthaes T. 23	27	Oldenburg	69-0292
GREININGER, Georg	35	Marquette	70-1023
GREINKE, Jul.	23	Scherwilowke	71-0479
GREISINGER, Cath.	31	Neumark	68-0957
GREISS, Wilhelm	30	Roesberg	70-0148
GREITHE, Wilhelmine	23	Lingen	69-0968
GREITZ, Joh.	26	Staussenberg	70-1142
GRETEMEYER, Anna	23	Herzfeld	68-0820
GRETEN, Carl	52	Bremen	69-1309
GRETH, Johanna	13	Pfeil	70-0259
GRETZLER, Barbara	59	Schrozberg	68-1027
GREUBEL, Barbara Joseph 21	26	Arnshausen	68-0707
GREULING, Ludwig Helene 24	31	Wiesbaden	70-0728
GREVE, Friedrich	19	Luebecke	69-0576
GREVE, Henry	16	Unterluebbeke	68-0957
GREVE, Marie	20	Huesede	68-0852
GREVERIUS, Ernst	20	Oldenburg	68-0786
GREWE, Clara	16	Bohmte	71-0521
GREY, Dorothea	28	Creuzburg	68-0820
GREYER, John Eva 20, Georg 16	27	Muntingen	69-0841
GRIEB, Joseph	21	Wuerzburg	68-0014
GRIEBE, Joh.	17	Bremen	71-0167
GRIEBEL, Louis	25	Coblenz	68-0647
GRIEBEL, Sarah	18	Alsenz	68-0786
GRIEBLING, Joh.	19	Ewighausen	71-0581
GRIEDER, V.	30	Basel	71-0712
GRIESCHE, Anna	20	Braach	68-0707
GRIESE, Aug.	30	Steinsdorf	69-1086
GRIESE, Chr. Emma 18, David 9	48	Cleveland	69-1086
GRIESE, Heinrich Hermine 31, Carline 39, Friederich 11 months	32	Oldenburg	70-0384
GRIESE, Herman	15	Quakenbrueck	68-1027
GRIESEL, Anna C. Adolph 9, Ottilie 4	36	Kurhessen	70-0443
GRIESHEIMER, Martin	22	Lampertheim	68-0957
GRIESING, Agnes Carl 18	17	Blankenbach	68-0820
GRIESS, Johann	19	Fuerth	71-0492
GRIESS, Wilh.	21	Erlangen	71-0821
GRIESSER, Berend	20	Wellendinger	70-0378
GRIESSER, Vincenz	17	Cappeln	69-1212
GRIESSNER, Eva	15	Pfalz	70-0508
GRIEVE, Elise Auguste 18	28	Hamelerwald	69-0848
GRIMLING, Max	23	Bonn	68-0957
GRIMM, Adolph	19	Aixheim	69-0923
GRIMM, Albin	15	Weimar	71-0429
GRIMM, Catherine	22	Deinfeld	71-0429
GRIMM, Died.	55	Hannover	70-1142
GRIMM, Elisabeth Friedr. 9, Heinr. 9, Dina 7	34	Frankfurt a/M	70-1142
GRIMM, Friedrich	21	Ebershausen	70-0355
GRIMM, Georg Carol 37, Georg 13	43	Reuss	69-1004
GRIMM, Heinr.	43	Zagenhausen	71-0393

NAME	AGE	RESIDENCE	YR-LIST
Marie 38, Kath. 19, Eva 17, Johannes 15, Karl 7, Nicolaus 6, Heinrich 9 mont			
GRIMM, Henry	37	Thueringen	70-1003
Sophie 37, Ferdinand 9, Max 8, Friedrich 6			
GRIMM, Ignatz	47	Oestreich	70-0728
Franziska 30, Franz 23, Anna 21, Ignatz 15			
GRIMM, Johann	22	Zollhausen	68-0661
GRIMM, Joseph	17	Zepfenhahn	69-0560
John 19			
GRIMM, Meta	19	Kuhstadtermoor	68-0907
GRIMM, Ph.	24	Niederroth	68-0753
GRIMM, Phil.	40	Cassel	71-0393
GRIMM, Therese	67	Speichingen	69-0841
GRIMM, Valentin	35	Gotha	68-0939
GRIMME, Aug.	22	Aurich	69-0490
GRIMME, Johann	41	Oestreich	70-0728
Cath. 46, Theresia 9, Joseph 7			
GRIMMEL, Louis	30	Hoya	71-0792
Auguste 27, Willi 11 months			
GRIMMELT, Leopold	20	Geeschen	69-1212
GRIMMINGER, Barbara	19	Bachzimmern	71-0429
GRIMPE, Gottlieb	29	Calbe	71-0643
Johanne 24, Marie 2, Friederike 11 m			
GRIS, Solem	25	Schwiezhausen	70-0569
GROBE, August	26	Bockenau	69-0208
GROBE, Christine	19	Meerdorf	68-0852
GROBE, Mathilde	30	Braunschweig	69-0560
Fred. 8, Ernst 6			
GROBERT, Louis	34	Mauerhardt	69-0798
GROCHOLSKI, Ant.	26	Exin-Esein	71-0684
Johann 6			
GRODE, Dorothea	22	Bibelnheim	71-0429
Magda. 24			
GROEBE, Elisabeth	23	Westhofen	69-0229
GROEBER, August	40	Magdeburg	68-0982
GROEGER, Brigitta	23	Steinau	68-0456
GROEHN, Joh.	25	Grabzonne	71-0581
GROENBECK, Gustav	32	Stockholm	69-0338
GROENBERG, Salomon	22	Assen	71-0712
GROENEWALD, Voelker	16	Aurich	68-0884
Broes 30, Wilh. 18			
GROENING, Wilhelmine	23	Bremen	68-0456
GROENINGER, Chas.	44	Birkenfeld	69-1011
GROESS, Johann	34	Weiberfelten	71-0492
GROH, Edw.	18	Bernsdorf	69-0100
GROMMEL, Marie	26	Leonberg	71-0581
Friedr. 17			
GRONEMEYER, Fr.	32	Buende	68-1006
Anna Marie 32, Mathilde 4			
GROOTHEER, Sophie	16	Bederkesa	69-1086
GROOTJOHANN, Marie	37	Wolgast	69-1086
GROSCH, Elise	37	Sulzbach	71-0521
Johann 15, George 11 months			
GROSCH, Friedrich	36	Armenhof	68-0314
GROSCH, Joh.	22	Hermerschen	71-0167
GROSCH, Marg.	21	Walzhenfeld	71-0363
GROSCH, Th.	19	Treisbach	71-0789
GROSMANN, Adolf	19	Obernkirchen	68-0957
GROSS, Adolph	45	Oldenburg	70-0204

NAME	AGE	RESIDENCE	YR-LIST
Helene 44, Marie 15, Anna 12, Catharina 9, Gesine 6, Hermann 3, Adolph 1			
GROSS, Bernhard	14	Affaltrach	68-0939
GROSS, C. G.	23	Karstadt	70-100
GROSS, Carl	30	Werdau	68-0939
GROSS, Caroline	22	Jastein	70-0378
GROSS, Caroline	42	Padunke	71-0821
GROSS, Catharina	25	Mainlins	68-0707
GROSS, Catharine	20	Scheckingen	71-0456
GROSS, Christine	52	Rottenberg	69-0771
Heinrich 23, Wilhelm 17			
GROSS, Emil	25	Erfurt	68-0625
GROSS, Emilie	28	Muenchen	70-0508
GROSS, Franz	29	Limburg	70-0204
GROSS, Fred.	30	Birkenfeld	70-0508
Jacobine 27, Edward 11 months, Ida 11 months			
GROSS, Friedrich	29	Niederbrombach	69-0848
GROSS, Heinrich	28	Mainleus	69-0848
GROSS, Johann	38	Langenwetzendf.	68-0760
GROSS, Julius	26	Bruchsal	69-0457
GROSS, Margreth	57	Mainbeus	69-0848
GROSS, Mathe.	24	R.B.Coblenz	68-1006
GROSS, Oswald	15	Berlin	69-1004
GROSS, Philippine	33	Rhein Pfalz	70-0355
GROSS, Rachel	25	Mertzviller	71-0581
GROSS, Robert	18	Giengen	68-0566
GROSS, Wilhelmine	21	Battenberg	68-0566
Henriette 18			
GROSSBUTEMAIER, Joh.	26	Schapen	68-0939
GROSSE, Carl	23	Coburg	68-0707
GROSSE, Julius	36	Eisleben	68-0707
GROSSE, Ludwig	23	Heidenheim	69-0572
GROSSMANN, Anna	27	Bremen	70-1142
GROSSMANN, Carl	17	Altenstaig	68-0852
GROSSMANN, Cathrine	65	Steinbach	71-0456
Cathrine 42, John 9			
GROSSMANN, Johann	29	Leupoldsgruen	69-0848
GROSSMANN, Louise	24	Kandel	71-0684
GROSSSTICK, Ernst	19	Rudolstadt	69-0429
GROSZEYK, Adalh.	24	Krojanke	71-0581
GROTE, August	28	Hannover	68-0707
GROTE, Carl	22	Bremen	68-0884
GROTE, Carl	16	Nienburg	68-1006
GROTE, Carl	23	Moringen	71-0712
GROTE, Heinr.	22	Ulrichshausen	68-0884
GROTE, Susanne	21	Bremen	71-0479
GROTELOESCHEN, Wilh.	14	Barglei	68-0610
GROTH, Eduard	30	Berlin	69-0784
GROTH, Georg	25	Neustrelitz	68-0707
GROTHE, August	27	Berlin	68-0753
GROTJOHAN, Johann	14	Heisenbuettel	68-0625
GRUB, Friedrich	23	Westbarthausen	68-0939
GRUBE, Andreas	16	Bremen	69-0572
GRUBE, Catharina	20	Bremen	69-0572
GRUBE, Friedrich	24	Frankfurt	69-1309
GRUBE, Henriette	16	Bremen	69-1319

NAME	AGE	RESIDENCE	YR-LIST
GRUBE, Johann	16	Bremen	71-0712
GRUBEL, Babette	23	Sondershausen	71-0681
GRUBER, Caroline	19	Bederkesa	68-0647
GRUBER, Dorothea	21	Coburg-Gotha	69-1212
GRUBER, Emilie	22	Wien	69-0542
GRUBER, Heinrich	29	Coburg-Gotha	69-1212
GRUBER, Johann	39	Nuernberg	68-1027
GRUBLER, Jacob	19	Aldingen	71-0492
GRUBLER, Veronica	32	Mittelkalban	68-0647
GRUBTA, Josef	26	Ibichau	69-0338
GRUDER, John	18	Boll	71-0643
GRUEBER, Friederike	23	Massenbach	68-0647
GRUEBER, Jacob	54	Koenigsberg	71-0681
Dora 52, Barb. 18, Jacob 14			
GRUEDER, Gottlieb	15	Schlaitdorf	68-0957
Elise 16			
GRUEFRER, Alb. Fr.	22	Varel	69-0079
GRUEN, Bertha	30	Frankfurt	70-0728
GRUEN, Christine	26	Osthofen	71-0821
GRUEN, Magda.	19	Diedesfeld	71-0429
GRUEN, Math.	27	Mainz	69-0050
GRUENBERG, Franz	22	S. Weimar	69-1309
GRUENBERG, Sophie		Assen	70-1142
GRUENBOEHMER, B.	28	R.B. Arnsberg	68-0884
GRUENE, Ludwig	28	Anholt	68-0661
GRUENE, Mathilde	15	Herford	71-0393
GRUENEFELD, Johann	28	Leer	68-0419
GRUENER, Lidia	28	Ronneburg	68-0625
GRUENES, Johann	54	Hochwarth,Austr	69-0547
Marie 55, Barbara 22, Mathias 13			
GRUENEWALD, Chas.	23	Schadwalde	69-1011
GRUENHAGE, Christian	28	Westerholz	68-0456
GRUENHAGEN, Henry	52	Hannover	70-0355
Minna 53			
GRUENHAUSER, Lisette	34	Paris	69-1212
GRUENSTEIN, L.	18	Altdorf	68-0456
GRUENWALDER, Emma	22	Gladbach	71-0643
GRUER, Friedr.	27	Tyrol	70-1142
GRUESBACH, Franz	25	Thierbach	69-0542
GRUETER, Bernhard	28	Brochterbeck	69-0429
GRUETZNER, Leopold	33	Muenster	68-0760
GRUHN, Gustav	26	Stauen	68-0661
GRUMERT, Julius	25	Leipzig	69-0784
GRUNBERG, Joh. H.	19	Norden	69-0576
GRUND, Maria	22	Niederauerbach	71-0492
GRUNDERMANN, T.	36	Altenburg	70-0569
Emma 13, Marie 8, Aug. 6, Anna 9 months			
GRUNDMANN, Carl Fr.	31	Osterode	69-0572
Wilhelmine 33, Anna Bertha 5			
GRUNDMANN, Fanny	30	Zerbet	71-0821
GRUNDMANN, Joach.	26	Stralsund	68-1006
GRUNDSCHOETTEL, M.	26	Bielefeld	71-0363
Alwine 9, Ernst 8, Mathilde 11 m.			
GRUNEBAUM, Auguste	27	Wuerzburg	68-0982
GRUNER, Anton	15	Tachau	68-0647
GRUNER, Aug.	17	Crispandorf	68-0820
GRUNEWALD, Gustav	23	Bremen	68-0314
GRUNEWALD, Ludwig	37	Waldeck	69-0592

NAME	AGE	RESIDENCE	YR-LIST
Cath. 35, Carl 7, Max 9 months			
GRUNNER, Caroline	16	Rudolstadt	68-1027
GRUP, Henriette	24	Neuenburg	69-0542
GRUPE, H.	26	Bremen	70-0170
GRUPPE, Amalie	20	Luckenwalde	70-0148
GRUPPE, Christoph	17	Alfdorf	69-1076
GRUS, Solam	25	Schwiezhausen	70-0569
GRUSE, Henriette	24	Neuenburg	69-0542
GRUSING, Teeke	20	Obermannsfehn	69-0672
GRUSS, Simon	54	Holybeck	69-0572
Catharina 50			
GSCHEIDLER, Friedrich	18	Wimpfen	68-0939
GUBA, Anton	24	Miltschowitz	71-0167
GUBENAU, Chr. Fr.	17	Goeppingen	71-0226
GUBIN, Iwanowitsch	25	Moscow	68-0820
GUBITZ, Elise	23	Neudrossenfeld	69-0848
Margreth 15			
GUCKELSBERGER, E.	25	Rockenberg	63-0296
John 2			
GUCKENHEIMER, Ester	18	Gera	71-0821
GUDEWELLE, G.	32	Bueckeburg	69-0292
GUDEWILL, Fred. W.	24	New York	69-1421
GUEBER, Heinr.	16	Ratgen	71-0684
GUEHRER, Jos.	30	Mainz	69-0559
Elise 24			
GUELDENPFENNIG, A.	19	Carons	68-0625
GUEMPEL, Bella	24	Harth	70-0682
GUENTER, Barbara	21	Aschach	68-0957
GUENTHER, Berthold	20	Marlishausen	69-0162
GUENTHER, Emilie	19	Detmold	69-1212
GUENTHER, Heinrich	18	Weimar	69-0208
GUENTHER, Hermann	17	Saalfeld	70-0816
Richard 14			
GUENTHER, Jacob	65	Cassel	71-0643
Philipp 21			
GUENTHER, Louis	39	Dortmund	69-1309
GUENTHER, Marie	27	Hilgersdorf	69-0559
Mathilde 16			
GUENTHER, Oscar	21	Bremen	69-0268
GUENTHER, Pauline	19	Gerasselwitz	69-0771
GUENTHER, Rudolph	22	Iber	71-0363
GUENTHER, Wilh.	20	Minden	68-1002
GUENZEL, Elisabeth	31	Einberg	69-0542
Caroline 2, August 1			
GUERTHER, Johann	37	Alton	71-0363
Marie 37, Arnold 9			
GUERTLER, Caroline	18	Stadtbingsfeld	69-0572
GUESSEL, Gottfried	53	Hellmersroh	69-0672
Fritz 52, August 20			
GUETH, Otto	16	Solingen	70-0272
GUETHE, Carl	15	Wangeritz	71-0581
GUETING, Elise	22	Licherode	71-0681
Marie 9 months			
GUETZKOW, Carl	24	R.B. Coeslin	68-0820
GUISE, Gottfried	26	Traumburg	68-0753
Florentine 26, Albertine 1			
GULAN, Johann	41	Rhadeeistedt	68-0852
Anna 44, Wilhelm 18, Peter 15, Catharine 9, Ludwig 5			

NAME	AGE	RESIDENCE	YR-LIST
GULDEN, Margarethe	34	Bandenbach	69-0079
GULEMANN, Gotthilf	23	Leipzig	68-1027
GULICH, John	44	Frankfurt	71-0167
GULL, Emilie	23	Reudnitz	71-0479
GUMBICH, Gerhard Hannchen 22	18	Rostadt	68-0939
GUMERICH, Marie	18	Bremervoerde	70-1003
GUMZ, Carl	23	Freist	69-0490
GUNDELACH, Heinr.	17	Coburg	71-0429
GUNDELL, Christian	20	Mangolhall	71-0643
GUNDERMANN, Joh. Katharine 52, Johannes 17	49	Rodenbach	71-0363
GUNDLACH, Aug.	32	Linningrode	68-0957
GUNDLER, Margar.	28	Schaffera	69-0542
GUNDMANN, Edward	18	Alsfeld	68-0534
GUNDRAM, Rudoph	18	Alsfeld	68-0852
GUNETH, Catharine	28	Kaltenhof	71-0429
GUNGLER, Cathar. Marg. 3	27	Ummenhofen	68-0610
GUNINGER, Mary	18	Bachzimmern	70-0308
GUNKEL, Julius	15	Magdeburg	70-0682
GUNKEL, Robert	17	Magdeburg	68-0625
GUNSOHR, Eva Eva 3, Anna 10 months	30	Riesenkirch	71-0789
GUNSSEN, Marie	21	Schorndorf	71-0479
GUNTERBERG, Michel Anna 35, Johannes 7, August 1, Cacilie 6	34	Dietz	68-0753
GUNTERMANN, Marg.	18	Wetzlar	68-1002
GUNTERMANN, Minn	23	Ziemeritz	70-0135
GUSE, August Hermann 25	26	Naseband	69-0338
GUSSMANN, August	20	Sindelfingen	68-0939
GUSTFAR, August	25	Lippe Detmold	70-0355
GUT, Heinrich	23	Wehr	69-1059
GUTBERLET, Fabian	16	Petersburg	68-0907
GUTER, Josef Elise 56, Johanne 21, Rosa 19, Josef 16, Theo 29, Anna 9, August 4	66	Pirsitz	71-0479
GUTERMUTH, Friedrich	27	Schluechtern	69-1212
GUTFREUND, Minna	22	Boehmen	70-0728
GUTHEIL, Erwin Ernst 23	23	Gunsdorf	69-0572
GUTHLAND, Therese	21	Carlsruhe	71-0815
GUTHORU, M.	26	Schwanheim	71-0643
GUTMANN, Bertha	18	Nordleda	68-0820
GUTMANN, Carl	30	Crimmitschau	69-0490
GUTMANN, Gg.	20	Boersdorf	71-0581
GUTMANN, H.	48	New York	69-1421
GUTMANN, Johann	45	Geyer	68-0014
GUTMANN, Philip	22	Verstadt	69-1212
GUTMANN, Seligmann Leopold 16	18	Heinfurth	71-0429
GUTMANN, Sophie Moses 11, Julie 9	14	Ulfenhausen	70-0682
GUTMANN, Wilhelm	23	Seibersbach	70-0223
GUTSZELL, Kilian	22	Pfaffenweiler	69-0583
GUTZAHN, Jacob	16	Maltendingen	70-0204
GUVOLLEK, Mathias Juliane 33	27	Danzig	69-0067

NAME	AGE	RESIDENCE	YR-LIST
GWINNER, Margarethe Martin 18	49	Coeln	69-0559
GYGI, Elisabeth baby girl 10	27	Schweiz	70-0378
Gemeinhart, Marg. Johanne 9, Christina 7, Lida 6, Andreas 4, Friedrich 6 months	33	Asch	71-0736
Georges, Friedrike Ida 14, Carl 6, Friedrich 4, Carline 9 months	32	Horsla	69-0848
HAAFLE, Friedrich	17	Rheinl.Hofsheim	71-0492
HAAG, Friedr.	20	Thalheim	71-0815
HAAG, Maria Christine 22	24	Wildbach	69-0100
HAAGA, Peter	24	Habenessel	71-0492
HAAGE, Charles Francisca 30	31	Laubheim	69-0560
HAAK, Wilh.	29	Gummin	68-0820
HAAKE, Justus	23	Wildetaube	69-1076
HAAR, Blasius	22	Tyrol	71-0167
HAAR, Joh.	28	Pfaeffingen	70-0089
HAARDICK, Heinrich	28	Greven	69-0429
HAAREN, Johann	23	Lehe	69-1086
HAARER, Mathilde	25	Tuebingen	69-0572
HAARMANN, Sophie Heinrich 9, Joseph 8, Gertrude 6, Wilhelm 3	28	St. Moritz	69-0015
HAARSCHNEIDER, Wm. Louise 39	37	Elberfeld	70-0006
HAAS, Carl	16	Freudenstadt	71-0792
HAAS, Catharine	39	Sulzbach	69-0784
HAAS, Heinrich	17	Darmstadt	71-0492
HAAS, Maria	23	Bunzlau	70-0443
HAAS, Marie	29	Nuertingen	69-1212
HAAS, Martha	19	Brennsbach	71-0821
HAAS, Regine	19	Ehrenfeldt	69-0592
HAAS, Theodor	16	Themar	71-0492
HAAS. Dorothea	20	Schweinfurt	69-1309
HAASE, Aug. Albertine 31, Albert 5, Otto 3	35	Stettin	68-0647
HAASE, Christine	22	Bederkesa	69-1059
HAASE, Ernst	43	Goettingen	71-0792
HAASE, Jacob	22	Elben	70-0052
HAATE, Friedr.	40	Berlin	69-0162
HAAVE, Albert	33	Breslau	69-0100
HABEKORN, Friderike	26	Eichholzheim	71-0393
HABEKOST, Charlotte	21	Erpen	68-0566
HABEKOST, Dorothea	18	Kl. Borstel	68-0610
HABEKOST, Franz	18	Dissen	68-0957
HABENER, August Marie 1	28	Blankensee	68-0770
HABENICHTS, Theodor	22	Leipzig	69-0542
HABER, Cathrine Carl 9 months, (born in Saaldorf)	26	Enzen	71-0643
HABER, Julius	21	Altschmeier	69-0050
HABERKORN, Marie	20	Oelsnitz	68-1027
HABERL, Johann Catharine 2	32	Woppenhof	70-0329
HABERMAHL, Johann	23	Willof	70-0378
HABERMANN, Martin	38	Gotha	68-0865

NAME	AGE	RESIDENCE	YR-LIST
Elise 35, Karoline 12, Ernestine 9, Ernst 7, Therese 5, Heinrich 2, infant boy			
HABERMANN, Phil.	46	Huettengesaess	68-0760
Anna 50, Mrgareth 24, Johann 8			
HABERSANA, H.	47	Salzungen	69-1011
HABERSTROH, Friedrich	56	Hecklingen	68-0707
Sophie 24, Josepha 20, Anton 17			
HABERSTRUMPF, J.	45	Meerane	68-0982
Emma 20, Augusta 9			
HABICHT, Andreas	66	Marjoss	68-0534
HABIK, Martin	14	Ziernau	71-0521
HACHE, Heinr.	19	Bellings	71-0479
HACHMANN, Eibe	20	Knull	70-0378
HACHMANN, Henriette	9	Cappeln	66-0734
HACHTMANN, Lena	57	Cappeln	66-0734
HACK, Elisabeth	21	Bruehl	68-0625
HACK, Ferdinand	31	Weidenau	68-0907
HACKBARTH, Friedrich	23	Preussen	69-0559
HACKBUSCH, Sophie	64	Wiedenhagen	70-0223
Friederike 23			
HACKE, Johann	17	Sosmer	68-1027
August			
HACKE, Margreth	23	Mistelgau	69-0848
HACKEBEIL, Gustav	29	Uechteruetz	70-0135
HACKELBERG, Wme.	25	Siekerode	68-1002
Alwine			
HACKELMANN, Jos.	34	Oberwyer	68-0939
HACKER, Heinrich	29	Friedland	68-1006
HACKER, Johanne	21	Fuerstenau	70-1161
HACKER, Paul	17	Lobau	71-0393
HACKMANN, Anton	18	Icker	71-0681
HACKMANN, Eva	18	Farmersheim	71-0429
HACKMANN, Friedr.	38	Oster Cappeln	68-1002
HACKMANN, Max	27	Grosvern	68-0939
HADEWIGS, Christine	29	Sengwarden	69-0229
Friederike 24			
HADLICH, Franz	22	Zeulenroda	68-0661
HAEAK, Hermann	19	Freiburg	70-0308
HAEBE, Heinrich	17	Braunschweig	70-0384
HAEBERLE, Caspar	25	Bernstein	68-1006
HAEBERLE, Ludwig	42	Ebersbach	69-0560
HAEBERLE, Marie	18	Ebersbach	69-0015
HAEDERLEIN, Georg	17	Buschdorf	71-0393
HAEFKE, Johann	29	Mecklenburg	69-0067
Caroline 27, Wilhelm 5			
HAEFNER, Marg.	24	Obernsen	71-0479
Barb. 22			
HAEGEBE, Wilhelm	20	Horlach	70-1003
HAEGELE, Johann	33	Neufra	69-0229
HAEGELL, A. W. H.	23	Grafenhausen	69-0050
HAEGEMANN, Cath.	23	Seestermuehl	68-0957
HAEGER, Johannes	20	Overlach	68-0625
HAEHRING, Therese	33	Muhlhausen	68-0939
HAERDTLE, Georg H.	23	Untersontheim	68-0610
HAERINGER, Maria	19	Hilzingen	68-1002
HAERTNER, Anna	17	Weisnach	68-0625
HAEUSER, Heinrich	18	Lautenhausen	71-0521
HAEUSLER, Mathilde	24	Heidersdorf	69-0672
HAFENA, Johann	16	Hannover	69-0672
HAFENBRACK, Gustav	25	Kirchheim	71-0821
HAFENDEUBEL, Jacob	23	Germersheim	69-0542
HAFFENFEFFER, R.	21	Schorndorf	68-0907
HAFFERKAMP, Cath.	15	Hahlen	68-0982
HAFFERKAMP, Johann	40	Menslage	68-0852
Diedrich 80			
HAFFNER, Emilie	19	Muehlhausen	71-0789
HAFFNER, Philipp	15	Asselheim	69-0457
Elise 17, Margarethe 14, Adam 10			
HAFKERS, Andreas	18	Eissel	68-0707
Doris 16			
HAFNER, Martin		Wiesenstetten	69-0798
HAFT, Wilhelmine	42	Homburg	70-0452
Marie 16			
HAGE, Friedrich	65	Braunschweig	69-0968
HAGEDORN, August	20	Stolzenau	71-0492
HAGEDORN, Christ.	21	Stockum	69-1086
HAGEDORN, Heinrich	27	Glandorf	69-0229
HAGEDORN, Joh. G.	29	Trienz	68-0647
HAGEDORN, Wilh.	28	Rodenberg	71-0681
HAGEL, Georg	29	Memingen	71-0821
HAGEMANN, Heinrich	39	Brakelsiek	68-314
Caroline 37, Heinrich 9, Hermann 7, Friedrich 3			
HAGEMANN, Josephine	23	Westfalen	70-0728
HAGEMANN, Louise	63	Segelhorst	69-0490
Sophie 30			
HAGEMANN, Mar.	25	Hohenzell	68-0753
HAGEMANN, Theodor	32	Minden	69-0429
HAGEMEYER, Elise	20	Nettelstedt	68-0957
HAGEMEYER, Fd.	16	Bremen	70-1066
HAGEMEYER, Ida	20	Deggingen	70-1035
HAGEMEYER, Menne	60	Visgnard	69-0429
Engel 64			
HAGEMUELLER, Caroline	19	Lichtenberg	69-0542
HAGEN, Dorothea	18	Wistelgan	68-0707
HAGEN, J.	19	Thunum	71-0363
Anna 16			
HAGEN, Michael	18	Altendorf	71-0712
HAGENBECHER, Pauline	27	Neuningen	71-0492
HAGENBRUK, Gottl.	24	Muehlhausen	68-0884
HAGENBUECHLE, Joh.	26	Messkirch	68-1027
HAGENBURG, Carl	40	Brochterbeck	69-0429
HAGENDORFF, E.	27	Oldenburg	69-0560
HAGENS, Arnold	21	Montreal	70-0378
HAGENSRAKER, Louise	16	Essen	71-0521
HAGENZO, Ebert	28	Wesguard	68-0456
HAGGE, Gesine	14	Wulsdorf	70-0384
HAGLER, Caroline	19	Muenchen	70-0184
HAGMANN, Dorothea	19	Weiler	71-0456
Catharina 33			
HAGS, Friedr.	16	Bremervoerde	71-0581
HAGSPIETE, Oscar	40	Hartum	68-0957
Caroline 34, Martha 8			
HAHMANN, Marie	19	Schluechtern	71-0479
HAHN, A.	29	Ober Samen	71-0643
HAHN, Adam	20	Gruenstadt	69-1076
HAHN, Alex.	27	Thuringia	69-1421

NAME	AGE	RESIDENCE	YR-LIST
HAHN, Aloys	28	Taurendau	71-0456
HAHN, August	31	Ramrod	68-0625
HAHN, August	23	Idar	71-0815
HAHN, Auguste	24	Berlin	71-0815
HAHN, Carl	43	Salzgitter	70-0184
HAHN, Carl	18	Boehmen	69-1309
HAHN, Elis.		.....rod	68-1002
HAHN, Elisab.	22	Freudenthal	71-0479
HAHN, Elise	28	Hessen	69-0672
HAHN, Elise	41	Selsungen	69-0968
Wilhelm 8, (died 8th Aug 1869 on voyage), August 6, Carl 4			
HAHN, Emilia	19	Blankwitt	71-0429
HAHN, Emma	16	Sauschau	70-1055
Lina 14			
HAHN, Fred.	20	Gruenstadt	68-0957
Cathar. 22			
HAHN, Friedrich	30	Hannover	70-1035
HAHN, Heinr.	20	Burgholz	68-0884
HAHN, Heinrich	22	Mar.	68-0770
HAHN, Jacob	19	Casel	69-0784
HAHN, Lina	35	Gruenberg	68-0534
HAHN, Marcus	14	Udenheim	70-0204
HAHN, Peter	30	Baden	70-0135
Adam 25, Marg. 18			
HAHN, Susanne	52	Landau	70-1161
Wilhelm 7, Friedrike 9			
HAHN, Victor	22	Minden	69-0457
HAHN, Willy	35	Ebersbach	71-0456
HAHNENFELD, Wilhelm	27	Otterndorf	70-0148
HAHNFELD, Marie	59	Ottensen	71-0736
HAID, Angelika	23	Imnau	69-0457
HAID, Jacob	30	Unterhausen	69-1076
HAID, Mathilde	10	Unterhausen	69-1076
HAIDT, Johann	18	Ulm	68-0786
HAIER, Anna	26	Markoebel	71-0581
Cath. 22, Anna 10 months			
HAINEMANN, Catharine	24	Rhausa	68-0625
Catharine 3 months			
HAINEN, Marie	23	Jever	68-0610
Johannes 14			
HAINIG, Barbara	30	Embrach	68-1027
Jacob 8, Armand 7, Anna 6, Beta 2			
HAISSCHELL, Rosine	24	Roethemeyer	71-0815
HAKE, Chr.	38	Braunschweig	69-0560
Dorothea 33, Minna 5, Caroline 8			
HAKENMOELLER, H.	19	Dorenkamp	69-0429
HALADA, Josefa	23	Kozin	70-0329
HALBACH, Anna	33	Barmen	68-0786
Laura 6, Carl 2, Hugo 8 months			
HALBBICH, Catharine	20	Unterfranken	69-0968
HALDEN, Henry	19	Frieburg	68-0456
HALEFELD, Hermann	26	Nassau	70-0384
HALESCHECK, Joh.	22	Vegesack	71-0300
HALFSEN, V. Ernst	31	Cleve	68-0760
HALL, Joh.	62	Frankfurt	71-0479
Pauline 52, Hermann 9			
HALL, Leonh.	20	Hall	71-0521
HALLA, Josef	35	Boehmen	70-0569

NAME	AGE	RESIDENCE	YR-LIST
Magdalene 33, Franciska 9, Josef 8, Joh. 6 months			
HALLE, Emanuel	14	Willmers	68-0707
Jettchen 19			
HALLE, Matthaeus	27	Aldingen	69-0771
HALLENPACH, Jacob	66	Thuringia	68-0456
Christine 80			
HALLER, Anna	18	Aldingen	70-0355
HALLER, J.	27	Eisenharz	70-0308
HALLER, Louis	9	Ottersberg	70-0378
HALLER, Marg.	30	Pirmasens	68-1027
HALLER, Ursula	22	Altingen	68-0625
HALLHEIMER, Aug	19	Crailsheim	71-0521
HALLMANN, Wilhelmine	22	Westercappeln	71-0736
HALLUEBER, Joseph	33	Kriegen	69-0079
HALLWEG, Marie	20	Lehe	68-0820
HALM, Marg.	31	Schneitach	71-0815
HALPE, Louis	17	Brochterbeck	71-0429
HALTER, Johanne	28	Aldingen	70-0031
HALTERMANN, Friedrich	39	Philadelphia	70-1003
Catharine 36, Fiedrich 6			
HAMANN, Adolf	19	Zeitz	71-0479
HAMANN, Anna	30	Trossingen	68-0957
HAMANN, Cacilie	23	Nassau	70-0384
HAMANN, Elisabeth	25	Darmstadt	70-0728
HAMANN, Ignatz	30	Seiferts	71-0684
HAMBAUER, Stephan	31	Forchheim	71-0684
HAMBRECH, Diedr.	17	Doertzbach	71-0521
HAMEISTER, Elise	30	Hildesheim	68-0939
HAMEL, Hermann	31	Biere	69-0848
HAMERLE, Barbara	30	Dornbirn	68-0610
HAMERSMANN, August	26	Oldenburg	71-0712
Auguste 23			
HAMISCHEN, Peter	16	Ostereistedt	68-0852
HAMJE, Anna Marg.	20	Sievern	68-0610
HAMMAN, Charlotte	18	Bremen	71-0581
HAMME, Carl	23	Tuebingen	68-0982
HAMMEL, Johanna	60	Forchtenberg	68-0610
Lisette 25			
HAMMEL, Masalla	16	Reinberg	69-0321
Jette 18			
HAMMEL, Michael		Havre	70-0259
Barbara, Margarethe, Katharine, Louise			
HAMMEL, Rosalie	22	Thiergarten	71-0521
Adolph			
HAMMER, Albert	10	Greiz	68-0534
Robert 8			
HAMMER, Anna	21	Schifferstadt	71-0393
HAMMER, Aug.	38	Offenburg	68-0534
Henriette 38, Catharina 7, Jos. 4			
HAMMER, David	26	Koenigswalde	71-0492
HAMMER, Elis.	16	Clausthal	69-1004
HAMMER, Herm.	12	Schriesshelm	70-0170
HAMMER, Wilhelm	24	Gr. Bruechter	71-0712
HAMMERERFEHR, A.	43	Pechausen	69-0672
HAMMERLE, Max	17	Orschwein	69-1396
HAMMERS, Emma	30	Bremen	68-1002
Louise 5, Helene 3, Fritz			

NAME	AGE	RESIDENCE	YR-LIST
HAMMERS, Wilh.	36	Bremen	68-1002
Sophie 35, Kunigunde 13, Frieda 8, Gust. 4, Johann 2, Anton			
HAMMERSCHMIDT, M.	22	Bielefeld	69-0583
HAMMERSKLAG, Franz	18	Tuetzlar	71-0581
HAMPE, Louise	23	Oldenburg	69-0457
HAMPEL, Otto	22	Meiningen	68-0566
HAMUTH, Caroline	25	Dettmold	69-0542
HANASCH, Pauline	36	Krotaschin	70-0583
Wilhelm 8, Leo 6, Gustav 4			
HANDEL, Caroline	25	Friedrichsdorf	71-0167
Ernst 2			
HANDEL, Johann	29	Dettingen	70-0378
Friedrich 23, Judith 20, Christ. 28, Elisabeth 23, Christ 1, Georg 4 months			
HANDER, Friedrich		Schmalkalden	69-0559
HANDRICK, Andr.	38	Berstelsdorf	69-1004
Mary 36, G. 13, H. 9			
HANFGARN, Cath.	17	Dissen	68-0884
HANFGAU, Louise	17	Bergholzhausen	71-0681
HANG, Christine	40	Trier	71-0492
Marie 9, Caecilie 5			
HANG, Elise	23	Gerolsheim	71-0363
HANKEN, Marianne	32	Bremerhaven	69-0592
Elise 8, Wilhelmine 6, Gottfried 3, Alma 4 months			
HANN, Cath.	20	Mainz	70-0443
HANN, Gottlieb	24	Niedergehen	69-1212
HANNALINA, Anton	42	Boehmen	69-0321
Barbara 38, Franz 13, Wenzel 9, Marie 5, Anton Josef 11 months			
HANNALINA, Franz	42	Boehmen	69-0321
Anna 31, Aloisia 9, Johann 7, Marie 5, Josef 3, Anna 6 months, Johann 70			
HANNE, Friedrich	24	Lueneburg	68-314
HANNE, Marie	30	Neu Hardenberg	71-0456
Helene 9, Louise 7			
HANNING, Diedrich	25	Hannover	69-1396
HANNING, Herm.	50	Diepholz	70-0378
Lisette 50, Hermann 26, Caroline 20, Friedrich 9, Diedrich 8, Caroline 80			
HANNSCHEN, Peter	16	Ostereistedt	68-0852
HANOLD, Siegmund	19	Birkenbuettel	71-0581
HANOW, Bertha	28	Schoenlanke	68-0786
Emma 21			
HANS, Ferdinand	30	Podelsig	68-0314
Johann 16			
HANSEL, Heinrich	27	Burkhardt	68-0760
HANSELMANN, John	18	Neumuehle	69-0560
HANSELMANN, Sim.	23	Mittfischbach	68-1298
HANSEN, Agnes	16	Coeln	68-0957
HANSEN, Emil	14	Hoboken	69-0338
HANSEN, Magnus	17	Seesterandeich	68-0957
HANSEN, Minna	21	Kehrwieder	69-0771
HANSHOLT, J. H.	17	Hoettandermuend	71-0521
HANSING, Julie	23	Bueckeburg	69-1004
HANSLICK, Martin	37	Domislitz	66-0623
Anna 35, Maria 9, Johann 7, Barbara 5, Martin 3, Catharina 1, Maria 19			
HANSSEN, Catharina	50	Hartwerden	71-0733
HAPPE, Friedrich	44	Goddelsheim	68-0786
Marie 43, Friedrich 15, Heinrich 9, Friedrike 8, Wilhelm 7			
HAPPEL, Christian	36	Palmira	70-100
HAPPEL, Reimund	63	Wildungen	70-100
Catharina 62			
HAPPESBERG, Nicolas	24	Alsheim	69-0229
HARBATSCHEK, Math.	31	Krenowa	71-0821
Catharina 25, Marie 9 months			
HARBERS, Chr.	23	Hammelwarden	68-1006
HARBERS, Gerhardine	20	Bremen	69-0429
HARBERTS, Bretje	23	Usshusing	69-0572
HARBURGER, Lorenz	16	Mainz	71-0792
HARDE, Wilhelm	28	L. Detmold	70-0272
HARDECKER, Clara	15	Kl. Heubach	71-0456
HARDEKOPF, Wilh.	28	New York	69-1086
Anna 28			
HARDELAND, Carl	10	Wunstorf	70-0355
HARDER, Sophie	40	Hannover	68-0534
Clemens 15			
HARDIEK, Maria	22	Ibbenbuehren	68-0456
HARDING, William	43	New York	70-0089
HARDKOPF, A. B.	33	Hannover	70-0170
HARDT, Adalbert	17	Eilpe	68-0982
HARDT, Jos.	24	Zagenhausen	71-0393
HARDT, Marg.	22	Marburg	69-1421
HARFST, Louise	19	Drielakermoor	71-0167
HARIES, Maria	18	Luedingwooth	70-0452
HARINA, Johannes	19	Bubsheim	70-0308
HARJES, Michel	20	Hoya	70-1161
HARKE, G.	21	Bremen	70-1066
HARKEN, Louise	24	Emiteck	70-1142
Aug. 1			
HARKEN, Reemts	28	Wesguard	68-0456
HARKER, Marg.	27	Wistelgan	68-0707
Magdalene 24			
HARLACH, Juliane	19	Rust	71-0492
HARLAND, Emily	37	Paddington	69-1086
Emily 1, John 4 months			
HARLING, Maria	29	Bremen	69-0798
HARLMANN, Alinia	18	Oppiny	69-1004
HARLOCH, Karoline	20	Rust	71-0492
HARMS, Adele	29	Darmstadt	71-0167
Franziska 9			
HARMS, Adelheid	48	Schweringen	69-0229
HARMS, Bertha	59	Hannover	69-1212
Emma 22			
HARMS, Cath.	28	Oberdorfmark	68-1002
HARMS, E.	16	Schweringen	70-0184
HARMS, Gerd	32	Wiesede	69-0338
Volina 33, Max 8, John 6, Henry 3, Baby 8 months			
HARMS, Gerhard	53	Oldenburg	70-0204
Sophie 48, Heinrich 16, Friedrich 14, August 12, Cathrine 9			
HARMS, Gesche	17	Achim	69-0968
HARMS, Gesche	15	Hannover	71-0821
HARMS, Harm	60	Oldenburg	69-0457
Catharina 57, Garrick 27, Hinka 20, Bernhard 12, Hermann 8			

NAME	AGE	RESIDENCE	YR-LIST
HARMS, Heinrich	34	Aurich	68-0419
HARMS, Henry	16	Hoya	68-0957
HARMS, Herm.	21	Oldenburg	69-0292
HARMS, Heyke	20	Kepsholt	69-0338
HARMS, Johanna	18	Hopert	68-0982
HARNISCHFEGER, Peter	30	Marborn	69-1319
HARNITZ, Johann	30	Beutschen	70-0508
HARNKOHL, August	45	Arendshausen	68-0625
Wilhelmine 45, August 19, Johanna 9			
HARPE, V. Carl	30	Livland	68-0566
HARR, Christine	27	Glatten	70-0329
HARRA, Josef	25	Vienna	68-0760
HARRING, John	24	Hoboken	71-0521
HARRIS, Amalie	21	Darmstadt	70-1142
HARSANEK, Anna	25	Boehmen	70-0728
Joseph 2, Maria 11 months			
HART, Aug.	21	Dinkelsbuehl	71-0681
HARTFELDER, Michael	40	Wuessingen	69-0321
HARTH, Ferd.	43	Mariazell	70-0728
Wendelin 34			
HARTH, Friedr.	20	Steinbach	71-0521
HARTING, Friedrich	22	Preussen	68-0456
HARTING, Wilhelmine	25	Bremen	69-1076
HARTJE, Anna	18	Groten	69-0457
HARTJE, Heinrich	51	Morschhausen	68-0534
Elisabeth 52, Conrad 22			
HARTLET, Auguste	22	Hinternach	69-0338
Emma 22			
HARTLOEHNER, Anna	27	Tuebingen	69-0229
Catharina 19			
HARTMANN, A. Elise	17	Herweiler	69-0572
HARTMANN, A. H.	19	Eichenfeld	71-0789
HARTMANN, Albert	23	Solingen	71-0479
HARTMANN, Alinia	18	Oppiny	69-1004
HARTMANN, Anna	22	Hemburger	69-0429
HARTMANN, Anna	43	Hildesheim	68-0625
Anna 15, Crescens 13, Antonia 9, Agnes 6, Georg 6, Julia 6, Mathilde 3			
HARTMANN, Carl	24	Niederorschel	69-0182
HARTMANN, Carl	17	Werdau	68-0610
HARTMANN, Cath.	20	Raibreitenbach	69-0560
HARTMANN, Catharine	23	Ditzingen	70-0148
HARTMANN, Chr.	25	Hannover	69-0229
HARTMANN, Christ.	50	Carlsruhe	71-0815
Fried. 30, Marie 26, Baby-girl 3 m.			
HARTMANN, Elisa	30	Etmansweiler	68-0534
HARTMANN, Ernst	24	Oppurg	71-0226
HARTMANN, Franz	25	Glachau	69-0542
HARTMANN, Fred.	45	Petershagen	69-1421
HARTMANN, Friedrich	58	Minden	68-0786
Louise 59			
HARTMANN, Gerh.	16	Ufermoor	71-0300
HARTMANN, Heinrich	33	Suhlingen	69-0079
HARTMANN, Heinrich	38	Westfalen	70-0728
Dorette 30, Minna 9, Louise 6, Sophie 4, Heinrich 3, Caroline 9 months			
HARTMANN, Heinrich	17	Langons	68-0625
HARTMANN, Hugo	34	Minden	69-1309
HARTMANN, Johann	26	Eisenach	69-0672
HARTMANN, Johann	24	Ladenburg	68-0786
HARTMANN, Johann	27	Gadheim	71-0712
Hortensia 39, Sophia 9, Conrad 3			
HARTMANN, Louise	42	Koenigsbronn	69-0490
HARTMANN, Margarethe	19	Soegeln	68-0647
HARTMANN, Mariette	25	Ludwigsburg	69-0784
HARTMANN, Otto	28	Greifswald	71-0363
HARTMANN, Sabine	20	Gmuenden	69-0457
HARTMANN, Theodor	26	Siegen	68-1006
HARTMANN, Theresa	23	Eissen	68-0957
Fr. 21			
HARTMANN, Wilh.	30	Verlosen	68-0957
HARTMANN, Wilhelm	22	Albershausen	68-0820
HARTMANN, Wilhelm	26	Biebelnheim	71-0429
HARTMANN, Wilhelmine	18	Lehe	68-1298
HARTMEYER, Sophie	18	Auerbach	68-0456
HARTSTEIN, Catharine	28	Unterhausen	69-1076
HARTSTEIN, Mathilde	15	Unterhausen	69-1076
HARTTE, Ferdinand	22	Mariazell	70-0728
Wendelin 34			
HARTUNG, August	18	Salmuenster	71-0456
HARTUNG, Helene	22	Bremen	70-0443
HARTUNG, Marie	50	New York	69-0672
HARTUNG, Meta	18	Bremen	71-0479
Lisette 15			
HARTUNG, Paul	21	Weierrohde	68-0770
HARTUNG, Wilhelmine	30	Langula	69-0560
Barbara 4			
HARTWIG, August	37	Leese	69-0968
HARTWIG, Clara	16	Bremen	71-0521
HARTWIG, Emma	20	Warzen	68-0939
HARTWIG, Friedrich	25	Henkenhagen	71-0456
Emma 18, Wilhelm 11 months			
HARTWIG, Rosalie	26	Sachsen	70-0089
HARTWIG, Wilhelm	46	Sondershausen	69-0672
Auguste 37, Anna 16, Ida 13, Carl 5, Anna 2			
HARTZ, Johann	20	Omersheim	71-0429
HARWALD, Georg	53	Deuerberg	68-0852
HASCHERN, Herm.	15	Bremervoerde	71-0581
HASEBROK, Wm.	32	Bentheim	69-0841
Helene 36, Wilhelmine 9, Hendrick 11 months			
HASEDENZ, Mathias	27	Schaffhausen	71-0643
Marie 24			
HASEL, Johann	23	Linz	71-0521
HASELBAUER, Joseph	53	Reichenau	68-1002
Catharine 55, Anton 29, Mathaus 19			
HASELEDER, Joseph	22	Wuerttemberg	68-0456
HASELMANN, Christian	21	Schuesbitz	70-0523
HASEMANN, Emma	26	Bremen	71-0581
Helene 6, Carl 4, Marie 3, Eduard 9 months			
HASEMEYER, Heinrich	16	Stockum	69-0672
HASENCLEVER, M.	24	Remscheid	68-0760
HASENKAMP, Clemens	19	Vechta	71-0581
HASENMAILE, Ant.	34	Ringschneit	70-1055
HASENZAHL, Theodor	17	Mehrfelden	68-1002
HASFELD, Creszenia	18	Huehlen	69-0338
HASHAGEN, Claus	17	St. MAgnus	71-0172

NAME	AGE	RESIDENCE	YR-LIST
HASHAGEN, Diedrich	54	New York	69-1396
Anna 50, Frank 11, Lili 4			
HASITZ, Hel.	22	New York	69-0490
Meta 1			
HASLER, Francisca	28	Vorarlberg	69-0560
HASLER, Jos.	26	Vorarlberg	69-0560
HASLOOFE, Caroline	22	Dorum	69-0429
Emma 4			
HASMEYER, Friedrich	23	Vaihingen	69-1319
HASS, Hr.	15	Hannover	70-0378
HASS, Moritz	18	Leipzig	69-1319
HASSE, Catharine	21	Fritzlar	68-1027
HASSE, Heinrich	24	Bueckeburg	69-0292
HASSE, Heinrich	17	Johannesroth	70-0378
HASSELBACH, Ernst	24	Solingen	69-0015
HASSELBACH, Wilh.	22	Dorum	71-0821
HASSELBAUER, Anna	58	Endchenreuth	71-1046
HASSELBAUM, Christ.	18	Secheim	71-0479
HASSELHORST, Peter	45	Oldenburg	68-0770
HASSEMEIER, Dorothea		Gadesbuenden	69-0338
HASSENPFLUG, Joh.	29	Barmen	71-0363
HASSENPFLUG, Nicolas	18	Rohrbach	71-0643
HASTERT, Heinr.	16	Hattenhof	71-0300
HATKOWRE,	18	Senojat	70-0329
HATT, Joh.	62	Frankfurt	71-0479
HATTER, Carl	25	Wallmerod	70-0076
HATZFELD, Julius	31	Louisville	69-1076
HATZFELD, Louis	34	Mannheim	69-1076
C. 30			
HAU, Christian	16	Sievern	69-0848
HAUB, Nicolaus	24	Bodenheim	70-0135
HAUBER, Mary	17	Nufringen	70-0170
HAUBER, Wilhelmine	31	Basel	69-0100
Carl baby, Marie baby			
HAUCH, Bernhard	22	Aixheim	69-0923
HAUCH, Heinrich	23	Lentwein	68-0534
HAUCK, Christoph Adam	27	Oeschelbronn	68-1006
HAUCK, Magdalene	37	Jersey City	69-1212
HAUDENMEYER, Conrad	20	Neuningen	69-0229
HAUENSTEIN, Elise	22	Manckenheim	71-0429
HAUENSTEIN, Reint	24	Hinte	68-0760
John 18			
HAUENSTEIN, Veronica	28	Endingen	68-1002
Heinr. 6, Ernst 5, Gottwald 1			
HAUER, Caroline	48	Roda	71-0492
Anna 4			
HAUER, G.	52	Altbreisach	69-0229
Catharina 50, Wilhelm 8			
HAUER, Mathilde	24	Windsbach	68-0865
HAUF, Marie	20	Kniedlingen	71-0167
HAUFF, Elise	19	Meiningen	68-314
HAUFF, Wilhelm	18	Kirdorf	71-0736
HAUFFLE, Gottlieb	29	Nawisky	69-0547
HAUG, Catharine	15	Oberifflingen	71-0456
HAUG, Michael	27	Diedlingen	69-1309
HAUG, Theresia	23	Eggingen	70-0443
HAUHUTH, Engel	34	Neuhaus	70-1003
HAUK, Jos.	32	Sigmaringen	68-1298

NAME	AGE	RESIDENCE	YR-LIST
HAUKE, Franz	37	Peitz	71-0712
Auguste 39, Robert 13, Emilie 11, Bertha 9, Maria 8, Pauline 7, Louise 5			
HAUKER, Louise	21	Crailsheim	71-0643
Marie 22			
HAUN, Martin	25	Trepsum	70-0384
HAUPE, Hermann	15	Hoexter	70-0259
HAUPT, C.	30	Untermutschl	69-1004
HAUPT, Philipp	31	Birkenfeld	68-0907
HAUPTLE, Anna	23	Billafingen	69-0923
Carl 19			
HAUS, Elisabeth	23	Bielefeld	70-0272
Math. Augustin 27			
HAUSEMANN, Joseph	20	Baltimore	69-1076
HAUSER, Albert	17	Radowitz	68-0820
Sigmund 15			
HAUSER, Andreas	20	Weigheim	71-0521
HAUSER, Cathrine	18	Seikershausen	69-1059
HAUSER, Chr.	23	Aldingen	70-1035
Matth. 20			
HAUSER, Christine	55	Aldingen	70-0355
HAUSER, Friederike	25	Goeppingen	71-0521
HAUSER, Ignatz	24	Wien	71-0226
HAUSER, John	18	Aldingen	70-0355
HAUSER, Michel	20	Aldingen	69-0771
HAUSER, Ursula	21	Wendlingen	70-0728
HAUSER, Ursula	18	Adingen	70-0355
HAUSHAELTER, Julie	34	Meiningen	69-1076
Carl 9			
HAUSINGER, Georg	40	Madison	70-0170
HAUSINGER, Marg.	77	Hammerbach	70-0170
HAUSKEER, Adolph	17	Zug	70-1055
HAUSMANN, August	33	Oldenburg	68-0456
HAUSMANN, Fr.	24	Liechow	69-0490
HAUSMANN, Friedr.	22	Dahlinghausen	71-0581
HAUSMANN, Gottlieb	44	Nuertingen	68-0566
HAUSMANN, Hermann	26	Lippe Detmold	70-0223
HAUSMANN, Jacob	71	Darmstadt	70-0052
HAUSMANN, Lina	15	Wachenheim	71-0521
HAUSMANN, Ludes	27	Burghaus	71-0479
HAUSMANN, Margaret	30	Obersontheim	69-0229
HAUSMANN, Mary	18	Marburg	69-1011
HAUSMANN, Peter	29	Westum	69-0229
HAUSSER, Anna Marg.	61	Aldingen	69-1212
Jacob 23			
HAUSSMANN, A.	50	Hannover/Hannov	69-0547
Everhardine 43, Carl 20, Marie 19, Fritz 17, Anna 13, Agnes 7, Helene 3			
HAUSSNER, Anna	17	Parkstein	71-0226
HAUSSUNGER, Paulus	19	Neudrossenfeld	69-0848
HAUSTEIN, Herman	25	Giessen	68-1027
HAUSTEIN, Minna	34	Berlin	68-1027
Oswald 8			
HAUSTEIN, Schafte	19	Richelsdorf	68-1027
HAUSWIRTH, Louis	21	Carlsruhe	70-0184
HAVBLICK, Magdalena	19	Boehmen	68-0456
HAVEMANN, Jacob	34	Nordleda	68-0625
Nicolas 25, Rebecca 27			
HAVEMANN, Margareth	22	Otterndorf	68-0625

NAME	AGE	RESIDENCE	YR-LIST
HAVEMEYER, Meta	31	New York	70-1055
HAVERDIECK, Anna	46	Osterwald	68-1002
Swenge 21			
HAVERKAMP, Marg.	18	Oldenburg	69-0542
HAVERKAMP, Wilhelm	34	Landbergen	69-0572
HAVERLAND, Heinr.	23	Ilbenbueren	71-0581
HAVERLANDT, Friedrich	28	St. Paul	69-0784
Alwine 26, Carl 30			
HAWLIECK, Franz	37	Kohsanjezd	68-0770
Maria 33, Maria 11, Franz 8, Edalbert 6, Joseph 4, Carl 1			
HAY, Barbara	20	Darmstadt	71-0363
HAY, Mathilde	20	Steinau	71-0363
HAYA, Michael	18	Laubheim	69-0079
HAYER, S.F.	49	Buffalo	69-1076
Amalie 44, Adele 16			
HAYS, Torgeline	26	New York	70-1161
Fanny 6, Willy 4, Emma 10 months			
HAZEL, Cathr.	22	Kirchenhausberg	69-1011
Dorothea 16			
HEATHER, Ferd.	29	Stettin	70-0223
HEBBELER, Eduard	24	Osnabrueck	69-0771
HEBBIG, August	39	Koerner	71-0643
Johanne 36, Emil 13, August 10, Ernestine 9, Liebreich 6, Gustav 6 m.			
HEBEBRANDT, Eva	23	Hessen	70-0178
HEBENBROCK, Frdr.	32	Berlin	69-1004
HEBERLEIN, Georg	51	New York	70-1003
HEBERLING, Jacob	27	Coblenz	68-0456
Eleonore 29, Wilhelm 6 months, Catharine 20, Wilhelm 17			
HECH, Henry	33	Albany	69-0672
HECHT, Abraham	23	Wartenberg	71-0684
HECHT, Elise	16	Frankfurt a\ M	69-0968
HECHT, Franx.	32	Gohles	71-0684
HECHT, Helene	20	Coblenz	68-0661
HECHT, Jacob	25	Wartenberg	71-0643
HECHT, Lene	17	Lemgo	70-0452
HECHT, Louis	14	Hamburg	68-0884
HECHT, Pauline	18	Hofgeismar	68-0884
HECHTS, Gertrude	25	Coblenz	71-0712
HECK, Anna	22	Ermereuth	71-0727
HECK, Aug.	26	Solingen	68-0647
HECK, Carl	24	Edenkoben	69-0182
HECK, Mar. Cath.	29	Coesfeld	68-1002
HECKEL, Alois	24	Brake	68-1002
Emma 25			
HECKEL, Johann	32	Menota	69-0572
HECKER, Andr.	64	Bilizingsleben	68-0820
HECKER, Catharina	21	Oberkochen	70-0508
Baby 4 months			
HECKER, H.	17	Falkenstein	70-0308
HECKER, Heinrich	33	Coeln	68-0760
HECKER, Johann	17	Oberkirchen	69-0208
HECKER, Louise	19	Gr. Neuhausen	71-0492
HECKING, J. H.	50	Hoboken	70-100
HECKLER, Bernhard	32	Hensbach	69-0321
HECKMANN, Fritz	28	Guetersloh	68-0707
HECKMANN, Heinr.	17	Wietersheim	71-0521

NAME	AGE	RESIDENCE	YR-LIST
HECKMANN, Magd.	17	Brechingen	69-0592
HECKMANN, Wilh.	53	Wietersheim	71-0521
Eleonore 48, Friedrich 17, Anton 15, Marie 9, Louise 8			
HECKMANN, Wilhelm	40	Stolzenau	69-0429
HECKMANN, Wilhelmine	25	Potsdam	68-1002
HECKROTH, Martha	31	Cassel	70-0682
HECTOR, Christ.	16	Walsrode	69-1086
HEDDE, Heinrich	39	Oppendorf	71-0300
Elise 49, Louise 7, Henriette 4			
HEDECKE, Heinrich	45	Alfeld	70-1142
HEEGEN, Sophie	26	Langenholz	71-0492
Caroline 21, Lina 6 months			
HEEGER, Helene	27	Ubstadt	68-1006
HEEGER, Marg.	55	Hermannshain	71-0363
HEER, Joh.	46	Erbach	68-0314
Helene 38, Daniel 9, Johann 7, Peter 6			
HEER, Joseph	17	Waexbenhausen	69-0968
Aloys 14, Max 31			
HEEREN, Friedrich	16	Soest	69-0784
HEEREN, Johann	44	Wiesederfehn	68-0907
Trientje 44, Harm 18, Frank 7, Hermann 5			
HEERHABER, Franz	29	Zerbst	68-0770
HEERING, Wilhelm	15	Falken Gesaess	70-0508
Henry 9			
HEERMNN, Casp.	17	Dohna	68-0884
HEES, Franz	26	Kirchweiler	70-0308
HEFEL, Catharina	18	Schwabing	68-0907
HEFENTHAL, Johann	69	Assenheim	70-0204
Henriette 33			
HEFFNER, Fried.	5	Asselheim	70-1066
Ludw. 3			
HEFKE, Ernst	24	Wetschen	69-1059
HEFTEN, Auguste	22	Muehlhausen	71-0167
Marie 17			
HEFTIG, And.	60	Leuchsingen	71-0789
Elis. 58, Rosine 16, Marg. 7			
HEFTIG, Fried.	20	Zinsingen	71-0789
HEGEL, Ad.	16	Reuss	69-1004
HEGELHEIMER, Joh.	20	Frankfurt	71-0479
HEGELHEIMER, Joh. Chr.	16	Nuernberg	71-0684
HEGERMANN, Heinrich	16	Hannover	71-0821
HEGERT, Georg	31	Altvorstetten	71-0492
Catharine 27, Josef 9 months			
HEIDBREDER, Amalie	24	Menninghueffen	68-1006
HEIDE, Louise	28	Sabbenhausen	68-0820
HEIDE, Therese	22	Hanau	69-0268
HEIDECK, Theresia	36	Langenhausen	70-0508
William 13, Hermann 12, Chls. 9, Franziska 8, Auguste 6, Louise 3			
HEIDEL, Adolph W.	21	Falkenstein	70-0006
HEIDEL, Emil	31	Lossnitz	68-0707
HEIDELBERGER, Carl	45	Glachau	70-0384
HEIDELBERGER, Wilh.	22	Landshausen	70-0052
HEIDELMARK, Johann	38	Rheinprovince	69-1076
HEIDEN, Carl	25	Baldekow	68-0884
Caroline 21, baby 3 months			
HEIDENREICH, Catharine	17	Klingenmuenster	68-0852
HEIDENREICH, Charles	24	Rheinberg	70-0508
HEIDEPOHL, Fritz	28	Bremen	70-0204

NAME	AGE	RESIDENCE	YR-LIST
HEIDINGER, Therese	54	Elinstein	70-1055
HEIDLE, Barbara	23	Koenigswart	68-0566
HEIDLER, Eleonore	16	Prague	68-0534
HEIDLER, Georg	17	Auenheim	71-0643
HEIDMANN, Henry	34	Columbia	69-1076
Louise 19			
HEIDSEIK, Franz	14	Oldendorf	71-0581
HEIDT, Johann	48	Hannover	69-1396
HEIGER, Elise	60	Hermannstein	71-0643
Catharina 30			
HEIL, Anna	54	Fuerste	69-0572
HEIL, Antonie	22	Weidenau	71-0456
HEIL, Barbara	22	Klosterhausen	68-0957
HEIL, Joseph	28	Neustadt	70-0135
HEIL, Wilhelmine	26	Bruechs	68-0786
HEILBRONN, Regina	21	Heilbronn	71-0712
Gustav 5 months			
HEILBRUNN, Helene	50	Fuckhofen	71-0581
Gilda 15, Leopold 12, Moses 11, Her. 7, Hermann 6			
HEILEFELD, Margarethe	16	Hatmann	69-0208
HEILEMANN, Joh. Gg.	25	Weiler	68-1002
Regina 33, Marg. 9, Julius 4, Wilh. 6 months			
HEILEMANN, John	29	Willingshausen	68-0534
Barbara 32, John 5, Elisabeth 2, Martha 2 months			
HEILGEIST, Charles	43	Preussen	68-0456
HEILHOFF, Heinr. Gottfr.	20	Lingen	68-0647
HEILIG, Sebastian	9	Neuningen	69-0229
HEILING, Wilhelm	28	Dortmund	69-0321
HEILMANN, Cath.	45	Darmstadt	70-1142
Franz 9, Herm. 11 months			
HEILMANN, Helene	55	Vollmers	71-0736
HEILMANN, Louise	20	Bruesken	71-0736
HEILMANN, Ph.	41	Baden	70-0170
Cath. 38, Franz 4, Phil. 2			
HEILMANN, Ursula	15	Harthausen	71-0521
HEILMEYER, Lenchen	19	Frankenthal	71-0736
HEILS, Joseph	17	Merzen	68-1002
HEILSHORN, Joh.	17	Schadinbeck	71-0521
HEILSHORN, Margreth	19	Ritterhude	71-0456
HEILSHORN, Meta	20	Oldenbuettel	71-0521
HEILWAGEN, Heinrich	25	Koerner	68-0786
HEIM, Carl	29	Cannstadt	71-0521
HEIM, Ernst	22	Lippe	69-1004
HEIM, Heinr.	15	Gudensberg	71-0684
HEIMANN, Herm.	31	Hannover	70-0384
HEIMBACH, Sali.	17	Niederwerbe	69-0321
HEIMBECKER, Wilhelm	54	Bielefeld	69-1309
HEIMBERG, Babette	25	Zeisendorf	70-1035
HEIMBERG, Jeremias	18	Podberg	68-0982
HEIMER, Anna B.	16	Neufang	71-0521
HEIMER, Heinrich	34	Brandenburg	68-0872
HEIMER, Hermann	28	Lauenheim	69-0572
HEIMES, Theodor	30	Feldbecke	68-0939
HEIMLER, Xaver	39	Muenchen	68-0314
Therese 45			
HEIMROTH, Wilh.	28	Nordcampen	68-0566
HEIMSOTH, Cathar.	20	Ahneberg	68-0610

NAME	AGE	RESIDENCE	YR-LIST
Marg. 18			
HEIN, Helene	16	Schwenstein	68-0982
HEIN, Maria	49	Hannover	68-0760
HEIN, Otto	22	Breslau	68-0770
HEIN, Peter	52	Cumberland	70-0523
Mathilde 43			
HEINCE, Christine	21	Waldeck	68-0753
HEINCKEL, Georg	40	Crailstein	68-0939
Theodor 7, Heinrich 6, Chatharina 73			
HEINDEL, Caroline	19	Muehlen	71-0456
HEINDL, Johann	30	Benking	69-0457
HEINE, Bernhard	18	Detmold	68-0939
HEINE, C.	27	Cannstadt	69-0338
HEINE, Carl	17	Ilserheide	68-0625
HEINE, Friedrich	16	Hannover	70-0682
HEINE, Gottl.	23	Schlesinghausen	68-1002
HEINE, Hermann	32	Hannover	69-0067
William 28			
HEINE, Hermann	16	Stadthagen	70-0355
HEINE, Ilse	30	Meiningen	69-0560
Dina 8, Minna 4			
HEINE, Peter	27	Hamschen	68-0456
HEINE, Wilh.	34	Kleinern	68-0566
Catharine 20, Wilhelm 11 months			
HEINECK, Friedrich	43	Thueringen	70-1003
Catharine 51, Henriette 29, August 16			
HEINECK, Otto	17	Alsfeld	68-0314
HEINECKE, Carl	40	Braunschweig	68-0707
HEINECKE, Heinrich	26	Roessing	68-1298
HEINEL, Johann	16	Lichtenberg	69-0542
HEINEMANN, Anna	20	Westfalen	70-0728
HEINEMANN, Catharine	24	Rhausa	68-0625
Catharine 3 months			
HEINEMANN, Christoph	14	Freinhagen	68-0661
HEINEMANN, Ferd.	35	Oldenburg	70-0452
HEINEMANN, Gerh.	15	Oldenburg	70-0452
HEINEMANN, Helene	20	Kirchheim	68-0786
HEINEMANN, Ph.	26	Alsfeld	71-0393
HEINEMANN, Wilhelmine	27	Zaasch	68-0647
HEINEMEYER, Aug.	18	Bueckeburg	70-0384
HEINEMEYER, Heinrich	30	Berlin	68-0872
HEINEN, Gertrude	30	Dueren	68-0566
Anna 11 months			
HEINENRATH, Abr.	18	Gilsenberg	71-0815
HEINERBERG, Friedrich	19	Ringstedt	71-0429
HEINERO, Gust.	32	Breslau	70-0523
HEINFURTER, Hirsch	53	Muehringen	69-0229
Fanni 59			
HEINGER, Carl	46	Idar	71-0815
HEINHOFF, Bernh. Fr.	4	R.B. Muenster	68-0610
HEINKE, Franz	28	Saarlouis	68-0456
HEINKE, Joh.	36	Hannover	70-0443
HEINL, Andreas	31	Boehmen	69-1004
Marie 27, Marie 10 months			
HEINLE, Wilhelm	29	Gmuend	69-0923
HEINMUELLER, Johann	17	Wiera	70-1035
HEINMUELLER, Johanne	17	Cassel	69-0457
HEINRICH, Albert	20	Stuttgart	69-0672

NAME	AGE	RESIDENCE	YR-LIST
HEINRICH, Anna	18	Hagenau	71-0581
HEINRICH, Auguste	22	Hassloch	71-0821
HEINRICH, Carl L.	16	Fuerth	69-1059
HEINRICH, Christian	21	Finsterroth	71-0643
Louise 15			
HEINRICH, Christine	46	Strutz	68-0939
Margarethe 7, Catharine 6, Dorothea 6, Mathilde 5, Anna 1			
HEINRICH, Fr.	25	Seiddorf	68-0820
HEINRICH, Friedrich	26	Wrisbach	68-0707
HEINRICH, Heinrich	37	Grossalmerode	69-0182
Catharine 36, Carl 15, Anna 12, Louis 9, Anna 7, Elisabeth ?			
HEINRICH, Joh.	39	Franken	70-0378
Catharine 25, Christine 4, Caroline 3			
HEINRICH, Louise	19	Baalbern	69-0029
HEINRICH, Peter	27	Altenkirchen	69-0572
Caroline 28			
HEINRICHER, Franz	28	Creefeld	71-0815
HEINRICHS, George	23	Susstron	68-0939
HEINRICHS, Tina	23	Marx	71-0492
HEINS, Diedrich	25	Marschkamp	69-0968
HEINS, Nicolaus	17	Lehe	71-0429
HEINSOHN, Cathrine	33	Hannover	70-1161
HEINSOHN, Henriette	40	Bederkesa	68-1006
HEINSOHN, Hermanna	18	Burgdorf	68-1006
HEINSOHN, Marie	24	Huebstadt	69-0229
HEINTARDT, Robert	19	Tribes	68-0852
HEINTEL, Jacob	35	Metzingen	69-0592
Marie 24			
HEINTZ, Catrine	26	Darmstadt	69-1059
HEINTZ, Laura	38	Eger	68-1006
HEINWETTER, George	23	Dingelstadt	71-0712
Therese 16, Dorothea 16, Louise 8, Catharina 14			
HEINZ, Anna	23	Baiern	69-1076
HEINZ, Carl	19	Irmenach	68-0786
HEINZ, Joseph	25	Lorch	69-0542
HEINZ, Leop.	18	Burgstadt	70-0308
HEINZ, Magdalaine	19	Kork	71-0581
HEINZE, Gottl.	22	Schwarzburg	69-1004
Ernst 24			
HEINZE, Rosine	17	Homberg	69-0592
HEINZER, Peter	47	Gemuenden	71-0456
HEINZMANN, John	23	Taurendau	71-0456
HEIS, Johann	28	Zerzin/Boehmen	69-0576
Barbara 24, Marie 9 months			
HEISE, Caroline	27	Bialken	71-0521
HEISE, Catharina	31	Eschershausen	68-0566
Caroline 7			
HEISE, Fritz	18	Cassel	69-0457
HEISELBAUER, Heinich	39	Wacher	71-0712
Catharina 37, Hermann 3, Anna 67, Elisabeth 9 months			
HEISER, Wilhelm	48	Detroit	69-1076
HEISING, Elise	19	Wiedenbrueck	71-0733
HEISMANN, Rosalie	63	Polna	70-0443
HEISSE, Carl	20	Fritzlar	70-0135
HEISSENBUTTEL, Meta	18	Bremen	69-0547
HEISSMEYER, Carl	36	Bodenbeck	69-0848
Louise 19			
HEISTERHAGEN, Emilie	18	Diekbergen	71-0736
HEIT, Emil	23	Langensalza	71-0712
HEITHANS, Hermann	14	Bersenbrueck	69-0208
HEITKAMP, Herm.	36	Luebbecke	71-0681
Charlotte 40, Louise 16, Carl 13, Heinr. 11, Gottl. 8, Wilhelm 6, Charlotte 3			
HEITMANN, D. H.	16	Engeln	71-0581
HEITMANN, Ida	28	Greifswalde	71-0736
Otto 2, Carl 6 m., Mathilde 6 m.			
HEITMANN, Joh.	18	Heiligenberg	71-0581
HEITMANN, Lidda	19	Altenburg	69-0672
HEITMANN, Wilhelm	23	Bielefeld	69-1396
HEITMEYER, Wilh.	14	Nettelsack	68-0957
HEITZ, Franziska	26	Griesheim	71-0363
HEITZ, George	26	Kork	71-0581
HEITZHUSEN, Johann	45	Oldenburg	69-0268
Ahke 34, Anna 9, Gesine 8, Diedrich 6, Georg 4, Catharina 2, Mathilde 1			
HEKERT, Louise	31	Gehlenbeck	69-0542
Ernst 5, Heinrich 10 months			
HELBACH, Kilian	24	Solingen	70-0308
HELBING, Carl	47	Grossbruechter	68-0625
Louise 47, Friedrich 16			
HELD, Andreas	25	Gossweinstein	69-0784
HELD, Carl	29	Langenargen	69-0848
HELD, Christ,	17	Imhof	68-0957
HELD, Franz	20	Hirschberg	69-1059
HELD, Georg	27	Scharkenberg	68-0707
HELD, Georg	18	Darmstadt	68-0939
HELD, Wilhelm	39	Berlin	69-0572
HELDENWANG, Imanuel	28	Dagersheim	70-0223
HELDER, Jacob	28	Birkenfeld	70-0508
HELDMANN, L.	32	Detmold	68-0014
HELDMOLD, Joseph	23	Seeburg	68-0314
HELFRICH, Andreas	9	Loehrbach	71-0643
HELFRISCH, Cacelie	25	Mainz	70-1035
HELGENBERG, Marie	18	Ziegenhain	70-1035
HELL, August	28	Treptow	68-0770
Albertine 34, Emilie 1			
HELL, Dora	32	St. Gallen	71-0479
HELLEMANN, Cord	18	Krotheim	68-0907
HELLENBERG, Georg	38	Schmalkalden	71-0479
Cacelie 44			
HELLER, Caroline	24	Bremen	69-0457
HELLER, Ernestine	17	Schoenwerder	68-1298
HELLER, Heinrich	18	Hannover	69-0583
HELLER, Lisette	21	Faurbach	68-0760
HELLER, Mathias	19	Aldingen	71-0492
HELLER, Wilhelm	38	Braunschweig	69-1059
HELLFARTH, Franz	18	Gotha	69-0784
HELLGUTH, Peter	68	Nordhalben	69-0592
Cath. 66			
HELLING, Joh.	31	Hinteburg	68-0566
HELLING, Sophie	25	Haldern	71-0821
HELLMANN, August	21	Braunschweig	71-0736
HELLMANN, Christine	22	Niederkainsbach	69-1319
HELLMANN, Doris	17	Rothenburg	69-1059

NAME	AGE	RESIDENCE	YR-LIST
Fallingbostel			
HELLMANN, Johanna	25	Oldenburg	71-1046
HELLMANN, Marie	26	Moelle	71-0643
HELLMANN, Max	20	Fuerth	71-0736
HELLMANN, Mich.	25	Wollstein	70-0308
HELLMERS, Tiebke	22	Nordhausen	70-0378
HELLMICH, Wilhelmine	24	Forthheim	68-0661
HELLMUTH, Carl	17	Saalfeld	71-0363
HELLSTERS, Victoria	40	Empfingen	69-0338
Hermann 9, John 11 months			
HELMANN, Bertha	22	Brake	69-0560
HELMANN, John	29	Neuenkirchen	69-0338
Carolina 25, Catharina 59, Fred 11 months			
HELMEKE, Charlotte	23	Wilnhaus	68-1006
HELMERICHS, M.	42	Gotha	68-0939
Heinrich 9, Friedrich 8			
HELMERS, Peter	35	Marienhafe	68-0707
Jabetje 39, Dirk 12			
HELMES, Caroline	20	Seesbach	68-0661
Jacob 16			
HELMES, Marianne	53	Bawinkel	69-0968
Johannes 29, Hermann 16			
HELMETAGE, Louis	21	Buhlen	68-0647
HELMICH, Henry	39	Laubach	70-0355
HELMICH, W.	52	Bohmte	68-0647
Heinr. 12			
HELMIG, Carl	18	Camen	68-0661
HELMKE, Bernhard	10	Osterholz	68-0760
HELMKE, Friedrich	30	Wenzen	68-0625
HELMKE, Herm.	56	Ehlden	68-0647
Sophie 52, Soph. Cath. 24, Wilh. 14, Dorette 8, Herm. Chr. 7			
HELMSTAEDT, Georg	74	Neuenkirchen	69-1004
HELVES, Friedr. Aug.	34	Wolfenbuettel	68-1049
HELWIG, Barth.	39	Oberjofsa	71-0684
Anna 36, Johannes 14, Georg 11, Christian 7			
HELWIG, Heinrich	31	Brochterbeck	69-0429
HEMANN, Clara	40	Buer	70-1055
HEMFF, Armin	25	Reval-Rival	70-1161
HEMKES, Wilke	27	Lubbertsfehn	69-0208
HEMMEL, Marie	17	Unterreningen	69-0672
HEMPEL, Bernh.	16	Meiningen	69-0583
HEMPEL, Catharina	24	Gelnhausen	68-0760
HEMPEL, Ernst	26	Gossitz	69-0457
Louis 25, Christ. 17			
HEMPEL, Gustav	20	Eulenberg	68-0852
HEMPEL, Heinr.	28	Lengenbrueck	71-0479
Johanne 32, Heinr. 2, Johanne 3 m.			
HEMPEL, Johannes	17	Borkum	70-0204
HEMPERSCH, Johann	27	Fladingen	69-0798
HEMPFER, Anna	36	Eschingen	71-0733
HEMPFLING, Lorenz	17	Burghaig	71-0363
Johann 14			
HENAL, August	32	Annaberg	70-0378
HENDRICH, Ignatz	27	Niederorschel	71-0643
HENDRICH, John	31	Niederorschel	71-0643
Friedrike 31, Marie 9, Ottilie 8, August 6, Rose 9 months, Marie 60, Franziska			

NAME	AGE	RESIDENCE	YR-LIST
HENDRICHS, Johann	41	Gladbach	68-0820
HENDRICHS, Maria	18	Niederoschel	69-0572
HENDT, Carl	41	Anhalt	70-0135
HENERMANN, H.	19	Neuenkirchen	69-0338
HENGEMUESCHLE, M.	55	Oldenburg	69-1086
HENINGER, Joseph	28	Beck	71-0521
Maria 30			
HENJE, Linder	35	Sandstedt	69-0457
HENJES, Hinrich	21	Neustadt	69-0429
HENKE, Adolph	15	Oldenburg	69-0572
HENKE, Joh.	37	Hannover	70-1066
Maria 30, Joh. 17			
HENKE, Wilh.	36	Kirchdorf	71-0363
HENKEL, Balthasar	28	H. Darmstadt	70-1003
HENKEL, Charles	43	New York	70-1142
HENKEL, Elisabeth	56	Wollmar	71-0821
HENKEL, Rosalie	20	Cassel	71-0521
HENKEL, Sophie	27	Gartenau	70-0443
HENKEL, Winfrieda	20	Wickers	68-0610
HENKELMANN, Friedrich	49	Bialken	71-0521
Anna 57			
HENKELMANN, Wm.	18	Kl. Bauken	69-1421
HENKEN, Betty	20	Geistendorf	71-0456
HENKEN, Margarethe	21	Papenburg	69-0572
HENKES, Ed.	26	Weimar	68-0820
HENN, Jacob	28	Walbenabs	68-0456
HENN, Johanne	18	Waldhausen	69-0429
HENNEKE, Heinrich	29	Arnstadt	68-0770
HENNEMANN, A.	31	Muenchen	71-0681
HENNES, Peter	49	Bos	68-0625
Anna 42, Jacob 17, Josef 9, Gertrud 2			
HENNIG, Gust.	33	Magdeburg	68-0760
HENNIG, Josephine	30	Unterfranken	69-0321
HENNIGES, Frdke.	18	Wenzen	68-0610
Dorette 17			
HENNING, Chr.	21	Eisenach	69-0560
HENNING, Christ.	4	Potsdam	68-1002
Augusta 1			
HENNING, Joh. Christ	50	Potsdam	68-1002
Johanna 38, Bertha 10, Marie 9, Johnna 8			
HENNING, Mary	20	Manrode	69-1086
HENNING, Rebecca	21	Oppeln	68-0566
HENNING, Valentin	18	Unterstoppel	68-0939
HENNINGES, Johanna	18	Gronau	70-0272
HENNINGS, Diedrich	14	Ottersberg	68-0770
HENNISCH, Johann	14	Ansbach	69-1011
HENRICH, Carl	20	Stuttgart	68-1027
HENRICH, Christ.	23	Merxheim	69-0490
HENRICH, Gustav	27	Sulzbach	71-0492
HENRICH, He.	27	Griflitz	69-1011
HENRICH, Johann	24	Herlebach	69-0229
HENRICHS, Georg	24	Otterndorf	71-0429
Meta 22			
HENRICI, Caroline	18	Sonderhausen	69-0672
HENSCHE, Wilhelm	16	Hagen	69-0457
HENSCHEL, Pauline	39	S. Gotha	69-0572
Helene 4			
HENSE, Anna	19	Wiedenbrueck	71-0479

NAME	AGE	RESIDENCE	YR-LIST
HENSE, Eduard	28	Elberfeld	69-0457
HENSE, Heinr.	38	Seringhausen	71-0815
Henriette 32, Theodor 9, Elisabeth 6, Bernhardine 5, Heinrich 3, Josef 9 months			
HENSEL, Gottlieb	36	Dubberow	69-0182
HENSEL, Heinr.	16	Hannover	71-0479
HENSEL, Joh.	29	Fischbach	71-0521
HENSEMANN, Marie	16	Bremen	68-0865
HENTZE, Auguste	18	Bremen	69-0321
HENTZEL, Joh.	22	Gommersheim	69-0100
HENZE, Felix	20	Volkmarssen	71-0821
HENZE, Wilhelm	25	Halle	68-0419
HENZEL, Maria	22	Eich	68-0786
HEPNER, Charlotte	56	Bellin	69-1309
Herman 14			
HEPP, Caroline	16	Muehlhausen	69-0321
HEPP, Heinr.	29	Weier	71-0581
Elise 19			
HEPPE, Louis	12	Salzwedel	71-0712
HEPPE, Martha Helene	23	Niedermoellrich	68-1002
HERB, Frdr.	20	Hochdorf	68-0610
HERBER, Christine	19	Momberg	68-0957
HERBOLD, Marg.	26	Machtlos	68-0647
Marie 7, Conrad 11 months			
HERBRECHT, A.	19	Druffach	71-0581
HERBST, Adam	26	Antenhausen	68-0957
HERBST, August	40	Braunschweig	68-0907
HERBST, August	21	Lauenberg	71-0581
Friedrich 23			
HERBST, Casp.	51	Boden	69-0490
Anna 48, Anna 21, Cath. 19, Marie 16, Caspar 8			
HERBST, Heinr.	15	Arzell	71-0300
HERBST, Johann	30	Tauchingen	70-0329
HERBST, Louise	21	Meckenbach	68-0661
Margarethe 17			
HERBST, male	28	Braunschweig	69-0100
HERBSTRITT, Theodor	20	Ettenheim	68-0625
HERCHENBACH, Franz	26	Eischeid	68-314
HERDEL, Jacob	24	Allertshofen	69-0572
HERDLINGER, John A.	38	Indianapolis	70-1035
Marg. 33, Joh. 10, Robert 9, Flora 7, Emma 4			
HERDRICH, Peter	31	Rust	71-0300
Marie 24			
HERDT, Hedwig	28	Werbachhausen	68-0647
HERFORTH, Louisa	29	Callies	68-0957
Gustav 7, Emil 5			
HERING, Elise	25	Ricken	69-1086
HERING, Emil	44	Reichenwalde	71-0684
Alma 30, Alma 6, Paul 5, Max 2, Elisabeth 9 months			
HERING, Peter	16	Benfelden	71-0167
Marie 20			
HERKER, J.	25	Dinkelbuehl	71-0582
HERLAN, Christine	20	Friedrichsthal	63-0244
Baby 6 months			
HERLAN, John	44	Friedrichsthal	63-0244
Christine 43, Wilhelmine 22, Martha 18, Pauline 15, William 9, Bertha 6, Carol			
HERLAN, Magdalene	54	Friedrichsthal	63-0244
Isaac 16, Lewis 20, William 24			
HERLEYN, Wilhelm	40	Breitenbach	69-0542
Elisabeth 38, Helene 7			
HERLIN, Marie	18	Wimpfen	68-0939
HERMANN, Adam	39	Queck	70-0508
HERMANN, Andreas	16	Kurhessen	70-0355
HERMANN, Anna	22	Katzenelnbogen	68-0982
HERMANN, Aug.	24	Leun	68-0760
HERMANN, Barb.	25	Kirchdorf	71-1046
Wilhelmine 2			
HERMANN, Berend	17	Otterndorf	69-0268
HERMANN, Carl	20	Meissen	69-1319
HERMANN, Carl	17	Ottersmeier	69-0050
HERMANN, Cathrine	37	Hessen	70-1066
Cathrine 9, Marie 5			
HERMANN, Christian	33	Wernshausen	68-0770
Christiane 26			
HERMANN, Eduard	52	Dresden	68-1006
Maria 19, Emma 17			
HERMANN, Elisa	17	Niederweimar	68-0534
HERMANN, Emil	21	Dresden	68-1006
Gustav 16			
HERMANN, Fritz	16	Suelbeck	68-0534
HERMANN, Georg	23	Waiblingen	69-0672
HERMANN, Gustav	28	Zemmen	69-0576
HERMANN, Gustav	24	Margoninsdorf	68-0456
HERMANN, Johann	22	Erstetten	69-0672
HERMANN, John	44	Berlin	69-0841
HERMANN, Leonhard	40	Kettmannsdorf	68-0907
HERMANN, Louise	20	Boehmen	69-0784
HERMANN, Louise	21	Crimmitschau	70-0508
HERMANN, Marie	61	Schnellenwelde	68-0707
HERMANN, Martin	24	Gruenstadt	69-0592
HERMANN, S.	44	New York	69-0923
O. 8			
HERMANN, Theresia	57	Baden	69-0841
Albert 16			
HERME, Philipp	17	Doerzbach	68-0760
HERMER, Emilie	23	Scheidt	68-1006
Mathilde 2			
HERMIS, Frd. Aug.	30	U Scheidt	68-0820
HERMLE, Rosa	18	Wilflingen	69-0429
HERMS, Otto	24	Berlin	70-1161
HERMSMAIER, Fr.	19	Lippe Detmold	70-0355
HERNIES, Theodor	30	Feldbecke	68-0939
HEROKWITZ, Emil	24	Lemesch	71-0681
HEROLD, Agnes	45	Kahla	70-0272
HEROLD, Barbara	20	Oberaislach	70-0355
HEROLD, Elisabeth	19	Goellheim	69-0592
HEROLD, Franz	22	Rothenkirchen	68-1006
HEROLD, Friedrich	31	Langenbernsdorf	71-0226
HEROLD, Heinr.	25	Adelsheim	69-0923
HEROLD, Wilhelmine	17	Rothenkirchen	68-1006
HERPICH, Heinrich	30	Thierbach	68-0907
HERR, Adolf	18	Kniebis	69-0429
HERR, Aug.	19	Emmendingen	68-0884
HERREWIG, John	45	Knesebeck	68-0907

NAME	AGE	RESIDENCE	YR-LIST
Dorothea 46, Carl 19, Wilke 17, Hermann 15, Adolph 7, Louis 6, Anna 5			
HERRIG, John	46	Trier	63-0244
Miss. 35, Angela 25, John 6, Andreas 4, Nicolaus 11 months			
HERRKE, Henriette	32	Danzig	68-0820
Carl 9, Arthur 7, Robert 5, Max 3			
HERRMANN, Jacob	31	Kirchstadt	69-0457
HERSCH, Lud.	22	Langenburg	68-0753
HERSCHEL, Albert	18	Stuttgardt	71-0736
HERSCHLEF, Albin	31	Sonderhausen	68-1049
HERSEN, Diedrich	19	Friedeburg	71-0492
HERSMEIER, Carl	17	Harverstedt-Wes	70-0006
HERTEL, Adam	26	Nordhalben	69-1319
HERTEL, Andr.	15	Asch	68-0610
HERTEL, Louise	34	Greiz	69-0560
Henry 4, Louis 8			
HERTER, Carl	35	Baden	70-0148
Emilie 14			
HERTKORN, Pauline	30	Hessbach	70-1035
HERTOLD, Johanna	47	Wenzen	68-0625
Herman 18, Augusta 9			
HERTSCH, Wilhelmine	30	Crimmitschau	68-0760
Anna 7, Johann 3			
HERWIG, Conrad	15	Friedewaldt	69-0572
HERWIG, Heinrich	19	Lautenhausen	71-0521
HERWIG, Otto	23	Bieberach	69-0592
HERZ, Anne E.	58	Kl. Heubach	71-0456
HERZ, Emil	20	Wiesbaden	70-0031
HERZ, Eva Barb.	32	Malzstadt	69-0182
HERZ, Joseph	39	Krumbach	68-0820
HERZ, Robert	17	Elberfeld	70-0728
HERZ, Simon	20	Birkenfeld	69-0923
HERZBERG, Diedrich	46	Hogerhagen	68-0907
Margarethe 44, Louise 18, Anna 16, Hermann 7, Diedrich 6, Hermann 2			
HERZEL, Friedrich	18	Koeplitz	69-0208
HERZFELD, Virginia	9	Carlshofen	68-0939
HERZOG, Augusta	15	Rinteln	68-0647
HERZOG, Christoph	43	Lobenstein	68-0760
Gustav 15			
HERZOG, Rosina	20	Steinenbronn	71-0712
HERZOG, Sophie	50	Lobenstein	69-0229
Lina 12			
HERZOG, Wilhelm	16	Verden	69-0672
HESPE, Heinr.	17	Faehr	71-0581
HESS, Alois	20	Unterwald	69-1309
Marie 21, Anna 5			
HESS, Anna	31	Entlebusch	69-0100
HESS, Anna	21	Fritzlar	71-0429
HESS, Balthasar	17	Hersfeld	68-1002
HESS, Carl	17	Riedlingen	69-0429
HESS, Carl	15	Weiten-Gesaess	69-1059
HESS, Catharina	19	Adenbach	69-0490
HESS, Daniel	20	Ehweiler	71-0226
Elisabeth 17, Adolph 3 months			
HESS, Emil	28	Heulbach	68-0770
Christiane 29, Hulda 4, Edwin 1			
HESS, Friederike	25	Stuttgart	69-1212

NAME	AGE	RESIDENCE	YR-LIST
HESS, Friedrich	34	Groetzingen	69-0229
Elisabeth 32			
HESS, H.	17	Cramfeld	70-1142
L. 15			
HESS, Hermann	26	Homburg	68-1027
Sophie 19			
HESS, Hermann	16	Stuttgart	68-0907
HESS, Jacob	47	Armershausen	68-0625
Anna 20, Martha 17, Magdalena 9			
HESS, Joh.	24	Hessen	70-0178
Engelh. 17			
HESS, John	32	Hollstadt	70-0355
HESS, Katharina	24	Darmstadt	71-0393
HESS, Lena	18	Suzdorf	68-0939
HESS, Lina	19	Gotha	70-0355
HESS, Margarethe	20	Heubach	70-0355
HESSBACHER, A.	65	Bretten	70-0308
Johanna 64, Charles 9			
HESSBERG, Ferd.	22	Schleusingen	68-1002
HESSE, Bernh. Joh.	25	Teiston	68-0770
HESSE, Christ.	41	Mehbra	71-0581
Fritz 17, Maria 15, Christiane 8, Ida 6, Emil 4			
HESSE, Daniel	16	Langenheim	68-0534
HESSE, Fr. Dorothea	22	Minden	69-1212
HESSE, H. H.	13	Rodenburg	70-0204
HESSE, Heinr.	17	Krempe	70-1066
HESSE, Heinrich	16	Ahausen	68-0939
HESSE, Heinrich	36	Gr. Bruechter	71-0712
Auguste 31, Minna 5, Emma 3			
HESSE, Louise	60	Liebenrode	68-0760
William 23			
HESSE, Pauline	19	Wiehe	68-0456
HESSE, Wilh.	57	Stottersheim	68-0884
Louise 33, Carl 8, Ida 7, Minna 5, Ernst 4, Reinh. 3, Friederike 6 months			
HESSEL, Carol	17	Darmstadt	69-1004
HESSEL, Hermann	27	Lette	69-0229
HESSELBACHER, Joseph	20	Bretten	68-0534
HESSELBERGER, J.	22	Pfedersheim	69-1212
HESSER, Johann	26	Sulzbach	68-0852
HESSING, Richard	31	Leipzig	69-0798
HESSINGER, John	17	Armsheim	69-1396
HESSLER, Michael	18	Harxheim	69-0542
HETEK, Jos.	49	Boehmen	70-1066
Rosalie 50, Anton 20, Jos. 3			
HETTERLING, Susanne	22	Carlsstaedt	71-0581
HETTINGER, CHr.	21	Urphar	71-0581
HETZ, Christian	34	Schwarzenbach	68-0907
Johanna 30, Johanna 7, Adelheid 3			
HETZER, Adolf	28	Hildesheim	69-0542
HEUAL, August	32	Annaberg	70-0378
HEUBACH, Philipp	16	Untertuerkheim	71-0521
HEUCHLING, Carl	20	Seibach	70-0728
HEUER, Alexander	16	Sudweyhe	68-0982
HEUER, Carten	27	Westerholz	68-0456
HEUER, Conrad	16	Wilhelmsdorf	71-0492
HEUER, Henriette	16	Grahn	70-0052
HEUER, Johanne	24	Grahn	70-0052
HEUERMANN, Emilie	20	Lennep	71-0736

NAME	AGE	RESIDENCE	YR-LIST
HEUERMANN, Emma	27	Freiburg	70-0728
HEUERMANN, Otto	15	Freiburg	70-0728
HEUKMANN, Michel	30	Reading	69-1396
Elise 20			
HEULOTH, Anton	18	Muenchen	70-0148
HEUMANN, Adolph	25	Hagen	69-1396
August 19			
HEUMANN, Carl	45	Soehlde	69-1309
Christine 27, Wilhelm 4			
HEUMANN, Emma	18	Fuerth	69-0848
HEUMANN, Franz	17	Schwarzbach	68-0753
HEUMANN, Richard	21	Jena	68-0647
HEUMANN, Sophie	29	Knesebeck	68-0534
Maria 8, Dorothea 6, Heinrich 4, baby-son 11 months			
HEUN, Josephine	22	Hartheim	68-1298
HEUSCHMANN, Anna	25	Boehmen	70-0728
HEUSER, Catharina	18	Progans	68-0661
HEUSER, Henriette	25	Schwelm	68-1027
HEUSLER, Chr.	20	Cincinnati	70-1023
HEUSS, Mathilde	19	Lendershaus	71-0521
HEUTER, Therese	26	Muenchen	70-0272
HEUTERICH, Heinrich	14	Unhausen	69-0208
HEWMANN, Joh.	17	Hollich	71-0226
HEXAUER, Johanna	24	Mainz	68-1027
HEY, Johann	20	Badingbuettel	69-1076
HEY, Wilh.	40	Hannover	71-0479
Anna 31			
HEYD, Susanne	15	H. Darmstadt	70-1003
HEYDA, Franz	36	Prosec	68-0770
Maria 27, Franz 5, Marie 2, Barbara 26			
HEYDE, August	28	Heinrichau	71-0581
HEYDER, Friedmann	26	Ludwigstadt	69-0784
HEYDT, Conrad	18	Gruenberg	68-0534
HEYE, Albert	25	Bremen	70-0443
HEYE, August	22	Bremen	68-0456
HEYE, Jacob	23	Sersheim	68-0907
Friedrich 7			
HEYEN, Isaac	37	Egichenberg	68-0456
HEYER, Ernst	24	Neu Dambach	68-0456
HEYER, Madga.	27	Zbitka	71-0479
Marie 3, Joh. 11 months			
HEYER, Trina	18	Strutz	68-0939
HEYL, Georg	15	Umstadt	71-0363
HEYLMANN, Carl	16	Bruecken	69-0572
HEYLMANN, Carl	30	Gelnhausen	69-0592
HEYMANN, Jonas	32	Frederiksburg	71-0363
HEYMANN, Pauline	25	Tribes	71-0363
HEYMER, Amalie	34	Gauchau	68-0786
Clara 7			
HEYN, Caroline	23	Bialosliwe	71-0492
HEYN, Emilie	32	Chersdorf	69-0798
HEYN, Friedrich	19	Breinen	70-0683
Wilhelm 13, Gustav 9			
HEYNE, Johann	25	Oldenburg	69-0268
Gerhard 22			
HEYSAR, Lina	23	Brake	71-0815
HEYSES, Heiko	60	Hannover	70-0378
Rieke 54, Alberdina 18, Reunda 9			
HEYSING, Gretedina	28	Hannover	70-0378
Baby daughter 10 months			
HEZEL, Wilhelm	18	Ilshafen	70-0378
HIBBE, J. Sophie	28	Hannover	69-1212
HIBBE, Marie	24	Neustadt	71-0479
HIBBELER Alb.	25	Westerburg	69-1004
HIBBELER, Herm.	38	Westerburg	69-1004
Marie 36, Meta 19			
HIBBELER, Hermann	39	Oldenburg	70-0523
Caroline 59			
HICHLER, Wilhelmine	35	Unterjesingen	70-0089
Johann 5, Wilhelmine 6 months			
HIEBER, John	19	Herzthal	69-1421
HIEBER, John	30	Muenster	68-0982
HIEBLE, Anna Maria	50	Boehmen	69-0559
Anna Maria 26, Barbara 25			
HIERONYMUS, Filian		Havre	70-0259
HIFENER, Bast.	21	Philadelphia	69-1363
Magdalene 21			
HILBERS, Heinr.	14	Bockhorn	70-1142
Anna 15			
HILBERS, Oltmann	60	Oldenburg	70-0204
Margarethe 54, Gerhard 19			
HILD, Paulus	45	New York	63-0244
Kunigunde 33			
HILD, Phil.	16	Cassel	71-0363
Marie 24			
HILDEBRAND, Anna	14	Frankenhausen	68-0707
HILDEBRAND, August	28	Bremen	71-0736
HILDEBRAND, Cathar.	17	Frankenhausen	69-1212
HILDEBRAND, Conrad	17	Hausen	68-0661
HILDEBRAND, Elise	26	Schuechtern	68-0760
HILDEBRAND, Jacob	32	New York	70-1003
Anna 28, Bab. 9 months			
HILDEBRANDT, Aug.	32	Rudolstadt	71-0300
HILDEBRANDT, Charles	17	Hessen	70-0508
HILDEBRANDT, Christ.	30	Neu Hardenberg	71-0456
Sophia 32, Ferdinand 9, Marie 7, Carl 5, Marie 28, August 9 months			
HILDEBRANDT, Elisabeth	22	Epferode	68-0786
HILDEBRANDT, Emilie	17	Orchofky	69-1076
HILDEBRANDT, Fritz	14	Sandstedt	68-0760
HILDEBRANDT, Heinrich	36	Querfort	69-0923
HILDEBRANDT, Heinrich	21	Reilos	71-0429
HILDEBRANDT, Herm.	15	Grohn	69-1086
HILDEBRANDT, Kathrine	22	Bederkesa	70-1003
HILDEBRANDT, Sophie	21	New York	69-1076
HILDEBRANDT, Wme.	26	Latten	71-0479
HILDEN, Henriette	46	Bielefeld	69-1309
HILDENBRAND, Barbara	18	Pflummern	68-0625
HILDENBRAND, Elisabeth	34	Rheinsberg	71-0521
Carl 6			
HILDNER, Nicolaus	15	Unterbrumberg	68-0661
HILFLINGER, Friedrich	19	Ballrechten	71-0581
HILGEMEIER, Eduard	24	Offenbach	69-1086
HILGENSTEIN, Heinr.	44	Hadamer	71-0479
Josef 35			
HILGERT, Joseph	36	Trier	68-0884
Johanna 31, Joh. 4, Joseph 2, Maria 11 months			

NAME	AGE	RESIDENCE	YR-LIST
HILGERT, Mathias	27	Frommersbach	69-0457
HILKE, Caroline	22	Neuenlandermoor	69-0848
HILKE, Theo.	30	Wadersloh	68-0314
HILKEN, Johannes		Huttbergen	68-1002
HILKER, Christian	54	Bogo	69-0968
Minna 47, Wilhelm 15, Louise 12, Minna 8, Louis 6, Lina 4			
HILKER, Heinrich	31	Lemgo	71-0736
HILKER, Lisette	20	Humersbergen	69-0490
HILL, Fried.	18	Waldeck	70-0384
Christine 23			
HILL, Julius	27	Berten	70-0089
Friederike 45			
HILL, Marie	20	Hannover	70-0378
HILLE, M.	19	Leideringen	70-0308
HILLE, Otto	25	Siesen/Seesen	69-1076
HILLE, Philipp	48	Rudolstadt	68-0647
Wilhelm 15			
HILLEBRAND, Chls.	15	Fritzlar	69-0338
Henriette 17			
HILLEBRAND, Therese	22	Brosewitz	71-0393
HILLEMANN, Henriette	32	Goettingen	68-0753
HILLEMEYER, August	26	Elberstahl	69-0182
HILLENS, Emma	21	Bremen	68-0661
HILLENS, Wilhelmine	23	Drakenburg	68-0661
Otto 4 months			
HILLER, Christ.	34	Norwegen	70-0569
HILLER, Jacob	29	Nabern	70-0259
HILLER, John	39	Donauschingen	68-0014
HILLER, Robert	45	Silberberg	69-1309
HILLER, Wilh.	35	Ilfeld	68-0610
Sophie 35, Wilhelmine 13, Julius 7, Fritz 5, Lina 11 m.			
HILLIG, Julius	25	Oldenburg	70-0728
HILLMANN, Cath.	24	Intschede	69-1086
HILLMANN, Heinrich	19	Delmhorst	68-0760
HILLMER, Heinrich	49	Neustadt	69-0429
Christine 42, Elise 18, Anton 16, Helene 11, Diedrich 8, Georg 5, Mathilde 3			
HILLRICHS, Remmers	47	Werdum	71-0363
Marg. 36			
HILMER, Chr.	37	Sabbenhausen	68-0884
Caroline 38, Chr. 8, Caroline 4			
HILMER, Heinrich	31	Bueckeburg	71-0712
HILS, Eva	31	Breitzbach	69-0572
Nicolaus 9 months, Anna M. 25			
HILSENT, Wilhelmine	29	Danzig	70-1142
HILSPERGER, Theodor	25	Freiburg	71-0429
HILT, Ludwig	25	Bidenfeld	68-0770
HILTEMEYER, Joh.	15	Cappeln	70-0569
Georg 19			
HILTER, Peter	27	Nessmersiel	71-0789
HILTERMANN, H.	26	Osnabrueck	68-1006
Josepha 17			
HIMELA-CAROSELLI, L.	22	Elberfeld	71-0363
HIMMELREICH, Emil	26	Rudolstadt	69-0542
HIMMELREICHER, G.	21	Forchtenberg	68-0610
HIMMELSBACH, Gallus	20	Schatterthal	71-0429
HIMMER, Fr. Aug.	27	Oberlosa	69-0079
HIMMES, Michael	29	Kissingen	68-0456

NAME	AGE	RESIDENCE	YR-LIST
Antoinette 26			
HINCK, Adolph	22	Hannover	70-0443
HINDENBERGER, Anton	19	Waexbenhausen	69-0968
HINDERER, Johann	19	Welzheim	68-0786
HINDERER, Matthaeus	28	Hillnhof	68-0884
HINDERK, Anne	25	Trepsum	70-0384
HINDERKS, Hinderk	24	Manslagt	68-0820
HINDRICHSMEYER, Ernst	21	Volmerdingen	68-0566
HINGST, Eduard	25	Bitow	69-0547
HINK, Christian	18	Hannover	69-0559
HINK, Georg	17	Zeven	71-0479
HINKE, Georg	42	New York	69-1086
Mary 35, Mary 8			
HINKELDAY, Rosa	32	Galveston	69-1086
Julia 17, Rosa 15, Augusta 9			
HINKEN, Emma	38	New York	69-1011
Henry 6, Anna 4, William 11 months			
HINNERS, Peter	34	Greytsyhl	68-0456
Antje 39			
HINRICHS, Albert	24	New York	69-0923
HINRICHS, Albert	54	Walle	68-0566
Petje 50, Heinr. 19, Wemka 18, Toelke 16, Amalia 8			
HINRICHS, Bernhard	15	Goedekenhausen	70-0523
HINRICHS, Carl	15	Cuxhaven	71-0492
HINRICHS, Charles	19	Paris	69-0672
HINRICHS, Hinrich	25	Walle	68-0566
HINRICHS, Johann	20	Ostfriesland	70-0184
HINRICHS, Mary	17	Ostereistedt	68-0534
HINRICHS, Oltm.	64	Hannover	70-0308
Sofia 56, Hinr. 30, Mary 27, Sofia 10 months			
HINSATEN, Anna	40	Otterndorf	71-0821
Wilhelmine 9, Marie 9 months			
HINSCHING, Christian	37	Immenrode	68-0566
HINSCHKA, Franz	34	Boehmen	69-1076
Catharina 39, Maria 14, Antonia 12, Barbara 7, Franz 5, Johann 3, Anastasia 3			
HINTERHALTER, Louis	49	Kischlingspeen	70-0259
Eduard 9			
HINTERMANN, Henry	55	Lueneburg	71-0456
Marie 50, Minna 19			
HINZ, Adolph	14	Smiskanowo	69-0547
HINZ, Meta	22	Bademuehlen	69-0592
HINZE, Rosalie	30	Kaleinerhausen	70-0006
Sophie 18, Loui 15, Georg 12, Philip 7, Carl 4, Charlotte 6 months,(Hessen)			
HINZLER, Carl	25	Goeppingen	68-1002
HIPP, Andreas	29	Nackenheim	69-1309
Margarethe 34			
HIPP, Catharina	27	Pflummern	68-0625
HIPP, Magdalene	17	Duerkheim	70-0508
Mary 17			
HIPPEMAYER, Rud.	21	Lindau	71-0456
HIPPEN, Cornelius	18	Aurich	68-1027
HIPPERT, Joseph	15	Germsheim	69-0067
HIPPOLSTEINER, Wilh.	21	DDirmstein	69-0229
or Duemstein			
HIRDTFELDER, Wilhelm	22	Balingen	69-0848
HIRN, Louisa	44	Ludwigsburg	68-0957

NAME	AGE	RESIDENCE	YR-LIST
HIRN, Ludwig	34	Zweibruecken	71-0821
HIRSCH, Andr.	46	Suchel	70-0272
HIRSCH, Caecilie	23	Gneien	69-0672
HIRSCH, Fred.	16	Wagenstadt	68-0957
HIRSCH, Josef	36	Markeisenstein	70-0384
Catharine 29, Mathias 2			
HIRSCH, Leonore	17	Emden	70-100
HIRSCH, Max	60	Bruesken	71-0736
HIRSCH, Moses	20	Steinfurt	68-0939
HIRSCH, Nathan	57	Darmstadt	69-1059
Roeschen 56, Josef 27, Samuel 9, Dora 19, Rika 8			
HIRSCH, Siegmund	25	Altona	71-0581
HIRSCH, Thekla	28	Bernearth	71-0643
Johanna 27			
HIRSCHAUER, S.	26	Grosseier	71-0226
HIRSCHBERG, David	28	Zwerten-Zwesten	69-1396
HIRSCHBERG, Gustav	20	Berlin	68-0456
HIRSCHBERGER, Heinr.	29	Thorn	70-0569
HIRSCHELMANN, Anna	22	Weimar	69-1076
HIRSCHFELD, Elisabeth	41	Colima	70-0452
Johannes 4, Hermann 2			
HIRSCHFELD, Marcus	17	Loebau	68-0760
HIRSCHFELD, Theodor	25	Bremen	70-0223
HIRSCHI, Rosine	18	Matrisch	68-0610
Christine 20			
HIRSCHING, Gerhard	45	Urbach	71-0684
Friederike 40, Julius 17, Hermann 15, Wilhelmine 8, Conrad 4			
HIRSCHMUELLER, Georg	24	Biechheim	70-0148
HIRSCHSPIEL, Martin	27	Baiern	69-0559
Elisabeth 25, Elisabeth 11 months			
HIRSEKORN, Paul	20	Stargard	69-1004
HIRT, Therese	18	Dietingen	70-0223
HIRZ, Conrad	55	Eichelsachsen	69-0015
HISCHE, Fritz	20	Linden	69-0015
HISS, Peter	22	Leitgettern	69-1319
HITTNER, Joseph	26	Mocknitz	70-0329
HITZ, Jos.	20	Schmeissingen	69-0490
HITZEMANN, Ernestine	14	Bueckeburg	69-0292
HITZEROTH, Wilh.	19	Dittershausen	68-0982
HOBBIE, Gerdt	60	Etzel	68-0907
HOBELBOLD, William	57	Heimarshausen	69-1212
Magdalena 56, Elise 28, Gertrude 26, Wilh. 24			
HOBELMANN, Friedrich	28	Boerninghausen	68-0566
Caroline 28, Friedrich 7, Louise 1			
HOBELMANN, Wilhelmine	12	Hannover	71-0479
HOBENSTREIT, Hermann	39	Weimar	70-0355
HOBERT, Johann	65	Weimar	69-1319
Elisabeth 48, Bernhard 11, Heinrich 7			
HOBISCHKE, Caroline	38	Leekatz	69-0592
HOCH, Jacob	16	Sprendlingen	69-0923
HOCH, Martin	28	Boll	69-0162
HOCHEISEN, Marie	37	Stuttgart	69-1086
Ferdinand 12			
HOCHHAUSS, Emilie	20	Clausmarbach	70-0204
HOCHKIRCH, Friederike	20	Leipzig	68-0566
HOCHMUTH, Christine	23	Detmold	69-0572

NAME	AGE	RESIDENCE	YR-LIST
Friedrich 14			
HOCHREIN, Anna	22	Grossbrach	68-0957
HOCHREITER, Georg	22	Clausen	71-0456
Anna 19			
HOCHSCHILD, Mich.	15	Darmstadt	70-0170
HOCHSTADT, Friedrich	26	Grimminghausen	71-0736
HOCHSTELTER, Herm.	21	Ulm	68-1002
HOCHSTRASSER, And.	23	Erzingen	71-0492
HOCHT, Isaac	15	Birkenfeld	71-0492
HOCHWART, Franc.	21	Teuz	71-0581
HOCHWEBER, Engel	25	Leustetten	69-0490
Balbina 28, Bernhard 9 months			
HOCK, Mary	16	Pfaeffingen	70-0089
HOCKENTIED, Josef	27	Teichdorf	69-0229
HOCKER, Henriette	28	Dielingen	69-0583
HODDE, Henriette	16	Westrup	71-0821
HODDEN, Johann	27	Horsten	71-0492
HODDERSEN, Hg.	14	Brake	69-1011
HOECHE, Guenther	33	Schernberg	68-0625
Augusta 32, Antonia 9, oscar 8, Louis 7 months			
HOECHNER, Joh.	26	Schoelbach	68-0770
HOECHST, Carl	12	Sandenbach	71-0363
Math. 9			
HOECHT, Johann	16	Hagenach	69-1076
HOECK, Rud.	36	Goettingen	70-0178
Anna 23			
HOECKELBERG, C.	25	Schwarzdorf	70-0204
HOECKELMANN, Carl	18	Schwaigstorf	68-0852
HOECKER, Joh. Wilh.	16	Versmold	68-1002
HOEDT, Fridr.	21	Heidelberg	69-1004
HOEFER, Emilie	21	Ottowind	68-0786
HOEFLER, Melchior	20	Duschhausen	68-0957
HOEFLING, Johann	27	Ostfriesland	70-0184
Catharine 23, Johanne Elise 23, Jacob 22			
HOEFNER, August	27	Meiningen	71-0429
HOEFNER, Wilhelm	16	Meiningen	68-0852
HOEFS, Mathilde	19	Wangeritz	71-0581
Anna 16, Julius 14			
HOEFT, August	19	Bremen	69-0798
HOEFT, Claus	17	Essel	70-0452
HOEFTMEYER, Friedrich	54	Hannover	71-0429
Anna 56, Charlotte 15, Margarethe 15			
HOEGER, Christiane	20	Helmbrecht	71-0821
HOEGER, Johannes	20	Overlach	68-0625
HOEGERT, Ludwig	25	Dessau	68-0707
HOEHL, Johann	53	Geismar	68-0786
Elisabeth 52			
HOEHL, Veronica	17	Steinwand	68-0610
HOEHLE, Auguste	17	Erlangen	71-0429
HOEHLE, Louise	29	Waldeck	68-0566
Rosine 4, Friedrich 3			
HOEHLITZ, Carl	23	Sachsen Meining	69-0321
Wendelina 19			
HOEHN, Ch.	24	Eppelsheim	70-0170
HOEHN, Christine	17	Zillbach	68-0661
HOEHNE, Carl	34	Waldeck	68-0566
HOEHNE, Christ.	26	Hessen	70-0508
Wilhelmine 25, Christ. 3, Louise 9 months			

NAME	AGE	RESIDENCE	YR-LIST
HOEHNE, Minna	18	Weimar	69-1059
HOELDER, Georg	22	Grabenstetten	69-1086
HOELE, Minna	23	Ruhla	68-0707
Selmi 2, Anna 11 months			
HOELLER, Ernst	19	Sulingen	69-0162
HOELMKE, Dorette	20	Lemstedt	71-0581
Carl 14			
HOELSCHER, Joseph	17	Esse	68-0982
HOELTKE, Carl	18	Wietersheim	71-0521
HOELZER, Christine	25	Mergentheim	71-0456
HOENE, Hermann	27	Oete	69-0547
HOENINGER, Leonhard	15	Oberndorf	71-0736
Veronica 12			
HOEPER, Julius	30	Bremen	69-1309
HOEPFLINGER, Emma	18	Ludwigsburg	70-1035
HOEPFNER, Emilie	24	Oldenburg	71-1046
HOEPKEN, Henriette	20	Bielefeld	69-1309
HOEPPNER, Elise	17	Bremen	69-1396
HOEPPNER, Ferdinand	18	Wetterborn	69-0429
HOEPPNER, Gustav	24	Ahsen	68-1298
HOERETH, Albrecht	19	Pechgraben	68-0707
Elisabeth 13			
HOERIG, Ernst	17	Gohlis	71-0681
HOERLEIN, Ulrich	70	Hermersheim	69-0572
HOERLER, Christian	28	New Orleans	69-0672
HOERR, John	19	Kl. Heubach	71-0456
HOERSCH, Peter	16	Boxheim	68-0939
HOERSTER, Caroline	59	Solingen	71-0733
Georg 22			
HOESCHLE, Julie	19	Untertuerkheim	68-0907
HOESLI, Jost	30	of the Pluthe	68-0661
Catharina 24			
HOESSNER, Johann	37	Haiterbach	68-0456
Sophie 37, Augusta 9, Elisabeth 7, Sophie 9 months			
HOETTGER, Simon	18	Schieda	68-314
HOEVER, Mathilde	20	Lemwerder	70-1066
HOEYER, Christiane	20	Helmbrecht	71-0821
HOF, Eduard	38	Berlin	69-0542
Friedrich 9			
HOF, Gottlob	24	Oettisheim	68-0610
HOFBAUER, Andreas		Oberschulz	69-0771
HOFEMANN, Johann	26	Coburg	69-0672
HOFER, Adolf Joh.	34	Arni	71-0226
Cath. 37, Ida 5, Gottlieb 3, Johannes 2, Catharina 6 months			
HOFER, Andreas	21	Wien	69-0560
HOFERER, Gustav	20	Ottenhoefen	69-1076
Fidel 24			
HOFFARTH, Anna	43	Molsberg	71-0581
Philipp 17, Anna 15, Johann 9, Ernst 5			
HOFFERBERTH, Jacob	29	Guenterfuerth	69-0968
HOFFERT, Eva Marie	24	Darmstadt	69-1212
HOFFMANN, Andreas	37	Schlakenrentz	68-0707
HOFFMANN, Anna	28	Birkenreuth	68-0907
Anna 9 months			
HOFFMANN, Anna	16	Reichenberg	68-0661
HOFFMANN, August	48	Halle	68-0419
Charlotte 40, Karl 17, Louise 13			

NAME	AGE	RESIDENCE	YR-LIST
HOFFMANN, Carl	19	Koeinigsberg	70-0443
HOFFMANN, Catharine	17	Oberkolzau	68-0852
HOFFMANN, Catharine	18	Romersreck	68-0939
HOFFMANN, Catharine	18	Cassel	71-0521
HOFFMANN, Christine	47	Leipzig	71-0733
HOFFMANN, Conrad	20	Baden	70-1161
HOFFMANN, David	19	Rieden	69-1086
HOFFMANN, Elisa	25	Rieden	69-1086
HOFFMANN, Emil	20	Chemnitz	71-0456
HOFFMANN, Franz	17	Scharmbeck	71-0521
HOFFMANN, Friedr.	20	Erfurt	68-0753
HOFFMANN, Friedrich	28	Haidengruen	69-0162
HOFFMANN, Friedrich	22	Gempertshausen	68-0566
HOFFMANN, Georg	33	Darmstadt	68-1298
HOFFMANN, Georg	30	Altenstein	68-0014
HOFFMANN, Georg	24	Goeritz	68-0907
Louise 19			
HOFFMANN, Gustav	30	Jassy	68-0884
HOFFMANN, Heinrich	12	Mittelseeman	70-1035
HOFFMANN, Helene	56	Niemburg-Nienbu	69-0162
HOFFMANN, Helene	52	Dorum	68-0566
HOFFMANN, Henriette	44	Greiz	69-0968
Anna 17, Richard 15, Erwin 13, Wilhelm 9, Paul 8, Hermine 6, Theodor 5			
HOFFMANN, Hilma	20	Berlin	71-0582
HOFFMANN, J. Dorothea	49	Christes	68-0610
Joh. Aug. 16, Joh. Gg.Theod. 16			
HOFFMANN, Jacob	31	Ruith	69-1059
HOFFMANN, Jacob	21	Bonfeld	68-0661
HOFFMANN, Joh.	30	Muenchhausen	71-0821
HOFFMANN, Joh. H.	23	Richstein	69-1212
HOFFMANN, Johann	26	Coburg	69-0672
HOFFMANN, Johann	31	Schaitz	69-0848
HOFFMANN, Johann	33	Neustadt a/H.	68-1006
HOFFMANN, Johann	21	Wistelgan	68-0707
HOFFMANN, Johann	44	Perseberg	68-0820
Catharina 44, Johann 15			
HOFFMANN, Johann	77	Steinsdorf	71-0429
HOFFMANN, Johannes	24	Bodewitz	68-0820
HOFFMANN, John	33	S. Weimar	69-0848
Elise 23, Johann 3, Heinrich 9 months			
HOFFMANN, Joseph	58	Krautheim	68-0939
Anastasia 58			
HOFFMANN, Julius	23	Stollberg	68-0939
HOFFMANN, Louis	17	Herborn	68-0982
HOFFMANN, Louise	21	Nassau	69-0559
HOFFMANN, Margarethe	24	Steinheim	69-0848
HOFFMANN, Maria	17	Sachsen Meining	69-0321
Juliane 23, Georg Johannes 34, Friedrich 17			
HOFFMANN, Martin	24	Loschenrod	69-1309
Marie 21			
HOFFMANN, Mathilde	22	Dieppigheim	71-0581
HOFFMANN, Max	15	Walldorf	68-0939
HOFFMANN, Paul	47	Valparaiso	69-0079
HOFFMANN, Philipp	43	Darmstadt	69-0321
HOFFMANN, Regina	21	Bachen/Buchen	68-0456
Julius 16			
HOFFMANN, Rosa	46	Gramaden	71-0479

NAME	AGE	RESIDENCE	YR-LIST
Pauline 5			
HOFFMANN, Wendelin	21	Neustadt	69-1076
HOFFMANN, Wilhelm	46	Gosslar	68-0707
HOFFMANN, Wilhelm	17	Else	68-0753
HOFFMANNS, Louis	17	Hildburghauen	70-0178
HOFFMEISTER, Anton	43	New Haven	70-0031
Amalie 39			
HOFFMEISTER, Dorothea	63	Lesse	70-1035
HOFFMEISTER, Friedrich	53	Dransfeld	68-0939
Dorette 13			
HOFFMEISTER, Heinrich	38	Essen	69-1059
Caroline 39, Cathrine 22, Mathilde 9			
HOFFSTAEDLER, Georg	25	Luebbeke	68-0884
HOFGESANG, John	27	Essen	70-0170
HOFHEINZ, Jacob	24	Guglingen	68-0647
HOFING, Jacob	30	Hopert	68-0982
Anna 20			
HOFINGER, Andr.	28	Scharding	69-0292
HOFLING, Julius	25	Thueringen	69-0848
HOFMANN, Alb.	16	Erlangen	71-0681
HOFMANN, Amalie	19	Bayern	70-0148
HOFMANN, August	30	Fotha\ Gotha	68-0852
HOFMANN, Cacelia	18	Heimbrechts/Bay	69-0547
HOFMANN, Caroline	29	Frautzenbach	69-0592
HOFMANN, Caroline	34	Zuerich	70-0355
HOFMANN, Catharine	17	Helmbrechts	69-0923
HOFMANN, Christine	24	Solms	68-0852
HOFMANN, Conrad	22	Bieberbach	71-0429
HOFMANN, Emilie	23	Raasdorf	71-0363
HOFMANN, Flore	16	Obersosolau	70-0508
HOFMANN, Geo.	36	Oberschmitten	69-1011
HOFMANN, Georg	24	Trichenhoefen	69-1076
Catharine 27, Sophie 1, Rosina 4			
HOFMANN, Georg	24	S. Meiningen	69-0848
HOFMANN, George	38	Heringen	68-0661
Anna 34, George 9 months			
HOFMANN, Joh.	20	Neusler	71-0363
HOFMANN, Johann	32	Niederohmen	69-0592
HOFMANN, Johanna	23	Katzenelnbogen	68-0982
HOFMANN, Joseph	19	Dittlofrod	68-1002
HOFMANN, Mar. Th.	17	Fulda	68-0610
HOFMANN, Meta	18	Scharmbeck	68-0957
HOFMANN, Peter	25	Darmstadt	69-0923
HOFMANN, Phil.	26	Weisbach	71-0300
HOFMEISTER, Anton	23	Osterburgen	71-0492
HOFREITER, Gg.	22	Sandshut	71-0581
HOFSCHULTE, Bernhard	28	Hannover	70-0178
HOFSTETTER, Catharine	23	Brueckenau	68-0760
HOGE, Friedrich	39	Wittichow	68-0314
Sophie 34, Bertha 9, August 7, Wilhelm 4, Ferdinand 2			
HOGESTRAAT, Diedrich	14	Au	68-1027
HOGREFE, Heinrich	16	Rotenburg	68-0939
HOGREFE, Johannes	17	Nedderavebergen	68-0566
HOGREFE, Wilh.	17	Oyle	71-0300
Marie 9			
HOH, Auguste	25	Hohenlenben	71-0581
HOHEISEL, Hinr.	49	Schellendorf	71-0363

NAME	AGE	RESIDENCE	YR-LIST
Katharina 49, Marie 22, Floria 18, Anna 14, Heinrich 9, Franz 6			
HOHENBIESTER, Ernst	17	Buer	69-0542
HOHENSEE, Theodor	18	Konari/Prussia	69-0547
HOHENSTEIN, Carsten	17	Brakenheim	70-0223
HOHER, Theresia	17	Schoenbach	68-0661
HOHL, Christian	18	Hohenbrach	69-0592
HOHLEN, Behrend	32	Hohenkirchen	68-0314
HOHLWEG, H. F.	17	Bruchhausen	70-0443
HOHM, Heinrich	23	Staeten	68-0770
Marie 26, Appolonia 3			
HOHM, Lucas	23	Eisenbach	69-0162
HOHMANN, Caspar	18	Unsleben	68-1298
HOHMANN, Eduard	28	Rudolstadt	71-0429
Henriette 23, Therese 61, Therese 5, Carl 3			
HOHMANN, Felix	27	Cassel	69-0771
HOHMANN, Ferd.	47	Dessau	71-0733
HOHMANN, Ferd.	47	Gr. Lubs	71-0733
Anna 13, Wilhelmine 11, Emilie 9			
HOHMANN, Friedrich	15	Borstel	69-0229
Heinrich 16			
HOHMANN, Hermann	25	Waldeck	71-0821
HOHMANN, Isidor	30	Lambach/Lausbac	69-0583
HOHMANN, Johanna	18	Wickers	68-0610
HOHMANN, Pauline	20	Grossheppach	71-0492
HOHMANN, Walpurga	26	Vallenda	71-0581
HOHMANN, Wilhelm	25	Bruch	69-0015
HOHMEIER, Louis	28	S. Francisco	71-1046
HOHN, Babette	20	Unterfranken	69-0798
HOHN, H.	22	Mecdorf-Meidorf	70-1035
Anna 24, Baby 6 months			
HOHN, Herm.	23	Repplin	68-0314
HOHNBAUM, Emma	25	Geisenhoehn	69-1004
HOHNBRINK, Joh.	17	Osnabrueck	69-1319
HOHNER, Johann	29	Oberfranken	70-0523
HOHNER, Philipp	49	Treichlingen	68-0852
HOHNLIN, Barbara	32	Mundingen	68-0884
HOHREIS, Julius	20	Ludingwoerth	71-0363
HOHWIESNER, Clemens	24	Bremen	70-0148
HOITZ, Adelheid	24	Roemdorf	71-0712
HOLB, Gottlob	20	Raidewangen	69-0338
HOLB, Philipp	15	Muensterappel	70-0443
HOLBORN, Carl	19	Goettingen	69-0672
HOLDERHUS, Christine	28	Langen	69-0292
HOLGER, Johannes	17	Habenessel	71-0492
Maria A. 25			
HOLKENBRINK, Franz	19	Winkelstetten	68-0852
HOLL, Cathrine	55	Scheckingen	71-0456
HOLL, Hermann	27	Homburg	71-0821
HOLL, Kath.	22	Wickenrode	71-0363
HOLLANDKUNTZ, Marg.	24	Oberschonau	68-0661
HOLLE, Caroline	17	Cadenhagen	71-0429
HOLLE, Catharine	20	Ellenberg	68-1027
HOLLE, Johann	40	Hohenzollern	70-0031
HOLLE, Johanne	24	Cloppenburg	69-0208
Louise 2			
HOLLE, Louis	18	Cassel	70-0204

NAME	AGE	RESIDENCE	YR-LIST
HOLLEN, Marten	47	St. Francisco	69-1004
Babette 37, Cary 12, Saul 11, Clara 5, Sigi 3			
HOLLENBACH, Adam	22	Wertheim	68-0820
HOLLERBUSCH, Elise	20	Fuerth	71-0479
HOLLERMANN, Auguster	19	Schoenlanke	71-0821
HOLLEROTH, Anna	22	Jade	69-0542
HOLLKAMP, Caroline	27	Quelle	69-1086
HOLLMANN, Heinrich	25	Brake	69-0592
HOLLMANN, Marie	21	Lage	68-1027
HOLLMANN, TH.	11	Seidenburg	71-0393
HOLLMANN, Wilhelm	28	Mueschen	68-0939
HOLLMICH, Joh.	38	Bremen	70-1142
HOLLSCHER, Wilhelm	25	Herben	68-0939
HOLLSTEIN, Georg	32	Dettensee	71-0792
Therese 31, Justine 3			
HOLLWEDEL, Johann	27	Bremen	71-0643
Louise 25			
HOLLWEDEL, Wm.	30	Bremen	69-0841
Anna 32			
HOLLY, Anna	22	Neustadt	71-0479
HOLM, Gust. H.	29	Dresden	68-0820
HOLM, Johann	20	Bremen	70-0272
HOLSCHER, Joseph	16	Hannover	68-0907
HOLSTEIN, Joh. D.	18	Gilfershausen	68-0610
HOLSTEN, Diedr.	17	Warpsdorf	70-0223
HOLTEN, Georg	19	Oberschupt	69-1059
HOLTERMANN, H.	36	Hannover	70-0308
Anna 33, John 9, Mary 2			
HOLTHAUSEN, Hermann	34	Werden	68-0907
Henriette 30, Elise 3, Hermann 10 months			
HOLTHUSEN, Arend	16	Brinkum	69-0457
HOLTHUSEN, Margarethe	16	Leeste	69-0457
HOLTHUSEN, Wilhelm	23	Masel	68-0820
HOLTHUUS, Diedrich	28	Hannover	68-0625
Margaret 28, Louise 5, Baby daughter 6 months			
HOLTJE, Herm	15	Rechsum	71-0736
HOLTKAMP, Engelina	22	Muehlendorf	69-0429
HOLTKAMP, Joh. Cath.	24	Dono	68-0820
HOLTMANN, Anna	25	Steinfeld	69-1004
HOLTMANN, Anton	12	Laufenselden	68-1027
HOLTZ, Adolph	23	Steinstrass	68-0661
HOLTZ, Carl August	26	Treptow	68-0419
HOLTZ, Peter Alb.	28	Guszen	68-0661
HOLWEDEL, Aug.	23	Bremen	70-1066
HOLZ, Franz	27	Duesseldorf	68-0707
HOLZ, Mathilde	27	Henkenhagen	71-0456
HOLZAPFEL, Wilh.	23	Wetzlar	68-0786
Elisabeth 26, Elisabeth 6 months			
HOLZER, Adele	22	Wien	68-0982
HOLZER, Wilhelmine	49	Lahr	69-0784
Max 17, Marie 9, Emil 5			
HOLZHAUSEN, Mart.	40	Naumburg	71-0363
Elisabeth 42, Catharina 16			
HOLZINGER, Anna	23	Hundsbach	71-0789
HOLZINGER, Joseph	34	Unterfranken	69-1309
Therese 25, Michael 5, Johann 3			
HOLZKAMP, Bertha	22	St. Gallen	71-0492
Lidia 9 months			
HOLZKAMP, Carl	24	Oerlinghausen	68-0661
HOLZNER, Carl	26	Amorbach	68-1002
HOLZSCHNEIDER, Will.	50	Crefeld	63-0244
Agnes 40, Adolph Charles 18, Francis Joseph 17, Johanne M. 16, John E. 8, Hein			
HOLZTRAUER, Carl	52	Volmerdingen	70-1035
HOLZWARD, D.	49	Soest	68-1027
HOMANN, Adolph	37	Hoerde	69-0559
HOMANN, Josef	34	New York	69-0560
HOMANN, Meta	21	Brake	70-1003
HOMBERG, Carl	35	Alfeld	70-1142
HOMBERG, Helena	31	Barmen	69-1309
HOMEYER, Carl	57	New Haven	69-0572
HOMEYER, Herm.	19	Lippe Detmold	70-0223
HOMEYER, Johanne	21	Bederkesa	69-1059
HOMPE, Friedrich	18	Hannover	71-0821
Charlotte 20			
HOMUTH, Aug.	26	Traumburg	68-0753
Wilhelmine 32, Charlotte 53, Ernestine 17, Carl 12, Emil 11 months			
HOMUTH, Carl	17	Sonneborn	68-0456
HONES, Ludwig	15	Creuznach	69-0457
HONS, Johann	48	Hustede	69-0229
Becka 45, Adelheid 22, Margaret 9			
HONZ, Bertha	27	Basel	68-0456
HOOFF, Wilhelm	31	Barntrup	69-0968
Charlotte 29, Hermann 3, August 9 months			
HOOG, Aug.	30	Sulbach	71-0393
HOOK, Albert	34	Berlin	71-0684
HOOLZER, John	26	Saarbrueck	63-0244
Margarethe 26, John 4, Magdalene 3, Charles 7 months			
HOOPS, Geesche	22	Stellenfelde	68-0707
HOOS, Johann	56	Steina	70-0204
HOPET, Mathias	34	Boehmen	70-1161
Therese 38, Thomas 7, Wenzel 6 months			
HOPF, Anna	20	Hannover	70-0378
HOPF, Georg Peter	33	Hirschendorf	68-0419
HOPF, Julius	35	Berlin	69-0771
Auguste 29, Bernhard 5, Hermann 3, Hedwig 11 months			
HOPFENGAERTNER, A.	30	Bremen	68-0647
Bertha 2			
HOPFENMUELLER, L.	18	Mainroth	71-0429
HOPMANN, John	16	Eitzendorf	70-1003
HOPP, Christine	27	Neufringen	71-0643
HOPP, Henriette	23	Dolgen	69-0560
Gustav 5			
HOPPA, B.	23	Wittenssen	70-1142
HOPPE, Charlotte	60	Leseringen	71-0581
Louise 27			
HOPPE, Johannes	16	Heimarshausen	70-0523
HOPPE, Mathilde	26	Solingen	70-1055
HOPPE, Theresia	31	Bremervoerde	68-0456
HOPPE, Wilhelmine	21	Fritzlar	71-0736
Elise 9			
HOPPENSTROCK, G.	19	Luegde	68-1027
HOPPER, Marie	20	Geestendorf	69-0968
HOPPNER, Albert	33	M. Friedland	68-0907
HOPS, Joh.	17	Hagenah	69-0321

NAME	AGE	RESIDENCE	YR-LIST
HOPSIKER, Fried.	18	Ueppentrupp	70-0443
HORA, Wenzel	35	Boehmen	69-1309
HORAK, Pauline	23	Caslau	71-0643
Carl 11 months			
HORCHLER, Wilhelmine	22	Landau	68-0566
Marie 11 months			
HORCPI, Mathaus	35	Neudorf	70-0329
HORDE, Wilhelm	28	L. Detmold	70-0272
HORENMANN, Johanne	24	Blexen	69-1396
HORG, Joseph	26	Gmuend	69-0208
HORIG, Carl	24	Braunschweig	68-1006
HORKEDER, Magd.	54	Tyrol	70-1011
Mary 19, Alisia 17			
HORLACHER, Michel	18	Wolpersdorf	69-0560
HORLINGS, Anna	18	Tedinghausen	68-0647
HORMACHER, Marie	20	Schwaben	69-1309
HORMANN, Wilh.	16	Stolzenau	68-0786
HORMANN, Wilhelm	14	Nenndorf	69-0268
HORMEL, C.	26	Roth	69-0338
HORMEL, Ernst	21	Roth	70-0170
Cathr. 19			
HORMEL, Georg	27	Schweinsburg	69-0321
HORMEYER, Marie	20	Ellwuerden	68-0884
HORMUELLER, Eugen	39	Muenchen	70-1003
HORN, Anna	20	Leipzig	68-1298
HORN, Carl	28	H. Darmstadt	70-1003
HORN, Christ.	18	Sontra	68-0820
HORN, Engel	30	Herford	71-0492
Heinrich 11 months			
HORN, Franz	56	Germersheim	71-0429
Marie 58			
HORN, Friedrich	19	Hannover	70-0682
HORN, Fritz	14	Emden	70-0508
HORN, Johanna	30	Boehmen	68-0456
HORN, Johannes	32	Schwaben	70-0816
Magdalena 33			
HORN, Oscar	19	Halle	70-0308
HORN, Pauline	17	Steinau	71-0363
HORN, Peter	25	Alsenz	68-1002
HORN, Reinh.	55	Elbing	69-1363
HORN, Sophie	32	Stedesdorf	68-0907
Minna 7, Heinrich 6, anna 5, Bernhard 3, Hermann 2			
HORNBERGER, Gottlieb	23	Kirchheim	68-0534
HORNBERGER, Math.	25	Aaich	69-1421
HORNEFF, Martha	48	Rothenburg	68-0907
HORNFINCKER, Henriette	22	Steinbach	71-0643
HORNICH, Wilhelm	28	Barmen	68-1006
HORNIKEL, Lorenz	38	Dittmar	70-0508
HORNUNG, Wilhelm	17	Friedrichsthal	68-0456
HORROWITZ, Leopold	26	Durmaul	70-1003
HORSCHSCHRAER, H.	35	Bochterbeck	69-0429
HORSMEIER, Carl	17	Harverstedt-Wes	70-0006
HORST, Wilhelmine	18	Gelnhausen	68-0707
Ludwig 2			
HORSTERINK, Johanne	27	Bielefeld	71-0363
HORSTMANN, Aug.	20	Niese	68-0610
HORSTMANN, August	30	Bremen	69-0268

NAME	AGE	RESIDENCE	YR-LIST
HORSTMANN, Gerhard	14	Cloppenburg	68-0661
HORSTMANN, Gustus	12	Burgdam	68-0760
HORSTMANN, Heinr.	18	Osnabrueck	68-1002
HORTERMANN, Martin	54	Thueringen	69-0848
Elise 45			
HORTH, Ludwig	17	Hasselbach	68-0707
HORVIND, Sophie	26	Gronau	70-0272
Christ. 24			
HORWISCH, F.	24	Bautzen	70-0523
HOSI, Johann	14	Cuxhaven	71-0492
HOSINER, Jos.	30	Freistadt	69-0050
HOSNEBER, Ferd.	28	Vogtreichenb.	68-1006
HOSPACH, Johann	23	Herlingen	70-0184
HOSS, Johann	23	Coblenz	69-0784
HOSSAESS, Christian	19	Almersbach,Wuer	69-0547
HOST, Magdalene	20	Westernhausen	70-0223
HOTING, Diedrich	29	Oldenburg	70-0308
HOTOP, Heinrich	18	Gifhorn	69-0560
HOTTER, Franz	28	Mayrhofen	69-0338
HOTTER, Mich.	24	Austria	70-0170
HOTTINGER, Joh.	34	Vixburgh	69-1363
HOTTINGER, Philippine	26	Waldshut	68-0314
HOTZEN, Maria	24	Stolzenau	68-0786
HOTZMANN, Marie	17	Domnitz	71-0581
HOVERKAMP, Friedr.	52	Borgholzhausen	71-0393
Caroline 61, Marie 16			
HOWENER, Gerh.	60	Hannover	69-1004
Elise 55, Heinrich 20, Gerh. 12			
HOWERMEYER, Therese	29	Meddingen	68-0982
HOYER, August	14	Coxhafen	69-0672
HOYER, Christian	16	Bremen	69-0182
HOYER, Johann	15	Molbergen	69-0968
Elisabeth 18			
HOYER, Wilhelmine	23	Bremerhaven	70-0031
HRUSCHKA, Adalb.	28	Babina	71-0393
Anna 28, Barb. 9 months			
HUBER, Anna	21	Wagenstadt	71-0226
HUBER, Anton	41	Baiern	69-0559
Elisabeth 37, Anna 20, Catharina 15, Christian 7, Elisabeth 2, Magdalene 10 mo			
HUBER, Babette	24	Schweiz	70-1066
Jacob 8			
HUBER, Bonifacius	37	Tuttlingen	69-0923
HUBER, Carl	14	Muenchen	69-0015
HUBER, Carl	21	Eggenstein	69-1396
HUBER, Conrad	66	Neudingen	68-0625
Conrad 27, Joachim 13, Franziska 18			
HUBER, Georg	26	Hamweiler	71-0684
HUBER, Johann	25	Warschau	69-0050
HUBER, Johannes	36	Zuerich	71-0363
Barbara 30, Gotthelf 5, Mathilde 3, Gotthold 2, Frida 11 months			
HUBER, Josef	19	Falkenstein	71-0393
HUBER, Kilian	26	Waldshut	68-0314
Constancia 24			
HUBER, Magdalena	35	Muenchen	69-0542
HUBER, Martin	30	Sartein	71-0581
HUBER, Rosa	22	Mannheim	70-0148
HUBER, Therese	26	Waldkirch	69-0229

NAME	AGE	RESIDENCE	YR-LIST
HUBERICH, Rud.	23	Gschwend	68-0957
HUBERT, Henriette	20	Erpolzheim	71-0429
HUBERTH, Marg.	26	Tuchensfelden	69-0784
HUBY, Carl	39	Boehmen	70-0184
Dorothea 37, Barbara 14, Katharina 9, Carl 7, Anna 3, Mariea 11 months			
HUCHTHAUSEN, Friedr.	32	Wangelstedt	68-0647
HUCKE, Minna	22	Buer	69-0542
HUE, Sophie	16	Rothenburg	68-0939
HUEBEL, Peter	18	Leimbach	69-0798
HUEBNER, Barbara	26	Gmuenden	69-0457
HUEBNER, Carl	23	Libau	69-0784
HUEBNER, Catharine	32	Siewershoefe	69-0784
Caroline 18			
HUEBNER, Johann Bapt.	35	Oberfranken	70-0523
HUEBNER, Julia	27	Naseband	69-0338
HUEBSCH, Sophie	21	Krasolup	71-0479
HUEBSCHER, Louise	39	Nuernberg	68-1027
HUEFFEMEIER, Christ.	27	Wesenstedt	68-0884
HUEFNER, Josefine	25	Homburg	70-0148
Scholastica 23, Marie 21			
HUEGEL, Johann	19	Krautheim	71-0736
HUEHMANN, Johann	21	Altenmanborg	71-0712
HUEHNEL, Gust.	20	Dittersbach	70-0170
HUEHNER, Georg	50	Buchholz	71-0492
HUEHNER, Wilhelmine	16	Buchholz	71-0492
Heinrich F. 15			
HUEHNKEN, Meta	28	New York	69-1004
Anna 7, Chr. 10 months			
HUEHNKEN, Meta	22	Hannover	69-1004
HUELLE, Ernst	42	Erfurt	69-1212
HUELLE, Meta	20	Wersabe	68-0884
HUELLER, Johann	26	Gr. Zappel	69-0547
Pauline 20			
HUELS, Fr.	32	Wiesens	68-0884
HUELS, Heinrich	25	Lette	69-0229
HUELSEMANN, Marie	26	Cantrup	69-0771
Anna 4			
HUELSMANN, Anna	29	Ostfriesland	69-0771
Marie 3, Gertrude 11 months			
HUELSMANN, Franz	24	Wewelsburg	68-1002
HUELSMANN, Minna	16	Wesenstedt	68-0884
HUELSMANN, Sophie	28	Blasheim	69-0771
HUELSMEYER, John	20	Buer	68-0957
HUELSTEBERG, Johann	40	Vollersode	71-0429
HUEMER, Johann G.	22	Nuernberg	71-0492
HUEMERLIN, Louise	54	Berlin	69-0050
Hedwig 16, Pauline 18			
HUEMMLER, Joseph	25	Wadersloh	68-0982
HUENCKE, Friedr.	25	Helgendorf	71-0581
HUENECKE, Marie	24	Holtrup	69-0162
HUENEKE, Marg.	24	Okel	68-0884
Adelh. 18			
HUENIKE, Margarethe	37	Thedinghausen	68-0661
Hermann 76, Hermann 8			
HUESENER, Friedrich	17	Halden	69-0429
Hermann 15			
HUESER, Mathilde	45	Hennhut	70-1023
HUESGEN, Peter	40	Leavenworth	63-0244

NAME	AGE	RESIDENCE	YR-LIST
Lena 30, Catharina 6, Kathi 4			
HUESING, Bertha	14	Loxstedt	71-0643
HUETHER, Maria	18	Hochheim	68-0566
HUETTEL, Elise	20	Carlsruhe	69-0798
HUETTENHAUSEN, Anna	18	Hamburg	69-0560
HUETTENMUELLER, C.	38	Frankfurt/M	71-0363
Johannette 36			
HUETTER, Caroline	14	Gerahausen	69-1212
HUETTIG, Juliane	30	Zittau	68-1027
HUETTNER, Emma	24	Regensburg	68-1002
HUETZEL, Reinhd.	20	Deggingen	68-0610
HUFE, Heinrich	30	Cantrup	68-0456
HUFLINGER, Marie	29	Nuernberg	68-0770
HUG, Edw.	22	Erlangen	71-0143
HUG, J.	22	Luzern	71-0479
HUG, Maria	31	Altsimonswald	68-0786
HUGE, Heinrich	16	Babber	71-0429
HUHN, August	18	Ahl	71-0456
HUHN, Georgine	22	Liebenstein	68-0534
HUHN, Heinrich		Grossmansrode	69-0457
HUHN, Ottilie	17	Amoeneburg	68-0939
HUHWALKER, H. G.	50	Hamburg	68-0610
HULDA, Antonia	34	Kuttenberg	71-0789
Francisca 27			
HULL, Johann	16	Steinau	69-0457
HULLER, Hermann	23	Lengelsheim	69-0547
HULS, Ad. Gottfr.	23	R.B. Coeln	68-0610
Cater. 18, Sybilla 16			
HULSMANN, Johann	45	Waren	69-0923
Marie 32			
HUMANN, Ernst	26	Goeditz	71-0681
HUMBERG, Adolph	21	Mastricht	69-0583
HUMMEBERG, Babette	25	Zeisendorf	70-1035
HUMMEL, Anton	17	Weissenstein	69-1004
HUMMEL, Aug.	26	Weissenberg	68-0820
HUMMEL, Elisab.	29	Duerkheim	71-1046
HUMMEL, Kunigunde	24	Weier	68-0852
Therese 1			
HUMMEL, Ludwig	53	Oberlenningen	68-0456
Christiane 56, Christiane 19, Jacob 11, Catharine 11			
HUMMELKENBERG, C.	24	Guetersloh	71-0456
HUMMER, Michael	31	Unterfranken	69-0321
HUMMERL, Francisca	24	Weissenstein	71-0429
HUMMLER, Martin	35	Stuttgardt	69-0457
Heinrich 9			
HUMPFELD, Simon	28	Dettmold	69-0542
Anna 54, Hermann 7			
HUMRICH, Susanne	19	Wietselters	69-0015
HUND, Louis	52	Oelpe	70-0329
HUND, Xaver	32	Sachsbachwalden	71-0456
HUNDECEK, John	31	Boehmen	70-0508
Anna 27, Barbara 6, Frantz 11 months			
HUNDERTMARK, Eduard	34	Danzig	71-0167
Henriette 24			
HUNECKE, Herm.	19	Lienen	68-0566
HUNEL, Johann	16	Lichtenberg	69-0542
HUNGER, Hermann	24	Ostkilver	68-0786

NAME	AGE	RESIDENCE	YR-LIST
Anna 19			
HUNING, Elisabeth	58	Buer	68-0939
Heinrich 24, Margarethe 24, Heinrich 35, Louise 27, Heinrich 6, Marie 2, Heinr			
HUNOLD, Mathilde	31	Graefrath	68-1006
Ernst 6, Walter 3, Gustav 11 months			
HUPE, Louise	20	Verden	68-0661
HUPFSCHMIDT, Aug.	28	Kalk	69-1086
Auguste 25, Adele 3, Carl 6 months			
HUPKA, Caecilia	23	Kralowitz	71-0429
HUPPE, August	38	Reitz	69-0672
HUPPERTS, Friedrich	29	Solingen	71-0492
HUPPRICH, Johann	43	Holperath	68-314
Catharine 42, Elisabeth 9, Peter 5, Maria 2			
HURECKER, Louise	24	Menningen	71-0821
HURLBRINK, Ernst	18	Buende	68-0534
HURST, C. F.	27	Freiburg	68-0884
HUSA, Martin	16	Dobregitz	70-0329
HUSBACH,Anna Elis.	25	Grossbuschla	68-0770
HUSEMANN, August	19	Detmold	70-0308
HUSEMANN, Joh.	16	Hinnebeck	68-0982
HUSER, David	32	Meissenheim	71-0492
Christiane 30, David 8, Theodor 7, Andreas 6, Christine 5, Adam 3, Gottlieb 2			
HUSFELDT, Anna	18	Eitzendorf	71-0581
Bremervoerde			
HUSMANN, Christine	24	Hollich	69-0208
Anna 18			
HUSMANN, Herm.	25	Hastrup	71-0792
HUSS, Meta	18	Bremen	71-0429
HUSSEMANN, Gustav	19	Hannover	70-1055
HUSSMEYER, Carl	36	Bodenbeck	69-0848
Louise 19			
HUSTEDT, Margareth	17	Hustede	69-0229
HUSTER, Anton	23	Gescher	68-0884
HUSTING, Berh.	17	Oldenburg	70-1023
HUTH, Gust.	19	Nassau	70-0308
HUTH, Henriette	22	Ronneburg	68-0760
HUTH, Mathilde	37	Altenburg	68-1002
Maria 6			
HUTH, Michael	19	Roethemeyer	71-0815
HUTHWALKER, Peter	14	Luedingworth	71-0821
HUTSCHLIN, Johanne	20	Braugarten	71-0521
HUTWALKER, Wilhelm	19	Altenbruch	68-0661
HUVENDIEK, Wilh.	19	Westerwinner	68-1006
HUXHALL, Aug.	24	Lehmkuhle	71-0479
HUXOLL, H.	26	Hohenhausen	70-0308
HUZER, Elisabeth	26	Weissenstein	69-0338
HYDE, Maximilian	23	Ranshausen	68-0456
Heinstaeter, Trina	21	St. Francisco	69-1004
Huber, Magd.	24	Obrigheim	71-0521
IBA, Elisabeth	20	Ellenbach	70-0184
Anna S. 18			
IBACH, Juliane	54	Heilbronn	68-1027
Pauline 24, Bertha 7			
IBELINGS, Helena	62	Hannover	69-1059
ICHLE, Catharina	16	Harsheim	69-0672
IDA, Gottlieb	29	Romenshoef	71-0643
Marie 26, Hermann 6 months			

NAME	AGE	RESIDENCE	YR-LIST
IDEKER, Dorette	34	Neustadt/R	68-0647
Christine 6			
IDEKER, Herm.	22	Schneeren	68-0647
Louise 22, baby daughter 10 months			
IDEN, Gottfried	20	Pitsburg/Hannov	69-1004
Elise 16, Herm. 9			
IFFLAND, Peter	29	Rentweinsdorf	69-1011
Elise 58			
IGERMEYER, Elise	14	Wehrendorf	71-0456
IGLBERGER, Franziska	28	Wallersdorf	71-0643
Johanne 4, Cathrine 10 months			
IGNOSKA, Franz	22	Sirzkowo	71-0456
Anna 20			
IHE, Otto	28	Kissingen	69-0841
IHLE, Fred.	37	Balz	69-1011
IHLE, Fritz	26	Hannover	71-0456
IHLE, Otto	15	Rauschenberg	71-0712
IHLER, Regine	23	Hannover	69-1212
IHNENFELD, Wilhelm	54	Duesseldorf	69-0559
Louise 58			
IHRIG, Elisabeth	24	Rothenberg	68-0661
IKATULLA, Carl	39	Ellgoth	69-0784
IKLER, Johannes	18	Altendorf	68-1027
ILG, Marie	32	Jaxtroth	71-0521
Caroline 9			
ILGEN, Babette	44	New York	70-1003
Ernst 7, Anna 3			
ILGHOLZ, Mrs.	22	Calbe	70-1066
Hermann 10 months			
ILLE, Jos. Jac.	24	Fritzlar	68-0884
ILLFELDER, Regine	23	Fuerth	68-0957
ILLGAS, Georg	24	Heimersbach	69-0771
ILLIES, Burghard	15	Hannover	69-0771
ILLMANN, Caroline	16	Einod	71-0492
ILMLAND, August	18	Hannover	71-0736
ILO, Carl	15	Kirchdorf	69-0672
IMDICKE, Bernhard	28	Graudorf	68-1002
IMHOF, Theodor	23	Basel	69-0490
IMHOF, Wilhelmine	36	Schwarzemann	69-0672
Christine 27			
IMHOFF, Anna	23	Sohr-Sehr	70-0031
IMHOFF, U.	13	Rastatt	70-1142
IMKER, Herm.	20	Groenenberg	68-0957
IMMIG, Catharina	17	Holler Wuestig	70-0204
IMMOHR, Herm.		Wildeshausen	70-0443
IMSCHWEILER, Maria	18	Niedermoschel	71-0226
INDERHEES, Heinr.	19	Osnabrueck	68-1006
INERLE, Joh.	18	Wollmar	71-0821
INKEN, Diedrich	21	Esens	68-0314
Theda 27, Aug. 3, Johanna 1			
INNERBUECHER, T.	24	Tyrol	70-1011
INNHOF, Wilhelmine	36	Schwarzemann	69-0672
Christine 27			
INTEMANN, Dorette	22	Helwege	69-1059
INTEMANN, Gesche	22	Hellwege	71-0479
Cath. 19			
INTEMANN, Hermann	22	Hannover	69-0771
INTERMANN, Fritz	15	Hakendorf	71-0789
INWALLE, Margarethe	66	Hannover	70-0259

NAME	AGE	RESIDENCE	YR-LIST
IPPENSEN, Christ.	29	Stoeckheim	68-0610
IPPENSEN, Wilh.	14	Edemissen	68-1002
IRGANG, Elisabeth	19	Weisenthal	69-0576
IRING, Oskar	17	Guetersloh	71-0456
IRION, Christian	27	Theningen	68-0820
ISAAC, Babette	26	Pfingstadt	70-0355
ISAAC, Isaac	20	Sausenheim	70-1055
ISAAC, Moritz	19	Frankfurt a/M	69-1396
ISAAK, Isidor	19	Landsberg	71-0821
ISAAK, Jacob	21	Flaxland	69-0079
ISEMANN, Catherine	24	Bayern	70-0148
ISENBURG, Barbara	15	Frankfurt	69-0968
ISENGART, Marie	21	Hannover	69-0015
ISENSEE, H.C.	15	Bremen	68-0820
ISER, Johann	30	Altstadt	71-0226
Anna 38, Caroline 11 months, Amalie 11 months			
ISER, Wilke	20	Darmstadt	69-1309
ISERMANN, Christian	32	Aerzen	71-0492
ISRAEL, Nathan	18	Burgdorf	69-0429
ISSLER, Rud.	14	Warmbrunn	71-0581
ITJEN, Elise	19	Cappel	68-1049
ITTIG, Mara	23	Hollinde	69-1086
Pauline 15			
ITZEL, K.	22	Halversdorf	71-0643
ITZEL, Marie	23	Frankfurt a/M	70-1142
ITZEN, Anna	59	Bremerhaven	69-0490
Louise 16			
ITZEN, Harm	24	Norddeich	69-1004
ITZENHAUSER, Joh.	26	Merghausen	70-1035
Caroline 21, Mathias 7 months			
JACHENS, Anna	16	Lehe	68-0957
JACHMANN, Otto	23	Berlin	68-0534
JACKLE, Julius	26	Riedheim	68-0647
JACOB, Adolph	24	Huefler	69-0321
JACOB, Caspar	54	Obersetzbach	68-0907
Margarethe 51, Peter 7, Caspar 6			
JACOB, Catharina	18	Altendorf	68-1027
JACOB, Christian	39	Oberoppurg	69-1396
JACOB, Georg	17	Hohenhausen	69-0182
Margarethe 16, Dorothee 14			
JACOB, Lina	36	Kleinsheim	70-100
Lina 5, Heinrich 3, from America			
JACOB, Sophie	23	Rehnen	71-0643
JACOB, Therese	37	Heckgenstadt	69-0798
Dorothea 15, Carl 9, Anton 6, Juliane 2			
JACOBI, Johanne	22	Gehrde	69-0923
JACOBI, Magdalena	21	Bremen	68-0625
JACOBI, Maria	21	Radolin	69-0592
JACOBI, Wilhelm	32	Brunswick	70-0076
JACOBS, Benjamin	31	Bielefeld	69-0079
Caroline 28			
JACOBSON, Christine	17	Bremen	71-0479
JACOBUS, Gottlieb	26	Gilgenburg	70-0184
JACOBUS, Samuel	30	Zempelburg	69-0968
JAECHER, Franz	25	Sachsen	69-1004
JAECKEL, Gust.	18	Schmichaw	71-0479
JAECKLE, Mary	46	Schwenningen	68-0760
JAECKLE, Seb.	18	Springfeld	71-0736
JAEGELE, George	20	Kensingen	71-0712
JAEGER, Andreas	47	Oberschonau	68-0661
Margarethe 42, Theodor Hermann 18, Caroline 16, Aminda 7, Alwine 6, Ernestine			
JAEGER, Anna	17	Breitenfeld	68-0707
JAEGER, Anna Maria	19	Nuernberg	68-1006
JAEGER, Carl	29	Mahlberg	69-1212
JAEGER, Carl	36	Oberschoenau	68-0610
JAEGER, Cath.	21	Einartshausen	69-0592
JAEGER, Cathar.	22	Beinstein	68-0957
JAEGER, Conrad	30	Waldeck	69-0583
JAEGER, Elise	19	Treppendorf	71-0456
JAEGER, Ernestine	39	Roschitz	68-0647
JAEGER, Eva	20	Kirdorf	71-0821
JAEGER, Franz	23	Leopoldsgruen	71-0300
JAEGER, Friedrich	21	Reuss	68-0872
JAEGER, Friedrich	27	New York	68-0661
Helene 18, Johann 14, Gesche 16			
JAEGER, Fritz	20	Beverstedt	68-0647
JAEGER, Georg	32	Niederorschel	69-0182
JAEGER, Heinrich	27	Treysa	69-0547
JAEGER, Joh.	22	Bellings	71-0479
Nicol. 18			
JAEGER, Johann	31	Brocklyn	69-0321
JAEGER, John	42	Asch	68-0957
Elisabeth 36, Gustav 8, Andrew 6, Baby daughter 2 months, Catharine 74			
JAEGER, Louise	17	Schweiz	70-1023
JAEGER, Meta	23	Hellwege	69-1004
JAEGER, Oscar	17	Weimar	70-0178
JAELINGER, Caroline	33	Leipzig	70-0508
JAENCHEN, Herm.	22	Leipzig	69-0572
JAENICKE, Meta	25	Etelsen	68-0852
JAGADZINSKI, Josef	24	Wirsitz	71-0643
JAGER, Gustav	11	Wennings	70-0683
JAGG, Andr.	52	Philippsburg	71-0792
Regina 50			
JAHN, Aloysius	31	Almus	68-0661
Veronica 22			
JAHN, Aug.	22	Dessau	68-0872
JAHN, Carl	34	Buchholz	68-1002
JAHN, Chrs. B.	24	Witzendorf	69-0572
JAHN, Richard	29	Weimar	69-1076
JAHN, Wilhelm	29	Dresden	69-1212
JAHN, Wilhelm	41	Berlin	68-0820
JAHNKE, Emma	20	Berlin	71-0736
JAHNKE, Ferd.	37	Burhaw	69-1004
Friederike 36, Ferd. 11 months			
JAHNKE, Ferd.	24	Zablmowa	70-0308
JAHNS, Johannes	18	Hannover	70-0178
JAHR, Georg	35	Kochheimbol	69-0798
JAIVA, Michael	33	Rehbach	70-0223
Christine 25, Phillip 11 months			
JAKOB, Anna	18	Rothweil	69-0798
JALENKE, Bertha	18	Corlin	71-0479
JAMBERG, Aron	37	Fannington	70-1023
JAMMUNSCH, Joh.	40	Gilizier	70-0204
Eva 26, N. 9 months			

NAME	AGE	RESIDENCE	YR-LIST
JAMUREK, Johanne	34	Lauenburg	71-0479
Albert 2 months			
JAMUSCH, Josef	35	Niezyhow	70-0204
Michael 35, Antonne 23, Baby son 6 months			
JANDA, Paul	39	Spititz	70-0329
Veronika 29			
JANDHOFF, Ernst	47	Frankfurt	69-0576
Johanne Charlotte 58, Emma 19, Betha 13			
JANDT, Carl	31	Seege	68-0770
Emilie 20, August 9 months			
JANECKI, Theo	34	Gollnancz	68-0957
JANKE, Carl	22	Berlin	69-0672
JANKENDORFF, Oscar	29	Rahmberg	69-1319
JANNING, Gertrude	26	Schoeppigen	71-0456
JANS, Herm. W.	19	Wuellen	68-1002
JANSEN, Carl	22	Herzborn	68-1006
JANSEN, H.	16	Lehe	69-0490
JANSEN, Janna	20	Emden	68-0852
JANSEN, Luebbe	31	Werdum	71-0363
JANSON, Louise	18	Hannover	70-1066
JANSSEN, A. C. U.	31	Hinte	68-0884
JANSSEN, Ad.	23	Sterling	68-0957
JANSSEN, Anna	18	Greetsyl	68-0982
JANSSEN, Anna	19	Boerger	68-0939
JANSSEN, Bernhard	17	Lehe	69-0321
JANSSEN, Chls.	16	Jever	68-0957
JANSSEN, Cornelia	17	Goettingen	68-1027
JANSSEN, Diedr.	19	Aurich	68-1027
JANSSEN, Emilie	30	Aurich	68-0982
Emilie 11 months			
JANSSEN, Engelbert	44	Sengwarden	69-0490
Agena 54, Louise 22, August 26			
JANSSEN, Friedr.	16	Jever	69-0572
JANSSEN, Gerh.	22	Oldenburg	68-0786
JANSSEN, Gesche	27	Varel	68-0534
JANSSEN, Harm	32	Burforde	69-0841
JANSSEN, Harm	19	Upschoert	68-0982
JANSSEN, Hato	14	Hannover	70-0329
Richard 7, Hilka 6			
JANSSEN, Heinrich	31	Fuechtorf	68-0907
JANSSEN, Jeraphje	78	Victorbur	68-0707
JANSSEN, Joh. W.	43	Tassens	68-0884
Nanke 53, Sibelt 18, Heinr. 14, Marie 8			
JANSSEN, Johann	32	Oldenburg	70-0728
Cath. 34, Helene 5 months			
JANSSEN, Johanna	21	Wremen	68-0566
JANSSEN, Pauline	19	Jever	68-0707
JANSSEN, Rixt. Mar.	22	Thunum	68-1002
JANTZ, Adolph	28	Kl. Volz	68-0707
JANZ, Jacob	40	Breitenbach	69-0572
Charlotte 20, Caroline 10 months, Carl 25, Juliane 24, Adolph 11 months			
JAPHA, Jacob	37	Berlin	69-1309
JAQUET, August	19	Homburg	71-0712
JARGER, Catharina	23	Volkartshain	68-0760
Maria 8 months			
JARNISCH, Joseph	19	Michelsdorf	68-0770
JAS, Friederike	22	Heilbronn	69-1309
Amalia 9 months			
JASIEK, Jac.	24	Sossnow	68-0314
Marianne 18			
JASPER, Catharina	25	Luedingworth	68-0661
Wilhelm 6 months			
JASPER, Emil	24	Cothen	69-0208
JASPER, Heinr.		Altenbruch	68-1002
JASSEN, Heinrich	17	Langwedel	69-0576
JASTER, Ludwig	27	Koenigsdorf	68-0907
JAUCH, Brigitta	21	Schwenninger	68-1002
Friedr. 9 months			
JAX, Carl	31	Obernenkirchen	70-0031
JEDLITZKA, Leopold	13	Mainz	71-0643
JEHLER, Paul	17	Cresbeck	68-0456
JEHN, Paul	18	Markneukirchen	68-0760
JEK, Adolf	5	Immendingen	68-0534
JEMMING, Heinrich	24	Pfalzdorf	69-0490
JEMMING, Jacob	24	Louisendorff	69-0490
JENDERMANN, Johann	40	Borken	68-0625
JENNINGS, Charles	29	Threwsburg	70-0355
Delaide 25			
JENTZEN, Nicolaus	18	Osterende	68-0786
Anna 20			
JERICHO, August	25	Sterbfritz	68-1002
JERICHOW, Marhilde	26	Magdeburg	68-0884
Gustav 9 months			
JERINGER, Lucas	27	Cleveland	69-0784
JERKE, Lorenz	42	Stettnetz	69-0576
Auguste 14			
JERONEK, Antonie	23	Sibi	71-0456
JESCHKE, Anna	35	Krakau	69-0547
Auguste 4, August 1			
JESSEN, H.	30	Reepsholt	70-0308
JETTER, Anna	22	Engstadt	69-0848
JEZHOEFER, Max	19	Aalen	71-0521
JILECEK, Maria	20	Wodnau	70-0329
JIRA, Johann	32	Neuzerecka	68-0770
Anna 31, Marie 11 months, Mathias 53, Josepha 50, Catharina 35			
JIRA, Marie	17	Protiwin	70-0329
JIRANCH, Franz	34	Boehmen	70-0384
Josefa 30, Emanuel 2, Josefa 6 months, Feska 29			
JIRNA, Aug.	27	Nakel	70-100
JOA, Serophine	18	Wuerzburg	69-1059
JOACHIMI, Julius	31	Nordhausen	69-0841
JOAS, Maria	21	Rottweil	70-1142
JOB, Julius	21	Lippe	71-0681
JOCHENS, Trientje	22	Ochtersum	69-0547
JOCHIM, Heinrich	28	Einartshausen	69-0592
Christina 25, Heinrich 4, Georg 2			
JOCHMANN, Joseph	26	Weingarten	71-0521
JOEDE, Carl	28	Stettin	70-1003
Albertine 26, Bertha 4, Auguste 3, Wilhelm 6			
JOERDEN, Bernhard	50	Osterwieck	71-0643
Antoni 35			
JOERDEN, Maria	19	Hannover	70-0378
Johanne 17			
JOERG, Elsbeth	32	Trins	71-0226

NAME	AGE	RESIDENCE	YR-LIST
Johann 8, Hans 2			
JOERGES, H.	22	Schiefhahn	69-0841
JOESTING, Gustav	21	Absen	68-0852
Marie 48, Elise 15, Johann 12, Marie 5, Johanna 2			
JOHANNES, Julia	20	Bremen	69-0015
JOHANNESMEYER, F.	28	Volmerdingen	69-0572
JOHANNING, Volker	30	Berlin	71-0456
JOHANNING, Wilhelm	19	Werste	68-1027
JOHANNINGMEYER, G.	16	Ost Kilver	68-1027
Catharina 20			
JOHANNINGSMEIER, H.	18	Westkilver	68-1027
JOHANNPETER, Gustav	17	Brackwiede	69-0429
JOHANNS, Anna	60	Altenbruch	68-0661
JOHANNS, Carl	17	Muenchen	69-0050
JOHANNSEN, Catharina	32	Mildstedt	68-0566
JOHANNSON, Nils	28	Kalmar	68-0647
Anna 23, Sarah 6 months			
JOHLER, Herm.	34	Stadtoldendorf	68-0534
Traugott 19			
JOHN, Adolph	27	Berlin	69-0542
JOHN, August	28	Krakau	70-1035
JOHN, Ernestine	70	Lincenfels	69-1212
JOHN, Paul	18	Peitz	68-0647
JOHN, Robert	34	Rosenthal	68-1027
JONNY, Peter	24	Sorl	71-0789
Marie 23, Magd. 3, Casp. 2			
JOOS, Friederike	21	Heilbronn	68-0566
JOOST, Cornel	25	Heinrichsfeld	69-0542
JOOST, Hans	50	Hannover	70-0355
Wilhelmine 48, Anne C. 19, Anna 11, Marie 4, John 5,			
JOPPEL, Constantin	22	Boehmen	69-0592
JORDAN, Ferdinand	28	Friedrichsdorf	69-0576
JORDAN, Georg	18	Offstein	68-0707
Philipp 17			
JORDAN, Margaret	22	Weichersbach	71-0643
JORDAN, Ottilie	42	Bueren	69-1059
JORDAN, Wilhelm	23	Solingen	70-0308
JORDAN, Wilhelm	52	Frankfurt	71-1046
JORDEN, Peter	24	Hannover	70-0378
JORDON, Ottilie	42	Bueren	69-1059
JOSEFA, Maria	40	Olpe	71-0712
Virginia 16, Maria 14, Adam 9			
JOSEPH, Lea	30	Darmstadt	70-0728
Moritz 9			
JOSEPH, Max	23	Michelstadt	70-0031
JOSEPHSEN, Louis	15	Altlueneburg	68-0647
JOSSI, Friederike	15	Schweiz-Saulgau	70-1142
JOST, Adam	18	Hesse Darmstadt	69-1059
JOST, Carl	26	Hermannsstein	71-0643
JOST, Christine	20	Pforzheim	68-1002
JOST, Eva	20	Loehrbach	71-0643
JOST, Johann	51	Darmstadt	69-0672
Catharina 46, Valentin 19, Catharine 16, Caroline 9			
JOST, Josef	27	Omersheim	71-0429
Marie 21			
JOST, Julius	19	Ixheim	71-0479

NAME	AGE	RESIDENCE	YR-LIST
JOST, Maria	22	Buedingen	68-0786
JOST, Michael	28	Mandern	68-1002
JOUNG, Elise	56	Giessen	68-0610
Lina 18			
JUCHNE, August	19	Goettingen	69-0429
JUD, Louise	16	Mezingen	70-1035
Pauline 19			
JUDE, Johanna	20	Gr. Marienau	69-0321
JUDT, Susanna	59	Darmstadt	69-1212
Margaretha 16			
JUECHTER, Franz	23	Emsteck	68-0625
JUENEMANN, Dorothea	29	Nordhausen	68-1002
JUENGEL, Mathilde	29	Delitsch	71-0821
JUENGER, Cath.	24	Schweighafen	69-1363
JUENGERT, Margarethe	24	Gerstfeld	68-0786
JUENGET, Fanny	18	Cloppenburg	69-0841
JUENGLING, Henry	15	Verden	68-1027
JUENGST, Carl	18	Herborn	68-0982
JUENGST, Louis	18	Herborn	68-0982
JUERGENS, Anna	25	Bremen	68-0625
JUERGENS, Antonie	35	Herford	71-0821
Ottilie 9			
JUERGENS, Caroline	17	Braunschweig	70-0683
JUERGENS, Cath.	21	Oldenburg	71-0736
JUERGENS, Claas	28	Utarp	68-314
JUERGENS, Efke	20	Ostfriesland	70-0384
Minna 17			
JUERGENS, Grete	24	Hannover	70-0384
JUERGENS, Seleste	26	Memel	69-0771
Ella 11 months			
JUINGER, Cath.	24	Schweighafen	69-1363
JUKIES, Ulrich	28	Esens	71-0300
Friederike 27, Beta 3			
JULIEN, Marie	33	Strassburg	71-0643
JULIUS, Carl	33	Braunschweig	70-0329
Juliane 28, Auguste 7, Ferdinand 5, Caroline 45, Heinrich 9			
JULIUS, Gesche	33	Sued-Georgsfehn	68-0610
Heinr. 6, Lambert 5 months			
JULIUS, Waldemar	25	Wetzlar	68-0820
JULY, Louis	27	Bramberg	71-0479
JUMP, Johann M.	44	Ollendorf	70-0006
Christiane 50, Ricke 19, Carl 16, Wilhelm 13, Heinrich 11			
JUNA, H.	27	Paris	69-1011
Mary 22			
JUNCK, Herm.	30	Hannover	70-1161
JUNG, Amalia	24	Delmhorst	68-0939
JUNG, August	39	Hannover	70-0355
Regine 39, Wilhelm 9, Christel 7, August 5, Henry 1			
JUNG, Christian	18	Lich	69-0672
JUNG, Elise	31	Reilsheim	69-0672
Minna 3, August 7 months			
JUNG, Elise	56	Giessen	68-0610
Lina 18			
JUNG, Friedrich	19	Muehlbach	70-0135
JUNG, Fritz	16	Meiningen	71-0456
JUNG, Joh. Georg	29	Eschwege	68-0753
Elisabeth 25, Adam 4, Baby-Boy			

NAME	AGE	RESIDENCE	YR-LIST
JUNG, Johann	16	Birkenfeld	69-0079
JUNG, Johannes	37	Megesheim	68-0610
JUNG, Marie	18	Nassau	70-0384
JUNG, Nicolas	26	Wiltingen	69-0457
Peter 28			
JUNG, Paul	23	Frankfurt/O	68-0753
JUNG, Rosine	21	Reichenbach	71-0815
JUNG, Wendelin	23	Gruenmettstette	71-0821
JUNGBLATE, Adam	52	Holtenbach	69-0672
Caroline 9			
JUNGE, Fr.	26	Erlangen	71-0143
JUNGE, Friedr.	18	Erlangen	69-0542
JUNGE, Heinrich	46	Gr. Bruechter	71-0712
Caroline 47, Pauline 14			
JUNGE, Meta	26	Cadenberge	68-0566
JUNGE, Severus	18	Trommlitz	68-0456
JUNGEN, Nic.	23	Dreis	69-1011
JUNGER, J.	19	Hinterweiler	68-0566
JUNGILAS, Caroline	25	Treysa	69-1076
JUNGMANN, Gustav	28	Altenburg	70-0148
JUNGNICKEL, Charles	29	Oberpretzschend	69-0560
Herm. 32			
JUNKE, August	26	Enstthal	71-0792
Itta 24, Clara 3, Minna 11 months			
JUNKER, Bertha	29	Berlin	69-1011
Clara 5 months			
JUNKER, Herm.	50	Bremen	69-0338
Maria 47, Friederike 22, Maria 14, Hermann 8, Hilbert 7, John 6, Betty 6, Ludw			
JUNKER, Wilhelmine	22	Goersbach	68-0566
JUNKERMANN, Herm.	18	Stemmen	68-0647
JUNKERS, Heinrich	32	Berlin	69-0572
JUNKERSTAFF, Adolf	29	Duesseldorf	71-0681
JUPPERT, Margareth	35	Wohnfort	69-1059
Therese 24			
JURS, Heinrich	21	Hannover	70-0443
JUSEL, Georg	25	Olingen	69-0490
JUTEMANN, Cord	16	Winningen	71-0521
JUTT, Marg.	15	Butzbach	71-0581
JUTTE, Heinrich	48	Rosenbeck	69-1086
Minna 9, Marie 8, Josephine 6, Mathilde 4, Josef 26			
JUTTMANN, Catharine	53	Badberg	71-0429
Catharine 24			
JUTZ, Anna	17	Heldkirch	69-1059
JUTZE, Louise	36	Sachsen Meining	69-0798
Hermann 4			
KAATZ, August	32	Fritzow	68-314
Wilhelmine 26, Otto 4, Reinhold 2, Franz 6 months			
KAATZ, Henriette	20	Gr. Rotten	71-0712
KABER, Adolf	15	Elpershausen	71-0681
KACHEL, Anna	26	Nussloch	69-0429
David 3, Maria 3			
KACHNE, Elise	22	Berlin	70-0052
KACKEIS, Magdalene	30	Vorarlberg	69-0560
KADAU, Carl	19	Flatow	69-0583
KAELBERER, Ludwig	42	Veit	68-0566
KAEMMERLING, Fer.	23	Coeln	70-0308
KAEMPF, Carl Ludwig	22	Waldmohr	68-1006
KAEMPFE, Caroline	66	Sachsen	69-1059
Clara 18			
KAEMPFER, Joachim	30	Callehoan	69-1212
KAEPPLINGER, Benedicta	25	Muenchen	70-100
KAERMNES, Margareth	48	Neustadt	71-0456
KAESE, Johannes	25	Landenbach	69-0429
KAESHEIMER, Magda.	25	Weyhl	71-0429
KAESMANN, Richard	20	Eiterfeld	69-0208
KAESTNER, August	36	Utstadt/Boehmen	69-0321
Caroline 32, Ernst 9, Robert 8, Erna 7, Theresa 3, Carolina 8 months			
KAEUFER, Johann	17	Albrehtitz	70-0329
KAFFENBERGER, Wilh.	24	Hessen	70-0204
KAFTEIN, Emilie	19	Triergarten	69-0321
KAH, Marg.	22	Gemuend	68-0957
KAHL, ANton	30	Boehmen	69-1004
Cath. 30, Cath. 6, Helene 5, Oleva 2, Anton 6 months			
KAHL, Aug.	28	Ohlau	71-0143
KAHLHAMMER, Friedr.	22	Frauenzimmern	71-0167
KAHN, Bhd.	19	Frielendorf	68-0534
KAHN, Friederike	20	Speyer	69-0229
KAHN, Gretchen	18	Homburg	69-1212
KAHN, Jeanette	21	Aschenhausen	71-0429
KAHN, Lippmann	17	Diedenbergen	71-0429
KAHN, Maria	24	Birkenfeld	69-0923
KAHN, Michel	19	Lothringen	71-0736
Jacob 17			
KAHN, Rebecca	30	Oberstein	69-0560
KAHN, Wilhelmine	18	Lichtenau	71-0712
KAHNE, Hr.	22	Belhusen	71-1046
KAHRS, Heinr.	28	Baschel	71-0736
Margareth 28, Anna 9 months			
KAHRS, Johann	16	Vorwerk	71-0521
KAISER, Albert	15	Herstelle	70-0443
KAISER, Andreas	63	Rudolstadt	70-0378
Ernestine 60			
KAISER, Caroline	28	Welzheim	68-0852
KAISER, Christine 47	47	Grumbach	68-0884
KAISER, Emil	19	Penig	70-0204
KAISER, Joh. D.	39	Bremervoerde	69-0100
KAISER, Johann	27	Lichtenstein	68-0939
KAISER, Joseph	20	Bauholz	70-0184
KAISER, Louise	12	Hohewart	68-0707
Georg 8			
KAISER, Margaretha	21	Rodesgrun	68-0939
Wolfgang 19			
KAISER, Marie	18	Dresden	68-0625
KAISER, Moritz	29	Neustadt	69-0208
KAISER, Servatin	26	Brudern	71-0479
KAISER, Traugott	47	Soemmerda	71-0363
KAISER, Wilh.	44	Pirsitz	71-0479
Susanne 42, Ernestine 11, Caroline 9			
KAISLE, Joseph	30	Holz	68-0770
KALB, Emil	15	Stuttgart	71-0684
KALB, Therese	33	Neukelheim	69-0848
Joseph 12, Joachim 8, Ignatz 6, Johann 5, Anton 2, Mathias 6 months			
KALCHTHALER, Math.	13	Endingen	71-0393

NAME	AGE	RESIDENCE	YR-LIST
KALKE, Johann	26	Zittlan-Pommern	70-0006
KALKWARF, Jan D. Metje 27, Dirk 9	28	Rechtsupweg	68-1002
KALLENBENZ, Rudolpf	23	Neuenstein	71-0492
KALLENBERG, Auguste	19	Goettingen	70-1035
KALLER, Joh. Fr.	28	Wedelfingen	70-0204
KALLINA, Anton	25	Kralowitz	71-0429
KALSEN, Joseph Thomas 33	41	Lienz	70-0135
KALSER, Andrae	45	Lienz	70-0135
KALTENBACH, Herman	20	Altenstaig	68-0625
KALTENBORN, Carl Catharina 35, Carl 9, Franz 5, Louise 3, Heinrich 11 months	27	Clausthal	70-0184
KALTENBORN, Nicolas	60	Breidenheim	69-1319
KALTWASSER, Jacob	44	Darmstadt	70-1161
KALVERKAMP, Anton	19	Enningen	69-0572
KAMBERS, Marie	25	Barkhausen	68-0939
KAMCKE, Edgard	18	Berlin	69-1319
KAMINSKI, Johann	25	Gerlin	71-0429
KAMM, Christine	27	Melzow	68-0786
KAMM, Marga	26	Lichhausen	71-0821
KAMMEA, August	17	Ramrod	68-0625
KAMMERICH, Louise	27	Engelsberg	70-1055
KAMMERZELL, Lisette	32	Coburg	69-1076
KAMMEYER, Heinrich	25	Westschalen	70-0384
KAMMHOLZ, Hermann	27	Clotzen	69-0429
KAMP, Dorothea	21	Muenden	69-1076
KAMP, Johann Catharina 45	50	Wiltingen	69-0457
KAMP, John	36	Colonia	69-0798
KAMPER, Heinrich	17	Amdorf	68-0852
KAMPF, Gesine	22	Oldenburg	69-0268
KAMPFHOEVENER, H.	17	Holsen	68-1027
KAMPFT, Jacob Sophie 20, Ludewig 15, Christian 9	17	Beerfelden	69-0771
KAMPHAUSEN, Emil	19	Barmen	71-0521
KAMPHEMANN, Wilh.	18	Dissen	68-0566
KAMPMANN, Christine Louise 3 months	18	Muenster	68-0314
KAMPMEIER, Ernst	27	Betzen	68-0534
KAMPS, Anna Georg 16	20	Luedingworth	71-0821
KAMPSHOFF, Emil	24	Bocholt	69-1059
KANIS, Ferd. Wilhelmine 15	18	Sorge	71-0479
KANITZ, Paul Ida 26	26	Leipzig	68-0014
KANNENGIESSER, F.	26	Steinfurt	68-0707
KANNGIESSER, Johanne Wilhelm 9, nna 3, Baby 11 months	30	Vilsdorf	70-1035
KANOP, Georg	15	Raute	68-0625
KANTNICK, Rosa	23	Brandlies	68-0534
KANZ, Catharina Joh. 7	32	Fruchtelfingen	68-0566
KANZLER, Carl Friederike 25	32	Lessa	68-0456
KANZLER, Klara Rosette 11 months	3	Lossa	68-0456
KAPLING, Ludwig Elisab. 34, Bernhardine 11 months, Sophie 3	45	Seidberge	71-0581
KAPPEL, Philipp	60	Celle	68-1006
KAPPER, Jette	18	Kl. Heubach	68-0957
KAPPES, Joseph	26	Mittenberg	69-0208
KAPPLIN, Johanna	50	Preussen	68-0456
KAPPLIN, Leo	50	Preussen	68-0456
KAPS, Friedrich Hermann	23	Leipzig	68-0865
KAPSCH, Ernst Johanna 29, Hermann 4, August 1	34	Borkau	68-314
KARACK, Herm. Wilhelmine 30	24	Strammer	69-0576
KARAFFA, Johann Jacob 14	17	Biebelnheim	71-0429
KARCH, Mary	31	Raulbach	71-0479
KARCHER, Albert	16	Sternenfels	71-0479
KARCHER, Louise	22	Michelbach	68-0610
KARE, Margarethe	16	Erbezhausen	68-0534
KARELA, Wenzel	30	Boehmen	69-1363
KARENKE, Aug.	34	Friedland	69-0162
KARFERLE, Marie	22	Moessingen	69-0784
KARKREUTZER, female	25	Sulzberg	69-0182
KARL, Eleonore Philippine 19, Anna 9, Mathias 7, Sophie 17	54	Darmstadt	70-0378
KARLE, Friedr.	22	Eichenthal	71-0521
KARLSTADTER, Aug.	48	Paderborn	69-0798
KAROLIN, Magdalena	57	Boehmen	69-1076
KAROW, Angelika	22	Damburg	68-0456
KARRASCH, Rosalie	23	Gerasselwitz	69-0771
KARREL, Alois	48	St. Gallen	71-0492
KARRENBERG, Aug.	23	Ovelgoenne	68-1027
KARRENBRUCH, Therese	22	Laer/Bad Laer	69-0429
KARRUS, Jos.	17	Endingen	71-0393
KARSCHMOCK, Frd. Dorothea 35, Wilhelm 17, Hermine 14, Ernst 11, Heinrich 7, Alwine 5, Aline 2	48	Launburg	68-0753
KARSTEN, Claus Anna M. 32, Matth. H. W. 3	33	Ottendorf	68-0820
KARSTENS, Anna	20	Bederkesa	69-0457
KARY, Friedrich		Darmesheim	69-0229
KARZ, Wilhelmine Paulie Johann 57, Julius 15, Wilhelmine 20, Pauline 10 months	57	Jankendorf	71-0492
KASACK, Herm. Wilhelmine 30	24	Strammer	69-0576
KASOLD, Friedrich	37	Gera	68-0314
KASPAR, Anna Johann 6	36	Kozin	70-0329
KASPAR, Joseph	28	Wirschheim	69-0583
KASSAU, Carl	51	Schlarpe	71-0581
KASSEL, Catharina	16	Oberschulz	69-0771
KASSING, Johanna	15	Westerenge	68-0939
KASSLING, Fried.	7	Ladbergen	71-0581
KASSNER, Ottilie	22	Preussen	69-0559
KAST, Elise	17	Carlsruhe	68-0884
KASTEN, Wilhelm	24	Robe	69-0457
KASTENDYCK, John Rebecca 26, Johann 6, Ellis 10 months	34	Brooklyn	69-1059

NAME	AGE	RESIDENCE	YR-LIST
KASTENS, Marga	23	Oldenburg	69-1086
KASTNER, Johann	23	Mittelfranken	69-1309
KASTNER, Walburga	23	Grossbellenfeld	68-0566
KASTROSCHE, Marie	18	Goettingen	71-0736
KATER, Conrad	27	Lippe Detmold	70-0355
KATER, Wilhelm	40	Burg	69-0968
KATEWOPSKY, Justine	22	Albrechtshof	69-0049
KATH, Georg	15	Reuteremsdorf	71-0479
KATH, Wilhelm	52	Lustebuhr	68-0661
Maria 52, Carl 15, Wilhelmine 19, Friederike 13, Caroline 25, Henriette 7, Ber			
KATT, Anna	17	Bremervoerde	71-0429
KATTEIN, Eleonore	53	Thiergarten	71-0521
Auguste 23, Oscar 11 months			
KATTERMANN, Sophie	20	Sehstadt	68-0707
KATTKAMP, Marie	53	Nettelstedt	69-0542
KATZ, Abraham	18	Jesberg	68-0939
KATZ, Betty	21	Malzfeld	68-0661
KATZ, Charles	14	New York	69-1363
A. 21			
KATZ, Elisabeth	22	Nackenheim	69-0923
KATZ, Francisca	30	Mannheim	68-0566
KATZ, Isaac	18	Erdmannsrode	68-0760
KATZ, Max	19	Minden	69-0050
KATZ, Meta	21	Braunschweig	71-1046
KATZ, Sophie	17	Walldorf	69-0784
KATZENBERG, Adolph	15	Elmshagen	70-0508
KATZENBERGER, Joh.	33	New York	69-1421
KATZENBUEHLER, R.	48	Ottersheim	68-0014
KATZMANN, Heinrich	18	Blankenbach	68-0820
KATZOR, Friedrich	24	Danzig	69-1309
KATZWINKEL, Wilhelmine	28	Schilleningken	71-0167
Carl 4, Marie 11 months			
KAUFER, Fritz	13	Gr. Weissand	71-0643
Carl 9			
KAUFFELD, Ida	18	Chemnitz	71-0479
KAUFFELD, John	20	Bremen	70-1023
KAUFFMANN, Julius	17	Gr. Holzheim	68-0456
KAUFMANN, Alois	20	Buedderlaun	69-1004
KAUFMANN, Amalie	45	Worms	68-0566
Livia 14, Rosalie 12, Caecilia 9, Sophie 8, Alexander 6			
KAUFMANN, Andreas	71	Arnstadt	68-0852
Wilhelmine 53, Joseph 23, Adalbert 17			
KAUFMANN, Bab.	22	Rimbach	71-0521
KAUFMANN, Caspar	36	Tuttlingen	68-0625
KAUFMANN, Cath.	20	Rimbach	71-0479
Cath. 62			
KAUFMANN, Falk	17	Mannheim	70-1003
KAUFMANN, Georg	24	Dornbirn	71-0643
KAUFMANN, Isaac	17	Nimheim	69-0542
KAUFMANN, Joh.	39	Niederzell	71-0393
KAUFMANN, Julius	18	Melsungen	69-0784
KAUFMANN, Louise	20	Hessen	69-1086
KAUFMANN, Martha	17	Kurhessen	69-1086
KAUFMANN, Sarah	20	Neustadt	68-0566
KAUFMANN, Wm.	21	Goettingen	68-0957
KAUFURT, Caspar	31	Fischbach	71-0479
KAUKA, Joef	54	Boehmen	70-0384
Anna 54, Valen. 22, Marie 16			
KAULBERSCH, Carl	22	Darmstadt	69-0592
KAUTER, Joh.	24	Boehmen	70-1035
KAUTNER, Heinr.	22	Derschenmuehle	71-0479
C. 19			
KAWARICK, Johann	30	Boehmen	70-0384
Jaufa 30, Johann 2, Josef 2 months			
KAYMANN, Arnold	50	Westerwicke	70-0728
Gertrud 46, Heinr. 13			
KAYSER, Carl	36	Lahde	69-0229
KAYSER, Christine	47	Grumbach	68-0884
KAYSER, John	24	Deilesheim	68-0760
KAYSER, Nicolaus	58	Dreyburg	69-0572
KAYSER, Wilhelm	25	Ulm	70-0031
KAZMIERSKY, Apollonia	23	Barndeis	71-0681
Anton 17			
KEBEL, Marie	52	Bremen	70-0452
Lina 9			
KECHE, Nathalie	23	Altenburg	71-0792
KECK, Andreas	30	Ober Iflingen	68-0786
KEFERSTEIN, Emil	22	Liegnitz	68-0456
KEFFENBURG, Johannes	25	Hammwiede	68-0566
KEHL, Caroline	24	Northeim	70-0204
KEHLE, Herman	18	Altenstaig	68-0852
KEHLE, Margaretha	46	Ragatz	69-0321
Benedict 18			
KEHLENBACH, Anna	49	Holperath	68-314
KEHLER, Maria	22	Lampertheim	69-0338
KEHM, Wilh.	17	Mainz	71-0789
KEHN, Carl	25	Arnstadt	68-1027
KEIBER, Adam	25	Villingen	68-0884
KEICKER, Heinr.	68	Dissen	71-0821
Marie 68			
KEIF, Chas.	26	Glauchen	70-0170
KEIFER, Johann	23	Langons	68-0625
KEIL, Aug.	52	Beildorf-Bieldo	70-1055
Dorothea 45, Friedrich 19, Hermann 9, Friedrike 7, Otto 11 months			
KEIL, Christian	42	Emartshausen	68-1027
Louise 19			
KEIL, Elise	20	Ennetshausen	69-0208
KEIL, Georg	15	Laisa	71-0821
KEIL, Gustav	22	Leipzig	68-0566
Marie 16			
KEIL, Kunigunde	53	Roth	68-0852
KEILER, Samuel	31	Berlin	71-0492
KEIMER, Georg	25	Welschingen	69-1212
KEIMICH, Severin	22	Gross Ostheim	68-0014
KEINATH, Johann	17	Winterlingen	70-0148
KEINERKAMP, Gertrude	25	Muenster	69-0968
KEIP, Heinrich	16	Storndorf	68-0852
KEIPP, Magdalena	28	Meisenheim	68-0939
KEITEL, Julius	38	Funzenhausen	68-0707
Henriette 34, Hermine 9, Clara 7, Lina 5			
KEITZ, Robert	36	Marienwalde	69-0848
KELINSKY, Sam.	36	Neudorf	69-1011
KELLAR, Ursula	10	Rottweil	70-0508
KELLE, Michael	33	Baiern	69-0559

NAME	AGE	RESIDENCE	YR-LIST
KELLER, Carl	19	Tuebingen	69-0229
KELLER, Carl	30	Ingelheim	71-0226
KELLER, Christine	28	Oberschuetz	68-0939
KELLER, Conrad	65	Seesbach	68-0661
Catharine 53, Sophie 30, Jacob 23, Elisabeth 16, Helene 7			
KELLER, Elisa	23	Katzenfurth	68-0647
KELLER, Elisabeth	24	Mainz	71-0429
KELLER, Ernstine	18	Pirsitz	71-0479
KELLER, Gottfried	22	Wald	68-0820
KELLER, J.	16	Druffach	71-0581
KELLER, Jacob	18	Hattenhofen	69-0542
KELLER, Jacob	24	Zuerich	69-0572
KELLER, Johann	28	Unterfranken	69-1309
Catharine 21			
KELLER, John	33	Gr. Lussen	71-0456
KELLER, Louise	25	Enzweihingen	70-0443
KELLER, Ludwike	22	Hannover	70-0178
Marie 17, Herm. 16, Herm. 35			
KELLER, Magdalene	28	Rhein Pfalz	70-0355
KELLER, Marie	20	Ibbenbuehren	68-0982
KELLER, Mathias	19	Rhein Pfalz	70-0355
KELLER, Max	17	New York	69-0572
KELLER, Robert	21	Pforzheim	71-0521
KELLER, Sophie	35	Nuernberg	68-1006
KELLER, Theresia	18	Riedheim	68-1002
KELLERMANN, Henriette	50	Gruenrade	68-0566
KELLERMANN, Jacob	61	Weinheim	69-0015
KELLERS, Meta	22	Wittstedt	71-0479
KELLERWESSEL, H.	33	Ibbenbueren	69-0429
KELLNER, Johannes	31	Kreuzeber	68-0786
Christine 31, Ludgardis 3, Pauline 11 months, Martin 68			
KELLNER, Louise	18	Bremen	70-0076
KELLNER, Theo.	25	Zofingen	68-0957
KELNER, Johannes	26	Birkungen	68-1002
KELPIN, Friedrich	26	Mariendorf/Prus	69-0547
KEMMLEIN, Julius	24	Stettin	69-1309
KEMMLER, August	28	Meton	69-0798
KEMMLER, Marie	19	Friedwald	71-0681
KEMMNER, Jacob	21	Unterensingen	69-1309
KEMPEN, August	35	Erklenz/Kansas	69-1059
KEMPFLE, Francisca	21	Ichenhausen	68-0014
KENESS, Henriette	22	Lugau	69-0798
KENETH, Wilhelm	31	Berlin	69-0542
Caroline 26, Otto 6, Anna 29			
KENZ, Marg.	25	Kirchberg	69-0490
KEPF, Catharine	30	Geislingen	68-0820
Joh. C. 2			
KERGER, Aug.	45	Gruenrade	68-0566
Wilhelmine 40, Augusta 12, Emma 9, Minna 2			
KERKHOFF, Anton	34	Frille	68-0625
Wilhelmine 29, Christian 4, Anton 9 months, Louise 21			
KERKHOFF, Eleonore	40	Eichendorf	68-0786
Sophie 17, Louise 14, Carl 9			
KERL, Fritz	25	Hameln	70-0148
KERL, Maria	23	Stavetitz	70-0329

NAME	AGE	RESIDENCE	YR-LIST
KERN, Alois	23	Grossweier	71-0456
KERN, Anna	23	Besenfeld	68-0456
KERN, Anna	24	Schleiz	68-0625
KERN, Anna	23	Hannover	68-1027
KERN, C.	19	Heilfingen	71-0681
KERN, Carl	40	Northeim	69-0559
Carl Wilhelm 10, Christian Wilhelm 7, Wilhelmine Louise 3			
KERN, Dorothea	54	Windischbuch	71-0226
Margarethe 18, Georg 9			
KERN, Elisabeth	23	Eberstadt	71-0429
KERN, Franz	23	Pest	70-0355
KERN, Fred.	17	Darmstadt	70-0308
Charles 16			
KERN, Hartmann	27	Meiches	68-1002
KERN, Heinr.	24	Stomdorf	69-0572
KERN, Jacob	50	Hueffler	71-0712
Catharina 44, Philippine 9			
KERN, Jos. Christian	24	Wuerttemberg	69-0559
KERN, Louis	30	Sondershaus	68-0852
Francisca 24			
KERN, Mathias	40	Lawenworth	68-0939
Aloisa 30, Amalia 24			
KERN, Richard	32	Riedern	69-0560
KERN, Valentin	44	Ladeburg	69-0559
Juliana 27, Barbara 7, Catharina 6, Carl Wilhelm 5, Georg 1, Friedrich 3 months			
KERNA, Hermann	16	Saxe-Mein.	68-0456
KERND, Auguste	31	Weimar	69-0592
Gustav 6			
KERNER, Friedericke	59	Aschaffenburg	69-1309
KERNERT, Carl Aug.	18	Dresden	70-0523
KERNWEIN, Louise	18	Wuerzburg	70-0728
KERSEN, Heinrich	30	Cassel	68-0852
KERSTEN, A.	32	Danzig	69-0079
KERSTEN, Emilie	31	Glauchau	68-0786
KERSTER, Ernst	48	Treutan	69-0542
KERSTIN, Alois	21	Rees	68-0707
KERT, Wenzel	30	Opolschitz	71-0429
KERTSCHER, Emilie	23	Hartha	68-0786
Emil 18			
KERTZNER, Karl	24	Hundsbach	71-0789
KERWER, Heinrich	30	Weissenthurm	69-0079
KESSEL, Helene	22	Duerkheim	69-1059
Baby 9 months			
KESSEL, Joseph	15	Oppenheim	68-0760
KESSENS, Nicol.	67	Esterwegen	68-0610
Gesine 58, Gesine 32, Anna 9, Christian 7, Gesine 5, Wilhelm 9 months			
KESSING, Lisette	18	Oldenburg	70-0683
KESSLER, Ernst	25	Roecklegen	69-0798
KESSLER, John	34	Brueckenau	70-1161
KESSLER, Louis	26	Stadilin/Stadli	69-0923
Adelheid 21, Anna 2, Lina 3 months			
KESSLER, Mathilde	37	New York	69-0798
Georg 7, Louise 1 months			
KESSLING, Aug	37	Cincinnati	70-1023
KESTNER, Christian	32	Friesau	68-0770
Friedericke 29, Hermann 4, Lina 2, Emma 4 months			

NAME	AGE	RESIDENCE	YR-LIST
KETHER, Joh.	26	Duesseldorf	70-0569
KETHMANN, Fr.	30	Oldenburg	69-0490
KETTENBURG, Johannes	25	Hammwiede	68-0566
KETTENRING, Cath.	23	Hochfraschen	71-0681
KETTER, Jacob	62	Croen	69-0321
Clara 57, Philipp 23, Clara 18, Margaret 15			
KETTERER, John	17	Oberwisheim	68-1006
Anton 23			
KETTERER, Prima	21	Schoenwald	69-0672
KETTLER, Ad.	22	Diepholz	71-0815
KETTLER, Agnes	22	Haldern	71-0821
KETTLER, Na.	23	Untermutschbach	69-1004
KETTNER, Albert	38	Hergisdorf	69-0162
KEUCH, Elisabeth	15	Koenigswalde	71-0815
KEUFER, H. F.	18	Duesseldorf	68-1006
KEULING, Julius	24	Waldeck	70-0259
Johanna 23			
KEUSCHER, Rud	24	Marburg	69-1421
KEUTER, Elisabeth	25	Barmen	68-0625
Baby daughter 11 months			
KICHERER, Christ.	25	Nuertingen	69-0560
Mar. 23			
KIEB, Ant. Jos.	25	Worbis	68-0610
KIEFER, Emilie	21	Erfurt	71-0492
KIEFER, Johannes	17	Baden	69-0559
Catharine 22			
KIEFER, Johannes	25	Altershausen	68-0907
KIEFER, Magdalene	22	Basel	71-0492
KIEFERLE, Carl	20	Rotenburg	69-1319
KIEFNER, Josef	39	Boehmen	69-1004
Anna 35, Franz 6, Anna 4, Marie 5			
KIEGELE, Wilhelm	18	Mainz	70-1161
KIEHERER, Friedke.	23	Grosskeppach	71-0789
KIEHNE, Bernhard	20	Quakenbrueck	69-0923
KIEL, ELISUS	24	Hessen	69-0771
Barbara 20			
KIELKOPF, Christ.	18	Albershausen	68-0820
KIENBAUM, Friedr.	28	Wittichow	68-0314
Aug. 29, Marie 23, Augusta 2, Hermann 6 months			
KIENE, Heinrich	49	Halberstadt	69-0208
KIENEMANN, Fried.	49	Stolzenau	70-0569
KIENETH, Elisabeth	22	Gefrees	70-0508
KIENLE, Friedr.	18	Magstadt	71-0736
KIERST, Carl Georg	37	Niedersohl	70-0006
Catharine E. 37, Catharine E. 9, Ottilie 5, Adam Henrich 7, Elise 2			
KIES, Gottlieb	50	Schorndorf	71-0363
KIESCHKE, Michel	24	Williamsburg	69-1421
KIESEL, Eva	26	Salesch	68-0786
KIESEL, Stephan	27	Niedlingen	70-0184
KIESELBACH, Maria	28	Elbing	68-0534
KIESER, Bertha	25	Stuttgart	71-0167
KIESER, Carl	28	Grossimpheim	71-0712
KIESEWETTER, Hugo	28	Breslau	69-0182
Anna 28			
KIESS, Heinricke	28	Schorndorf	71-0363
Nathaniel 16, Marie 13			
KIESSELBACH, Carl	20	Bremen	69-0067

NAME	AGE	RESIDENCE	YR-LIST
KIEWITT, Cath.	26	Holtern	71-0479
KIFFE, F. Wilh.	45	Bremen	69-0079
KILGUSS, Friedrich	17	Dottenweiler	69-0321
KILIAN, Marga.	17	Ginseldorf	68-0786
KILLIAN, Marga.	17	Ginseldorf	68-0786
KILLINGER, Friederike	20	Beinstein	68-0957
KILLIUS, Magdalena	28	Altenheim	71-0363
Wilhelm 10 months			
KILLNER, Wilhelmine	19	Lippe Detmold	70-0223
KIMBAL, Dorothea	22	Langenschwarz	70-0378
KIMBER, Karsten	65	Hofe	70-0508
Johanne 13, Henriette 16			
KIMMEL, Conrad	45	Moskeden	69-0079
KIMPEL, Johannes	32	Neukirchen	71-0363
KINDER, Hermine	17	Bremen	70-0148
Adolf 17			
KINDERMANN, Caroline	46	Meppen	70-1003
Henry 18, Louis 12			
KINDESVATER, Carl	30	Schlattstedt	71-0643
KINDGEN, Antonia	23	Sobernheim	70-0728
KINEMANN, Fried.	49	Stolzenau	70-0569
KING, Elisabeth	33	Bergzell	70-0728
Benjamin 1 months, Anselm 24			
KINGELING, Bessi	40	St. Louis	69-1212
Franz 7, Alex 6			
KINKEL, Jacob	27	Wiesenbach	68-0884
KINKEL, Johannes	23	Darmstadt	69-0576
KINKELE, Joh. G.	15	Groezeingen	68-0957
KINOWSKY, Joseph	33	Ostadomir	69-0547
Victoria 26, Augustine 5, Stephan 3, Theophil 10 months			
KINSKE, Leopold	26	Lech	69-0542
KINTZEL, Henriette	25	Vlotho	69-0572
Louise 11 months			
KIPKE, Anna	16	Blumenthal	70-0204
KIRAL, Eduard	18	Michelsdorf	71-0492
KIRCHBERG, Charles	26	Seifertsbach	68-0760
KIRCHBERGER, Rob.	21	Weilberg	71-0582
KIRCHER, Albert	17	Altenburg	69-0592
KIRCHER, Karl	28	Boitzenburg	71-0393
KIRCHGESSNER, Mattias	18	Kirchzell	71-0736
KIRCHHOFF, Carl	21	Wien	68-0647
KIRCHHOFF, Chls.	31	Schnathorst	68-0957
KIRCHHOFF, Fried.	22	Osnabrueck	70-0728
KIRCHHOFF, Friederike	18	Delmenhorst	68-0534
KIRCHHOFF, Friedrich	30	Goersbach	68-0566
Johanna 30, Augusta 7			
KIRCHHOFF, Gustav	15	Barmen	68-0939
KIRCHHOFF, Heinrich	26	Kirchberg	71-0492
KIRCHHOFF, Johann	17	Amelungen	69-0542
KIRCHHOFF, Ottilie	19	Nieder Opel	68-0907
KIRCHMEYER, Catharine	26	Thalkirchen	71-0643
KIRCHNER, Alexandrine	24	Coburg	69-1086
KIRCHNER, August	20	Worms	69-0968
KIRCHNER, Auguste	25	Schoenlanke	71-0712
KIRCHNER, Christiane	36	Pfeddersheim	70-1055
KIRCHNER, Ferdinand	34	Sievern	68-0566
Dorothea 31, Friedrich 9, Carl. 8, Aug. 6, Ferdinand 6 months			

NAME	AGE	RESIDENCE	YR-LIST
KIRCHNER, Gg.	28	Lauscha	68-0610
KIRCHNER, Johannes	25	Westerhaun	70-0378
KIRCHNER, Marie	15	Brakel	68-0982
KIRCHNER, Marie	21	Oberleimingen	71-0521
KIRCHNER, Phil	71	Darmstadt	70-0052
KIRIAM, Margarethe	25	Tarfirst	71-0643
KIRKEL, Wilhelm	31	Hannover	69-0672
Sophie 27, Sophie 9 months, Dorothea 22			
KIRSCH, August	38	Eilau	68-0770
KIRSCH, Henriette	31	Striegau	69-0182
Emma 4			
KIRSCH, Philippine	20	Sausenheim	69-1309
KIRSCHTOHR, Magd.	25	Offenbach	69-0542
Friedr. 2			
KIRSTEN, Louis		Erfurt	69-1363
KISCH, Rosalie	18	Dornbach	68-0610
KISCHEL, Wilhelmine	46	Saalfeld	68-0753
Emil 14, Otto 12, Emma 7			
KISLING, Christine	22	Schwakendorf	69-0321
KISOW, Louise	50	Fuersteusa	69-0547
August 18, Michael 16, Wilhelm 13, Caroline 7			
KISSIG, Emil	20	Bischofswerder	69-0229
KISSNER, Carl	28	Maylar	68-0939
Franziska 53, Heinrich 11 months			
KISTER, Adam	52	Burgham	69-0798
Amalia 42, Auguste 9, Joseph 7			
KISTINGER, Ludwig	25	Hahn	69-1076
KISTUR, Friedrich	32	Rastenberg	70-0384
KITTEN, Therese	22	Ibbenbuehren	68-0456
KLAAR, Josef	18	Wien	70-0378
KLAAS, Lambert	32	Schaale	70-0452
Cathy 30, Lambert 6, Johanne 4, Bernhard 11 months			
KLAASSEN, Catharina	22	Wrisse	69-0208
KLAASSEN, Jacob	69	Visgnard	69-0429
Anna 64, Ettje 21, Trientje 19			
KLAEBER, Conrad	43	Ebergoens	71-0492
Anna E. 32			
KLAER, Louise	17	Birkenfeld	70-0508
KLAGES, Caroline	48	Oldenburg	70-0452
Friedr. 9			
KLAGES, Friederike	71	Nienburg	71-0521
KLAGHOLZ, Johann	19	Oberaula	69-0798
KLAIBEN, Anna	19	Schwemmingen	69-0229
KLAIBER, Anna	27	Enzthal	68-0610
Louise 19			
KLAIS, Mich. Fr.	57	Woenersberg	68-0820
Margarethe 48, Anna 20, Eva 13, Gertrude 18			
KLAM, Michel	51	Niederzehren	69-0672
Eleonore 48, Justine 21, Michel 16			
KLAMETH, Franz	49	Schnellendorf	71-0363
Maria 45, Maria 17, Caroline 15, Mathilde 12, Herta 9, Therese 8, Josef 5			
KLAMPNER, David	45	Wien	68-1002
KLANG, Rosine	27	Owen	70-0378
KLAPINSKE, Mar.	52	Sommerklings	69-1011
KLAPPROTH, Heinr.	29	Mattorf	69-1212
KLAREMEYER, S.	24	L.Detmold	71-0789

NAME	AGE	RESIDENCE	YR-LIST
KLARMANN, Johann	32	Oberfranken	69-0784
Anna 32, Anna 24, Johann 3, Georg 9 months			
KLARNER, Herm.	20	Lichtenstein	70-0384
KLASS, Susanne	57	Heiligenkreuz	68-0760
Anna 27, Helena 16			
KLASSMEYER, Hermann	26	Wiedenbrueck	68-0014
KLATTE, John	15	Bremen	70-0508
KLATTE, Meta	19	Bremen	71-0736
KLAUBER, David	65	Feuerschau	69-1212
Julie 60			
KLAUS, August	45	Reichenbach	68-0786
Johanna 45, Amalie 16, Emma 12, Alfred 14, Hugo 9, Otto 5, Anna 7, Ida 3			
KLAUS, Cath.	16	Unterschmitten	68-0982
KLAUS, Justine	68	Winschendorf	68-0534
KLAUS, Katharina	18	Asmushausen	71-0363
KLAUS, Rosm.	15	Bueckershagen	71-0492
KLAUSMANN, Anna	23	Engerte	71-0643
KLAUSPRECHT, Gustav	30	Mainz	70-0259
KLAUSS, Jacob	26	Kemingen	69-0338
Bernhard 25			
KLAWOLZ, Martin	31	Gr. Teyopel	69-0547
Gr. Teyspel			
KLAWON, Caroline	26	Marienwerder	68-0786
KLAZEL, Franz	61	Bruenn	69-0841
KLEBE, Cath.	11	Schifferstadt	71-0393
KLEBERGER, Louise	23	Hannover	68-0456
KLEE, Carl	18	Bielefeld	68-0610
KLEE, Lina	36	Bielefeld	71-0363
KLEE, Wilhelm	9	Bremen	69-0050
KLEEMANN, Auguste	21	Korrbus	71-0226
Marie 16			
KLEEMANN, Joh.	26	Goersbach	68-0566
Amalie 21			
KLEEMEYER, August	37	Bremervoerde	68-0456
KLEFF, Emanuel	20	Untergussringen	71-0300
KLEFFEL, Henriette	20	Wichtshausen	70-0355
KLEFKER, Louis	18	Muenster	68-0760
KLEHNERS, Gesine	17	Deichhorst	69-1309
KLEIBER, Anna	22	Hosenpferrena	68-0770
KLEIDER, Christian	19	Ersingen	70-1003
KLEIMANN, Peter	32	Hohenzollern	70-0031
KLEIN, Adalbert	24	Koenigsberg	69-0015
KLEIN, Alwine	26	Gilgenburg	70-0184
KLEIN, Amalie	35	Liegnitz	68-0786
Emma 9, Emilie 5, Max 2, Rosa 11 months			
KLEIN, Anna	72	Ostfriesland	70-0378
Budingen			
KLEIN, August Ludwig	29	Unterfranken	69-0321
KLEIN, Bernh.	17	Bergreichenstei	71-0581
Therese 14			
KLEIN, Carl	17	Berndorf	71-0733
Wilhelm 14			
KLEIN, Caroline	20	Boehmen	70-1035
KLEIN, Cath.	20	Sickenhofen	71-0363
KLEIN, Christian	17	Sindelfingen	68-0534
KLEIN, Elisab.	23	Arenshain	71-0815
KLEIN, Eva	35	Galszeseg	71-0521

NAME	AGE	RESIDENCE	YR-LIST
Raj. 9, Cath. 8, Rosi 6, Adolph 4, Hani 2			
KLEIN, Fr.	30	Newark	70-0728
KLEIN, Franz Josef	68	Croen	69-0321
KLEIN, Friedrich	22	Ludwigstadt	69-0784
KLEIN, Gertrude	24	Dreis	71-0581
KLEIN, Heinrich	34	Unterfranken	69-1059
KLEIN, Hermine	23	Oldenburg	68-0647
KLEIN, Jacob	30	Binstadt	70-0135
KLEIN, Jacob	44	Cairo	69-0229
Marg. 46, Elise 15			
KLEIN, Jacob	16	Dettingen	68-0760
KLEIN, Joh.	20	Hoerdt	68-0982
KLEIN, Johann	69	Niederhochstadt	71-0492
Friederike 39, Friederike 5			
KLEIN, Johannes	18	Wangen	71-0492
KLEIN, Lazarus	14	Grimstadt	70-1055
KLEIN, Lisette	22	Ilvese	69-0457
KLEIN, Marie	19	Malmedy	70-0378
KLEIN, Martin	25	Hechtsheim	69-0572
KLEIN, Max	35	Karlsdorf	70-0076
Marie 30, Rosa 6, Anna 11 months, Luer 5			
KLEIN, Ulrich	32	Stockheim	69-0268
KLEINCKE, Carl	40	New York	69-0672
KLEINE, Anna	28	Ottersweier	71-0456
KLEINE, Friedrich	22	Wuelferdingen	68-0566
KLEINE, Heinrich	33	Winckelstetten	69-0321
KLEINE, Marie	44	Wulferdingen	69-0771
Caroline 13, Louise 8			
KLEINEMANN, Marie	36	Erlangen	71-0429
KLEINEMEYER, Heinrich	17	Spradow	68-0566
KLEINEMEYER, Johanna	23	Volmerdingen	68-0566
KLEINER, Gesine	31	Papenburg	69-1076
KLEINERT, Louise	32	Uckermuende	69-1319
Ottilie 19, Georg 11 months			
KLEINEWILKE, Heinrich	33	Winckelstetten	69-0321
KLEINHAUS, Anna	51	Bechtoldsheim	69-1396
Elise 20, Ferdinand 8, Georg 7			
KLEINMEYER, Johann	58	Wahrendorferber	71-0429
Marie 53, Louise 17, Ernst 12			
KLEINORDINGER, Elias	14	Ichenhausen	71-0712
Bertha 22			
KLEINSCHMIDT, Ernst	24	Isenstaedt	68-0907
KLEINSCHMIDT, widow	58	Cassel	68-0957
KLEINSORGE, Johanna	27	Voersten	68-0939
KLEINSTISCH, Franz	26	Bucharest	68-0661
KLEISER, Caroline	26	Vorarlberg	69-0560
KLEIST, Carl Fr.		Neuenhagen	69-0321
KLEMAN, Casp.	35	Brake	70-0308
Wilhelmine 27			
KLEMANN, Jacob	15	Osthofen	71-0821
KLEME, Friedrich	48	Iiserheide	68-0625
Louise 52, Wilhelmine 20			
KLEMENS, Michel	35	Wiltingen	69-0457
Barbara 48, Catharina 9, Johann 8, Michel 7, Peter 5			
KLEMENT, Simon	39	Frankfurt	69-0968
KLEMM, Jacob	26	Heslach	70-0443
KLEMM, Mathias	23	Obergrimpen	69-0229
KLEMME, Frdr.	25	Niese	68-0610
KLEMME, Hugo	23	Heidelbeck	68-0534
KLEMME, Robert	14	Lemgo	69-0457
KLENCK, Heinr.	16	Altenbruch	68-314
KLENCK, Louise	21	Sulzbach	69-0784
KLENCKE, Aug.	18	Altenbruch	71-0821
KLENDERMANN, Heinrich	44	Magdeburg	71-0736
KLENER, Sophie	24	Bremen	68-1027
KLENK, Rosine	19	Nitzenhausen	68-0786
KLENK, Rosine	20	Hall	70-0523
KLENNER, Rosalie	20	Freiburg	68-1002
KLEPFER, Gottlob	22	Grossheppach	71-0492
KLEPP, Barbara	18	Bischofsheim	71-0712
KLESENS, Wilhelmine	27	Gr.Umstadt	68-0907
KLESIUS, Wilhelmine	27	Gr.Umstadt	68-0907
KLESSA, Marianne	27	Usez	71-0684
KLETT, Friedrike	32	Dusslingen	69-1212
Wilhelm 7			
KLETT, Gottlieb	57	Steinberg	69-0592
KLEY, Val.	30	Boehmen	70-1142
KLEYMANN, Carl	35	Buende	68-0534
KLEZAK, Anna	27	Boehmen	69-1396
KLIE, Elisabeth	32	Heckgenstadt	69-0798
Franz 6			
KLIEGEL, Konrad	27	Grafmuehle	69-0592
Jacob 23			
KLIEKA, Marie	33	Klattau	68-0314
Catharine 16, Rosalie 3 months			
KLIMMER, Victoria	35	Muenchen	68-0760
Josef 14			
KLINDWORTH, John	19	Sellhorn	69-1011
Herm. 16			
KLING, Johannes	57	Gr. Bieberau	70-1035
Elisb. 50, Aderm. 35, Margr. 23, Johann 16, Philipp 14, Marie 9, Wilhelm 8, Fr			
KLINGE, Conrad	27	Roda	68-0456
KLINGE, Moritz	16	Hertinghausen	71-0456
KLINGELE, Heinr.	30	Todtnauberg	68-0566
KLINGEMAIER, Melchior	27	Hecklingen	68-0707
KLINGEMANN, Elise	18	Dallau	69-0848
KLINGEMAYER, Melcher	23	Hecklingen	68-0707
KLINGENBERG, Albert	18	Rosen	71-0733
KLINGENER, August	16	Achim	69-0268
KLINGHO'RST, Friederike	20	Hannover	71-1046
KLINGMANN, Georg	29	Heidelberg	69-0162
Johanna 35			
KLINKERFUSS, Emilie	39	Kurhessen	69-1212
Louise 7, Wilhelm 5, Carl 3			
KLINTWORTH, Margaret	18	Rhade	68-0625
KLINZEL, Babette	20	Volkach	68-0534
KLIPP, Georg	21	Melsungen	69-0572
KLIPPEL, Marie	16	Wendelsheim	71-0429
KLOBEDANZ, Siegm.	27	Magdeburg	68-0753
KLOCKE, Franz	16	Bremen	71-0684
KLOCKE, Henriette	19	Dettmold	69-0542
KLOCKE, Ignatz	29	Hampenhausen	68-0982
KLOCKSIN, Emilie	24	Samarthin	68-0753
Berta 2			
KLOEPPER, Christ.	34	Wietersheim	71-0521

NAME	AGE	RESIDENCE	YR-LIST
Sophie 48, Friedr. 5			
KLOEPPER, Marie	18	Friedewalde	71-0521
KLOEPPING, Fred.	28	Detmold	70-0308
KLOMANN, Charles	48	Washington	69-0784
KLOMANN, Frederik	42	Baltimore	69-0784
Caroline 54			
KLOPF, Margret	22	Oberlauchringen	68-1298
KLOPFER, Auguste	17	Hannover	71-0733
KLOPKE, Louise	21	Lehe	68-0610
KLOSA, Guenther	37	Berlin	70-1142
KLOSS, Gustav	36	Polisch Lissa	69-0268
KLOSS, Theodor	45	Hamburg	68-0760
KLOSTER, Jacob	28	Trepsum	70-0384
KLOSTERMANN, B.	24	Dargast	68-0852
KLOTZ, Arnold	15	Bargcyk	68-1027
KLOTZ, Friederike	28	Grossbettingen	68-1027
Friederike 16, Gottlob 28			
KLOTZ, Hugo	19	Marburg	71-0712
Carl 3			
KLOTZ, Pauline	27	Lahr	69-0583
KLOTZ, Sophie	18	Ruppau	68-0786
KLOTZBACH, Caspar	50	Bengendorf	68-1002
Eva Elis. 35, Johannes 9, Peter 7, Elisabeth 5, Eva Marg. 3, baby girl 5 months			
KLOTZE, Ernst	31	Weimar	69-1076
KLUBERTANZ, Elisabeth	58	Thuelb	71-0821
KLUCK, Louis	34	Muenster	70-0583
KLUERER, Ludowik	65	Vegesack	70-0148
KLUETER, Heinrich	19	Noerten	69-1059
KLUETZ, Carl	47	Preussen	68-0456
Charlotte 49, August 14, Friedrich 9, Otto 7, Ulrike 5			
KLUG, Christine	26	Unterfranken	69-1059
KLUG, Mathilde	18	Eschenring	68-0661
KLUGATH, Carl	31	Eschenring	68-0661
KLUGER, Wenzel	42	Neumark	71-0736
KLUGERSTEIN, Carl	45	Braunschweig	70-0329
Henriette 39, Theodor 18, Carl 15, Anna 7, Richard 5			
KLUGHERZ, Johann	39	Putzbrun	70-0329
Barbara 8, Georg 5, Johanne 4, Maria 2			
KLUGHERZ, Minna	18	Offenbach	68-0852
KLUGKIST, Fentje	36	Weener	69-1363
Gretje 5, Johann 3, Hermann 6 months			
KLUMP, Anton	26	Lauf	71-0226
KLUMP, Bernhard	26	Heslach	70-0443
KLUMP, Wilh.	27	Ramstadt	68-0786
KLUMPP, Burchard	32	Lautenbach	68-314
Balbine 26, Max 3, Peter 11 months, Michael 19			
KLUMPP, Friedr.	32	Baiersbronn	69-1059
KLUSMEYER, Sophie	18	Wersebe	71-0429
KLUSSMANN, Carol.	21	Holzhausen	71-0363
KLUTE, Doris	20	Bremervoerde	71-0456
KNAAK, Augusta	53	Berlin	68-1049
Joseph 20			
KNACK, Anna	24	Volmirtz	69-0848
KNACKE, Sophie	28	Lippe	69-1004
Heinrich 11 months			

NAME	AGE	RESIDENCE	YR-LIST
KNACKSTEDT, Helene	38	Hannover	69-1421
KNADEL, Emil	33	Hacheim	69-0292
KNAEBEL, Johanna	32	Magdeburg	68-0760
KNAKE, Margarethe	29	Hannover	70-0148
KNANTH, Philipp	34	Darmstadt	70-0308
KNAPP, Anna	14	Ems	69-1086
KNAPP, Carl	26	Rammelsbach	69-0572
KNAPP, Ernst	25	Karlsruhe	71-0521
KNATZ, Louis	28	Wahlershausen	69-0583
KNAUER, Caroline	34	S. Gotha	69-0572
Bianka 14, Valeska 6			
KNAUER, Conrad	25	Fuerth	68-0707
KNAUER, Ludwig	48	Groitsche	68-0760
Sophie 52, Emilie 14			
KNAUFF, Heinrich	15	Steinau	68-0456
KNAUL, Adolph	47	Berlin	68-1002
Rudolph 16			
KNAUS, Anna	32	Mainz	68-1027
Barbara 34, Jacob 9, Franz 7, Heinrich 4, Anna 9 months			
KNAUSS, Barbara	23	Asch	68-0786
KNAUSS, Charlotte	19	Betzenhein	70-0308
KNAUST, Heinrich	25	Dente	68-0820
KNEBEL, Adolf	26	Barmen	69-1086
KNEBEL, Amalie	32	Isselhorst	68-0760
KNEBELKAMP, Wilhelm	26	KlosterGauersch	68-0566
KNECHT, Carl	26	Dietz	68-0982
KNECHT, Elise	17	Mainz	70-0683
KNECKER, Friedrich	19	Mandelsloh	68-1027
KNEDES, Simon	14	Grengen	69-1086
KNEER, Xaver	19	Westernheim	68-0610
KNEF, Andreas	16	Wuerzburg	69-1059
KNEHL, Adolf	34	Elbing	68-0534
KNEIP, Conrad	27	Volkartshain	68-0760
Maria 23, Baby daughter 6 months			
KNEIPP, Otto	24	Dresden	69-0572
KNELL, Marie	23	Arnsheim	69-0268
KNELTER, Sophie	30	Zeiten	68-0456
KNERBLE, Eva	25	Woernersberg	68-0820
KNERR, Ludwig	19	Zweibruecken	68-0647
KNEU, Josef	35	Sultz	68-0566
KNICHEL, Joh.	25	Walhausen	70-0452
KNIEBEL, Nicolaus	28	Weimar	68-0872
KNIEF, Al.	17	Einlinghausen	71-1046
KNIERIEM, Cathar.	25	Kurhessen	69-1212
KNIERIEM, Just.	27	Rauschenberg	70-0170
KNIERIEM, Vincenz	54	Solz	68-0625
Sidonia 51, Elisabeth 19, Catharina 17, Heinrich 15, Vincenz 13, Dorothea 9			
KNIERION, Melchior	37	Altenburg	69-1086
KNIES, August	24	Regenswalde	69-0292
KNIFF, Heinr.	19	Brinkum	71-0821
KNIFFLER, Rud.	30	Crefeld	71-0736
KNIPFER, Auguste	26	Remsa	69-0079
Oscar 4, Mathilde 2, Agnes 3 months			
KNIPPE-OMEYER, Wilh.	26	Graul	71-0821
Marie 24, Heinr. 3, Wilhelm 10 months			
KNIPPENBERG, Eduard	17	Osnabrueck	68-0907

NAME	AGE	RESIDENCE	YR-LIST
KNITTER, Michael	30	Neu Subeza	71-0521
Auguste 19, Betha 18 months, Karl 6 months, Anna 51			
KNOBEL, Joh.	17	Leupelbach	71-0789
KNOBLAUCH, Franz	40	Frankfurt	68-0939
KNOBLAUCH, Jos.	17	Bohmenkirch	71-0581
KNOBLOCH, Helene	20	Mauchenheim	71-0429
KNOCH, Fr. Wilh.	21	Oelsnitz	69-0079
KNOCHE, Joh.	24	Wundershausen	68-0982
KNOCKE, Ludw.	29	Bremen	70-0170
KNOCKE, Wilhelm	28	Holzminden	69-0182
KNODEL, Jacob	20	Knittlingen	69-0182
KNODEL, Mathias	35	Vaichingen	69-0784
KNOEBLE, Alb.	18	Urach	68-0884
KNOEDLER, Josef	20	Iggingen	68-1298
KNOERIG, Herm.	49	Fuchel	69-0576
KNOERR, Georg	50	Cassel	68-0014
Ottilie 31, Georg 9, Gottfried 7, Christiane 6, Adam 4			
KNOESS, Conrad	31	Sellnrod	69-0592
KNOFFLER, Wilh.	29	Glaushau	71-0393
Hugo 4, Helene 9 months, Georg 9 months			
KNOLL, Catharina	29	Marbach	71-0492
KNOLL, Ed.	16	Altstudlen	71-0393
KNOLL, Elis.	16	Ahlenbach	71-0393
KNOLL, Johann	23	Moosbach	68-0314
Ferdinand 18, Margarethe 57			
KNOLL, John	32	Wertahune	68-0884
Sophie 26			
KNOLL, Nicolas	31	Trier	68-0852
KNOLL, Reinhard	17	Bresen	69-0229
KNOOP, Theodor	18	Cassel	68-0647
KNOPF, Henriette	43	Eberdorf	69-0547
KNOPP, Jacob		Sontheim	69-0162
Joh. 9			
KNORR, Susanne	54	Weikersheim	71-0226
Georg 21, Martin 13			
KNORR, Wilhelm	18	Hof	68-0907
KNORTZ, Catharina	32	Coblenz	68-0884
Joh. 3			
KNOTH, Catharine	20	Mandel	70-0452
KNUEBEL, Johann Fr.	16	Delmenhorst	71-0492
KNUEPFER, Martin	22	Osnabrueck	69-0050
KNUPPENBERG, Georg	26	Rabber	69-0572
KNUSPER, Reinh.	27	Rhena	71-0479
KNUTH, Carl	31	Riesenburg	71-0479
Cacelie 24			
KNUTH, Joh.	33	Marienwerder	68-0786
Elisabeth 28, Mathias 7, Augusta 5, Henriette 19, Johann 60, Anna 56			
KOBB, Ludwig	18	Menzingen	69-0572
KOBELE, Mathias	43	Cast Spring	69-0798
Catharine 42, Maria 9, Lena 8, Anton 6, Carl 4, Barbara 9 months			
KOBER, Auguste	22	Liechow	69-0490
KOBER, Conr.	43	Stengelheim	70-0178
KOBER, Gottlieb	30	Schleiz	70-0204
KOBERSTEIN, Catharina	22	Volkersbier	68-0625
Johann 12			
KOBIERZINSKA, J.	34	Stettnitz	69-0576
Peter 17, Barbara 14			
KOBITER, Wilhelm	35	Coeslin	69-0182
KOBOLD, Marie	23	Thueringen	70-0443
Christiane 17			
KOCH, Abolene	24	Leubach	71-0521
KOCH, Albert	34	Meisinke/Musink	69-1011
KOCH, Andreas	16	Hundeshagen	69-0771
KOCH, Andreas	14	Wollmer	68-0707
KOCH, Anna	26	Mittelseeman	70-1035
Mathilde 2			
KOCH, Barbara	21	Heppenheim	69-1086
KOCH, Carl	16	Wommen	69-0592
KOCH, Caroline	36	Greifenthal	69-0672
Hedwig 13, Albert 9			
KOCH, Caroline	19	Villingen	68-0884
Wilhelmine 17			
KOCH, Cath.	30	Loeben	71-0479
KOCH, Catharina	26	Flehingen	68-0760
KOCH, Christine	48	Trossingen	68-0957
KOCH, Dorothee	18	Amelitz	69-1086
KOCH, Elisabeth	34	Beelen	68-314
KOCH, Elisabeth	20	Niederweimar	71-0712
KOCH, Elise	60	Werthausen	70-1161
Margrethe 19, Anton 23			
KOCH, Emil	36	Wagenstadt	71-0226
KOCH, Emma	19	Ammelitz	68-0760
KOCH, Emma	20	Chemnitz	71-0521
KOCH, Ewald	23	Barmen	68-0647
KOCH, F.	33	Bremerhafen	69-1212
KOCH, FR.	24	Stolberg	70-0223
KOCH, Florentine	24	Osnabrueck	69-0559
KOCH, Franz	43	Bawinkel	69-0968
Margarethe 43, Franz 9, Angela 7, Agnes 6			
KOCH, Georg	48	Coburg	69-0572
Elisa 32, Friedrich 18, Georg 17, Barbara 13, Dorothea 8, Andreas 6, Nicolaus			
KOCH, Gertrude	21	Steinbach	68-1027
KOCH, Gustav	19	Hannover	69-1363
KOCH, Gustav	27	Leipzig	69-1212
KOCH, Gustav	17	Aschersleben	68-0865
KOCH, Heinr.	26	Buickborn	71-0815
Frau 25			
KOCH, Heinr.	39	Meiningen	71-0429
Christiane 30, Ida 5, Emilie 2			
KOCH, Heinrich	17	Eschersleben	68-0865
KOCH, Heinrich	16	Zweidorf	68-0852
Conradine 18			
KOCH, Henrich	23	Unterkatz	70-0076
KOCH, Henry	15	Bremen	70-1003
Doris 9			
KOCH, Henry	28	Rinteln	68-0982
KOCH, Jac.	26	Alsfeld	70-0308
Ernst 17			
KOCH, Jette	18	Wollbrechthause	68-0770
KOCH, Joh.	26	Weimar	70-0569
KOCH, Johann	23	Frankfurt	69-0592
KOCH, Johann	17	Egenhausen	69-0848
KOCH, Johann	58	Hamschen	68-0456
Barbara 58, Anna 25, Barbara 26, Marie 49			

NAME	AGE	RESIDENCE	YR-LIST
KOCH, Johann	56	Pfaffenhofen	68-0760
Sophie 43, August 23, Sophie 14			
KOCH, Johann	42	Diedingen	71-0492
Caroline 52			
KOCH, Johanne	52	Hausberg	69-1086
KOCH, Johannes	18	Weyher	68-0907
Joseph 16			
KOCH, Jos.	23	Schwarzenbach	69-0050
KOCH, Just.	16	Kurhessen	70-0355
KOCH, Justine	59	Soemmerda	68-0661
KOCH, Lazarus	46	Bermastel	71-0456
KOCH, Magdalene	24	Baikensahl	71-0492
KOCH, Marie	20	Herweiler	69-0572
KOCH, Marie	86	Darmstadt	71-0643
Cathrine 21			
KOCH, Mary	53	Fort Wayne	70-1003
KOCH, Mary	20	Niederweimar	68-0534
KOCH, Matthilde	16	Wollgast	71-0479
KOCH, Moritz	39	Paris	69-0321
KOCH, Nanny	28	Bremen	70-0089
Ernst 9, Jonny 7, Willy 5, Helene 3			
KOCH, Pauline	26	Berlin	68-1006
KOCH, Philippine	64	Steinbach	71-0456
KOCH, Sophie	33	Bremen	70-1003
Meta 14, Wilhelm 9, Carl 8, Johanna 6, Fritz 5, Gottfried 3, Lucie 9 months			
KOCH, Sophie	18	Borum	70-0204
KOCH, Sophie	32	Doertel	68-0852
KOCH, Wilhelmine	26	Bremen	71-0456
KOCHANSKA, Anila	19	Dombina	69-0547
KOCHDUMPE, Therese	26	Steinwiesen	69-1059
KOCHENDOERFER, Elise	24	Magdeburg	70-0682
KOCHER, Daniel	20	Bayreuth	71-0712
KOCHER, Louise	51	Kirchheim	69-0429
Margarethe 21			
KOCHSMEIER, Friedrich	17	Detmold	69-0457
Wilhelmine 22			
KOCK, Anna	30	Altenbachen	69-0771
KOCKORATZ, H.	38	Paderborn	69-1004
KODAD, Franz	35	Woperum	71-0581
Barbara 35, Josef 9, Vincenz 9, Franz 4, Carl 10 months			
KODER, Bekka	59	Mulsum	68-0820
KODISCH, Margarethe	26	Kupferberg	68-0872
KOEBB, Johann	58	Feldkirch	68-0884
Anna 23			
KOEBER, August	40	Kleina	68-1027
KOECHEL, Victor	20	Ulm	71-0643
KOECHELE, Alois	21	Erbach	69-0067
KOEHLE, Catharine	31	Herzogenweiler	68-0707
KOEHLER, Albert	17	Sandstedt	68-0939
KOEHLER, Aug.	31	Ziegenhain	70-1035
KOEHLER, August	48	Kraschen	70-1003
KOEHLER, August	16	Coeln	68-0939
KOEHLER, Auguste	32	Marienwalde	69-0848
Paul 9, Minna 5, Anna 2, Otto 6 months			
KOEHLER, Carl	50	Goeditz	71-0681
KOEHLER, Christine	22	Rebgestain	68-0982
KOEHLER, Christine	15	Coblenz	71-0456

NAME	AGE	RESIDENCE	YR-LIST
KOEHLER, Christoph	17	Schwalingen	68-0820
KOEHLER, Eduard	20	Bersdorf	70-0031
KOEHLER, Elise	30	Villingen	71-0300
KOEHLER, Gretchen	24	Hannover	70-0384
KOEHLER, Henriette	50	Bremen	68-0661
KOEHLER, Joh.	24	Altenburg	69-0592
KOEHLER, Johann	28	Wolfemuenster	71-0712
Rosalie 24			
KOEHLER, Josef	26	Schoenewalde	69-0848
KOEHLER, Juliane	21	Hamm	68-0014
KOEHLER, Katharina	20	Homberg	71-0363
Elise 16			
KOEHLER, Louis	25	Rebgeshain	68-1002
Marie 26, Augusta 9 months			
KOEHLER, Marie	25	Zimmern	71-0521
KOEHLER, Meta	18	Sandstedt	69-1011
KOEHLER, Michael	27	Elsendorf	71-0736
KOEHLER, Ottomar	19	Schalkan	68-0647
KOEHLER, Paul	20	Duschhausen	68-0957
Ursula 19, Barbara 17, Gertrud 16			
KOEHLER, Pauline	33	Leipzig	69-0229
KOEHLER, Reinhard	36	Pferdsdorf	68-0661
Dorothea 30, Maria Elis. 6			
KOEHLER, Sophie	43	New York	70-1142
KOEHLER, Therese	26	Koenigsberg	68-0534
Wilhelmine 55			
KOEHLER, Valentin	14	Altendorff	68-0456
KOEHLER, Wm.	40	Renningen	70-0170
C. 27			
KOEHM, Elise	28	Mainz	68-1027
Catharina 4, Johann 5 months			
KOEHN, Aug.	18	Wittichow	68-0314
KOEHN, Gottfried	54	Carolinenhorsch	71-0736
Hanne 52, August 21, Hanne 19, Hermann Franz 17, Hanne 14			
KOEHNE, Elise	51	Koeln	71-0479
KOEHNE, Friedr.	32	Rudolstadt	70-0378
KOEHNE, Henriette	23	Haldern	69-0848
KOEHNE, Johann	27	Luegde	69-0592
KOEHNE, Johanna	18	Bremen	68-1006
KOEHNKEN, Friedrich	16	Altbullstadt	70-0378
KOEHSING, Heinrich	39	Gr. Bruechter	71-0712
Friederike 35, August 15, Caroline 12, E. 9 months			
KOELBLIN, Carl	17	Baden	70-1161
Richard 21			
KOELKEBECK, Carl	24	Vegesack	70-0355
KOELLER, Carl	18	Detmold	70-0148
KOELLING, Christine	18	Wietersheim	68-0625
KOELLING, Friederich	17	Wiebersheim	69-1212
KOELLISCH, Jacob	16	Dittelsheim	71-0681
KOELN, Anna	26	Koehnholz	68-0957
KOELN, Louis	26	Bremen	71-0821
KOEMMICH, Phil.	39	Edenkoben	68-0534
KOENCHEL, Valentin	38	Czienowiser,Pru	69-0547
Barbare 30, Juliane 7, Joseph 10 months (Czianowisa,Prussia)			
KOENCKE, Wilh.	22	Hannover	71-0821
KOENEMANN, Ad.	17	Dortmund	70-0378

NAME	AGE	RESIDENCE	YR-LIST
KOENEMANN, Wilh.	49	Stolzenau	71-0821
Friedr. 14, Meta 9			
KOENIG, Anna	35	Schwarzenreuth	68-0939
Therese 9			
KOENIG, Anna	26	Altvorstetten	71-0492
KOENIG, Ant.	34	Luxemburg	68-0610
Anora 21			
KOENIG, Cath.	18	Dreis	71-0581
KOENIG, Elisabeth	33	Bergzell	70-0728
Benjamin 1 months, Anselm 24			
KOENIG, Elise	21	Bodenwyl	68-0786
KOENIG, Friedr.	20	Diepholz	71-0143
KOENIG, Georg	35	Galveston	70-1003
Marie 30			
KOENIG, Georg	25	Bergheim	68-0314
KOENIG, Georg	19	Asbach	68-0534
KOENIG, Heinrich	33	Hildburghausen	69-1212
Adolphine 31			
KOENIG, Heinrich	49	Borgentruck	70-0443
KOENIG, Heinrich	23	Hannover	71-0736
KOENIG, Heinrich	23	Hannover	71-0736
KOENIG, Hermann	19	Osterbruch	69-0572
KOENIG, Jacob	49	Hoffenheim	71-0684
Catharina 48, Minna 18, L. 16, Jacob 9, Catharine 7			
KOENIG, Johann	22	Magdeburg	69-0490
KOENIG, Julchen	24	Deut	71-0792
KOENIG, Leopold	38	Prag	70-0443
Gella 39, Regina 8, Frieda 7, Alfred 6, hugo 4, Rudolph 3, Wilhelm 11 months			
KOENIG, Math.	16	Dreis	71-0581
KOENIG, Minna	32	Guetersloh	71-0456
KOENIG, Nicol	13	Pfaffschwende	70-0569
KOENIG, Therese	52	Zeitz	68-0566
KOENIGSBAUM, Moritz	39	Pest	70-0031
KOENITZER, Malwina	23	Danzig	68-0957
KOENKER, Jobst H.	19	Ennigloh	68-1002
KOENNECKE, Anna	27	Berlin	71-0792
KOEPCKE, Herm.	16	Bockhorn	68-0957
KOEPER, Heinrich	20	Bremen	69-0559
KOEPKEN, Friederike	63	Schlagentin	68-0770
KOEPLIN, Eva	32	Flatow	71-0736
Reinhard 7, Anna 5, Ernst 2			
KOEPP, August	39	Boninen	68-0770
Caroline 34, Augusta 13, Marie 11, Franz 7			
KOEPPEN, Carl	28	Moellitz/Meckle	69-0547
Sophie 25, Wilhelm 4, Emilie 9 months			
KOEPPEN, Ludwig	55	Moellitz/Meckle	69-0547
Minna 49, Wilhelm 24, Fritz 22, Auguste 20, Adolph 17			
KOEPPER, Friedr.	29	Minden	68-0786
Christine 28, Christine 6 months			
KOEPPER, Wilh.	30	Minden	68-0786
Lisette 20			
KOERBER, Carl	17	Frankfurt	68-0786
KOERL, Johann	18	Rodesgrun	68-0939
KOERNER, Heinrich	21	Detmold	69-0457
Wilhelmine 21			
KOERNER, Joseph	24	Paderborn	68-0314
KOERNER, Marg.	27	Endchenreuth	71-1046

NAME	AGE	RESIDENCE	YR-LIST
KOERNER, Wilhelmine	20	Weimar	71-0429
Ernestine 18			
KOERPER, Adolf	28	Nuertingen	68-0566
KOERSCHNER, Mary	21	Coburg	68-0760
KOERTING, Clara	28	Berlin	71-0821
Paul 5, Otto 30			
KOERTZCHER, Gustav	16	Eisenberg	68-0884
KOESTER, August	25	Woerderfeld/Lip	69-0547
Wilhelm 18			
KOESTER, Catharina	13	Otterndorf	71-0429
KOESTER, Heinr.	27	Luebeck	70-1055
KOESTER, Heinr.	41	Sudweyerheide	68-0884
Adelh. 40, Anna M. 13, Adelheid 12, Claus H. 10, Elisabeth 8			
KOESTER, John	16	Loxstedt	71-0643
KOESTER, John H.	25	Boversen	68-0957
KOESTER, Ludwig	18	Corbach	71-0643
KOESTER, Wilhelm	15	Westrup	71-0821
KOESTERING, Marie	26	Dahlinghausen	68-0982
KOESTERS, Joh.	25	Delbruck	68-314
KOESTLER, Barbara	20	Bleistadt	71-0521
KOESTLER, Josef	19	Bleistadt	69-0208
KOETH, Ottilie	15	Krzurouke	71-0300
Mathilde 8			
KOETHE, Christian	50	Gr. Turra	71-0712
Christine 50, Carl 12, Hermann 9, Emilie 7			
KOETHE, Louis	33	Grossen	68-0939
Hugo 14			
KOETTER, Fr.	35	Krollage	68-0820
Ilsabein 36, Louise 9, Franz 6,, Heinrich 3, Ilsab. 9 months, Louise 60			
KOFIG, Friedr.	41	Eglert	71-0581
KOGGE, Louise	21	Bremen	69-1076
KOHAUT, Theresia	19	Putlitz	68-0566
KOHL, Andreas	28	Sausenheim	69-0162
KOHL, Anna	27	Noischeid	68-0982
KOHL, Caspar	24	Unterschneidhei	68-0534
KOHL, Cath.	17	Darmstadt	70-0728
KOHL, David	14	Rauschenberg	71-0712
KOHL, Friedr.	16	Wagnersfehn	71-0363
KOHLBACHER, Jacob	26	Darmstadt	69-1212
KOHLBECK, Georg	34	Grossaigen	71-0429
Barbara 28			
KOHLER, Emil	19	Berlin	69-0292
KOHLER, Heinr.	16	Quernheim	68-0610
Frdr. 15			
KOHLES, Andreas	30	Oberfranken	70-0508
KOHLHAAS, Casper	24	Bensendorf	69-0321
KOHLHAGEN, Adolf	19	Soest	71-0643
KOHLHEIM, Julius	18	Stettin	69-0848
KOHLHEIM, Louise	43	Stettin	69-0848
Emil 11, Max 7, Oscar 1			
KOHLHEPP, Johann	25	Gundhelm	68-0566
Henriette 19			
KOHLHORST, Heinr.	24	Sielhorst	71-0300
KOHLIDKA, Franz	31	Boehmen	70-0728
KOHLMANN, Johann	17	Hannover	69-0029
KOHLMEYER, Catharina	22	Lauscheid	68-0939
KOHLMEYER, F. H.	61	Hankenberg	68-0957

NAME	AGE	RESIDENCE	YR-LIST
Anna M. 18, Henry 18			
KOHLTFERBER, Louise	14	Hannover	71-0821
KOHN, Anna	40	Muttersdorf	68-1006
Jeanette 18, Friedrich 12, Fritz 13			
KOHN, Bertha	20	Steinbach	68-0456
KOHN, Caroline	37	Muehlhausen	68-0760
KOHN, Catharina	19	Boehmen	69-1076
KOHN, Catharine	26	Lancaster	63-0244
William 6, Catharine 4			
KOHN, Emma	18	Buchau	71-0492
KOHN, Josef	18	Weseritz	70-1161
Emanuel 16, Jacob 10			
KOHNLIE, Carl	18	Welzheim	71-0712
KOHRING, Heinrich	38	Osnabrueck	69-1059
Johanne 35, Alex 3, Carl 9 months			
KOHRS, Hermann	15	Otterstedt	68-0707
KOHRS, Theodor	18	Gross Sottrum	71-0712
KOHTE, Heinrich	26	Herzfeld	68-0820
KOINKE, Carl L.	36	Hofgeismar	68-0884
KOINKE, Maria R.	65	Moys	68-0884
Johanna A. 27			
KOKE, Louise	25	Krautheim	68-0939
KOKESCH, John	28	Boehmen	70-1035
Marie 21, Joseph 11 months			
KOLADZECK, Herm.	22	Goeschen	68-1027
KOLANDER, Johann	41	Dembentke	68-0770
Wilhelmine 42, Wilhelm 16, Johannes 12, Ferdinand 9, Louise 6, Otto 3			
KOLB, Cath.	20	Cassel	71-0143
KOLB, Johannes	16	Lorch	68-1027
KOLIHA, Theresia	25	Dotronitz	70-0329
KOLISCHA, Theod.	21	Wien	71-0581
KOLKMANN, Diedrich	17	Langwedel	70-1003
KOLKMANN, Wilhelmine	50	Kuppendorf	70-0683
KOLLAR, Johann	32	Rackowitz-Bohem	70-0006
Anna 31, Johann 5, Marie 6 months			
KOLLARSCHICK, Anna	23	Wien	71-0479
KOLLATZ, Albertine	36	Berlin	71-0712
Anna 8, Robert 5			
KOLLATZ, Anna	21	Piepenburg	70-0378
KOLLER, Dorothea	25	Luedersfeld	71-0363
Heinrich 15, Conrad 6			
KOLLERMANN, Auguste	19	Schoenlanke	71-0821
KOLLINSKA, Arnold	24	Wien	70-0683
KOLLMANN, Anna	22	Stockhausen	68-0753
Joh. 6 months			
KOLSCH, Louis	33	Greitz	70-0148
KOLWEG, Heinrich	35	Ortmanbocholt	69-0429
KOMATRIENS, John	15	Meckelstedt	69-0560
KOMER, Emma	33	Kensingen	71-0712
KOMKE, Marga.	32	Nuernberg	69-1086
KOMMER, Friedr.	45	Imheiden	69-0923
Margarethe 53, Henrich 19, Carl 17, Martin 14			
KOMPTER, Johanna	40	Rottweil	69-0848
Wilhelm 14			
KOMWELL, Joh.	24	Reusten	70-0089
KONBA, Marhias	16	Boehmen	70-1161
KONDEL, Josef	46	Losa	70-0329
Theresa 37, Maria 17, Wenzel 13, Anna 6, Petronella 3, Anton 3 months			
KONERT, Heinr.	30	Nowack	70-0452
KONICZENY, Albertina	32	Berlin	68-0820
Adelheid 11 months			
KONKE, B.	25	Hinchau	70-1066
KONNEMANN, Wilhelm	23	Hamburg	68-0907
KONRAD, Friedr.	19	Carlsruhe	68-0786
KOO, Hermann	44	Settlage	69-0560
Elisabeth 43, Hermann 8, Gerhard 6, August 11 months, Engeline 11 months			
KOOB, Anna	24	Speyer	69-1011
Sofia 32			
KOOB, Joh.	62	Duerkheim	70-0728
KOOP, Friedrich	19	Dielingen	69-0542
KOOP, Friedrich	50	Dielingen	69-0583
Sophie 46, Engel 16, Wilhelm 9, Wilhelmine 5, Heinrich 3			
KOOP, Johann	14	Scharmbeck	69-0583
KOOP, Louise	28	Paris	68-0907
KOOP, Sybille	54	Speyer	69-1011
KOOPMANN, August	25	Fladderlohausen	69-1059
KOOPMANN, Diedrich	63	Warnow	69-1076
KOOPMANN, Heinr.		Verden	71-0226
KOOPMANN, Maria	21	Dalum	68-0907
KOPELKA, Sophie	56	Behle	68-1002
Augusta 21, Marie 19			
KOPF, Claus	14	Johannesroth	70-0378
KOPF, Ernest	16	Belum	69-1086
KOPF, Fr. Wilh.	15	Steinau	71-0363
KOPF, Joh.	24	Johannesroth	70-0378
KOPF, Martin	16	Luedingen	71-0521
KOPF, Peter	20	Ihlienworth	68-0760
KOPISCH, Gottlieb	9	Reuss	69-1004
KOPLIEN, Julius	26	Kappe	68-0865
KOPP, Anna	16	Hannover	69-1076
KOPP, Anton	17	Kamischbach	70-100
Apollonia 13			
KOPP, Catharina	23	Constanz	69-0672
KOPP, Charles	17	Drake	70-0508
KOPP, Christine	27	Neufringen	71-0643
KOPP, Dorette	19	Moeneheim	71-0712
KOPP, Joh.	35	Darmstadt	70-1142
Elise 37, Cath. 6, Elise 3			
KOPP, Mary	29	Nafringen	70-0170
M. 17			
KOPP, Pauline	28	Wasseraltingen	68-0534
KOPP, Wilhelm	34	Knatterheide	68-1006
Justine 32, Wilhelm 11 months			
KOPPARS, Gabriel	42	Boehmen	70-0728
Rosalie 44, Josef 9, Amalie 8, Wilhelm Heinrich 9 months			
KOPPEN, Cath.	36	Gross Almerode	68-1002
Oscar Theodor 14, Carl W. A. D. 13, Elise A. 11, Augusta Ch. 9, Herm. W. C. E.			
KOPPENHOFER, Wilhelm	19	Sulzbach	69-0784
KOPPERMANN, John	16	Verden	70-1003
KOPS, Joh. Fr.	20	Drege	68-0760
KORBELT, Jocunde	52	Bischofsheim	69-0592

NAME	AGE	RESIDENCE	YR-LIST
Marga. 36, Anna 2, Adam 9 months			
KORBMACHER, Wilhelm	35	Coeln	70-0523
Catharine 28, Louis 5, Theodor 3, Pauline 3 months			
KORDES, Paul	31	Neu Subeza	71-0521
Marie 27, Johann 6 months			
KORDING, Christ. Fr.	15	Hiddengswarden	69-0321
Joh. 14			
KORFF, August	24	Bremen	70-0089
KORFF, Christ.	18	Huelsen	68-0566
KORFFAGE, Max	30	Loningen	70-1003
KORKER, Heinrich	36	Hannover	69-1059
Christine 36			
KORMEYER, Henry	27	Hilter	68-0957
KORN, Albrecht	16	Tarocin	68-0982
KORN, Elisabeth	18	Neumorschel	71-0363
KORN, Ignaz	29	Schelekrippen	71-0789
S. 24, Anna 21, Phil. 26, Martha 30, Bernhard 15			
KORNAU, Margarethe	24	Kl. Borstel	70-0523
Johann 26			
KORNBOSKI, Andr.	52	Nakel	71-0581
KORNCKE, Carl	25	Buende	68-0939
Marie 27, Johanna 4, Carl 9 months			
KORNDNER, Lina	38	Erlangen	71-0521
KORNELSEN, Pauline	23	Saalfeld	68-0753
Georg 1, Max 6 months (died on board)			
KORNKUMPF, Adolf	17	Gosslar	68-0566
KORNREICH, Eduard	25	Cochem	68-0647
KORNSTEDT, Louis	30	Sondershausen	70-0728
KORST, John	23	Waldmoor	69-0841
KORTE, Heinrich	44	Kutenhausen	69-0798
Christine 46, Johann 19, Heinrich 9, August 6			
KORTE, Heinrich	59	Stavern	69-0229
Bernhard 20, Johann 18, Tecla 27			
KORTELE, Catharina	32	Nordheim	68-0939
KORTEN, August	34	Wesel	69-0592
KORTH, Gerhard	19	Grosvern	68-0939
KORTHALS, Paul	16	Zirkwitz	68-0786
KORTHE, Wilh.	24	Ebeleben	71-0479
KORTMANN, Rosine	36	Steinbach	71-0456
KORTMEIER, Louise	59	Oberwuesten	68-1006
KORZMEIER, Therese	30	Brochterbeck	69-0429
KOSCHE, Johann	32	Sudejov	70-0329
KOSNER, Christian	16	Mainz	71-0429
KOSS, Moritz	27	Lawenworth	68-0939
KOSTER, Anna	46	Kenn	68-314
Peter 7, Mathias 5, Marie 11 months			
KOSTER, Ernst	20	Midlum	68-0982
KOTEISDORF, J.R.	53	Hartford	69-0841
Bertha 57, Robert 20, Hans 19, Marie 10, Franz 8			
KOTHE, Chr.	16	Bremervoerde	71-0581
KOTHE, Wilhelm	33	Hannover	70-0728
Anna 31			
KOTHE, Wilhelmine	17	Kurhessen	70-1142
Wilhelm 19			
KOTHMANN, Heinrich	31	Osnabrueck	68-0939
KOTSCH, Tjark	31	Wangerooge	69-0923
KOTTKE, Daniel	23	Wittenssen	70-1142
KOTTKE, Julius	13	Neu Subeza	71-0521
KOTTLER, Heinrich		St. Gallen	69-0572
KOTTMEYER, Ernst	37	Holsen	68-0566
Anna 27, Sophie 57, Friederike 25, Sophie 3, Anna 9 months			
KOTTMEYER, Wilh.	17	Holzhausen	68-0566
KOTZHAMMER, David	30	Wien	69-0572
KOWALSKI, Antonia	26	Zurnwia	68-0707
Joseph 9 months, Catharina 24, Maria 9 months			
KOY, Aug.	39	Ciessau	70-1055
Anna 24, Tecla 11 months			
KRAATZ, Marie	25	Seesen	69-0429
KRABATH, Franciska	34	Zarmarta/Polen	69-0576
Johann 3			
KRACHER, Georg	29	Rueckersdorf	69-1076
KRACK, Georg	30	Wesseserode	69-0771
KRACK, Heinr.	20	Grauel	71-0821
KRACK, Heinrich	16	Dorum	71-0521
KRACK, Sybilla	41	Salmuenster	69-0560
KRACKE, Marie	24	Bremen	69-0457
KRACKOWSKY, Caroline	37	Lauenburg	71-0479
Marie 3, Johanne 10 months			
KRAEGEL, Johann	30	Schoenewald	69-0542
KRAEGER, Heinr.	33	R.B.Coblenz	68-0647
Marie 34, Heinrich 7, Elisabeth 5, Peter 3			
KRAEMER, Carl	22	Wingershausen	69-0321
KRAEMER, Elise	24	H. Darmstadt	70-1003
KRAEMER, Ferd.	19	Schriesheim	70-0170
KRAEMER, Franz	25	Nierding	68-0753
Anna 24, Nicolaus 9			
KRAEMER, Friederike	18	Sperrge	68-0939
KRAEMER, Friedrich	16	Breitenbach	68-0820
KRAEMER, Heinrich	49	Liekwegen	68-0534
Augusta 48, Karl 18, Wilhelmine 16, Ferdinand 13			
KRAEMER, Johann	22	Allershausen	68-0625
KRAEMER, Nicol.	35	Derkweiler	70-0308
Christine 36, Hubert 6, Michael 4, baby daughter 11 months			
KRAEMER, Peter	29	Albershausen	68-0625
KRAEMER, Phil.	24	Mertesheim	68-0957
KRAENER, Carl	27	Bueckeburg	69-1004
KRAENER, Frdr.	59	Bueckeburg	69-1004
Sophie 50, Ferd. 35, Ernst 14, Aug. 12, Heinr. 9, Heinr. 16			
KRAENKEL, Gustav	23	Magersbach	68-0770
KRAEPFEL, D. Gustav	27	Tuebingen	70-0184
KRAETEL, Barb.	32	Rosshaupt	70-0308
Anna 5, Catharina 3			
KRAETER, Andreas	18	Hargelin	69-0547
KRAEUSER, Geo.	21	Marten-Marlen	69-1421
KRAEUTHLE Friedl.	26	Lauterbach	71-0815
KRAFFT, Aloys	39	Spessart	68-0786
KRAFT, Apolonia	22	Nierstein	69-0457
KRAFT, Elise	36	Botenhausen	70-0384
KRAFT, Heinrich	26	Rebgesheim	68-0456
KRAFT, Jac.	16	Muehlbach	71-0393
KRAFT, Joh.	25	Lauffen	71-0681

NAME	AGE	RESIDENCE	YR-LIST
KRAFT, Johann	32	Kleinselheim	68-0661
KRAFT, John	17	Schmittau	71-0456
KRAFT, Magdalena	27	Lautenbach	68-314
Helene 25, Benedict 18			
KRAFT, Otto	16	Darmstadt	68-1027
KRAFT, William	18	Heilbronn	70-1003
KRAFTHOEFER, Carl	29	Allendorf	71-0226
KRAFTS, Minna	23	Wuerzburg	69-0542
KRAHN, August	22	Parsin	69-0321
KRAICH, Reinhold	29	Unterfranken	68-0786
KRAIZ, Barbara	17	Buda/Austria	69-0547
KRALL, Catharine	50	Gladerau/Bohemi	69-0049
Jacob 17			
KRAMBACH, Jacob	54	Katzenheim	68-0770
Catharina 58			
KRAMER, Albert	18	Braunschweig	70-0682
KRAMER, August	20	Webedingen	69-1212
KRAMER, Cacilie	15	Riedlingen	69-1396
KRAMER, Cathrine	26	Graben	71-0456
Louise 24			
KRAMER, Elisabeth	40	Vohrum	68-0852
Carl 12, Emma 8, Heinrich 27, Johanna 30, Carl 9 months, Albert 9 months			
KRAMER, Elise	18	Bremen	71-0643
KRAMER, Helene	40	Lippstadt	70-0523
KRAMER, Hermann	27	Grosvern	68-0939
KRAMER, Hermann	24	Quakenbrueck	71-0521
KRAMER, Johanne	28	Obernhofen	69-1004
Friederike 23			
KRAMER, Joseph	24	Rosenthal	70-0452
KRAMER, Marie	22	S.C.Gotha	70-0728
KRAMER, Marie	23	Eppelsheim	71-0429
KRAMER, Sophie	20	Bueckeburg	69-0292
KRAMER, Willem	22	Weitenhagen	69-0771
KRAMFUSS, Gerh.	17	Brachterbeck	69-0583
KRAMPEL, Wilhelm	27	Himkirchen	70-0223
Friedrich 20			
KRAMPF, Adolf	19	Mecklar	68-0534
KRANE, August	32	Lippe Detmold	70-0384
Anna 11 months			
KRANICH, Franz	18	Breitenbach	69-0542
KRANICH, Wilhelmine	20	Rudolstadt	71-0736
August 15			
KRANTZ, Rudolph	21	Heilbronn	70-0076
KRANZ, Alwine	25	Berlin	70-1023
KRANZ, Franziska	16	Kirchland	68-0753
KRANZ, Georg	35	Hessen	70-0178
Anna 29, Adam 7, Joh. 77			
KRANZ, Herm.	27	Rietburg	68-0982
KRANZ, Joh.	31	Neukirchen	71-0815
KRANZEN, Gretje	28	Akelsberg	68-0884
KRANZER, Wilhelm	27	Boehmen	70-0728
KRANZUSCH, Wilh.	29	Gleischow	69-0321
KRAPPE, Elise	20	Wickenrode	71-0363
KRATHKY, Anna	73	Gruenewald	68-0770
KRATZ, August	28	Halberstadt	69-0848
KRATZ, Christ.	30	Darmstadt	70-0355
KRATZ, Friedrich	32	Schwarzb.Rudols	71-0492
Minna 29, August 9, Emilie 9 months			
KRATZ, Simon	17	Dudenhofen	71-0456
KRATZSCH, Peter	39	Nienburg	68-0786
KRAUCHER, Philipp	37	Mainz	69-1059
KRAULL, Fritz	26	Otterndorf	69-1396
KRAUS, Carl	21	Muenster	68-314
KRAUS, Carl	20	Wien	71-0736
KRAUS, Friedr.	24	Frankfurt a/M	70-0135
KRAUS, Georg	37	Jarkoits	68-1006
Caroline 25			
KRAUS, Heinrich	23	Appenhagen	69-1076
KRAUS, Joh.	18	Schwurbitz	68-0820
KRAUS, Joh.	12	Mitteldorf	71-0167
KRAUS, MArgarethe	21	Eppelsheim	68-0534
KRAUS, Melchior	24	Sachsen Meining	69-0321
KRAUS, Philipp	34	Boehmen	68-0456
KRAUSCH, Joh. Dan.	19	Coblenz	68-1002
KRAUSE, Amalie	9	Zeven	71-0479
KRAUSE, August	33	Rudolstadt	68-0760
Christine 27, Charles 5, Gustav 3, Philipp 59, Maria 59, Louise 34, Augusta 21			
KRAUSE, August	61	Pummelwitz	71-0643
Charlotte 60			
KRAUSE, Ernst	25	Friedrichshuett	68-0982
KRAUSE, Franz	18	Niederfrankenh.	68-0907
KRAUSE, Friedrich Th.	29	Erfurt	68-0661
KRAUSE, Julius	37	Rudolstadt	70-0378
Friederich 38			
KRAUSE, Kilian	24	Sisstingen	68-0982
KRAUSE, Magdalena	18	Duerkheim	68-1027
KRAUSE, Sophie	24	Hensfeld	69-0542
Christine 5 months			
KRAUSE, Wilh.	40	Vechta	68-1002
Antoinette 40, Widow 60, Wilhelm 16, Louis 11, Anton 8, Bernhard 4, Lisette 6,			
KRAUSHAAR, August	21	Hanau	69-1076
KRAUSS, Carl	33	Mark Neukirch	71-0712
KRAUSS, Carl Th.	26	Bremen	70-0223
Catharina 26, Eduard 8 months			
KRAUSS, Christian	28	Schoenbrunn	71-0684
KRAUSS, Friedr.	16	Richelkirchen	71-0521
Heinrich 15			
KRAUSS, Joseph	30	Coeln	70-100
KRAUSS, Louis	17	Westernach	69-1212
KRAUSS, Sophie	25	Aalen	69-0429
KRAUTLEHNER, Caroline	27	Ernsbach	69-0592
KRAUTLER, Albert	26	Cannstatt	68-0647
KRAUTWUSEN, Heinr.	43	Saargsund	71-0792
Susanne 45, Theodor 14, Caroline 9, Rudolph 8, Bernh. 6, Philipp 4, Alwine 11			
KRAY, Georg	47	Lehmen	71-0429
Anne 41, Gertrude 13, Jacob 11, Magdalene 9, Johann 6, Marie 2			
KREBS, Adolf	32	Hardenbeck	68-0566
Johanna 29, Albert 9, Anna 3, Johanna 10 months			
KREBS, Anna	24	Badbergen	69-0968
KREBS, Catharina	30	Selzen	68-0707
KREBS, Heinr.	24	Oldendorf	71-0226
KREBS, Lisette	27	Heilbronn	71-0456
KREBST, Georg	36	Darmstadt	69-1059

NAME	AGE	RESIDENCE	YR-LIST
Sarah 34			
KRECH, Friedrich	30	Meiningen	71-0736
Auguste 28, Antonia 7, Bernhard 3			
KREFT, Hann.	30	Wallenbrueck	71-0393
KREFT, Wilhelm	24	Sperrge	68-0939
KREGE, Johann	18	Bromberg	68-0865
Gottlieb 18			
KREGEL, Louise	19	Hannover	68-0647
KREGEL, Marie	27	Hannover	69-1004
Marie 9 months, Leon. 9			
KREGEL, Peter	24	Hoerdt	68-0982
KREHRER, John	32	Dornstetten	69-0560
Catharina 27, John 9 months			
KREIDEL, Jacob	31	Lammsberg	71-0456
KREIDEL, Val.	23	Offenbach	68-0939
KREIDENWOLFF, H.	17	Treysa	69-0029
KREIENJOBST, Amalie	24	Langenholzhause	68-0647
KREIMEYER, Adolph	26	Rischenau	68-0884
KREINBERG, Marie	26	Rockenhausen	70-0355
KREISEL, Friedrich	46	San Francisco	69-1059
KREISEL, Pauline	21	Mieczkow	69-0572
KREITER, Ferdinand	18	Merzhausen	68-0566
KREJCI, Josef	53	Boehmen	70-1161
Cathrine 48, Josefa 23, Marie 9, Anton 7			
KREKOW, Wilhelmine	21	Schuerenfeld	71-0429
Maria 17			
KREMBEL, E.		Schifferstadt	71-0393
KREMER, Wilhelm	39	Siegen	68-0456
Catharine 39, Wilhelm 7, Elisabeth 3, Philipp 11 months			
KRENNING, Heinrich	23	Hilter	68-0647
KRENSCH, Heinr.	35	Muenster	68-0982
KRENSKE, Gustav		Rohrsdorf	69-0182
KRENZ, Julius	16	Lippe-Col., Pol	69-0547
Wilhelm 25, Wilhelmine 60			
KREPPEL, Peter	18	Oberselters	68-0314
Clara 19			
KRESS, Christ.	34	Nendingen	68-0820
Marie 39, Wilhelm 15, Amalie 12, Barbara 10, Josefa 9, Emma 5, Fidel 2			
KRESS, Franz E.	26	Reuss	70-0178
Wilhelm 16			
KRESS, Hermann	19	Greiz	71-0733
KRESS, Ottilie	21	Unterfranken	69-0968
KRESS, Otto	15	Altjendorf	71-0733
KRESSER, Caroline	24	Schernberg	68-0625
KRETER, Friedrich	20	Cleveland	69-0490
KRETSCH, Wilhelmine	69	Bieberich	69-1319
KRETSCHMER, Franz	20	Meissen	69-1004
KRETTA, Wilh.	27	Horst/Russia	69-0049
KREULEIN, Conrad	41	Michelfeld	68-0982
KREUSCH, Heinr.	35	Muenster	68-0982
KREUSSEL, Magda.	32	Unterruesselbac	68-0982
KREUTER, R.	19	Coblenz	68-0884
KREUTZ, Jacob	42	Haschbach	71-0363
KREUTZER, Bernh.	16	Duesseldorf	69-0841
KREUZ, Oswald	28	Podarewa	70-0223
KREUZER, Christian	25	Nofelden	69-0015
KREUZER, Johann	56	Stawochin	69-0672

NAME	AGE	RESIDENCE	YR-LIST
Florentine 55, Henriette 20, Albert 13, Caroline 9, Auguste 7			
KREUZMANN, Marie	25	Frankfurt a/M	69-0672
KREY, Dorothea	26	Rheinfels	68-0872
KREY, Henrich	34	Oldenburg	69-0268
KREY, Henry	28	Oldenburg	70-0452
Wife 22			
KREY, Wilhelm	28	Neukirchen	68-0852
KREYENBERG, Carl	24	Barmen	69-1086
KREYER, Conrad	44	Rudolstadt	69-0547
Johanne 46, Carl 18, Hermine 15, Berthold 7, Edmund 6, Antonie 4, Johann 20			
KREYMBORG, Louis	17	Horumersiel	69-0490
KREYMBORG, Sophia	26	Hommersiel	68-0957
KREYNEKE, Rob.	31	Nakel	69-1421
Ernestine 25, baby 4 months			
KRICK, Andreas	17	Bingen	68-0760
KRICKMEYER, Anton	20	Bueren	69-0572
KRIEBEL, Nicolaus	28	Weimar	68-0872
KRIEBIATKOWSKY, John	29	Laaske	69-0338
KRIECHMANN, Wilhelm	36	Lutzlow	70-0006
KRIECK, Louis	22	Rudolstadt	71-0736
KRIEG, H.	19	Speyer	69-1011
KRIEG, Jacob	28	Altdorf	69-0162
KRIEG, Joh.	40	Kommbach	71-0792
Anna 38, Elisabeth 9, Johann 7, Michael 5, Justus 4, Jacob 9 m.			
KRIEG, Martin	63	Northeim	71-0521
Johanne 60, Franz 27, Sophie 25			
KRIEGER, Carl	37	Blasheim	69-0771
KRIEGER, Caroline	20	Wolf	68-0939
KRIEGER, Christoph	20	Ahl	69-0429
KRIENSICK, Heinrich	14	Neuenkirchen	70-0523
KRIETE, Louise	25	Vegesack	68-0939
KRIETEMEYER, Friedrich	56	Schnathorst	68-0566
KRIETENSTEIN, Amalie	22	Detmold	69-0583
Friedrich 16			
KRIM, Carl	17	Denhendorf	68-0982
KRIMMER, Caroline	35	Oberweissach	68-0820
KRINGHOFF, Catharine	25	Tuchtorf	69-0429
KRINGS, Jos.	23	Erkelenz	68-0610
KRIPPENDORF, Cath.	21	Pforzheim	71-0521
KRIZL, Peter	34	Kralowitz	71-0429
Anna 23, Dorothea 11 months			
KROBSKY, Johann	28	Morabec	68-0770
Marie 35, Johann 11 months			
KROCKEL, Adam	30	Thuelb	71-0821
KROEBER, male	51	Leipzig	71-0582
Amalie 48, Maria 20, Johannes 17			
KROEGER, Anna	24	Rotenburg	68-0939
KROEGER, Elis.	24	Cloppenburg	69-1004
KROEGER, Helene	37	Cloppenburg	71-0456
KROEGER, Hermann	16	Weimar	69-1076
KROEGER, John H.	16	Sievern	70-0452
KROEHLE, Magd.	26	Darmstadt	68-1027
KROELL, Peter	23	Niedermendig	68-314
KROEMER, Carl	34	Ilserheide	68-0625
Sophie 36, Minna 11 months, Wilhelmine 60, Caroline 58, Hanna 13			

NAME	AGE	RESIDENCE	YR-LIST
KROENER, Lisette	20	Lengerich	68-0982
Friederike 25			
KROENKE, Barthold	49	Luedingworth	68-0786
Sophie 46, Johann 19, Sophie 12, Barthold 11, Catharina 9, Wilhelmine 2			
KROETSCH, Georg	57	Tiefenillen	71-0226
Margarethe 25			
KROEZEL, August	16	Muehlhausen	70-0308
KROGE, Heinrich	60	Westerholz	68-0456
Dorothea 46, Heinrich 26, Friedrich 15, Dorothea 23, Sophie 18			
KROL, Johann	26	St. Catharina	71-0363
KROLL, August	30	Smilowo	69-1086
KROLL, Carl	24	Heilbronn	68-0566
KROLL, Friedr.	24	Berlin	69-0268
Max 7, Maria 2, Adolph 1			
KROLPHEIFER, August	18	Notzemger	68-0707
KROMER, Edmund	40	Towante	68-0939
KROMM, Ludwig	39	Kissingen	69-0015
Anna 38, Caspar 2, Carl 10 months			
KRON, Elisabeth	22	Harringen	70-0443
KRONBERG, Victor	16	Goettingen	68-1006
Anna 24			
KRONECK, MAthias	18	Boehmen	69-1309
KRONENBERGER, T.	25	Hoppstetten	71-0429
KRONER, Bertha	22	Zempelburg	68-0707
Fritz 26			
KRONHEIM, Moritz	16	Guttstadt	68-0534
KROOS, Christ.	24	Offenbach	70-0452
KROPEROW, Pauline	31	Potsdam	69-0050
KROPFELD, Mary	21	Oberfranken	69-1011
KROPP, Fried.	31	Markoebel	71-0581
Minna 27, Anna 6			
KROPP, Isabella	40	Sourheim	69-1011
Barbara 16, Jacob 15, John 8			
KROSCH, Anna	14	Loxstedt	71-0643
KROSS, Anna	22	Ellenberg	68-1027
KROSS, Heinr.	73	Bederkesa	68-1006
KROSS, Hermann	40	Kronach	68-0456
KROTTE, Christ.	16	Tuttlingen	68-0647
KROTZ, Friederike	39	Eschelbach	71-0643
KROTZ, Josefine	18	Carlsruhe	71-0429
KRUCKE, Heinr.	32	Stroehen	68-0982
Sophie 32, Wilh. 7			
KRUCKMANN, Christine	20	Spedra	69-1059
KRUDOP, Henry	47	Bramstedt	70-0308
Christine 46, Diedrich 9, Anna 6, Magdalena 8			
KRUEDENER, Hinrich	17	Meckelstedt	68-0770
KRUEDNER, John	18	Gerstenreth	70-1003
KRUEGER, Albert	37	Bialken	71-0521
Mathilde 37, Emil 9, Ewaldine 8, Hedewig 10 months			
KRUEGER, Albertine	21	Bramstedt	69-1011
baby daughter 4 months			
KRUEGER, August	24	Pietronke	68-0456
KRUEGER, Bernhard	43	Herzfeld	68-0820
Sophie 44, Christoph 4, Catharine 2, Franz 10 months			
KRUEGER, Carl	21	Reinersdorf	70-0148

NAME	AGE	RESIDENCE	YR-LIST
KRUEGER, Carl	19	Semmerbusch	68-0770
KRUEGER, Carl	39	Smirdowo	71-0521
KRUEGER, Christoph	25	Grunau	68-0865
KRUEGER, Emilie	26	Gr. Rotten	71-0712
KRUEGER, Franz	22	Schlagenwald	71-0712
KRUEGER, Franzisca	22	New York	69-0321
KRUEGER, Friedrich	29	Thurn	70-0135
KRUEGER, Friedrich	34	Jammerrauhorst	69-0547
Justine 35, Justine 7, Elisabeth 5, Wilhelm 1			
KRUEGER, Friedrich	25	Fuerstenwerder	68-0770
Friederike 23, Anna 10 months			
KRUEGER, Friedrich	34	Niederzehren	68-0770
Augustina 35, Friederike 4, Friedrich 11 months			
KRUEGER, Friedrich	62	Lippe Detmold	70-0223
Louis 26			
KRUEGER, Friedrich	25	Kennelmoor	68-0534
KRUEGER, Fritz	22	Berlin	71-0226
KRUEGER, Georg		Dresden	69-0100
KRUEGER, Hermann	21	Schneidemuehle	68-0907
KRUEGER, Johann	64	Aarhorst	69-0592
Christine 57, Christiene 24, Christian 18, Franz 16, Marie 11			
KRUEGER, Johann	53	Marienfelde	69-0321
Friederike 51, Maria 22, Wilhelmine 18			
KRUEGER, Josephine	24	Wittkow	69-0848
KRUEGER, Marianne	25	Flatow	68-1002
Baby girl 11 months			
KRUEGER, Marie	18	Menninghueffen	68-1006
KRUEGER, Wilh.	34	Mecklenburg	69-0592
Johanne 28, Hermann 7, Johanne 8 months			
KRUEGER, Wilhelm	16	Zatten	71-0492
KRUEGER, Wilhelmine	9	Mecklenburg	70-1023
Friedrich 6, C. 6 months			
KRUEMMEL, Friedr.	36	Metze	68-0647
KRUESEL, Friedrich	35	Twiram	68-0770
Albertine 24, Augusta 3, Pauline 6, Wilhelm 2			
KRUG, Eva	24	Walzhausen	71-0736
KRUG, Johanna	14	Crumstadt	68-0707
KRUKE, Marie	24	Hertlinghausen	71-0581
KRUKEMEYER, Ernst	14	Essen	68-0647
KRUKENBERG, Chr.	16	Melzingen	69-0338
KRULL, Benedict	16	Delhofen	71-0643
KRUMBECK, Christine	18	Bederkese	69-0457
KRUMHOLZ, Friedrich	34	Nauenburg	69-1212
Pauline 33, Otto 7, J. 5, Helene 4, Hedwig 2, Max 9			
KRUMLAND, Gerhard	33	Doehlen	68-1027
KRUMME, Marie	46	Calbe K.	69-1396
Albert 12, Fritz 9			
KRUMMSIECK, Friedrich	53	Sonneborn	68-0456
Wilhelmine 45, Caroline 9, Louise 6, Marie 4, Wilhelm 13			
KRUPE, Adolph	24	Muehlhausen	71-0226
KRUSE, Adelh.	19	Bremen	69-0490
KRUSE, Anton	18	Bremen	69-0457
KRUSE, Anton	18	Bremen	69-0457
KRUSE, Dorette	21	Dueste	70-0508

NAME	AGE	RESIDENCE	YR-LIST
KRUSE, Ernst	18	Diethe	69-0429
KRUSE, Gerhard	27	Hastrup	69-0208
Marie 54			
KRUSE, Gesche	61	Intschede	68-0707
KRUSE, Johann	57	Heuthen	68-0907
Catharine 57, Magdalene 21			
KRUSE, Johanna	29	Surhausen	68-0625
KRUSE, Margareth	20	St. Louis	69-1059
KRUSE, Margarethe	63	Neuenkirchen	68-0786
Henriette 32, Caroline 6			
KRUSE, Marie	21	Bokel	68-0820
KRUSE, Martin	23	Cadenberge	68-0661
KRUSE, Meta	16	Hannover	69-0572
KRUSE, Wilhelm	27	Friedewolde	68-0456
KRUTHAUPT, Heinrich	16	Danne	68-0939
KRUTHOFFER, Emil	19	Samarang	68-1006
KRUZKY, Franz	28	Rachnowitz/Bohe	69-0049
KRZEWITZ, Otto	22	Breslau	69-0848
KSCHIER, Mathias	69	Pilsen	69-1309
KUBAT, Franziska	37	Chikowitch-Bohe	70-0006
Joseph 18, Marie 16, Carl 8, Franz 5, Anna 11 months			
KUBESCH, Marie	22	Boehmen	70-1035
Barbara 17			
KUCERA, Wenzel	29	Boehmen	69-1363
KUCH, Martin	19	Schwarzenhassel	69-0321
KUCHS, Carl	56	Sachsen	69-1004
Henriethe 51, Emma 26, Max 16, Georg 14, Agnes 9, Johanne 8			
KUCHS, Paul	16	Zeven	71-0479
Pauline 15			
KUCK, Anna	22	Hannover	68-0982
KUCK, Gesche	21	Worpswede	71-0581
Meta 17			
KUCK, HAnnchen	20	Blexen	71-0521
KUCK, John	47	Friedeburg	68-0760
Sophia 45, John 16			
KUCKWIED, Carl	18	Darmstadt	70-1035
KUDLICH, Hermine	26	Troppau	71-0643
KUDRNA, Franz	18	Mirowitz	68-1006
KUEBELE, Anna	25	Ravensberg	71-0300
KUEBLER, Eva	20	Bruchsal	70-0728
KUEBLER, Rosina	22	Huetten	71-0736
KUEBRICH, Johann	16	Steinsdorf	68-1006
Peter 17			
KUECHLE, Clemens	29	Leutkirch	71-0581
Caroline 28, Clemens 10 months			
KUECK, Christian	38	Neckarthalfinge	69-0542
KUECK, Gesche	18	Ottersberg	71-0429
KUECK, Heinr.	17	Hannover	71-0479
KUECK, John	17	Glinstedt	69-0560
KUECK, Ludwig	30	Lubs	68-0786
Emilie 20, Carl 9 months			
KUECKEN, Marie	44	Gottesbunden	71-0300
Mary 9			
KUECKING, Johann	24	Seeburg	68-0314
KUECKNER, Carl	30	Wiesbaden	69-1212
Elise 24, Georgine 2, Carl 9 months			
KUECKS, Johann	38	Zeven	68-0707
Catharina 16			
KUEFFNER, Wolfgang	26	New York	70-0170
KUEFNER, Conrad	18	Pechgraben	69-0848
Elise 15			
KUEHLE, Louise	24	Berlin	68-1027
KUEHLKE, Anna	14	Offenwardenermo	69-0542
KUEHLKE, Gerh.	15	Sandstedt	68-0884
KUEHLMANN, Christ.	39	Pente	68-0884
Caroline 40, Caroline 17, Rudolph 7, Anna 3, Her. 10 months			
KUEHLMANN, Fritz	39	Oberweimar	69-0848
KUEHLWIND, Lad.		Poggenmuehlen	69-0560
KUEHMUND, Wilhelmine	18	Hannover	71-0479
KUEHN, Aug. C.	28	Mausbach	69-1212
KUEHN, Bertha	17	SSchwarzb. Rude	69-0672
KUEHN, Carl	37	R.B. Potsdam	68-0820
KUEHN, Eloise	20	Manebach	69-0229
Carl 19			
KUEHN, Henriette	28	Grossbocka	71-0429
KUEHN, Lorenz	33	Ludwigshafen	68-1002
KUEHN, Marg.	31	Breitenworbis	68-1002
Dorothea 10 months			
KUEHN, Philipp	25	Bremen	69-0968
KUEHN, Sal.	22	Seligenstadt	68-0753
KUEHN, Wilhelm	28	Fischbach	71-0521
KUEHNE, Aug.	31	Bremen	69-0321
KUEHNE, Celestin	27	Jochenheim	68-0770
KUEHNE, Heinrich	42	Landau/Landan	69-1309
KUEHNERT, Hermann	24	Oberwinkel	70-0135
KUEHNHOPP, Robert	18	Niewinko	68-0707
KUEHNLE, Gottlieb	30	Hochdorf	69-0029
KUEHNLEIN, John	26	Mandersteinach	69-0338
KUEHSEL, Max	20	Leipzig	70-0683
KUEKRAL, Adalbert	16	Stavetitz	70-0329
KUELBS, Bertha	21	Kusel	69-0848
KUELKAMP, Fr.	44	Cincinnati	70-1023
August 7, Edward 9			
KUELLMER, Cath.	15	Hadamar	69-0771
KUELZ, Fried.	23	Rockenhausen	69-0457
KUEMMEL, Cha.	16	Wilhelmsburg	69-1011
KUEMMEL, Marie	29	Giessen	71-0167
KUEMMLER, Adele	18	Brinkum	71-0821
KUENDIGER, Sigmund	26	Rosstadt	68-0820
KUENNETH, Jean	20	Culmbach	69-0592
KUENSTLE, Carl	17	Neufra	69-1004
KUENSTLER, Auguste	24	Reuss	70-0178
KUENSTLER, Catharine	34	Neuenkirchen	69-0572
KUENZEL, Andreas	21	Absroth	71-0226
Lorenz 25			
KUENZEL, Gottlieb	38	Kesswill	71-0363
KUENZER, Johann	28	Thueringen	69-0559
KUENZLE, Caroline	21	Esslingen	70-0308
Charles 10 months			
KUERTZ, Wilhelm	20	Gr. Asbach	69-0848
KUERTZHAHN, Wilhelm	24	Meseritz	69-0547
KUESEL, Johann	16	Ottersberg	71-0521
KUESTER, Bernh.	25	Plankauth	71-0479
KUESTER, Heinrich	15	Burgdamm	68-0566
KUESTNER, Gustav	30	Frankfurt a/M	70-0443

NAME	AGE	RESIDENCE	YR-LIST
KUET, Flora	20	Matten	69-0208
KUETEMEYER, Fried.	19	Dennebeck	71-0521
KUETTLER, Richard	21	Arolsen	68-0314
KUGEL, Emilie	20	Fahlenwerder	69-0542
KUGLER, David	20	Aichstruth	69-1059
KUGLER, Jacob	28	Sanzenbach	69-1086
KUHFUSS, Friedrich	24	Heustdorf	69-0968
KUHHAUPT, Christine	24	Waldeck	70-0355
KUHL, Adolph	17	Schwarzenhaus	68-0707
KUHL, Catharina	59	Huettengesaess	68-0760
KUHL, Emma	21	Altenbruch	70-0006
KUHL, Georg	31	Suettrup	68-1002
KUHLEMANN, Bernh.	26	Brake	69-0592
KUHLMANN, Diedrich	53	Oldenburg	69-0268
Catharine 40, Johann 15, Diedrich 9, Johann 8			
KUHLMANN, Florentine	65	Lahe	69-0968
KUHLMANN, Fred.	25	St. Huelse	69-1011
KUHLMANN, Friedr.	17	Herdecke	68-0982
KUHLMANN, Fritz	16	Achim	68-0707
Doris 25			
KUHLMANN, Gustav	19	Detmold	69-0457
KUHLMANN, Johann	17	Barkhausen	69-0923
KUHLMANN, Joseph	19	Ankum	68-0939
KUHLMANN, Louise	22	Bollenzen	71-0643
KUHLMANN, Wilhelm	14	Schaumburg	69-0542
Gesine 20			
KUHLMANN, Wilhelm	25	Nullhoff	68-0456
KUHLMANN, Wilhelm	38	Coblenz	68-0456
KUHLMANN, Wilhelm	17	Albasloh	71-0712
KUHLMEIER, Jacob	30	Baden	70-0135
Marie 28			
KUHN, Carl	34	Landau	68-0707
Minna 35, Heinrich 6, Angelika 4, Carl 1			
KUHN, Christian	50	Marienwerder	68-0865
Ernestine 18, Friedrich Heinrich 15			
KUHN, Ferd.	40	Krzurouke	71-0300
Justine 27			
KUHN, Heinrich	15	Landau	68-0707
KUHN, Joh. G.	20	Mezingen	70-1035
KUHN, Margarethe	17	Milkbach	68-0456
KUHN, Mathilde	18	Vloto	68-0647
KUHN, Philipp	16	Oberzwehren	68-1006
KUHNGERNSBERGER	23	Empfingen	70-0355
KUHWAND, Claus	24	Otterndorf	68-314
KUISLE, Joseph	30	Holz	68-0770
KUJAWA, Peter	36	Powolla/Polen	69-0576
Marie 26, Wodja 4, Joseph 6 months, Thomas 31			
KUKLENS, Augustine	30	Oschich	71-0733
Hermann 9, Emil 3, Johann 11 months			
KUKUK, Friedrich	15	Isenstaedt	68-0907
KULAND, Marie	32	Ehnstein	71-0821
KULHANEZ, Anna	52	Boehmen	70-1035
KUMHEFF, Cath.	54	Darmstadt	69-0771
Elisa 25			
KUMMER, Karl	28	Berlin	71-0712
KUMMER, Ludw.	16	Hindena	71-0815
KUMMERIK, Theresia	46	Altendorf	69-0560
KUMPF, Barbara	27	Hammelbach	71-0821
KUNDE, Auguste	36	Neuvalm	69-0560
Hulda 5			
KUNDE, Hermann	34	Buletitz	71-0684
Johanne 30, August 9, Wilhelm 6, Ernst 5, Hermann 11 months			
KUNDMUELLER, Henry	34	Halversdorf	71-0643
M. 34, Albert 12, Michel 6			
KUNKEL, Anna	35	Cammin	70-0052
Friedr. 14, Carl 9, Reinh. 4, Ottilie 3			
KUNKELMANN, Anton	66	Frankfurt	71-0456
Clara 20			
KUNKER, Eli	20	Schelekrippen	71-0789
Ludw. 17			
KUNLEIN, Christine	56	Themar	71-0492
Eduard 18, Dorothea 32, Elise 9, Christine 5			
KUNN, Fried.	22	Siegen	70-0728
KUNOLD, Christ.	16	Wahlershausen	68-0884
KUNOLD, Ludwig	19	Breitenbach	68-0786
KUNOTH, Anna	27	Bremen	68-0884
KUNOTH, Martin	51	Lauenburg	68-0884
KUNST, Auguste	50	Brunswick	69-0542
Auguste 24, Carl 22, Anna 7, Louise 6			
KUNST, Ottilie	26	Magdeburg	70-0682
Anna 9 months, Hermann 21			
KUNTH, Theodor	20	Bremen	69-1396
KUNTZE, Eberhard	25	Hildesheim	68-0534
KUNTZE, H. A.	45	Dresden	70-0259
KUNZ, Albert	19	Arisdorf	71-0492
KUNZ, Alex	21	Chemnitz	68-1006
KUNZ, Barb.	20	Zeuthen	70-1142
KUNZ, Carl	28	Marienwerder	68-0786
Anna 30, Wilhelmine 6 months			
KUNZ, Catharine	21	Mutterstadt	69-0784
Marie 16			
KUNZ, Ferdinand	48	St. Paul	70-0076
KUNZ, Jac.	23	Ruppertshofen	68-0820
KUNZ, Johann	27	St. Gallen	71-0712
KUNZ, M.	20	Groetzingen	71-0681
KUNZ, Sebastian	28	Elmstein	70-0170
KUNZ, Sophie	36	Schuttenthal	71-0429
Otto 3			
KUNZ, Susanna	23	Diemstigen	69-0338
William 2, Sofia 6 months			
KUNZ, Susanne	23	Schweiz	70-0272
KUNZE, Bernh. Aug.	35	Altenburg	68-1006
KUNZE, Carl	32	Strehlen	70-0384
KUNZE, Ferd.	43	Magdeburg	68-0820
KUNZE, Louise	16	Anzefahn	69-0162
KUNZEMANN, Heinrich	15	Buhlen	69-0592
Friederike 18			
KUNZER, Joh. Mart.	27	Speyer	68-1002
KUNZER, Valentin	25	Herbolsheim	71-0521
KUNZLER, Carl	25	Tachau	68-1006
KUNZMANN, Friedr.	25	Eibensbach	71-0521
Ferdinand 19			
KUNZMANN, Heinr.	28	Halle	68-0707
KUNZMANN, Lisette	30	Sulzbach	71-0792
KUPER, Friedr.	28	Eickeln	69-1086
KUPFER, Elisabeth	15	Leipzig	68-0625

NAME	AGE	RESIDENCE	YR-LIST
KUPFER, Hermann	15	Neustadt	69-0457
KUPFERER, Josef	24	Stuhrberg	69-0338
KUPHAL, Herman	30	Stuchow	69-0429
Wilhelmine 27, Friedrich 9, Anna 6, Ida 3, Albert 11 months			
KUREHANS, Gottlieb	28	Rommelshausen	69-0560
Phil. 24			
KUREK, Georg	41	Schoenlaube	71-0456
KURFUERST, Anna	17	Dresden	63-0296
KURFUERST, Ida	22	Neustadt	63-0990
KURSTRIN, Eduard	25	Glauchau	69-0784
KURTZ, Joh.	17	Exhenau	71-0789
KURZ, Ferdinand	30	Nassau	68-0534
KURZ, Gg.	9	Unter Aulenbach	70-1055
KURZ, Jacob	20	Engelhufen	69-1004
KURZ, Jacob	15	Meysberg	68-0456
KURZ, Johann	48	Hochdorf	69-1059
KURZ, Josepha	29	Hirrlingen	68-0939
Carl 3, Pauline 23, Lorenz 28, Marie 24, Joseph 4 months			
KURZ, Marie	22	Brettenfeld	68-0610
KURZ, Wilhelm	31	Neubornin	69-0923
August 27			
KURZ, Wilhelmine	48	Jankendorf	71-0456
Ottilie 8			
KURZE, Ad.	25	Oberndorf	68-0647
KURZEKNABE, Hch.	16	Fritzlar	68-0753
Hellwig 15			
KURZEKNABE, Wilh.	17	Moenckehof	68-0884
KURZNER, Charlotte	26	Buzien	71-1046
William 9			
KUSCHMANN, Caroline	34	Grottkau	68-0610
KUSEMEGGER, Caroline	45	Tyrol	70-1035
Carl 19, Felix 18, Betty 16, Marie 14,August 12, Adolph 9, Kunigunde 7, Frnaz			
KUSSEROW, Bertha	18	Rugenwalde	68-0982
KUSSEROW, Joh.	36	Potsdam	69-0050
KUSTER, Johann	28	Stetten	68-314
KUSTER, Wilhelm	21	Bueckeburg	68-0786
KUTFELD, Aug.	28	Alt Glietzen	68-0957
KUTHE, Andreas	25	Germesheben	69-1363
KUTSCHER, Ida	22	Schulenburg	71-0429
KUTTLER, Heinrich	27	Ulm	69-0208
KUTTNEER, Regina	25	Warsaw	68-0707
KUTZ, Albertine	26	Simatzig	69-0848
KUTZLEB, August	28	Leipzig	71-0712
KWIETIK, Johann	39	Merdaken/Boeh.	69-0576
Marianne 39, Dorothea 4, Catharina 25, Barbara 25			
KYBER, Theda	20	Altenburg	68-1006
KYRISS, Christian	28	Nordheim	71-0643
LAAGER, Kasjen	45	St. Glarus	68-1006
LAAKER, Therese	28	Conary	69-1004
LAATENSCHLAEGER, C.	18	Einbeckheim	70-0569
LABADI, Veronica	60	Hirschau	71-0492
LABATKA, Josef	24	Chicago	70-0329
LABATKA, Josef	56	Albrechtitz	70-0329
Maria 52, Johann 18, Maria 26, Anna 15, Maria 77, Katharina 41, Johanne 16, An			

NAME	AGE	RESIDENCE	YR-LIST
LABBI, Elise	28	Steinfeld	70-1142
Carl 9, Marie 7, Amalie 4, Carl 3			
LABIG, Magnus	26	Marbach	68-0661
LABITZKY, Auguste	33	Breslau	71-0492
LABOHM, Carl	31	Oldenburg	70-1142
LABUDDA, Jacob	27	Lamblewa	69-1076
LACH, Elis.	21	Cassel	71-0393
Aug. 19, Jac. 7			
LACHER, Franz	40	Nimpfenburg	68-0661
Theresia 30, Franz 5			
LACHER, Rud.	18	Rudolstadt	71-0789
LACHSE, Christine	24	Radewell	69-1363
Reinhard 6, Carl 4			
LACHTRUP, Johannes	17	Scharmbeck	71-0143
LACINA, MAth.	64	Boehmen	70-0443
Marie 62, Josef 27, Anna 24			
LACK, Ibbe	44	Pekin	69-1004
LACKMANN, Anna	16	Mahadorf	71-0429
LACKMANN, Christine	48	Inschede	68-0707
LACKNER, Ernst	28	Koenigswalde	71-0492
Wilhelmine 28, Anna 6, Anton 4, Arnold 2			
LADBERG, Wilhelm	16	Aachen	68-0939
LADERER, Johs.	22	Westernheim	68-0610
Crescentia 23, Bab. 9 months			
LAECHER, Georg	39	Kandel	71-0429
Veronica 35, Anna 9, Amalie 24			
LAEMMER, Peter	18	Niederweimar	68-0534
LAESKER, Joh. Heinrich	25	Erfurt	68-0661
LAESSER, Juliane	15	Oberbach	71-0521
LAETZLER, Carol	20	Schweigern	69-1004
LAG, Zerephine	15	Hirschthal	71-0684
LAGEBIEL, Wilh. Carl	35	Bremen	71-0172
LAGEMANN, Charlotte	37	Ziegenhain	70-1035
Otto 3			
LAGEMANN, Gerhard	29	Oldenburg	71-0429
Sophie 26			
LAGEMANN, Mr.	40	Bielefeld	70-0204
LAGEMANN, Rud.	26	Gaste	68-0534
Elisa 21, Maria 11 months			
LAGING, Marie	47	Lemcke	68-0610
LAGMANN, Dorothea	21	Wittorf	71-0492
LAHMANN, Louise	18	Dielingen	69-0583
LAHR, Elise	25	New York	70-1055
LAHR, Joh.	21	Freudenthal	71-0479
LAHR, Martha	26	Schrecksbach	68-0852
LAHRMANN, Heinrich	25	Wallenhorst	68-0661
LAMB, Caroline	26	Beckerbach	68-0939
LAMBERT, Ottolie	14	Ruebesheim	69-0672
LAMBINUS, Margarethe	24	Wertheim	68-0786
LAMBRECHT, Ferd.	23	Zimdorsen	70-100
LAMBRECHT, Richard	22	Halberstadt	68-0957
LAMBRECHT, Wilhelm	24	Zimdarse	68-0014
LAMM, Johann	22	Meinetshausen	71-0733
LAMMERT, Herm.	25	Hinteburg	68-0566
LAMPART, Julie	18	Obergunzburg	69-0798
LAMPE, Christ.	24	Deets	68-0760
LAMPE, Eduard	28	New York	69-0923
Helena 22			
LAMPE, Gerhard	28	Westeroden	68-1002

NAME	AGE	RESIDENCE	YR-LIST
Maria 25			
LAMPRECHT, Carl	47	Wangrow	71-0733
LAMSCHA, Anton	39	Danzig	68-0610
Rosalie 34, Johanna 3			
LANDAU, Joel	16	Krakau	68-0786
LANDAUER, Caroline	18	Schwaben	71-0363
LANDAUER, Nanette	26	Echtersheim	71-0521
LANDECK, Johann	17	Hermersheim	69-0572
LANDECKER, Alex	37	Dessau	69-0784
LANDEFELD, Anna	15	Oberthalhausen	68-0534
LANDEFELD, Bernh.	57	Licherode	71-0681
Martha 46, Johanne 17, Christ. 9, Georg 8, Carl 7, Maria 9			
LANDGRAF, Dorothea	22	Fehlheim	68-0014
LANDGRAF, Mathis	45	Wolfenbuettel	69-0841
LANDGRAFE, Justus	24	Blankenheim	69-0229
LANDGRAP, Caroline	15	Oberkatz	70-0076
LANDGREBE, Rick	19	Merseburg	71-0681
LANDHERR, Lina	55	Eichstaedt	68-0610
LANDMANN, Sigm.	21	Muenster	71-0681
LANDMANN, Xaver	38	Koenigsbach	69-0100
Helene 38			
LANDWEHR, Herm.	17	Doehren	69-0338
LANDWEHR, John	26	Hoyer	69-0182
LANDWEHR, Wilhelm	30	Schinkel	68-0907
LANE, Antonia	38	Markvippach	68-0647
Therese 16, Max 11, Herm. 8, Reinhard 6			
LANG, Adam	26	Selchenbach	69-1319
LANG, Anna	34	Vechta	70-0135
Wilhelm 7, Lina 5, Anna 3, Christian 11 months			
LANG, Anton	16	Schlatt	70-0135
LANG, Balthasar	34	Buch	69-0338
LANG, Bernh.	52	Hilsbach	69-1421
Elisab. 50, George 15, Anna 9			
LANG, Betty	16	Meiningen	68-0707
LANG, Carl	16	Riegel	69-0923
LANG, Carl	27	Geyer	68-0534
LANG, Caspar	58	Boehmen	69-1363
Josef 16			
LANG, Caspar	37	Tenkseufen	68-0661
Anna 31, Bertha 4			
LANG, Catharine	68	Wungendorf	71-0736
LANG, Christoph	41	Kerbersdorf	70-0443
Elisabeth 44, Helene 9, Wilhelm 7, Conrad 5, Marie 3, Catharine 11 months			
LANG, Conrad	16	Steinsdorf	68-1006
Margaret 14			
LANG, Daniel	24	Osterbruecken	68-0820
Catharina 23, Carl 9 months, Ludwig 14, Theobald 12, Caroline 25, Caroline 9			
LANG, Elisabeth	25	Oberfranken	69-0321
LANG, Fanny	31	Hochheim	71-0363
LANG, Ferdinand	20	Fladingen	69-0798
LANG, Franz	22	Schifferstadt	71-0393
LANG, Friedrich	19	Steinbach	69-0784
LANG, G. W.	39	Worms	71-0789
LANG, Georg	26	Verdorf	69-0771
LANG, Joh. Jac.	40	Zuerich	70-0223

NAME	AGE	RESIDENCE	YR-LIST
Barbara 33, Heinrich 4, Pauline baby			
LANG, Jos.	22	Schifferstadt	71-0393
LANG, Justus	19	Dillichhausen	70-1142
LANG, Kunigunde	21	Bamberg	71-0479
Jofefine 24, Auguste 23, Hermi. 19			
LANG, M.	20	Spiek	71-0521
LANG, Maier	23	Bieswangen	69-0542
LANG, Margreth	20	Fehlheim	71-0643
Philipp 16			
LANG, Maria Barbara	29	Truchtelfingen	68-0647
LANG, Michael	38	Doettingen	69-0798
LANG, Reinhard	17	Wien	69-0771
LANG, Rosa	20	Rust	71-0300
LANG, Simon	65	Lohma	71-0429
Kunigunde 66, Magda. 27			
LANGBECKER, August	26	Zetzin	69-0429
LANGBEIN, Jacob	29	Friolsheim	69-0592
Caroline 26, Jacob 3, Caroline 2, Christian 3 months			
LANGE, Anna	24	Sekenhausen	70-1035
Heinr. 11 months			
LANGE, Anna	18	Suderleda	68-0314
LANGE, Anna	19	Wardenberg	68-0852
LANGE, Auguste	36	Halberstadt	69-1319
LANGE, Auguste	7	St. Crone	69-1212
LANGE, Carl	16	Berndorf	71-0479
LANGE, Christ.	33	Hallensen	63-0244
Dorothea 21			
LANGE, Dorette	70	Hastedt	71-0821
LANGE, Edmund	32	Plietwitz	69-1212
Marie 7, Johann 4, Hermann 11 months			
LANGE, Ewald	19	Sooden	70-0443
LANGE, Friedr.	32	Berlin	71-0479
Mathilde 24, Mathilde 9 months			
LANGE, Friedrich	49	Bremervoerde	70-0031
LANGE, Gerhard	23	Heidhofen	70-0682
LANGE, Heinrich		Ahlhausen	69-1363
LANGE, Heinrich	27	Berge	69-0559
LANGE, Heinrich	15	Mussendorf	68-0982
LANGE, Henry	24	Buschschade	68-0852
LANGE, Joh.	28	Langenbach	68-0982
Cath. 22			
LANGE, Johann	15	Herun	69-0672
LANGE, Johann	52	Riede	69-0968
Be. 48, Anna 15, Adelheid 5, Meta 15, Johann 15			
LANGE, John	26	Barrien	68-0534
LANGE, Ludwig	25	Cammen	68-0625
LANGE, Maria	60	Wisbach	68-0456
LANGE, Marie	17	Gollnow	69-0672
LANGE, Marie	20	Hannover	69-1004
LANGE, Marta	19	Rodenburg	70-0204
LANGE, Minna	20	Hereringen	68-0456
LANGE, Mrs.	32	New Orleans	70-0170
LANGEMEIER, Carl	27	Kempten	68-0770
LANGEMEYER, Friedrich	30	Wallenhorst	68-0661
LANGENBACH, Julius	28	Frankfurt/M	68-0820
LANGENBERG, Fritz	32	Berlin	69-0848
Pauline 29			

NAME	AGE	RESIDENCE	YR-LIST
LANGENER, Sophie	39	Breslau	68-1027
LANGENHAHN, Bernh.	32	Springfield	70-0355
LANGENHAHN, Emanuel	26	Wichtshausen	70-0355
LANGENHAHN, Seb.	62	Wachshausen	71-0521
Elisabeth 52, August 16, Theodor 9, Bernhardine 8			
LANGENHEBER, Friedrich	27	Buer	69-0672
Marie 25			
LANGENMANN, Louise	18	Hannover	70-1055
LANGER, ALb.	21	Obergrund	71-0581
Johann 55			
LANGER, Anton	31	Oestreich	70-0728
Johanne 31, baby 6 months			
LANGER, J.	17	Friedland	71-0521
LANGER, Josefa		Obergrund	71-0581
Daniel 26, Marie 24			
LANGGUTH, Wilhelm	15	Meiningen	71-0429
LANGHOF, Wilhelm	38	Mecklenburg	69-0542
Emilie 17, Sophie 54			
LANGHOLTZ, Marie	24	Niedertolla	70-0523
LANGHORST, Wilh.	42	Rhaden	71-0479
LANGHORST, Wilhelmine	24	Stroehen	68-0982
August 15			
LANGKES, Marie	23	Wetterfeld	71-0681
LANGLITZ, Anna	13	Darmstadt	69-0672
LANGLOTZ, Johann	26	Thueringen	70-0523
Anna 23			
LANGMEISTER, Johann	19	Koenigswald	68-0707
LANGMUESTER, D.	19	Rotenburg	68-0456
LANGOHR, Elisabeth	20	Niederohmen	69-0592
LANGSCH, Joseph	47	Zduny	68-1027
Caroline 42, Hedwig 18, Carl 9, Marie 7, Robert 4, Paul 2			
LANIS, Agnes	62	Cincinnati	70-1023
LANK, John	22	Ohio	66-0576
LANKENAU, Died.	18	Steinfeld	69-1004
LANKMAN, Johann	28	Achim	69-0968
Catharine 16			
LANKMANN, Claus	17	Hortum	71-0521
LANNINGER, Franz	36	Altwiesloch	68-1027
Catharina 30			
LANTE, Ernst	16	Bremen	69-1011
LANTZ, Ernst	50	Bremen	69-1011
Ernst 16			
LANZ, Elise	17	Arnshain	69-0592
LANZER, Caroline	26	Bockenhausen	68-0939
LAPP, Anna	15	Cassel	69-0457
LAPPE, Pauline	22	Goettingen	69-0672
LARDON, Ferd.	27	de Feut/Switzer	69-0049
LASAMNIK, Wilhelm	24	Neu Markgrafpie	68-0647
LASCHEN, Gerh.	17	Norden	69-1004
LASIUS, Louis	36	Riga	68-1027
Anna 30			
LASKYWITZ, August	30	Edinghausen	68-0907
Friederike 28, Caroline 7, Minna 4, August 9 months			
LASSMANN, Johanne	47	Braunschweig	70-100
LATERMANN, Bhd.	50	Peine	68-0534
Elisa 51			
LATERMANN, Dorette	19	Jeinsen	69-0848
LATJEN, Christ.	53	Langenhausen	68-0982
Anna 41, Joh. 14, Hinr. 9, Carl 6			
LATTER, Carl	26	Zeulenrode	71-0789
LATZ, Marg.	16	St. Steinach	71-0479
LATZKE, Maria	13	Roberullersdorf	69-0798
LAU, Georg	27	Hundshausen	70-0508
LAU, Gust.	28	Gardelegen	71-0300
Marie 33, Gust. 2, Franz 9 months			
LAU, Samuel	28	Posen	68-0957
LAUBENHEIMER, Carl	33	Berlin	68-0884
LAUBER, Henriette	26	Gustendorf	71-0789
Wilh. 7, Bertha 5, Aug. 10 months			
LAUBER, J.	39	Oberohmbach	71-0393
Kath. 27, Wilh. 6, Daniel 3, Jacob 5 months, Ludwig 13, Elise, Elise 10 mon			
LAUCHHEIM, Henry	38	New York	70-1003
Caroline 30, Jacob 9, Mat. 16 months, Hugo 6 months			
LAUENSTEIN, Friedrich	40	Nienburg	70-0682
LAUENSTEIN, Wilhelm	29	Elbingerode	68-0939
LAUENWALD, Marg.	17	Obenasphe	71-0681
Catharine 19			
LAUER, Julius	20	Tuebingen	68-1027
LAUER, Margaret	27	Orb	68-0852
Franz 5			
LAUER, Nicolaus	28	Trier	68-0907
Helene 23			
LAUFENBERG, Julius	44	Blankenberg	69-1309
LAUFER, Agnes	34	Wetterweil	71-0712
LAUFER, Anna	23	Furingen	71-0492
LAUFERSWEILER, L.	44	Mainz	68-1027
LAUGGER, Eduard	52	Schwenningen	71-0521
Anna 53, Georg 29, Catharine 25, Anna 21, Eduard 17, Johannes 14, Martin			
LAUN, Anna Rosina	23	Friedensdorf	69-0321
LAUPP, Adolph	18	Tuebingen	68-0907
LAURER, Josef	24	Grossaigen	71-0429
LAUT, Susanne	27	Buerrstadt	69-0429
Joseph 4			
LAUTERBACH, F.	22	Altenkenstadt	68-0625
LAUTERBACH, Georg	23	Trebgost	68-0707
LAUTERBACH, Heinrich	19	Beesten	69-0848
LAUTERBACH, Johann	19	Oberfranken	69-0798
LAUTERMILCH, Barbara	25	Ittingen	69-0457
LAUTNER, Max	17	Freiburg	71-0363
LAUTS, Ulrich	46	Hommersiel	68-0957
Anke 44, Ulrich 8, Heinr. 1			
LAUX, Wilhelm	16	Sperrge	68-0939
LAUZ, Elise	17	Arnshain	69-0592
LAW, Maria	17	Elmenloh	70-0523
LAWAN, Wenzel	44	Zerzin/Boehmen	69-0576
Veronica 44, Anna 20, Johann 19, Wenzel 15, Barbara 13, Joseph 12, Veronica 10			
LAZANSKI, Fanny	22	Lockkow	68-0786
LAZINSKY, Const.	18	Jadtorowo	68-0647
LEBER, Joseph	57	Tenkseufen	68-0661
Josepha 56, Josepha 22			
LEBERENZ, Heinrich	29	Berlin	71-0492
Friederike 30, Max 4, Agnes 3			
LEBERMANN, Adolph	27	Untermerzbach	69-0923

NAME	AGE	RESIDENCE	YR-LIST
LEBLING, Hugo	25	Muenchen	70-0052
LECHEL, Johann	20	Podzermin	68-0625
LEDERER, Ignatz	30	Bremen	69-0923
LEDERER, Juliane	25	Darmstadt	69-0560
LEDERER, Simon	22	Egelsbach	69-0572
LEDERHAUS, Conrad	58	Hannover	70-0148
Witty 16, Betty 9			
LEDERHOSE, August	15	Frankenberg	71-0456
LEDERHOSE, Emil	17	Frankenberg	71-0456
LEDERKANS, Betty	43	Hannover	70-0148
Emilie 6			
LEERKAMP, Heinrich	23	Ludendorf	69-0572
LEFERS, Margaretha	19	Eissel	68-0707
LEFORE, Elisabeth	20	Bielefeld	70-1066
LEGLER, Louisa	23	Groitsche	68-0760
LEGRO, Johann	42	Kralowitz	71-0429
Anna 30, Josefa 9, Juliana 6, Anna 11 months			
LEGRO, Therese	47	Schau\Schan	69-1086
Antonie 16, Anna 14			
LEGRON, Babette	24	Heidelberg	68-1298
LEHEBERGER, Lilly	19	Fuerth	71-0479
LEHM, Peter	29	Mauresmuenster	71-0521
LEHMANN, Carl	35	Braunschweig	69-0542
Marie 31, Wilhelm 7, Auguste 2, Marie 6 months			
LEHMANN, Carl	25	Torgau	69-1309
LEHMANN, Cath.	19	Hannover	70-0052
Louis 15			
LEHMANN, Christine	25	Fuerssbronn	69-1011
LEHMANN, Ernstine	22	Petiztuland	71-0581
LEHMANN, Ferdinand	59	Peitz	69-0672
Catharina 59			
LEHMANN, Franz	26	Gilgenburg	70-0184
LEHMANN, Frke.	43	Strehlitz	68-1006
LEHMANN, Jac.	16	Breifurth	71-0393
LEHMANN, Joh.	15	Nuernberg	71-0521
LEHMANN, Josefa	25	Harthausen	69-1363
Ant. 2			
LEHMANN, Lisette	20	Zittlingen	68-0982
LEHMANN, Marie	18	Hallnengen	69-0429
LEHMANN, Mary	16	Zweihachen	68-0534
LEHMANN, Sophie	24	Chrodrziesen	71-0736
LEHMBERG, Heinr.	39	Bremen	69-1212
LEHMEYER, Christ.	40	Herichbach	71-0479
LEHMKUHL, Caroline	23	Oldenburg	71-0429
LEHMKUHL, Emilie	19	Schluesselburg	68-0957
LEHMKUHLE, Elise	28	Twistringen	69-1059
LEHMKUHLE, Heinrich	45	Aachen	70-0583
LEHNING, Adam	25	Merkensfritz	68-0884
Eva 57			
LEHR, Andr.	15	Hornhofen	71-0581
LEHR, Jacob	22	Finthen	68-0982
LEHR, Johann	22	Darmstadt	70-0204
LEHR, Johann	19	Heiligenstein	68-0566
LEHR, Marie	30	Hanau	68-0753
LEHRSTOFF, Hinrich	24	Wichens	69-0208
LEIB, Johannes	30	Bernkastel	68-0820
Heinrich 34			

NAME	AGE	RESIDENCE	YR-LIST
LEIBEL, Veronica	29	Leimersheim	71-0521
LEIBLEIN, Joseph	30	Hardheim	69-0182
LEIBOLD, Anselm	13	Lauttingen	69-0672
LEIBOLD, Christine	18	Waexbenhausen	69-0968
LEIBOLD, Leopold	15	Margrethhausen	69-0338
LEIBROCK, Wilhelm	25	Duschroth	68-1027
LEICH, Friedrich	27	Woelferlingen	68-0939
LEICHNER, Carl	25	Bonstadt	69-1396
Catharine 28			
LEICHTFUSS, Emilie	23	Eiersberg	68-0760
LEIDE, Antonie	18	Ismaning	71-0643
LEIDER, Christian	36	Pommern	69-0672
Louise 34, Friedrich 6, Carl 3, Maria 2			
LEIDGEN, Gerhard	30	Wieskirchen	68-0707
LEIDHOLDT, Franz	30	Greiz	68-0907
Marie 27, Moritz 11 months			
LEIDINGER, Johanna	35	Hohenbrunn	68-1027
LEIFELD, Heinrich	25	Liesbonn	68-0314
LEIM, Heinrich	35	Wohnfeld	69-0592
Elisabeth 35, Cath. 9, Carl 3, Marie 9 months			
LEIMBACH, Fred.	17	Cassel	70-0308
LEIME, Louise	18	Hardegsen	70-0384
Adolf 15			
LEIMKUEHLER, Caspar	33	Gaste	68-0534
Maria 27, Friedrich 7, Wilhelm 4			
LEINEMANN, Heinrich	16	Kemme	68-1027
LEINEWEBER, C.	19	Lippe Detmold	70-0355
LEINGANG, Barb.	42	Buelzheim	70-1035
Cath. 9, Elis. 9, Marie 8, Franz 7, Anna 3			
LEINPEST, Heinrich	15	Gaisa	71-0821
LEINWEBER, Friedrich	45	Parchem	71-0492
Louise 36, Friedrich W. 9, Auguste 7, August 4			
LEIPING, Franz	44	Mauritz	71-0712
LEIPOLD, Johann	36	Unterfranken	70-0523
Margarethe 30, Elisabeth 6, Agnes 9 months			
LEIPZIGER, Roeschen	15	Schneidemuehle	68-0456
LEIS, Wilhelm	28	Bromberg	69-1363
LEISE, Herm.	45	Cladow	71-0681
Cath. 43, Emilie 20, Axel 18, Pauline 15			
LEISER, Simon	17	Coeln	68-0760
LEISS, J.	16	Langeroog	70-0089
LEISSER, Carl	33	Bayern	70-0148
Catharina 26, Henriette 15, Julius 24, Adolf 20			
LEIST, Anna	28	Regensburg	69-0015
Fanny 8, Emmy 4			
LEIST, Anna	23	Trier	69-0229
LEISTHEUSER, Friedrich	23	Altenheim	71-0456
John 18			
LEISTOR, Emma	23	Cassel	68-0625
LEITEMEYER, Margreth	26	Muenchen	69-1059
LEITENMEYER, Lorenz	23	Unterroth	68-0014
LEITNER, Georg	14	Brimbach	69-0182
LEITNER, Heinrich	27	Frankfurt	70-0148
LEITNER, Michel	40	Bundenthal	71-0479
LEITZ, Margareth	38	Hanau	71-0226
LEITZMANN, Cath. Mar.	53	Fallingbostel	68-1002

NAME	AGE	RESIDENCE	YR-LIST
Marie 18, Wilhelm 8			
LEIVERMANN, Aug.	19	Legden	69-0771
LELLMANN, Michael	47	Cobern	71-0429
Marie 47, Mathias 17, Peter 15, Marga. 9			
LEMCKE, Marie	24	Bederkesa	69-0542
LEMCKE, Max	22	Carlsruhe	69-0592
LEMKE, Doris	17	Bremervoerde	68-1006
LEMKE, Friedrich	30	Winterhagen	71-0736
LEMKE, Gretchen	18	Koehlen	69-1076
LEMKE, Johanne	33	Lauenburg	70-0443
LEMKE, Matthilde	21	Eylau	70-0052
LEMKE, Rudolf	43	Berlin	71-0736
LEMKE, Wilhelmine	36	Burhaw	69-1004
LEMM, Dorethea	36	Mainz	70-1161
LEMME, Anna Elise	23	Benkendorf	69-0321
LEMMERMANN, Elise	18	Ottersberg	69-0672
LEMP, Pauline	25	St. Gallen	69-0572
LEMPKE, August	18	Nossow-Rossow	71-0712
Hermann 16			
LENCHS, Johann	14	Lautenbach	68-1006
LENCKENHEIMER, Marg.	19	Wallhausen	70-0452
LENE, Gustav	28	Wittenberg	68-1006
LENGERICH, Bernhard	27	Handorf	68-1006
LENGERT, Wilhelm	17	Osterode	68-1027
LENGSTOCK, Adolf	25	Warsau	69-0457
LENK, Ludwig	26	Muehlheim	70-0682
LENNEMANN, Theodor	31	Habbecke	68-0314
LENNING, Margaret	39	Schottens	68-0625
Anna 9, Carl 7, Georg 5, Heinrich 2			
LENSKE, Hermann	16	Osterode	71-0712
LENTHAUSER, Arthur	16	SSchwarzb. Rude	69-0672
LENTSCH, August	19	Muehlheim	69-0572
LENTZ, Mathilde	18	Gnesen	71-0300
LENTZ, Theobald	28	Naersheim	70-0308
LENTZE, Johann	55	Lienzingen	68-0852
Elisabeth 53, Caroline 25, Pauline 18			
LENZ, Carl	22	Maeschenfelde	71-0492
LENZ, G. Fr.	18	Schnaith	70-0135
LENZ, Johann	34	Madison	69-0457
LENZ, Louise	23	Schnaith	68-0907
LENZ, Michel	58	Schlienstadt	69-1363
LENZ, Sofia	35	Altena	69-1421
Amalia 8, Wilhelmine 6, Adolf 4			
LENZ, Wilhelm	18	Dortmund	69-1076
LENZ, Wilhelm	25	Freiburg	71-0429
Ida 22			
LENZE, Barbara	37	Eningen	68-0907
LENZEN, H.	38	Kayserswerth	69-0560
LENZING, Agnes	23	Schwemmingen	69-0229
LEONHARD, Fer.	18	Croen	69-0321
LEONHARD, Henry	21	Bremen	68-1298
LEONHART, Rudolf	37	Pittsburg	69-1086
LEOPOLD, Amalie	24	Tuttlingen	70-1023
LEOPOLD, Anna	18	Hannover	70-1035
LEOPOLD, Carl	17	Baden	70-0148
LEOPOLD, Catharine	19	Endingen	70-0508
LEOPOLD, Phil.	24	Darmstadt	69-1011

NAME	AGE	RESIDENCE	YR-LIST
LEPPER, Carl August	16	Bederkesa	68-1006
LERCH, Peter	62	Darmstadt	68-0610
LERYKAM, Caspar	30	Wuerzburg	69-0321
LESCHKE, Johann	48	Hahlenhardt	68-1027
Catharine 45, Catharine 15, Marie 9, Johann 6, Elise 2			
LESCHORN, Alex	24	Aachen	71-0821
LESEBERG, Friedrich	22	Sonneborn	68-0456
LESEKE, Johann	48	Hahlenhardt	68-1027
Catharine 45, Catharine 15, Marie 9, Johann 6, Elise 2			
LESING, Mar. Cath.	32	Coesfeld	68-1002
LESKE, F. W.	16	Margonin	71-0736
LESSENKUP, Mar.	24	Bueren	71-0521
Louise 24			
LESSMANN, Heinrich	24	Detmold	68-0314
LETAH, J.	28	Boehmen	70-0569
Barb. 24			
LETENHOF, Adam	25	Buchenberg	71-0681
LETKE, Emilie	22	Salakowo	71-0521
LETTERMANN, Christiane	24	Darmstadt	71-0492
LETTNER, Caroline	21	Kappelrodeck	71-0456
LETTRE, Catharine	32	Hanau	71-0712
LEU, Johanna	19	Nikosken	68-0786
LEUBCHEN, Heinrich	32	Guenthers	68-0939
LEUKE, Georg	17	Aerzen	71-0492
LEUPOLD, Babette	19	Lichtenberg	71-0479
Sophie 17			
LEUPOLD, Elisabeth	22	Haid	71-0821
LEUPOLD, Georg	19	Lichtenberg	69-0542
LEUT, Caroline	36	Chicago	70-1023
Arnold 9			
LEUTER, Theodor	22	Oberrossau	68-0770
LEUTHAEUSER, Peter	15	Mittwitz	68-0534
LEUTHERER, Catharine	29	Hassmacheim	71-0736
Carl 19			
LEUTWEIN, Gotthold	24	Eisingen	68-0534
LEUTZ, Julius	28	Danzig	68-0884
LEVI, Carl	23	Brusnath	71-0581
LEVI, Hermann	15	Osthofen	69-1059
LEVI, Jetta	19	Burgbaum	69-0968
LEVI, Leopoldinge	18	Cassel	69-0029
LEVIN, John	33	Elbersheim	69-0338
Mary 27, Margareth 22			
LEVY, C.	25	Achim	70-0583
LEVY, Calmar	15	Dresden	68-0982
LEVY, Chs.	22	Mannheim	70-0170
LEVY, Josef	25	Sontra	71-0643
LEVY, Leon	20	Mertzviller	71-0581
LEVY, Leon	23	Wingersheim	71-0581
LEVY, Mas	18	Kreuznach	68-0456
LEVY, Minna	26	Ronshausen	68-0534
LEVY, Rosa	23	Jeesen	69-0560
LEVY, Simon	17	Hachingen	70-0031
LEWIG, Johanne	42	Muenster	71-0736
Elisab. 20, Anna 9, Jacob 8			
LEWIN, Adolf	25	Halle	71-0429
LEWIN, Heinr.	18	Minden	68-0786
LEWIS, Alex	27	London	70-0204

NAME	AGE	RESIDENCE	YR-LIST
Louise 27			
LEWKOWITZ, Abraham	31	Namslau	68-0661
Rosalie 21			
LEWKOWITZ, Bertha	40	Kempen	68-0534
LEY, Christian	15	Neudorf	68-1006
LEYDIG, Caroline	20	Hall	70-0682
LEYH, Christian	59	Gelnhausen	70-1055
LEYH, Wilhelm	27	Kattnitz	70-0683
Bertha 22, Richard 5 months			
LEYSER, Ernst	17	Herbein	71-0363
LIBEGOTT, Heinrich	18	Bergheim	70-0452
LICHOWSKY, Lorenz	22	Camnitz	69-0547
LICHOWSKY, Michael	26	Camnitz	69-0547
Elisabeth 25			
LICHTE, Andreas	24	Hessen	70-0508
LICHTEN, Georg	18	Kirchwistedt	69-0429
LICHTENBERG, Bernhard	28	Rocholl	70-0355
LICHTENBERG, Fr.	32	Wiezen	70-0170
Elise 28			
LICHTENBERGER, A.	19	Germersheim	68-0760
LICHTENWALDE, Joseph	37	Wien	71-0363
LICHTI, Barbara	12	Duttweiler	71-0429
Magda. 17			
LIEB, Johanna	21	Neuenhaus	68-0957
LIEB, Maria	26	Flehingen	68-0760
LIEBARTH, Eduard	36	Veronica	69-0457
Wilhelmine 30, Baby 11 months			
LIEBENOW, Julius	43	Wordel	69-0162
LIEBERMANN, Bertha	22	Coburg	69-1086
LIEBERMANN, Franz	17	Duerkheim	71-0393
LIEBERMANN, Meta	22	Nenzinen	69-0672
LIEBERMANN, Veronica	20	Czarnikau	68-0566
LIEBHABER, Anton	40	Oberasberg	69-1212
LIEBIG, Philipp	14	Nildenhausen	68-0707
LIEBLER, Mary	20	Gamberg	70-0508
LIEBMANN, Siegmund	18	Dirmstein	69-0208
LIEBNER, Hugo	30	Shebrygan	69-1076
LIEDEKE, Elise	20	Frankfurt a/M	70-0135
LIEDERWALD, Richard	35	Aux.Pajes	69-1076
LIEDKE, Andreas	58	Dallenheim	68-0707
Wilhelmine 58			
LIEDTKE, Marie	31	Bramberg	71-0479
Louise 2			
LIEHAU, Elise	26	Cassel	68-0884
LIEHECKA, Joh.	47	Boehmen	70-1142
Maria 47, Barbara 18, Magdalena 9, Maria 6			
LIEHR, Emilie	29	Bleicherode	71-0363
LIENAU, Anna	22	Niederzehren-Pr	70-0006
Caroline 18			
LIERSCH, Fr.	60	Apolda	68-0884
LIES, Wilhelmine	21	Oberellenbach	69-0429
LIESE, Abraham	53	Arnstedt	68-0625
Anna 43, Marie 18, Franz 17, Angela 15, Marie 13, Emil 9, Joseph 7, Augusta 6			
LIESE, George	17	Rotenburg	68-0456
LIESENBEIN, Catharine	20	Frauensheim	71-0429
LIESKE, Franz	17	Odargau	69-0457
LIETH, Jacobine	20	Neuenkirchen	71-0429
LIETHMANN, Joh.	33	Oldenburg	70-0089
LIETZKE, Carl	19	Traumburg	68-0753
LILIENKAMP, Friedrich	16	Walle	68-0566
LILIENTHAL, Cathrine	35	Hannover	69-1059
Meta 12			
LILIENTHAL, Dr.	18	Osterholz	68-0957
Metta 21			
LILIENTHAL, Friederike	25	Charleston	69-1059
LILL, Ferd.	19	Sassen	68-0566
LILLER, Rosalie	25	Rastadt	68-1027
Anna 3			
LIMARUTTE, Lorenz	33	Wolfsberg	68-1006
Lorenz 9			
LIMENSKY, Aug.	38	Squirawen	68-0753
Catharina 34, August 7, Franz 5, Peter 11 months			
LIMPRECHT, Elisabeth	27	Graefenthal	68-0625
LIN, Catharine	26	Neidenbach	68-0939
LIND, Johann	19	Maachenheim	71-0712
LINDAU, H. R.	35	Japan	69-1396
LINDAUER, Christ.	19	Eberhardsweiler	68-0884
LINDEMANN, Fritz	59	Mecklenburg	69-0067
Anna 53, Elise 19, Johann 33, Elise 28, Anna 3			
LINDEMANN, Joh.	25	Dorum	68-0820
Anna 54			
LINDEMANN, Ludw.	27	Bremen	69-0162
LINDEMANN, Marie	52	Bramsche	68-1006
Elise 17			
LINDEMANN, Marie	19	Hannover	71-0456
LINDEMANN, Meta	20	Schwarme	68-0610
LINDEMEYER, Ernst	50	Wehringsdorf	69-0923
Cathrine 45, Ernst 26, Heinrich 24, Florentine 20, Catharine 17			
LINDEMEYER, Gottl.	39	Woadville	71-0815
LINDENAU, Anna	15	Horst-Bohemia	70-0006
Catharina 40, Thomas 8, Marie 6, Addalbert 3,			
LINDENAUER, Clemens	42	Vorarlberg	69-0560
LINDENER, Maria	23	Turkheim	68-0707
LINDENLAUB, Ferd.	50	Gotha	69-1011
Mary 44, Valentin 21			
LINDENSCHMIDT, A.	24	Mengshausen	68-0852
LINDER, Aug.	20	Ehingen	70-0259
LINDERER, Ernestine	22	Roschwitz	69-0229
LINDERER, Joh.	69	Gallschuetz	71-0581
Christiane 68, Ernestine 30, Maria 26			
LINDERS, Anna	20	Westner	71-0821
LINDES, Marie	17	Ottersberg	68-0982
LINDHOFF, Catharine	20	Pellen	69-0208
LINDHORN, Emma	14	Offenwalder	68-0566
LINDHORST, Johann	25	Bremen	70-0523
LINDSTAEDT, Paul	27	Muenster	69-0208
LING, Christian	24	Grutlmerode	71-0456
LINGNER, H.	22	Kaemmerod	71-0643
LINK, Armin	19	Cassel	69-1011
LINK, Bertha	22	Schlirstadt	68-1002
LINK, Caroline	31	Golnau	70-0006
Franz 12, Hedwig 8, Max 5, Emma 6, Marie 11 months			

NAME	AGE	RESIDENCE	YR-LIST
LINK, Charles	24	Madan	68-0760
LINK, Crescentia	21	Duerheim	71-0521
Emil 2 months			
LINK, Elise	17	Wallroth	71-0393
LINK, Johann Georg	22	Unterfranken	69-0321
LINK, John	38	Gockendorf	71-0456
LINK, Maria	22	Neuenkirchen	71-0789
LINK, Pauline	29	Wuerzburg	68-0852
LINK, Rudolf	28	Uickenrode/Wick	70-0170
LINKE, Anna	28	Glatz	70-0308
LINNEMANN, Friederike	20	Wuelfer	68-1006
LINNI, Peter	24	Horschbach	70-0308
Elise 30, Jacob 19			
LINS, Hermann	34	Naumburg	68-0982
Anna 30			
LINSKY, Carl	27	Bitow	69-0547
LINTARDE, Barbara	23	Graefenberg	68-1006
LINX, Joh.	17	Ahlenbach	71-0393
LINZ, Anton	18	Boehmen	70-1142
LINZIG, Louise	18	Haagen	71-0363
LION, Caroline	42	Goettingen	68-0786
Adolph 13			
LIPGRAAF, Herm.	24	Wissel	69-1086
LIPMANNSOHN, Elias	27	Oberstein	68-0939
Ernestine 28, Georg 10 months			
LIPP, Barbara	19	Offenheim	71-0712
LIPP, Peter	46	Steinsfurth	68-0786
Marie 45, Peter 22, Helene 14, Caroline 9, Regine 24, Franz 3 months			
LIPPARD, Henry	19	Kleba	68-0534
LIPPAUER, Catharina	42	Wien	68-0661
LIPPE, Abraham	18	Lippe	71-0789
LIPPE, Joseph	23	Hoxter	70-0728
LIPPERT, Herm.	25	Bleistadt	71-0521
LIPPERT, Moritz	22	Meissen	69-0784
LIPPERT, Peter	38	Raimar	69-1363
LIPPMANN, Henry	17	Hemlingen	68-0957
LIPPOLD, Louis	27	Mulsum	69-0542
Wilhelmine 26, Richard 9 months			
LIPPOLD, Louis	18	Braunschweig	70-0272
LIPPOLDT, Christian	25	Dohrlitz	69-0968
LIPPSTADT, Sebastian	41	Merzhausen	68-0760
LISE, Heinz	46	Olsen	69-0049
George 12, A. Elisabeth 10, John Heinrich 7, Katharine 45, Elisabeth 17, Catha			
LISKA, B.	57	Boehmen	70-1066
LISS, Benedict	35	Augsburg	68-0939
Margaretha 32, Alwisius 9			
LISS, Georg		Hamelingen	71-0456
LISSER, Friedrich	28	Dessau	68-0939
LIST, Carl	46	Glauchau	68-0456
Caroline 49, Wilhelmine 16			
LIST, Catharine	30	Niederbeerbach	68-1002
Christine 9, baby 11 months			
LISTMANN, Anna	19	Almenrod	68-0884
LISY, Franz	24	Boehmen	70-0569
LITCH, Anna	16	Badelitz	70-0329
LITGENS, Robert	19	Wieden	68-1298
LITTIG, Wilhelm	9	Bremen	69-0923
LITTLE, Joh.	22	Pittsburgh	70-0569
LITTON, James	42	New York	69-0572
Caroline 38			
LITZENBAUER, Joh.	16	Rotenburg	71-0363
LITZENBAUM, Friedrich	15	Rosenberg	68-0456
LITZENBERGER, Magd.	32	Langenlausheim	71-0363
LIZUIS, Marie	45	Waldeck	71-0456
Amalie 16, Bernhard 17, Gerhard 9, Bertha 3			
LOCHMANN, Joh.	30	Hartershausen	68-0884
LOCHNER, Nicolas	29	Leupoldsgruen	69-0848
LOCKE, Christian	22	Meissen	69-0182
LOCKER, George	17	Hobhausen	71-0712
LODE, Jacob	30	Vallendar	68-0647
LODERER, Benedict	15	Kallin	70-1023
Cath. 23			
LOEB, Benedict	22	Weisenheim	68-1002
LOEB, Julius	15	Bechtheim	69-1004
LOEB, Michael	59	Kettstadt	71-0581
Sara 24			
LOEB, Zerlina	20	Schweppenhaus	68-0852
LOEBE, Fanny	18	Such	69-0771
LOEBE, Lina	18	Muenden	68-0753
Luise 15			
LOEBENSTEIN, Pauline	20	Muehlhausen	68-0610
LOEBER, Elise	22	Niedenstein	71-0821
LOEBL, Bertha	21	Boehmen	69-0784
LOEBNER, Max	22	Schulin	70-1003
LOEBSACK, Heinrich	50	Hessen	69-0559
Elisabeth 49, Gerhard 13, Wilhelm 11			
LOEFFEL, Anna	24	Kenzingen	68-0820
LOEFFEL, Euphrosine	46	Kenzingen	69-1421
LOEFFERT, Anna	23	Bellings	71-0479
Cath. 20			
LOEFFERT, Jean	28	Breunings	68-1002
LOEFFERT, Joh.	20	Bellings	71-0479
LOEFFLER, Angon	19	Ballrechten	71-0581
LOEFFLER, Christ.	17	Hueninggen	70-0523
Jacob 12, Emilie 7, Sophie 5			
LOEFFLER, Friedr.	40	Primlas	71-0681
LOEFFLER, Ludwig	25	Bierbach	69-0798
LOEFFLER, Marie	56	Wetzekow	71-0581
LOEHNER, Andrea	17	Speyer	69-1076
LOEHNERS, Nicolas	29	Leupoldsgruen	69-0848
LOEHR, Barbara	19	Ruebesheim	69-0672
LOEHR, Christ.	22	Bruchmachtersse	71-0581
LOENI, Caroline	23	Wallesgruen	71-0821
LOENING, Sophie	23	Stolzenau	69-0572
LOER, Sophie	22	Oberschaffhause	71-0492
LOESCH, Bertha	29	Altenburg	69-0592
LOESCH, Eberhard	21	Danzig	68-0707
LOESCH, Elisabeth	20	Queidesbach	70-0508
LOESCH, John	25	Hannover	69-1421
LOESCHEN, Johann	17	Wichens	69-0208
LOESCHER, Louise	28	Loeban	68-0957
LOESCHHORN, John	5	Villingen	69-0560
LOESCHHORN, Marg.	26	Villingen	68-0884
Louise 20			

NAME	AGE	RESIDENCE	YR-LIST
LOESER, Adolf	19	Muehlheim	69-0162
LOESER, Adolph	18	Cassel	69-0576
LOESER, Thomas	26	Obernberg	71-0712
Maria 26			
LOETSCH. Ludwig	20	Ostdorf	70-0569
LOETZERIG, Heinrich	19	Kleinern	68-0566
LOEVENSTEIN, Georg	56	Darmstadt	69-0576
Catharina 58, Elisabeth 21			
LOEWE, Herm.	21	Reichenbach	69-0771
LOEWEN, Petr	19	Darmstadt	70-0355
LOEWENBEIN, Regina	14	Prag	69-0050
LOEWENGARD, Joseph	16	Fuerth	71-0736
LOEWENSEIN, S.	15	Darmstadt	69-1059
LOEWENSTEIN, C.	20	Hannover	68-1298
LOEWENSTEIN, Gust.	17	Obrigheim	71-0521
LOEWENSTEIN, Julie	25	Coblenz	68-0647
LOEWENSTEIN, Julius	25	Bremen	70-0384
LOEWENSTEIN, Lena	24	Rhede	68-0939
LOEWENSTEIN, Sal.	38	Oberstein	69-0560
LOEWENSTERN, Heinrich	50	Paderborn	68-0314
LOEWENTHAL, Adolph	16	Althofen	70-1142
LOEWENTHAL, Heinrich	39	Neustadt	68-0661
Natalie 42, Max 7			
LOEWENTHAL, Sim.	19	Franken	70-0378
LOEWINGER, John	18	Himmelkron	71-0643
LOEWLEIN, Margareth	20	Zederritz	70-0329
LOEWY, Rudolph	13	Radnitz	68-1006
Aloys 9			
LOFFERS, Elisabeth	32	Vechtel	68-0786
LOFFLER, Anna	24	Schlenglengsfd.	68-0707
LOFFLER, Joseph	18	Schuetten	69-0268
LOGEMANN, Lucie	9	Nauenburg	70-0308
Mary 7			
LOGES, Dorothea	21	Aerzen	71-0492
LOH, Christian	25	Neuenkirchen	71-0643
LOHM, Henry	32	Meimbressen	68-1298
LOHMANN, Albert	30	Braunschweig	70-0683
LOHMANN, Anton	28	Rochlitz	69-0229
LOHMANN, Gesche	23	Taken	69-1004
LOHMANN, Johann	30	Hoboken	70-0355
LOHMANN, Wilh.	23	Muenchehof	71-0456
LOHMEIER, Ludwig	16	Braukamps	68-0707
LOHMUELLER, Friedrich	30	Buenos Ayres	69-1076
LOHMUELLER, Marie	51	Berghausen	71-0393
Wilh. 20, Cath. 7			
LOHN, Franz	38	Altona	70-0170
LOHNES, Catharine	25	Hessen	70-0204
LOHNSTEIN, Otto	20	Berlin	69-0067
LOHR, Ad. Doroth.	20	Wollin	71-0684
LOHRE, Joseph	14	Brakel	68-0982
LOHRMANN, Christine	24	Goeppingen	68-1006
LOHSEN, Joh. Christ.	16	Volkmant	71-0226
LOHSTROH, Heinrich	29	Varnhg.-Vornhg.	68-0534
Elisa 28, Dorette 2, baby-daughter 6 months			
LOLSCHERER, Philippine	37	Coburg	69-0784
LOMPARTER, Christian	28	Thornbach	71-0712
LONNAMANN, Rebecca	17	Altstadt	71-0821
LOOCK, Carl	23	Braunne	68-0566

NAME	AGE	RESIDENCE	YR-LIST
LOOS, Frd.	31	Doggingne	71-0393
LOOS, Friedrich	26	Tuesk	69-0490
LOOS, Philipp	25	Weinheim	70-0204
Gertrude 25			
LORCH, August	40	Meissen	71-0736
LORCH, Joh. H.	18	Bodenheim	70-0378
LORCHE, George	28	Hastrup	71-0792
LORENZ, Adam	33	Stubig	69-0182
LORENZ, Ferdinand	49	Bremen	69-1076
LORENZ, Frank	45	Berlin	68-1002
LORENZ, G.	22	Aixheim	69-0968
LORENZ, Henriette	38	Berlin	69-0848
Bertha 12, Henriette 58, Fanny 8			
LORENZ, Joh. G.	17	Lauschroeden	68-1002
LORENZ, Johann	28	Parchem	71-0492
LORENZ, Joseph	23	Pichelberg	68-0770
LORENZ, Mathilde	19	Heringhausen	68-0884
LORENZ, Minna	32	Stettin	69-1004
Hedwig 9			
LORSCH, Caroline	20	Heuchelheim	70-1003
LORSCHNEIDER, Anna	18	Oppen	71-0736
LOSCHETTER, Marg.	59	Neuhuetten	68-0314
Elisabeth 23			
LOSERT, Carl	28	Nautisheim	70-0204
LOSGAR, Joh.	27	Oberfranken	69-0321
LOSKE, Hedwig	23	Oppersdorf	68-0456
LOSSL, Carl	30	Heinrichsgau	68-0820
LOTZ, Catharina	30	Darmstadt	69-0583
LOTZ, Conrad	19	Harxheim	69-0542
LOTZ, Henry	33	Sonnendeich	68-0957
LOTZ, Johann E.	17	Benshausen	71-0712
LOTZ, John	30	Seestermuehl	68-0957
Sophia 31			
LOTZ, Wilh.	22	Kirchhain	71-0684
LOUX, Johann H.	54	Barmen	69-0576
Gertrude 56, August 17			
LUBKEMANN, Caroline	20	Hozhausen	71-0684
Wilhelm 17			
LUBLASSER, Leonh.	26	Tyrol	71-0167
LUBLINER, Dorel	29	Kempen	68-0534
LUCAS, Melchior	43	Grosshausitz	68-0760
Justine 41, Hermann 16, Emil 4, Augusta 6			
LUCAS, Peter	23	Hopstaedt	69-0457
LUCESI, Moris	16	Lucca	71-0363
Antono 14, Ispiridioni 12			
LUCHS, Renke	44	Hassebrok	69-0029
LUCIUS, Ernst	22	Darmstadt	69-1212
LUCK, Reimund	32	Weingarten	70-0076
LUCK, Wilhelmine	31	Preussen	68-0456
Louise 9 months			
LUCKA, Peter	19	Bremen	70-0308
LUCKHARDT, Adam	23	Trokenfurth	69-0672
LUCKHARDT, Ernst	65	Kirspenhausen	71-0456
LUCKHAUS, Ernst	23	Remscheid	69-1059
LUCKING, Anna	25	Wallenbruch	68-0939
LUDDE, Anton	28	Muenster	69-0968
LUDEMANN, Diedr.	31	Hannover	70-0355
LUDEMANN, John	27	Kuhstadt	69-1004

NAME	AGE	RESIDENCE	YR-LIST
LUDEWIG, Minna	23	Rochlitz	68-0625
LUDMANN, Christ.	25	Roggenburg	68-0820
Christ. 9, Minna 26			
LUDOLPH, Johann	56	Waldkappel	71-0684
Elisabeth 49			
LUDWIG, Adam	31	Neckerau	69-0229
LUDWIG, Andreas	61	Rossbach	70-1161
John 19			
LUDWIG, Anna	28	Braunschweig	69-1396
Baby 9 months			
LUDWIG, August	22	Nauenburg	69-1212
LUDWIG, Carl	25	Geislingen	68-0610
LUDWIG, Carl	28	Utrichshausen	71-0643
LUDWIG, Christ.	38	Lorsch	71-0167
LUDWIG, Emilie	19	Leipzig	70-0204
LUDWIG, Fr. W.	17	Coblenz	68-0820
LUDWIG, Friedr.	27	Weimar	68-1298
LUDWIG, Gottlieb	16	Asch	68-0957
LUDWIG, Heinrich	18	Otterndorf	69-0542
LUDWIG, Joh.	19	Marburg	68-0820
LUDWIG, Maria	48	Steinbach	71-0363
Joseph 21, Therese 18			
LUDWIG, Marie	29	Plogwitz	70-0204
LUDWIG, Mars	17	Leipzig	69-1212
LUDWIG, Oscar	23	Berlin	69-1059
LUDWIG, Reinhard	34	Greussen	68-0534
LUDWIG, Wilhelm	17	Landenbach	69-0429
LUDWIGS, Catharine	21	Zetel	68-0566
Georg 18			
LUEBBE, Fritz	27	Strohen	71-0479
Caroline 29, Sophie 3, Wilh. 11 m.			
LUEBBE, John	41	Scharnerwisch	68-0957
LUEBBEN, Clemens	23	Hannover	70-0728
LUEBBEN, Elise	38	Hannover	70-1142
Eduard 9, Antonie 7, Johanna 7, Caroline 5, Dorothea 9 months			
LUEBBEN, Juergen	14	Schirum	69-0208
LUEBBERT, Louise	21	Huelsen	68-0566
Marie 15			
LUEBKE, Aug.	25	Schesindebeck	70-0443
LUEBKE, Fritz	30	Balfanz	69-0429
Auguste 28			
LUEBKEMANN, Meta	32	Gustendorf	69-0923
Anna 4			
LUEBKER, Friedrich	60	Quelle	69-1086
Louise 55, Hermann 27, Marie 27, Henriette 9, Eduard 3 months			
LUEBKER, Heinrich	25	Quelle	69-1086
LUEBKING, Friedrich	18	Minden	68-0939
LUECK,Carl	34	Kerchenburg	70-0378
LUECKE, Johann	43	Haast	68-1027
Anna 43, Carl 8, Anna 3, Louise 17			
LUECKE, Peter	46	Brastawo	71-0681
Wilhelmine 36, Gust. 9, Aug. 8, Wilhelmine 5, Albertine 10 months			
LUECKEL, Louise	18	Aue	69-0968
LUECKEN, Mary	21	Alde	68-0760
Adelheid 25			
LUECKEN, Mary	21	Alde	68-0760
Adelheid 25			

NAME	AGE	RESIDENCE	YR-LIST
LUECKER, Friedrich	48	Isenstaedt	68-0907
Sophie 46, Wilhelm 22, Caroline 17, Friedrich 13, Anna Sophia 7			
LUECKERT, John	21	Volkershausen	68-0534
LUECKING, Anton	14	Borgentreich	68-0760
Margarethe 16			
LUEDEMANN, Joh.	40	Blankenhain	68-0786
Marie 28, Marie 9, Anna 7			
LUEDER, Gustav	30	Osterhagen	68-0852
LUEDERS, Heinr.	38	Leisten	69-0321
Marie Sophie 30			
LUEDIKE, Fr.	19	Meinsdorf	69-1011
LUEDKE, Emilie	19	Moschuetz	71-0521
LUEHLER, Thomas	28	Boehmen	70-1161
LUEHR, Anton	29	Pfaffenweiler	70-0031
LUEHRMANN, Diedr.	14	Hannover	70-0443
LUEHRMANN, J.	30	Nienburg	68-0884
LUEHRS, Anna	20	Stoteln	71-0456
LUEHRS, Christian	34	Ostfriesland	70-0329
Antje 35, Vollant 7, Harinke 3, Wessel 9 months			
LUEHRS, Heinrich	26	Oldenburg	70-0204
Friedrich 20			
LUEHRS, Johanna	15	Lehe	68-0786
LUEHRSEN, Aug.	32	Heepen	69-0338
LUEK, Reimund	32	Weingarten	70-0076
LUEKEN, Chr. D.	26	Oldenburg	69-1421
Anna 27			
LUEKENBACH, Henriette	37	Salzburg	70-0682
LUELLMANN, Heinr.	30	Sabbenhausen	68-0884
Maria 28			
LUELWES, August	22	Osnabrueck	68-1006
LUENINGHAUSEN, N.	37	Bremen	70-0006
LUENZMANN, Julia	22	Bremen	69-0338
LUERDING, Diedrich	16	Kl. Minnelage	68-0939
LUERRBECK, Sophie	38	Buehl	71-0492
LUERSSEN, Anna	22	Bremen	69-0542
LUERSSEN, Meta	20	Scharmbeck	68-1006
LUESEM, John	18	Eyten	70-0508
LUESSER, Luer	58	Imsen	69-1212
LUETGE, Louis	22	Braunschweig	69-1059
LUETJE, Auguste	20	Hannover	70-1142
LUETJEN, Fritz	16	Osten	71-0363
Heinrich 15			
LUETJEN, Heinrich	16	Scharmbeckstote	68-0760
LUETJEN, Herm.	19	Hannover	69-1086
LUETJEN, John	14	Hambergen	71-0172
LUETJENS, Diedr.	27	Cadenberge	69-0560
LUETJENS, Heinrich	34	Vollen	68-0661
LUETJENS, Richard	23	Solingen	70-0508
Emma 25, Mathias 11 months			
LUETMANN, Joh.	16	Nedderavebergen	68-0566
LUETZKE, Carl	19	Traumburg	68-0753
LUFT, Carl Wilh.	22	Paetzig	70-0259
LUFT, Friedrich	27	Liepe	69-1212
LUFT, Joh.	20	Bombach	71-0789
LUFT, Johannes	16	Geiss Nidda	69-0490
LUFT, Otto	17	Weimar	69-0542
LUGELDER, Gustav	21	Bischoffsheim	69-0457

NAME	AGE	RESIDENCE	YR-LIST
LUH, Christine	18	Darmstadt	68-0957
Catharina 7			
LUHASCH, Rosalie	16	Zetiar	70-0329
LUHMANN, Anna	19	Elsdorf	68-0456
LUHMANN, Wilhelmine	28	Stuttgart	71-0643
LUHRS, Conrad	32	Zesern	70-0006
LUHRS, Sara	21	Spandau	70-0052
LUISE, Carl	26	Maulin	69-0490
Auguste 27, Wilhelm 11 months			
LUITEN, Gerhardine	58	Schwafheim	71-0815
Gerhardine 14, Marie 26, Johann 6 m.			
LUITEN, Jacob	27	Schwafheim	71-0815
Johannes 22, Gerhard 20, Joh. 17			
LUITER, Herm.	25	Schwafheim	71-0815
LUKISCH, Anton	21	Boehmen	70-0569
Josef 24, Emmanuel 18			
LUKTERHAND, Carl	30	Cutzhof	68-0753
Friederike 27			
LULEY, Elisabeth	24	Darmstadt	70-0204
LUMANN, Cath.	21	Merbaum	71-0479
LUNG, Marie	19	Forchtenberg	68-0982
LUNTJE, Johann	42	Erlangen	71-0429
LUNZMANN, Anna	17	Rodenburg	70-0204
LUPPOLD, Catharine	19	Endingen	70-0508
LUSCH, Joh.	30	Berlin	70-0384
LUSTHOFF, Henriette	34	Drakenburg	68-0661
Fritz 3			
LUTCH, Justus	35	Hansen	71-0681
Anna 27, Joh. 9, Claise 7, Reinhard 6, Catharina 4, Gertrud 9 m			
LUTHER, Julie	19	Brastawo	71-0681
LUTHMANN, Louise	26	Aldermissen	68-0456
Wilhelmine 15, Friedrich 16, Doris 13			
LUTNER, Heinrich	27	Frankfurt	70-0148
LUTTER, Maria	21	Niederauerbach	71-0492
LUTTMANN, Johann	29	Sage	68-1027
LUTZ, Bath.	26	Gerdringen	68-0753
Barbara 28, Catharina 3, Johannes 4			
LUTZ, C.	25	Wildbad	63-1003
F. 29, F. 5			
LUTZ, Heinrich	17	Nacha	69-1319
LUTZ, Heinrich	28	Heidenheim	69-0572
LUTZ, Jacob	58	Baden	70-0148
LUTZ, Wilh.	24	Hemberg	71-0300
LUTZEN, Hermann	17	Aurich	68-0419
LUX, Anna	25	Unterfranken	69-0968
LUX, Hermann	27	Uelzen	71-0429
LUZ, Friedericke	21	Altenstaig	68-0852
Dorothea 2			
LUZER, Johann	41	Altensteig	68-0456
Catharina 38, Friedrich 14, Christian 9, Gottfried 8, Wilhelm 6, Catharine 4			
MAAR, Fr.	27	Steibra	68-0820
Margaretha 29, Ferdinand 5, Catharina 11 months			
MAAS, Aug.	48	R.B. Coeslin	68-0820
Amalie 39, Friederike 15, Albert 3, Friedrich 9, Ferdinand 9			
MAAS, Frd.	28	Oldenburg	70-0452
MAAS, Gesche	16	Barrien	68-0957
MAAS, Heinr.	30	Altenhuntorf	71-0581
Gesine 19			
MAASS, Ulrich	20	Henkenhagen	71-0456
MACDONALD, Emil	27	Swinemuende	69-0542
MACH, Eleonore	25	Karlov	70-0329
MACHEDANZ, Georg	30	Vacha	68-0820
MACHELEIDT, Linda	32	SSchwarzb. Rude	69-0672
Henriette 26, Tecla 22			
MACHENIUS, Wilhelm	18	Frankenberg	71-0712
MACK, Christ.	18	Bayreuth	70-0569
MACK, Urban	57	Bilfingen	69-0015
MACKE, Caroline	14	Hemdorf	69-0208
Bernhard 17			
MACKE, Caroline	24	Damme	68-0939
MACKE, Werner	59	Ossenbeck	68-1002
MADER, Carl	13	Edemissen	68-1002
MADER, Christ.	22	Rotheil	69-0841
MADER, Jacob	50	Oberasberg	69-1212
Theresa 35, Theodor 5			
MADER, Simon	29	Bruck	71-0521
Theresia 22			
MADICKE, Wilhelmine	21	Gr. Lubs	71-0733
MAECHTLE, Jacob	23	Pfaffenhofen	68-0760
MAEDER, Albrecht	35	Sondershausen	68-0014
MAEDER, Emil	30	Sondershausen	68-0707
MAEDER, Julie	24	St. Gallen	69-0672
MAEDER, Robert	18	Burkheim	71-0733
MAEDER, Rosalie	63	Rolla	71-0581
MAEDLER, Anna	28	Lanz	68-0770
MAEHRENS, Anna	16	Stofel	69-0429
MAELZER, Ernst	25	Gotha	70-0384
MAENLET, Georg	31	Pforzheim	70-1003
MAENOLEN, Rosa	22	Stuttgart	69-0542
MAESCHER, Catharine	14	Melle	68-0939
MAESS, Hermann	47	Schale	68-0786
Anna 32, Heinrich 8, Anna 5, Johann 11 months			
MAESTING, Jacob	26	Bondorf	69-0583
MAETTER, Wilhelm	48	Kirchdorf	71-0684
MAGDEFRAU, Mart.	30	Soul	68-0753
Eleonore 24			
MAGEN, And.	14	Rockenfeld	71-0789
MAGG, Gustav	30	Neresheim	68-0884
Amalie 28, Heinr. 3			
MAGNUS, David	17	Berlin	68-0456
MAHENKE, Heinrich	25	Detmold	71-0429
MAHLER, Friederike	50	Isenstaedt	68-0907
Friedrich 16, Gottlieb 12			
MAHLER, Heinrich	69	Gunderbunden	70-0184
MAHLER, Sophie	22	Vegesack	69-0784
MAHLER, Sophie	21	Sielstadt	68-0907
MAHLMANN, Carl	25	Braunschweig	68-0786
MAHLMANN, Hermann	14	Johannesroth	70-0378
MAHNKE, Friedrich	31	Altmersleben	69-0321
Marie Elisabeth 50, Marie Elisabeth 29, Fr. Wilhelmine 23			
MAHNKE, Wm.	26	Pommern	69-0841
Wilhelmine 51, Friedrich 28, Hermann 20			
MAHNKEN, Herm.	31	Ottersberg	70-0378

NAME	AGE	RESIDENCE	YR-LIST
MAHNKEN, Johann	15	Hannover	69-0672
MAHNKEN, Louis	25	Lilienthal	69-1059
MAHNKER, Catharina	20	Osterholz	69-1212
MAI, Catharina	33	Densborn	68-0939
MAI, Herz	19	Darmstadt	70-0170
MAI, Max	30	Berlin	68-0456
MAI, Robert	32	Bergen	68-0625
Pauline 27, Robert 4, Hermine 2			
MAI, Robert	27	Wasmegen	68-0707
Amalia 26, Amalia 3 months			
MAICHLE, Stephan	9	Margrethhausen	69-0338
MAIER, Christine	18	Gomaringen	68-0566
MAIER, Constantin	25	Rottweil	69-0592
MAIER, Crescenz	33	Irslingen	69-0490
MAIER, Elisabeth	23	Hainshaim	69-1212
MAIER, Heinrich	14	Reuthlingen	70-0523
MAIER, Henn. H.	16	St. Magnus	68-0707
MAIER, Isidor	18	Carlsruhe	68-0884
MAIER, Jacob	19	Dornham	69-0784
MAIER, Joh. Anton	36	Muenchen	68-1002
Josepha 26, Joseph 3			
MAIER, Joseph	34	Aixheim	69-0923
Magdalena 35, Melchior 9, Johannes 7, Marie 6, Therese 2, Susanne 9 months, Mag			
MAIER, Levi	17	Frankenhausen	70-1003
MAIER, Louise	35	Urach	71-0479
MAIER, Pauline	36	Schorndorf	71-0363
MAIER, Wilhelm	18	Neuhausen	69-0672
MAIKER, Christ.	33	Sulzungen	71-0393
MAIKRANZ, Christine	53	Breitzbach	69-0572
Anna Marg. 16			
MAILE, Joh.	46	Nessmersiel	71-0789
Jac. 35, Antje 35, Joh. 7, Joh. 3, Hermann 6, Doreth. 5			
MAIMANN, Marg.	19	Nafringen	70-0170
O. 14, G. 9			
MAIMANN, Marie	55	Andewenne	68-0907
Caroline 18, Hermann 14			
MAIMHERZ, Cath.	22	Meinzeschein	70-1035
MAIN, Barbara	22	Waldau	69-0848
Dorette 1, Margreth 6 months			
MAINER, Catharina	17	Klenkheim	69-0968
MAISCH, Andreas	16	Nuernberg	71-0684
MAISCH, Magdalena	18	Grafenberg	70-1003
MAISENHELDEN, Marga.	22	Kirchhausen	69-0784
Caroline 17, Jacob 25			
MALCH, Carl	38	Birkenfeld	70-0308
MALECHA, Franz	50	Boerkowitz,Aust	69-0547
Catharina 29, Johann 26, Franz 17, Elisabeth 14, Veronica 7			
MALICA, Anila	17	Sabelly/Prussia	69-0547
MALICZEWSKY, F.	26	Neulupsky	68-0760
Antonia 52, Franz 3, Maria 9 months			
MALKOWSKY, Wilh.	45	Tramnau	71-0479
Ida 55, Albert 9			
MALL, Georg	22	Doernstetten	69-0490
MALLEK, A.	22	Waldau	71-0226
MALOWSKY, Fr.	25	Borgholzhausen	70-0135
MALSCHECK, A.	32	Altstaden	71-0792
MALT, Joh.	20	Krebstein	69-1086
MALTRIG, Conrad	20	Leidelheim	70-0204
Margarethe 23			
MALTZAHN, Georg	26	Darmstadt	68-0753
MAMELSDORF, Edward	18	Mannheim	68-0534
MAMMANGER, Jacob	24	Surhessen	68-0456
MAMMEN, Frerich Johan	17	Oldenburg	70-0329
MAN, Kunigunde	35	Zimmerau	69-0784
MANDEL, Emma	21	Zwickern	69-1011
Adolf 4 months			
MANDEL, Joseph	30	Hagen	71-0815
MANDELBAUM, J.	17	San Francisco	69-1212
MANDER, Dorothea	24	Giebelstadt	71-0492
MANDER, Joh.	14	Unterfranken	68-0566
MANDT, Johann	27	Kell	69-0923
MANE, Georg	60	Pittsburg	69-1076
MANEGOLD, Johann	26	Keller	70-0031
MANERT, Franz	18	Buerten	68-0770
MANGELS, Alb.	22	Neulininingen/Neu	69-1309
Wilhelm 14			
MANGELS, Geschels	56	Alfstedt	68-0456
MANGELS, Heinr.	9	Hannover	70-1035
MANGELS, Johann	26	Stade	69-1309
MANGELS, Marg.	20	Hannover	69-1086
MANGER, John	22	Weidehesch	69-0560
MANGHERS, Maria	28	Hamburg	68-0884
Gustav 4, Helene 3, Elise 3 months			
MANGLIERS, Maria	28	Hamburg	68-0884
Gustav 4, Helene 3, Elise 3 months			
MANGOLD, Marg.	21	Liebersbronn	71-0363
MANN, Christ.	18	Cassel	71-0393
MANN, Juliane	48	Lissberg	68-0610
Theod. 9, Heinrich 8			
MANN, Peter	60	Worms	70-0308
Christine 61			
MANNER, Wilh.	22	Wien	70-1055
MANNS, Cath.	16	Niederaula	71-0429
MANNS, Heinrich	46	Assmannshausen	68-0820
Catharina 42, Heinrich 16, Georg 9, Johannes 14, Anna 50			
MANNSBERGER, Ludwig	4	Iffenbach	70-0523
MANNWAL, Chrs.	27	Gross Umstadt	66-0221
MANSER, Franz	32	Mainz	71-0479
MANSIR, Elise	58	St. Steinach	71-0479
Elise 14			
MANSMANN, John	22	Elmstein	70-0170
MANSNEST, Jacob	28	Albershausen	68-0820
MANTEIS, Aug.	25	Pansin	68-0610
MANTHEY, Johann	22	Neustettin	68-0625
MARBERG, Francis	38	Frankfurt	68-0957
MARBURGER, Wilhelm	28	Herbertshaus	68-0625
Elise 34, Luise 6			
MARBUSE, Georg	27	Berlin	71-0712
MARCUS, Rudolph	27	Darmstadt	68-0456
MARCUS, Sophie	16	Rhaden	71-0479
MARCUS, Therese	35	Kansas	69-0672
Rebecca 9			
MARDER, Florian	30	Albany	70-0204
Helene 23, Therese 6, Marie 4			
MARGER, Jacob	29	Sommerloh	70-0204

NAME	AGE	RESIDENCE	YR-LIST
Catharina 27			
MARGGRAF, Julius	18	Kusel	70-0135
MARGMANN, Rieke	18	Dissen	70-1035
MARGRAFF, Wilhelm	19	Melsungen	68-1002
MARGUARZ, Wilh.	26	Horst/Russia	69-0049
MARK, Louis	21	Havre	68-0939
MARKERT, Adam	58	Dernbach	68-1002
MARKERT, Elise	19	Kaltensunsheim	69-1363
MARKERT, Georg	26	Meiningen	70-0178
MARKIEWIEZ, Charlotte	20	Kulm	69-0784
MARKS, Herm. Alb.	38	Rahde	68-1002
Elisab. 23, Joh. H. 5, Bernhd. 3, Marie 3 months			
MARKS, Margaretha	23	Coeln	68-0760
MARKS, Wilh.	59	Breslau	68-0884
MARKS, Wilh.	59	Breslau	69-1011
MARKSTEINER, Mich.	32	Austria	70-0170
MARKT, Anna	24	Solingen	71-0479
MARKWERT, Louis	25	Iburg	69-0229
MARMANN, Marie	55	Andewenne	68-0907
Caroline 18, Hermann 14			
MAROLD, Marga	15	Dresden	69-0592
MARONEK, Amalie	21	Wien	68-1002
MARONEK, Wenzel	25	Wien	68-1002
Cath. 31			
MARQUARD, Eduard	26	Lebarnke	68-0770
MARQUARD, Engelb.	20	Gunzheim	68-1298
MARQUARDT, Hermann	16	Wittorf	71-0492
MARQUARDT, Joh.	17	Stettnetz	69-0576
Wilhelmine 20			
MARQUARDT, Johann	25	Wien	70-0031
MARQUARDT, Julius	23	Zwangsbruch	68-0786
MARQUARDT, Julius	35	Granow	68-0647
MARQUARDT, Wilhelmine	20	Wysgneedorf	71-0492
Emma 9 months			
MARSCHBRUCK, Sophie	20		71-0581
MARSHACK, Josephine	27	Mengerden	68-0939
Rosine 22, Georg 7			
MARSHALL, Fred.	28	New York	69-1421
Mary 22			
MARTENS, Betty	15	Bremervoerde	68-1006
MARTENS, Claus H.	33	Bramel	68-0647
MARTENS, Dorothea	18	Dorum	68-0647
MARTENS, Friedr	25	Hannover	69-1086
MARTENS, Heinrich	25	Oldenburg	69-0162
MARTENS, Henry	16	Fissherhude	71-0456
MARTENS, Marcus	7	Altenbruch	68-0661
MARTENS, Margarethe	16	Bramel	68-0456
MARTENS, Theresia	25	Bersenbrueck	68-1002
MARTI, Jacob	38	Othmersingen	71-0492
Anna 59, Anna 23			
MARTI, Laurenz	25	Kienberg	69-0338
MARTIN, Adolf	25	Duisburg	70-0031
MARTIN, Adolf	20	Bischoffsheim	69-0457
Caroline 22			
MARTIN, Andr.	36	Hoefles	68-0884
MARTIN, Caroline	25	Carlsruhe	69-0923
MARTIN, Christine	18	Eimsheim	68-0786
MARTIN, Elisabeth	48	Kurhessen	70-0443
Emilie 19			
MARTIN, H.	26	Dunnern	70-1035
MARTIN, Joseph	21	Eschingen	71-0684
MARTIN, Jules	34	Paris	69-1363
MARTIN, Maria	19	Ihringen	71-0492
MARTIN, Nicolaus	49	Creen	68-0707
Mathias 20, Margaretha 17			
MARTIN, Sabine	21	Obermillrich	69-0576
MARTIN, Werner	15	Ermethies	68-0314
MARTINECK, Johann	57	Techin	70-0329
Anna 39, Wenzel 7, Josef 3, Marie 3			
MARTUSZACK, Ignatz	28	Bromberg	69-0029
MARUM, Carl	25	Frankenthal	71-0363
MARUM, Simon	30	Frankenthal	71-0363
MARX, Aug.	36	Latdorf	68-0820
Marie 30, Emilie 7, August 6, Ferdinand 2, Baby 7 months			
MARX, Barbara	23	Bummelsheim	68-0852
MARX, Hermann	24	Bruchsal	69-0457
MARX, Johanne	28	Creuznach	70-1055
Moses 7, Ludwig 5, Simon 3, Hermann 9 months			
MARZEL, John	52	Weiler	71-0456
Barbara 55, Dorothea 15			
MASCHALL, Franz	29	Berlin	70-0272
wife 29, Carl 4			
MASCHAUER, Samuel	59	Werkel	71-0521
Anna 30			
MASCHEK, B.	31	Kewanner	69-1421
MASER, Georg	19	Peterzell	71-0736
MASSEY, Georg W.	32	New York	69-0321
J. Edward 30			
MASSMANN, Sophie	25	Mittwitz	68-0534
MAST, Amalie	18	Marbach	71-0643
MASWA, Moritz	20	Seeps/Russia	69-0547
Louis 24			
MATAK, Joh.	27	Boehmen	70-1142
Marie 5			
MATHAI, Daniel	16	Marburg	68-0907
MATHDOSAK, Peter	18	Albrechtie	69-0848
MATHES, Sophie	36	Mierane	71-0479
Laura 6, Gustav 9 months			
MATHEY, Alfred	18	Zadelsdorf	68-1002
MATHIES, Friedr.	28	Stettin	69-0923
MATT, Julie	13	Zettingen	71-0681
MATTERN, Catharina	23	Kandel	68-0820
MATTERN, Friedrich	18	Finkenbach	69-0015
MATTFELD, Rudolf	21	Nordlitz	71-0492
MATTHAEI, Julius	23	Redenberg	69-0771
MATTHEIS, Judith	18	Hendelsheim	71-0681
MATTHES, Franz	45	Pansa	69-1004
MATTHEWS, Christian	22	Schoenlanke	69-0457
MATTHEY, Wm.	30	Nothwendig	69-1421
Emilie 29			
MATTHIEXEN, Herm.	18	Merbaum	71-0479
MATTMUELLER, Georg	22	Theningen	69-0490
MATUSCH, Therese	25	Friedland	71-0521
MATZ, August	27	Hammer	68-0770

NAME	AGE	RESIDENCE	YR-LIST
MATZ, Carl	20	Eisenach	68-0820
MATZ, Franz	32	Waldau	71-0226
MATZENBACHER, J.	21	Kusel	69-0848
MATZENBACHER, P.	41	Cassel	69-0923
Wilhelmine 32			
MATZINGER, Alois	40	Pilsen	69-0841
MATZKE, Aug.	32	Gruenbaum	71-0479
Louise 21			
MATZNER, Rosalia	29	Schnellenwelde	68-0707
MAUCH, Joh.	24	Dummingen	69-1212
MAUCH, Paul	19	Neukirch	71-0521
MAUCH, Pripa	45	Aixheim	69-0923
Mathias 18, Gertrud 15, Therese 9			
MAUER, Catharina	17	Faehr	71-0712
MAUER, Edw.	21	Kettenheim	70-0170
MAUERSBERG, Wilhelm	37	Werdau	69-0182
MAUGOLD, Jacob	34	Blaubeuren	69-0784
MAUL, Barbara	31	Gernsheim	68-0314
MAULBETZSCH, Friedr.	17	Berneck	68-0456
MAUNZ, Leonhard	20	Wangen	71-0456
MAURER, Caspar	31	Lingefeld	68-0939
MAURER, Cath.	20	Gerswalde	71-0581
MAURER, Gottfried	67	Wiesbaden	69-0798
MAURER, Heinrich	19	Vinnsbach	71-0429
Louise 17			
MAURER, Joh.	32	Althuetten	71-0681
MAURER, Magd.	20	Kleinbundenbach	71-0393
MAURER, Marie	24	Oberscharbach	71-0492
MAURER, Ursula	20	Tuerkheim	68-0820
MAUS, Amalie	58	Laufersweiler	70-0569
Rosette 17, Babette 16			
MAUS, August	18	Schoenstadt	71-0456
MAUS, Diedr.	23	Buergel	71-0684
MAUS, Johann	14	Gerresheim	68-0786
MAUS, Ludwig	23	Philippsburg	71-0792
Hermine 20			
MAUSBACH, Gustav	29	Judrea	70-0184
MAUSCHUND, Heino	25	Hessen	70-0178
Elise 25, Elise 6 months			
MAUSER, Anna	18	Muehlhausen	69-0338
MAUSSEN, Elise	26	Juelich	71-0167
Math. 3, Franz 8 months			
MAUTE, Gottlieb	22	Tiggingen	70-0184
MAUTHE, Martin	16	Schwemmingen	71-0521
MAY, Adam	32	Langenthal	71-0429
MAY, Joh.	18	Tressa	68-0820
MAY, M.	17	Lobau	71-0393
MAY, Marens	19	Steinbach	69-0784
MAY, Minna	27	Troge	68-0625
MAY, Siegf.	16	Schuppach	71-0582
MAYEN, Clementine	25	Nesselwangen	68-0566
MAYER, Alfred	18	Weisenheim	69-1004
MAYER, Anna	68	Neustadt	68-0852
MAYER, Apollonia	23	Kotzle	69-0798
MAYER, Babette	20	Culmbach	70-0204
MAYER, Carl.	27	Neuhausen	68-0982
MAYER, Catharine	22	Mittelfischbach	69-0229
MAYER, Conrad	35	Ebergoens	71-0492

NAME	AGE	RESIDENCE	YR-LIST
MAYER, Friedrich	25	Neustadt	69-0208
MAYER, Friedrich	21	Manheim	69-0067
MAYER, Friedrich	19	Mutterholz	71-0643
Charles 16			
MAYER, Friedrich	17	Kirchheim	71-0226
MAYER, Georg	21	Seligenstadt	68-0753
MAYER, Isaac	18	Valaenz	69-0162
MAYER, Jacob	30	Dietingen	70-0223
MAYER, Joh. Frdr.	18	Mittelfischbach	68-0610
MAYER, Joh. G.	18	Aufhausen	70-0204
MAYER, Johann	30	Michelbach	71-0733
MAYER, Johanne	17	Koenigsbronn	69-0490
MAYER, Leonhard	28	Henfeld	68-1006
MAYER, Moritz	17	Creuznach	68-0982
MAYER, Pauline	18	Markdorf	71-0456
MAYER, Philip	29	Waldernbach	69-0229
Angelica 23, Josef 1			
MAYER, Regine	20	Oberaichen	69-0268
MAYER, Rudolf	20	Riedlingen	68-0852
MAYER, Valentin	23	S. Meiningen	69-0848
MAYER, W.	17	Wittenwater	71-0581
MAYER, Wilh.	20	Bubendorf	68-0786
Louise 18			
MAYER, Wilhelm	22	Lauffen	70-0031
MAYER, Wilhelm	25	Waiblingen	71-0643
MAYER, Wilhelmine	19	Tuebingen	70-1142
MAYERHOFER, Franz	30	Stadtbergen	68-0753
Anna 28			
MAZANCE, Jacob	18	Pruidrazko	69-0672
MAZIER, Johann	24	Holybeck	69-0572
Michael 4, Josefa 20, Agnese 22, Josefa 3 months			
MECHT, Mathilde	18	Wremer	71-0581
MECHWARD, Johann	22	Baiern	69-0559
MECKBACH, Heinrich	31	Wehrda	69-0592
Elisabeth 28, Marga 5, Friedrich 19, Adam 25, Marga 25			
MECKLENBURG, Female	18	Emden	68-1006
MEDINGER, Lisette	21	Speyer	69-1011
MEENES, Marie	30	Hannover	69-1396
Henry 3, Baby 7 months			
MEENTS, Meent	17	Hannover	69-0457
MEESEL, Martin	23	Lerchenfeld	69-0848
MEESLER, Harm.	18	Werdum	68-0610
Jan 25			
MEESTER, Wilh.	6	Wildeshausen	71-0581
MEG, Agnes	16	Neukirch	70-0329
MEHLBRECHT, Margreth	19	Stadingen	69-0848
Elise 60, Johann 21			
MEHLER, Engel	17	Bingen	69-0229
MEHLER, Josephine	33	Rheinpfalz	69-1076
MEHLER, Sophie	20	Schiffdorf	71-0429
MEHLHOP, Anna	23	Danelsen	71-0226
MEHLHOP, Margaretha	22	Blendern	68-0707
MEHLHORST, Gustav	21	Jena	68-0456
MEHMANN, male	35	Grafeld	69-0292
Elisabeth 41, Bernhard 9, Joseph 7, Elisabeth 11 months, Engel 21			
MEHNKEN, Gesche	22	Sottrum	68-0982

NAME	AGE	RESIDENCE	YR-LIST
MEHRENS, Friederike	19	Rechtebe	69-0576
Meta 7			
MEHRHOFF, Therese	23	Ostercappeln	68-0647
Herm. 16			
MEHRINGS, Johanna	25	Bremen	68-0314
MEHRTENS, Anna	19	Stenstedt	70-0378
MEHRTENS, Mary	18	Hannover	70-0170
John 16			
MEHSING, Ida	20	Friedland	69-0798
MEI, Caspar	20	Kepsholt	69-0338
MEIER, Andr.	36	Sammersdorf	71-0479
Emilie 34, Emilie 8, Bertha 7, Hermann 5			
MEIER, Anna	25	Oldenburg	69-0268
MEIER, Carl	16	Drakenburg	69-0429
MEIER, Carl	18	Hoboken	69-0923
MEIER, Elise	25	Bremen	68-0647
MEIER, Ernst	42	Jeinsen	69-0592
Gesine 31, Heinrich 9, Dorette 8, Carl 5, Fritz 3, Ernst 6 months, Elisabeth 62			
MEIER, Heinrich	17	Groenloh	69-0923
MEIER, Jette	60	Rostadt	68-0939
MEIER, Johann	19	Merkowitz	70-0728
MEIER, Johanna	25	Frankfurt\ M	68-0625
Bertha 20, Sophie 19, Josephine 17			
MEIER, Josephine	20	Loehne	71-0581
MEIER, Marg.	26	Steinborn	71-0581
MEIER, Paulina	22	Esslingen	71-0581
MEIER, Peterdina	23	Leer	68-0419
MEIER, Wilh.	33	Wuesten	71-0581
MEIERBOECKE, Carl	28	Lippe Detmold	70-0355
MEIERCORD, Conrad	56	Westerwinner	68-1006
Louise 50			
MEIERCORDT, Marie	30	Stapelage	71-0479
Elise 6			
MEIERHORD, Wilhelm	47	Lippe Detmold	70-0355
Friederika 46, Wilhelmine 23, Henriette 15, Sophie 9, Simon 7			
MEIHEL, Friedr.	23	Urbach	71-0581
MEILENDER, Louise	27	Schrottinghause	70-1055
Ernst 4, Louise 11 months			
MEINBERG, Georg	23	Holtensen	68-1002
MEINBRANT, Fritz	15	Lamstedt	69-0457
MEINECKE, Anna	20	Neustrelitz	68-0707
MEINERS, Gebke	54	Akelsberg	69-0208
Gretje 19, Fueller 14, Menne 9			
MEINERS, Gerhard	32	Schale	68-0647
Anna 67f			
MEINGAST, Jos.	21	Taschau	68-0647
MEINHARD, Max	57	Ellerstadt	69-1396
MEINHARDT, Anna	26	Leipzig	69-1086
Max 9 months			
MEINHARDT, Friedrich	32	Zoerbig	68-0786
Wilhelmine 35, Emma 6, Louise 3, Carl 11 months			
MEINHARDT, Hermann	26	Leipzig	69-0560
MEINHEIM, Adelheid	22	Oyten	69-0560
MEINHOLD, Wilhelmine	36	Zwankau	69-1319
Anna 9, Bernhard 8, Theo 7, Minna 4			
MEINICKE, Carl	25	Voerden	68-0610
MEINKE, Christian	14	Franzenberg	68-0852
MEINKEN, Hermann	20	Bremen	68-0865
MEINSCHIN, Dora	28	Wersahl	71-0479
Minna 4			
MEINTHEN, Frauke	21	Hannover	70-0384
MEINTS, Jann	63	Palswitz	69-0208
Engel 52, Meints 29, Ahltje 22, Maria 16, Harm 12, Garrelt 9, Antje 7			
MEINTS, Meint	27	Beersum	68-1027
Johann 28			
MEINZERT, Anna	25	Schwarzenbach	70-0329
MEISE, Friedrich	18	Rheda	68-314
MEISEL, Karoline	21	Achern	71-0363
MEISENHAEDER, Gottl.	15	Olhausen	70-0223
MEISS, Caroline	21	Coburg	69-1319
MEISSBERGER, Arnold	16	Collin	69-0848
MEISSNER, Alvine	32	Elberfeld	68-0820
Baby daughter 9 months			
MEISSNER, Georg	27	Leuchtenberg	68-1002
Elisabeth 21			
MEISSNER, Hermann	25	Grossenhain	68-0707
MEISSNER, Joseph	17	Steinau	71-0363
MEISTER, Julius	15	Wabern	68-0820
MEISTER, Paul	7	Biesendorf	68-0786
MEITZEN, Wilh.	47	Treptow	68-0647
MEKS, Philipp	24	Weinbach	71-0429
Cath. 30, Cath. 9 months			
MELCHERS, Edward	30	Prussia	69-0923
MELCHIORS, Friedr.	32	Krainel	71-0521
MELCK, Peter	25	Austria	70-0170
MELIN, Albert	38	Zarbatowo	69-0672
MELKMUS, Friderika	54	Heinfeld	69-1004
MELKOP, Joh.	19	Ardinghausen	71-0581
Albert 17			
MELSHEIMER, Jos.	19	Dosenbach	71-0581
Barb. 17			
MEMEINEKE, Friedr.	35	Velgau	69-1212
Wilhelmine 3, Friedrich 7, Wilhelm 5			
MEMKEN, Ede G. J.	14	Thunum	68-1002
MENCKE, Johann	33	Treckenhorst	69-0429
MENCKE, Marie	34	Oldendorf	68-0566
MENDE, Ad.	37	Greiz	69-0560
MENDEL, Meyer	23	Steinfurt	68-0939
MENDER, Claus	19	Hannover	70-0308
MENFEN, M.	21	Speckendorf	69-0208
MENGE, Franz	25	Lingen	69-0572
MENGEL, Georg	14	Cusel	70-0452
MENGEL, Heinr.	17	Eschwege	71-0521
MENGEL, Jacob	47	Rosenthal	71-0736
Catharina 9			
MENGELING, Karl	23	Liekwegen	68-0534
MENGELS, Anton	16	Bliane	69-1076
MENGER, Cath.	26	Muehringen	69-0490
MENGERS, Peter	28	Zwingenberg	71-0712
MENK, Catharine	15	Neukirch	70-0682
MENKE, Anna	18	Leute	71-0479
MENKE, B.	21	Zitten	69-1004
MENKE, Fritz	26	Hannover	69-1319
Marga. 28			
MENKE, Heinr.	45	Hatten	68-0884

NAME	AGE	RESIDENCE	YR-LIST
Marg. 42, Friedr. 16, Ang. 8, Wilh. 7			
MENKE, Hy. H.	37	Clarensville	70-0355
MENKE, Jobst	35	Hannover	71-0792
Anna 31, Heinr. 9, Anna 3			
MENKE, Joseph	25	Wallenbruch	68-0939
MENKE, Meta	14	Oldenburg	70-0204
MENKE, Nicl.	19	Scharmbeck	68-0957
MENKEN, Friedr.	16	Holsel	68-0786
MENNECKE, Auguste	18	Homburg	69-0490
MENSEL, Andr.	58	Steibra	68-0820
Barbara 58, Frd. 25			
MENSLAGE, Christian	48	Hannover	71-0429
Elise 42, August 9, Wilhelm 7			
MENTNISEN, Albert	16	Hamswehem	71-0479
MENTZ, Fr.	40	S. Francisco	69-1004
MENTZE, Anna	16	Asendorf	71-0581
MENTZEN, Marg.	28	Goldinstedt	69-0490
MENZEL, August	20	Spiller	69-0798
MENZEL, Georg	14	Cusel	70-0452
MENZEL, Helena	34	Schwelm	69-0490
Clara 5			
MENZEL, Helene	18	Breslau	68-0625
MENZEL, W.	27	Friedland	71-0521
R. 17			
MENZEN, Hermann	24	Oldenburg	70-0378
Friedrich 16			
MENZLER, Conrade	19	Frankenburg	70-0259
Christian 23			
MERBITZ, Fritz	42	Hoexter	70-0355
MERBITZ, Maria	18	Herzberg	70-0184
MERFELD, Franz	25	Halsdorf	69-0229
Anna 25, Heinrich 4, Catharine 2, Johann 3 months			
MERIAN, Albert	28	Basel	68-1298
MERK, Baptist	28	Benhau	70-0204
MERK, Catharine	38	Mainz	68-1027
Michael 38			
MERK, Conrad	22	Deggingen	71-0736
MERKE, Captan	18	Waldeck	69-1309
MERKEL, Elise	22	Eisenach	70-0006
MERKEL, Margarethe	23	Elsendorf	71-0736
MERKLE, Jacob	48	Beinstein	71-0643
MERL, Therese	19	Gladbach	70-0223
MERLAN, Con.	56	Arenhain	69-1011
Mary 56, Elisabeth 31, John 28, Conrad 25, Anna 16, Henry 9			
MERLE, Peter	18	Altenburg	68-0852
MERSEBERG, Heinr.	15	Meienburg	70-0052
MERTELBRUNN, Berta	27	Mertelbrunn	71-0456
MERTEN, August	19	Osterode	68-0661
MERTENS, B.	26	Albig	68-1006
MERTENS, Doris	18	Schiffdorf	71-0681
MERTENS, Fr.	16	Waldeck	68-0820
MERTENS, Georgine	16	Cassel	68-0820
MERTOFF, Elisabeth	57	Osterkappeln	68-0647
MERTZ, Anna	25	Hanau	71-0643
MERTZ, Wendelin	26	Pergau	68-0770
MERZ, Anna	20	Ruetheim	71-0643
Marie 26			

NAME	AGE	RESIDENCE	YR-LIST
MERZ, Christian	19	Klemmenau	68-0661
MERZ, Elise	30	Ramstadt	69-1059
Cathrine 5			
MERZ, Lisette	24	Mannheim	68-0661
Otto 3, Louise 9 months			
MERZ, Louise	27	Reuss	69-1076
Lene 4, Maria 11 months			
MESCH, Michel	24	Schwarzburg	69-0672
MESCHKE, Gust.	17	Werdau	71-0681
MESLOH, Fritz	28	Neuenlande	68-0456
MESMER, D.	26	Mainz	71-1046
Christine 57, Victoria 15,			
MESS, Anna	21	Arenhain	69-1011
MESS, Anna	50	Arenhain	69-1011
F. 49, Conrad 8, Henry 9 months			
MESS, Anna M.	19	Lauffen	69-0268
MESSAL, Gottlieb	25	Posen	68-0707
Wilhelmine 18, Wilhelmine 24, Arthur 2, Otto 9 months			
MESSER, Christine	20	Trossingen	68-0957
MESSER, J. Wessel	43	Hannover	70-1003
Cathrina 41, Diedrich 4, Minna 9 mo			
MESSERSCHMIDT	60	Falkenburg	69-0542
Marie 36, Mathilde 22			
MESSLOH, H.	36	Gr. Mimmelage	68-1006
MESSNER, Bernhard	17	Kurhessen	70-0443
MESSNER, Emil	18	Cassel	69-0457
MESSNER, Maria	20	Tuttlingen	68-0852
METEK, Marie	63	Boehmen	70-1142
METTE, Fritz	19	Dorlars	69-1059
METTGER, Heinrich	17	Speyer	69-1076
METTICH, Wilh.	17	Wehden	71-0300
METTING, Johanna	16	Cloppenburg	68-0661
METZ, Amalia	28	Laufen	68-0907
METZ, Friedr.	27	Altenstaig	69-0100
METZ, Henry	30	Schiplage	69-0338
Caroline 40			
METZEN, Mich.	25	Steinborn	70-0308
METZGER, Barbara	23	Alzenrod	69-0490
METZGER, Carl	23	Mittelfranken	70-1055
Emilie 25, Max Otto 21			
METZGER, Caroline	23	Asperg	70-1035
METZGER, Fr.	20	Hechingen	68-0610
METZGER, Ignatz	17	Muenchen	70-0148
METZGER, Jacob	27	Dettingen	68-0610
METZGER, Julie	40	Frankfurt	68-0884
Henry 8, Johanna 7			
METZGER, Karl	30	Neuchingen	71-0736
METZGER, Matthilde	27	Dinckelsbuehl	71-0492
Elise 20			
METZLAR, Johann	31	Orb	68-0852
METZLER, Carl Wilhelm	19	Dillenburg	70-0378
METZMACHER, Louise	45	Berlin	70-0443
METZNER, Fr.	17	Rothenhof	71-0684
METZNER, Johann	17	Limbach	69-0592
MEUGSDOHL, Theodor	25	Bruntrup	69-0798
MEURER, Friedrich	48	Spangenberg	69-0848
MEUSEL, Ernst	24	Sonneberg	68-0661
MEUSSEN, Siebert	19	Speckendorf	69-1421

NAME	AGE	RESIDENCE	YR-LIST
MEWES, Adolph	25	Altona	69-0067
Ida 32			
MEXMEL, Paula	34	Steinbach	71-0643
MEY, Bertha	20	Loebau	71-0736
MEY, Friedrich	40	San Franzisco	69-0672
MEYBERG, Peter	35	Otterndorf	69-0542
Cath. 33			
MEYEM, Georg	26	Rostock	71-0456
MEYENBURG, Chs.	16	Hannover	70-0170
Auguste 21			
MEYER, Adelheid	22	Bremen	71-0456
MEYER, Adolph	15	Ansbach	69-0672
MEYER, Albert	18	Untersigmaringe	69-0771
MEYER, Albert	19	Kolmsdorf	71-0643
MEYER, Andr.	25	Guenzbach	70-0178
MEYER, Anna	27	Stadt	69-0182
Amalie 24			
MEYER, Anna	22	Waldernbach	69-0229
MEYER, Anna	18	Wulsten	68-0566
MEYER, Anna	56	Zeven	68-0625
MEYER, Anna	21	Ritzebuettel	71-0712
MEYER, Anna	15	Breisach	71-0492
MEYER, Anna	24	Rulle	71-0429
MEYER, Anna	25	Brinkum	71-0521
Albert 3, Anna 11 months			
MEYER, Anton	28	Gruenmettstette	71-0821
Caroline 22, Agathe 5, Anna 2			
MEYER, Aug.	39	Weilburg	71-0363
Jeanette 40, Margareth 9, Christ. 8, Louis 6, Franziska 4, Anna 2			
MEYER, August	15	Hannover	70-1003
MEYER, August	26	Renlage/Reselag	69-0429
MEYER, Augusta	27	Hessen Darmstad	70-0076
MEYER, Augusta	19	Grohnde	68-0661
MEYER, Bernh.	26	Arsten	69-1086
Heinr. 23			
MEYER, Bertha	15	Negenborn	70-0523
MEYER, C. P.	31	Fuerth	70-0170
MEYER, Carl	30	Osnabrueck	69-0050
Adam 27			
MEYER, Carl	24	Kollerbeck	69-0429
MEYER, Carl	28	Basel	71-0226
MEYER, Carl Edw. jr.	26	Bremen	70-0076
MEYER, Carol	27	Neuenkirchen	69-0542
MEYER, Caroline	26	Biere	70-1003
Marie 6, Louise 5, Carl 3, Ernst 2			
MEYER, Caroline	44	Trutzweiler	71-0521
MEYER, Cath.	18	Jettenburg	71-0789
MEYER, Cath.		Schifferstadt	71-0393
MEYER, Catharina	30	Jarlingen	68-0760
Doris 25			
MEYER, Charles	38	Paxten	69-0798
MEYER, Christ.	36	Uehlede	70-0384
MEYER, Christian	16	Minden	68-0939
MEYER, Christine	39	Untergrombach	68-0760
MEYER, Christoph	45	Soltau	68-0820
Anna C. 42, Claus H. 20, Friedrich W. 17, Johannes W. 8			
MEYER, Clara	25	Bremen	70-1003
John 7, Emil 3, Baby 6 months			
MEYER, Claus	18	Cadenberge	69-0560
MEYER, Claus	20	Anderlingen	68-1027
MEYER, Conrad	18	Egenhausen	68-314
MEYER, Cord	16	Hannover	71-0792
MEYER, Diedr.	17	Hannover	71-0792
Meta 20			
MEYER, Diedrich	29	Bremervoerde	68-0625
MEYER, Dorette	22	Mulsum	68-0820
Carl 2			
MEYER, Doris	20	Hannover	71-1046
MEYER, Dorothea	27	Barmenensiek	71-0492
MEYER, E.	21	Lehe	71-0681
MEYER, Eleonore	18	Bremen	69-0542
Friederike 20			
MEYER, Elisabeth	60	Schweeringen	69-0229
MEYER, Elisabeth	16	Friedewald	70-0272
MEYER, Elise	28	Wilhelmshagen	71-0821
MEYER, Elise	20	Emden	71-0712
MEYER, Franz	39	Berlin	69-0338
Pauline 30			
MEYER, Frdr.	35	Geyer	68-0610
MEYER, Fried.	17	Osnabrueck	70-0728
MEYER, Friedr. P.	25	Emden	69-0182
MEYER, Friedrich	19	Detmold	70-0728
MEYER, Friedrich	43	Nenndorf	69-0268
Maria 38, Wilhelm 7, Caroline 15			
MEYER, Friedrich	35	Wesenstedt	68-0884
Anna 30, Heinr. 8, Sophie 7, Doris 5			
MEYER, Friedrich	25	Altenbruck	69-1086
Heinrich 24			
MEYER, Friedrich	18	Minden	68-0907
MEYER, Geo. (Glinstedt)	29	Philadelphia	69-0560
MEYER, Georg	27	Osnabrueck	70-0682
MEYER, Georg	20	Gessken	71-0733
MEYER, Gesine	18	Leste	71-0581
MEYER, Gottfried	54	Heilbronn	68-0566
Florentine 48, Julius 20, Frierich 17, Augusta 10, Pauline 7			
MEYER, Gottlieb	41	Posen	69-0559
Juliana 34, Emilie 13, Minna 9 months			
MEYER, Gottlieb	17	Flienworth	71-0492
MEYER, Greg.	21	Neustadt	68-0753
MEYER, Harriet	22	Bremen	68-0957
MEYER, Heinr.	16	Lilienwoerth	69-0542
MEYER, Heinr.	15	Otterndorf	68-0982
MEYER, Heinr.	15	Twistsingen	68-0982
MEYER, Heinr.	25	Hannover	71-0429
MEYER, Heinrich	33	Kleinenkneben	69-0798
Helene 25, Anna 4, Helene 2, Friedricke 6 months			
MEYER, Heinrich	39	Minden	70-0006
MEYER, Heinrich	27	Bannelze	69-0490
MEYER, Heinrich	45	New York	69-1076
Mrs. 32			
MEYER, Heinrich	22	Heppens	68-0852
MEYER, Heinrich	12	Breitenkamp	68-0610
MEYER, Heinrich	23	Feuchtwangen	68-0625

NAME	AGE	RESIDENCE	YR-LIST
MEYER, Heinrich	56	Sulingen	71-0792
MEYER, Heinrich	17	Sievern	71-0492
MEYER, Henrich	20	Ostercappeln	69-0798
MEYER, Henry	27	Cincinnati	69-1212
MEYER, Henry	15	Leeste	68-0957
MEYER, Henry	20	Bremen	71-0456
MEYER, Herm.	18	Weisenheim	70-1055
MEYER, Hermann	18	Detmold	70-0148
MEYER, Hermann	26	Halberstadt	69-1396
MEYER, Hermann	26	Glinstedt	69-0560
MEYER, Hermann	34	Oldenburg	70-0204
Marie 36, Catharine 9, Marie 6, Hermann 11 months			
MEYER, Hermann	34	Oldenburg	70-0204
MEYER, Hermann	19	Scholl	68-0456
MEYER, Hermann	16	Ahnberg	68-0707
MEYER, Hy.	47	Strohin	69-1011
MEYER, J. H.		Obelenburg	69-0321
MEYER, Jacob	49	Hirschfeld	68-0419
Anna 47, Heinrich 19, Cathrina 17, Johannes 13			
MEYER, Jette	15	Kirchgans	69-0542
MEYER, Joh.	27	Oldenburg	69-1363
MEYER, Joh.	23	Steckborn	70-0272
MEYER, Joh.	26	Bevern	68-0647
Ilse Metta 32			
MEYER, Johann	26	Duingdorf	68-0786
Marie 25			
MEYER, Johann	25	Bremen	68-0957
MEYER, Johann	17	Bremen	69-1309
Hermann 9, Catharina 7, Louise 4			
MEYER, Johann	29	Bevensen	68-314
Anna 26, Anna 6 months			
MEYER, Johann	31	Otterndorf	68-0625
MEYER, Johann	32	Hannover	68-1006
MEYER, Johann	62	Rauschenberg	68-0661
Elisabeth 62, Elisabeth 23			
MEYER, Johann	25	Hannover	71-0643
Sophie 11 months			
MEYER, Johann	50	Neu Subeza	71-0521
Wilhelmine 46, Wilhelm 16, Wilhelmine 15, Auguste 14, Male 9, Charlotte			
MEYER, Johann J.	25	Albershausen	68-0820
MEYER, Johanna	50	Eisenheim	68-0625
Maria 15, Friedrich 9, George 9, Catharina 7, Carl 6			
MEYER, Johanne	18	Groenheim	69-0208
MEYER, Johanne	24	Bremerhaven	70-0355
MEYER, Johannes	14	Buer	68-1027
MEYER, John	19	Deedendorf	71-0456
MEYER, Julius	17	Hannover	70-0443
MEYER, Karoline	17	Wittenssen	70-1142
Daniel 22			
MEYER, Lazarus	17	Secheim	71-0479
MEYER, Leopold	25	Zell	69-0429
Amalie 22, Rosine 52, Gustav 15			
MEYER, Leopold	18	Lothringen	71-0736
MEYER, Lied.	49	Campen	71-0300
Grete 49, Sabine 22			
MEYER, Lina	21	Ilsenburg	70-0523

NAME	AGE	RESIDENCE	YR-LIST
MEYER, Louise	34	Hannover	71-0736
MEYER, Louise	53	Bramsche	71-0479
MEYER, Louise	20	Aplern	71-0479
MEYER, Ludwig	59	Hannover	70-1055
Henriette 56, Wilhelmine 22			
MEYER, Luetje	29	Meckelsen	68-0625
MEYER, M.	37	Giessen	71-0681
MEYER, Marg.	18	Rodenburg	70-0204
MEYER, Marg.	30	Asendorf	71-0581
MEYER, Marg.	38	Ulm	71-0521
Albertine 6, Friederike 11 months			
MEYER, Margareth	72	Eschenfelde	68-0760
MEYER, Margarethe	20	Kausenbock	70-0523
MEYER, Margarethe	37	Bremen	69-0968
Heinrich 9, Louise 14			
MEYER, Maria	16	Hannover	69-1086
MEYER, Maria	61	Elsdorf	68-0456
MEYER, Maria	17	Oesen	71-0492
MEYER, Marie	17	Systedt	70-1035
MEYER, Marie	16	Muenchen	68-0884
MEYER, Marie	24	Beverstedt	69-0592
MEYER, Marie	20	Borstel	69-0229
MEYER, Marie	28	Hannover	70-0443
MEYER, Marie	23	Haplinghausen	71-0581
MEYER, Marie	21	Botel	71-0492
MEYER, Martin	30	Bremen	69-0321
MEYER, Mary	38	Buffalo	70-1003
Barbara 4			
MEYER, Mathias	18	Arenlah	69-0292
MEYER, Meta	22	Landstedt	70-0031
MEYER, Meta	34	Bremen	69-0067
MEYER, Meta	18	Osterholz	70-0443
MEYER, Meta	15	Langen	71-0521
MEYER, Meyer	20	Steinfurt	68-0939
MEYER, Michael	16	Rhade	68-0625
Cord 14			
MEYER, Moses	16	Grebenau	69-0968
Hermann 15			
MEYER, Moses	20	Soest	68-0625
MEYER, Pauline	38	Kirchberg	71-0712
Rudolph 9, Reinhard 7, Louise 3			
MEYER, Sara	16	Herenberg	70-0184
MEYER, Sarah	60	Gedern	71-0643
MEYER, Sophie	26	Eisenach	68-0786
MEYER, Sophie	25	Oldenburg	69-0848
MEYER, Sophie	19	Bremen	68-0852
MEYER, Sophie	21	Kl. Borstel	68-0610
MEYER, Steffen	25	Neuscharrel	68-0957
MEYER, Wilh.	31	Lueneburg	70-0583
MEYER, Wilh.	30	Dehringhsen	69-0572
MEYER, Wilh.	16	Hannover	69-1004
MEYER, Wilh.	24	Krimetsgrun	71-0581
MEYER, Wilhelm	16	Otterstedt	69-0798
MEYER, Wilhelm	17	Osnabrueck	70-0728
MEYER, Wilhelm	15	Trestorf	68-0610
MEYER, Wilhelm	24	Goslar	68-0939
MEYER, Wilhelm	19	Oldendorf	71-0581
Charlotte 17			

NAME	AGE	RESIDENCE	YR-LIST
MEYER, Wilhelm	17	Bremen	71-0429
MEYER, Wilhelm	18	Hannover	71-0456
Otto 15, Wilhelm 26			
MEYER, Wilhelmine	23	Altenbruch	68-0625
MEYER, Wilhelmine	18	Hannover	71-0429
MEYER, Wm.	18	Unterluebbeke	68-0957
MEYER,, Therese	25	Hildesheim	70-0204
MEYERDING, Marie	19	Plattendorf	68-0820
MEYERHEINRICH, H.	35	Lippe Detmold	70-0223
MEYERHENRICH, Wm.	32	Lippe Detmold	70-0223
Aug. 29			
MEYERHOFF, Friedrich	16	Teufelsmoor	68-0566
MEYERHOFF, John	15	Hannover	70-0355
MEYERHOLZ, Anna	28	Bremen	70-0355
MEYERKORD, Wm.	48	Hoya	69-0338
MEYERS, Carl	33	Hamburg	69-1396
MEYERSIEDK, Sophie	17	Bohmte	69-0968
MEYINHOF, Salomon	19	Medebach	68-0939
MEYMANN, Bernhardine	19	Bokel	69-0208
MEYNER, Anna	15	Altenburg	71-0736
MEYRON, Louise	21	Wehstein	69-0560
MEYSE, Hein.	55	Neufehn	71-0681
MICHAEL, Catharina	24	Geismar	69-0798
MICHAEL, Conrad	18	Gifhorn	69-0560
MICHAEL, Kilian	20	Igerstein	68-0707
MICHAELIS, Cathrine	23	Trute	71-0456
MICHAELIS, Max	29	Berlin	69-0208
MICHAELIS, O.	26	Zempelburg	71-0684
Ernestine 30, Baby-girl 9 months			
MICHAELSEN, Wilhelmine	23	Nordleda	71-0429
MICHALOWSKY, H.	20	Bodschwingken	68-0907
MICHALOWSKY, Marie	24	Glinau	71-0479
MICHALOWSKY, Moritz	29	Sabbawitz	68-0907
Dorothea 29, Felix 2			
MICHATSCH, Hieron.	24	Costenthal	68-0647
MICHEL, A. Cath.	17	Lenderscheid	71-0792
MICHEL, Babette	18	Nordhalben	69-0592
MICHEL, Conr.	17	Waldeck	70-0384
MICHEL, Heinrich	17	Hopstaedt	69-0457
MICHEL, Heinrich	32	Borgloch	69-0457
Catharine 55			
MICHEL, Joh.	15	Franken	70-0378
MICHEL,Wilh.	17	Chur	68-0982
MICHELFELDER, Julie	22	Wasungen	71-0456
MICHELIS, Marg.	18	Bettstedt	69-1004
MICHELOWSKY, Josef	29	Kruschwitz	69-0848
MICHELS, Carl	28	Barmen	71-0363
MICHELS, Josef	43	Schillingen	71-0736
Christine 43, Susanne 20, Josef 8, Barbara 17, Susanne 12, Peter 5, Johann 3,			
MICHLER, Emil	18	Heppenheim	69-1086
MICHOT, A. Marie	67	Habenbubach/Bai	69-0049
Margaretha 26			
MIDDENDORF, Catharine	26	Bielefeld	69-0784
Catharine 9			
MIEHE, Caroline	45	Salzgitter	71-0429
Louis 9			
MIELE, Heinrich	43	Salzgitter	70-0184
Louise 16			
MIESCH, Carl	15	Hambach	69-0672
MIESCHEN, Karl	16	Steinau	71-0363
MIESELER, Friedrich	27	Dessau	71-0492
MIESMER, Marie	26	Endingen	71-0393
MIESNER, Claus	32	Zeven	68-0456
Anna 28			
MIESNER, Heinrich	35	Meckelsen	68-0625
Marie 29			
MIESSNER, Johann	46	Hagenah	68-1002
Anna 41, Johann 15, Gretchen 12, Heinrich 9, Jacob 8, Meta 6, Fieken 3, Diedr.			
MIETENKOTTE, B.	19	Lienen	71-0492
MIETHE, Bernhard	37	Ibbenbueren	69-0429
MIETKE, Mathilde	22	Bankwitt	71-0429
Emilie 19			
MIHM, Theodor	23	Zella	68-0939
MIKOLAJEWSKI, Josef	19	Chelmie	69-0848
MILKE, Aug.	20	Traumburg	68-0753
MILKE, Christine	42	Steinbach	68-0534
Libette 13, Ferdinand 9, Elise 5, Gustavus 3			
MILKOUSKI, Marie	25	Merdrowiz	71-0479
Anna 9, Andr. 7, Victorette 3			
MILLER, Alois	22	Lienz	70-0135
MILLER, Asmus	30	Jersey City	69-1309
MILLER, Caspar	40	New York	63-0244
Victoria 29			
MILLER, Elisa	24	Argenstein	68-0534
MILLER, Johann	15	Dernbach	69-1212
MILLER, Joseph	31	Dornweiler	69-0182
MILLION, Johann	26	Lixheid	69-1309
MILLITZER, Christ.	52	Ramspach	68-0907
Ernestine 44, Christian 18, Ernestine 12, Louise 7, Minna 7			
MILS, Louise	21	Schlawen	71-0736
MILTE, Johann	34	Paderborn	68-0707
MILTNER, Marie	28	Wien	71-0821
Emilie 9 months			
MIN, Marie	26	Blankwitt	71-0479
Marie 8, Julius 1 months			
MINDAK, Peter	27	Crone	71-0300
MINDERMANN, Diedrich	29	Winkeldorf	71-0492
MINDERMANN, Herm.	17	Rudolstadt	71-0363
MINDERMANN, Johann	16	Fischerhude	68-0661
MINGES, Andreas	18	Burrweiler	69-1396
MINGST, Marie Reb.	24	Ledau	68-0770
MINGST, Peter	36	Nordleda	69-0592
Angela 28, Minna 4, August 2			
MINIAZWSKI, Clemens	18	Stonary	68-0707
MINK, Wilhelm	35	Minden	69-1212
MINKEMILLER, Friedr.	39	Herford	71-0681
MINLINGER, Henricus	42	Emden	69-1076
Frauke 36, Heike 9, Fanni 8, Hilgine 7, Jacobine 3, Thakenna 61, Pauline 8 mon			
MINNCH, Leonhard	24	Hoechst	68-0707
MINNEMANN, Diedrich	32	Meckelstedt	69-0560
Marie 31, Marie 11 months, Gesine 11 months			
MINTKENSOELLER, J.	31	Buer	69-1011
Anna 31, Fritz 5, William 2			
MIRATZKY, Anna	40	Boehmen	70-1161

NAME	AGE	RESIDENCE	YR-LIST
Anna 5			
MIRBACH, Carl	37	Raeren	69-0457
MIRKS, Johann	60	Sinzfelt	69-0672
MIRLAN, Cath.	17	Arnshain	69-0592
MISCHENICH, Wm.	25	Dormagen	69-0841
MISCHLER, Andr.	21	Heppenheim	71-0581
MISKOWSKY, Otto	18	Minden	70-0308
MISPOTZIANY, male	27	Fletz	68-0753
Josepha 58			
MISTERER, Caroline	17	Kratzungen	71-0492
MITTEL-HOKAMP, Hanne	31	Stedefreund	63-1010
Wilhelmine 28			
MITTELSTEDT, Mathilde	26	Ascherhude	69-0542
MITZICHKE, Carl	28	Torgau	71-0643
MIX, Margaretha	20	Abtswind	69-1309
MIXDORF, Carl	36	Wisba	71-0581
Emilie 28, Robert 6, Anna 4, Hermann 11 months			
MOBUS, Louisa	22	Gundesberg	70-0184
MOCK, Eugen	22	Rielsingen	68-0647
MODENBACH, Marg.	23	Niederstoll	68-0884
MODER, Carl	29	Schreidach	71-0643
MODROW, Julius	20	Leppi	70-0683
MOEBUS, Fred.	28	Lauterbach	68-0760
MOECKEL, Balthasar	19	Steinberg	69-1319
MOECKEL, Maria Elise	16	Langenheim	70-0443
MOEHA, Peter	26	Eschenthal	69-0268
MOEHL, Ernst	15	Riedlingen	69-1396
MOEHLE, Frid.	14	Egershausen	70-0508
MOEHLENFELD, Anna	15	Bremen	70-0148
MOEHLENFELS, Anna	15	Bremen	70-0135
MOEHRING, Carl H.	28	Altenburg	69-0583
Ida 16			
MOEHRING, Friederike	35	P. Friedland	70-0178
Ottilie 19			
MOEHRING, Joh.	30	Uhlstaedt	68-0786
Marie 31, Hermann 14, Augusta 9, Emma 8, August 4			
MOELLER, Barb.	21	Ronshausen	71-0581
MOELLER, Carl	28	Destel	70-1003
MOELLER, Christine	23	Breitzbach	69-0572
MOELLER, Christoph	47	Mecklenburg	69-0923
Marie 43, Johann 22, Friedrich 21, Heinrich 7, Wilhelm 4			
MOELLER, Elisabeth	27	Frauenzimmern	69-0229
MOELLER, Emma	30	Gotha	69-0490
MOELLER, Friederike	42	Rohrbach	68-0661
MOELLER, Heinrich	33	Detmold	68-0314
Amalie 29, Heinrich 4, Fritz 1			
MOELLER, Heinrich	37	Minden	68-0820
Anna 35, Friedrich 7, Hermann 6, Catharina 2			
MOELLER, Hy.	53	Bueckeburg	69-1011
Philippine 47, Herm. 8, Sofia 4, Engel 11 months			
MOELLER, Johann	20	Stotterzheim	68-0456
MOELLER, Marie	19	Schwenstein	68-0982
MOELLER, Minna	23	Eitzendorf	68-0707
MOELLER, Vincent	29	Friesenhausen	68-0610
MOELLERING, William	35	Buffalo	69-0798
MOELLERMANN, Rud.	34	Hollich	69-0208
MOELLING, Heinrich	17	Gnernheim	68-0647
MOEMMEL, Friedrich	27	Keukkopf	68-1027
Henriette 26, Robert 11 months			
MOENCH, Bernhard	17	Sonnefeld	71-0643
MOENCH, H.	24	Hamburg	70-1066
MOENCH, Heinrich	19	Osterrode	68-314
MOENCH, Louise	24	Wuestenberg	71-0792
MOENKEMUELLER, Hch.	25	Bielefeld	68-0753
Marie 26			
MOENNCH, Julie	35	Osterode	68-0939
Heinrich 11 months			
MOERLING, Carl	39	Magdeburg	69-0208
Therese 34, Emma 16, Minna 9, Alma 6, Mathilde 9 months			
MOESENKRUG, M.	19	Bremervoerde	69-0560
MOESSNER, Gerh.	70	Diedelsheim	68-0647
MOESSURY, Eva	25	Wallerfangen	68-0939
MOHLER, Carl	25	Udenheim	70-0031
MOHN, Leopold	37	Hobooken	70-1055
Cornelia 32, Cornelia 9, Lina 5, Carl August 3			
MOHNKE, Albert	27	Satznick	69-0457
MOHR, Anna	20	Hannover	69-1086
MOHR, Anna	13	Petersberg	71-0456
MOHR, Catharine	36	Darmstadt	68-1298
Charles 9, Georg 7, Amalia 5, Catharina 9 months			
MOHR, Friedrich	30	Wittenhausen	68-0852
MOHR, Georg	32	Markhausen	69-0182
MOHR, Hermann	22	Mannheim	68-1006
MOHR, Jacob	56	Coblenz	68-0456
Jacob 23, Wilhelm 16, Wilhelmine 9			
MOHR, Johann	29	Herzborn	68-1006
MOHR, Peter	16	Annelsbach	71-0736
MOHR, Peter	43	Muenster	71-0712
MOHR. Nicolaus	17	Obermennig	69-0457
Heinrich 28, Margareth 33, Johann 11 months			
MOHRMANN, Heinrich	29	Lenzinghausen	68-0939
Anna 29, Anna 3, Johann 7 months			
MOHRMANN, Henry	32	Visselhoevede	68-0786
Marie 23			
MOHRMANN, Wilhelm	16	Johannesroth	70-0378
MOLDER, John	18	Praest	68-0957
MOLITOR, Catharina	25	R.B.Coblenz	68-1006
MOLL, Apollonia	48	Pittsburg	69-0672
Carl 12			
MOLL, Gust.	22	Dessau	68-0753
MOLL, Justine	24	Russmannshaus.	71-0792
MOLL, Lisette	42	Barmen	68-0566
Auguste 9, Mathilde 8, August 7, Hulda 6			
MOLLE, August	28	Langensalza	68-0786
Constanze 26, Roeschen 3, Clara 10 months			
MOLLENHAUER, Grete	18	Weden	71-0492
MOLLENI, Franz	25	Italien	69-1059
MOLLER, Johann	25	Niederhellersch	69-1059
MOLLER, Mart.	28	Essingen	70-0308

NAME	AGE	RESIDENCE	YR-LIST
MOLLETOR, Joh.	16	Dreis	71-0581
MOLT, Caroline	18	Lorch	69-0542
MOLTER, Johann	34	Eversten	69-0015
MOLZAHN, Ludwig	27	Putchow	68-0314
Albert 30			
MOMBERG, Carl	38	Alfeld	69-1086
MOMBON, Heinrich	25	Altendorf	69-0771
MONAT, Babette		Strumpelbronn	69-0429
MOND, Lena	29	Koeningshofen	69-0923
Apollonia 11 months			
MONKE, Sophie	23	Herford	68-0707
MONTAG, Christ.	45	Heuthen	71-0521
Anna 44, Christ. 18, Friederike 4, Anna 9 months			
MOOR, Elisabeth	30	Leopoldsgruen	71-0792
MOORHAUS, Anna	20	Menslage	68-0852
MOORHUSEN, Diedr.	26	Rodenkirchen	68-0534
Adelheid 25			
MOORMANN, Auguste	23	Metingen	70-0178
MOORMANN, Heinrich	16	Hagen	68-0625
MOORMANN, Louise	28	Voerden	68-0610
MOOS, Therese	30	Daxlanden	68-0014
Gottfried 3 months			
MORCHWINSKY, Vincent	30	Posen	68-0647
MORELL, Georami	80	Italia	69-1309
Louise 24, William 28, Jannett 22			
MORESSE, Elisabeth	29	Neustadt	70-0682
MORGEN, Peter	24	Mannebach	68-0647
MORGENROCK, Friedrich	16	Gr. Breitenbach	68-0939
MORGENROTH, Emil	23	Koenigser	71-0167
MORGENROTH, Hermann	25	Bamberg	71-0492
MORGENSCHWEISS, J.	26	Herschbach	68-0610
MORGENSTEIN, Johann	27	Guckelsberg	71-0429
MORGENSTERN, P.	40	Quimbach	68-0820
Jacob 11 months			
MORING, Therese	50	Niederorschel	71-0581
Adam 24, Carl 9			
MORITZ, Casp.	30	Krebsfeld	71-0393
MORITZ, Gerd.	18	Ottum	70-0170
MORMELSTEIN, Jette	18	Daubringen	68-0534
MORRIS, S.	29	Dalmation	70-1055
MORT, Fracisca	14	Renchen	71-0821
MORTFELL, Richard	20	Goerlitz	68-1027
MOSBACHER, Samuel	17	Mittenberg	69-0208
Joseph 15, Regine 21, Cathinka 19			
MOSCHAYSKY, Ivan	25	St. Petersburg	68-0939
MOSCHIKAU, Lina	18	Lobau	71-0393
MOSE, Willy	7	Quakenbrueck	69-1076
MOSER, Elise	47	Amsterdam	71-0681
MOSER, Fred.	42	Cincinati	69-1363
MOSER, Louis	28	Strassburg	68-0770
MOSER, Louis	19	Gotha	68-0872
MOSES, Julia	20	Oberndorf	68-0957
MOSES, Levy	32	Cleveland	69-0784
Levi Bloch 9			
MOTSCH, Julius	17	Gernsbach	68-314
MOTSCHLER, Jos.	16	Hechingen	68-0610
MOTTCHENBACHER, M.	31	Kronach	68-0456
Johann 9, Baptist 5			

NAME	AGE	RESIDENCE	YR-LIST
MOTTEL, Maria	18	Seefeld	71-0712
MOTZ, Alwine	22	Bremen	69-1212
MOTZ, Ferdinand	22	New York	69-1212
L. 22			
MOTZ, Johann	21	Altenstaig	68-0852
MOTZ, Marie	58	Kappeln	71-0429
MOTZ, Rennigius	27	Wuerzburg	69-1086
MOYER, George	24	Eastbourne	70-0148
Harry 12			
MRAZEK, Joseph	54	Kallin	70-1023
MRODROW, Carol.	20	Radolin	71-0581
MUCK, Johann	32	Bernfeld	68-0852
MUCK, Michel	21	Mellrichstadt	68-1298
MUEHLENBROCK, J.	78	Engstlath	70-0523
MUEHLENFELD, Carl	16	Hannover	70-0443
MUEHLENHARDT, Maria	20	Strohen	68-0456
Wilhelmine 16			
MUEHLENSTADT, H.	47	Eggeberg	68-0957
Catharina 34, Henry 7, Fred. 11 months			
MUEHLHAEUSER, Paul	21	Hatzheim	70-0378
MUEHLKE, Wilhelmine	20	Stolzenau	68-0786
MUELDER, Gretchen	20	S. Francisco	69-0923
MUELDNER, Pauline	16	Hannover	71-0363
MUELKEN, Friedrich	20	Volmerdingen	68-0566
MUELLER, Abraham	35	Erfurtshausen	69-0592
Regine 30, Regine 11 months			
MUELLER, Adelh.	34	Thedinghausen	68-0884
MUELLER, Adelheid	20	Bremervoerde	68-1006
MUELLER, Adolf	17	Ahlfeld	69-1319
MUELLER, Adolph	19	Marzhausen	70-0223
MUELLER, Adolph	45	Schwarzenbach	68-0707
Johanna 41, Frank. 9, Richard 8, Ida 7, Emilie 4, Angelica 23, Rosa 17, Caroli			
MUELLER, Agnes	27	Berlin	71-0792
MUELLER, Albert	48	Gotha	69-0049
MUELLER, Albert	19	Waldsee	69-0429
Georg 25			
MUELLER, Albert	17	Wuerttemberg	69-1004
MUELLER, Albin	23	Heibolzheim	69-1319
MUELLER, Alex	16	Sondershausen	70-0728
MUELLER, Alt.	14	Elmlohe	69-0560
MUELLER, Amalia	41	Hattenheim	68-0625
Johanna 14, Gustav 12			
MUELLER, Amalie	30	Leer	70-0683
MUELLER, Andr.	39	Heicklingen	69-1363
Eva 40, Franz 9, Leopold 4			
MUELLER, Andreas	52	Wingen	68-0625
Caroline 47, Heinrich 24, Johanna 26, Wilhelmine 18, Caroline 15, Wilhelm 11 m			
MUELLER, Andreas	38	Pforzheim	71-0226
Cath. 35			
MUELLER, Anna	24	Coeln	69-0079
MUELLER, Anna	46	Dusslingen	68-0982
MUELLER, Anna	31	Hetzbach	69-0338
Mary 5			
MUELLER, Anna	17	Rottweil	69-0429
MUELLER, Anna	25	Tevel	68-0610
MUELLER, Anna	18	Wohra	68-0661
MUELLER, Anna	17	Kalup	71-0479

NAME	AGE	RESIDENCE	YR-LIST
MUELLER, Anna	18	Barchel	71-0300
MUELLER, Anna	19	Pempertin	71-0429
MUELLER, Anna Elise	18	Stellenfelde	68-0770
MUELLER, Ant.	26	Havre	69-1363
MUELLER, Anton	36	New York	70-1003
Anna 26			
MUELLER, Anton	17	Ueberlingen	69-1011
MUELLER, Aug.	29	Lippe	69-1004
Sophie 26			
MUELLER, Aug.	18	Nordheim	68-0610
MUELLER, August	30	Schwarzburg-Rudolstadt	69-0015
MUELLER, August	16	Wallenhorst	68-0907
MUELLER, August	16	Bodenfelde	71-0712
MUELLER, Augusta	31	Borchholz	68-0786
MUELLER, Auguste	19	Marienwalde	69-0848
MUELLER, Babette	25	Franken	70-0378
Johann 6, Conrad 2			
MUELLER, Barth.	25	Etsikow/Switzer	69-0049
MUELLER, Bernh.	20	Endenbach	69-0162
MUELLER, Bernhard	16	Dormattingen	70-0728
MUELLER, Carl	32	Saalstedt	69-0968
MUELLER, Carl	36	Berlin	68-1027
MUELLER, Carl	19	Gr. Bocke	68-0820
MUELLER, Carl	32	Breslau	71-0712
Anna 24, Carl 11 m., Martha 1 m.			
MUELLER, Carl	48	Vegesack	71-0643
Catharine 41			
MUELLER, Carl	26	Wurmlingen	71-0226
MUELLER, Carl	34	Ermschwert	71-0429
Friedrike 35, Sophie 4			
MUELLER, Caroline	14	Muehringen	71-0456
MUELLER, Caroline	25	Altmersleben	69-0321
MUELLER, Caspar	29	Meiningen	70-0148
Marie 19			
MUELLER, Caspar	36	S. Meiningen	69-0848
MUELLER, Caspar	29	Wolfstein	68-1027
MUELLER, Cath.	58	Nassau	69-1363
MUELLER, Cath.	23	Oberzell	71-0815
Johann 6 months			
MUELLER, Cath.	21	Alsfeld	71-0393
MUELLER, Cathar.	16	Gruenstadt	68-0957
MUELLER, Catharina	20	Zeven	68-0456
MUELLER, Catharina	41	Zeven	68-0625
Elise 17, Heinrich 23			
MUELLER, Catharina	19	Altenkirchen	68-0820
MUELLER, Catharine	32	Finsterroth	71-0643
Rosine 9, Carl 7, Christian 5			
MUELLER, Cathrine	29	Flonheim	71-0643
Friedrich 5, Franz 4			
MUELLER, Ch.	23	Orsingen	71-0479
MUELLER, Christ.	44	Truchtelfingen	69-0321
Joh. 16			
MUELLER, Christian	17	Remmelshausen	71-0643
John 7			
MUELLER, Christiane	21	Meiningen	69-0592
MUELLER, Christoph	31	Heusen/Hensen	69-0321
MUELLER, Chrs.	27	Iserlohn	69-0338
MUELLER, David	23	Eiderfeld	68-1002
Caroline 25, Ida 21, Isaac 18			
MUELLER, Diedrich	22	Oldenburg	69-0268
MUELLER, Doris	45	Hersbruch	69-0572
MUELLER, Doris	18	Dorum	69-0576
MUELLER, Dorothea	61	Katzhuette	70-0308
MUELLER, Dorothea	28	Eichenberg	71-0363
MUELLER, Eduard	27	Coburg	69-0672
MUELLER, Eduard	37	Magdeburg	71-0821
MUELLER, Edward	28	Kirchberg	69-0784
Ernestine 28, Carl 5 months			
MUELLER, Eilert	36	Hudermoor	69-0321
Meta 25, Hermine 2, Anna 6 months			
MUELLER, Eilert	32	Hannover	70-0329
MUELLER, Elisa	16	Birkenau	71-0456
MUELLER, Emil Hermann	14	Zillerfeld/Harz	69-0559
MUELLER, Emilie	17	R.B. Potsdam	68-0820
MUELLER, Ernestine	28	Altenburg	71-0172
Richard 6, Baby-girl 6m., Caroline 24			
MUELLER, Ferd.	33	Joachimsthal	68-1027
MUELLER, Ferd.	28	Schlatt	71-0581
MUELLER, Fr.	32	Woerperdorf	71-1046
MUELLER, Franz	31	Obermaisberg	68-1027
Meta 26			
MUELLER, Franz	27	Berleburg	68-0939
MUELLER, Franziska	21	Bodenweis	69-0542
MUELLER, Franziska	23	Wasseraltingen	68-0534
MUELLER, Friederike	28	Grossbottwar	70-0523
MUELLER, Friederike	24	Osterode	68-0939
MUELLER, Friedr.	40	Grauel	71-0821
Marie 35, Diedrich 9, Heinrich 7, Friedrich 10 months			
MUELLER, Friedr.	74	Dedesdorf	71-0733
MUELLER, Friedr.	20	Kirberg	71-0684
MUELLER, Friedrich	30	Chemnitz	69-0784
Juliane 30, Louise 5, Anna 4, Clara 3, Betha 11 months			
MUELLER, Friedrich	16	Lahnsen	69-0457
MUELLER, Friedrich	16	Darmstadt	70-0355
MUELLER, Friedrich	29	Eisenach	68-1049
MUELLER, Friedrich	42	Heinichen	68-0770
MUELLER, Friedrike	45	Magdeburg	71-0456
MUELLER, Fritz	29	Bombach	71-0789
MUELLER, Georg	27	Coburg	69-0572
MUELLER, Georg	27	Essingen	69-0457
Susanne 21			
MUELLER, Georg	25	Ober Ramstadt	71-0736
Rosine 22, Regine 17			
MUELLER, Georg	16	Schaffhausen	71-0643
MUELLER, Georg	38	Weisbach	71-0479
MUELLER, Georg	19	Lohr	71-0429
MUELLER, Gottfr.	54	Colbitz	70-1055
Anna 54			
MUELLER, Gottfr.	48	Buenerode	71-0733
Christiane 47, Hermann 13, Emma 17, Friedrich 15, August 12, Wilh. 12, Louis 9			
MUELLER, Gottlieb	28	Borsen	71-0429
MUELLER, Gust.	16	Samoehlenek	71-0815
MUELLER, Gustav	28	Goldorf	69-0457
MUELLER, Hedwig	18	Rudolfzell	71-0456

NAME	AGE	RESIDENCE	YR-LIST
MUELLER, Heinr.	15	Allendorf	69-0592
MUELLER, Heinr.	29	Frankfurt/M	71-0167
MUELLER, Heinrich	23	Lamstedt	69-0457
MUELLER, Heinrich	15	Darmstadt	69-0576
MUELLER, Heinrich	39	Antwerpen	70-0569
Emilie 40			
MUELLER, Heinrich	30	Reddighausen	69-0968
MUELLER, Heinrich	61	Stein	69-1086
MUELLER, Heinrich	65	Wesenstedt	68-314
MUELLER, Heinrich	16	Walle	71-0712
MUELLER, Heinrich	21	Moringen	71-0712
MUELLER, Heinrich	15	Lippe	71-0226
MUELLER, Helena	18	Bremen	71-0733
MUELLER, Henriette	20	Dorum	71-0681
MUELLER, Henriette	16	Radenkirchen	71-0581
MUELLER, Henry	28	Sellenrod	68-0534
Susanna 27, Catharina 5, Charles 3			
MUELLER, Herm.	25	Bremen	69-0050
Johann 35			
MUELLER, Herm.	16	Gr. Sutrum/Lutr	69-1004
MUELLER, Herm.	30	Hakendorf	71-0789
MUELLER, Hermann	16	Freiburg	68-0456
MUELLER, Hermen	17	Kolding	69-0029
MUELLER, Hinrich	19	Melle	68-0625
MUELLER, Hubert	24	Ahrdorf	69-1363
MUELLER, Hugo	27	Allstedt	68-1027
MUELLER, J.	16	Primanens	71-0681
MUELLER, J. M.	22	Wohlenbeck	71-0736
MUELLER, Jac.	15	Stuttgart	70-1055
MUELLER, Jacob	22	Hasselbach	68-0707
MUELLER, Jacob	25	Auw	71-0226
MUELLER, Jacobine	24	Ziershausen	69-0229
MUELLER, Joh.	25	Rahringmoor	69-1363
MUELLER, Joh.	27	Schwemingen	68-0884
MUELLER, Joh.	33	Nuernberg	70-0443
MUELLER, Joh.	63	Rudolstadt	71-0300
Herm. 16			
MUELLER, Joh.	50	Falkenstein	71-0393
Caroline 43, Caroline 7, Joh. 3			
MUELLER, Joh. Jac.	26	Otterndorf	69-0583
Caroline 18			
MUELLER, Johann	23	Oberfranken	69-0798
MUELLER, Johann	18	Deisslingen	70-1142
MUELLER, Johann	23	Wertheim	68-0786
MUELLER, Johann	26	Gr. Zappel	69-0547
Pauline 20			
MUELLER, Johann	23	Braunweille/Aus	69-0547
MUELLER, Johann	28	Pracht	68-0770
MUELLER, Johann	26	Fischerhude	68-0982
MUELLER, Johann	40	St. Louis	69-0490
MUELLER, Johann	24	Huebertushuette	69-1076
MUELLER, Johann	22	Meiningen	68-0852
MUELLER, Johann	25	Langons	68-0625
Heinrich 28, Anton 19			
MUELLER, Johann	62	Schnellenwelde	68-0707
Pauline 31, Emma 24, Bertha 3			
MUELLER, Johann	30	Bremervoerde	71-0521
MUELLER, John	40	Westphalen	70-1161

NAME	AGE	RESIDENCE	YR-LIST
Josephine 35, Franz 9, Anton 8			
MUELLER, John	32	Lippstadt	69-0457
MUELLER, John	43	Lechenich	68-0957
Louisa 38, Franz 8, Josephine 6, Ella 9 months			
MUELLER, John	37	Neuhaus	68-0760
Ida 4, Augusta 25, Maria 3, Emma 11 months			
MUELLER, John	57	Carlsruhe	71-0643
MUELLER, John	16	Heilsdorf	71-0456
MUELLER, Jos.	18	Borgenstreich	71-0581
Theresia 17			
MUELLER, Joseph	52	Gelingen	68-0770
MUELLER, Justus	16	Bremen	69-1076
MUELLER, Katharina	35	Darmstadt	68-0865
Conrad 13, Anna Maria 15, Elisabeth 3			
MUELLER, Katharine	25	Zoelingen	69-0049
MUELLER, Lina	23	Danzig	69-0968
Anna 15, Lina 12, Antonie 10, Clara 9, Hermann 2, Gretchen 1, Helene 3 months			
MUELLER, Louis	19	Leipzig	69-0771
MUELLER, Louis	23	Koenigsberg	71-0681
MUELLER, Louise	24	Basel	69-0572
MUELLER, Louise	59	Zweibruecken	69-0429
Pauline 36			
MUELLER, Louise	39	Niedernau	69-0583
Friederike 34, Christian 13			
MUELLER, Louise	19	Wuelferdingen	68-0566
MUELLER, Louise	18	Quirnbach	71-0456
MUELLER, Ludw.	26	Waldeck	68-0647
MUELLER, Lueder	16	Lesnig	70-0076
MUELLER, Lueneburg	33	Ploenjeshausen	68-0647
MUELLER, Margareth	18	Croen	69-0321
MUELLER, Margareth	22	Grebenau	71-0684
Sophie 18, Adam 14			
MUELLER, Margarethe	19	Schluesselburg	69-1309
MUELLER, Margarethe	27	Coblenz	68-0456
MUELLER, Maria	19	Philippsthal	69-0182
MUELLER, Maria	25	Rattelsdorf	69-0321
MUELLER, Maria	18	Kirchen	69-1086
MUELLER, Maria	22	Strohen	68-0456
MUELLER, Maria	16	Dornsieders	68-0760
MUELLER, Marie	22	Otterndorf	69-1004
MUELLER, Marie	19	Coburg	69-1309
MUELLER, Marie	20	Bremerhaven	70-0329
MUELLER, Marie	22	Bechtelsheim	68-0852
MUELLER, Marie	18	Metzingen	71-0479
MUELLER, Marie	56	Germersheim	71-0429
MUELLER, Martin	25	Sachsen Meining	69-0321
MUELLER, Martin	16	Heissenbuettel	70-0355
MUELLER, Martin	20	Hannover	68-0456
MUELLER, Meyer	60	Eiderfeld	68-1002
Betty 60			
MUELLER, Michael	20	Westenhausen	68-0939
MUELLER, Michael	25	Forchheim	71-0684
MUELLER, Michel	42	Steinau	70-0355
Cathrine 32, Nicolas 5, Sebastian 11 months			
MUELLER, Nic.	30	Jettersdorf	71-0581

NAME	AGE	RESIDENCE	YR-LIST
MUELLER, Oscar	16	Meiningen	69-0560
MUELLER, Peter	25	Wiersheim	68-314
MUELLER, Peter	55	Darmstadt	68-0314
Juliane 53, Juliane 23, Rudolph 17, Therese 9			
MUELLER, Peter	25	Coelbe	68-0707
Marie 24			
MUELLER, Philipp	18	Thallichtenberg	71-0456
MUELLER, Philippine	21	Ditschweiler	71-0479
MUELLER, Rebecca	21	Entzendorf	71-0643
MUELLER, Rosine	35	Stuttgart	70-0204
Anna 5			
MUELLER, Rudolf	24	Hopsten	69-1086
MUELLER, Rudolph	24	Carbach	69-1059
MUELLER, Theodor	20	Nuernberg	69-0572
MUELLER, Theodor	20	Wien	68-0456
MUELLER, Theodor	22	Hanau	71-0643
MUELLER, Valtin	18	Dilkirchen	71-0363
MUELLER, Wilh.	28	Oldenburg	69-0321
Helene 28, Carl 3, Wilhelm 10 months			
MUELLER, Wilh.	20	Nuernberg	71-0681
MUELLER, Wilh.	20	Stotternheim	71-0479
MUELLER, Wilhelm	26	Schleiz	70-0178
MUELLER-WOLSEIFER	35	Duesseldorf	69-0457
Fanny 3, Elly 2, Marie 9 months			
MUELLERSOHN, Chr.	24	Grafenberg	70-0089
MUENCH, Eduard	28	Klengen	71-0521
MUENCH, Elisabeth	58	Wuerzburg	68-0566
MUENCH, Joh.	26	Steinbach	68-0982
MUENCH, Johanne	17	Schluchtern	70-0259
MUENCH, Ludwig	21	Wimpfen	68-0939
MUENCH, Martha	60	Waldeck	69-0672
MUENCH, Peter	28	Bruern	71-0521
Cath. 15			
MUENCH, Robert	29	Giebeckenstein	70-0682
MUENDERMANN, Friedr.	28	Schierneichen	68-0786
MUENTZ, Ludewike	9	Vegesack	70-0148
Carl 6 months			
MUENZ, Barbara	23	Schriessheim	70-0170
MUENZEBROCK, C.	16	Neuenburg	70-0259
MUENZER, Bernhard	32	Ostratz	69-0841
MUENZNER, H. F.	31	Reichenbach	70-0089
Wilhelmine 32, Clara 9, Emma 8			
MUERDTLER, Thomas	25	Gr. Lussen	71-0456
MUES, Ernst	36	Bremen	70-1003
MUES, Ernst	37	Bremen	71-0643
MUESER, Heinrich	59	Daxburg	70-0523
Eva Catharine 58, Theresia 30, Wilhelm 4			
MUESING, Wilhelm	31	Liekwegen	68-0534
Anna 30, Baby-daughter 9 months			
MUESS, Friedericke	30	Warfleth	70-0682
MUETSCHLER, Christine	22	Dornhain	69-1212
MUETZ, H.	23	Verden	69-1004
MUETZE, Carl	17	Frankenberg	71-0456
MUETZE, Joh.	29	Warzenbach	71-0821
MUHLMEYER, Franz	21	Kemnath	71-0581
MULDENDORF, Heinr.	26	Breslau	71-0300
MULE, Friederike	77	Hohe	68-0610
Frdr. 26			

NAME	AGE	RESIDENCE	YR-LIST
MULL, Aug.	39	Braunschweig	69-1011
Dina 55, Wilhelmine 8, August 5, Flitz 4, Caroline 9 months			
MULL, Heinrich	20	Ohr	68-0661
MULLERT, Carl	21	Berlin	69-0182
Paul 19			
MULTER, Johann	59	Doebeln	69-0229
MULTHAUSS, Margarethe	15	Heiligenstadt	69-0572
MUND, Guenther	23	Goersbach	68-0566
MUNDEL, David	18	Obrigheim	71-0521
MUNDERLOH, J.	17	Oldenburg	70-0204
MUNDIG, Georg	42	Regensburg	69-0672
MUNDINGER, Carl	17	Sandeck	70-0204
MUNDINGER, Leonh.	16	Warbrunn	71-0581
MUNGER, Magd.	22	Chur	70-1055
Marie 2, Ludwig 9 months			
MUNK, Rosina	20	Waiblingen	69-0338
MUNSTERICH, Gottfried	19	Buttenhausen	71-0821
Wilhelmine 17, Elisabeth 42, Barbara 14, Friedr. 9, Johannes 8, Christiane			
MUNSTERMANN, Elenore	60	Drentsteinfurt	68-0907
MUNZ, Gottlieb	19	Stocksberg	69-0457
MURHOFF, Engel	16	Bueckeburg	69-1011
MURICH, Anton	40	Boehmen	70-0384
Ludewika 33, Anna 11 months			
MURZSICH, Arneseto	33	Dalmation	70-1055
Anna 22, Antonie 9, Raymus 8,			
MUSCH, Diedr.	37	Gropfelden	70-0272
Anna 39, Heinr. 13, Bernh. 7			
MUSCH, Gottlieb	17	Esslingen	71-0643
MUSCHENHEIMER, Ernst	24	Hannover	68-0647
MUSEK, Gottlieb	17	Esslingen	71-0643
MUSELMANN, Michel	28	Unternfeld	68-1298
Christine 24			
MUSIAL, Florentine	22	Szacimirowa	69-0547
MUSMANN, Cord	19	Schwarme	69-0547
MUSOLF, Carl	39	Cascin/Boehmen	69-0576
Marianne 30, Franz 8, Marianne 6, Anilla 9 months			
MUSSEL, Katherine	19	Eichloh	70-0148
Christine 17			
MUSSGILLER, Geo.	32	Heroldsberg	68-0982
MUSSMANN, Friedr.	16	Brokoleh	70-0452
MUSTER, Christ.	38	Schweiz	70-1161
MUTERT, Lotte	40	Tecklenburg	68-0566
Marie 13, Wilhelmine 9, Hermann 7, Catharine 4, Wilhelmine 10 months			
MUTH, Friedr.	18	Obrigheim	71-0521
MUTH, Johann	34	Obrigheim	69-0583
MUTH, John	65	Wiesbaden	70-0355
Cathrine 58			
MUTING, Heinrich	36	Harren	71-0300
MUTTER, Wilh.	19	Lichtenhain	71-0681
MUTTHAUPT, Lucas	46	Heiligenstadt	69-0572
Margaretha 54, Christoph 17			
MUTZ, Marie	23	Manheim	68-0786
Anna 9 months			
NABELL, Wilh.	23	Dresden	71-0684
NABER, Christian	21	Bremen	69-0182
NACHBAR, Elisa	23	Wulsdorf	68-1298

NAME	AGE	RESIDENCE	YR-LIST
NACKENHORST, Justine	20	Wagenfeld	68-0661
NADELFEST, Regine	17	Prag	68-0982
NADERMANN, Engel	20	Hannover	70-1142
NAEBE, Hugo	25	Dresden	71-0815
NAECHTER, Johann	28	Reuss	68-0872
NAEFER, Friedrich	53	Trebes	71-0681
Auguste 58			
NAEGELE, Carl	48	Muehlhausen	69-0321
NAEGELE, John	34	New York	69-1059
Catharina 27			
NAGEL, August	39	Lilz	71-0684
NAGEL, Franz	19	Camberg	68-0314
NAGEL, Heinr.	23	Minden	71-0521
NAGEL, Louise	21	Herzfeld	70-0728
NAGELMANN, Auguste	19	Gr. Zappel	69-0547
NAGENGAST, Joh.	26	Stuermich	71-0581
Marg. 22, Johann 3			
NAGLER, Wilhelmine	30	Zeulenroda	71-0429
Marie 9 months			
NAHLE, Andreas	40	Berlin	68-0661
NAHM, Heinr.	16	Sinsheim	69-0592
NAHSER, Barbara	29	Braunsberg	69-0923
Rosa 18			
NAHSER, Bertha	17	Braunschweig	71-0479
Auguste 23			
NAKATH, Johann	41	Aspel	71-0363
Johanne 22			
NAMANN, Ottilie	22	Berlin	71-0681
NANERT, Franz	18	Meinsdorf	69-1011
NAPPER, Therese	23	Herbolsheim	71-0521
NAPPERELL, Julius	36	Oldenburg	70-0148
NARR, Johann	42	Schlegel	68-0907
NARRJES, Wilh.	42	Hannover	69-1004
Marie 50			
NASMANN, Amalie	33	Lauenstein	71-0300
Emil 9, Martha 3, Carl 1			
NASS, Catharina	23	Treysa	69-0547
NASSAUER, Doris	23	Frankfurt	68-0610
NASSEN, Wilhelmine	19	Trebes	71-0681
NASTOLL, Geo.	25	Mertesheim	68-0957
NATHAN, Emil	35	Memphis	70-1003
Sophie 29, Hugo 4, Ernst 9 months			
NATHANSEN, Julius	19	Berlin	71-0167
NATHER, Henrich	39	Cottleben	69-0268
NATHHAUSEN, R.	25	Bach	70-0384
NATMANN, Gerhard	16	Lastrup	69-1004
NATZ, Christine	29	Wetterdingen	68-0534
Willy 4, Caroline 3, Peter 2, Lorle 6 months			
NAU, Gertrude		Parkstein	71-0226
NAU, Gottlieb	24	Schoenbrunn	68-0760
NAUDIT, Carl	27	Schinkenberg	70-0204
Auguste 25			
NAUKE, Maria	18	Rothenburg	68-0707
NAUKEMANN, Hermann	30	Duethe	68-0939
NAUMANN, Anna	20	Goosfelden	68-1027
NAUMANN, Friedrich	19	Rieste	69-0208
NAUMANN, Henriette	29	Ilfeld	68-0610
Heinr. 5			
NAUMANN, Pauline	28	Leipzig	71-0456

NAME	AGE	RESIDENCE	YR-LIST
NAUMBURG, Wolf	14	Treichlingen	68-0852
NAUNINGGER, Maria	24	Breisach	71-0492
NAUSS, Kunigunde	28	Oberfranken	69-0968
NEBE, Maria	28	Themar	69-1309
NEDDERMEYER, August	16	Doehren	68-0314
NEDENMEIER, Georg	26	Anderten	69-0321
NEEB, Heinrich	51	Oetzen	68-0707
NEEMANN, Anna	26	Etzel	71-0492
NEERMANN, Heinrich	24	Bunde	70-0135
NEES, Anna Mary	29	Hensbach	69-0321
NEFF, Caroline	28	Bretzingen	71-0712
NEHER, Franz	28	Binsdorf	68-0534
NEHER, Louise	22	Stuttgart	69-0784
NEHER, Marie	22	Harthausen	68-0786
NEHLS, Heinr.	30	Mariendorf	68-0884
NEHR, Johanna	39	Pest	68-0786
NEHRBACH, Jacob	26	Schwabsburg	70-0204
NEIDHARDT, Joh. P.C.	19	Flieden	68-0610
NEIDHARDT, Maria	33	Darmstadt	68-0707
NEINASS, Wilhelmine	28	Peutzedin	71-0521
NEISEL, Catharina	17	Niederwellen	68-0707
NEITHAMMER, Mary	19	Rohrau	70-0170
Andrew 21			
NEITZKE, Ernst	17	Stolp	68-1298
NELKE, Emil	15	Smiskanowo	69-0547
NELLE, Joseph	18	Muenster	69-0079
NELLER, Gerson	21	Bessenhessen	71-0643
NEMANN, Theodor	18	Kalveslage	68-0610
NEMECECK, Johann	26	Kamena	69-0229
Franz 6			
NEMECK, Jonas	29	Seltschau	71-0393
Anna 27			
NEMICH, John	44	Eberdieffen	68-0957
Caroline 43, Elisabeth 12, Catharine 10, Hermann 8, Adolph 4, Jacob 9 months			
NEMITZ, August	27	Schurow	69-0784
NEMITZ, Otto	17	Doehringen	71-0792
NEMMERT, Doris	17	Coburg	71-0429
NENECKER, Wilhelm	36	Holzhausen	71-0681
Christ. 28, Christine 13			
NENNER, Joh.	27	Gschand	68-0982
NERZ, Walburga	20	Beuren	69-0321
NESEN, Gertrud	47	Hegensdorf	69-0079
Therese 16, Dina 6			
NESTLE, Cath.	28	Ebhausen	69-1363
NETTEBROCK, Anna	25	Herben	68-0939
NETTER, Carl	18	Mannheim	70-1003
NETTZE, Minna	23	Holzminden	71-0456
NETZKE, August	23	Rahmel	69-0338
NEUBAUER, Andreas	45	Thueringen	70-0443
Christine 45, Carl 18, Caroline 17, Friedrich 15, Marie 13, Wilhelm 9, Wilhelm			
NEUBAUER, Ant.	25	Semoschitz	71-0393
Marg. 22, Katharina 6 months			
NEUBAUER, Barb.	64	Pegnitz	71-0393
Marg. 31, Marg. 5			
NEUBAUER, Caroline	52	Mechoezyn	71-0581
Franz 22, Reinhold 16, Emil 14, Gustav 9			
NEUBAUER, Joseph	49	Ringelberg	68-0661

NAME	AGE	RESIDENCE	YR-LIST
Catharina 45			
NEUBAUER, Mary	30	Nordhalben	70-0170
NEUBERGER, Clara	36	Hainstadt	68-0786
NEUBERT, Friedrich	27	Hanau	70-0148
Albertine 26, Albertine 3			
NEUBERT, Johanne	42	Rudolphstadt	71-0712
NEUBRANDT, L.	19	Ochsenbuch	69-1421
NEUENBURG, John	25	Seesterandeich	68-0957
NEUENBURGER, C.	16	Bremen	71-0363
NEUENFELD, Auguste	28	Berlin	70-1023
NEUENKIRCH, Christian	50	Potsdam	68-0661
Dorothea 50, Carl 13, Marie 7			
NEUFALE, Christ.	15	Blaubichren	69-1004
NEUFELDT, Friederike	22	Gilkenburg	70-0184
NEUFERT, Herm.	39	Muehlhausen	68-0610
Bertha 29, Eduard 6, August 4, Emilie 6 months			
NEUFFLER, Johann	32	Neckarems	71-0643
NEUGASS, Wilhelm	27	Frankfurt	69-1319
NEUGEBAUER, Carl	19	Massbruch	68-0852
NEUGEBAUER, Clara	29	Schweiz	71-0736
Regine 27			
NEUGESCHWENDLER	18	Kufstein	70-0184
NEUHAUER, Josef	28	Lind	69-1011
Barbara 24			
NEUHAUS, Heinrich	16	Oldenburg	70-0523
NEUHAUS, Henry	50	Halberstadt	71-0456
NEUHAUS, Minna	23	Wollin	71-0684
NEUHAUSER, Emilie	24	Schwaben	71-0172
Veronica 11 months			
NEULING, Elisab.	25	Liepe	69-1212
August 11 months			
NEULING, Marie	25	Luebbars	69-1212
Wilhelm 6 months			
NEULING, Wilhelm	51	Luebbars	69-1212
Marie 46, August 17, Albert 7, Gustav 5			
NEULING,Ernst	21	Luebbars	69-1212
NEUMANN, A.	26	Zeittingen	71-0792
NEUMANN, Alfred	17	Frankfurt a/M	70-0443
NEUMANN, August	22	Eberdorf	69-0547
NEUMANN, Augusta	18	Kucherson	68-0820
NEUMANN, Carl	41	Detroit	69-1004
NEUMANN, Caroline	21	Hannover	69-1004
NEUMANN, Charles	27	San Francisco	69-1212
Henry 29			
NEUMANN, Elise	20	Nesselbaum	69-1059
NEUMANN, Emilie	35	Posen	68-0647
Augusta 5, Emma 9 months			
NEUMANN, Gottlieb	26	Zachatberg	69-0162
NEUMANN, H. Magd.	52	Wacha	69-0049
A. Elisabeth 14, Anna 8			
NEUMANN, Johann	28	Rosenfeld	69-0429
NEUMANN, Johannes	49	Schwarzenberg	68-1002
Martha 42, Heinrich 13, Adam 9			
NEUMANN, Josef	46	Boehmen	70-0569
Marie 50, Magdalene 21, Gerry 6 months			
NEUMANN, Julius	19	Ebertsheim	70-1142
NEUMANN, Loeb.	18	Darmstadt	70-0170
NEUMANN, Lother	29	Goeditz	71-0681
NEUMANN, Ludwig	16	Muttersdorf	68-0566
NEUMANN, Maria	24	Kleistadt	69-1076
NEUMANN, Pet.	16	Derkweiler	70-0308
NEUMANN, Sophie	28	Sagefumme	69-0968
NEUMANN, Therese	20	Berlin	71-0581
NEUMEISTER, Georg	27	Lichtenberg	69-0542
Zacharias 34			
NEUMEISTER, Johanne	59	Lichtenberg	71-0479
NEUN, Georg	20	Wennings	69-1319
NEUNECECK, Friedrich	31	Kuttenberg	71-0492
Anna 24, Alois 10 months			
NEUSCH, Oscar	23	Strassburg	68-0566
NEUSE, August	21	Cassel	70-0682
NEUSTADT, Hek.	24	Liechow	69-0490
NEUSTAEDTER, Julius	22	Oldendorf	70-0089
NEUSUESS, Conrad	27	Oberdunzelbach	68-0707
NEUSUESS, Friedrich	9	Oberdinzenbach	69-1363
NEUTZEL, D.	54	Schoenfeld	71-0300
Joh. 23, Dora 20, Johann 17, Franz 9, Barb. 8			
NEVEKE, Marie	51	Lehna	69-1004
Helene 9			
NEYMANN, Clara	30	New York	70-1142
Olga 9, P. 7,			
NICHALEWSKY, Ignatz	32	Patzem/Austria	69-0547
NICKEL, Bertha	21	Fitzerie	69-0457
Emil 16			
NICKEL, Conr.	31	Bramstedt	68-0647
Elisabeth 53			
NICKEL, Heinr.	23	Resengarden	71-0479
NICKEL, John	17	Cassel	68-0760
NICKEL, Marie	25	Rappenhausen	71-0479
NICKEL, Peter	30	Winden-Minden	68-0534
Elisabeth 22, Anna 11 months			
NICKERT, Catharine	19	Meisenheim	71-0733
NICKLAS, Peter	17	Darmstadt	69-1212
NICOLA, Francisca	34	Villingen	70-0443
NICOLAI, Friedr.	30	Koenigser	71-0167
NICOLAUS, Louise	20	Ottersberg	68-0820
NICOLAUS, Margarethe	15	Ostheim	63-0015
NIEBAUER, Franz	29	Wien	68-0982
NIEBLING, Kath.	15	Untherthal	71-0821
NIEBUHR, Johanna	17	Paris	68-0907
NIEBUHR, Mathias	17	Hannover	70-0508
NIECOLEI, Adeline	28	Holler Wustig	70-0204
NIED, Friedr.	42	Duisburg	71-0681
Anna 38, Louis 18, Mathilde 9, August 8, Adolf 4			
NIEDERHOEFER, H.	26	Lippe Detmold	70-0223
NIEDERHOMMERT, I.	20	Dueme	69-0848
NIEDERWERFER, Franz	39	Glachau	70-0384
NIEDZINSKI, Franz	28	Gasmirow	70-0204
NIEGALDT, Franz	17	Gera	68-0456
NIEHAUS, E.	17	Ibbenbrunn	69-0338
NIEHOFF, Anna	23	Laxten	69-0968
NIEKAMP, Herm.	17	Buende	68-0534
NIEKAMP, Sofia	28	Bentheim	69-0841
NIEM, Wilh.	16	Berndorf	68-0982
NIEMANN, Aug.	26	Bethem	69-0338

NAME	AGE	RESIDENCE	YR-LIST
NIEMANN, August	27	Oldenburg	68-0852
Marie 24			
NIEMANN, Carl	41	Bremen	69-1363
NIEMANN, Ferdinand	47	Osnabrueck	69-1059
NIEMANN, Franz	27	Oesede	68-0957
Louise 22			
NIEMANN, Geert	38	Deegveld	68-0566
NIEMANN, John	23	Bremen	70-1023
NIEMANN, Louise	18	Dissen	68-0957
NIEMANN, Wilhelm	17	Hannover	70-100
NIEMEC, Johann	32	Jernowitz	68-0770
NIEMEIER, Christ.	43	Sabbenhausen	68-0957
Mary 36, Mary 8, Anna 6, Louisa 3, Christine 2			
NIEMENZ, Ang.	17	Warendorf	71-0736
NIEMES, Georg	18	Sausenheim	69-0162
NIEMEYER, Carl	43	Milzow	71-0733
Carl 38, Louis 9, Hermann 8			
NIEMEYER, Friedrich	26	Braunschweig	69-1309
NIEMEYER, Marie	17	Lueckeberge	69-0429
NIEMEYER, male	28	Hannover	70-100
NIEMUTH, Johann	57	Karwenbruch	69-0672
Henriette 40, Rudolph 16, Carl 9, Johann 7, Wilhelmine 4, Johann 6 mo.			
NIENBURG, Hr.	17	Hannover	70-0308
NIERCKE, Christ.	35	Stettin	68-0566
Augusta 33, Caroline 13, Emilie 8			
NIERMEYER, Friedrich	15	Minden	68-0907
NIERSTE, Heinrich	18	Huellhorst	68-314
NIES, Metha		Marienborn	69-0592
NIESMANN, Hermann	29	Bodense	69-0672
NIESSEN, Joh.	37	Berlin	68-0820
NIETEBOCK, Albert	39	Hanibal	70-0452
NIETEBOOK, F. W. C.	17	Bremen	71-0226
NIETFELD, Diedr.	23	Mainschhorn	68-1027
NIETHOLD, Christiane	58	Schoelm	69-0542
NIETLING, Mary	31	Stuttgart	68-0534
Friederike 21			
NIEWEG, Conrad	31	Lahe	69-0968
NIEWISCH, Heinr.	16	Hasbergen	71-0479
NIEZHORN, F. W.	21	Muehlhoff	70-0728
NIFF, Georg	22	Mochelstock	68-1002
NIGAULT, Julius	22	Bremen	69-0457
NIGGEMANN, Sophie	21	Lippe Detmold	70-0223
NIGLEMEYER, Cath.	16	Ostkilver	68-0786
NILOLITZ, Victor	22	Wien	69-1396
NIMTZ, Carl	18	Flatow	71-0429
NINEMANN, Celeste	35	Rehme	69-1004
Bertha 3			
NIPPERT, Juliane	29	Breslau	69-1011
NIPPS, Margarethe	27	Reinbach	68-0661
Catharina 20, Elise 18			
NISSING, Peter	36	Lahnstein	71-0172
NISTAL, Jacob	34	Wallersdorf	69-0798
NITCHKE, Marie	24	Breslau	69-0576
NITSCH, Ed.	28	Krakisch	68-0820
NITSCHE, Ernst	30	Sachsen	69-0559
NITSCHMANN, Oscar	28	Chemnitz	68-0939
NITZ, Auguste	22	Bukowitz	69-0547
NITZ, Ludwig	22	Eschenring	68-0661
NITZECHI, Sophie	55	Rasephus	70-0178
Emilie 21, Alwine 16			
NITZEL, Kunigunde	22	Stockau	69-0560
NITZOLD, Otto	28	Altenburg	71-0167
NITZSCHKE, Moritz	30	Hartha	68-0661
NOACK, Paul	17	Hirschberg	68-0907
NOBBE, Frdr.	17	Destel	68-0610
W. Ludw. 20			
NOBER, Auguste	22	Liechow	69-0490
NOBMANN, Johanna	21	Bremen	68-1006
Caroline 18			
NOCHEM, Hannchen	25	Wronke	69-0162
NOCKIN, Geo.	34	Speyer	69-1011
NODLBICHLER, Anna	24	Muenchen	68-0907
NOELKER, Bernhard	27	Osnabrueck	69-0560
Johanna 25, Lor. 11 months			
NOELL, Elisabeth	20	Zwersten	68-0647
NOELLE, Gustav	21	Osnabrueck	68-0907
NOELTING, Friedr.	23	Rischenau	68-314
NOETHINGER, Daniel	42	Werkheim	71-0521
Marie 24, Theoph. 8, Hermine 7			
NOETHLICH, Silvia	19	Unterwellenborn	71-0733
NOETZELMANN, Ferd.	22	Gr. Lubs	71-0733
NOFF, Christiane	51	Waldenburg	68-0661
Anna Julie 17, Gustav Emil 28			
NOLD, Peter	25	Fulda	68-1049
NOLKENS, Conrad	14	Dinkelhausen	68-0707
NOLL, August	17	Neuningen	69-0229
Carl 14, Georg 12			
NOLL, Christian	24	Singlis	68-0707
NOLL, Emma	47	Landau	69-0229
Emil 9			
NOLL, Eugen	29	Mainz	69-0784
NOLL, Friedr.	18	Teufelsmuehl	71-0456
NOLTE, Anton	37	Berlin	69-0321
NOLTE, August	57	Evansville	70-0135
Dorette 26			
NOLTE, Carl	57	Borstel	68-0661
Maria 58, Carl 27, Lina 24, Sophie 20, Doris 18			
NOLTE, Conrad	18	Hohenhausen	70-0308
NOLTE, Friedrich	29	Ottbergen	69-1309
NOLTE, Heinrich	15	Goettingen	68-0820
NOLTE, Joh. H.	17	Kl. Borstel	68-0610
NOLTE, Louis	30	Dekorah	68-0456
NOLTEMEYER, August	36	Lippe-Detmold	69-0429
NOLTER, Anton	27	Greffern	70-0148
NOLTING, Gerh.	18	Neufiggebruch	69-0784
NOLTING, Gerhard	41	Bueckeburg	71-0226
Sophie 41, Sophie 9, Friedrich 8, Caroline 3			
NOLTING, H.	16	Bueckeburg	70-0308
NOLTING, Simon	30	Lippe Detmold	69-0268
NOLTZ, Peter	25	Obernthal	68-0625
NONN, Friedrich	20	Wichtshausen	68-0852
NONN, Josef	34	Coblenz	69-0015
NOR, Joseph	31	Wallhausen	71-0792
NORDEN, Diedrich	24	Nordcampen	68-0566
Heinrich 17			

NAME	AGE	RESIDENCE	YR-LIST
NORDEN, Herm.	26	Suedwalsede	68-0566
NORDEN, Hermann	14	Potsdam	68-0707
NORDENSCHILD, Tina	30	Boston	70-1003
Fanny 8, Sarah 6, Babette 9 months			
NORDHAUSEN, Johann	17	Hannover	69-0672
NORDMANN, Betha	23	Horst/Russia	69-0049
NORDMEYER, Anna	21	Hatten	68-0884
NORDMEYER, Heinrich	17	Heidhausen	68-0786
NORDSIECK, Herm.	16	Oldendorf	70-1055
NORDWALD, H.	30	Alverdissen	70-0728
NORT, Philipp	28	Luxemburg	68-0939
NORTHOFER, W.	25	Freistadt	69-0050
NORWEG, Conrad	15	Frielendorf	69-0798
NOSTER, Gottlieb	18	Neudorf/Prussia	69-0547
NOTHNAGEL, Ernestine	30	Radolin	71-0479
NOWACK, Peter	31	Niezyhow	70-0204
NOWATNY, Antonie	37	Adony	71-0815
Antonie 5, Johann 3, Anna 7 months			
NOWETRY, Wenzel	20	Boehmen	69-1309
NRIEMANN, Geert	38	Deegveld	68-0566
NUEFNER, Johann	23	Oberschulz	69-0771
NUERNBERG, Bertha	20	Berlin	71-0479
NUERNBERG, Carl	21	Mellenau	71-0521
NUERNBERG, Heinrich	27	Mecklenburg	68-0770
NUERNBERGER, Emil	21	Lohsa	68-0456
NUERNBERGER, Emilie	27	Greiz	68-0907
Ida 7			
NUESE, Franz	24	Arnsberg	68-1027
NUESSE, Anna	29	Lohne	71-0581
NUHN, Heinrich		Grossmansrode	69-0457
NUHN, Justus	20	Reckrod	68-0534
NULSEN, Johanna	22	Hannover	68-0610
NUNNENMANN, J.	24	Paderborn	68-0852
NUSS, Anton	29	Towolla/Polen	69-0576
Catharina 27, Pauline 1, Stanislaus 2			
NUSSBAUM, Christine	28	Plochingen	70-0170
NUSSBAUM, Imanuel	18	Edersbach	70-0170
NUSSBAUMER, Peter	25	Lingenau	68-0534
NUTTELMANN, Marie	20	Hannover	71-0736
Niewoehner, August	18	Duisburg	68-0760
OBENKACK, Johann	23	Hartershausen	69-0208
OBERCOCK, L.	26	Paris	69-1076
Alexander 4			
OBERHAUSEN, Ludw.	33	Wien	69-1212
OBERLAND, Friedr.	30	Grossgartach	71-0789
Julie 7			
OBERMEYER, Josef	58	Muenchen	70-0569
Johanne 26, Friedrich 29			
OBERMEYER, Ludwig	17	Huellhorst	68-0566
Carl 40			
OBERNDORF, Gust.	16	Rimbach	71-0521
OBERNDORF, Hermann	18	Reimbach	69-0268
OBERNDORF, Minna	25	Rimbach	71-0521
OBERSTELLER, L.	26	Koadjuethen	68-0820
OBERT, Rosine	43	Steinach	68-0786
Veronica 23			
OBERWOEHRMANN, A.	14	Dehlinghausen	71-0456
OBROCK, Casper	28	Eicken	69-1004

NAME	AGE	RESIDENCE	YR-LIST
Catharine 29, Louise 2, Caroline 6 months			
OBSTFELDER, Carl	37	Weimar	69-1319
OCH, Catharina	42	Hinhahn	68-0647
OCHS, Barb.	21	Kirchheim	71-0167
OCHS, Elisabeth	28	Babenhausen	69-1212
OCHS, Josef	24	St. Ingbert	70-1003
OCHS, Minna	21	Oberzell	68-0939
OCKINGA, Dirk	56	Manslagt	68-1027
Peilje 54, Hankea 18, Tomke 11			
ODEMOELLER, J.	59	Friedrichsthal	71-0363
ODENWELLER, Cath.	20	Friedrichsthal	68-0957
ODERMANN, Stephan	45	Bernkastel	68-0820
Alexandrine 25, Anna M. 4, Franziska 2, Theodor 10 months, Joseph 17			
OECHLA, Kath.	24	Darmstadt	71-0393
OECHLIESS, Johann	29	Wonsowin	70-0308
OECHSLER, Apollonia	60	Reutli	68-0707
OECKLER, Carl	24	Gera	69-0848
OECTERING, G.H.	24	Reissebeck	69-1212
OEFFINGER, Matheus	23	Trossingen	68-1006
OEFINGER, Anna	40	Oldingen	70-0452
OEFINGER, Friedrich	27	Adingen	70-0355
Marie 54, John 19			
OEHL, Leonhard	34	Dorsheim	68-0907
OEHLER, Alois	42	Laas	68-0647
OEHLER, Anton	30	Rudolstadt	68-0872
OEHLER, Carl	16	Grochwitz	69-1396
OEHLMANN, Conrad	43	Louisville	71-0821
OEHLSCHLAEGER, Carl	24	Cronstadt	69-1309
OEHM, Anna	19	Ersrode	68-0534
OEHME, Christ.	56	Allstedt	68-0534
Wilhelmine 48, Charles 22, Wilhelmine 19, Hermann 15			
OEHME, Christine	32	Allstedt	68-0534
Therese 9 months			
OEHNE, Theodor	20	Frankfurt	71-0456
OEHRING, Bernhard	52	Manebach	69-0229
Therese 53, Hannibal 14, Ferdinand 9, Robert 19			
OEHRUNG, Friedrich	22	Ohrauf	68-0314
OELERICH, John	37	Wanna	71-0643
OELERICH, Wilhelmine	27	Holte	68-0647
OELKRUG, Wilhelm	23	Nuertingen	69-0457
OELRICH, Carl	26	Rethem	68-0884
Augusta 23			
OERKE, August	30	Brockeln	68-0661
OERTEL, Louise	24	Ribera	68-0456
OERTEL, Marie	21	Lobenstein	71-0681
OESTERHAUS, Wilhelm	29	Lippe Detmold	70-0378
OESTERLE, Josepha	26	Hechingen	68-0610
Recentia 5			
OESTERREICHER, D.	21	Alsheim	68-0566
OESTLER, Martin	54	Winzoefer	68-0707
OESTREICHER, Caroline	22	Primanens	71-0681
OETJEN, Cord	16	Sudweihe	71-0521
OETTER, Conrad	20	Pechgraben	68-0707
Johann 21			
OETTER, Johann	49	Pechgraben	69-0848

NAME	AGE	RESIDENCE	YR-LIST
Barbara 51, Adam 26, Margreth 17, Margreth 15			
OETTIG, Lu.	37	Leipzig	71-0681
Christine 31, Auguste 9, Jacob 8, Hulda 5, Ernstine 3			
OETTING, Carl	15	Bremen	69-0162
OETTING, Heinrich	34	Borstel	69-0229
Christian 34, Dorothea 35, Wilhelmine 3, Marie 1			
OETTING, Wilhelm		Harrienstadt	69-1319
OETTINGER, Jacob	27	Marienbronn	71-0712
OETZEL, Elise	26	Cassel	69-0050
OETZEL, Jacob	22	Breitenbach	68-0939
Elizabeth 18			
OETZEL, John	28	Breitenbach	70-0223
OEVERMANN, H.	20	Wehbergen	69-0100
OFF, Pauline	30	Sellbach	71-0363
OFFENBACHER, Otto	17	Ober Ohnen	71-0681
OFFENSANDT, Marie	22	New York	69-0923
OFFERMANN, Johann	20	Ringstedt	71-0429
OFTRING, Marg.	22	BUEHLER	70-0170
OHDEN, Freerk Peters	23	Canhusen	69-0572
Pauline 50			
OHL, Adam	16	Dudenhofen	71-0456
OHL, Cath.	24	Semt	68-0566
OHLAND, Agnes	25	Bederkesa	69-0542
OHLE, Johannes	29	Brunswick	70-0523
Helene 3			
OHLENDORF, C.	56	Braunschweig	68-0610
Christine 52, Johanna 17, Louise 9			
OHLENDORF, Fritz	27	Gitter	69-0208
OHLENDORF, Heinrich	47	Peine	68-0314
Marie 42, Louis 9, Anna 8, Willi 6			
OHLENDORF, Wilhelm	24	Braunschweig	69-1212
OHLMANN, Magd.	28	Schwiezhausen	70-0569
OHLMEYER, Ferdinand	21	Kopenhagen	69-0208
OHLSEN, Carl	22	Hamburg	70-0184
OHLSEN, Lueder	17	Hagen	68-0456
OHLWEHRTES, Franz	19	Mittelfranken	69-1011
OHM, E.	56	Terre Haute	71-0815
OHM, Louise	22	Minden	69-0029
OHM, Wilhelmine	20	Blumenthal	68-0820
OHMSTEDE, Bernhard	17	Lippe Detmold	69-0268
OHNEN, Heinrich	42	St. Joost	69-0490
Cath. 37, Marie 8, Rudolph 6, Johanne 3			
OHNMACHT, Math.	26	Dummingen	68-0566
OHRENSCHALL, Johanna	26	Treffert	69-0457
OHRMUND, Carl	40	Golz	68-0753
Henriette 41, August 8, Anna 6			
OHRT, August	42	Ottendorf	68-0820
OHSEE, Anna	9	Delmenhorst	69-0841
Fritz 12			
OHSEL, Anna	9	Delmenhorst	69-0841
Fritz 12			
OKEN, Ida E.	32	Antwerp	68-1049
Johanna 1			
OLDAG, Maria	19	Hannover	68-0456
OLDENBUETTEL, Ber.	19	Hannover	71-0479
OLDENBURG, Carl	26	Mecklenburg	70-1023
Caroline 24, Carl 3 months			
OLDENBURG, H.	15	Sandstedt	69-0429
OLDIGES, Angela	28	Asthendorf	68-1006
OLDING, Emilie	15	Lastrup	71-0521
OLDING, Wilhelm A.	35	Lastrupp	68-1006
OLINGER, Franz O.	20	Solingen	68-1049
OLK, Lucia	23	Neidenbach	68-0939
OLLERICH, Maria	17	Schellendorf	71-0363
OLLIGS, Imke	44	Ihrhove	69-0229
Etje 14, Belke 11, Johanne 8, Wilhelmine 5			
OLM, Marie	22	Jezzyn	68-0625
Helene 3, Max 9 months			
OLMLAND, August	18	Hannover	71-0736
OLPP, Herm.	18	Urach	68-0884
OLSCHUNSKI, Caroline	29	Ciganer	71-0479
Auguste 4, Carl 2			
OLTE, Friedr.	34	Rodenberg	69-0576
Sophie 35, Louise 7, Sophie 9 months			
OLTHAUS, Helena	26	Stavern	69-0229
OLTMANN, Mary	22	Oldenburg	69-0841
OLTMANN, Wilhelm	44	Reipstrolt	69-0784
OLTMANNS, Heinrich	32	Westerhauderfeh	71-0429
Wilhelmine 36, Eilert 8, Theda 4, Friedrich 6 months			
OLTMANNS, Juergen	36	Oldenburg	68-0314
Marie 18			
OLWEGER, Fr	27	Austria	70-0170
John 24			
OLWEZER, Fr.	27	Austria	70-0170
OMASCH, Alb.	23	Salakowo	71-0521
ONKEN, Sophie	16	Abbehausen	68-0625
OPAL, Cath.	30	Weissenberg	71-0521
OPEL, Christian	23	Offenbach	71-0429
OPITZ, Christine	23	Merchingen	69-1086
OPITZ, Friedrich Bernhard	21	Chemnitz	68-0865
OPPATTVIN, Wenzel	40	Kralowitz	71-0429
Anna 35, Anna 14, Marie 9, Anton 8			
OPPEL, Dorothea	24	Ober Franken	69-1086
OPPEL, Guido	16	Meiningen	68-0852
OPPEL, Theodor	48	Rudolstadt	71-0429
Octavia 46, Anna 22, Albin 16, Edwin 8, Louise 6			
OPPENHEIM, Anna	70	Anweneburg	68-0534
OPPENHEIMER, Babette	47	Rimbach	70-1003
OPPENHEIMER, Ester	26	Mittenberg	69-0208
OPPENHEIMER, Heinrich	49	Mannheim	69-1309
Rose 49, Sieger 19, Sophie 17, Minna 9, Julius 8, Adelheid 7, Ludwig 5			
OPPENHEIMER, Herm.	27	Hannover	70-1142
Henriette 23			
OPPENHEIMER, S.	19	Mannheim	69-1319
OPPENHEIMER, male	19	Fuerth	69-0490
Charlotte 3			
OPPENNAUER, Cath.	30	Katzenheim	68-0770
Catharine 10			
OPPERMANN, Carl	16	Hannover	69-0771
OPPERMANN, David	44	Harbke	68-0707
Friedrike 37, Elise 13, Wilhelm 11, Carl 7, August 5, Georg 10 months, Anna 2			
OPPERMANN, Louis	38	Hannover	70-0170

NAME	AGE	RESIDENCE	YR-LIST
OPPERMANN, Marie	16	Alfeld	68-0314
OPPERMANN, Philipp	19	Mannheim	70-0329
OPPERS, Peter	19	Uluyn	69-1396
Marie 26			
ORDENSHEIM, Joseph	22	Nuerenberg	69-0067
ORENSTEIN, Salomon	70	Hammerstadt	71-0429
Anna 50, Elisabeth 15, Carl 9			
ORLEMANN, Magda.	39	Philadelphia	70-1003
Philipp 9			
ORMILECKI, Anton	42	Camin	69-0547
ORTBRING, Elise	15	Badbergen	71-0226
Hermann 13, Anna 9			
ORTBRINK, Johann	16	Grothe	69-0968
Helene 18			
ORTH, Wilhelm	26	Siegen	70-0329
ORTLOFF, Anna	22	Coburg	70-1003
ORTLOFF, Edward	31	New York	70-1003
ORTMANN, Maria	18	Westfalen	70-0728
ORTMEIER, Christ.	44	Calldorf	68-0610
Christine 34, Simon 17, Conrad 9, Marie 13, Anna 7, Sophia 4, Friedrich 6 mont			
ORTON, William	43	New York	70-0089
ORZEL, Johann	28	Lupkau	69-0457
Anna 20			
OSBERGHAUS, Aug.	24	Solingen	68-0647
OSCHMANN, Nicol	35	Steinbach	71-0479
Friederike 31, Lina 8, August 6			
OSENBRUECK, Maria	27	Tuetzlar	71-0581
Heinrich 3, Helene 10 months			
OSER, Johann	30	Altstadt	71-0226
Anna 38, Caroline 11 months, Amalie 11 months			
OSING, J. H.	52	Kl. Mimmelage	68-1006
Cath. 54, Diedrich 20			
OSMERS, Fritz	16	Brauen	69-0798
OSOLA, Marie	29	Boehmen	69-1363
Josefa 6, Anton 11 months			
OST, Joh.	24	Alsbach	69-0162
Georg 21			
OSTARP, Joh.	27	Beelen	68-314
Anna 19			
OSTENDORF, Josef	15	Oldenburg	71-0821
OSTENDORF, Joseph	28	Mettingen	69-0583
OSTERBRINK, Georg	27	Ibbenbuehren	68-0456
OSTERHOLZ, Joh.	33	Nordholz	71-0821
Marie 33, Heinr. 4, Anna 11 months			
OSTERHUSEN, Diedr.	26	Munderlah	69-1363
OSTERLAND, Theo	29	Cantzan	71-0479
Minna 31, Minna 9, Carl 7, Anna 2			
OSTERLOH, John	22	Hannover	69-1212
OSTERLOH, Wilhelm Ch.	28	Bremen	70-0816
OSTERMEYER, Wme.	18	Kohlenfeld	68-0534
OSTERNDORF, Sofia	18	Luedelehde	69-0338
OSTERRITTER, Barthel	40		70-0223
OSTERTAG, Jacob	23	Gmuend	69-0848
OSTERTAG, Victoria	24	Mogglingen	71-0429
Johanne 23			
OSTERTHUN, Diedr.	34	Munderlah	69-1363
OSTHOLTHOFF, Selmus	36	Andervenne	68-1002
Marianne 33, Gerhard 2, Anna 9 months			

NAME	AGE	RESIDENCE	YR-LIST
OSTMANN, Bernhard	18	Hagen	68-1002
OSWALD, Therese	21	Hamelburg	68-0707
OSWALD, Wilhelm	36	Fladingen	69-0798
Louise 34, Maria 9, Johanne 8, Franz 3			
OTERIEN, Meta	29	Achim	69-0079
OTT, Anna	19	Rothenburg	69-0560
OTT, Barb.	20	Neuenkirchen	71-0581
OTT, Caroline	20	Gera	69-1309
OTT, Chls.	18	Rothenburg	69-0560
OTT, G.	18	Mittenberg	71-0789
OTT, Gottlieb	26	Adelmannfelden	69-0429
OTT, Joh.	25	Eichenbuehl	68-0647
OTT, Johann	31	Hetschigen	69-0457
OTT, Ludwig	18	Wuenzenweiler	69-0560
OTT, Magd.	21	Aschstetten	69-1059
Anna 1			
OTT, Margreth	22	Hochstadt	71-0643
OTT, Mathias	41	Kell	68-0760
Elisa 45, Margaretha 18, Johann 14, Susanna 9, Anna 7, Elisa 5, Peter 3, Matth			
OTT, Paul	19	Kirchheim	69-0182
OTT, Wilhelm	22	Fuerth	68-1006
OTTE, Diedrich		Verden	71-0226
OTTE, Johann	14	Nuernberg	69-0321
OTTE, Wilhelm	51	Braunsberg	69-0771
Dorothee 44, Hermann 17, Emilie 16, Franz 12, Albert 9, Edmund 6, Bertha 4			
OTTEMANN, Anne	17	Oldenburg	70-0204
OTTEN, Hannah	24	Lehe	68-0820
OTTEN, Heinrich	21	Koehlen	71-0429
OTTEN, J. C.	17	Meyersburg	68-1006
OTTEN, Joh.	15	Horstedt	69-1004
OTTEN, Johann	18	Grossenhain	69-0672
OTTEN, Johann	26	Krautheim	68-0939
OTTEN, Meta	32	Hagen	69-1011
OTTEN, Meta	21	Hannover	69-1086
OTTENBACHER, Eva	50	Muschardt	71-0479
Cath. 20			
OTTENHEIMER, Mr.		Havre	70-0259
OTTERSOESER, David	16	Fuerth	71-0172
OTTERSTADT, Johann	17	Otterstedt	68-0707
OTTERSTEDT, Catharine	22	Sottrum	71-0429
OTTERSTEDT, Christine	14	Winningen	71-0521
OTTERWIESS, Bernhard	25	Sevelden	70-0682
OTTMANN, Franz	18	Hammelburg	68-0647
OTTMANN, Johann	19	Clevers	69-0784
Gerhard 17			
OTTO, Auguste	34	Greitsch	71-0712
Minna 32, Pauline 26, Richard 22			
OTTO, Friederich	34	Renzkau/Prenzla	69-0968
Henriette 34, Anna 11 months			
OTTO, Georg	33	Hannover	68-0456
OTTO, Gertrud	25	Dula	68-1006
OTTO, Guenther	30	Meiningen	69-1076
OTTO, Heinrich	16	Eberschuetz	68-0820
OTTO, Hermine	22	Bremen	68-0820
OTTO, Ida	23	Berlin	70-1035
Martha 2			
OTTO, Peter	38	Pacussen	69-1363

NAME	AGE	RESIDENCE	YR-LIST
OTTO, Sophie	17	Hannover	68-0456
OTTO, Wilhelm	47	Nienburg	69-0015
OTTO, Wilhelmine	29	Neustaedle	69-0015
OTZELER, Joh.	29	Lossburg	69-1363
OVERHAGE, Arnold Heinrich 31	32	Luedinghausen	68-0625
OVERLAMM, Hermann	21	Coeln	69-1076
OVERMANN, Anna	18	Albershoh	68-0907
Omeyer, Wilh. Knippe Marie, Heinr. 3, Wilhelm 11 months	26	Graul	71-0821
Otte, Carl	24	Hetlerje	68-0820
PABST, Caroline	15	Rudolstadt	68-0625
PABST, Friedrich	26	Braunschweig	70-0683
PABST, Magdalene	18	Darmstadt	70-0378
PABST, Mathilde	19	SSchwarzb. Rude	69-0672
PACHE, Carl	32	Leipzig	68-0820
PACHER, Anna	32	Tenkseufen	68-0661
PACHNER, Adolf	18	Bamberg	69-0848
PACOWSKY, Wenzel	20	Kuttenberg	71-0492
PADEWITZ, Peter Anna 27	30	Neuenkirchen	69-0542
PAECHTER, Marie Anna 9	51	Sedlitz	69-1004
PAEPKE, Heinr. Wilh. 17	19	Otterndorf	68-0982
PAESOLD, Johann	18	Fleissen	69-0848
PAETZ, Andreas	17	Dehren	71-0492
PAETZ, Erich	20	Bueckeburg	71-0821
PAETZ, Minna	16	Lobke	70-1035
PAGEL, Alwine	18	Claushagen	71-0684
PAGEL, Dorothea	53	Gr. Wachlin	69-0672
PAGEL, Joh.	71	Colberg	70-0272
PAGEL, Johann	66	Rosenhagen	70-1055
PAGELER, Gerd Johann 25	18	Marx	68-0907
PAHE, Hermine	28	Birlingen	69-0292
PAHL, Friedrich	17	Margonin	71-0736
PAHL, Heinrich	28	Alfeld	69-1319
PAHL, Herm.	28	New York	69-1363
PAHLMANN, Willy	25	Greifwalde	69-0672
PAHR, Joseph Ernestine 31	31	Halberstadt	69-0576
PAIDLER, Friedr.	36	Metzbruch	71-0821
PALENTE, Hermann Marie 28, Herm. 5 months	33	Elberfeld	70-0569
PALLICH, Christian	32	Berlin	69-0542
PALM, Bernhard	26	Heinsheim	69-0490
PALM, Jacob	27	Nassau	69-0672
PALM, Richard	22	Breslau	69-0542
PALMER, Chr. S.	30	Aurich	68-1027
PALMER, Ferdinand	47	Bremel	69-0771
PALMERT, Eugen	20	Hardheim	69-0182
PALS, Dirk	26	Bunderheimik	69-0429
PAMPLUM, Joh.	27	Ratzgrund	68-0786
PANNNENBORG, Rud.	22	Ostfriesland	70-0378
PANTHOF, Gronewald	31	Holtrop	69-0208
PANZER, Johann	29	Hirschheide	69-0321
PANZMEYER, Wilh.	25	Gottwald	71-0789
PAPE, August	17	Hambergen	71-0456
PAPE, Elise	18	Drackel	71-0429
PAPE, Ferdinand Therese 24, Anna 15, Peter 7, Joseph 5, Franz 6 months, Elisabeth 37	34	R.B. Arnsberg	68-0884
PAPE, Joh.	30	Lindheim	70-1066
PAPE, Leopold	19	Lemgo	69-0457
PAPE, Lewis	40	Bremen	69-0050
PAPE, Louise	26	Warendorf	68-0534
PAPKEN, Peter	26	Hannover	71-0429
PAPST, Minna	18	Markoldendorf	71-0581
PARADIES, Cath.	23	Everstein	70-0728
PARADIES, Marie	21	Oldenburg	70-0178
PARCHMANN, Carl	18	Liepen	69-0547
PARDAU, Mary	23	Laaske	69-0338
PARDON, Charlotte	24	Wittenssen	70-1142
PARIS, Justus	28	Koenigser	71-0167
PARISETTE, Henry Sophie 17	14	Duelmen	70-1003
PARTKUM, Christine	23	Krumbach	68-0456
PARTMANN, Herm. Adelheid 18	26	Wietmarschen	71-0581
PASCAL, Emil Martha 3	40	Berlin	68-0939
PASCHKE, Johann Henriette 45, Friedrich 16, Gustav 4	51	Ledwiskowo	69-0457
PASNANSKI, Henriette	21	Lissa	69-0560
PASSMANN, Franz	28	Aachen	69-0268
PAST, Elisa	21	Oberselters	68-0314
PASTLE, Rud. Dorothee 33, Otto 11, Anna 9, Lina 8, Albert 7, Mathilde 5, Friedr. 4, Oscar 1	39	Hannover	70-1142
PATENDEICH, Brigitte	28	Schellendorf	71-0363
PATERS, Johann Anna 9, Carl 7, Helene 5	37	Lippe Detmold	69-0268
PATHE, Carl	22	Bolkenhain	68-1002
PATRY, Georg	17	Bortzheim	69-0429
PATZELT, Joseph	26	Kortez	69-0547
PATZER, Friedrich August 22	25	Bagnitz	71-0456
PAUK, Caroline	20	Laer	69-0229
PAUK, Heinrich	18	Laer	69-0429
PAUL, Albert	30	Pommern	69-0672
PAUL, Carl	26	Potsdam	68-0625
PAUL, Chr.	24	Villingen	68-0884
PAUL, Friedrich Louise 27	30	Sichow	69-0672
PAUL, Rudolph	24	Lubeza	68-0707
PAUL, Wilhelm	25	Schadeleben	69-0672
PAULI, Heinrich	58	Gera	68-0456
PAULI, Ma.	40	Bremen	70-0378
PAULICH, Carl	28	Prosec	68-0770
PAULSCHEN, Jacob	16	Donnern	69-0968
PAULSEN, Ernestine	20	Barntrup	68-0982
PAULSEN, Heinr.	16	Altenbruch	68-314
PAULUS, Anna Wenzel 9 months	29	Koenigswart	68-0566
PAULUS, Heinrich	39	Coblenz	68-0456

NAME	AGE	RESIDENCE	YR-LIST
Catharine 42, Elise 13, Friedrich 9, Gottfried 9			
PAULY, Emma	17	Darmstadt	70-0308
PAUR, Caroline	19	Tuchsenfeld	69-0429
PEBLER, Valentin	29	Bonn	68-0760
Maria 31, Peter 8 months			
PECH, Anna	22	San Francisco	69-1212
PECHER, Elisabeth	67	Waldeck	71-0429
PECK, August	23	Oldenburg	69-0592
PECKCHOW, Albertine	24	Klokow	69-0572
PEDERSON, Christian	15	Otterndorf	69-0542
PEDRAGLIA, Johane	30	Mainz	69-0162
Bertha 8, Johanne 7			
PEDROWITSCH, Nicolaus	25	Hardt	70-0184
PEEPIANG, Anna	20	Loebenstein	68-0939
Hermann 18			
PEIK, Caroline	23	Lippe Detmold	70-0355
Friedrike 18, Friedrich 9			
PEINZIG, Pauline	15	Heilbronn	68-0852
PEISAR, Maria	21	Opolschitz	71-0429
PEITZ, Johann	25	Moellitz/Meckle	69-0547
PEK, Christine	22	Iserheide	68-0625
PELEKAN, Maria	55	Boehmen	69-1363
Josefa 33, Anton 9 months			
PELIKAN, Johann	36	Pilsen	69-0592
PELLENS, John	16	Burgdamm	68-0957
Mary 20			
PELLHORST, Franz	19	Riefberg	70-0184
PELMAN, Mathilde	18	Philadelphia	70-1003
Louise 19			
PELSTER, Emilie	20	Warendorf	69-1076
PELTZ, L.	27	Detmold	71-0521
PELZER, And.	21	Alsfeld	71-0393
PENN, Auguste	21	Gr. Lubs	71-0733
PENNING, Albert	28	Halten	71-0479
Teke 26, Peter 11 months			
PENNING, Eilert	19	Hannover	69-1004
Dielke 19, Amke 33			
PENSHORN, Georg	50	Marklendorf	68-0456
Catharine 46, Gustav 12			
PENSOLDT, Hermann	21	Priesen	69-0182
PENZ, John	34	Austria	70-0170
PEPER, Cord	17	Fissherhude	71-0456
PEPER, Johann	24	Fischerhude	68-0786
PEPPLER, Henriette	30	Darmstadt	69-1059
Christine 33, Wilhelm 9 months			
PERANT, Anton	42	Grunda	70-0329
Barbara 36, Pauline 5			
PERAUTKA, Josef	50	Boehmen	70-0384
Catharina 49, Franz 18, Tilemann 16, Wenzel 13, Se. 9			
PERJON, Maria	36	Unterkrain	68-0707
Johann 15, Andreas 7, Jacob 2, Josef 6 months			
PERNISS, Theodor	19	Weimar	68-0872
PERRET, Cecilie	29	Oeschelbronn	68-1006
PERSATZ, Christ.	26	Hesslingen	68-0566
Caroline 19			
PESCH, Barbara	40	Bos	68-0625
Jacob 15, Caspar 8, Mathias 6, Catharine 8 months			
PESCHEL, Hermann	23	Neuschuetz	69-0321
PESEL, Anton	30	Trieste	68-1027
Marie 25			
PESSEFALL, Minna	13	Mellsheim	71-0643
PETA, Fred.	50	Charlesten	69-1011
Mary 40			
PETA, Joseph	17	Rielingen/Rieti	68-0957
PETER, Christian	50	Schwarzenborn	68-0707
PETER, Christian	19	Babenheim	71-0429
PETER, Daniel	27	Friedewald	68-0625
Caroline 24			
PETER, Elisabeth	23	Friedewald	71-0736
PETER, Gertraud	45	Kurhessen	69-0672
Meta 17, Johann 15, Jacob 13, Gustav 9			
PETER, Heinr.	25	Densberg	68-0982
PETER, Johann	25	Ichstaedt	69-0848
PETER, Louise	29	Tennstedt	68-0534
PETER, Magdalena	40	Nievernheim	68-0707
Joseph 16, Jacob 7, Gerhard 6, Philipp 3, Gottfried 11 months, Margaretha 59			
PETER, Nicolaus	45	Maltendingen	70-0204
Marie 42, Louise 15, Wilhelm 9, Caroline 7			
PETER, Ursula	24	Fuerth	70-0178
PETERKA, Wenzl	25	Saarbruecken	68-0534
PETERLEIN, Joh. Gottl.	55	Hermsdorf	71-0736
Marie 50, Reinhard 17, Traugott 13, Eduard 12, Rosine 21			
PETERMANN, Anna	27	Lehe	70-0329
PETERMANN, Friederike	60	Frankfurt a/M	69-1212
Louise 20			
PETERMANN, Jacob	18	Frankfurt a/M	69-1212
PETERMANN, Margarethe	17	Thedinghausen	68-0939
PETERS, August	31	Sachsen	69-0559
PETERS, August	21	Hannover	71-1046
Emilie 20, Emma 10 months			
PETERS, Carl	22	Sulingen	69-0162
PETERS, Carl	18	Wellendingen	70-0223
PETERS, Friedrich	17	Osterhorn	69-0784
PETERS, Heinrich	30	Essens	68-0707
PETERS, Heinrich	66	Leeste	68-0661
Anna 64			
PETERS, Johann	32	Wiedenhagen	70-0223
Henriette 34, Christian 30			
PETERS, Maria	9	Prim	71-0581
PETERS, Marie	23	Hannover	68-1027
PETERS, Peter J.	30	Weishosen	69-0798
Gertrude 25, Christine 2, Maria 9 mo			
PETERS, Robert	33	Sachsen	69-1004
PETERSEN, Antje	22	Ostfriesland	69-1011
PETERSEN, Joh. W.	18	Luedingworth	68-0647
PETERSEN, Lauritz	22	Copenhagen	68-0647
PETERSEN, Pet. H.	20	Schleswig	70-0223
PETERSHAGEN, A.	26	Hannover	70-0728
PETERSOHN, Aug.	34	Neuschoenefeld	68-1298
Friederike 30			
PETERSSEN, Joh.	16	Lankenau	71-0479
PETRAS, Heinr.	26	Bueden	71-0821

NAME	AGE	RESIDENCE	YR-LIST
PETRI, Georg	26	Mosbach	71-0363
PETRIE, Jacob	29	Berkach	68-0907
PETRIE, Thomas	39	Kallin	70-1023
Anna 40, Arnold 9			
PETRITZ, Matth.	19	Krain	70-0384
PETRY, Helene	27	Darmstadt	70-0378
PETRY, Philip	40	Reichenborg	71-0479
PETRZILKA, Anna	55	Boehmen	69-1076
Anton 7, Emanuela 5			
PETSCH, Adolph	16	Frankfurt a/M	69-1212
PETTERS, Sophie	17	Lienen	69-0968
PETTIG, Heinrich	20	Kluckhof	69-0268
PETZ, Anna	16	Schwarzenborn	71-0479
PETZ, Barbara	14	Edesheim	71-0429
PETZGER, Christian	56	St. Louis	70-1055
PETZOLD, Barb.	21	Schneitach	71-0815
PETZOLD, Emil	20	Mulsewitz	71-0733
PETZOLD, Gottlieb	22	Eisenach	69-1363
PETZOLD, Paul Joh.	19	Kirchberg	69-0321
PEUBERT, John	19	Jesserndorf	70-1161
PEXAS, Georg	30	Gorjenow	69-0547
PFAB, Wilhelmine	18	Roschau	68-0982
PFAFF, Friedrich	56	Grebenstein	68-0939
PFAFF, Georg	36	Sonnenkahe	71-0733
Pauline 24			
PFAFF, Georg	27	Rothenburg	71-0363
PFAFF, Maria Cath.	17	Hirschfeld	68-0770
PFAFF, N.	36	Zimmern	71-0521
PFAFF, Ottilie	24	Harthausen	69-1086
PFAFF, Peter	24	Darmstadt	69-1212
PFAFFENBACH, John	51	Hessen	70-0508
Guenter 51, Anna 17, Daniel 15, August 15, Catherine 11, Diedrich 9			
PFAFFENBERGER, Joh.	46	Bayreuth	71-0521
Elisab. 48, August 17			
PFALZ, Joseph	39	Fegernbach	71-0736
Regine 39, Stephan 9, Walpurga 3, Joseph 11 months			
PFALZGRAF, Anna	28	Zella	70-0452
PFANDTNER, Carl	31	Leipzig	70-0384
PFANDTNER, Rud.	38	Leipzig	70-0384
Wilhelmine 25, Hermann 5			
PFANKUCHE, Wilhelm	26	Braunschweig	69-0672
PFANNENSTIEHL, Theo	17	Memphis	70-1055
Marie Eva 48			
PFARRER, Conr.	73	Villingen	68-0884
PFEFF, Rosa	24	Ubstadt	68-1006
PFEFFER, Carl	20	Schluechtern	69-0592
PFEFFER, Carl	29	Bossleben	69-0429
Bertha 26, Richardt 5, Ida 9 months			
PFEFFER, Georg	21	Sommerau	68-0566
PFEIFFELMANN, Oscar	15	Stuttgart	69-0268
PFEIFFER, Aug.	17	Bombach	71-0789
PFEIFFER, Barbara	27	Erfurt	69-0229
Albert 2			
PFEIFFER, Bernhard	64	Waibenabs	68-0456
Barbara 59, Dorothea 24, Barbette 11 months			
PFEIFFER, Carl	28	Walrabs	68-0456
PFEIFFER, Caspar	15	Bergfelden	69-0798
PFEIFFER, D.	20	Bombach	71-0789
Mag. 20			
PFEIFFER, Fr.	27	Klein Sachsenhe	69-0100
Marie 24			
PFEIFFER, Francisca	26	Kaiserslautern	71-0429
PFEIFFER, Friedr.	55	Rotenburg	71-0363
PFEIFFER, Friedr.	55	Rotenburg	71-0363
PFEIFFER, Georg	40	Pensygola	69-0968
Henry 9			
PFEIFFER, Georg	16	Mannheim	70-0329
PFEIFFER, Giselle	14	Asselheim	69-0798
PFEIFFER, Heinr.	31	Darmstadt	71-0581
Magda. 21			
PFEIFFER, Herm.	24	Zeitz	69-0576
PFEIFFER, Ignatz	37	Buchen	68-1002
PFEIFFER, Jacob	18	Alsfeld	69-0229
PFEIFFER, Johann	18	Wiesenbach	68-0884
PFEIFFER, Marianne	33	Werbach	69-1396
PFEIFFER, Marie	67	Oldenburg	69-0162
Allendorf			
PFEIFFER, Marie	38	Doebeln	69-0229
Auguste 4, Marie 4			
PFEIFFER, Philipp	32	Goettelfingen	68-0456
PFEIFFER, Tugand	18	Krysgahnen	71-0479
PFEIFFER, W.	17	Bombach	71-0789
Pauline 24			
PFEIL, Anna	29	Barmen	70-0583
Emma 24			
PFEIL, Catharine	19	Pleidenroth	69-0672
PFEIL, Fried.	57	Hannover	71-0479
Gesine 52, Carl 16, Anna 14			
PFEIL, Ludwig	64	Reichelsdorf	69-0429
Georg 20, Ludwig 17, Johannes 13			
PFEITZ, Jacob	15	Klems	69-0672
PFENDER, Maria	20	Neustadt	71-0479
PFENNIGER, Johann	64	Zuerich	69-1076
PFEUFER, Theod.	20	Wetzendorf	69-1011
PFINGSTEN, August	26	Horsten	69-1396
PFINGSTEN, Carl	32	Rannenberg	71-0479
Wilhelmine 23, Heinrich 10 months			
PFINGSTEN, Herm.	16	Rotenburg	68-0753
PFISTER, Georg	50	Braunschweig	69-0229
Elisabeth 52, Elisabeth 19			
PFISTER, Jacob	29	Schweiz	69-1076
PFISTER, Jos.	19	Bachingen	71-0581
PFITZENREUTHER, Ign.	41	Doerrebach	69-0841
Catharine 35, Kilian 42, Anna 9, Heinrich 7, Friedrich 5, Louis 3			
PFITZMANN, Otto	20	Leipzig	68-1049
PFLASIEN, Therese	16	Wuerzburg	69-1059
PFLEGER, Franz	14	Heimkirchen	70-1142
PFLEGING, Julius	17	Cassel	69-1086
PFLUGER, El.	23	Volkardinghause	69-0560
PFORR, Elise	32	Prutzbach	71-0300
Elise 8, Johann 10 months, Elisab. 9			
PFORTNER, Jacob		Havre	70-0259
PFREUDER, Johann	17	Aixheim	69-0923
PFROMM, Heinrich	58	Schlenglengsfd.	68-0707
Anna 57, Heinrich 24, Johann 14			

NAME	AGE	RESIDENCE	YR-LIST
PFRUENDER, Marie	23	Aixheim	69-1309
PFUENDER, Carl	33	Nordhausen	68-0852
PFUENDER, Justine	26	Richnowfeld	68-0566
PFUFF, Michael	22	Wernshausen	68-0770
PFUND, Minna	34	New York	71-1046
Dora 5, Alfred 9 months			
PFURR, Marg.	18	Rosbach	68-0753
PHANNENSCHMIDT, Phil.	49	Bummenbach	70-0178
Rosine 43, Renni 9, Lina 11 months			
PHILIPP, Albert	29	Berlin	69-0542
Therese 26, Olga 6 months			
PHILIPP, Johann	33	Kl. Hessen/Saxo	69-0547
PHILIPPS, Eva	47	Saalfeld	68-0753
Julius 13, Marie 16			
PHILIPS, Louise	28	Bremen	69-0923
PHILIPSTHAL, Moritz	28	Raegelin	68-0625
PHILLIPS, Wm.	28	New York	69-1421
PIASETER, Christ.	30	New Bedford	69-1076
PIATH, Carl	15	Michelstadt	68-1298
PICHELBAUER, John	48	Kirchschlag	70-0355
Marie 43, Carl 9			
PICK, Rosa	28	Moldautein	68-1002
baby girl 8 months			
PICKEL, Anna	18	Liebles	71-0643
PICKEL, Bruno	5	Hohenlenben	71-0581
PIEGER, Emma	22	Guetterlitz	68-0647
PIEHLER, Fritz	29	Hahn	69-1076
PIEL, Anton	23	Neuss	69-1363
PIEPER, Arnold	16	Lippe Detmold	70-0355
PIEPER, Carl	31	Boitzenburg	71-0479
Wilhelmine 25			
PIEPER, Carl	1	Boitzenburg	71-0479
PIEPER, Heinrich	24	Ottendorf	68-1006
PIEPER, Hermann	34	Moenkehofen	71-0521
Elisabeth 20, Hermann 6 months			
PIEPER, Louise	39	Waldenhausen	68-0534
PIEPER, Louise	21	Soest	71-0363
PIEPER, Wilhelm	33	St. Mauritz	71-0684
PIEPHOFF, Marg.	25	Willstedt	71-0521
PIERING, Amalia	28	Markenkirchen	68-0661
Oswald 6,I Mathilde 3, Emma 2, Pauline 9 months			
PIGAN, Marie	22	Braunschweig	70-1003
PIGGE, Heinrich	24	Oldendorf	68-0939
PILCK, Georg	40	Boehmen	70-0178
Marie 34, Marie 8, Anna 7, Catharina 5, Georg 6 months			
PILGER, Joseph	18	Poland	68-0820
PILGERN, Marie	20	Oldendorf	71-0479
PILGRAM, Johann	29	Cassel	70-100
PILL, Anton	34	Nittenau	71-0792
PILZ, Franz	18	Reichenberg	68-0661
Robert 15			
PINKERT, Otto	32	Weissenfels	70-0308
PINNCKE, Friedrich	32	Willensen	69-0208
PINNER, Charlotte 48	48	Egichenberg	68-0456
Philipp 36			
PINNER, Franz	28	Cammin	69-0457
PINNER, Max	18	New York	69-0457

NAME	AGE	RESIDENCE	YR-LIST
PIPERLING, Franz	18	Westfalen	70-0728
PIPPEL, Christ.	50	Goersbach	68-0566
Henriette 41, Johanna 18, Johann 14, Joh. 9, Friederike 2			
PIRINGER, Alois	22	Wien	70-0682
PISACEK, Josef	16	Horti	70-0329
PISAWSKY, Valentin	33	Leszeze	69-0848
PISCH, Wilhelm	31	Berlin	68-0647
PISCHERT, Moritz	23	Lichtenberg	69-0542
PISTNER, Ottilie	21	Sonnenkahe	71-0733
Johann 24			
PISTORIUS, Friedrich	17	Waldeck	70-0259
PITSCH, Julius	17	Cassel	69-0560
PITZEN, Anton	50	Dreis	71-0581
Anna 47, Marie 18			
PIXMEYER, Wilhelmine	28	Wimmers	69-0572
PLACKUTER, Elise	22	Delmenhorst	70-0135
PLAGGE, Johann	59	Bockel	68-0625
PLANDER, Sophie	26	Bremen	70-1142
PLATE, Henry	14	Hambergen	71-0456
PLATE, Segelke	55	Anriede	69-0784
PLATH, Wilhelm		Butzfletherm.	68-0707
PLATHNER, Therese	46	Zellerfeld	68-0939
Louise 17			
PLATZ, Heinr.	24	Lemesch	71-0681
PLATZ, Leo	28	Woerth	68-0314
PLATZ, Margareth	25	Frankfurt a/M	69-0798
PLAUT, Liebman	32	Nordhausen	71-0167
PLENDEL, Joseph	19	Regensburg	69-0268
PLETTNER, Johanne	26	Bremen	69-1396
PLEUSEL, Christ.	24	Feinbreitenbach	69-1363
PLEWE, Jacob	40	Langendorf	68-0707
PLOCHAE, Josef	17	Boehmen	70-1161
PLOEGER, Christ.	17	Lippe Detmold	70-0355
PLOEGER, Josefine	50	Nieheim	71-0643
Albert 18, Therese 16			
PLONSKA, Ernestine	14	Gullub	69-1076
Adolph 9			
PLUEDDEMANN, Fried.	40	Stettin	69-0182
Caroline 31, Richard 13, Ernst 11, Anna 9, Maria 5			
PLUESKE, Louise	17	Herford	68-1027
PLUKAR, Magdalena	18	Boehmen	69-1309
PLUNTKI, Elise	32	Fuerth	68-0625
PLUSCHKE, Johanna	57	Falkenberg	68-0661
PLUTZ, Johann	32	Blottnitz	68-0707
Barbara 32, Margaretha 21, Johann 9 months, Elisabeth 3			
PODDEISEN, Eduard	28	Braunschweig	69-0968
Minna 27			
POEGER, Eduard	17	Lippe-Detmold	69-0429
POEHLMANN, Simon	24	Oberfranken	69-0798
POELKER, Simon	18	Lippe Detmold	70-0355
POELLING, Heinrich	28	Killerbeck	71-0712
POETKER, Caspar	17	Huesede	68-0647
POETTGEN, Ferd.	46	Aachen	70-0583
POGGENPOHL, August	15	Versmold	68-1002
POGGENWELLER, H.	55	Schnatthorst	68-0566
Catherine 48, Louise 19, Marie 9			

NAME	AGE	RESIDENCE	YR-LIST
POHL, Fr. Wilh.	30	Erzhausen	69-0321
POHLE, Wilhelm	17	Dueme	69-0848
POHLKAMP, Joh.	30	Telgte	68-1006
POHLMANN, Martin	17	Schoenwald	68-1027
POHMELL, Alex	25	Schleiz	69-0672
POKRZYWINSKI, Capetan	32	Nakel	68-1027
Julie 27, Baby daughter 6 months			
POLACK, August	47	Hamburg	71-0821
Dorothea 42, Gustav 16			
POLACK, Josef	17	Seltschau	71-0393
POLAREK, Franz	36	Polzin	71-0643
POLASCHINSKI, Andr.	32	Nakel	71-0581
POLATZKI, Ottilie	24	Eperies	68-0786
POLENSKA, Anna	15	Roznowo	68-0610
POLINSKY, Julius	30	Luckowo	68-0534
Julia 24			
POLINSKY, Wenzel	42	Boehmen	70-0728
Franziska 32, Maria 9, Antonia 6			
POLLACH, Siemon	25	Pest	70-0204
POLLAK, Jos.	38	Friedland	68-0610
Richard 16			
POLLERT, Wilh.	24	Schroetinghause	68-0566
POLLERT, Wilhelmine	17	Pr. Oldendorf	68-0647
POLLMANN, Joh. August	30	Essen	68-0419
Sophie 24			
POLLMER, Gustav	27	Magdeburg	70-0682
POLSKA, Catharine	25	Posen	69-0559
Antonie 5, Josepha 3, Ignatz 11 mo			
POLSTER, Babette	16	Erlangen	71-0429
POLTIMER, Georg	16	Bamberg	69-0848
POLZER, Vinzentine	20	Tropplowitz	70-1003
POMMER, Wilh.	27	Sulzbach	69-0542
POMMERENING, C.	38	Eschenring	68-0661
Henriette 48, Mathilde 18, Ida 12, Theodor 16, Wilhelm 48			
POMMERING, John	53	Wusterhausen	69-0338
Carolina 53, Louise 69, Wilhelmine 20, Charles 16, Frederic 14			
POMOWITZ, Ferd.	55	Breslau	71-0363
PONTWIG, Heinrich	24	Landersbergen	68-0314
POOHN, Therese	27	Oberoffhausen	70-0204
POPA, Franz	44	Krojank	71-0581
Anna 44, Nic. 5, Valentin 3			
POPA, Pauline	18	Blankwitt	71-0581
POPA, Stephan	20	Krojahnke	70-1035
POPE, John	16	Lintel	71-0456
POPE, Margaret	44	Zeven	68-0625
POPKES, Reemt	16	Hinte	70-0443
POPOWITZ, Jauke	27	Krain	70-0384
POPP, Andreas	22	Bamberg	69-0229
POPPE, Christine	15	Lossa	68-0456
POPPE, Ernst	30	Lipz	70-1161
POPPE, Herm.	32	Gruppenbuehren	71-0167
POPPE, Johann	21	Hermelingen	69-1059
Georg 19			
POPPE, John	19	Hannover	70-0308
POPPEL, Conrad	27	Darmstadt	69-0672
PORAK, Ernst	18	Trautenau	68-0610
PORTH, Carl	17	Duschroth	68-1027

NAME	AGE	RESIDENCE	YR-LIST
Christine 21			
PORTHESIUS, Julius	13	Gemuenden	71-0456
PORZ, Adam	23	Obernedig	71-0681
POSCHEDAG, Wilhelm	28	Herford	71-0492
POSCHEL, Marie	27	Unterkrain	68-0707
Maria 4, Anna 11 months			
POSES, Christian	26	Albersdorf	69-0968
POSS, Ignatz	27	Wojkowitz	69-0229
Rosalie 17, Albertine 1			
POSSNER, Ernst	30	Schemeritz	68-0760
POST, Johann	59	Roth	68-0982
POSTELS, Peter	24	Willstedt	71-0521
POTCHEN, Anna	30	Dreis	71-0581
POTRYKUS, August	28	Okurnirow	69-0672
Pauline 24			
POTT, Johann	55	Steiermark	71-0712
Pl. 56			
POTT, Wilhelm	29	Bielefeld	69-0162
POTTBERG, Friedrich	31	Drakenburg	69-0547
Wilhelmine 31, Friedrich 6, Elise 11 months			
POTTEBAUM, Carol.	26	Melle	68-0534
POTTHOFF, Heinrich	24	Gr. Aschen	68-1027
POTZ, Louise	26	Obersorpe	71-0492
PRACH, Maria	18	Oberaula	68-0661
PRAGER, Joseph	35	Nuernberg	68-0820
Therese 30			
PRAISSER, Carl	23	Wilsdorf	70-0378
PRANGE, Diedrich	16	Seppenhausen	68-0770
PRASSE, Julius	30	Rudolstadt	68-0625
PRASUHN, Friedrich	60	Maysville	70-1035
PRATZMANN, Adolf	27	Anderhausen	69-0490
PRECHEL, Ferd.	49	Fuhlen	68-0610
Wilhelmine 47, Wilhelmine 19, Charles 17, Friedrich 8, Anna 6, August 2			
PRECHT, Hermann	16	Droegenbostel	71-0643
PREISS, Susanne	17	Springstiller	69-0229
PRELL, Karoline	23	Hessen	69-0672
Karoline 6 months			
PRELLER, Andreas	24	Hof	69-0572
PRESCH, Ernst	27	Zeugfeld	68-1002
PRESS, Theodor	24	Tuebingen	68-1027
PREUSS, Traugott	29	Gratz	70-100
PREVOT, Mary	60	Paris	69-1011
PREZEL, Selma	23	Schwetz	70-1023
PRIBNAW, Christian	61	Brunswic	69-0771
Willemi 48, Carl 21, Bernhard 19, Johann 15, Louisa 9, Emillie 6, Marie 4			
PRICO, Wilhelmine	23	Ploenzig	69-0672
PRIEBE, August	50	Niewinko	68-0707
Wilhelmine 38, Wilhelm 19, Gustav 16, August 14, Emil 7, Paul 6, Bertha 4, Alw			
PRIEBE, Wilhelm	40	Bevensdorf	70-0569
Auguste 33, Bertha 3			
PRIECHEDA, Wenzel	18	Gall	68-0456
PRIETSCH, Fredr.	19	Untermutschl	69-1004
PRIFFE, Heinrich	17	Ziegenrueck	69-0457
PRIGGE, Emilie	16	Uthlede	70-1055
PRILLER, Max	25	Dernbach	68-0760
PRINZ, Caspar	18	Frankenberg	71-0712

NAME	AGE	RESIDENCE	YR-LIST
PRITSCH, Charlotte	26	Niederfeerbach	68-1002
PROBST, Chr.	21	Bechtheim	71-0393
PROBST, Crescenz	26	Deckendorf	71-0684
PROBST, Edward	33	Aschersleben	69-1059
Marie 25			
PROBST, Gustav	46	Bernburg	68-0625
Gustav 14			
PROBST, Heinrich	35	Mehren	68-0852
Anna 32, Catharina 5, Barbara 6 months			
PROBST, Wilh.	23	Ockenhausen	69-0162
PROEGLER, Marie	26	Nuernberg	69-0560
PROEHL, Heinrich	26	Dushhorn	68-0456
PROEHLE, Matthilde	19	Oestreich	71-0581
Ida 17, Mariane 15			
PROEPPER, Marie	22	Goldhausen	68-0786
PROKOSH, Josef	32	Hamschen	68-0456
Anna 29, Georg 5, Johann 2			
PROLLE, Georg	17	Hannover	71-0456
PROMMEYER, Arnold	18	Neuenkirchen	71-0521
PROSCHEK, Anton	41	Senojat	70-0329
Katharina 37, Anna 19, Johann 17, Franz 15, Maria 7, Anton 6, Katharina 11 mon			
PROSPER, Jac.	16	Bechtheim	71-0393
PROSS, Carl	23	Wildenfels	70-0355
PROTIVA, Mathaeus	57	Wodnau	70-0329
Katharina 58			
PROTT, Agnes	23	Magdeburg	71-0821
PROTZ, H. M.	35	Hergestfeld	71-0581
PRUEFER, Ernst Traug.	31	Gingenberg	68-1002
PRUEGER, Catharina	43	Krena	70-0204
PRUESS, Cath.	19	Zeven	71-0479
Barb. 26			
PRUESSING, Joh.	21	Freudenthal	71-0479
PRUN, William	30	Schamoder	69-0798
PSOTA, Anna	37	Kuttenberg	71-0492
Carl 9, Anna 7			
PUCHANG, Marie	22	Kuttenberg	71-0167
PUERS, Caspar	58	Warndorf	68-0760
Ida 40, Caspar 15, Bernhard 12, Gertrude 6, Anna 9, Heinrich 4			
PUESCHEL, Edw.	24	Carlsruhe	69-0923
PUESCHEL, Moritz	42	Jittau	70-0355
PUETZ, Laurenz	33	Dueren	71-0712
PUETZ, Nic.	25	Dreis	69-1011
PUFAHL, Gotthard	27	Owierzek	68-0770
PUFAHL, Marcel	16	Monkawarsk	68-0770
PULS, Wilh.	16	Altendanap	71-0681
PULVERMUELLER, B.	23	Geggingen	70-0204
PUNSNEK, Christine	24	Kallin	70-1023
PUPP, August	37	Mellen-Pommern	70-0006
PURE, Wilh.	40	Luebbecke	71-0681
Charlotte 39, Wilhelmine 15, Lisette 15, Carl 9, Caroline 7, Ernst 5, Louise			
PURNCHER, Elisabeth	34	Thierstein	69-1076
Johann 8, Joseph 3, Carl 11 months			
PURNKER, Johanne	29	Thierstein	69-1076
PUSTKUCHEN, Louise	24	Detmold	69-0457
PUTER, Otto	27	Berlin	69-0429
PUTTER, Friedrich	17	Kandern	69-0429
PZIBYL, Anna	54	Boehmen	68-0456
QUAADE, Margaretha	34	Bremen	68-1006
QUABECK, Johann	17	Elberfeld	70-0006
QUADE, Catharine	16	Cassel	68-0865
QUADE, Meta	18	Hannover	69-1076
QUADL, Henry	17	Muenchen	69-0923
QUANST, Elisabeth	21	Bahlen	68-0566
QUANTMEYER, Carl	9	Bremen	68-0939
QUATLAENDER, Marg.	23	Schoeningen	69-1212
QUELLE, Anna	47	Westheim	71-0684
QUENENGAESSER, Carl	24	Kelba	69-0457
QUERFELD, Heinrich	34	Mandelsloh	68-1027
Christine 34, Wilhelmine 9, Sophie 8, Marie 11 months			
QUEST, Louise	18	Petershagen	68-0314
QUILLE, Wilhelm	32	Ledde	68-0820
QUINDEL, Heinrich	44	Jeinsen	69-0592
Marie 42, Johanne 18, Lida 9, Carl 8, Heinrich 4			
QUOBOF, Franz	23	Neuschatel	68-0566
RAAB, Elise	20	Trais Horloff	68-0014
RAAB, Jac.	49	Oberstetten	71-0393
Elisa 44			
RAABE, Alexander	40	New York	69-0923
RAABE, Carl	20	Herford	69-1004
RAABE, Carl	41	Waltersdorf	68-0753
Johanna 45, Christian 19, Louis 16, Wilhelmine 14, Carl 12, Heinrich 10, Fried			
RAABE, Franz	34	Breitenworbis	69-0572
Charlotte 30, Adolph 2			
RAABE, Heinrich	21	Diedotz	68-0456
RAAKE, Wilhelmine	30	Vieden	68-0957
Julius 4, Baby son 4 months			
RAASE, Christian	30	Pommern	69-0672
Dorothea 59, Wilhelm 25, Ernestine 23			
RABANUS, Henry	42	Naumburg	71-0456
Helene 41, Anton 8, Helen 3, Franz 6 months			
RABASOWA, Barbara	20	Kralowitz	71-0429
RABE, Georg	19	Hannover	70-1003
RABE, Heinrich	25	Verden	69-0559
RABE, Louis	23	Lugau	69-0798
RABE, Philipp	56	Solz	71-0712
RABEL, Jacob	33	Dettingen	68-0610
Christine 30, Joh. M. 7, Joh. Jac.4			
RABIEN, Helene	20	Oldenburg	69-0771
Hanna 20			
RABING, Franz	22	Stadtbingsfeld	69-0572
RACCO, Alb.	22	Tasso	69-0490
RACHTERMANN, Fr.	50	Menden	71-0736
Julie 48, Adolf 8			
RACK, Robert	20	Heilbronn	69-0490
RADE, August	17	Nordleda	71-0429
RADECKE, Johann	64	Greifenberg	68-0939
RADEFELD, Louis	14	Dissen	71-0393
RADEMACHER, Folkert	17	Groothusen	68-0982
Sophie 26			
RADEMACHER, Hans	27	Uttum	68-0456
RADEMACHER, Tobias	50	Hannover	69-0229

NAME	AGE	RESIDENCE	YR-LIST
Nauke 25, Tobias 6 months, Dietje 46, Wuebke 26			
RADEMACHER, Wme.	21	Hannover	71-0492
RADKE, Gust.	19	Schneidemuehl	68-0753
RADKE, Gust.	17	Friedland	71-0479
RADKE, Wilhelm	25	Rienekow	68-0770
RADLER, Valentin	42	Breslau	68-0419
Gertrude 48			
RADTKE, Gottlieb	45	Ledwiskowo	69-0457
RADTKE, Julius	31	Stettin	68-0625
RADUENZEL, Wilhelmine	24	Carlsburg	68-0786
RAEBEL, Heinrich	18	Frankfurt	68-0982
RAEDER, Heinrich	19	Gollheim	69-0968
Heinrich 17			
RAEHN, Gustav	19	Bukowitz	69-0547
Auguste 24			
RAEKER, Aug.	16	Hannover	69-1004
RAEKER, Friedr.	53	Brakelsiek	68-314
Friedrich 18, Heinrich 16, Wilhelm 24			
RAEL, Daniel	28	Dettingen	68-0760
RAEMPF, Carl Ludwig	22	Waldmohr	68-1006
RAENSCHER, Philipp	25	Kriegsheim	68-0647
RAEPLE, Friedrich	18	Wittorf	71-0492
RAFFEL, Ferd.	40	Koenigsberg	69-1363
RAFFMANN, August	18	Sassmar	70-0178
RAFORT, Herman	16	Damerow	68-0625
RAGOTZKY, F.	28	Osnabrueck	69-0050
RAHDE, Cath.	21	Hatten	68-0884
RAHDE, Georg Franz	18	Kierpen	70-0272
RAHE, Minna	20	Dissen	71-0821
RAHM, Margarethe	31	Schlossborn	71-0492
RAHM, Marie	20	Hilschbach	68-0610
Joseph 22, Georg 13			
RAHMER, Friedrich	31	Offenberg	69-0542
RAHMOELLER, Heinrich	52	Holsen	68-0566
Louise 50, Christian 19, Anna 18, Heinrich 9			
RAHMS, Bernh.	25	Schoeppingen	71-0479
RAHN, Carl	23	Mirchau	69-1212
Louise 22, Minna 2, Therese 9 months			
RAHOLZ, Kunigunde	17	Pechgraben	69-0848
RAIBLE, Carl	16	Barmen	69-1212
RAIBLE, John	17	Zepfenhan	68-0534
RAICHEL, Barbara	17	Sauerhof	71-0492
RAIMBOTH, Rosalie	34	Berlin	71-0712
RAISCH, Friederike	23	Asperg	70-1035
RAISER, Gottfr.	26	Albersweiler	71-0393
RAITER, Conrad	17	Osstergen	71-0681
RAITHEL, Elise	13	Oberfranken	69-0784
RAIZNER, Josefa	39	Mestisko	71-0479
Antoniette 10 months			
RAKEJEN, Heinrich	17	Zesen	71-0712
RAKEL, Johann	24	Obergrimbach	69-0015
RALF, Heinrich	39	Hollmdorf/Russi	69-0049
Dorothea 39			
RAMM, Caroline	29	Knesebeck	68-0907
RAMME, Maria	18	Altenbruch	68-0661
RAMPA, Mary	22	Bernaditz	68-0957
RAMPENDAHL, Auguste	18	Engerte	71-0643

NAME	AGE	RESIDENCE	YR-LIST
RAMSDORF, Wilhelmine	50	Elberfeld	71-0581
RAN, Philipp	28	Hahn	69-1076
RANDEK, Franz	27	Bernburg	69-0100
RANG, Heinrich	28	Freiburg	68-1027
RANK, Georg	18	Lichtenberg	71-0479
Henriette 21			
RANK, Johanne	20	Lichtenberg	70-0443
RANK, Leonhard	24	Neuhausen	68-0786
RANKE, Elise	41	Darmstadt	69-1309
RANKE, Ernst	17	Frankfurt	71-0643
RANNER, Peter	57	Sahren	71-0300
Susanne 55, Marie 18, Charlotte 16, Caroline 9			
RANNKE, Auguste	42	Reitz	69-0672
RAPP, Andreas	20	Laufen	69-0784
RAPP, Carl	35	Giesen	71-0429
RAPP, Conrad	18	Kirnbach	68-0760
RAPPACHER, Johannes	30	Pfalheim	69-0968
RAPPE, Mathilde	31	Birlingen	69-0292
Marie 1			
RAPPER, Carl	25	Hannover	70-0089
RAPS, Sofia	33	Letten	69-0560
Barbara 6, Rebecca 11 months			
RARAJCZAK, Joseph	28	Sielex	68-0456
Antonia 26, Xaver 9 months			
RASCH, Nicolaus	16	Pfeddersheim	69-0572
RASCHE, Friedr.	27	Hille	69-0583
RASCHEN, John	59	Oldenburg	70-0355
Anna 56			
RASENBAUM, Elke	49	Aurich	69-1004
RASENFELD, Helene	24	Benyen	69-1004
RASSFELD, Georg	61	Schwetzingen	69-1363
Otto 5			
RASSNER, Fr.	28	Schwiezhausen	70-0569
RASTEDE, Johanna	18	Twelbaeke	68-0884
RASTHAUSEN, Aug.	16	Bremen	69-0841
RATEHIS, Moritz	19	Nuernberg	71-0581
RATENHOF, Joh.	20	Stutenhof	71-0815
RATH, Anna	41	Wien	71-0363
Anna 23, Barbara 19, Marie 16, Johann 14, Adolph 3			
RATH, Barbara	35	Darmstadt	70-0308
RATH, Theodor	41	Schotten	69-0542
Catharine 44, Louise 7			
RATHENKE, Adeline	17	Rudolstadt	71-0429
RATHERT, Eleonore	23	Wietersheim	71-0521
RATHGEB, Xaver	20	Buechlertann	68-0610
RATHGEBER, Georg	23	Saxthausen	68-0647
Friedrich 20			
RATHJEN, F.	16	Rastede	69-0100
RATHKAMP, Friedrich	34	Oeflinghausen	68-0884
Doroth. 31, Hanna 11 months			
RATHMANN, Valentin	30	Hessen	70-0508
RATJEN, Johann	17	Borstel	68-0786
RATKE, Friedr.	50	Britzig	69-0576
Johanne Louise 48, Carl Gustav 25, Caroline 19, Otto Albrecht 16, Marie Friede			
RATSCH, Hermann	18	Stecke-Pommern	70-0006
RATSEMEN, Wilhelm	20	Duesseldorf	71-0643
Cathrine 55			

NAME	AGE	RESIDENCE	YR-LIST
RATTE, Fr. Chr.	44	Duesseldorf	68-0647
Elise 35, Bernhard 76			
RATZEK, Lina	18	Wien	68-0982
RATZER, Liddi	20	Vogelsang	68-0647
RAU, Adelheid	18	Ludwigsburg	69-0542
RAU, Elisabeth	19	Wieseck	68-0907
RAU, Engelbert	18	Waldkirch	69-0321
RAU, Eug.	20	Hesloch	68-0982
RAU, Joh.	15	Nuertingen	68-0566
RAUCH, Georg	21	Mittenberg	71-0789
RAUCH, Georg	31	Tyrol	71-0167
RAUCH, Jost	23	Kurhessen	70-0355
RAUCH, Moritz	38	Wiehe	69-0457
Rosine 31, Marie 6 months			
RAUCH, Peter	29	Lochau	70-0135
RAUH, Anton	52	Hasloch	71-0479
RAUP, Joh.	34	Kurzel	71-0393
RAUSCH, Antonia	42	Oberndorf	70-0728
Josef 32			
RAUSCH, Clara	57	Lengsfeld	68-0661
RAUSCH, Emma	16	Stadtbingsfeld	69-0572
RAUSCH, Eva	22	Baden	70-1161
RAUSCH, Friedrich	18	Vecherhagen	69-0457
RAUSCH, John	51	Gr. Siesen	71-0456
Georg 16			
RAUSCH, Reinh.	21	Langenschwarz	70-0378
RAUSCHENBERG, L.	17	Rauschenberg	70-0031
RAUSCHENBERGER, C.	24	Gottelfingen	68-0707
Friederike 2			
RAUSCHENBERGER, M.	25	Wittenweiler	69-0583
RAUSCHER, Gottlieb	24	Niederbeerbach	68-1002
RAUSCHMANN, H.	14	Lobasch	68-0625
Pauline 23			
RAUSWEILER, Wilhelmine	23	Obermoschel	70-1003
RAUTE, Martha	47	Ruckshausen	68-0770
Anna Cath. 24, Anna Elisabeth 15			
RAVERSON, Sophie	32	Bueckeburg	69-0292
REBBER, Claus	38	Hannover	69-1004
Engel 31, Gerh. 8, Heinr. ;6, Friedr. 4, Gerh. 6 months			
REBER, Johann	23	Steinaet	69-0457
REBER, John	18	Otterbach	69-0560
REBHORN, Regine	10	Stuttgart	71-0456
REBION, Cathar.	17	Beinstein	68-0957
REBMANN, Christine	29	Schonaick	71-0456
REBSTOCK, Engelb.	17	Hausen	68-0534
RECH, Fr.	17	Kirchweiler	69-0292
RECHT, Elise	28	H. Darmstadt	70-1003
RECHT, Jos.		Schaffhausen	71-0581
RECHT, Peter	31	Ludingwoerth	71-0363
Marie 27, Peter 3, Baby 6 months			
RECHT, Rachel	20	Schaffhausen	71-0581
August 17			
RECHTEN, Margarethe	17	Fischerhude	68-0786
RECK, Maria	24	Wiltingen	69-0457
RECKOW, Ernestine	20	Samotschin	68-1002
RECOFF, Otto	21	Altenburg	68-0456
REDEHASE, Sophie	17	Dielingen	69-0542
REDEMEYER, Wilh.	28	Hilter	68-0957
REDENSKI, A.	17	Giesebitz	71-0736
REDER, Christ.	32	Bruesinhagen	69-0583
REDLICH, H.	27	Wien	69-0592
Isidor 7			
REDLLICH, Elise	15	Hof	70-1003
REEBER, Albert	24	Frautzenbach	69-0592
REEDE, Conrad	16	Reisefoerth	69-0592
REEMTS, Johann	25	Petersburg	71-0492
Lina 25			
REENTS, Joh.	22	Horsten	68-1006
REERMANN, Margarethe	21	Hammingen	69-0798
REES, Johann	44	Sachsen Meining	69-0321
Johanna 46, Gertrude 21, Maria 9, Agnes 8			
REES, Wilhelmine	16	Ludingwoerth	71-0363
REESE, Frdr.	40	Rambin	68-0610
Christine 36			
REESE, Henry	20	Lamstedt	68-0957
REESE, Sophia	19	Koenigswald	70-0443
REETZ, Christian	50	Karzig	68-0770
Emilie 24, Ernst Wilhelm 7			
REETZ, Joh.	24	Sossnow	68-0314
REGEL, Wilhelmine	19	Badegant	71-0479
REGENSBURGER, David	17	Kissingen	68-1002
REGENTER, Wilhelm	31	Hannover	70-0148
REGENUTH, J. B.	43	Kirchheimboland	71-0736
REGER, Friedrich	23	Burg	70-0523
REGER, Hironimus	30	Wieflingen	70-0135
REGIA, Heinrich	27	Lankendorf	71-0479
REGLIEN, Carl	53	Boitzenburg	71-0479
Dora 50, Friederike 16			
REH, Wilhelmine	28	Trutzweiler	71-0521
Ludwig 8, Elisab. 4, Amalie 11 months			
REHBOCK, Eduard	29	Papenburg	70-0184
REHFUSS, Gottfried	17	Waelde	69-0321
REHLER, Franz	28	Westfalen	70-0728
REHM, Christian	23	Hieller-Huller	70-1003
REHM, Katharina	15	Breitenbach	71-0363
REHM, Maria	26	Birkach	69-1076
REHMEIER, Heinr.	16	Cappeln	71-0300
REHMSTEDT, Fritz	27	Hannover	70-0148
Louise 21			
REHMSTEDT, Maria	16	Ardinghausen	71-0581
REHOZ, Felix	27	Boehmen	70-0569
Franziska 25, Rosa 3, Felix 9 months			
REIBERT, Babette	27	Windsheim	68-0647
REICH, Aust.	38	Wiesenstetten	69-0798
REICH, Bertha	20	Miloslewitz	70-1161
REICH, Elisabeth	20	Steinheim	70-1055
Catharine 14			
REICH, Gottfried	18	Ludge	69-0542
REICH, Hannchen	15	Zeitloss	69-0592
REICH, Henriette	23	Friedrichshorst	68-0610
REICH, Rebecca	19	Bederkesa	68-0566
REICHARD, Joh.	32	Esens	71-0300
REICHARDT, Heinr.	39	Meinsbiessen	71-0479
REICHEBUSCH, Gust.	23	New York	69-1363
REICHEL, Anna	19	Marienberg	69-0572
REICHEL, Carl	20	Marienbad	68-0884

NAME	AGE	RESIDENCE	YR-LIST
REICHELS, Ernst	35	Heinichen	68-0770
Anna 33			
REICHENBACH, Simon	27	Ulm	70-0683
REICHENECKER, Ludwig	17	Serchingen	70-1003
REICHER, Ferd.	38	Dresden	69-0490
REICHERT, Anna	26	Kell	69-0457
REICHERT, Caroline	33	Zimmern	71-0681
Andr. 29			
REICHERT, Cathr.	22	Pfaeffingen	70-0089
REICHERT, Christ.	15	Ebhausen	69-1363
REICHERT, Jacob	28	Flacha	68-0939
REICHERT, Johann	31	Flacht	71-0712
REICHERT, Johannes	19	Eschelbronn	68-1006
REICHERT, Louise	20	Heilbronn	71-0479
REICHERT, Marg.	20	Odelshofen	71-0521
Elisabeth 21			
REICHERT, Marie	30	Pfacksingen	71-0300
REICHERT, Marie Anna	38	Neumark	71-0736
Margarethe 16			
REICHERT, Philippine	28	Eberbach	68-0647
REICHL, Johann	19	Boehmen	68-0456
REICHMANN, John	29	Aixheim	69-0583
REICHMANN, Joseph	32	Dottenheim	68-0939
Joseph 17			
REICHMANN, Medarel	32	Polschwein	69-1363
REICHMOLD, Friederike	21	Schotten	69-0542
REIDMUELLER, Marg.	73	Crailstein	68-0939
REIF, Conrad	29	Hoefler	71-0521
REIF, Ernst	17	Kandern	69-0429
REIF, Georg	14	Windischenhg.	68-0707
Andreas 23			
REIFF, Johann	40	Elsoff	68-0760
REIFF, Pauline	17	Unterhausen	69-1076
REIFFERT, Heinr.	19	Mecklan	68-0884
REIFMANN, Ernstine	18	Asch	70-0452
REIGER, Marie	22	Waldhausen	71-0815
REIGERSBERG, Hugo	20	Muenchen	70-0148
REIL, Karl	24	Neuchingen	71-0736
REIM, Florenz	30	Meerane	69-0542
REIMANN, Carl	49	Schwarzbg.Sonde	70-1023
Hugo 17, Reinhard 14			
REIMANN, Charlotte	20	Carlshafen	68-0610
REIMANN, Claus W.	24	Ihlienworth	68-0753
REIME, Carl	26	Suebberk	69-0429
REIMER, Barbara	22	Schlemesitz	68-0456
Elisabeth 28, Joseph 24, Margaretha 22			
REIMER, Dora	35	Alzei	70-0355
REIMER, Franz	25	Schlenzig	70-0378
REIMER, Heinrich	16	Bremen	68-1006
REIMERS, Christ.	36	Bremen	71-0681
REIMERS, Jacob	30	Seesterandeich	68-0957
Anna 26			
REIMLER, Louis	14	Hille	69-0560
REIMLER, Louise	14	Minden	68-0907
REIN, Dorothea	25	Darmstadt	68-0786
Johanna 5, Cornelia 10 months			
REINACK, Caroline	20	Homburg	70-0443
REINAR, Emanuel	25	Pest	70-0204
REINEBOK, Rich.	16	Apolda	68-0884
REINECK, Adam	25	Darmstadt	69-0923
Pauline 28, Heinrich 6 months			
REINECKE, Dorothea	28	Stollberg	68-0939
REINECKE, Friedr.	28	Hackenberg	69-0162
REINEKE, Christine	55	Hoerde	70-0523
Antonie 15			
REINEKE, Heinrich	16	Hannover	69-1076
REINEKE, Mr.	16	Hannover	70-0443
REINEKING, Ernst	38	Frille	68-0625
Wilhelmine 36, Carl 15, Christian 9, Christine 7, Anton 4			
REINER, Christian	22	Leutenbach	70-0272
REINER, Elvira	16	Dresden	71-0167
REINERS, Berend	63	Blexen	69-1396
REINERS, Joh.	42	Hannover	70-1035
REINERS, Maria	22	Heppens	68-0707
REINERS, Meta	19	Ostechersen	68-1002
REINERT, Anna	19	Lockhausen	71-0456
REINERT, Franz	38	Unterwald	69-1309
Franciska 28, Joseph 7			
REINERT, Louise	18	Bohmte	68-0852
REINFELD, J.	58	Lifland	69-0560
REINGANZ, Cath.	23	Bernbach	71-0300
REINHARD, Barbara	21	Gruenheim	69-0784
REINHARD, Caroline	25	Wachbach	71-0736
REINHARD, Friedrich	29	Berlin	68-0647
Caroline 32			
REINHARD, Helene	27	Worms	71-0492
REINHARDT, Aaron	16	Wachenbuchen	70-0508
REINHARDT, Amanda	15	Zillbach	68-0625
REINHARDT, Anna	26	Deidesheim	70-0682
REINHARDT, Catharina	44	Krumbach	68-0820
REINHARDT, Christian	25	Gotha	70-0329
Emilie 28, Louise 4, Bertha 11 months			
REINHARDT, Ludwig	25	Berlin	68-1027
REINHOLD, E. G.	30	Bremervoerde	70-1035
REINHOLD, Robert	23	Meerane	68-0534
REINKE, August	21	Drausnitz	68-0786
REINKE, Emilie	20	Rothenburg	68-0939
REINKE, Renke	16	Himsbeck	69-0572
REINKER, Jacob	25	Lena	68-0852
Elisabeth 21, Wilhelm 16			
REINKING, Ferdinand	25	Hannover	70-0443
Fritz 16			
REINKOBER, Johann	38	Schweinsdorf	68-0760
REINKOSTER, Florentine	59	Buer	70-1055
REINNER, Heinrich	40	Herford	71-0492
Anna 36			
REINSCH, Joseph	19	Breslau	68-0419
REINSCH, William	38	Neusalz	68-0534
REINTGES, Marie	28	Dollendorf	69-1363
REIS, Barb.	26	Zagenhausen	71-0393
REIS, Marie	20	Gandelsheim	69-0292
REIS, Wolfgang	31	Waldmuehle	68-0566
REISER, John	26	Mantel	69-0338
REISER, Otto	21	Elberfeld	70-0355
REISS, Anna	18	Kusel	69-0848

NAME	AGE	RESIDENCE	YR-LIST
REISS, Joseph	24	Ruessingen	68-0852
REISSERT, Aug.	12	Kleinostheim	71-0363
Carl 12, Louise 9			
REISSIG, female	17	Zillbach	70-0223
REISSING, Caroline	19	Leteln	68-0625
REISSING, Sophie	8	Doehren	68-1027
Wilhelmine 6			
REISSING, Wilhelm	36	Doehren	68-1027
Sophie 40, Wilhelmine 9			
REISSINGER, Johann	33	Darmstadt	69-0923
REITELBACH, Franz	32	Mellrichstadt	68-0753
REITER, Wille	14	Deverden	70-0384
REITH, Alois	27	Hachilstuhe	69-0292
REITHER, Wilhelmine	18	Baehrwalde/Prus	69-0547
REITHWIESSNER, Niclas	35	Modschidel	69-0848
REITTER, Justine	25	Hammelburg	71-0363
REITZ, Elisabeth	15	Friedlas	69-1363
REITZENBERGER, Caroline	20	Friesen	
REIZ, Christine	46	Zwingenberg	68-1298
Catharine 16, Philipp 14			
RELKE, Will.	30	Gine/Russia	69-0049
REMESCHAHS, Carl	42	Bremen	71-0363
Metta 38, Gottlieb 12, Joh. Fried. 11, Catharina 9, Hermann 6, Mathilde 2			
REMGO, August	35	Stettnetz	69-0576
Karoline 36, Hermann 6, Albert 3, Auguste 1			
REMICHEN, Georg	19	Schwiburg	71-0300
REMKE, Georg	18	Wildheim	68-0707
REMMEL, Julius	24	Merklingen	69-0848
REMMERS, Hannchen	15	Bremen	71-0712
REMMERS, Heinr.	16	Sievern	70-0452
REMTS, Jan	23	Hannover	68-0707
RENDA, Philippine	33	Kappebodeck	71-0492
Johann 2			
RENDER, Andreas	26	Seefeld	71-0712
RENDHEIM, Carl	16	Darmstadt	69-0572
Heinrich 15			
RENETH, Wilhelm	31	Berlin	69-0542
Caroline 26, Otto 6, Anna 29			
RENIER, Mary	23	Tuemau	68-0534
RENKEN, Joh.	32	Hannover	70-1142
Maria 30			
RENKENS, Gietje	20	Canhusen	69-0572
RENNDIER, Johann	53	Brinkum	71-0521
Meta 50, Elisa 16, Karl 13, Anna 8			
RENNE, Adolf	26	Cassel	69-0923
RENNEMANN, Mathias	21	Walbenabs	68-0456
RENNER, Philipp	31	Eschberg	69-0268
Ludwig 19			
RENSING, Bernhard	30	Hollwick	69-0268
RENSKE, Marie	16	Hopert	68-0982
RENTER, Anna	33	Hoboken	69-0229
George 9 months			
RENTER, Wilhelmine	34	Nienburg	71-0521
Heinrich 35, Wilhelm 5, Adolph 10 m.			
RENTSCH, Ferd.	25	Werther	68-0610
Robert 17			
RENTZEL, Susanna	40	Keferod	68-0852
Elisabeth 19, Margareth 18, Marie 9			
RENZ, Johann	25	Hinterweile	68-0566

NAME	AGE	RESIDENCE	YR-LIST
RENZ, Marg.	25	Kirchberg	69-0490
RENZ, Marie	18	Meichingen	71-0479
Gottlieb 8			
RENZ, Sophie	18	Marbach	69-0784
Carl 3			
RENZ, Wilhelm	17	Zell	68-0852
REOHRDT, Johann	20	Koehlen	71-0429
REPHEIM, L.	19	Leipzig	71-0681
REPP, Charlotte	19	Darmstadt	70-1023
Christine 15, Adam 14			
REPP, Rosine	30	Wellersdorf	70-0508
REPPE, Diedrich	31	Etelsen	69-1011
Anna 25, Becca 5, John 11 months			
REPPIER, Hermine	17	Leipzig	68-0820
REPSTEIN, Mathias	32	Sand	68-0852
RESAG, Ferdinand	23	Luebenau	68-0786
REST, Joh.	34	Volkmarsen	68-0753
RESTON, Louise 70-0452	50	Schubin	69-0968
Emilie 19			
RETHENBURGER, Josefa	56	Frankfurt	71-0681
Frieda 56			
RETHERATH, Friedr.	28	R.B.Coblenz	68-1006
RETHORST, Catharine	40	Watertown	69-0923
Louise 17			
RETTIG, Elisab.	17	Reidesbach	71-0521
RETTWEGEN, Adolph	21	Lengsfeld	68-0661
RETZBACH, Josepha	25	Baden	70-1161
RETZLER, Ferdinand	38	Schlagentin	68-0770
Wilhelmine 33, Friederike 8, Wilhelm 7, Augusta 5, Hermann 1			
REUBER, Catharina	16	Assmannshausen	68-0820
REUBERG, Pauline	23	Oldenburg	70-1066
Bertha 18			
REUKEN, Trina	21	Huettenbasch	71-0492
REULING, Peter	32	Hanau	71-0226
REUNEN, Cathrine	16	Handelshausen	69-1059
REUTELSBERG, Friedrich	26	Obermendig	68-314
REUTER, August	21	Kleinsheim	70-100
REUTER, Diedrich	47	Barke	68-0610
Margarethe 48, Heinrich 14, Sophie 9, Wilh. 8			
REUTER, Gottl.	20	Chrenstunfeld	70-0052
REUTER, Heinr.	16	Heppenheim	71-0521
REUTER, Hermine	54	Heslingen	68-0957
Hermine 28, Hermann 18			
REUTER, Jansen	19	Loppersum	69-0576
REUTER, Johann	31	Heppach	70-1055
REUTER, Ludwig	58	Heslingen	68-0957
REUTER, Marie	52	Nersiel	68-0770
REUTER, Peter	26	Gallersheim	68-0786
REUTHER, Luise	22	Jeesen	69-0560
REUTHER, Nicol.	51	Hof	70-0728
Hermann 9			
REUTSCHLER, Anna	22	Goettelfingen	68-0456
REUTSCHLER, Anna M.	24	Woenersberg	68-0820
REVERS, Eduard	51	Berlin	70-1035
Emelie 26			
REWOLINSKY, John	26	Lobsens	71-0456
REX, Joh. Mich.	52	Bennington	69-0583

NAME	AGE	RESIDENCE	YR-LIST
REY, Andreas	16	Hertinghausen	71-0456
REYMER, Rebec.	18	Neuenkirchen	69-0542
REYSEN, Adolph	14	Altenbruch	68-0661
REYSEN, Claus	19	Altenbruch	68-0707
REZNIER, Mich.	17	Darmstadt	70-0308
REZNIK, Wenzel	46	Boehmen	70-0443
Anna 44, Magdalene 14, Catharine 5			
RHEDEMEYER, Wilh.	34	Waldick	71-0167
RHEINHOLD, Wilhelmine	45	Irchwitz	71-0363
Robert 17, Franz 14, Hermann 9			
RHEYDT, Ferdinand	56	Preussen	68-0456
Caethe 30			
RIBERS, Rebecca	25	Achim	68-0865
RICHARD, Heinr.	28	Walshausen	71-0789
RICHARD, Henriette	22	Mosebeck	68-0786
RICHARDT, Louis	24	Iburg	68-0456
RICHARTZ, Auguste	40	Rastedt	71-0815
RICHBERG, Angelica	25	Chrintwoda	69-0672
RICHBERG, Anna	35	Kurhessen	70-0443
Elisabeth 17, Emilie 14, Karl 14			
RICHEL, Julia	23	Lengerich	68-0982
RICHELSKY, Franz	27	Kuttenberg	71-0456
Rosalie 21			
RICHERS, Anna	17	Fr. Leinberg	70-0523
RICHERS, Walter	29	Hildesheim	68-0566
Johanne 20			
RICHTBERG, Christ.	24	Romrad	71-0815
RICHTER, Alwin	13	Lobenstein	68-0760
RICHTER, Anna	18	Eubach	71-0363
RICHTER, Aug.	25	Cadenberge	70-1142
RICHTER, Carl	38	Leipzig	70-0178
Louise 22			
RICHTER, Carl	18	Woebbel	68-314
RICHTER, Carl	36	Limbach	68-0707
RICHTER, Emilie	28	Doebeln	69-0229
Emilie 4, Marie 3			
RICHTER, Fritz	27	Luckau	69-0338
RICHTER, Gustav	30	Hamburg	69-0848
Marie 24			
RICHTER, H.	29	Obernkirchen	71-0789
RICHTER, Henriette	54	Valenza	68-1002
RICHTER, Hugo	27	Leipzig	69-0672
RICHTER, Louise	44	Issiglen	71-0479
Heinr. 17, Friedr. 13, Christ. 9			
RICHTER, Louise	17	Calbe	71-0226
RICHTER, Ludw.	27	Heiningen	68-0982
RICHTER, Ludwig	19	Huelscheid	71-0363
RICHTER, Maria	15	Sterndorf	69-0208
RICHTER, Minna	19	Danzig	68-0760
Martha 7 months			
RICHTER, Moritz	23	Greiz	68-0884
RICHTER, Rud.	16	Neuenstein	71-0789
RICHTER, Therese	22	Thierbach	69-0542
RICHTER, Trebbedina	21	Aurich	69-1309
RICHTER, Wenzel	31	Gr. Lippen	69-0429
Mathilde 20			
RICHTERS, Rosa	53	Hocherjagd	69-1421
Katty 17			
RICK, Carl	40	Parlin/Russia	69-0049
Caroline 38, Emilie 7, Wilhelm 5, Carl 4, Anna 6 months			
RICK, John	36	Oberdreis	70-0355
Anna 21, Bernhard			
RICKENBERG, Heinrich	14	Ottersberg	70-0378
RICKERS, Nic.	22	Buer	69-1011
RICKERT, Marie	16	Berlichingen	69-1309
RICKERT, Wilhelm	32	Billerbeck	69-0229
RICKEY, Louis	25	Braunschweig	70-0148
RICKHAUS, Heinrich	43	Gr. Mimmelage	68-1006
RICKLER, Claus	18	Ottersberg	68-0939
RICKMERS, P.	30	Bremerhaven	68-1006
RICKMERS, R. C.	62	Bremerhaven	69-0321
Etta 62			
RIDDER, Heinrich	22	Olfen	69-0798
RIDELER, Paul	30	Ulm	68-1006
Marie 19			
RIEB, Johannes	26	Stetten	68-0820
RIEBELING, Elisabeth	20	Merscheid	68-0982
RIECHMANN, Friedrich	50	Ilserheide	68-0625
Louise 46, Wilhelmine 15, Heinrich 12, Louise 8, Carl 4			
RIECKE, Charlotte	16	Dissen	70-1035
RIEDE, Chst.	23	Neuenstein	71-0789
RIEDE, Wilh.	25	Riedheim	68-1002
RIEDEBUESCH, Marie	23	Jever	69-0559
RIEDEL, Friedrich	42	Neustadt	69-0923
RIEDEL, J. F.	35	Braunschweig	70-0272
Emilie 11			
RIEDEL, Paul	16	Chemnitz	69-0771
RIEDELMANN, Johann	15	Brinkum-Rettenh	69-0672
Gerhard 14			
RIEDEMEYER, Anna	25	Langenstrass	71-0821
RIEDENHARDT, Hermann	31	Wien	69-0542
RIEDERMANN, Franz	23	Bugzell	69-1059
RIEDESCH, Cath.	22	Sendebach	69-0542
RIEDINGER, Christ.	26	Dessenheim	71-0456
RIEFENSTAHL, Clemens	23	Muenster	69-0067
RIEFFER, Dor.	17	Hohenzell	68-0753
RIEFSTAHL, Friedrich	30	Neusommerthal	68-0770
Elisabeth 35, Friedrich 8, Caroline 3 , Carl 9 months			
RIEG, Sebastian	31	Mogglingen	71-0429
RIEGEL, Carl	40	Everbach	69-0547
RIEGELE, Wilhelm	18	Mainz	70-1161
RIEGELSBERGER, A.	19	Fautenbach	71-0226
RIEGEN, Johann	15	Hanstedt	68-0625
RIEGER, Barb.	24	Buchold	71-0681
RIEGER, Caroline	26	Oblenz	71-0393
Carl 2, Aug. 4 months			
RIEGER, Caspar	29	Bohlingen	69-0968
RIEGER, Johann	29	Grossersdorf	70-0204
Johann 14			
RIEGER, Johann	18	Oberweiler	68-0456
RIEGER, Leopold	28	Meiselbach	71-0712
RIEGER, Marie	25	Schweinsdorf	68-0456
RIEGERT, Emil	21	Stuttgart	71-0815
RIEGFELD, Wm.	23	Bremen	71-1046

NAME	AGE	RESIDENCE	YR-LIST
RIEGGER, Anna	58	Ditishausen	68-0982
RIEGGER, Conr.	28	Riedbahringen	69-0079
RIEGGER, Genovefa	21	Hirslingen	68-0820
RIEKE, Emil	31	Neuffen	68-0760
RIEKE, Heinrich	52	Brakelsiek	68-314
Friederike 55, Louise 19, August 9			
RIEKE, Louise	24	Detmold	71-0429
RIEKE, Ludwig	17	Brakensiek	68-314
RIEKEMANN, Marie	19	Hoysighausen	68-0982
RIEKEN, Anton	37	Wittmund	69-1011
RIEMANN, Carl 49	47	SSchwarzb.Sonde	70-1023
Hugo 17, Reinhard			
RIEMEL, Maria	69	Neu Ruppin	69-0798
RIEMENSCHNEIDER, Ludwig	49	Wenzen	
Friederike 45, Ferdinand 21, Wilhelm 18, August 12, Herman 9, Lina 7, Albert 4			
RIENS, Grethe	53	Thunum	71-0363
Grethe 19, Anna G. 15, Antke 9, Johann 6			
RIEPELMEYER, Friederich	55	Wulferdingen	70-1035
Christine 50			
RIEPKE, Marie	25	Halbrueck	68-0982
RIES, Catharine	31	Koenigsbach	69-0457
RIES, Jeanette	22	Baden	66-0221
Theodor 17			
RIESBERG, Mathilde	31	Fuerstenwalde	69-0672
RIESINGER, Agnes	24	Klein Zimmen	69-0771
RIESNER, Anna	19	Schwarzkostelen	68-0770
RIESS, August	14	Gotha	68-0939
RIESS, Chs.	28	Bebra	68-0760
Christine 37, Henriette 15			
RIESSER, Vitus	23	Tyrol	71-0167
RIESSICK, Wilhelm	27	Lippe Detmold	70-0355
RIESSINGER, Mich.	40	Waldmichelbach	68-1002
Eva 30, Peter 7, Christina 9 months			
RIETTGER, Georg	36	Steinau	69-1076
Elisabeth 34, Maria 9, Johannes 4, Baby 11 months			
RIETZ, Emil	24	Wuestfalke	68-1027
RIEWERSI, Johann	49	Wiltingen	69-0457
Barbara 55, Anna 18, Peter 15			
RIFAER, Magdalena	50	Muenchen	70-0259
RIFLE, Pauline	17	Kappel	70-1161
RIGELMANN, Julie	26	Prag	68-0770
RIKKERS, Gertrude	25	Muenster	68-0786
RIMKE, Ernst	36	Bueckeburg	69-1011
Dorothea 34, Christian 7, Charlotte 11 months			
RINDELTS, Agnete	16	Greetziel	69-0429
RINDFUSS, Barbara	25	Ingenheim	68-0786
Valentin 17			
RINEKE, Ernst	36	Bueckeburg	69-1011
Dorothea 34, Christian 7, Charlotte 11 months			
RINGBER, Peter	56	Friedewald	69-0572
Anna Catharina 43, Justine 14, Catharina 9, Peter 7, Anton 5, Elisabeth 9 mont			
RINGE, Albert	23	Schoenebeck	69-0771
RINGE, Albert	23	Schoenebeck	69-0771
RINGE, John	16	Rade	70-0308
RINGELSBACHER, P.	27	Weisenheim	71-0712

NAME	AGE	RESIDENCE	YR-LIST
Magdalene 28, Catharine 3, Jacob 10 months			
RINGEN, Claus	16	Hanstadt	71-0429
RINGENBERG, Joh.	27	Coeln	68-0647
RINGENBERG, Joh.	39	Regensburg	71-0300
RINGNELDT, Elise		Havre	70-0259
RINGS, John	40	Dreis	69-1011
Magdalene 38, John 2			
RINGSWALD, Sezilia	20	Bieberach	69-0321
RINKE, Carl	23	Steinau	68-0456
RINKE, Philipp	28	Lemm	68-0456
RINKEL, Heinrich	17	Gravenhorst	69-0672
RINKEN, Franz	16	Oldenburg	68-0707
68-0625			
RINKER, Caroline	17	Hochberg	69-1309
RINKER, Georg	19	Detmold	68-0314
RINKER, John	16	Weidenhausen	68-0534
RINNE, August	19	Enger	68-0647
RINNE, Friederike	26	Bremke	68-0566
RINNE, Heinrich	57	Enger	68-0647
Engel 55, Wilhelm 14, August 7, Rieke 6, Hermann 5, Friedrich 10 months			
RINNENSLAND, Conr.	16	Gleichen	68-0647
RINSBACH, Casp.	21	Nesselroden	69-0560
Sofia 23, Henry 4 months			
RINSCHEID, Franz Ant.	29	Bilsheim	68-1006
RINTJE, Johanna	9	Kirchbauer	68-0456
RIPHOFF, Maria W.	23	Altenbruch	68-0661
RIPKA, Johann	25	Wigstadt	69-0542
RIPP, Anton	18	Mainz	68-0456
RIPPBERGER, Marie	26	Neuenkirchen	71-0789
RIPPENS, Marie	30	Aixheim	69-0583
Joseph 4			
RISCH, Anna	22	Berlin	71-0581
RISCHERGER, Adolf	53	Treinschein	70-0384
Elise 21			
RISCHMOELLER, Wilh.	55	Hesslingen	68-0566
Wilhelmine 59, Anton 24, Wilhelm 22, August 18, Justine 16			
RISCHMUELLER, August	34	Eissel	68-0707
Metta 31, Adolph 9, Marie 3, Minna baby			
RISCHMUELLER, Carl	25	Durmersheim	69-1004
MENTZ, Fr.			
RISKE, Heinrich	19	Buer	68-0760
RISKRER, Max	70	Mannheim	70-0170
RISO, Gustav	16	Scharmbeck	68-0852
RIST, Johannes	26	Engesblatt	69-0321
RISTAU, Johann	16	Ruehden/Bavaria	69-0547
RISTER, MAthias	14	Wuelflingen	70-0508
RITHMEYER, Georg	20	Goettingen	69-0672
RITTER, Anna	22	Pickliessen	68-0661
RITTER, Auguste	22	Fulda	68-0534
RITTER, Carl	58	Bonville	68-0820
RITTER, Carl von Schauer	16	Creins	68-0610
RITTER, Christine	25	Druisbach	68-0534
RITTER, Dorothea	22	Seesen	68-0610
RITTER, Emma	17	Winnenden	71-0363
RITTER, Fritz	24	Ohlendorf	69-1363
RITTER, Joseph	22	Darmstadt	69-1212

NAME	AGE	RESIDENCE	YR-LIST
RITTMANN, Carl	21	Schweke	68-0707
RITZ, Adolph	24	Steinbach	69-0208
RITZ, Aloys	17	Bohnenkirch	71-0521
Marianne 19			
RITZ, Joseph	18	Steinbach	70-0204
RITZAU, Elis.	26	Herper	71-0792
Doretta 4			
RITZDORF, Joseph	23	Koehlerhof	68-0770
RITZENHOFF, Wilh.	18	Gelsenkirchen	69-0050
RITZENTHALER, Georg	19	Hartheim	71-0736
Johann 19			
RITZER, Fidel	26	Vorarlberg	69-0560
RITZIG, Konrad	23	Sasbachwalden	71-0492
RIXEN, Christian	29	Feidelhausen	69-0923
RIXMANN, Friedr.	60	Fuerstenau	68-1002
Maria 66, Diedr. 29			
RIZIUS, Rudolph	20	Marburg	68-0014
ROBECK, August	28	Samotschin	68-1002
ROBEL, Philipp	30	Kirchberg	71-0492
ROBER, Edward	24	Bamberg	69-0292
ROBER, Fr.	40	Walsrode	69-0490
ROBERT, Karl	28	Marienberg	69-0572
ROBERT, Nicolaus	29	Barkhausen	68-0939
ROBITEK, J.	53	Boehmen	70-1066
Gesefa 50, G. 28, Anton 9			
ROCH, Pauline	26	Berlin	68-1006
ROCHENBACH, Gustav	37	Merxheim	70-0204
ROCHER, Louise	51	Kirchheim	69-0429
Margarethe 21			
ROCKER, Johann	22	Haubern	69-0798
ROCKMANN, Hermann	58	Kemme	68-1027
Christine 44, Louise 25, Johanna 18, Wilhelm 13, Carl 9, Emma 4, Minna 3, Augu			
ROCKSTROH, Wilh.	19	Lehesten	68-0566
RODE, August	17	Nordleda	71-0429
RODE, Elise	56	Grunstadt	71-0167
Regine 20			
RODE, Louis	28	Goddelshaim	68-0786
Cath. 26, Marie 11 months			
RODE, Wilhelmine	16	Oeynhausen	68-0647
RODEKUHR, Johann	16	Heuerhagen	71-0643
Doris 26			
RODENBECK, Conradine	21	Bremen	70-0355
RODENBURG, Hermann	16	Fischerhude	68-0661
RODENBURG, Matths.	69	Ottendorf	68-0820
RODER, Xaver	19	Geisslingen	68-0534
Crescentia 21			
RODEWALD, Florentine	30	Hannover	69-0067
ROEBBING, Christoph	51	Luthe	68-0534
Sophia 51, Friedrich 22, Minna 20, Christoph 16, August 14, Dorette 8			
ROEBEN, Werner	22	Leer	68-0753
ROEBER, Emma	15	Stettin	69-0672
Pauline 14			
ROEBER, Ernst	47	Walsrode	69-1004
Dor. 33, Magdalene 6, Justine 5, Marie 3, Wilhelmine 6 months			
ROEBKE, Carl	19	Wietersheim	71-0521
Christ. 17, Christiane 21, Sophie 13, Louise 9, Marie 7			

NAME	AGE	RESIDENCE	YR-LIST
ROEBKE, Jacob	24	Wolffenhausen	69-0784
ROEDE, Wilhelm	17	Hainburg	68-0872
ROEDECKER, Bernhard	28	Laer	68-0770
ROEDEL, Friedrich	47	Altenburg	69-0542
Wilhelmine 38, Hermann 15			
ROEDEL, Louise	32	Heilbronn	68-0566
Martha 4			
ROEDER, Adam	30	Guentersleben	68-0982
ROEDER, Andreas	37	Kronach	69-0229
ROEDER, Franz Johann	28	Augsburg	68-0865
Anna Maria 2			
ROEDER, Friederike	22	Leu	68-0647
ROEDER, Georg	32	Niederohmen	69-0592
ROEDER, Julius	25	Oberfranken	68-0610
ROEFSEN, Johann	50	Hannover	69-0457
Antje 40, Johanna 21, Christine 18, Hindertje 16, Tenna 13, Ferdinand 9, Marga			
ROEGE, Adelheid	19	Glenstadt	69-0798
ROEHDE, Heinr.	17	Neuenkirchen	71-0429
ROEHL, Jacob	26	Coblenz	68-0456
ROEHL, Joh. Fr.	36	Kuhdamm	68-0647
Wilhelmine 30, Emilie 6, Augusta 4, Marie 2			
ROEHLING, Fr.	50	Bokel	68-0820
Dorothea 47, Dorothea 21, Sophie 17			
ROEHMANN, Hermann	39	Petershagen	68-0625
ROEHMS, Johann	15	Schwitschau	71-0492
ROEHR, Frank	23	Brooklyn	69-0560
ROEHRICH, Aug. Chr.	21	Oberndorf	68-0647
ROEHRIG, August	58	Oberfranken	69-1076
Elisabeth 62			
ROEHRS, Friedr.	16	Otterstedt	68-0707
ROEHRS, Heinr.	19	Satbeum	69-1004
ROEHRS, Heinrich	16	Stokenborstel	69-0672
ROEHRS, Hermann	17	Willstedt	69-1076
ROEHRS, Hermann	26	Wettringen	68-0939
ROEHRS, Meta	17	Rodenburg	70-0204
ROELKER, Josefine	25	Bremen	71-0429
ROELKER, Otto	16	Bremen	69-0067
ROELKER, Theobald	16	Osnabrueck	70-0355
ROEMELBERG, Ferd. Theodor	24	Nutzungen	70-1023
ROEMER, Carl	25	H. Darmstadt	70-1003
Henry 16, Louise 18			
ROEMER, Catharina	28	Croen	69-0321
ROEMER, Charlotte	46	Minden	71-0479
Anna 9, Luise 9, Wilh. 6			
ROEMER, Georg	18	Gruenberg	68-0534
ROEMEYER, Anna M.	23	Essen	68-0647
ROENIGK, Gottl.	55	Ufkoven	71-0456
Marie 44, Anna 16, Richard 14, Julius 14, Auguste 11, John 3			
ROENNEBERG, Bertha	22	Leese	68-0907
ROEPKE, Bernh.	9	Aumund	70-0355
ROEPKE, Friedrich	35	Hannover	70-0076
ROEPKE, Heinrich	39	Mandelsloh	68-0907
Maria 39, Heinrich 19, Fritz 7, August 6, Minna 4, Wilhelm 3, August 32, Marie			
ROEPKE, Heinrich	26	Fischerhude	68-0661
ROEPKE, Lena	15	Morsum	68-0707

NAME	AGE	RESIDENCE	YR-LIST
ROEPKE, Marie	24	Hahlen	71-0789
Anna 9 months			
ROEPKE, Meta	35	Vegesach	71-0821
ROEPKE, male	7	Vegesack	69-0208
ROEPKEN, Cathrina	39	Hotten	68-0707
ROES, Elisabeth	16	Altendorf	68-1027
ROES, Gerh.	28	Mannheim	70-0089
ROES, Heinrich	17	Allendorf	69-0457
ROES, Johann	16	Hannover	69-1396
ROES, Wilh.	22	Ritzebuettel	69-0100
ROESCH, Caroline	42	Poemeck	70-0308
Bernhard 4			
ROESE, Elisa	25	Wiedeshausen	68-0314
ROESENER, Wilhelm	46	Frille	69-1004
Eleonore 46, Eleonore 18, Christ. 15, Friedr. 9, Sophie 7, Marie 5, Christ. 2,			
ROESER, Joh. D.	17	Loehlbach	71-0736
ROESING, Johannes	35	Bremen	68-1006
Clara 25, Johannes 2, Clara 6 months			
ROESLER, Martin	29	Darmstadt	68-0707
ROESLER, Minna	26	Neuwedel	68-0760
ROESSER, Barbara	20	Pforzheim	68-1002
ROESSIG, Carl	48	Alfeld	69-1086
ROESSLEIN, Barg.	20	Oberfranken	69-1004
ROESSLER, John	20	Kantenheim	70-0378
Catharina 16			
ROETLEIN, Josef	30	Rattelsdorf	69-1059
ROETTNER, Herm.	37	Altenburg	68-0610
Frdrke. 20			
ROEVER, Friedrich	16	Wellen	68-0907
Anna 19			
ROEVERS, Heinrich	26	Varnhg.-Vornhg.	68-0534
Justine 26, Justine 3, Baby-daughter 9 months			
ROGERS, William	25	Dover	69-1086
Mary 25			
ROGGE, Franz	26	Birkungen	68-1002
ROGGE, Franz	31	Eppau	70-0569
ROGGE, Fritz	32	Bassel	68-0820
Anna M. 28, Heinrich Friedrich 4, Georg Friedrich 9 months			
ROGGE, Louise	21	Bremen	69-1076
ROGGE, Wilhelm	30	Salzgitter	69-0208
ROGGE, Wilhelm	21	Rodenkirchen	68-0625
ROGLERS, Ferdinand	34	Asch	69-0457
Marie 22			
ROGOLT, Peter H.	17	Ihlienworth	68-0661
ROGUER, Martin	22	Reuss Schleiz	69-0583
ROGURZKA, Franz	46	Gembitz	69-0547
Antonie 5, Mariane 48, Juliane 16			
ROHDE, August	23	Neustadt	71-0792
Hermann 16			
ROHDE, Auguste	32	Deutschkrone	69-1086
Bertha 9 months			
ROHDE, Eugen	19	Stuttgart	69-0784
ROHDE, Ferd.	29	Padbus	70-0569
ROHDE, Frdr.	27	Bremen	71-0456
ROHDE, Johann	51	Trockenerfurth	69-0672
Heinrich 13, Wilhelm 9, Georg 8, Elise 6			
ROHDE, Wilhelmine	17	Ludingwoerth	71-0363
ROHLFS, Christoph	26	Okel	68-0534
Dorothea 17			
ROHM, Johann	34	Wangen	69-0029
ROHN, Felix	20	Fuerth	69-0429
ROHN, Heinr.	18	Einartshausen	69-0592
ROHR, Ernst	17	Lehe	69-0321
ROHRBACH, Abraham	18	Fuerth	71-0172
ROHRBACH, Elise	28	Thina	71-0581
ROHRBACHER, Louise	21	Watteneffingen	68-0707
ROHRBECK, Aug.	31	Magdeburg	70-0728
ROHRER, Leopold	20	St. Peter	71-0492
ROHRIG, Julius	28	Goettingen	69-1076
ROHRISCH, Carl	16	Goettingen	68-0753
ROHRKASTE, Carl	6	Helpsen	68-0852
ROHRN, Ludwige	16	Neuchingen	71-0736
ROHRWASSER, Albert	22	Freiburg	71-0226
ROHSTENSCHER, Gotth.	16	Veisdorf	69-0490
ROHWEL, Theodor	17	Oldenburg	69-0572
ROISSIERE, Julie	20	Elberfeld	69-0572
ROKUSECK, Carl	34	Wednand	68-0770
Marie 27, Adalbert 9, Ladislaw 4 months			
ROLFES, Gerhard	25	Brickwedde	69-0208
ROLFF, Carl	16	Aschaffenburg	69-0162
ROLFS, Diedrich	16	Bresel	68-0939
ROLFS, Heinr.	26	Weyerheide	68-0884
ROLFS, Heinrich	16	Eschold	68-0610
ROLFS, Jenne	27	Vechta	68-1002
ROLL, Johanna	16	Weimar	71-0521
ROLL, Marie	34	Dettingen	70-0259
ROLLING, Heinrich	26	Bulsten	68-0760
ROLOFF, Charles	52	Allstedt	68-0534
Augusta 45, Friederike 12, Therese 7, Friedrich 5			
ROMAN, Jonas	19	Knibis	71-0792
ROMANN, Friedrich	16	Heilbronn	68-1006
ROMERKAMP, Marie	24	Hagen	68-0625
ROMMEL, Christoph	40	Sachsen Meining	69-0559
Catharina 40, Marie 7			
ROMMEL, Johannes	19	Waexbenhausen	69-0968
ROMMELMEIER, Cath.	52	Oberfranken	69-0784
ROMMIG, Joh.	20	Forchtenberg	68-0982
ROMPF, Hermann	18	Ferna	68-0770
RONBAL, Maria	10	Chadenitz	69-1076
RONDEBROCK, Mrs.	48	Lennep	68-0957
Anna 15, Ernst 14, Otto 12, Augusta 8, Wilhelm 6, Charles 1			
RONNENBERG, Augusta	17	Einbeck	68-1002
RONSHEIM, Joseph	14	Meltingen	68-0456
ROOS, Carl	18	Ebersbach	71-0643
ROOS, Jacob	28	Hessen Darmstad	70-0076
ROOS, Jacob	18	Kerspenhausen	71-0456
ROOS, Peter	29	Ohlweiler	68-0852
ROOS, Sophie	13	Schoppenizehr	69-0457
ROPETER, Heinr.	18	Veckerhagen	68-0786
ROPP, Catharine	23	Constanz	69-0672
ROPPELT, Joh.	28	Wetzow	68-0820
RORRACHER, Johann	39	Lienz	70-0135
Helene 45			

NAME	AGE	RESIDENCE	YR-LIST
ROSASCO, Guiseppe	24	Maconiese	69-0015
ROSCH, Anna	17	Mulsum	68-0820
ROSCH, Julie	21	Offenheim	71-0393
ROSE, August	40	Noehne	68-1027
ROSE, Gustav	18	Eisenach	70-0031
ROSE, Hermann	28	Holtensen	68-0534
ROSEBROCK, Marie		Vedderaverberge	68-1002
ROSELINS, F.	23	Bahlum	71-0581
ROSELIUS, Hinrich	24	Tedinghausen	68-0647
ROSEMANN, Friedrich	38	Niedergehen	69-1212
Anna 38, Caroline 12, Gustav 5, Wilhelmine 3, Friedrich 9 months			
ROSEMANN, Wilhelmine	19	Grossbruechter	68-0625
ROSENAU, Friedrich	25	Althof	68-0786
Alma 24, Wilhelmine 9 months			
ROSENAU, Jos.	24	Sossnow	68-0314
ROSENBAUM, Augusta	20	Driesen	68-0820
ROSENBAUM, Bluemlein	22	Naumburg	68-0982
ROSENBAUM, Georg	15	Loenig	68-0566
ROSENBERG, Henriette	19	Kruft	71-0581
ROSENBERG, Salomon	16	Gr. Buseck	71-0167
ROSENBERGER, Cath.	18	Sendelbach	69-1011
ROSENBERGER, Heinr.	17	Lichtenberg	71-0479
ROSENBERGER, Hirsch		Reckendorf	68-0625
Adelheid 17			
ROSENBLATT, Maria	20	Mansbach	68-0760
ROSENBOHM, Adele	40	Hagen	71-0456
Diedrich 18			
ROSENBOHN, Sophia	23	Rhaden	68-0957
ROSENBREITNER, Julie	27	Hollanderdorf	71-0393
Emma 2, Emilie 6 months			
ROSENBROCK, Gesche	19	Fischerhude	71-0429
ROSENBROCK, Heinrich	30	Hannover	69-0672
Minna 29, Carl 4, Fritz 2, Minna 1, Henriette 1 months			
ROSENBROCK, Johann	18	Adelsdorf	71-0429
ROSENDAHL, Helene	35	Luebbertsfehn	69-0229
Ubbe 5, Tjede 1			
ROSENHEIM, Rosalie	36	Berlin	71-0492
Paul 9, Max 8, Siegfried 7			
ROSENHEIMER, Jul	17	Deren	71-0363
ROSENHEIMER, Laemle	39	Steinbach	68-0610
ROSENKRANZ, August	42	Warbelow	69-0547
Friederike 41, Friedrich 18			
ROSENSTEIN, Theodor	32	London	69-0592
ROSENSTENGEL, Julius	28	Hannover	71-0733
Mathilde 42			
ROSENSTRIER, Andreas	25	Brauningen	68-0939
ROSENTHAL, Alexander	16	Ziegenhaim	69-0672
ROSENTHAL, Carl	59	Richnowfeld	68-0566
Christine 47, August 35, Sophie 22, Henriette 17			
ROSENTHAL, Carl	28	Breslau	71-0429
ROSENTHAL, Dorette	24	Imbshausen	68-1002
Johanna 19			
ROSENTHAL, H.	17	Muehsingen	69-0841
ROSENTHAL, W.	20	Goeppingen	71-0521
ROSENWINKEL, Mathilde		Nassenerfurth	71-0581
ROSNAWSKY, Therese	39	Wien	69-0848
ROSS, Aug.	16	Vockenrode	71-0479
ROSS, Francisca	43	Denkingen	68-0852
Maria 70, Maria 9			
ROSS, Heinrich	34	Thangenburg	69-0292
Anna 32, Dorothea 9, Heinrich 4			
ROSS, James	28	S. Francisco	69-1421
ROSS, Therese	28	Ihlbenstedt	70-0523
ROSSARD, Jacob	21	Nusshof	71-0733
ROSSE, Gerh.	51	Hoerdinghausen	71-0789
Marie 54, Marie 26, Elise 22, Clara 17			
ROSSE, Gustav	38	Braunschweig	70-0682
Juliette 34, Marie 7			
ROSSFELD, Rudolph	33	Eisenach	70-1142
ROSSIN, Joh.	24	Launburg	68-0753
ROSSKAMP, Sophie	27	Oldenburg	70-0523
Anna 24			
ROSSNER, Catharina	27	Friedersreuth	68-0566
ROSSNER, Chr.	16	Darmstadt	70-0204
ROST, Carl	28	Hohenfeld	68-0707
ROST, Christine	31	Leipzig	71-0681
Gustav 9, Oswald 8, Otto 6			
ROST, Magd.	22	Arzberg	71-0479
Jette 17			
ROSTOCK, Marie	21	Berlin	71-0582
ROTENBERG, Louise	18	Lenzinghausen	68-0939
ROTERMUND, Joh.	29	Harstedt	71-0736
ROTERS, Wilh.	15	Hagen	71-0521
ROTH, Anna	23	Hausen	68-0566
ROTH, Anna Mar.	24	Dermbach	69-0321
Wilhelm 11 months			
ROTH, Barbara	23	Waldmichelbach	68-1002
ROTH, Barbara	21	Roth	69-0848
ROTH, Carl	22	Wallhalben	68-314
ROTH, Carl	23	Tribes	68-0852
ROTH, Christine	45	Meichingen	71-0479
ROTH, Clara	37	Brooklyn	69-1212
Alex 7, Julie 6			
ROTH, Elise	15	Cassel	71-0643
ROTH, Emil	19	Muester	71-0581
ROTH, Franz	25	Zell	69-0429
ROTH, Franz	41	Birkenried	68-0314
Marie 35, Catharine 9, Albert 6, Ludwig 3, Mathilde 10 months			
ROTH, Georg	27	Miehlen	70-0508
ROTH, Georg	17	Westheim	71-0684
ROTH, Gottl.	20	Reusten	70-0089
ROTH, Gottlob	22	Zeulenroda	71-0429
ROTH, Gustav	25	Plauen	70-1003
Marie 23			
ROTH, Helene	33	Bubenheim	68-0884
ROTH, Hermine	33	Goettingen	69-0572
ROTH, Iwan	35	Bremen	70-0308
ROTH, Johann	52	Delphie	68-0625
ROTH, Johann	23	Wachenroth	71-0736
ROTH, Juliane	30	Staufenberg	68-0907
ROTH, Magdalena	18	Abenthauer	69-0583
ROTH, Marie	21	Bremen	69-1363
ROTH, Marie	25	Merscheid	68-1027
ROTH, Metta	25	Seestermuehl	68-0957

NAME	AGE	RESIDENCE	YR-LIST
ROTH, Peter	42	Nassau	69-0672
Elise 31, Carl 8, Wilhelm 5, Carl 10 months			
ROTH, Sebastian	16	Astrimsum	69-0542
Andreas 18			
ROTH, Sebastian	17	Harthausen	70-0223
ROTH, Valentin	41	Birkenried	68-0314
Catharine 42, Louise 14, August 9, Hermann 6, Josepha 3			
ROTH, Wilhelm	23	Gnels	71-0456
ROTHAMEL, Anna	22	Landefelde	71-0815
Sophie 17			
ROTHE, Fried.	22	Gotha	70-0384
ROTHE, Johanne	53	Doebeln	69-0229
ROTHEMEYER, Wilhelm	23	Minden	68-0907
ROTHENBERGER, Aug.	17	Butzbach	71-0492
ROTHENBURGER, Julius	20	Fuerth	68-0852
ROTHENFELS, Otto	29	Fechenbach	70-0378
ROTHFUSS, Anna	18	Erzingen	71-0429
ROTHGEISER, Herm.	14	Cassel	71-0681
Bertha 21			
ROTHSCHILD, Heinrich	18	Nordstetten	69-1059
ROTHSCHILD, Sal.	45	New York	69-1421
ROTTE, Heinrich	20	Trichenhoefen	69-1076
ROTTMANN, Carl	22	Gotha	70-0076
ROTZIN, Michael	42	Ternowke	68-0770
Eva 32, Carl 8, Ida 6, Emil 2			
ROUSSION, Anne	18	Bielefeld	70-0184
ROVER, Heinrich	40	Oberhausen	69-0292
Anna 32, Amelia 9, Hermann 7, Georg 6 months			
RUBEN, Gustav	22	Bielefeld	68-0884
Nathan 17			
RUBEN, Jacob	58	Posen	68-0760
Wilhelmine 48, Johanna 21, Henriette 18, Rosalia 15, Bertha 14, Rachel 7, Doro			
RUBES, Rosalie	28	Kralowitz	71-0429
RUBINE, Marie	26	Ziegenhaim	70-0452
RUBINO, Rudolph	66	Frankfurt a/M	69-1309
RUBINSTEIN, Meyer	44	Berlin	71-0736
Rosalia 48, Ida 16, Isidor 14, Zerline 9, Joseph 5			
RUBSEM, male	15	Getmold	71-0789
RUCK, Carl	16	Hannover	71-0681
RUCKENHOFER, Heinrich	20	Ulm	69-0672
RUCKES, Wilh.	20	Oberroth	71-0300
RUDELIN, Franz	18	Ballrechten	71-0581
RUDER, Franzisca	18	Cappel	69-0338
RUDERT, August	32	Mainsdorf	68-0907
Reince 7, Lina 6, Gustav 4, Max 3			
RUDLOFF, Eduard	24	Halle	69-0923
RUDOLF, Wilhelmine	39	Suederstede	68-0760
RUDOLFS, Carl	16	Elberfeld	70-0728
RUDOLPH, Carl	25	Altenburg	69-0592
RUDOLPH, Henry	17	Elgershausen	70-0508
RUDOLPH, Joseph	20	Mergentheim	68-1006
RUDOLPH, Joseph Anton	17	Hensbach	69-0321
RUDOLPH, Margaretha	24	Aalen	68-0707
Wilhelmine 60, Carl 7			
RUDOLPH, Martha E.		Leimbach	68-1002
RUDOLPH, Renate	23	Kettenacker	69-1086

NAME	AGE	RESIDENCE	YR-LIST
RUDOWSKY, Carl	16	Pausa	69-0029
RUEBENICHT, Heinrich	22	Seesbach	68-0661
RUEBHAUSEN, Gottfried	34	Preussen	68-0456
Adelheid 29			
RUEBMANN, Wilhelm	36	Hattorf	71-0736
RUEBSAM, Blasius	28	Borsch	68-1006
RUEBSAM, Emil	27	Cassel	68-0982
RUEBSON, Carl	31	Steinau	68-0456
RUECHE, Rupert	19	Ewattingen	71-0815
Wilhelm 30, Sophie 19			
RUECK, Elisabeth	20	Steinheim	70-1055
Catharine 14			
RUECK, Marg.	17	Gross Steinheim	69-1363
RUECKEL, Kunigunde	22	Illstadt	71-0479
RUECKERT, Philipp	21	Crummstadt	68-0707
RUEDEBUSCH, Heinrich	16	Delmhorst	71-0492
RUEDEMANN, Johanna	20	Flechtorf	68-0884
RUEDER, Carl	26	Wallert	71-0733
Helene 18			
RUEDIG, Peter	52	Altenkirchen	68-0820
Catharine 54, Elise 17, Catharine 9, Philippine 8, Margarethe 7			
RUEDIGER, Reinhard	24	Breslau	69-1212
RUEDLINGER, Catharine	20	Kirchheim	71-0643
RUEDLINGER, Josef	22	Kirchheim	71-0643
RUEF, Friedrich	19	Hallingen	69-0229
RUEFLI, Anna	30	Langnau	71-0681
RUEGE, Augustine	26	Neuhoff	69-0490
RUEGER, Cathar.	24	Frankfurt	69-0560
RUEGER, Marie	22	Waldhausen	71-0815
RUEGER, Sebastian	38	Griessen	71-0456
RUEGER, Willy	18	Petersberg	71-0456
RUEGGE, Adolph	22	Rahr	71-0492
RUEGNER, Caroline	26	Radeweiler	71-0712
RUEHL, Adam	26	Darmstadt	69-0592
RUEHL, Chr. Jos.	22	Oberndorf	68-1002
RUEHL, Reinhard	30	Detmold	68-0939
RUEHL, Wilhelm	23	Ramrod	68-0625
RUEHMANN, Hermann	42	Rhaeden	68-0625
Doris 42, Louise 9, Hermann 4, Louis 1 months			
RUEHREN, Ch.	17	Wagenstadt	70-1066
RUEKNICH, Wilhelm	31	Worstad	68-0647
RUELING, Georg	60	Aerzen	71-0492
Caroline 50, Maria 23, Emma 5			
RUEMPING, Heinrich	17	Osnabrueck	71-0821
RUEMPLER, Wilhelm	19	Niederwoehren	68-0456
RUENZI, Caspar	18	Allenschwand	68-0647
RUEPE, Marie	19	Aschen	68-0820
Hermann 11 months			
RUEPEINSKI, Josef	46	Schneidemuehle	69-0229
Wilhelmine 43, Francisco 9, Josef 7, August 4			
RUEPPE, Johann	36	Verden	68-1049
Catharine 34, Marie 14			
RUEPPEL, Catharina	28	Weidenhausen	69-1212
RUEPPEL, Elisa	17	Bernsdorff	68-0534
RUEPPEL, Fred.	76	Danzig	69-1421
RUESCH, Anna	35	Lehe	71-0521

NAME	AGE	RESIDENCE	YR-LIST
Heinrich 15, Anna 9			
RUESCH, Wilh.	16	Groden	68-0647
RUESSELER, Carl	24	Berndorf	68-0982
RUESSINGER, A.	17	Oberbach	71-0521
RUEST, Carl	58	Darmstadt	69-0672
RUETER, Casper	17	Suedlengern	69-1076
RUETTGER, Georg	36	Steinau	69-1076
Elisabeth 34, Maria 9, Johannes 4, Baby 11 months			
RUETTLER, Marianne	22	Lautenbach	68-1006
RUETTNER, Peter	19	Somoczyn	71-0643
RUF, Elis.	9	Seebach	71-0581
RUF, Heinrich	37	Niederauerbach	71-0492
Katharina 37, Friederich 29			
RUFF, Aug.	20	Nueslingen	68-0647
Julius 22			
RUFF, Barbara	17	Deggingens	70-1035
RUFF, Carl A.	22	Hamburg	71-0521
RUFF, Catharine	19	Zimmern	69-0182
RUFF, Gottl.	32	Gattenberg	71-0167
RUFF, Wilhelmine	30	Nuertingen	69-0229
RUGE, Catharina	17	Gestdorf	68-0770
RUGEN, Friedrich	19	Lauffen	71-0681
Caroline 17			
RUGEN, Herm.	16	Neuenbuelstedt	71-0300
RUGER Joh.	29	Grossersdorf	70-0204
Johann 14			
RUGER, Diedrich	16	Kirschsink	69-1076
RUGTER, Christian	18	Ihlienworth	68-0907
RUH, Anna Maria	51	Worms	68-1006
Catharine 17, Charlotte 13, Franz 9, Margaretha 8			
RUHE, Cath.	23	Ziegenhain	68-0753
RUHE, Jos. Ed.	15	Herbstein	68-1006
RUHL, Adolph	26	Reichenbach	68-0456
RUHL, Emma	21	Altenbruch	70-0006
RUHL, Friedrich	26	Bremen	68-0456
RUHL, Johann	27	Kissingen	68-0456
RUHL, Johannes	39	Hoezburg-Holzbu	70-0204
Anna 38, Catharina 5, Heinrich 3, Maria 6 months, Catharina 27			
RUHLAND, Martin	16	Oberelbesheim	68-0786
RUHMKE, Albert	20	Krojanke	71-0736
RUHRHEINE, Carl	21	Hundelshausen	68-0753
RUILMANN, Bernhard	28	Theine	68-0907
RUITER, Jansen	19	Loppersum	69-0576
RUK, John	36	Oberdreis	70-0355
Anna 21, Bernhard			
RULAND, Marie	32	Ehnstein	71-0821
RUMLAND, Carl	15	Buttstadt	71-0456
RUMME, Henry	25	Rothlachen	69-0572
RUMMEL, Friedr.	29	Helmighausen	68-0884
Louise 25, Caroline 2			
RUMMLER, L.	24	Goerlitz	71-0521
RUMP, Carl	25	Fuerstenau	68-0314
RUMP, Johanne	15	Quakenbrueck	69-0923
RUMPF, Louis	25	Giessen	68-0610
RUMPFF, Sophie	30	Oberhammelwd.	68-0760
Johann 8, Fred. 6, Augusta 10 months			

NAME	AGE	RESIDENCE	YR-LIST
RUMPKEN, Marg.	23	Wahn	68-1002
RUMPLER, Anton	21	Berlin	71-0821
RUNGE, August	29	Luebbars	69-1212
Dorothea 25, Helene 2			
RUNGE, Christine	26	Abbensen	69-0592
Friedrich 24			
RUNGE, Friedrich	24	Abbensen	68-1006
RUNGE, Heinrich	26	Hannover	70-0076
Georg 16			
RUNGE, Meta	17	Hannover	69-1212
RUNGE, Sophie	18	Lehe	68-0456
RUNGE, Wilhelm	16	Hannover	70-0184
RUNTZ, Catharina	24	Crosewick	68-0884
RUNZE, Bernh. Aug.	35	Altenburg	68-1006
RUOFF, Barb.	19	Bachingen	71-0479
RUPP, Barbara	20	Frauensheim	71-0429
RUPP, Catharine	16	Alsenz	68-0786
RUPP, Frdr.	37	Untermutschl	69-1004
RUPP, Isidor	20	Hahlheim	71-0363
RUPP, Marie	18	Frauensheim	71-0429
RUPP, Reinhard	21	Oehringen	69-0457
RUPP, Theresia	30	Unterrodach	69-0572
RUPPEL, Jos.	34	Oberndorf	71-0581
Marg. 33, Anton 19, August 9, Magdalene 3			
RUPPEL, Marie	28	Darmstadt	69-0672
RUPPEL, Marie	20	Odensachsen	69-1059
RUPPERT, Anna Cath.	20	Obermillerich	69-0576
RUPPERT, Aug.	30	Mittelfranken	70-1142
RUPPERT, Barbara	21	Armenhof	68-0314
RUPPERT, Elis.	20	Alsfeld	71-0393
RUPPERT, Jetchen	30	St. Lengsfeld	69-1212
RUPPERT, Johann	26	Schiernitz	70-0204
RUPPERTI, Valentin	13	Fulda	68-0865
RUPPRECHT, Joh.	27	Zahlbach	70-0384
MAUCH, Anton			
RUPRECHT, Sophie		Salzungen	66-0412
Michael 18			
RUSH, J.E.C.	24	Schuettdorf	69-0572
RUSS, Leonhard	60	Arnegg	70-0443
Catharina 45, Marie 18, Wallburga 15, Catharine 14, Justine 8, Ursula 7			
RUSS, Mary	23	Doerzbach	68-0760
RUSS, Oscar	20	Breslau	70-0259
RUSSDORF, Wilhelm	27	Coeln	68-0707
RUST, Gustav	32	Leipzig	70-0006
RUST, Johanna	24	Vegesack	68-0707
RUST, Julius	43	Heede	68-0939
RUSTENBACH, ANt.	21	Schoningen	71-0789
RUSTENBACH, Aug.	54	Schoeningen	68-0610
RUTH, Gottfried	28	Boesingen	69-0321
RUTH, Rosine	19	Michelfeld	70-0355
RUTHFER, Maria	17	Menslage	70-0728
RUTSCHMANN, Maria	52	Oberlauschingen	68-0661
Pauline 9, Johann 45			
RUTTMANN, Caroline	17	Uchte	71-0581
RUTZ, Conrad	21	Sulzbach	71-0363
RYSSEL, Franz	24	Weissenfels	68-0456
SAABE, Theodor	25	Hannover	71-0521

NAME	AGE	RESIDENCE	YR-LIST
SAAG, Marie	31	Hohenhausen	71-0226
August 8			
SAALBACH, Lebrecht	36	Graefendorf	69-0848
Gottlob 32			
SAAM, Anna Marg.	78	Friedewaldt	69-0572
SAAME, Catharine	25	Cassel	69-0672
SAAR, Adam	24	Baumersreuth	68-0610
SAAR, Carl	22	Achterbach	71-0736
SAARBOLDT, H.	27	Uffen	70-1066
SAATHOFF, Be.	38	Ludwigsdorf	69-1011
SAATHOFF, Jans	42	Norden	69-0576
Alberdine 41			
SABATKA, Josef	24	Chicago	70-0329
SABATKA, Josef	56	Albrechtitz	70-0329
Maria 52, Johann 18, Maria 26, Anna 15, Maria 77, Katharina 41, Johanne 16, An			
SACHHOFF, Christian	64	Lahde	69-1076
Friederike 34			
SACHS, Caroline	29	Stocksberg	70-1003
SACHS, Joh.	22	Boerlas	68-0982
SACHS, Maria	18	Ulm	68-1002
SACKEROSKA, Polagia	28	Polonia	69-1309
Pri. 8			
SACOLOWSKY, Heinrich	33	Bitow	69-0547
SADECKY, Magdalena	76	Kuttenberg	70-0329
Anna 7			
SADNAB, Friedr.	30	Aurich	68-1027
SAEGER, C. A.	24	Buehlerthal	69-0050
SAEGER, Karoline	23	Burkheim	71-0733
SAEHL, Marie	19	Hannover	69-1086
SAENGER, Carl	25	Hamm	68-0957
SAETTER, Henriette	23	Neuschoenewald	69-0560
SAEUGLING, Joseph	38	Meiningen	68-0820
SAFRANEK, Ignatz	33	Wien	69-0490
SAGEMUEHL, Warnecke	29	Hannover	69-0559
Catharine 29			
SAHL, Otto	19	Hannover	69-1086
SAILE, Johann	27	Weiler	69-0208
SAILE, P.	20	Herrlingen	69-1319
SALATHE, Christ.	32	Basel	71-0681
Verena 32			
SALEM, Catharina	24	Schillingen	69-0457
SALLER, Friederike	27	Mullenhagen	68-0534
Albert 6			
SALM, Bertha	17	Brandeisel	71-0479
Kati 24			
SALOMON, Robert	18	Muellheim	71-0167
SALOMON, Sigm.	17	Schoenfeld	69-0338
SALOMON, Sophie	20	Hannover	69-0672
SALZER, Wilhelm	25	Durlach	70-0308
SALZMANN, F.	24	Oberfranken	70-0508
SAMARRE, Heinrich	28	Oldenburg	69-1076
SAMENDINGER, Evert	25	Eisslingen	68-0566
SAMETZ, Rosalie	24	Woperum	71-0581
SAMINGHAUSEN, E.	21	Burhave	71-0521
SAMISCH, Moritz	16	Lichtenstadt	70-0508
SAMISH, Louise	27	Lichtenstadt	68-0610
Rose 16			
SAMMLER, Isaac	15	Ichenhausen	71-0479
SAMPON, Janna	18	Rysum	69-0490
SAMSON, Janna	18	Rysum	69-0490
SAMUEL, Ernestine	25	Czarnikow	69-0572
SAMUEL, Regina	23	Salzburg	71-0792
SANDEL, Carol.	26	Hirschhorn	70-0508
SANDER, Herm.	24	Wuerzburg	68-0982
SANDER, Hermann	56	Bremen	68-0707
SANDER, Jacob	12	Orbis	69-0457
SANDER, Johann	41	Goersbach	68-0566
Susanne 41, Johanna 17, Johanna 15, Augusta 12, Johanna Augusta 9, Johann 6, M			
SANDERGELD, Ed.	19	Oberuffhausen	71-0226
SANDERS, Catharine	38	Bremerhaven	69-0572
SANDERS, Tecla	27	Stavern	69-0229
SANDFORT, Marie	18	Laer	71-0429
SANDHOFF, Aug.	39	Potsdam	68-0566
SANDHOLZ, Soeren	17	Bodum	69-0338
SANDKUHL, J. H.	30	Luewste	68-1006
SANDKUP, Anna	20	Boehmen	70-0728
SANDMANN, Marie	60	Wurchow	68-0314
Mathilde 22			
SANDMEYER, Carenna	36	Benhau	70-0204
SANDNER, Therese	16	Gossengruen	71-0456
Elise 9			
SANERMANN, Carl	44	Luederswerder	69-0321
Anna Louise 38, Emilie 15, Mathilde 9			
SANGER, Ottilie	14	Altenburg	70-0569
Selma 14			
SANNING, Bernhard	24	Hannover	70-0178
SANSSEN, Reemt	32	Emden	69-0229
SANTER, Georg	25	Neustadt	70-0135
SAPPER, Ferd.	18	Nufringen	70-0170
SAROPSKY, Georg	18	Eperges	68-0647
SASSE, Louis	32	Moorsum	68-314
SASSENROTH, Wilhelm	27	Lohdorf	71-0643
SATORIUS, Cath.	18	Bremen	69-0490
Dieter 16			
SATTELMEYER, Hermann	22	Brockenheim	69-0079
SATTLER, Antonia	36	Koenigswart	68-0647
Amalia 2			
SATTLER, Hanna	21	Wailesgruen	71-0821
Bernh. 18			
SATTLER, Heinrich	16	Wallisgruen	69-1319
SATTLER, Henriette	25	Gollheim	69-0592
SATTLER, Jacob	22	Langenau	71-0492
SATTLER, Louise	20	Emmendingen	69-1319
SATTLER, Wilhelmine	19	Versmold	68-1002
SATTMANN, Claas	33	Hannover	70-0384
SAUER, Amand	46	Marbach	68-0753
Emilie 38, Ferdinand 16, Constant 14, Veronika 10, Joseph 9, Sabina 8, Augusti			
SAUER, Andrew	34	Hahlen	68-0534
SAUER, Anton	28	Forchheim	68-0770
SAUER, Dora	17	Herbfeld	71-0815
SAUER, Fried.	28	Kaisersbach	71-0815
Bertha 10 months			
SAUER, Friedr.	40	Zeisendorf	70-1035
Wilhelm 7			

NAME	AGE	RESIDENCE	YR-LIST
SAUER, Helene	19	Nackenheim	69-1309
SAUER, Jonas	30	Frankfurt	70-1003
Dorette 26, Hermann 3 months			
SAUER, Louise	18	Fladingen	69-0798
SAUER, Louise	34	Elberfeld	69-0457
Julius 10, Adele 8, Ernst 6, Paul 5, Emilie 3, Eduard 11 months			
SAUER, Martin	52	Kl. Wissek	69-0547
Ernestine 42, Wilhelm 22, Auguste 16			
SAUER, Mathias	35	Duermane	68-0456
SAUER, Ursula	19	Rothenburg	71-0581
SAUER, Wilhelm	15	Rieber	69-1059
SAUERLAND, Maria	7	Warburg	68-0907
Anna 5			
SAUERMANN, Carl	25	Hannover	70-0272
SAUERMANN, Johann	22	Muenichsroth	68-0661
Simon 23			
SAUERTEIG, Nic.	28	Meiningen	69-0338
SAUERWEIN, Heinr.	56	Alsenz	68-0786
Catharine 33, Friederike 21, Marie 19			
SAUERZOPF, Robert	23	Magdeburg	69-1086
Friedrike 31			
SAUFER, Hermann	17	Hahlen	70-0728
SAUHN, Ignatz	51	Boehmen	70-0569
Anna 51, Marie 21, Anna 17, Carl 15, Matthias 12			
SAUM, Peter	27	Anzefahn	69-0162
SAUMANN, Babette	27	Darmstadt	70-0728
SAUTER, Ba.	33	Nuernberg	71-0300
SAUTER, Eva	21	Sulzfeld	69-1396
SAUTER, Fred.	23	Grossaschenheim	69-0338
Christine 20			
SAUTER, Gebhard	18	Zepfenhan	71-0521
SAUTER, John	20	Muehlhausen	70-0508
SAUTER, John	19	Adingen	70-0355
SAUTER, Willibald	15	Rathshausen	71-0521
SAUTHOF, Wilhelmine	35	Holzminden	68-1006
Heinrich 14, Wilhelmine 9, Caroline 7, Christian 6, Friedrich 2			
SAUTTER, Andreas	20	Deisslingen	70-1161
SAUTTER, Christian	30	Teubingen	68-0852
Paul 32			
SAUTTER, Dorothea	29	Reusten	68-314
SAXER, Georg	31	Hochheim	68-0566
SCHAA, Heye H.	31	Westerrauderfeh	69-0572
Harm 8, Harm B. 7, Johann 4, Haye 2			
SCHAADE. Louis	37	Schwerin	68-0852
SCHAAF, Carl	17	Fischbach	69-0457
SCHAAF, Hugo	18	Coblenz	68-0884
SCHAAF, W.	21	Hamweiler	71-0684
SCHAAL, Gottlieb	20	Schorndorf	68-0852
Maria 21			
SCHAAL, Heinr.	19	Schorndorf	71-0479
Gottl. 17			
SCHAAL, Louis	27	Frankfurt	69-1396
SCHAAR, G.	26	New York	70-0170
SCHAAR, Theo.	23	Schoenlanke	68-0786
SCHAAR, Wilhelm	25	Rupertsburg	69-0592
Marga. 48, Cath. 22, Johanes 12			
SCHAATH, Henriette	19	Otterndorf	71-0479
SCHABATKA, Anna	17	Wotiez	70-1023
SCHABBEL, Friedrich	36	Zemmen	69-0576
Pauline 26, Carl 6 months			
SCHABE, Marie	18	Wittlage	71-1046
SCHACHART, Carl	26	Allgottesen	71-0712
SCHACHEL, Christ.	62	Sichau	71-0681
Elise 66			
SCHACHERT, Joh.	27	Wien	70-0443
SCHACHT, Ernst	32	Braunschweig	69-0592
SCHACKNAT, Friedr.	28	Dittwischen	68-1002
SCHAD, Bab.	18	Wulsdorf	70-0384
SCHADDE, Peter Th.	28	Duesseldorf	68-0610
SCHADDECKER, Frdr.	26	Ruedesheim	69-1004
SCHADDIN, Bertha	30	Drosedow	71-0521
Caroline 25			
SCHADE, Anna	15	Hannover	70-0682
SCHADE, Anna	19	Hannover	71-0479
SCHADE, Eduard	23	Langensalza	68-0753
SCHADE, Friedr.	23	Schweinfurt	71-0226
SCHADE, Robert	22	Breslau	71-0712
SCHADE, Sophie	27	Bebra	68-314
Justus 6, Barbara 4, Gertrud 3, Kunigunde 10 months			
SCHAECKELHOFF, F.	18	Osnabrueck	69-1319
SCHAEDLER, Cath.	23	Edesheim	71-0300
SCHAEFER, Abrah.	14	Obrigheim	70-1055
SCHAEFER, Albert	31	Pferdsdorf	68-0661
SCHAEFER, Anton	42	Altendorff	68-0456
Charlotte 39, Anne 14, Johannes 9, Martha 8, Elisabeth 3			
SCHAEFER, Carl	70	Goettingen	69-1212
Elise 62, Emilie 28			
SCHAEFER, Carl	20	Freiburg	69-0050
SCHAEFER, Carl	25	Gerchinghausen	69-0457
SCHAEFER, Catharina	19	Niederwellen	68-0707
SCHAEFER, Cathr.	22	Gastringen	70-0170
SCHAEFER, Charles	20	Berghausen	68-0760
SCHAEFER, Christine	42	Gundenheim	68-0566
SCHAEFER, Christine	28	Freisberg	71-0521
Robert 3			
SCHAEFER, Conrad	28	Lohe	69-0572
SCHAEFER, Conrad	17	Rennertshausen	68-0760
SCHAEFER, Elise	19	Coblenz	68-0760
SCHAEFER, Emilie	25	Baubeueren	69-1059
SCHAEFER, Ernest	16	Eschenbruch	68-0760
SCHAEFER, Ernst	25	Muenster	70-0052
SCHAEFER, Frdr.	17	Quernheim	68-0610
SCHAEFER, Friederike	20	Wuetferdingen	71-0479
SCHAEFER, Friedrich	18	Veldrum	70-0355
SCHAEFER, Georg	41	H. Darmstadt	70-100
Phil. 12, Dorothea 9			
SCHAEFER, Georg	44	Kirtorf	68-0610
Dorothea 19			
SCHAEFER, Gerd	36	Zetel	68-0907
Gesche 36, Anna M. 7, Hermann 7, Anna 11 months			
SCHAEFER, Heinr.	18	Hilter	71-0581
SCHAEFER, Heinr.		Altheim	71-0226
SCHAEFER, Heinrich	29	Detmold	69-0572

NAME	AGE	RESIDENCE	YR-LIST
Caroline 26, Heinrich 2, Friedrich 9 months			
SCHAEFER, Helene	26	Rittenau	68-0566
Marie 1			
SCHAEFER, Heye	14	Eidorn	68-0753
Juergen 12			
SCHAEFER, Johann	20	Osnabrueck	69-0208
SCHAEFER, Johann	28	Hillinghausen	70-0523
SCHAEFER, Johann	18	Oberzolbshs.	68-0707
SCHAEFER, Johannes	56	Rossbach	69-0798
Anna M. 58			
SCHAEFER, Juliane	41	Oleswald	70-0683
Ida 9, August 9, Gustav 8, Richard 6, Anna 3			
SCHAEFER, Louis	17	Afoltern	68-0566
SCHAEFER, Louise	29	Eibenbach	69-1004
Marie 27			
SCHAEFER, Ludwig	24	Villingen	68-0884
SCHAEFER, Ludwig	13	Rockenhausen	70-0355
SCHAEFER, Marie	29	Gengenbach	69-1319
SCHAEFER, Marie	24	Lienen	68-0982
SCHAEFER, Martin	25	Engschlah	69-0321
SCHAEFER, Meta	78	Blumenthal	69-0429
SCHAEFER, Peter	55	R.B.Coblenz	68-1006
SCHAEFER, Richard	20	Eibenstock	70-1035
SCHAEFER, Rosina	18	Hattenleidenhei	70-1055
SCHAEFER, Rosine	52	Engstlath	70-0523
Daniel 15			
SCHAEFER, Wilh.	17	Morbach	71-0581
SCHAEFER, Wilhelm	16	Marburg	70-0178
SCHAEFER, Wilhelm	36	Damastow	69-0542
Wilhelmine 33, Pauline 5, Ottilie 3, Auguste 9 months			
SCHAEFER, Wilhelmine	25	Burg	70-0523
SCHAEFER, Wilhelmine	40	Hasloch	68-0534
Mathilde 30			
SCHAEFER, male	30	Effenbach	69-0542
Mathias 28			
SCHAEFFER, Adolfine	22	Bremen	69-0338
August 20, Christian 17, Betty 15			
SCHAEFFER, Carl	46	Goettingen	68-0770
SCHAEFFER, Friedrich	25	Gruenstadt	69-1076
SCHAEFFER, Jac.	26	Frierichsthal	70-0170
SCHAEFFER, Johanne	27	Burg	70-0523
Friedrich 9 months			
SCHAEFFLE, Adam	25	Sickenhofen	71-0821
Cath. 25, Marie 11 months			
SCHAEKEL, Anton	23	Wietersheim	71-0521
SCHAEPERMEYER, H.	34	Heinbergen	69-0429
SCHAER, Maria	20	Stolzenau	71-0492
Heinrich 15			
SCHAETZLE, Franz	24	Muenchen	69-0923
SCHAEUFFELE, Wilh.	20	Gebersheim	69-1363
SCHAEUFLE, Barb.	38	Dettingen	71-0521
Carl 9, Gottfried 8, Catharina 4, Marg. 6 months			
SCHAF, Johannes	29	Bohlingen	71-0792
SCHAFER, Anna	26	Werkel	71-0521
SCHAFER, Caroline	21	Hessen	70-1066
SCHAFER, Christine	16	Darmstadt	70-0682
SCHAFFENBERGER, F.	57	Brucks	68-0647
SCHAFFERT, Joh.	42	Spechtsdorf	70-0384
SCHAFFERT, Marie	19	Plochingen	68-0647
SCHAFFNER, Catharina	22	Flehingen	68-0760
SCHAFFNER, Eva	19	Griselbach-Geis	70-0508
SCHAFT, Peter	50	New York	69-1212
David 16			
SCHAGETER, Joh.	18	Vettelbrun	71-0581
SCHAIBLE, Johann	15	Hochdorf	69-0592
SCHAICH, Gottl.	21	Leutenbach	71-0815
Johann 19			
SCHAICH, Peter	45	Flieden	71-0429
Louise 30, Anna 9			
SCHAIGER, Helene	31	Koadjuethen	68-0820
Hanna Ida 5, Emma 2			
SCHALE, Minna	18	Herford	71-0821
SCHALER, Johann	24	Deisslingen	69-0968
SCHALK, Catharina	20	Duerkheim	69-0429
SCHALKENSTEIN, Judith	38	Muttersdorf	68-0566
Jacob 3, Carl 2			
SCHALL, Paul	23	Oehringen	69-0457
SCHALLER, Eduard	28	Braunschweig	68-0661
SCHALLER, Franz	26	Schwarzenbach	68-0907
SCHALLER, Heinrich	17	Weimar	68-0661
SCHALTER, Eduard	32	Renss	70-0508
Rosine 57, Hulda 17			
SCHAMBER, Math.	19	Merghausen	70-1035
SCHAMBERG, August	19	Zemmen	69-0576
SCHAMBERGER, Marg.	18	Gustenfelsen	68-0647
SCHAMBURG, Marie	23	Bremen	71-0167
SCHAN, Bertha	20	Iduni	70-0569
SCHANILLE, Wenzel	25	Bohemia	69-0841
John 16			
SCHANK, MArie	36	Rast	69-0457
Ambrosius 9			
SCHANTZ, Agnes	25	Euxkloesterle	68-0884
SCHANZ, Abraham	25	Maessingen	71-0300
SCHANZ, Elise	20	Neuweiler	70-0355
SCHANZ, Eva	15	Gehaus	71-0581
SCHAPER, Catharina	32	Lichtenhagen	68-0884
Charlotte 27			
SCHAPER, Henry	16	Ritterhude	71-0456
SCHAPPER, Christian	18	Eschendorf	71-0727
SCHARDIN, August	24	Reckow	69-0457
SCHARENBERG, Ad.	18	Springe	68-0760
SCHARF, Babette	26	New York	69-0672
SCHARF, Herm.	25	Vlotho	70-0052
SCHARF, Johann	33	Rudolfstadt	69-0268
Mathilde 31			
SCHARFSCHEER, Adolph	46	Cassel	68-0753
Anna 25			
SCHARGERS, Therese	25	Suttrup	68-0760
SCHARM, John	27	Prague	68-0534
SCHARMER, Daniel	24	Friedland	71-0479
Carl 25, Emilie 24, Ida 3			
SCHARTENBERGER, A.	43	Bruecks	69-0923
SCHARWAECHTER, H.	24	Coeln	68-0865
SCHASSER, Chrph.	24	Braunschweig	68-0610
SCHATZ, Carl	21	Raedewill/Saxon	69-0547
SCHATZ, Elise	36	Hildburghausen	71-0363

NAME	AGE	RESIDENCE	YR-LIST
Mathilde 35, Catharine 66, Carl 3			
SCHATZ, Gregor	28	Goesslingen	70-0355
SCHATZ, William	39	Neukirchen	68-0786
Dora 20			
SCHAU, Carl	23	Roda	69-0592
SCHAUB, Wilhelm	29	Newark	70-0184
SCHAUBLE, Febronia	26	Hochsal	68-0625
Johanna 8			
SCHAUBOHM, Joh.	52	New York	69-1363
SCHAUENBERG, Auguste	27	Strelitz	71-0456
Wilhelmine 28			
SCHAUENBERG, Carl	16	Oldenburg	71-0681
SCHAUER, Magdalena	17	Mittelfranken	70-1142
SCHAUF, Wilh.	41	Weisteneulach	69-1004
SCHAUFFLER, Christine	24	Vaichlingen	68-0610
SCHAUING, Elisabeth	19	Trier	68-0982
SCHAUMBERGER, Clara	18	Coburg	70-0170
SCHAUMBURG, B. F.	19	Otterstedt	68-1006
SCHAUMBURG, Marie	16	Heimarshausen	70-0523
SCHAUMWECKER, L.	59	Worms	68-0456
SCHAUS, Bertha	25	Wiesbaden	68-0939
Hermann 18			
SCHAUSS, Catharina	18	Holzhausen	68-0647
SCHAWER, Paul	25	Jaschowo	69-0572
SCHECHINGER, J.M.	39	Sulz	68-0753
SCHECK, Adolph	18	Knibis	71-0792
SCHECK, Anna	21	Eisslingen	68-0566
SCHECK, Paulus	29	Sattendf.-Salte	70-0355
Anna 27, Barbara 6, Anna 3, Johanna 4, Andreas 9 months			
SCHEDEL, Magdalena	31	Beggingen	68-0566
Albert 11 months			
SCHEDLER, Ludwig	11	Markdorf	68-1027
SCHEELE, Friedrich	15	Rotenburg	68-0939
SCHEELE, Fritz	20	Hannover	68-0820
SCHEEMACHER, Marg.	29	Schonberg	69-0292
Michael 9, Jacob 4			
SCHEER, Frdr.	20	Reichenbach	69-0321
SCHEER, Gustavus	21	Goeppingen	68-0534
SCHEERER, Barbara	23	Dormettingen	69-1076
Anton 19			
SCHEERER, Sophie	16	Hallnengen	69-0429
SCHEFFELER, Anna	34	Waldeck	69-1309
Anna 9, Johanna 7			
SCHEFFLER, Amalie	25	Sangerhausen	68-0786
SCHEIBE, Caroline	19	Zeulenrode	71-0429
SCHEIBE, Franz	22	Manndorf	69-0338
SCHEIBE, Justus	40	Umysterode	69-0542
Martha 42, Elisabeth 15, Franz 7, Anna 6, Catharina 5, Marie 7 months			
SCHEIBLE, Rosine	18	Gangenwald	68-0820
SCHEID, Heinrich	15	Kaulbach	69-0321
SCHEIDEMANTEL, A.	30	St. Antonio	69-1011
SCHEIDER, Alfred	26	Dresden	71-0684
SCHEIDERMANTEL, Carl	25	Koenigsberg	70-0355
SCHEIDIG, Babette	26	Fuerth	68-0625
SCHEIDINGER, Joh.	26	Reudern	70-0089
SCHEIDLE, Auguste	23	Jungnau	71-0456

NAME	AGE	RESIDENCE	YR-LIST
SCHEIDLER, Elisabeth	27	Vorra	70-0204
SCHEIDT, Wilh.	17	Raulbach	71-0479
Mary 19			
SCHELING, Louis	16	Walsrode	69-0490
SCHELINSKI, Joh.	35	Russ	71-0479
Cath. 31			
SCHELL, Augusta	18	Treptow	68-0760
SCHELLE, Caroline	26	Allstedt	68-0534
Anna 6 months			
SCHELLENBERG, Adolph	26	Wasungen	69-0015
SCHELLENBERG, Bertha	16	Weissenfels	71-0733
SCHELLER, Richard	23	Leipzig	70-0508
SCHELLHAS, Julie	31	Ziegenhain	68-0647
SCHEMEL, Heinrich	48	Sassenburg	68-0770
Albertine 30, Anna 14, Mathilde 11, Ottilie 7, Ida 5, Albert 2			
SCHEMER, Tauf.	8	Lehna	69-1004
SCHEMMINGER, Ottmar	19	Lautlingen	69-0784
SCHENCK, Marie	44	Apolda	69-1076
SCHENECA, Max	38	Oberschulz	69-0771
Anna 35, Margretha 13			
SCHENK, Adolph	35	Gotha	69-1076
SCHENK, Christian	16	Hattenbach	69-0457
SCHENK, Elisa	30	Thueringen	69-1086
SCHENK, Georg	23	Knitzgau	71-0456
SCHENK, Leopold	28	Heidelberg	69-1086
SCHENK, Marie	42	Duenheim	68-1006
Anna 16, Philipp 7, Elise 2			
SCHENKER, Adolf	30	Gretzenbach	71-0226
SCHENNEMANN, Carl	31	Coslin	70-0076
SCHENNEMANN, Wme.	26	Coerlin	69-0429
August 9 months			
SCHEPER, Anna	23	Wulsten	68-0566
SCHEPMANN, Chr. Fr.	70	Heringhausen	68-0647
Marie E. 68, Herm. Friedr. 35, Christoph 30			
SCHEPPACH, Alfred	18	Chemnitz	71-0492
SCHERB, Caroline	23	Schweiz-Saulgau	70-1142
Eugenie 2			
SCHERDER, Lisette	23	Bersenbrueck	68-1002
Dina 19			
SCHERDIEN, August	26	Lustebuhr	68-0661
SCHERDIN, Gottfried	23	Hokow	70-0728
SCHERER, Catharine	27	Anriede	69-0784
SCHERER, Louis	21	Lobenstein	68-0707
SCHERER, Marie	26	Feideldorn	70-0728
Leonhard 2			
SCHERER, Peter	32	Kreimbach	69-0321
SCHERER, Wilhelmine	17	Birkenfeld	69-1004
SCHERF, Hulda	17	Werdau	71-0681
SCHERFF, Elisabeth	36	Schwarzenfels	71-0226
Anna 5, Christian 6 months			
SCHERMUND, Joh.	28	Rosenthal	70-0452
SCHERNICH, Franz	16	Hartheim	71-0521
SCHERP, Maria	19	Wichdorf	68-0707
SCHERP, Wilh.	20	Hadamar	68-1002
SCHERPICH, Friedrich	41	Wesel	68-0865
Antonia 36, Hugo 17, Ferdinand 11, Otto 9, Marie 7, Eugen 6, Emil 4, Franz 2,			
SCHERRE, Joh.	16	Ritzebuettel	71-0479

NAME	AGE	RESIDENCE	YR-LIST
SCHERRER, Emilie	22	Dettingen	70-0378
SCHERZBERG, Marie	***	Toba	69-0429
SCHESAP, Joseph	25	Hechingen	69-0784
SCHETTERER, Johann	18	Neulininingen/Neu	69-1309
SCHEU, Cath.	23	Villmar	71-0226
Anna 19			
SCHEU, Joh.	19	Hall	69-0162
SCHEUBAUM, Ernst	17	Lichtenberg	71-0479
SCHEUBNER, Anna	19	Goslar	71-0456
SCHEUER, Elisabeth	23	Muehlenbach	69-0923
SCHEUERMANN, Christ.	44	Bremen	69-0029
Helene 19, Ida 13			
SCHEUERMANN, Marie	27	Heilbach	70-1035
SCHEUFELE, Rosine	22	Wellheim	71-0226
SCHEUFFLER, Ludwig	37	Edingen	68-0982
Marie 33, Marie 8, Heinr. 6, Wilhelmine 4			
SCHEUFLER, Elias	29	Umysterode	69-0542
Christine 24, Otto 3 months			
SCHEULER, Elisabeth	19	Linne	68-0852
Ernst 32			
SCHEUNEMANN, C.	27	Mellenhoff-Pomm	70-0006
Auguste 32			
SCHEUNEMANN, Franz	34	St. Mauritz	71-0684
SCHEURIG, Carl	19	Waldain	68-0852
SCHEURMANN, Otto	18	Carlshafen	69-0162
SCHEUSSLER, Joh.	30	Celle	69-0050
SCHEWEMANN, Bernh.	18	Borghorst	68-0907
SCHEYERMANN, T.	16	Birkenau	71-0456
SCHIBLO, Joseph	36	Kuttenberg	68-0957
Barbara 30			
SCHICHTER, Wilhelmine	25	Markgroningen	71-0479
SCHICITER, Josef	52	Thein	70-0329
Theresia 50, Theresia 20, Franz 17, Katharina 14, Marie 12			
SCHICK, Const.	16	Seibelsdorf	71-0479
SCHICK, Eva	26	Hebsack	68-0786
Marie 8, Christian 7			
SCHICK, Jacob	17	Duerkheim	71-0821
SCHICK, Joh.	22	Bamberg	71-0789
Cath. 22			
SCHICKMANN, Anna	22	Laer	69-0429
SCHIEBERT, Marie	37	Wonnischen	68-0647
Josef 8			
SCHIECK, Caroline	40	Erfurt	68-0625
Albert 9, Caroline 8, Rudolf 7, August 5, baby son 9 months			
SCHIEDHELM, Joh.	38	Bechtheim	69-1004
Carol. 58, Eva 21, Cathar. 20			
SCHIEFELBEIN, Bab.	15	Falkenburg	69-0841
SCHIEFER, Christine	65	Dettingen	68-0534
Mary 2			
SCHIEFERDECKER	28	Neckargmuend	71-0712
SCHIEFFERDECKER	23	Schloeben	68-0770
SCHIEL, Augusta	24	Dresden	68-0314
SCHIEL, Ferdinand	17	Lautenbach	68-314
Mathias 22, Benedicta 46, Martin 17, Johann 22			
SCHIENE, Theodor	36	Osterrieden	68-0314
Elisabeth 30, Walburga 7, Therese 5, Gertrud 4, Marie 3, Elise 11 months, Franz			
SCHIENKE, John	27	Elbing	70-0170
SCHIENSTOCK, Friedrich	26	Wadersloh	68-0314
SCHIERENBERG, Gustav	50	Meyenberg	68-0982
SCHIERENBICK, John	17	Brinkum	70-0508
SCHIERENHOLD, Anna	28	Oldenburg	70-0523
SCHIERFELD, Tonjes	17	Ostfriesland	70-0329
SCHIERHOLZ, August	29	Enger	68-0456
SCHIERHOLZ, Maria	28	Stettin	69-0798
SCHIERMACHER, Anna	24	Wildungen	71-0456
SCHIEVENZ, Veronica	28	Freren	70-0508
SCHIFF, Bernh.	18	Detmold	70-0308
SCHIFF, Jacob	21	Langenschwarz	71-0712
SCHIFFER, Otto	19	Coeln	68-0707
Josepha 20, Sybilla 28			
SCHIFFERL, Ignatz	27	Feideldorn	70-0728
SCHIFFLER, Marie	15	Romelsbach	70-1035
SCHIKENDAM, Louise	26	Landau	68-0534
SCHILD, Elise	17	Marburg	68-0753
SCHILD, Sally	20	Corbach	70-0308
SCHILDBACH, Rosalie	22	Glauchau	68-0786
Hermann 3			
SCHILDBERG, Gustav	28	Kolata/Kotata	69-1309
Wanda 6, Friede 11 months			
SCHILDMANN, Anna	24	Besenkamp	68-0957
SCHILKE, Jacob	45	Gross Krebs	70-0204
Auguste 35, Emilie 15, Auguste 13, Henriette 7, Hermann 9 months			
SCHILL, Francisca	39	Vorarlberg	69-0560
SCHILL, Jacob	18	Frankenhain	69-0490
SCHILL, Marie	16	Unterleben	69-0542
SCHILLER, Carl	43	Friedland	68-0610
SCHILLER, Caroline	31	Ringelshain	68-0786
Reinhold 7, Carl 4			
SCHILLER, Pauline	26	Schniedeberg	68-0661
Robert 4			
SCHILLING, Adolf	13	Gera	71-0736
SCHILLING, August	26	Bebenstadt	69-1086
SCHILLING, Auguste	20	Bagnitz	71-0456
SCHILLING, Caroline	20	Neuenstein	71-0492
SCHILLING, Eduard	44	Gera	70-100
SCHILLING, Franz	35	Aachen	69-0268
SCHILLING, Heinrich	51	Leipzig	70-1055
SCHILLING, Margarethe	52	Coburg	69-0784
Julie 21			
SCHILLING, Maria	50	Geestendorf	71-0429
Conradine 23			
SCHILLING, Minna	20	Ruhba	69-0321
Ida 10 months			
SCHILLINGER, Joh.	27	Untermosbach	71-0521
SCHILP, Wilhelmine	15	Loewenstein	68-0661
SCHIMANECK, Johannes	28	Boehmen	69-0321
SCHIMBER, Minna	22	Marzhausen	69-1396
SCHIMECK, Franz	33	Raidreva-Bohemi	70-0006
Marie 33, Anna 6, Joseph 1			
SCHIMEK, Josef	36	Hlavatetz	70-0329
SCHIMMEL, Caroline	19	Rothselberg	71-0300
SCHIMMEL, Franz	26	Hain	68-0456
SCHIMMEL, Ludwig	27	Lippe-Col., Pol	69-0547
Wilhelmine 32, Wilhelmina 3 months			

NAME	AGE	RESIDENCE	YR-LIST
SCHIMMEL, Marg.	27	Rotselberg	68-1027
SCHIMMERLPFENNIG, C.	27	Schiesebern	70-0308
SCHIMON, Franz	30	Neuzerecke	68-0770
Catharina 35, Rosalia 8, Franz 6, Wenzel 3			
SCHIMPFF, Jac.	50	Lauterecken	68-0957
SCHINCK, Sophie	19	Wien	68-0820
Rosa 17, Sigmund 9, Catharina 14, Anna 42			
SCHINCKER, David	25	Tyrol	71-0167
SCHINDELAR, Johann	38	Rackowitz-Bohem	70-0006
Anna 28, Joseph 4			
SCHINDELMANN, Robert	38	Grengen	69-1086
Ursula 34, Sophie 7, Robert 5, Rudolf 5, Hermann 8 months			
SCHINDLER, Amalie	20	Waldkirch	70-0272
SCHINDLER, Anna	24	Berlin	69-0182
SCHINDLER, Friedrich	35	Wennings	69-1319
SCHINDLER, Ger.	31	Hannover	69-0841
SCHINDLER, K.	21	Fautenbach	71-0226
A. 19			
SCHINELLA, Michael	27	Rischwind	71-0712
Margarethe 36, Titus 9, Johann 6, Sabine 4, Vitus 11 months			
SCHINTZ, Nicolaus	47	Kell	68-0939
Anton 85, Anna Marie 45			
SCHIPPE, Wilhelmine	21	Rohma	68-0852
SCHIPPER, Jacob	28	Marientrave	69-1004
SCHIRLITZ, Julius	28	Erfurt	71-0456
SCHIRM, Rosa	34	Oehringen	69-0457
SCHIRMER, Franz	26	Stuttgart	69-0292
Marie 27			
SCHIRRMEISTER, C.	29	Dresden	68-1006
SCHIRRMOELLER, A.	60	Fischbach	69-0429
SCHIRZE, Johann	26	Trebnitz	69-0208
SCHITTGER, Louise	8	Oeynhausen	68-0647
SCHITTLER, Franz	44	Weinolzheim	68-0566
SCHLABOHM, Ludw.	32	Lehe	71-0479
SCHLADEMANN, John	50	St. Louis	70-1023
Doris 43, Hermine 18, Emma 6 months			
SCHLAEPFER, Ludw.	17	Speicher	70-0452
SCHLAGINTWEIB, J.	28	Villars	71-0429
Catharine 14			
SCHLAMBACH, Barbara	27	Poppenlauer	71-0821
SCHLAMM, Jette	36	Inowroclaw	68-0610
Rosalie 10 months			
SCHLAMP, Dorothea	23	Sentheim	70-0308
SCHLAMPP, Johann	39	Hockenheim	69-0572
Eva 30, Regina 5, Ludwig 11 months			
SCHLANDER, Anna Elis.	24	Oberkinzig	68-0884
SCHLANGENBACH, Carl	44	Bremen	71-0792
SCHLANK, Conrad	34	Hedisdorf	71-0815
SCHLATTAUER, Marie	17	Bettersheim	71-0479
SCHLAUCH, Adelheid	23	Rueppelso	69-1212
SCHLECHT, Franz	18	Guningen	68-0957
John 20			
SCHLECHT, Mag.	18	Breitenstein	71-0681
SCHLECHTER, Adolph	14		71-0727
SCHLEDORN, August	28	Elberfeld	69-0572
SCHLEGEL, Charles	22	Pforzheim	69-0771
SCHLEGEL, Heinrich	20	Naumburg	70-0355

NAME	AGE	RESIDENCE	YR-LIST
SCHLEGEL, Henriette	22	Fuerth	69-0490
SCHLEGEL, Josef	35	Cleveland	70-1003
Elise 25			
SCHLEGEL, Robert	14	Gera	70-0384
SCHLEGEMUEHL, Amalie	22	Suhl	68-0707
Emilie 16, Bruno 14			
SCHLEHUBER, Marie	37	Henfeld	68-1006
SCHLEI, Ludwig	22	Wien	70-0355
SCHLEICH, Balthasar	27	Hesse Darmstadt	70-0355
SCHLEICHARDT, F.	26	Toba	69-0429
Friederike 25, Auguste 3, Louis 6 months			
SCHLEICHER, HErm.	17	Markendorf	70-0569
SCHLEICHER, Lambert	25	Villingen	71-0492
SCHLEINITZ, W.	35	Paris	69-1004
Julie 25			
SCHLEIPER, Hermann	26	Lau	68-0939
SCHLEISS, Catharina	26	Baznitz	71-0429
SCHLEITER, Carl E.	21	Lippersdorf	69-0968
SCHLEITNER, Aug.	39	Landeck	68-0566
SCHLEMM, Gesine	20	Brinkum	68-0786
SCHLEMMING, Auguste	16	Bielefeld	70-1161
SCHLENK, Carl	25	Rust	71-0300
SCHLENK, Walburga	20	Diepoldsdorf	68-0982
SCHLENKER, Anna	33	Schwenningen	68-0760
Johann 8, Christian 6, Martin 3, Jacob 1			
SCHLENKER, Joh. 21	21	Schwenninger	68-1002
SCHLENSTEIN, Wme.	22	Goldlauter	69-0429
SCHLEPSTEIN, Anna	20	Hannover	71-0479
SCHLEPUETZ, W. H.	41	R.B. Coeln	68-0820
Sybilla 24, Johannes 12, Winard 9, Grete 6, Marie 6, Anna 5, Peter 10 m			
SCHLEUSKER, Maria	17	Minden	68-0907
SCHLEVE, Ludw.	23	Neisse	69-0490
SCHLEZEL, Leonh.	23	Langenfeld	69-0338
SCHLICHLEIN, Christ	16	Furth	69-1059
SCHLICHTHORST, F.	59	Dorum	63-0908
Hermine 24, Anna 22, Helene 21, Hermann 16			
SCHLICHTING, Bertha	30	Hannover	70-1003
SCHLICHTING, Georg	26	Mecklenburg	69-0067
SCHLICHTING, Henry	31	Hannover	69-0672
Johann 58, Rebecca 16, Anton 14			
SCHLICHTING, Nicolas	52	Langensalza	68-0786
Therese 59, Emma 19			
SCHLICK, Herm.	26	Zittay	69-1421
SCHLICKER, Edmund	24	Ludge	69-0798
SCHLICKWEIN, Christ.	17	Mannheim	69-0592
SCHLIK, Anna	27	Boehmen	70-1142
S. 9 months			
SCHLIKEISER, Rosine	50	Frankfurt	69-0576
SCHLIMME, Christian	46	Borstel	69-0229
Marie 44, Wilhelm 15, Minna 9, Louise 9, Marie 6			
SCHLIMME, Fritz		Borstel	69-0229
SCHLIMME, Heinrich	16	Borstel	69-0229
SCHLINGER, Johann	30	Wien	69-0559
Antonie 28, Rosa 11 months			
SCHLINGER, Ludwig	19	Heilbronn	69-1363
SCHLINGMANN, Friedrich	46	Buer	68-0786

NAME	AGE	RESIDENCE	YR-LIST
Caroline 45, Alwine 17, Otto 13, Hermine 9, Marie 6, Ottilie 2			
SCHLINGMANN, Heinrich	18	Dissen	68-0907
Fritz 18			
SCHLINGMANN, Henry	24	Bremen	69-1396
SCHLINGMANN, Marie	19	Bremen	68-0770
SCHLITTE, Adolph	31	Koethen	68-0661
SCHLITTING, John	34	Boehmen	70-1003
Alois 3			
SCHLITZBERGER, Hyethe	33	Hohenkirchen	69-1011
Anna 1			
SCHLOEMANN, Wilh.	44	Rabber	71-0581
Eleonore 18, Marie 11, Friedr. 9			
SCHLOENDORF, Gesina	16	Berne	69-0321
SCHLOENDORF, Mathilde	20	Oldenburg	70-0682
SCHLONDORF, Margreth	19	Lilienthal	71-0456
SCHLOO, Elisa	8	Ottersberg	69-0560
SCHLOO, Henry	19	Rothenburg	70-0355
SCHLOSHUSEN, John	22	Selsingen	69-0338
SCHLOSS, Anton	16	Jockim	68-0786
SCHLOSSER, August	33	Dittersbach	71-0429
SCHLOSSER, Johann	20	Borsitz,Austria	69-0547
SCHLOSSER, Marie	19	Lambrecht	69-1212
SCHLOSSER, Wm.	30	Bernstadt	69-1011
SCHLOSSMACHER, W.	38	Wesel	71-0429
Anna 28			
SCHLOTT, Wilhelm	14	Ziegenheim	69-0672
SCHLOTTAG, Wilh.	67	Neustadt	68-0753
Charlotte 64, Ferdinand 27, Henriette 25, Hermann 18			
SCHLOTTER, Elisabeth	18	Nidda	68-0786
SCHLOTTER, Prisca	16	Rastedt	68-1027
SCHLOTTMANN, Heinr.	39	Grossendorf	68-0982
SCHLUDE, Mathilde	25	Heinstetten	69-0672
Catharine 19			
SCHLUE, Friedrich	17	Detmold	69-0572
SCHLUE, Louise	20	Sonnebom	68-0456
SCHLUECHTER, Beta	20	Meyenburg	69-0572
SCHLUETER, Anna	22	Herzfeld	68-0820
SCHLUETER, August	16	Lehe	69-0848
SCHLUETER, Friedrich	16	Achim	71-0492
SCHLUETER, Fritz	39	Brakelsiek	68-314
Louise 34, Louise 13, Friedr. 4			
SCHLUETER, Heinrich	33	Wuelpe	69-0572
SCHLUETER, Henry	18	Neuenkirchen	69-0338
SCHLUETER, Herm.	17	Essen	69-0771
SCHLUETER, Hermann	23	Siesen/Seesen	69-1076
SCHLUETER, Julius	35	Treptow	68-0647
Alwine 35			
SCHLUETER, Julius	38	New York	71-1046
SCHLUETER, Marie	19	Bremervoerde	71-0479
SCHLUETER, Robert	15	Rietberg	68-0314
Anton 23			
SCHLUETTER, Justine	37	Zablmowa	70-0308
Wilhelmine 8, Alwine 4, Albert 11 months			
SCHLUTEN, August		Hanau?	69-0771
SCHLUTEN, Niclas	26	Neuboergen	69-0848
SCHLUTER, Friedr.	18	Wietersheim	71-0521
SCHLUTTER, Louis	78	Pyrmont	68-0982

NAME	AGE	RESIDENCE	YR-LIST
SCHMAEDEKE, Johann	16	Hasbergen	69-1309
SCHMAIDT, Friedrich	28	Altenstein	69-0429
SCHMAL, Jacob	17	Worms	68-0456
SCHMALE, Franz	44	Eininghausen	68-0566
Marie 42, Lotte 26, Friedr. 22, Marie 19			
SCHMALE, Johann	37	Boerninghausen	68-0566
Marie 33, Wilhelm 5, Catharine 9 months			
SCHMALLE, Herm.	45	Berghausen	71-0393
SCHMALRIEDE, W.	16	Mehnen	68-0610
Friedr. 15			
SCHMALZ, Charles	21	Limbach	68-0534
SCHMALZ, Georg	56	Dahlheim	69-1319
Magdal. 56			
SCHMALZ, Marga	19	Weisdorf	69-1319
SCHMAR, Friedr.	15	Riglashof	71-0521
SCHMAUCH, Jacob	65	Solz	68-0625
SCHMECK, Meta	19	Willendingen	71-0581
SCHMECKENBACHER	45	Hockenheim	71-0521
Catharine 44, Magdalene 19, Johanna 9, Elisabeth 7			
SCHMECKPEPER, J.	16	Hustede	69-0229
SCHMEIDER, Ferdinand	26	Goesslingen	70-0355
SCHMEISSER, Ad.	20	Siegen	68-0957
Ernst 17			
SCHMEISSER, Johann	33	Weiher	69-0848
Margareth 28, Margareth 9 months			
SCHMELZ, Heinr.	16	Cassel	68-0610
SCHMELZER, Georg	20	Ackerthausen	70-0052
SCHMERER, Jacob	20	Frielingen	69-0457
SCHMETZLE, Friederika	30	Knibis	71-0792
SCHMICKERLE, Gertrud	28	Westum	69-0229
SCHMID, Anna	26	Pappdan	69-0848
SCHMID, Anna	19	Uznuch	68-0534
SCHMID, August	35	Rudenweiler	69-0798
SCHMID, John	40	Rippoldsau	70-0355
SCHMID, Joseph	23	Habernitz	69-0015
SCHMID, Ma.	20	Stuttgart	70-1161
SCHMIDT, Adeline	20	Hannover	69-1421
SCHMIDT, Adolf	28	Cassel	70-0052
SCHMIDT, Adolf	15	Hall	71-0821
SCHMIDT, Agnes	30	Villmar	69-0321
SCHMIDT, Alfons	24	Hamburg	68-1298
SCHMIDT, Anna	25	Doningsdorf	68-0610
SCHMIDT, Anna	23	Koenigsworth	68-0534
SCHMIDT, Anna	24	Breitenbach	68-0939
SCHMIDT, Antony	36	Moys	68-0884
Henriette 32, Marie A. 8, Maria A. 3			
SCHMIDT, Aug.	28	Anhalt	69-1004
SCHMIDT, August	29	Hannover	71-0456
SCHMIDT, Auguste	17	Tadingbuettel	71-0521
SCHMIDT, Barb.	22	Auerbach	70-0384
SCHMIDT, Barbara	20	Bierstein	69-1011
SCHMIDT, Barbara	23	Grossueften	68-0566
Christine 19			
SCHMIDT, Barbara	54	Mannheim	68-0534
Anna 16			
SCHMIDT, Bhd.	14	Bremen	69-0338
Christ. 9			
SCHMIDT, Carl	40	Freistadt	69-0050

NAME	AGE	RESIDENCE	YR-LIST
SCHMIDT, Carl	40	Berlin	68-0770
SCHMIDT, Carl	28	Albenstadt	70-0523
SCHMIDT, Carl	25	Wolffenbuettel	70-0329
SCHMIDT, Carl	19	Fulda	68-0753
SCHMIDT, Carl	18	Herbolzheim	71-0581
SCHMIDT, Carl	19	Goeppingen	71-0521
SCHMIDT, Carl F.	39	Mellenau	71-0521
Henriette 39, Wilhelmine 11, Marie 9, Friederike 8, Pauline 3, Hermann 6,			
SCHMIDT, Carol.	54	Berlin	69-1363
SCHMIDT, Caroline	19	Muenchen	70-0378
SCHMIDT, Caroline	33	Gr. Mehmen	70-0223
Carl 8, Albert 6			
SCHMIDT, Caroline	20	Rodolin	71-0479
SCHMIDT, Caspar	27	Rickshofen	71-0684
SCHMIDT, Cath.	21	Hannover	70-1142
SCHMIDT, Catharina	29	Awigo	69-0338
SCHMIDT, Catharina	32	Besigheim	68-0760
Jacob 8			
SCHMIDT, Catharine	17	Espa	71-0492
SCHMIDT, Charles	18	Rothenburg	69-0560
Bertha 21			
SCHMIDT, Charles	48	Soltau	69-1011
Dorothea 47			
SCHMIDT, Charles	35	New York	69-1076
Catharine 35			
SCHMIDT, Charles	16	Lobenstein	68-0760
SCHMIDT, Charlotte	27	Wershausen	70-0355
SCHMIDT, Charlotte	24	Braunschweig	68-0610
SCHMIDT, Chr.	25	Owen	70-0378
SCHMIDT, Chr. E.	37	Wickenstedt	68-0610
SCHMIDT, Christ.	17	Darmstadt	68-0647
SCHMIDT, Christ.	17	Weimar	71-0821
Adam 14			
SCHMIDT, Christian	25	Steinberg	70-0184
SCHMIDT, Christian	22	Bremen	68-0907
SCHMIDT, Christine	20	Arnsheim	71-0643
SCHMIDT, Conrad	18	Eisenach	68-0852
SCHMIDT, Conrad	25	Bartshausen	68-0625
SCHMIDT, Died.	16	Grassander	71-0479
SCHMIDT, Diedrich	33	Uelzen	68-0707
Christine 30			
SCHMIDT, Ed.	22	Essen	68-0753
SCHMIDT, Egidius	41	Varnhalt	68-0014
Victoria 38, Catharina 15			
SCHMIDT, Eilert	21	Leeroth	69-0572
SCHMIDT, Eleonore	19	Davoerde	69-0771
SCHMIDT, Elisabeth	13	Oberfranken	69-0798
SCHMIDT, Elisabeth	19	Dexbach	71-0821
SCHMIDT, Elisabeth	29	Ilbesheim	71-0429
SCHMIDT, Elise	32	Darmstadt	70-0508
SCHMIDT, Elise	21	Oberohmbach	68-0820
SCHMIDT, Emil	7	Loerrach	70-0148
SCHMIDT, Emilie	20	Hannover	70-1142
SCHMIDT, Ernst	17	Davoerden	69-0771
SCHMIDT, Ernst	19	Cassel	68-1027
SCHMIDT, Eva	17	Staerklos	69-0457
SCHMIDT, F. A.	22	Clinton	70-0135

NAME	AGE	RESIDENCE	YR-LIST
SCHMIDT, Fr. Aug.	53	Clinton	70-0135
Johanne 60			
SCHMIDT, Franz	26	Coeln	68-0314
SCHMIDT, Franz	50	Waisenstaig	68-0852
SCHMIDT, Franz	32	Reichenau	71-0429
SCHMIDT, Frd.	67	Zweibruecken	71-0393
Karoline 57, Ferd. 30, Henriette 17			
SCHMIDT, Fred.	30	Wiesbaden	68-0534
SCHMIDT, Friedr.	23	Langensalza	68-0753
SCHMIDT, Friedrich	21	Unterjettingen	68-0566
SCHMIDT, Fritz	21	Esperke	68-0707
SCHMIDT, Fritz	25	Zeulenrode	71-0456
Lina 25, Otto 7			
SCHMIDT, Gabriela	35	Dresden	70-1142
Gabriela 4, Marie 9 months			
SCHMIDT, Gebhard	13	Neuhausen	69-0672
SCHMIDT, Georg	27	Wiesenbach	68-0884
SCHMIDT, Georg	45	Hoholz	70-0508
SCHMIDT, Georg	42	Saginan	69-1076
SCHMIDT, Georg	27	Rennfeld	68-1006
El. 24			
SCHMIDT, Georg	21	Oberiflingen	68-0534
Fabricius 17, Marian 22			
SCHMIDT, Georg	17	Magstadt	71-0684
SCHMIDT, George	28	Gangschweiler	70-0443
SCHMIDT, Gertrude	22	Siegen	68-0456
SCHMIDT, Gottl.	20	Rotenheim	69-1004
SCHMIDT, H. H.	26	Hannover	68-0647
SCHMIDT, Heinr.	18	Ringle	68-1002
SCHMIDT, Heinr.	27	Nenndorf	69-0572
Wilhelmine 27			
SCHMIDT, Heinr. P.	26	Darmstadt	68-0820
SCHMIDT, Heinrich	26	Zimmerscheid	68-0661
SCHMIDT, Heinrich	21	Bielefeld	71-0821
SCHMIDT, Henry	18	Bodenhausen	70-0508
SCHMIDT, Herm.	28	Talge	71-0479
SCHMIDT, Herm. Jul.	19	Eisenberg	68-0647
SCHMIDT, Hermann	22	Kahla	69-0067
SCHMIDT, Hermann		Sondershausen	69-0542
SCHMIDT, Hermann	23	Lippe Detmold	69-0268
SCHMIDT, Hermann	21	Lemgo	71-0733
SCHMIDT, Hermann	19	Heilbronn	71-0643
SCHMIDT, Hugo	17	Mannheim	70-0683
SCHMIDT, J. P.	36	Oldenburg	69-0560
Margarethe 31, Peter 8, Louise 5, Charles 3, Catharine 1 months, Peter 1 months			
SCHMIDT, J.B.	34	Pittsburg	71-1046
SCHMIDT, Jac.	45	Niedermendig	68-314
Maria 29, Catharina 6, Margarethe 11 months			
SCHMIDT, Jacob	23	Ingstingen	68-0786
SCHMIDT, Jacob	33	Aschstetten	69-1059
SCHMIDT, Jacob	18	Wiesentheid	69-1309
SCHMIDT, Jacob	25	Ruestenhausen	68-0647
SCHMIDT, Jacob	17	Siegmarswangen	71-0643
SCHMIDT, Joh.	25	Leer	68-1002
SCHMIDT, Joh. G.	30	New York	69-1421
SCHMIDT, Johann	18	Oberschulz	69-0771
SCHMIDT, Johann	30	Ober Iflingen	68-0786

NAME	AGE	RESIDENCE	YR-LIST
SCHMIDT, Johann	35	Doehlen	69-0490
Anna 29, Anna 8, Joseph 6, Catharina 10 months, Marie 64			
SCHMIDT, Johann	36	Franken	69-1059
Anna 30, Barbara 5, Gustav 1 months			
SCHMIDT, Johann	19	Baiern	70-0384
SCHMIDT, Johann	20	Igerstein	68-0707
SCHMIDT, Johann	47	Schmalkalden	68-0760
SCHMIDT, Johann	20	Helmbrechts	71-0643
SCHMIDT, Johann	35	Ebergoens	71-0492
Catharine 32, Martin 9, Catharina 5, Margarethe 11 months			
SCHMIDT, Johannes	14	Ebingen	70-0523
SCHMIDT, Johannes	19	Steinbach	71-0521
SCHMIDT, John	38	Duseun	70-1023
SCHMIDT, John	52	Ottersberg	69-0560
SCHMIDT, John	27	Doebra	69-0560
SCHMIDT, John	18	Weidenhausen	68-0534
SCHMIDT, Josef	23	Ramsdorf	69-1086
SCHMIDT, Josef	44	Kralowitz	71-0429
Josefa 33, Franz 9, Marie 8, Josefa 7, Josef 5, Johanne 11 months			
SCHMIDT, Julie	45	Torgau	70-0728
Bruno 15, Clara 12			
SCHMIDT, Kaethe	23	Rothenburg	68-1298
SCHMIDT, Kath.	20	Kurhessen	70-0443
SCHMIDT, Kunigunde	22	Nuernberg	68-0982
SCHMIDT, Kunigunde	30	Oberfranken	69-0321
SCHMIDT, Louise	25	Fokinghausen	68-0647
Dorothea 22			
SCHMIDT, Ludwig	57	Fuchel	69-0576
Cath. 54			
SCHMIDT, Ludwig	15	Oldenburg	69-0923
SCHMIDT, Magd.	17	Darmstadt	70-0378
SCHMIDT, Magdalene	19	Nussloch	69-0429
David 18			
SCHMIDT, Marga.	21	Marburg	71-0821
SCHMIDT, Maria	24	Hauben	69-0798
SCHMIDT, Marie	21	Handelshausen	69-1059
SCHMIDT, Marie	29	Leibhardt	68-0566
SCHMIDT, Marie	21	Muenchen	68-0566
SCHMIDT, Marie	26	Weikersheim	71-0226
Johann 2			
SCHMIDT, Martin	17	Darmstadt	70-0355
SCHMIDT, Martin	23	Ostfriesland	70-0329
SCHMIDT, Minna	23	Muehlen	68-0982
SCHMIDT, Moritz	32	Kirchberg	69-0784
SCHMIDT, Nicolas	28	Burgstall	69-0229
SCHMIDT, Pauline	31	Leipzig	71-0789
Clara 7, Martha 6, Ernst 9 months			
SCHMIDT, Peter	18	Lederbach-Liede	69-0798
SCHMIDT, Peter	18	Ottersmeier	69-0050
SCHMIDT, Peter	34	Aschbach	68-0419
SCHMIDT, Peter	23	Idar	71-0815
SCHMIDT, Philip	22	Geitmann	71-0681
Elise 24			
SCHMIDT, Philipp	16	Heppenheim	69-0672
Caroline 21			
SCHMIDT, Philipp	25	Einzelthurm	68-0852
SCHMIDT, Philippine	26	Dreisen	69-1396
SCHMIDT, Philippine	17	Dilkirchen	71-0363
SCHMIDT, Richard	36	Bloomington	70-1003
Josephine 32, Emma 5			
SCHMIDT, Rolf	25	Oldendorf	68-0707
SCHMIDT, Ruppert	20	Niederweimar	68-0534
SCHMIDT, Sextus	31	Flins	68-0852
SCHMIDT, Sophie	19	Frauenstein	70-0508
SCHMIDT, Sophie	27	Bremen	70-0452
SCHMIDT, Sophie	20	Lippstadt	71-0789
Elise 17			
SCHMIDT, Theo	19	Leipzig	69-0771
SCHMIDT, Theo.	19	Pruem	71-0143
SCHMIDT, Theobaldina	18	Frankfurt	68-1049
SCHMIDT, Therese	18	Langensalza	70-0443
SCHMIDT, Trientje	48	Bunde	71-0456
Jantje 4, Trientje 10 months			
SCHMIDT, Valentin	16	Unterstoppel	68-1002
SCHMIDT, Victor	26	Meiningen	68-0566
SCHMIDT, Wilh.	25	Rittersbrug	69-0592
Marie 17			
SCHMIDT, Wilh.	18	Hochdorf	71-0479
SCHMIDT, Wilhelm	38	Carolina	69-0338
Sofia 29, Ottilie 3, Auguste 2			
SCHMIDT, Wilhelm	15	Litterhof	69-1076
SCHMIDT, Wilhelmine		Nenndorf	69-0268
SCHMIDT, Wilhelmine	22	Reetz	68-0314
Emilie 24			
SCHMIDT, Wilhelmine	56	Neuwedel	68-0760
Augusta 23, Friedrich 17, Anton 14			
SCHMIDTBORN, Eduard	18	Giesen	68-0786
SCHMIDTS, Anna	25	Koenigswald	71-0581
SCHMIDTZINSKY, Carl	30	Hildesheim	71-0429
SCHMIEDER, Louise	20	New York	69-0457
Louise 8 months			
SCHMIEDER, Ludwig	16	Merane	70-0031
SCHMIEDEWOLF, J.	44	Frankenhausen	68-0707
Juliane 16, Wilhelmine 14, Marie 3, Therese 11 months			
SCHMIEDINGER, Joseph	23	Tirol	70-0523
SCHMIEDKE, Carl	26	Coslin	68-0939
Marie 26			
SCHMIERMUND, Adam	16	Wehrda	68-0939
SCHMIETZ, Joseph	16	Crefeld	69-0798
Maria 17			
SCHMINKE, Elisabeth	44	Umysterode	69-0542
Michael 45, Catharina 17, Georg 7, Otto 6, Wilhelm 3			
SCHMINKE, Johann	41	Umysterode	69-0542
Christiane 29			
SCHMION, Josepha	36	Neuzerecka	68-0770
SCHMIT, Marie	19	Leidenbach	71-0789
SCHMIT, P.	26	Echternach	69-1363
SCHMITT, Georg	20	Verden	70-1161
SCHMITT, Jacob	27	Kalbe	68-0760
SCHMITT, Ludwig	14	Ruedigheim	69-1319
SCHMITT, Michael	25	Rosstadt	69-0592
SCHMITT, Peter	33	Schafthausen	71-0643
Magdalene 30, Marie 5, Nico. 11 m.			
SCHMITTGES, Marg.	32	Fuerth	71-0712

NAME	AGE	RESIDENCE	YR-LIST
Babette 11 months			
SCHMITTKER, Elise	20	Rettinghausen	71-0456
SCHMITZ, Bernh.	49	Wellesberg	69-0338
Anna 49, Anna 20, Franz 19, Christiane 17, Elisabeth 12, Peter 8, John 6			
SCHMITZ, Henry	16	Wildshausen	70-0355
SCHMITZ, Jacob	24	R.B.Coblenz	68-1006
Johann 24			
SCHMITZ, Peter	18	Pfeffelbach	70-0452
SCHMITZ, W.	39	Gladbach	69-0798
SCHMITZ, Wilhelmine	25	Mettmann	69-0429
SCHMITZER, Jacobine	30	Ockending	69-1076
Emma 5			
SCHMOELZER, Ch.	23	Austria	70-0170
SCHMOERER, Louise	46	Rust	71-0492
Leopold 19, Victoria 17, Rosina 9			
SCHMOLAH, W.	69	Lahr	69-1004
Antoni 20, Richard 1			
SCHMOLL, Johann	18	Joachimsthal	69-0321
SCHMOLZER, Elise Marg.	21	Regensburg	69-1076
SCHMUCK, Fritz	28	Schoetmar	68-0625
Henriette 21			
SCHMUCK, Rosine	66	Neutlingen	69-0542
SCHMUDLACH, Ernestine	16	Lubs	68-0786
Wilhelmine 24			
SCHMUELLING, Carl	35	Coeln	68-0957
SCHMUER, Elise	21	Alt Schlunuf	71-0479
SCHMUPFLER, Heinr.	24	Mehringen	71-0681
SCHMUTZ, Gust.	27	Riskowitz	69-1004
SCHMUTZ, Maria	24	Weisshosen	69-0798
SCHMUTZ, Rupert	23	Sullixgen	71-0300
SCHNABEL, Catharina	26	Richelkirchen	71-0521
SCHNACKENBERG, D.	18	Groeplingen	69-0162
SCHNACKENBERG, J.	18	Westertimke	68-0770
Joseph 16			
SCHNACKER, Johann	30	Hannover	69-0923
SCHNADEL, Adam	24	Herweiler	69-0572
SCHNAKENBERG, H.	15	Tarmstadt	68-0625
SCHNAKENBERG, H.	18	Hannover	69-0208
SCHNAKENBROCK, C.	22	Wellingholzhaus	68-0957
SCHNARS, Wilhelmine	19	Wulferdingen	68-0786
SCHNECKE, Christian	36	St. Joseph	69-1212
Marie 19			
SCHNECKELHOF, W.	19	Schwege	69-0229
SCHNECKENBECHER	36	Dettingen	68-0014
SCHNECKENBURGER, C.	27	Tuttlingen	68-1298
SCHNEEBERGER, David	30	Tyrol	71-0167
SCHNEEMANN, Wm.	36	Neustadt	68-0760
SCHNEENK, Gustav	17	Lossberg	68-0647
SCHNEIDER, Ad.	27	Falkenstein	70-0308
SCHNEIDER, Anna	45	Frankin	69-0162
SCHNEIDER, Anna	20	Eberstadt	71-0429
SCHNEIDER, Anne	22	Volkertsbier	68-0625
SCHNEIDER, Anton	25	Dousenau	68-0661
SCHNEIDER, Aug.	38	Braunschweig	68-0647
SCHNEIDER, Bernhard	42	Attendorn	68-1006
Eugen 2			
SCHNEIDER, Bertha	12	Leipzig	70-0508

NAME	AGE	RESIDENCE	YR-LIST
SCHNEIDER, Carl	33	Wuerzburg	69-0784
SCHNEIDER, Carl	46	Thueringen	70-1003
SCHNEIDER, Carl	13	Frankenberg	70-0452
SCHNEIDER, Carl	19	Minden	68-0939
SCHNEIDER, Caroline	16	Rommelshausen	71-0643
SCHNEIDER, Cath.	14	Cusel	70-0452
SCHNEIDER, Catharina	19	Werda	70-0378
SCHNEIDER, Catharine	24	Biederbach	70-0452
SCHNEIDER, Cathrine	26	Frankfurt	70-1003
SCHNEIDER, Char.	22	Bernsburg	69-1011
SCHNEIDER, Conrad	25	Rotenburg	68-0314
SCHNEIDER, Eleonore	59	Kirchberg	69-1363
Carol. 14			
SCHNEIDER, Elisabeth	37	Gernsheim	68-0314
SCHNEIDER, Elise	17	Reichenbach	69-1059
SCHNEIDER, Erwin	28	Rudesheim	71-0492
SCHNEIDER, Fr.	20	Kaemmerzell	68-1002
SCHNEIDER, Franz	25	Baumgarte	69-0547
SCHNEIDER, Friedr.	50	Nedal	68-0982
Willy 6			
SCHNEIDER, Friedrich	59	Kirchberg	68-0907
SCHNEIDER, Georg	17	Berleburg	70-0728
SCHNEIDER, Georg	19	Galveston	70-1003
SCHNEIDER, Georg	17	Schwarzenborn	71-0479
SCHNEIDER, Gg.	18	Essingen	70-1035
SCHNEIDER, Gottlieb	27	New York	70-0508
SCHNEIDER, Gustav	43	Elenberg	69-0542
Ottilie 9 months			
SCHNEIDER, Heinrich	41	Wiedermuss	71-0492
SCHNEIDER, Helena	61	Zweibruecken	68-0456
Catharina 31, Franziska 25, Magdalena 11 months			
SCHNEIDER, Jacob	20	Kirchheim	69-0592
SCHNEIDER, Joh.	23	Mutterstadt	68-0786
SCHNEIDER, Joh.	22	Koenigsberg	71-0681
SCHNEIDER, Joh.	28	Wellingen	71-0479
Cath. 22			
SCHNEIDER, Johann	29	Emmershausen	69-0968
Margarethe 24, Anna 11 months, Heinrich 26, Georg 58			
SCHNEIDER, Johann	49	Erlau	71-0712
SCHNEIDER, Johann	26	Deissau	71-0581
SCHNEIDER, Johannes	18	Sondelfingen	70-0452
SCHNEIDER, Johannes	26	Schenklengsfeld	68-0820
SCHNEIDER, John	24	Schenklengsfeld	68-0534
SCHNEIDER, Josef	30	Kirchhain	69-0162
Louis 19			
SCHNEIDER, Josef	18	Schwarzelbach	71-0681
SCHNEIDER, Joseph	28	Solingen	70-1055
SCHNEIDER, Joseph	47	Birkenried	68-0314
Anna 46, Joseph 9, Christian 2, Heinrich 10 months			
SCHNEIDER, Joseph	19	Halden	71-0733
SCHNEIDER, Juerg	26	Niederfroschhei	71-0643
SCHNEIDER, Ludwig	15	Deisslingen	70-0308
SCHNEIDER, Magd.	19	Rathsweiler	68-1027
SCHNEIDER, Male	22	Ulm	69-0050
SCHNEIDER, Maria	17	Strothe	69-0268
SCHNEIDER, Marie	30	Bamberg	68-0884

NAME	AGE	RESIDENCE	YR-LIST
SCHNEIDER, Mathilde	21	Einmingen	71-0521
SCHNEIDER, Michael		Jaddowa/Boehm.	69-0576
SCHNEIDER, Nicol.	25	Kuernach	68-1002
SCHNEIDER, Ottilie	57	Kaltennortheim	68-0534
Valentin 22			
SCHNEIDER, Otto	14	Cusel	70-0452
SCHNEIDER, Paul	23	Enskirchen	68-0957
SCHNEIDER, Peter	23	Nehren	69-0208
SCHNEIDER, Philip	41	Manweiler	68-1298
Carolina 15, Philipp 13, Jacob 9, Magdalena 8			
SCHNEIDER, Raimund	46	Ulm	68-0852
SCHNEIDER, Reinhard	16	Neufra	68-0852
SCHNEIDER, Rosalie	24	Steinau	68-0456
SCHNEIDER, Rosine	60	Deisslingen	68-0982
Georg 39, Ursula 45			
SCHNEIDER, Rosine	22	Wichtshausen	70-0355
SCHNEIDER, Simon	18	Kempten	70-1003
SCHNEIDER, Theodor	26	Gonzeroth	69-0798
Elisabeth 24			
SCHNEIDER, Traugott	28	Gera	68-0625
Pauline 23			
SCHNEIDER, Wilh.	32	Bayreuth	69-1086
SCHNEIDER, Wilhelm	45	Rheinprovinz	69-1363
Marie 44, Gerhard 18, Wilhelm 16, Elisabeth 9, Marg. 7, Anton 5, Helene 2			
SCHNEIDER, Wilhelmine	16	Rommelshaus	69-0784
SCHNEIDIG, Joh.	27	Fuerth	69-0162
SCHNEIDLER, Elisabeth	24	Guenthers	68-0939
SCHNEIER, Heinrich	30	Uchte	68-1027
SCHNEING, Louise	22	Holland	70-0384
SCHNELL, Carl	16	Altenhuntorf	71-0581
SCHNELL, Heinrich	15	Rielingshausen	69-0798
SCHNELL, Joh.	21	Sprendlingen	71-0581
SCHNELL, Johannes	16	Friedingen	71-0712
SCHNELLER, Joseph	59	Saaz	68-0534
Josepha 59, Barbara 19, Rosalie 16			
SCHNELLER, Wm.	16	Wien	69-1011
SCHNELZLE, Wilhelm	23	Sasbachwelden	71-0821
SCHNEPF, Simon	32	Nuernberg	68-0820
Toni (female) 30			
SCHNEPPENDAHL, L.	19	Hagen a/W	69-0015
SCHNEPPENHEIM, H.	27	R.B. Coeln	68-0610
Catharina 54			
SCHNERLE, Barb.	19	Wettmannsweiler	71-0581
SCHNETZ, Wilhelmine	35	Pinnow	71-0733
August 9, Wilhelmine 4, Andreas 8			
SCHNIBBE, Louis	15	Vorbusch	69-0572
SCHNIEPF, Carl	21	Halle	69-0672
SCHNIRA, Dora	24	Hannover	70-1142
SCHNITGEN, Catharina	18	Croen	69-0321
SCHNITTCHER, Anna	25	Altenbruch	68-0661
SCHNITTER, Christine	18	Ebingen	68-314
SCHNITTGER, Friedrich	26	Bielefeld	69-1076
SCHNODHELM, Elise	26	Nesselroden	69-0229
SCHNUCK, Carl	14	Sobernheim	70-0728
Elisabeth 25			
SCHNUETGEN, Julius	31	Hueckerswagen	68-0982
Mathilde 27, Aug. 11 months, Friedr. 28, Wilhelmine 22, Ernst 3 months			
SCHNURR, Johann	4	Moehringen	69-0798
SCHOATSKIN, Adam	37	Merdaken/Bohem	69-0576
Dorothea 37, Joseph 7, Margaretha 6			
SCHOBEL, Rosa	17	Rothweil	70-0329
SCHOBER, Mathilde	30	Elberfeld	68-0907
SCHOCK, Alois	33	Hannover	71-0429
Josefa 27			
SCHOCK, Paul Ludwig	23	Dessau	70-0259
SCHODA, Elisabeth	46	Moorsum	69-1309
SCHODERER, Johannes	31	Donauwoerth	68-0770
Wilhelm 25			
SCHOEK, Barb.	24	Esslingen	71-0581
SCHOELHAMMER, Carl	18	Welzheim	69-0429
SCHOELKER, Konrad	25	Detmold	69-0672
Anna 24			
SCHOELL, Bernhard	27	Hudermoor	69-0321
SCHOELLER, Ad.	27	Frankfurt a/M	69-0100
SCHOELLER, Ferd.	33	Solingen	68-0753
SCHOELLER, Mary	14	Guetersloh	68-0957
SCHOELLHAMMER, C.	18	Nuertingen	68-0982
SCHOEMERNS, Gerhard	42	Huelbrunn	68-0456
SCHOEN, Bertha	20	Iduni	70-0569
SCHOEN, Georg	17	Cassel	70-1003
SCHOEN, Magreth	29	Walderssen	71-0643
SCHOEN, Reinhard	31	Woltershausen	69-0457
SCHOEN, William	20	Bischhausen	68-0534
SCHOENAUER, Anna	21	Neudrossenfeld	69-0848
SCHOENBERG, Herm.	23	Repplin	68-0314
SCHOENBERGER, C.	20	Sattendf.-Salte	70-0355
SCHOENBUSCH, Louise	34	Bilefeld	69-0798
Emilie 13, Carl 11 months			
SCHOENDECK, Amalie	27	Erfurt	71-0727
SCHOENDER, Hermann	12	Mittelstren	71-0521
SCHOENE, Carl	17	Zerbst	69-0968
SCHOENELING, Auguste	28	Rathe	71-0581
Therese 19			
SCHOENEMANN, Robert	14	Bielefeld	69-0583
Minna 2			
SCHOENFELD, Ernestine	32	Weida	68-0456
Ernst 9			
SCHOENFELD, H.	15	Hannover	69-0490
SCHOENFELD, Heinr.	19	Pest	70-0052
SCHOENFELD, Sophie	56	S. Weimar	70-1023
Joseph 16			
SCHOENFELD, Wilhelm	27	Dessau	69-1319
SCHOENHARDT, John	27	Marburg	71-0172
SCHOENHEIDT, Carl	44	Thueringen	69-0672
Friedrich 32, Adolph 9			
SCHOENHERR, An.	26	Tyrol	70-1142
SCHOENSTEIN, Friedrich	20	Hasselbach	68-0982
SCHOENTHAL, Abraham	29	Marienhagen	68-0707
SCHOENWERK, Otto	16	Cassel	70-0076
SCHOEPFER, Catharina	29	Obertuerkheim	68-0907
SCHOEPPE, Heinrich	13	Gerolsheim	71-0363
Barbara 20, Eva 23			
SCHOEPPMANN, Marie	26	Osnabrueck	70-0728

NAME	AGE	RESIDENCE	YR-LIST
SCHOEPSKE, Fr.	25	Gross Krebs	70-0204
SCHOETTELE, Sebastian	21	Westernhausen	69-0490
SCHOETTLER, Herm. Fr.	18	Wuergassen	69-1212
SCHOETTLER, Hermine	28	Lungwitz	69-1076
SCHOETTLER, Johann	55	Sellinghausen	71-0736
Anna 50, Franziska 18, Gertrud 14, Elisabeth 8			
SCHOETTLER, Marie	20	Elmlahr	71-0479
SCHOETTOBER, J.	36	Sasbach	71-0789
SCHOH, Betty	49	Ottersberg	71-0393
Marie 7			
SCHOLE, Wilhelm	24	Oberfeld	69-0268
SCHOLECK, Mathias	19	Zelibow	68-0770
SCHOLKEMANN, Aug.	16	Eschede	71-0684
SCHOLL, Charlotte	19	Darmstadt	70-1142
Joh. 22			
SCHOLL, Johann	31	Boehmen	70-0728
Maria 21, Anna 6, Paulina 11 months			
SCHOLL, Johanna	64	Heimbach	68-0852
Elisabeth 20, Catharina 23			
SCHOLL, John H.	53	Wuergendorf	68-0957
Mary 54, William 24, Henry 21, Christian 19, Christine 13			
SCHOLL, Magnus	14	Marbach	68-0661
Peter 26			
SCHOLLE, Auguste	20	Bremen	69-0457
SCHOLLERS, Gustav	19	Homburg	69-0848
SCHOLT, Wilhelmine	22	Werdau	71-0684
Franzisca 16, Selma 14, Clara 9, Rudolph 6			
SCHOLTER, Louise	24	Bremen	68-0456
SCHOLTZ, Louise	21	Glatz	68-0939
SCHOLZ, Doroth.	26	Breslau	71-0815
SCHOLZ, Franz	23	Steinsdorf	68-0456
SCHOLZ, Rudolph	36	Schweidnitz	71-0363
SCHOMAKER, Wilhelm	26	Mulsum	68-0534
Anna 27, baby-son 11 months, John 55, Anna 56			
SCHOMBURG, Ernst	19	Buehren	68-0786
SCHOMBURG, Fr.	16	Holzhausen	71-0363
SCHOMBURG, Ludwig	33	Oppenwede	69-0321
Wilhelmine 30			
SCHOMBURG, Ludwig	42	Carons	68-0625
Elisabeth 36, Carl 7, Friederike 4, Augusta 2			
SCHOMEHL, Heinr.	14	Wallhausen	70-0452
SCHOMERASKY, And.	25	Merdrowiz	71-0479
SCHOMERUS, W. L.	24	Neuland	71-0736
SCHONAK, Gottlieb	32	Lautern	69-1396
SCHONEBURG, Lina	17	Bueren	68-0625
SCHONIER, Hermann	27	Osterrieden	68-0314
SCHONLAU, Dina	28	Henkhausen	68-0314
SCHOON, Johann	26	Obergrimpen	69-0229
SCHOOR, Wilhelm	25	Zuerich	70-0443
SCHOOT, Bernadina	34	Eppe	68-0852
Marie 37, Bernhard 5, Joseph 3, Josephine 11 months			
SCHOPP, Therese	18	Oberdissen	69-0572
SCHOPPE, Aug.	25	Wenzen	68-0610
SCHOPPE, Henry	35	Lenne	70-1003
SCHORN, Maria	17	Abenheim	69-0229
Josef 13			
SCHORP, Franz	21	Fischbeck	69-0229
SCHORR, Conrad	29	Emskirchen	68-0625
Georg 20			
SCHOSSER, Gertrud	24	Weilhausen	71-0492
SCHOTTE, Cacilie	17	Nordhausen	71-0363
SCHOTTEN, Pauline	22	Allstedt	68-0534
SCHOVERTS, Theodor	61	Wolfenbuettel	70-0184
SCHRABER, Friedrich	57	Sachsen	70-1161
Auguste 55			
SCHRADER, August	26	Suederbrook	68-1027
SCHRADER, Carl	20	Northeim	69-1319
SCHRADER, Franz	29	Gr. Denkle	69-0321
SCHRADER, Friedr.	25	Buende	68-1002
SCHRADER, Friedr.	17	Goslar	71-0429
Elise 12			
SCHRADER, Hermann	30	Osterscheps	68-0939
Helene 28			
SCHRADER, Josef	17	Himmelsthuer	68-0760
SCHRADER, Wilhelm	23	Wollbrechthause	68-0770
SCHRADIN, Caroline	28	Stettin	69-1086
SCHRAEFER, Ulrich	70	Huetten	68-0865
SCHRAFF, Joh.	22	Tyrol	70-100
SCHRAG, Friedrike	29	Scheibeweiler	71-0821
Jacob 3			
SCHRAM, H.	17	Mestolz	70-0443
SCHRAMER, Friedrich	40	Hechingen	71-0727
SCHRAMM, Aug. Wilhelm	37	Luege	69-0321
Anna Elisabeth 35, Friedrich Wilhelm 9, Aug. Wilhelm 8, Anna Helene 5, Anna Fr			
SCHRAMM, Jac.	19	Buschdorf	71-0393
SCHRAMM, Magdalene	27	Breitbrunn	71-0712
SCHRAMM, Marg.	22	Bamberg	68-0760
SCHRAMM, Peter	25	Trost	70-0184
SCHRAMM, Valentin	44	Gotha	69-1011
Mary 31, Charles 8, Richard 7, Ernst 4, baby son 9 months			
SCHRAPFER, Joh.	19	Schoenewald	69-0542
SCHRECK, Rosine	26	Hasselbach	68-0982
Georg 15			
SCHRECKE, Wilh.	20	Stolzenau	68-0786
SCHREIBER, Carl	22	Cassel	71-0393
SCHREIBER, Elise	14	Jarbach	70-1161
SCHREIBER, Ernst	25	Skoenk	68-0647
SCHREIBER, Geo.	26	Mecklenburg	69-0841
Johanna 21, William 3 months			
SCHREIBER, Hulda	19	Heldrungen	68-1006
SCHREIBER, Jacob	26	Orb	68-0852
SCHREIBER, John	54	Grossenschwend	70-0355
Ursula 49, Margareth 8			
SCHREIBER, Marie	51	Cassel	69-0457
SCHREIBER, Regine	28	Zirkwitz	71-0479
Franz 9, Anton 7, Albert 3, Marie 10 months			
SCHREIBER, Theo.	24	Holzstadt	68-1298
SCHREIER, Gottlieb	25	Rexingen	69-0576
SCHREINER, Arnold	23	Darmstadt	69-0841
SCHREINER, Elisabeth	16	Germersheim	71-0581
SCHREINER, Margarethe	50	Badbergen	71-0226
SCHREINER, Wilhelm	21	Rechelndorf	71-0684

NAME	AGE	RESIDENCE	YR-LIST
SCHREINERT, Wilhelm	18	Prenzlau	68-0770
SCHREYER, Friederike	16	Alfeld	71-0456
SCHREYER, Georg	18	Hall	70-0682
SCHREYER, Joh.	40	Alsenz	68-0786
Marie 38, Elisabeth 9, Joh. 7, Catharine 3			
SCHREYER, Johannes	27	Suetz	68-1006
SCHREYER, Sophia	25	Alfeld	68-1298
SCHRICHER, Elisabeth	21	Thierstein	69-1076
SCHRIEFER, Diedr.	16	Huettenbusch	69-0572
SCHRIEFER, Diedr. Hein.	33	Hannover	70-0378
SCHRIEVER, Georg	17	Dingelfingen	68-0786
SCHRIMPER, Frz.	18	Vellage	68-0610
SCHRINK, John	18	Tolesla	69-1363
SCHROCK, Magda.	16	Boettingen	70-1161
SCHRODT, Rosina	58	Westhofen	69-0490
SCHROECK, Conrad	35	Bremen	70-1003
SCHROEDER, Alb.	24	Nuxei	69-1363
SCHROEDER, Anna	29	Volkmarsdorf	68-0957
SCHROEDER, Anna	18	Wietzen	71-0736
SCHROEDER, Carl	25	Barmen	71-0363
SCHROEDER, Caroline	24	Waldeck	71-0821
SCHROEDER, Chr. Aug.	36	Oldenburg	70-0355
Helene 33, Helene 6, Margreth 6, Baby daughter 6 months			
SCHROEDER, Conrad	53	Lieme	68-0534
Caroline 40, Johanna 17			
SCHROEDER, Diedrich	18	Jeddingen	71-0492
SCHROEDER, Elise	20	Alsbevern	68-0852
SCHROEDER, Emil	26	Darmstadt	69-1086
SCHROEDER, Ernestine	28	Chatchefse	71-0300
Wilhelmine 22, M. 5, Fr. 6 months			
SCHROEDER, Ernst	24	Petershagen	69-0559
SCHROEDER, Ernst	24	Oschatz	69-0229
SCHROEDER, Ernst	17	Soemmerda	71-0363
SCHROEDER, Francisca	28	Jever	69-1396
Johann 10 months			
SCHROEDER, Franziska	28	Hammelburg	69-1212
SCHROEDER, Friedrich	42	Hohenward	69-1212
SCHROEDER, Georg	48	Veerssen	69-0848
Sophie 56			
SCHROEDER, Gerd	40	Bremervoerde	71-0456
Anna 33, John 7, Margreth 6, Conrad 3, Claus 10 months, Anna 28			
SCHROEDER, Greetje	32	Hanstedt	68-0625
Anna 9, Adelheid 17			
SCHROEDER, Heinrich	24	Lienen	68-1006
SCHROEDER, Heinrich	14	Hannover	68-0820
SCHROEDER, Heinrich	25	Gilten	71-0492
SCHROEDER, Henriette	36	Iserlohn	71-0712
Dorothea 7, Heinrich 11 months			
SCHROEDER, Hermann	16	Barntrup	70-0148
Otto 23			
SCHROEDER, Immanuel	44	Thueringen	70-0443
Anna 37, Elisabeth 14			
SCHROEDER, J.	21	Bremen	71-0643
SCHROEDER, J.A.	50	Oldenburg	71-0521
Anna 45, Anna 22, Wilhelmine 20, Mariea 14, Heinrich 28, Anton 14, Johanne 9,			
SCHROEDER, Joh.	45	Lamstedt	69-1319
SCHROEDER, Joh.	43	Eichelsachsen	68-0314
SCHROEDER, Joh.	15	Bremen	71-0521
SCHROEDER, Johann	40	Hammelburg	69-1363
SCHROEDER, Johann	65	Hessen	69-0672
Konrad 26, Wilhelm 6			
SCHROEDER, Johann	25	Mecklenburg	70-1023
SCHROEDER, Johann	22	London	69-0490
SCHROEDER, John	15	Lockstedt	70-0355
SCHROEDER, Louis	40	Hudermoor	69-0321
Beta 38, Elise 6, Heinrich 5			
SCHROEDER, Louise	20	Gr.Bage	68-0884
SCHROEDER, Lucia	54	Arnhofer	68-0770
Catharine 19, Hubert 13			
SCHROEDER, Maria	18	Osthofen	71-0492
SCHROEDER, Martha	17	Cassel	68-0014
SCHROEDER, Mary	21	Hassel	68-0957
SCHROEDER, Mathias	35	Hannover	69-1086
Anna 30, Trina 3			
SCHROEDER, Meta	21	Scharmbeck	68-1006
SCHROEDER, Metta	20	Oldenburg	71-0492
SCHROEDER, Nicolaus	27	Hannover	69-1086
Aug. 25			
SCHROEDER, Oscar	23	Mittweide	71-0736
SCHROEDER, Peter	16	Glinstedt	69-0560
SCHROEDER, Peter H.	65	Nordletha	68-0610
SCHROEDER, Victor	36	Barmen	71-0492
SCHROEDER, Wilh.	16	Bremervoerde	68-0957
SCHROEDER, Wilh.	16	Lamstedt	71-0736
SCHROEDER, Wilh.	18	Soemmerda	71-0363
SCHROEDER, Wilhelmine	30	Stuchow	69-0429
SCHROEDER, Wilhelmine	32	Bremen	68-0957
SCHROEPFER, Adolf	33	Toutogany	69-0067
SCHROETER, Aug.	27	Sievern	68-0566
SCHROETER, Oscar	16	Salzungen	71-0681
SCHROFF, Konrad	18	Altheim	71-0226
SCHROLE, Martin	36	Christrinchen	70-0006
SCHROLL, Therese	38	Regensburg	69-0015
SCHROT, Susanne	26	Auru	71-0479
SCHROTH, Christian	24	Busenbarl	69-0268
SCHROTH, Gottlob	32	Puska	68-1006
Pauline 33, Hermann 8, Friedrich 3			
SCHRUFF, Friederike	32	Neuenhaus	68-0957
Wilhelm 8, Johanna 6			
SCHUBEL, Friedr. Johann	25	Watzkendorf-Mec	70-0006
Johanne 25, Wilhelm 6 months			
SCHUBERT, Adolf	15	Minden	69-1086
SCHUBERT, Auguste	19	Hannover	70-0355
SCHUBERT, Carl	24	Lauterbach	71-0789
SCHUBERT, Christine	19	Nuernberg	68-1006
Pauline 17			
SCHUBERT, Eduard	15	Eisenberg	71-0736
SCHUBERT, Ernst	30	Breslau	69-1011
SCHUBERT, Gustav	19	Wien	68-0456
Carl 18			
SCHUBERT, Henr.	32	Langweitzendorf	71-0733
SCHUBERT, Josephine	25	Boehmen	68-0456
SCHUBERT, Peter	48	Westertown	68-0566
Catharine 17			
SCHUBERT, Richard	23	Rothenkirchen	69-0015

NAME	AGE	RESIDENCE	YR-LIST
SCHUBERT, Stephan	36	S. Meiningen	70-1003
Eva 36, Henry 14, Louis 11, Anton 9, Ferdinand 8, Adam 6, Carl 18 months			
SCHUBERT, Ursula	35	Bollenheim	68-0982
SCHUBERTH, Hy.	30	Altenstein	68-0957
SCHUBINGER, Adolph	22	Uznuch	68-0534
SCHUCH, Aug.	23	Worms	68-0820
SCHUCHARDT, Carl	17	Keffahausen	69-0923
SCHUCHARDT, Michael	28	Keffahausen	69-0923
Magdalene 19			
SCHUCHART, Joh.	29	Heiligerstadt	70-0308
SCHUCHMANN, Gust.	25	Ravensburg	68-0982
SCHUCHMANN, Wilhelm	18	Sinsheim	69-0592
SCHUCK, Elisab.	20	Silhombach	70-0308
Silkombach			
SCHUCK, Peter	27	Siewershoefe	69-0784
SCHUCKART, Ernestine	18	Lehesten	68-0566
SCHUDER, Christoph	24	Sondershausen	68-1049
SCHUDT, Heinrich	16	Osterndorf	68-1027
SCHUEBE, Friederike	48	Neuwied	69-0771
SCHUEBEL, Christine	59	Goldlauter	69-0429
August 29, Emilie 24			
SCHUECHEL, Gustav	27	Reichenberg	68-0820
SCHUEFFNER, C.W. Jr.	30	Chemnitz	68-1006
SCHUELER, Andreas	28	Lengsfeld	70-0523
SCHUELER, Anna	54	Schlatz	69-0321
August 23, Anton 13, Caroline 20			
SCHUELER, Conrad	32	Ruppertshofen	68-0957
Barbara 28, Sophia 11 months, Marg. 3, Georg 31			
SCHUELER, Josef	35	Darmstadt	70-0384
Wilh. 8, Friederich 5, Sophie 9			
SCHUELKENS, Joh.	27	Lingen	68-0865
Anna Maria 44, Elisabeth 32, Elisabeth 6, Anna Maria 3, Johann Bernhard 7			
SCHUENEMANN, George	24	New York	69-1421
SCHUENHOFF, Sophie	28	Hannover	70-0443
Ernst 15			
SCHUEPLER, Julius	41	Braunschweig	69-0182
SCHUEPPEL, Ernestine	26	Flusspethgrube	71-0456
Friedrike 20, Wilhelmine 23			
SCHUERER, Magd.	25	Apfelbach	71-0736
SCHUERMANN, Bernhard	29	Billerbeck	69-0229
SCHUERMANN, Henriette	18	Bremen	69-0542
SCHUERMANN, Hermann	23	Buer	68-1027
Emilie 55, Louis 20, Robert 18			
SCHUERMANN, Mathilde	19	Schwarzbg.Sonde	70-1023
SCHUERMANN, Wilh.	28	Altschambrock	68-1002
SCHUERMER, Johann	31	Nuernberg	69-0572
SCHUESSLER, Georg	27	Schwarzenau	69-0229
SCHUESSLER, Hermann	17	Soegeln	69-0490
SCHUESSLER, William	24	Berlin	68-1027
SCHUETT, Anna	19	Otterndorf	71-0821
SCHUETTE, Anna	19	Friedburg	68-0939
SCHUETTE, August	17	Lippe	69-1086
SCHUETTE, Christel	50	Wesenstall	69-0798
SCHUETTE, Elise	26	Faehr	71-0712
Heinrich 8			
SCHUETTE, Franz	31	Wiggeringhausen	71-0815
Marie 19, Wilhelmine 3 months			
SCHUETTE, Friedrich	17	Wesenstedt	68-314
SCHUETTE, Friedrich	24	Nienburg	68-0661
SCHUETTE, Joh.	24	Hannover	71-0479
SCHUETTE, Johanne	54	Hannover	71-0479
Marie 5, Margarethe 3, Aug. 9 months			
SCHUETTE, Louise	24	Volmerdingen	68-0566
SCHUETTENBERG, J. J.	18	Buer	69-1011
Clena 23			
SCHUETTER, Wm.	35	Sondershausen	68-0014
SCHUETTLER, Friedrich	25	Strothe	68-0786
SCHUETZ, Alwine	21	Oberschlema	68-0907
SCHUETZ, August	32	Revier/France	69-0968
Wilhelmine 25, Anna 9 months			
SCHUETZ, Caroline	20	Solingen	69-0321
SCHUETZ, Catharina	24	Vorarlberg	69-0560
SCHUETZ, Catharine	17	Norderweidentha	71-0429
SCHUETZ, Mary	28	New York	69-1421
Charles 2			
SCHUETZ, Nicolaus	25	Trier	68-0884
Marie 30			
SCHUETZ, Sabine	16	Birkenfeld	70-0329
SCHUFF, Henry	26	Kreimbach	71-0643
SCHUH, Carl	17	St. Wendel	69-0321
SCHUH, Conrad	17	Hohenech	69-1363
SCHUHMANN, Abraham	39	Altenburg	68-0625
Sophie 38, Sophie 59, Valentin 9, Gottfried 7, Herman 5, William 9 months			
SCHUKOLZ, Andreas	22	Gingen	69-0771
SCHULENBURG, Lueder	17	Bremen	68-0884
SCHULENBURG, Phil.	22	Hannover	70-0178
SCHULENBURG, Sophie	22	Oerdinghausen	70-0148
SCHULER, Albert	25	Pflummern	68-0625
SCHULER, Elisabeth	21	Oggenhausen	68-0907
SCHULER, Jacob	26	Streichen	70-0355
SCHULER, Leopold	28	Schweiz	70-1142
SCHULES, Johann	24	Fuerssbronn	69-1011
SCHULKEN, Claus	29	Blumenthal	69-1076
SCHULKEN, Mathilde	20	Blumenthal	68-1002
SCHULT, Aug.	16	Obernkirchen	71-0789
SCHULT, Henry	51	Hannover	68-0456
Augusta 38			
SCHULTE, Anna	28	Aurich	68-1027
Friederike 7, Augusta 5			
SCHULTE, Arend Fokken	34	Klinge	68-1006
Meye Everts 34, Hinderika 7, Evert 5, Meike 6 months			
SCHULTE, Bernhard	16	Landwege	69-1059
SCHULTE, Dorothea	25	Osterbruch	69-0572
SCHULTE, Elisabeth	44	Altengesecke	70-1142
SCHULTE, Elisabeth	24	Hagen	68-0625
SCHULTE, Emilie	19	Berlin	69-0079
SCHULTE, Gerhart	14	Hastorf	69-0208
SCHULTE, Gertrude	54	Bentheim	71-0429
Friedrike 24			
SCHULTE, Henrich	39	Settlage	69-0560
Marianne 30, Henrich 8, Bernhard 6			
SCHULTE, Jan	22	Bunde	68-0852
Swaantje 23			
SCHULTE, Johann	38	Ostfriesland	68-0647

NAME	AGE	RESIDENCE	YR-LIST
Falke 33, Hinrica 11, Antje 8, Johanna 7, Theodor 2, Baby son 1 months			
SCHULTE, Johanna	30	Bentheim	69-0841
SCHULTE, Lina	17	Fechte	69-0490
SCHULTE, Marie	23	Aschen	68-0820
SCHULTE, Peter	43	Hoevel	71-0581
Franzca. 35, August 6, Franz 24			
SCHULTE, Therese	30	Kischilte	71-0736
SCHULTHEIS, Amarella	20	Marbach	68-0753
SCHULTHEIS, Catharina	21	Grossersdorf	70-0204
SCHULTHEISS, Cath	16	Albsheim	70-1055
SCHULTHEISS, Marie	18	Heiligersdorf	70-1161
SCHULTZ, August	38	Kamin/Boehmen	69-0576
Anna 38			
SCHULTZ, Carl	32	Damerow	68-0625
Ida 25, Marie 4, Hanna 2, Baby daughter 6 months			
SCHULTZ, Dorothea Fr.	25	Molitz	69-0321
SCHULTZ, Fritz	23	Werntgerode	71-0456
SCHULTZ, Nicolai	19	Petersburg	68-0661
SCHULTZE, Anna	46	Hitzacker	70-0076
SCHULTZE, Carl	22	Hamburg	69-1363
SCHULZ, Anna	24	Cottbus	71-0643
SCHULZ, August	27	Gr. Wachlin	69-0672
August 29, Charlotte 29, Albert 3, Friedrich 2, Louise 3 months			
SCHULZ, August	34	Niederscheeren	68-0770
Louise 34, Caroline 8, Mathilde 5, Louise 4, Albert 1, Hermann 14			
SCHULZ, Carl	35	Bremen	70-1003
SCHULZ, Carl	29	Greiz	68-0786
SCHULZ, Carl	22	Rewitzgruen	71-0643
SCHULZ, Carl	39	Danzig	71-0479
Franziska 40			
SCHULZ, Caroline	26	Moellitz/Meckle	69-0547
SCHULZ, Caroline	30	Greiz	68-1027
Anna 5			
SCHULZ, Catharine	21	Homburg	68-0852
SCHULZ, Conrad	27	Heimsweyer	71-0492
SCHULZ, Ed.	23	Neu Langsaw	69-1004
SCHULZ, Elise	28	Magdeburg	69-0672
Louise 2			
SCHULZ, Friedrich	52	Briesenhorst	69-0771
Christine 56, Marie 25, Ernestine 23, Friedrich 19			
SCHULZ, Friedrich	31	Betzendorf	68-0534
SCHULZ, Gertr.	25	R.B. Muenster	68-0610
SCHULZ, Gottfried	26	Bretzig	69-0576
Anna Regina 34, Joh. Friedr. 1			
SCHULZ, Herm. Julius	24	Neuenhagen	69-0321
SCHULZ, Hermann	26	Alfstedt	68-0456
Johanne 52			
SCHULZ, Hugo	29	Cassenhoefchen	70-0135
SCHULZ, Johann	22	Varel	69-0542
SCHULZ, Julius	33	Cammin	69-1363
Auguste 40, Rudolf 5, Louise 4, Emilie 2 months			
SCHULZ, Julius	24	Buzig	69-0547
Carl 28, Auguste 23, Augustine 58, Malwine 6, Hermann 3, Wilhelmine 10 months			
SCHULZ, Louis	34	Mackensen	70-0052
Carl 17			
SCHULZ, Louis	42	Clausthal	69-1004
Henriette 38, Julius 9, Wilhelm 8, Theo 4			
SCHULZ, Ludwig	14	Lueneburg	71-0643
SCHULZ, Michel	23	Marienwerder	68-0786
SCHULZ, Pauline	24	Boehmen	69-1076
SCHULZ, Peter	13	Oberamstadt	68-0820
Margarethe 35			
SCHULZ, Philipp	44	St. Martin	70-0184
Franz 9, Rosina 8			
SCHULZ, Robert	30	Karzig	68-0770
August 29, Louise 4, Betha 10 months			
SCHULZ, Rupert	16	Muenchen	71-0736
SCHULZ, Sophia	63	Dobbin	69-0592
SCHULZ, Sophie	27	Nassow	68-0566
Rosette 4, Hermann 11 months			
SCHULZ, Wilh.	30	Schweigern	69-1004
SCHULZ, Wilhelm	45	Buchholz	69-0672
Ernestine 39, Louise 16, Emilie 14, Carl 8, Wilhelm 5			
SCHULZ, Wilhelm	19	Hamburg	69-0182
SCHULZ, Wilhelm	46	Schneidemuehl	69-0542
SCHULZE, Aug.	25	Walsrode	69-1363
SCHULZE, Carl	29	Halle	70-0682
Anna 26			
SCHULZE, Carl	23	Riestedt	68-1002
SCHULZE, Carl	36	Goersbach	68-0566
Marie 29, Mathias 9, Gottfried 7, Ernestine 5, August 2, Emilie 54			
SCHULZE, Christine	23	Holzhausen	68-0610
SCHULZE, Friedrich	33	Berlin	68-1027
Emilie 35, Emma 8, Friedrich 7, Martha 5			
SCHULZE, Hedwig	29	Altenburg	68-0314
SCHULZE, Heinrich	36	Bokel	68-0820
Dorothea 32, Dorothea 9, Heinrich 3			
SCHULZE, Josephine	26	Paderborn	69-0672
Werner 2			
SCHULZE, Pauline	18	Glauchau	68-0786
Marie 15			
SCHULZE, Wilh.	28	Linnenkamp	68-0647
SCHUMACHER, Carsten	35	Vegesack	70-0052
Anna 5, Carsten 12, Meta 68			
SCHUMACHER, Ernst	27	Stuttgart	69-0784
SCHUMACHER, Friedrich	16	Rieden	70-1161
SCHUMACHER, Friedrich	59	Chicago	70-0184
SCHUMACHER, Friedrich	25	Ransweiler	69-1076
SCHUMACHER, Gottl.	17	Tuebingen	71-0581
SCHUMACHER, Gret.	18	Vilsen	71-0581
SCHUMACHER, Heinr.	31	Lengerich	71-0300
Pauline 33			
SCHUMACHER, Jacob	25	Hohenstein	69-0268
SCHUMACHER, Joh. H.	16	Sudweyke	68-0884
SCHUMACHER, Johann	24	R.B.Coblenz	68-1006
SCHUMACHER, Leopold	20	Carlruhe	69-0923
SCHUMACHER, Marg.	21	Widdern	68-0534
SCHUMACHER, Maria	17	Geestendorf	69-1076
SCHUMACHER, Marie	33	Oberensingen	69-1396
Dorothea 7, Christine 4			
SCHUMACHER, Pauline	25	New York	69-1363

NAME	AGE	RESIDENCE	YR-LIST
SCHUMACHER, Peter	50	Herdecke	68-0982
SCHUMACHER, Therese	20	Bremen	70-0259
SCHUMACHER, Victor	42	Solothurn	68-0014
SCHUMACHER, Wilhelm	17	Muenden	70-0031
SCHUMANN, Adam	24	Weissenbach	70-0569
SCHUMANN, Alex.	23	Ellernitz	68-1002
SCHUMANN, David	17	Heinsen	71-0167
SCHUMANN, Emil	16	Siegismundsburg	71-0736
SCHUMANN, Franz	30	Doebeln	69-0229
Marie 25, Theodor 1			
SCHUMANN, Johann	38	Berlin	68-0786
SCHUMANN, Johanna	29	Muenster	68-0534
Johanna 6, Clara 4, Engelbert 11 months			
SCHUMANN, Louise	50	Gamikaw	71-0479
Auguste 15			
SCHUMM, Adam	23	Koenig	68-0760
SCHUMM, Louise	14	Cappel	68-0647
SCHUMMELPFENNIG, E.	31	Lichtenau	68-0907
Eleonore 3			
SCHUNKE, Anton	37	Naumburg	69-0798
SCHUPP, Louis	15	Widdern	68-0534
SCHURBROCK, Conrad	27	Vechta	68-0939
SCHURMANN, Gottfried	15	Luzern	69-0923
SCHURR, Andreas	26	Hattenhofen	68-1298
SCHUSHARDT, Alb.	23	Greiz	69-0229
SCHUSS, Sophie	18	Wangen	71-0643
Andreas 24			
SCHUSTER, Bapt.	20	Risstingen	70-1035
SCHUSTER, Burghard	61	Mergentheim	68-0852
SCHUSTER, Heinrich	25	Ackelsberg	69-0208
Jann 22, Zeetje 20			
SCHUSTER, Henriette	28	Allertsheim	69-0572
Margarethe 61			
SCHUTTE, Marianne	23	Hardenstetten	69-0429
SCHUTTE, Rudolf	34	Lawell	69-0292
Arendarke 34			
SCHUTTENBERG, Z.	24	Altenberg	71-0479
Marie 18			
SCHUTZ, August	37	Reiskow	69-0079
SCHWAAB, Isaac	71	Gruenstadt	69-0592
Therese 47, Helene 20, Rosa 20, Max 16			
SCHWAB, Albert	19	Boehmen	69-1076
SCHWAB, Barbara	23	Scheringen	68-0820
Michael			
SCHWAB, Ernst	20	Roedelheim	69-1309
SCHWAB, Friedrich	20	Unterregenbach	69-0490
SCHWAB, HAnchen	26	Grebenau	69-0968
SCHWAB, Leonh.	23	Alfeld	71-0681
SCHWAB, Martin	19	Bamberg	69-0559
SCHWAB, Moritz	20	Gruenstadt	69-0592
Josef 59			
SCHWAB, Peter	24	Orbis	69-0229
SCHWABE, Gottfr.	66	Stotternheim	71-0479
Elise 60			
SCHWACH, Carl	26	Schoeneberg	69-1076
SCHWACHERT, Wme.	44	Radolin	69-1319
SCHWACKER, Johann	25	Heuthen	68-0907
SCHWAEBOLD, Robert	28	Golsdorf	70-0682
SCHWAGER, Joh. Hch.	30	Ihlendorf	68-1002

NAME	AGE	RESIDENCE	YR-LIST
SCHWAHN, Philipp	47	Worms	68-0014
SCHWAIBOLD, Ignatz	17	Hausen	68-0566
SCHWAIBOLD, Reinhard	19	Goelsdorf	69-0592
SCHWAKE, Joh.	58	Aplern	71-0479
SCHWALIN, Johannes	45	Mengsberg	68-0456
Anna 35, Martha 12, Anna 16, Louise 6 months			
SCHWALM, Barbara	16	Ibra	68-0852
SCHWALM, Marie	56	Treysa	68-0982
SCHWALM, Wilh.	14	Schmalkalden	68-0566
SCHWAN, Christian	42	Neundettelsau	70-1055
SCHWAN, Friederike	23	Detmold	70-0308
SCHWAN, Johanne	22	Bremen	69-1086
SCHWANCKE, Emma	34	Barmen	69-1212
SCHWANCKE, Joh.	48	Moschuetz	71-0521
Christine 50, Rosalie 18, Cacelie 16, Albert 9, Auguste 8, Hyronimus 8			
SCHWANECKE, Louis	17	Rothenfelde	69-1059
SCHWANIKE, Emma	34	Barmen	69-1212
SCHWANINGER, Paul	27	Bruchsal	68-0760
SCHWANT, Catharina	25	Schornheim	69-0457
Heinrich 27			
SCHWANTZ, Elise	19	Rothenburg	69-0560
SCHWARGELS, Johann	26	Oldenburg	69-0848
SCHWARS, Marie	20	Wietzen	71-0821
SCHWARTING, Johann	34	Oldenburg	69-0268
Anna 42, Johann 16, Anna 9, Diedrich 8, Gesine 5			
SCHWARTING, Magd.	32	Bischendorf	71-0492
SCHWARTJE, Marie	24	Vegesack	71-0821
SCHWARTZ, Eduard	35	Wien	71-0643
SCHWARZ, Adam	28	Wiesbaden	70-0384
SCHWARZ, Adam	44	Schwangen	71-0492
SCHWARZ, Adolf	25	Harpstedt	69-1059
SCHWARZ, Angela	18	Trier	71-0643
SCHWARZ, August	23	Weiler	68-0760
SCHWARZ, Barbara	22	Odenheim	69-0572
SCHWARZ, Barbara	18	Oberaula	68-0661
SCHWARZ, Catharina	16	Edelsheim	71-0733
SCHWARZ, Dorothea	21	Neuenhaus	68-0957
SCHWARZ, Emma	24	Elberfeld	69-0771
Adele 10 months			
SCHWARZ, Emma	22	Muden	71-0821
SCHWARZ, Francisca	32	Boehmen	71-0821
Marie 5, Anna 9			
SCHWARZ, Franz	21	Riedlingen	69-1396
SCHWARZ, G.	25	N. Dieffenbach	69-0841
SCHWARZ, Gerh.	21	Westerlade	69-1004
SCHWARZ, Gustav	24	Cannstadt	71-0736
SCHWARZ, Henriette	38	Reula	68-0647
Julius 6			
SCHWARZ, Henry	35	Baltimore	69-0572
SCHWARZ, Henry	24	Effingen	71-0456
SCHWARZ, Hermann	25	Preetz	69-0321
SCHWARZ, Jacob	30	Wenden	70-0728
Marie 25			
SCHWARZ, Jacob	22	Gruben/Prussia	69-0547
SCHWARZ, Johann	71	Grosenbader	69-0457
Anna 61, Marie 14			

NAME	AGE	RESIDENCE	YR-LIST
SCHWARZ, Johann	27	Prottenburg	69-0229
SCHWARZ, Julie	23	Kosalop	70-1142
SCHWARZ, Marg.	25	Nenndorf	70-1035
SCHWARZ, Pauline	24	Obergrund	71-0581
Anna 6 months			
SCHWARZ, Peter	26	Ebstadt	69-0338
SCHWARZ, Regine	20	Kreuznach	68-0456
SCHWARZ, Richard	18	Dessau	71-0456
SCHWARZ, Simon	39	Friesau	68-0770
Friederike 36, Heinrich 12, Caroline 4, Anna 2			
SCHWARZ, Theodor	19	Basel	71-0429
SCHWARZ, Therese	20	Himkirchen	70-0223
Anton 18			
SCHWARZE, Franz	32	Bigge	68-0610
SCHWARZE, Heinrich	18	Dielingen	69-0583
SCHWARZE, Jos.	25	Oestinghausen	68-0957
SCHWARZER, Dorette	22	Vegesack	70-1161
SCHWARZER, Joseph	28	Steinau	68-0456
SCHWARZFAERBER, C.	72	Beig/Beiz	69-1059
Elise 24			
SCHWARZMEIER, Georg	27	Neugehof	69-0229
SCHWARZWALDER, M.	35	Neustadt	70-0135
SCHWAT, Aug.	18	Burgstadt	70-0308
SCHWAUB, Catharina	25	Schornheim	69-0457
Heinrich 27			
SCHWEBEL, Marie	17	Gr. Bieberau	70-1035
SCHWECKENDIEK, J.	27	Vorbruch	69-0572
SCHWEDA, Lina	30	Bremen	68-314
SCHWEER, Herm.	16	Horsten	68-0753
SCHWEER, Otto	18	Hannover	70-0728
SCHWEER, Wilhelm	17	Wichte	69-0429
Hermann 11, Friedrich 8			
SCHWEERS, Heinrich	30	Neuenkirchen	68-0456
SCHWEERS, Marie	61	Varrel	71-0684
SCHWEGLER, Friedr.	21	Stuttgart	71-0521
SCHWEIGER, Jacob	21	Austria	70-0170
SCHWEIGER, John	28	Austria	70-0170
SCHWEIGER, Mary	23	Trossingen	68-0957
SCHWEIGERT, Georg	31	Oberfranken	69-0321
Elisabeth 30, Appollonia 9			
SCHWEIKERT, Cath.	19	Ehrstruehn	69-1004
SCHWEIKERT, Constant	19	Winzeln	68-0982
SCHWEIKERT, Paul	42	Oberstein	70-0508
Philippine 24, Line 4 months			
SCHWEIKHARDT, Jac.	35	Niederinzelheim	70-0170
SCHWEIKLE, John	35	Wittendorf	71-0456
SCHWEINFURT, Carl	19	Weingarten	71-0712
SCHWEINFURTH, Georg	40	Hilchenbach	71-0456
Lisette 38, Carl 9, Rudolf 7, Anna 4, Albert 3, Bertha 2, Emma 6 mont			
SCHWEITZ, Charlotte	27	Petershagen	69-1212
SCHWEITZER, Anna	23	Reichenbach	68-0647
SCHWEITZER, Christine	21	Gondelsheim	69-0457
SCHWEITZER, Josef	16	Sanderbuch	71-0681
SCHWEITZER, Paul	29	Thalheim	68-0907
SCHWEITZER, Sophie	1	Darmstadt	68-0456
SCHWEIZER, Carl	19	Nuestlingen	69-1004
SCHWEIZER, Carl	19	Oberwalden	71-0684

NAME	AGE	RESIDENCE	YR-LIST
SCHWEIZER, Fr.	24	Lippe Detmold	70-0355
SCHWEIZER, Georg	19	Waexbenhausen	69-0968
SCHWEIZER, Georg	35	Heitzenburg	71-0456
SCHWEIZER, Jac.	28	Austria	70-0170
SCHWEIZER, Joh. Jac.	46	Zuerich	71-0736
SCHWEND, Joh.	44	Moembers	68-0566
SCHWENHARD, Mehal	28	Etmansweiler	68-0534
SCHWENK, Christ.	22	Dieburg	68-0820
SCHWENK, Philip	16	Mensfelden	71-0226
SCHWENKA, Friedrich	16	Minden	68-0907
SCHWENKE, Bertha	26	Bukau	71-0300
Agnes 4, Gustav 2			
SCHWEPPE, Cath.	17	Laer	71-0429
SCHWER, Gertrude	20	Aspel	71-0363
SCHWER, Peter	32	Kreimbach	69-0321
SCHWERING, Sophie	34	Oberzenzheim	69-1086
Fritz 9			
SCHWERTFEGER, A.	17	Henkenhagen	71-0456
SCHWERTFEGER, Max	22	Crossen	68-0456
SCHWICKER, Carl	42	Osnabrueck	68-1006
SCHWIED, Berhardine	7	Bremerhaven	68-0907
SCHWIETERS, Anton	27	Leyden	68-0907
SCHWIND, Marg.	24	Darmstadt	70-0204
SCHWINDEL, Jacob	17	Hemmingen	71-0172
SCHWING, Conrad	23	Landenhausen	69-0968
SCHWINGLER, John	49	Rochester	70-0170
SCHWINN, Christine	23	Falkengerach	71-0643
SCHWINN, George	47	Kreuznach	68-0456
SCHWITZER, Carl	20	Obersieblingen	69-1309
SCHWOERER, Carl	17	Babenhausen	68-0610
SCIPIO, G. Ludw.	23	Rehburg	68-0647
SEBALD, Franz	30	Schwarzenbach	68-0566
SEBASTIAN, Magdalena	19	Jegendorf	68-0707
SEBBACH, Marie	21	Menningsroth	69-0572
SEDEL, Caroline	26	Bickenau	71-0456
SEDLACK, Ignatz	30	Schnieau-Bohemi	70-0006
SEDTMANN, Joseph	18	Muenchen	69-1086
SEEBA, Claas	40	Marienhafe	68-0647
Greetje 33, Juergen 8, Eylert 6, Ohne 3, Baby son 11 months			
SEEBASS, Theresia	33	New York	69-1212
Constanze 7, Helena 5			
SEEBECK, Friedrich	28	Meyenberg	69-0457
SEEBECK, Hermann	16	Sanstedt	69-0968
SEEBEN, Friedrich	32	Sachsen Meining	69-0559
SEEBER, Helene	20	St. Martin	69-0923
SEEDORF, Heinr.	16	Altstadt	71-0821
SEEFELD, Carl	25	Potsdam	68-1002
SEEGELKEN, Heinrich	30	Scharmbeck	68-0707
Rebecca 21			
SEEGER, Chr.	18	Oetisheim	71-0815
SEEGER, Dorothea	16	Spielberg	68-1027
SEEGER, Fred.	23	Bonitz	69-0338
SEEGER, Georg	30	Rothfelden	70-0728
SEEGER, Henry	39	Preussen	68-0456
SEEGER, Joh.	38	Untermutschl	69-1004
Andr. 41, Louise 17, Caroline 13, Christine 9, Caroline 7			

NAME	AGE	RESIDENCE	YR-LIST
SEEGER, Johann	19	Bremen	69-1396
Carl 16			
SEEGERS, Wilhelm	30	Hannover	69-1076
SEELER, Helene	20	St. Martin	69-0923
SEELIG, Albert	18	Heilbronn	71-0456
SEELING, Aug. Ferd.	34	Bialosliwe	68-0770
Wilhelmine 28, Emilie 8, Augusta 6, August 11 months			
SEELING, Christ.	64	Neuenburg	68-0760
Sophie 62			
SEELMANN, Catharine	24	Ober Franken	69-1086
SEEMANN, Ette	25	Sengwarden	69-0490
Johann 27, Anna 28			
SEEVERS, Albert	18	Hannover	70-1055
SEEWALD, Marie	23	Mergentheim	68-0852
SEFELD, Carl	24	Moenkiel	69-0547
SEGEBRUCH, Adolf	17	Bueckeburg	71-0681
SEGELKE, Anna	45	Hoboken	71-1109
Hans 7			
SEGELKE, Ed.	80	Otterndorf	71-0733
Anna 63, Wilhelm 30, Louise 25			
SEGELKE, John	17	Hambergen	71-0456
Otto 16			
SEGELKE, Theod.	22	Ihlienworth	69-0572
SEGELKEN, Fried.	25	Oldenburg	71-0815
Minna 19			
SEGELKEN, Heinr.	40	Grambke	68-0982
Gesine 20			
SEGELKEN, Julius	15	Bremen	71-0736
SEGEMUELLER, Johanne	46	Tamowitz	70-0728
Angelina 9, Clara 6			
SEGGERN, Heinrich	25	Oldenburg	69-0268
SEGIN, Johan	29	Wewelsburg	68-1002
SEGITZ, Andreas	18	Fuerth	71-0479
SEGLING, Dorothea	19	Nordholz	71-0821
SEHLECHT, Adolph	17	Bretten	70-0378
SEHLICH, Franz	14	Bitz	70-0523
Mathias 12			
SEHRAIT, Mathias	13	Boehmen	70-1161
SEHRT, Otto	25	Friedberg	69-1363
SEIB, Johann	44	Baerheim	71-0521
Simon 16			
SEIBEL, Peter	23	Paterson	70-1142
SEIBEL, Philipp	70	Waldeck	69-0672
Henriette 60, Christine 14			
SEIBRANDO, Johanne	33	Rhaude	71-0712
Caroline 6			
SEIBT, Josef	57	Halberstadt	68-1298
Frederika 57, Charlotte 30, Minna 28, Frederik 24, Louisa 22, Hermann 18, Marg			
SEIDE, Franz	19	Fuchsberg	71-0792
SEIDEL, Andreas	23	Oestreich	70-0728
Maria 23			
SEIDEL, Anna	28	Kocojeda	68-0534
SEIDEL, Carl	28	Frankfurt	69-1059
Margreth 20			
SEIDEL, Johann	18	Turnau	68-0770
SEIDEL, Wenzel	39	Wescheherd	71-0429
Anna 41, Josefa 18, Maria 14, Thomas 9, Anton 8, Wenzel 9 months			
SEIDEL, Xaver	36	Unterfranken	69-1309
Therese 19			
SEIDEL,Mary	19	Foerstenreuth	69-1004
SEIDENSPINNER, Maria	19	Wuestenberg	71-0792
SEIDENSTREICHER, A.	26	Bohrbrunnen	68-0625
SEIDLER, Julius	23	Drausnitz	68-0786
SEIDLER, Miss.	43	Braunschweig	70-0204
Wilhelmine 9, Marie 8, Auguste 11 months			
SEIDLER, Oscar	14	Eisenach	68-0707
SEIFERMANN, Aug	19	Legden	69-0771
SEIFERT, Carl August	25	Kettendorf	68-0770
Christ. Wm. 33			
SEIFERT, E.	35	Freistadt	69-0050
SEIFERT, Eleonore	29	Podebueh	71-0492
SEIFERT, Henriette	31	Schwarzbach	68-0610
Louise 5, Albert 2			
SEIFERT, Herm.	26	Koenigsberg	71-0681
Johanne 19, Fritz 9 months			
SEIFERT, Johann	30	Altenburg	69-0771
SEIFERT, Mrs.	50	Schmiedefeld	70-0452
SEIFERT, Oswald	16	Kuhschappel	68-314
SEIFERT, Wilhelmine	30	Sachsen	70-1161
Paul 3, Bruno 6 months			
SEIGLING, Eva	31	Thueringen	69-0848
Christian 6, August 4, Marie 10 months			
SEIGNER, August	22	Meseritz	69-0547
SEIKER, Heinr.	24	Stroehen	68-0982
Marie 28, Sophie 4, Wilh. 9 months			
SEIL, August	27	Bibke\ Bibbe	68-0456
SEILEN, Carl	24	Leymwyl	68-0534
SEILER, Barbara	67	Constanz	68-0625
SEILER, Bernhard	30	Pest	70-0184
SEILER, Catharine	25	St. Catharina	68-0770
SEILER, Franz	40	Pogkis	69-0457
SEIM, Johann	17	Erbenhausen	68-314
SEIMIG, Elise	21	Wehrda	69-0592
Friedrich 15			
SEINEKE, Adolph	15	Hannover	70-0523
SEINRUS, Angelika	51	Dessau	68-0456
SEIP, Catharine	17	Ruedesheim	70-0508
SEIPEL, Heinrich	51	Eichelsachsen	69-0672
Anna 48, Elise 7			
SEIPEL, Justine	31	Niederamstadt	69-0841
Wilhelmine 2, Elisabeth 2			
SEISSLER, Cath.	21	Sausenheim	70-1055
SEITER, John	23	Romberg	68-1006
SEITZ, Catharine	18	Olpfinger	71-0792
SEITZ, Geo.	19	Welkenbach	70-0170
SEITZ, Gust.	17	Chemnitz	71-0815
SEITZ, Jacob	15	Klems	69-0672
SEITZ, Martin	19	Winterbach	69-0771
SEITZ, Paul	14	Fuerth	68-1006
SEITZ, Rosa	12	Ober Schefflanz	71-0684
SEITZ, Tobias	30	Nuernberg	71-0479
SEIWERT, Jacob	30	Merxheim	69-1319
Johann 17			
SELDENECK, V. W.	34	Carlsruhe	68-0884
SELIG, Gotthel	28	Ehrbardorf	68-0770
Ernestine 28, Gustav 8 months, Anna Christ. 55, Wilhelm 35			

NAME	AGE	RESIDENCE	YR-LIST
SELIG, Joseph	16	Reichelsheim	71-0521
SELIG, Sophie	20	Schluechtern	69-0592
SELIGMANN, Conrad	26	Oberlengsfeld	68-0534
SELIGMANN, D.	28	Hamburg	70-1035
SELIGMANN, D. M.	40	Frankfurt/M	71-0363
SELIGMANN, Magdalena	20	Mertzviller	71-0581
SELL, Pauline	21	Lumau	69-0457
SELLE, Caroline	61	Bremen	71-0479
Auguste 19			
SELLE, Marie	23	Bremen	69-1076
SELLMANN, Georg	34	New York	70-0148
Elise 36, Louis 8			
SELLMANN, Wilhelm	36	New York	70-1003
SELTMANN, Emilie	22	Leesen	71-0479
SELTMANN, male	22	Kl. Lesen	69-1363
SEMAN, Valent.	29	Hammelburg	69-1363
Mary 29, Elise 6 months			
SEMMLER, Anton	19	Wittges	68-0610
Antonia 30			
SEMMLER, F. W.	47	Leipzig	71-0792
SEMMLER, Marg.	21	Bremen	70-1142
SEMPF, Maria	5	Zeitz	68-0566
SENDER, Israel	32	Birkenfeld	70-1142
SENF, Albertine	26	Hoboken	70-1003
SENFERT, Franz	42	Unter Franken	69-1086
Marie 33			
SENFFT, Wilhelm	38	Wiesbaden	68-0786
SENGLE, Bernhard	18	Stuttgart	69-0338
SENGSTAAK, Marie	28	Michelstedt	70-1003
SENGSTAK, Henry	26	Bremen	70-1003
SENK, Cath.	17	Diedrichsheim	71-0581
SENNECKER, Hugo	30	Culm	69-0292
SENSENBUTTS, E.	21	Bremen	70-1066
SETHMANN, Heinr.	16	Barchel	71-0300
SEUBERLING, Philipp	21	Unter Franken	69-1086
SEUBERT, Nicolas	28	Ober Franken	69-1086
SEUFERT, Cath.	14	Massenbachhaus	71-0521
SEUFTLEBEN, Louise	32	Berlin	68-0820
Hedwig 11 months			
SEULICH, Johanna	64	Voersten	68-0939
SEUMLER, Marg.	21	Bremen	70-1142
SEVERIN, Heinr.	41	Werther	68-0610
Augusta 30, Bertha 5, Laure 6 months			
SEVERING, Louise	21	Bremen	68-0610
SEYBALD, Christian	17	Nuertingen	68-0982
SEYDEL, Adolph	27	Hof	71-0492
SEYDEL, Max	44	Heseltown	68-1006
Minna 27			
SEYER, Joseph	17	Revingen	69-0576
SEYFERT, Andreas	41	Herzbrueck	68-0647
SEYL, Louis	23	Theisbergstegen	70-0378
SEYLING, Dorothea	19	Nordholz	71-0821
SIATS, A.	16	Lehe	69-0490
SICHEL, Auscher	17	Langenschwarz	68-1002
SICHLER, Magdalene	26	Tuttlingen	68-0957
SICKEL, Pauline	22	Grossbruechter	68-0625
Wilhelmine 16			
SICKEN, Carl	32	Muenster	68-0770

NAME	AGE	RESIDENCE	YR-LIST
SICKERS, L.	19	Schwickau/Zwick	70-0259
SICKERT, Catharine	23	Hesse Darmstadt	70-0355
SICKLER, Joh.	30	Eisslingen	68-0566
Agnes 31, Johann 11 months			
SIDLO, Wenzel	19	Klonk	70-0329
SIEBE, Friedrich	17	Levern-Westfale	70-0006
SIEBECKER, Maria	23	Arolsen	69-1076
SIEBELS, David	59	Sanshorst	69-1004
Julie 58, Thecla 16			
SIEBEN, Phil.	32	San Francisco	69-1011
Margarethe 35, Helene 2, Jacob 35			
SIEBENBORN, B.	25	Fuerstenberg	71-0736
SIEBER, Bernhard	50	Constanz	70-0728
SIEBER, Elise	29	Stettin	69-1396
SIEBER, Hugo	30	Bulen	71-0681
SIEBER, Johann	19	Oehningen	68-0456
Agnes 17			
SIEBER, Kranz	57	Borgloh	68-0957
Catharina 50, Ernst 22, John M. 19, Hermann 8, Wilhelmine 6, Henry 4, Charlott			
SIEBERGER, Sofia	64	Bueckeburg	70-1011
SIEBERT, Elisa	25	Eggersmuehlen	68-0982
SIEBERT, Georg	29	Mitteldachstett	71-0712
SIEBERT, Joh. M.	15	Naumburg	71-0363
SIEBERT, Johanna	38	Hamburg	69-0067
August 18, Dorothea 7, Antonie 6, Carl 2			
SIEBERT, Luise	34	Duisburg	69-0559
SIEBKE, Friedrich	41	Windhorst	68-0707
Sophie 34, Marie 7, Sophie 7, Friedrich 6, Margaretha 4, Heinrich 7 months			
SIEBOLD, Heinr.	29	Wollmershausen	70-0569
SIEBOLD, Johannes	27	Hindelshausen	70-0184
SIEBOLD, Meta	22	Grohn	68-1006
SIEBOLDT, Eva	52	Mellingen	68-0456
Maria 26, August 22, Hermann 20, Friedrich 18, Carl 13			
SIEBRECHT, Heinrich	52	Goettingen	71-0429
SIEBRECHT, Wilhelm	17	Goettingen	70-0135
SIEBURG, Sophie	19	Oldenburg	69-0559
SIEBUS, Ursula	61	Techtingen	68-1298
Stephan 25, P. 17			
SIECK, Johann	16	Ritterhude	68-1027
SIEDELER, Carl	37	Bremen	69-1309
SIEDENBURG, Gerhard	23	Hannover	69-1076
Anna 14			
SIEDLE, August	16	Furtwangen	68-0884
Lisette 17, Emma 15			
SIEDLE, Elias	50	Furtwangen	68-0884
SIEDLER, Mathias	23	Waldbuettelbrun	71-0521
SIEFKEN, Henriette	28	Hannover	70-0308
SIEFKES, Hermann	38	New York	69-0923
SIEGEL, Elise	18	Greden	69-1309
SIEGEL, Gottl.	19	Hofingen	69-1363
SIEGEL, Johann	19	Kirchheim	70-0089
SIEGEL, Louise	16	Kirchheim	70-0443
SIEGEL, Marie	17	Moxhuette	69-0923
SIEGEL, Marie 26	26	Bochterbeck	69-0429
Agnes 26			
SIEGEL, Oskar	13	Burglengenfeld	71-0226

NAME	AGE	RESIDENCE	YR-LIST
SIEGEL, Wm.	30	New York	69-1421
SIEGELE, Louise	16	Rauheim	69-0268
SIEGENER, Wilhelmine	18	Celle	71-0479
SIEGES, Ludwig	24	Hannover	70-0443
SIEGL, Rosine	34	Schoenbach	68-0661
SIEGLE, Emilie	15	Pforzheim	69-0923
SIEGMANN, Anna	30	Berlin	68-1027
SIEGMANN, Diedrich	17	Grassdorf	68-0661
SIEGMUND, Friederike	18	Langensalza	69-1004
SIEKMANN, Louise	22	Kampbugen	69-0968
SIEKMEIER, Conrad	23	Lippe Detmold	70-0355
SIELKEN, Louis	16		68-0982
SIEMENS, Johann	27	Tettons	69-0490
SIEMERN, Marie	22	Otterndorf	68-0566
SIEMERS, Cath.	17	Hannover	71-0479
SIEMERS, Wilhelm	19	Wolfenbuettel	68-0625
SIEMON, Ernestine	28	Melsungen	68-1002
SIEMON, Louise	21	Braukamps	68-0707
SIEMON, Marie Jacob 2	24	Oderherm	68-1027
SIEMS, Adeline	30	Bremerhaven	71-0429
SIEMS, Jacob	26	Hannover	70-0443
SIEMS, Johann	18	Fischerhude	69-0968
SIEMSON, Carl	35	Altona	71-0581
SIENER, Cathrine	24	Ruppersberg	69-0848
SIEPERT, Alwine	23	Dramburg	69-0798
SIESEL, B.	55	Frankfurt a/M	69-0100
SIESEL, Diedrich	28	Darmstadt	69-0592
SIESENOP, Caroline	22	Luette	68-0907
SIETING, Julius	18	Pottsdam	70-0682
SIETZINGER, MArie	15	Muester	71-0581
SIEVERING, Herm.	17	Dahlinghausen	71-0581
SIEVERS, August Christine 24	30	Westfeld	71-0684
SIEVERS, Rebecca	23	Intschede	69-0572
SIEVERS, Wilhelm Theodor 14	17	Lamstedt	69-1076
SIEWERT, Dorothea	20	Neu Hardenberg	71-0456
SIEWERT, Friedr.	33	Westercappeln	71-0821
SIHLBAUER, Peter Elise 26, Michel 3, Christine 9 months	31	Pfreindt	70-0355
SIKORA, Kovacek Johann 19	26	Wien	68-0661
SILBER, Joh.	17	Doerzbach	70-0089
SILBERHERZ, Bertha	20	Saarlouis	70-0683
SILBERMANN, Jacob	22	Bamberg	70-100
SILGER, Heinrich	25	Gohfeld	70-0148
SILGER, Heinrich	25	Gohfeld	70-0135
SILL, Amalie	16	Reuss Schleiz	69-0583
SILLER, Franz	25	Barmen	69-1086
SIMANDA, Simen	34	Weissenberg	68-0907
SIMMONIS, Barbara Peter 9 months	24	Quidersbach	69-0672
SIMMRING, J. P.	33	Emden	68-0884
SIMON, Anna	18	Buehl	68-0647
SIMON, Catharine	18	Lessenig	69-0321
SIMON, Christ.	16	Dermbach	68-0760

NAME	AGE	RESIDENCE	YR-LIST
SIMON, Franz Catharina 35, Rosalia 8, Franz 6, Wenzel 3	30	Neuzerecke	68-0770
SIMON, Heinrich	29	Neudorf	69-0292
SIMON, Jacob	48	Graubuenden	68-0957
SIMON, Louis	18	Stolp	69-1319
SIMON, Lucia	17	Sandernau	69-0798
SIMON, Michel	19	Bellings	71-0479
SIMON, Minna	19	Frankfurt	70-0148
SIMON, Sarah	71	Filehne	68-0534
SIMON, Valentin Caroline 54, Adam Ernst 25, Johannes 22	59	Sachsen Meining	69-0559
SIMON, Wilhelm	29	Nassau	70-0308
SIMON, Wilhelm	22	Ondernheim	68-0314
SING, Leop.	33	Carlsruhe	69-0100
SINGER, Christine	24	Oberfranken	69-0968
SINGER, Elisa	25	Eckenhaid	68-0982
SINGER, Ernestine Joseph 17	21	Revingen	69-0576
SINGER, Gottlieb	23	Rothenkirchen	69-0798
SINGER, Johann	25	Stebin	69-0542
SINGER, Michl	22	Rubenheim	69-1004
SINGERHOFF, Hch.	16	Dortmund	68-1006
SINGEWALD, Hermann	18	Falkenstein	68-0456
SINGLE, Ludwig	38	Frommern	69-0162
SINGRIEN, Friederike	24	Ettenheim	71-0300
SINKUHLE, Josef	16	Wescheherd	71-0429
SINN, Christine Christian 14	20	Neuhuetten	71-0429
SINNER, Johann	25	Steinberg	69-0490
SISTIERT, Caroline	65	Berlin	69-0771
SIXA, Johann Katharina 30, Marie 9, Victor 3, Anton 11 months	36	Kralowitz	71-0429
SKALA, Joh.	18	Elsawitz	69-1363
SKAWARA, Georg	19	Kauth	68-0610
SKIRRA, Jacob Dorette 31	28	Scheiz	69-0547
SKORING, Marie Carl 26, Johann 18, Anna 9, Paul 7	47	Reetz	68-0314
SLAETER, John Mary 17	15	Schwabach	70-0508
SLEEF, Johann	16	Blexen	69-0079
SLUDER, Sebastian Juliane 24, Wilhelm 7 months	24	Stein	68-0939
SLUKSPIEL, Joachim Lena 44, Johann 10, Heinrich 4, Joachim 13	45	Mecklenburg	69-0067
SLUND, Martin	24	Altendorf	69-0079
SMIT, Antje Gummel Gummel 7, Jacob 5, Maria 3, Friederika 10 months	25	Hannover	69-0559
SMITH, Isaac	36	Frankfurt a/M	69-1212
SMYZINSKY, Stanislaus Anna 7, Michalina 32	37	Zloschau	69-0547
SOBECK, Pauline	23	Lipin	69-0229
SOBECKE, Andreas Franciska 30, Marg. 9 months	33	Sukow	71-0363
SOBECKER, Maria Louise 19, Louise 17	51	Frankfurt/M	71-0712
SOBERNHEIM, Jac.	18	Bingen	69-0050
SOCHSE, Heinrich	24	Neuhaus	70-0523

NAME	AGE	RESIDENCE	YR-LIST
SOEFFLER, Anton	19	Ballrechten	71-0581
SOEFTJE, Caroline	42	Kirchweyhe	68-0610
Frdr. 6, Heinr. 4			
SOEHL, Claus	24	Steinau	69-1309
SOEHL, Metta	21	Gliede	71-0479
SOEHLKER, Adam	34	St. Paul	69-1086
SOELTER, Conrad	26	Braunschweig	70-0135
SOERGER, Joseph	50	Kippenheim	69-0923
Ursula 50, Xaver 9, Joseph 8			
SOERGER, Wilh.	26	Ottersmeier	69-0050
SOERTOFF, Jean	32	Bocholt	68-0566
SOESENBERG, Wolff	57	Nordhofen	71-0581
Elisabeth 57, Minna 22			
SOESSLER, Philip	20	Muehlheim	68-0760
Gottlob 17			
SOEST, Hugo	24	Lauenburg	68-0852
SOHDA, Phil.	25	Schweinfurth	71-0581
SOHNS, John	27	Schweigen	68-0957
SOLDAN, Fredr.	16	Frankfurt	69-1004
SOLLER, Friedr.	52	Munder	71-0581
Albert 16, Agnes 19, Marie 9, Arthur 8, Marie 40			
SOLMS, Theresia	22	Sehlau	68-0707
Bertha 2			
SOLZER, Hermann	30	Vockenrode	69-0798
SOMMER, Anton	16	Neustadt	71-0521
SOMMER, Aug.	25	Zimmerhof	68-0647
SOMMER, Bluemchen	20	Baumbach	71-0681
SOMMER, Cath.	24	Ernsthausen	71-0581
SOMMER, Gerhard	24	Neuschoenebeck	68-0314
Anna 27, Maria 9 months			
SOMMER, Gertrud	29	Darmstadt	69-1059
SOMMER, Johanna	20	Oberkolzau	68-0852
Babette 20			
SOMMER, Paul	29	Berlin	71-0792
SOMMER, Sebast.	27	Kaltenhofen	71-0479
SOMMER, Ursula	18	Flossenburg	71-0821
SOMMEREISEN, W.	40	St. Paul	71-0581
SOMMERKAMP, Cath.	60	Sudweyerheide	68-0884
SOMMERS, Johann	46	Doelzig	68-0884
Dorothea 42, Louise 19, Friedr. 3			
SONDERMANN, Marie	30	Erfurt	71-0581
Maria 25, Christina 13, Concordia 2, Heinrich 9 months			
SONDERMANN, Marie	17	Leipzig	71-0492
SONGELAUB, Catharina	54	Giltenberg	69-1086
Heinrich 24, Margarethe 16, Anna 14, Catharina 5, Cath. Willhelmine 16			
SONLIER, Carl	22	Balmbach	71-0581
SONLIK, Catharina	28	Mary 11 months	70-0508
SONN, isaac	18	Buettelborn	70-0728
SONNENBERG, Carl	21	R.B. Coeslin	68-0820
Augusta 20			
SONNENBORN, Conr.	21	Rotenburg	70-1142
SONNENBURGI, Cath.	20	Grabzonne	71-0581
SONNENHAMMER, Fritz	16	Numberg	70-1003
SONNTAG, W.	19	Solingen	71-0789
SONSECK, Johanna	21	Coeslin	70-0452
SOORHAGEN, Ludwig	36	Muehlhausen	68-0786
SORETH, Marie	30	Niedersobern	68-0982
Lorenz 14, Marie 3, Johann 2, Franz 2 months			
SORGE, Caroline	20	SSchwarzb. Rude	69-0672
SORKA, Wenzel	32	Gaug	71-0581
SORMS, Minna	24	Hoboken	69-0015
SOSNER, Julius	19	Glehn	69-1076
Julia 10			
SOSTER, Johann	32	Oberfranken	69-0968
SOSTMANN, Elise	40	Bramsche	70-0523
Ernst 15, August 13, Rudolph 7, Hermann 5, Auguste 3, Charlotte 6 months			
SPACHT, Johannes	17	Marburg	71-0736
SPADINGER, J. B.	28	Desslingen	69-1212
SPAEHLER, Barbara	27	Wiebaden	69-1212
SPAETH, Fritz	19	Sachsbachwalden	71-0456
SPAHN, Cath.	21	Altenburg	69-1086
Peter 4 months			
SPAHR, August	19	Forchtenberg	68-1006
SPAMER, Mathilde	24	Altenschlirf	69-0592
SPANBORN, August	31	Salz Ditforth	70-0148
SPANDAU, Christine	24	Braunschweig	70-0329
SPANGENBERG, Wilh.	29	Stolberg	68-0786
Amalie 28, Carl 3, Robert 11 months			
SPANGENMACHER, Mina	18	Osthofen	71-0521
SPANIER, Julius	31	Wunstorf	69-0798
SPANJOEL, Marg.	28	Schiffweiler	69-0029
Johann 7			
SPANKNEBEL, Jac.	27	Alzey	70-0204
Barbara 21, Johanna 9 months			
SPANNAGEL, C.	29	Siegen	69-1076
SPARK, Adelheid	25	Hannover	68-0647
SPATH, Fr. J.	26	Carlsruhe	70-0089
SPECHT, Carl	37	K. Hothel	68-0456
Maria 36, Heinrich 7, Carl 4, Bertha 9 months			
SPECHT, Carl.	16	Osnabrueck	70-0184
SPECHT, Friedrich	23	Forchtenberg	69-1212
SPECHT, Julius	45	Magdeburg	68-0419
Wilhelm 23, Otto 19, Carl 10			
SPECHT, Weert	16	Nordmoor	69-0490
SPECK, Joh.	16	Carlsruhe	68-0786
SPECK, Theod.	50	Wendlingen	70-0728
Franziska 15, Sophie 9			
SPECKERT, Joseph	20	Hambach	71-0712
SPECKMANN, Anna	15	Achim	69-0968
SPECKMANN, Friedrich	17	Versmold	71-0492
SPECKMANN, Sophie	16	Rheda	68-0647
SPEER, Francisca	28	Tauberbach	68-0610
SPEER, Friedrich	38	Chemnitz/Saxony	69-0547
SPEICH, Melch.	16	Leuchsingen	71-0789
SPEIDEL, Rosine	16	Moessingen	69-1363
SPEIER, Anna	21	Berlin	70-1003
Helene 20			
SPEIS, Carst.	16	Leimbach	71-0300
SPEISSER, Sophie	29	Sulzbach	68-0852
SPEKELS, Bernh.	35	Rodenkirchen	68-0534
Meta 37, Johann 9 months			
SPELLMANN, W.	34	Bielefeld	71-0789

NAME	AGE	RESIDENCE	YR-LIST
SPELLMEYER, M. H.	72	Wester Oldendor	68-1006
SPENGLER, Emilie	20	Altenburg	69-0672
SPERBER, Gustav	18	Rothenburg	68-0707
SPERRY, Julie	22	Ettenheim	68-0625
SPETH, Jacob	24	Ichenhausen	68-0014
SPICHER, Herm.	45	Muenster	68-0982
SPIECKEN, Cath.	23	Wersen	71-0821
SPIECKERMANN, Johann	64	Mildow	69-0672
Sophie 60, August 25			
SPIEGEL, Georg	17	Berlin	71-0492
SPIEGEL, Herm.	13	Camon	68-0982
SPIEGEL, Johanne	24	Hannover	69-0923
SPIEGEL, Louise	22	Parlin/Russia	69-0049
Fred. 11, Emilie 4			
SPIEGEL, Luisa	21	Soest	69-0798
SPIEGEL, Siegfried	13	Halverstadt	68-0707
SPIEGELN, Catharine	24	Schale	68-0647
SPIEGLER, Anna	12	Westphalia	69-0841
Henrich 14			
SPIEKER, Henry	58	Colonia	69-0798
SPIEKER, Kampe	24	Wuerdum	68-0852
SPIEKERMANN, Augusta	23	Posen	68-0707
Anton 27			
SPIELBERG, Emilie	25	Dietz	69-0542
SPIELBERG, Friedr.	37	Giesenbruegge	69-0542
Caroline 33, Albert 7, Emil 6, Emma 5, Minna 3			
SPIELER, Martin	36	Westerheim	71-0581
Anna 26			
SPIELMANN, Jos.	18	Pfanweisach	69-1011
SPIER, Carl	52	Willebadessen	68-0456
Theodore 58, Gertrude 20			
SPIER, Guste	20	Wellinghausen	71-0815
SPIES, August	29	Kirchheim	69-0429
Elisabeth 26, Ludwig 11 months			
SPIES, C.	23	Nufringen	70-0170
SPIES, Moritz	16	Bildweis	71-0581
SPIESS, Valentin	15	Pfiungstadt	69-1421
SPIETH, Wilhelm	87	Esslingen	71-0643
Chrisiane 30, Bertha 3			
SPILKER, Peter	16	Hueffen	71-0821
SPILLNER, Heinrich	48	Cassel	68-0661
Dorothea 48, Georg 7, Elisabeth 6, Justus 9 months			
SPINDLER, Carl	6	Gempertshausen	68-0566
SPINDLER, Caspar	49	Gempertshausen	68-0566
Lina 52, Maria 16			
SPINDLER, Catharina	25	Wangen	68-0939
SPINDLER, Dorothea	17	Benswangen	71-0521
Rosine 14			
SPINDLER, Edw.	25	Eisenberg	69-0572
SPINNER, Joseph	21	Buehe	68-0314
SPITTLER, Ant.	36	Breslau	71-0815
Auguste 31			
SPITZER, Rudolf	34	Peter	69-1319
Johanne 24			
SPITZMUELLER, Franz	27	Wien	69-0490
Marie 7, Franziska 5			
SPLITTORF, Johann	19	Schwarzenborn	69-0672
SPLONSKOWSKI, Martin	30	Zirkwitz	68-0786

NAME	AGE	RESIDENCE	YR-LIST
SPOCKEN, Therese	20	Bruchhausen	68-0907
SPOEHRER, Johannes	23	Hoergenau	68-0625
SPOEKEN, Therese	20	Bruchhausen	68-0907
SPOHN, Charles	20	Hausheim	70-0308
SPORLEDER, Marie	25	Langendorf	71-0456
SPOTEK, Valent.	31	Craejoze	71-0479
Anna 27, Bartol 58, Magdalene 57, Rosa 7 months			
SPRAUDEL, Rosine	25	Grafenberg	70-0089
SPRENGER, Carl	35	Sommerfeld	71-0792
Louise 30, Georg 10 months			
SPRENGER, Friedrich	29	Waldeck	70-0259
Elisabeth 28, Elise 3, Johanne 2, Friedrich 9 months			
SPRENGER, Wilhelm	33	Pankow	70-0204
Wilhelmine 33, Max 5, Emma 2, Paul 5 months			
SPRENGLER, Fr.	16	Darmstadt	69-0841
SPRETH, Franz	18	Hausbrunn	70-0308
Mathel 16			
SPRICK, Charlotte	18	Hannover	71-0821
SPRICKERMANN, A.	23	Posen	68-0707
Anton 27			
SPRINGBORN, Friedrich	35	Strelitz	69-0559
Sophia 40, Caroline 9, Wilhelm 7			
SPRINGHAGEN, Gesine	18	Arbergen	71-0429
SPRINGHORN, Doris	21	Wisselhoevede	71-0643
Catherine 18			
SPRINGMANN, Ferd.	26	Brueggen	69-0841
SPRINGMANN, Marie	28	New York	70-1003
SPRINZING, Catharina	27	Menningen	71-0821
SPRITZERBACH, Helene	21	Oberbieber	71-0733
SPROESSER, Andreas	20	BOEHLINGEN	69-0968
SPROSKY, Johann	38	Rekowitske/Boeh	69-0576
Franciska 38, Anna 7, Johann 3, Antonia 14			
SPRUCK, Friedr.	30	Barmen	69-1363
SPRUTE, Fred.	36	Detmold	70-0308
Sofia 36, John 18, Fred. 16, Caroline 9, August 6			
SPRUTE, Heinrich	48	Mosebeck	68-0786
SPUDEL, Agnes	25	Moeningen	69-0672
SPUERING, F. Marg.	59	Tedinghausen	68-0647
Cathrine 18, Wilhelm 21			
SPUHN, Peter	33	Steinheim	69-1363
STAAB, Anna	50	Solingen	69-0457
STAAB, Wilhelm	19	Kreuznach	68-0456
STAADTS, Johannes	80	Roemershausen	68-0456
Heinrich 38			
STAAK, Wilhelm	16	Treptow	68-0852
STAAKE, Erdmann	22	Pegan	68-0820
STAAR, Johann	16	Schmilsdorf	68-0707
STAAS, Fried.	25	Dahlinghausen	71-0479
Clara 22			
STAB, Wilhelmine	30	Bremen	68-0982
Johanna 6			
STACEK, Anna	21	Boehmen	69-1363
STACHELKER, Martin	30	Hargelin	69-0547
Catharine 24, Marianne 24			
STACHLE, Martin	17	Empfingen	69-0798
STADE, Bernhard	31	Apolda	68-0456

NAME	AGE	RESIDENCE	YR-LIST
STADELMANN, Conr.	26	Oberschendi	71-0736
STADLER, Jos. Anton	31	Welfensberg	68-0770
STADTHANDER, Gottl.	19	Gr. Drensen	69-1421
STAEB, Anna Wilhelmine 13	17	Emsdorf	71-0643
STAEBLEIN, Georg	24	Varrel	69-1396
STAEBLER, Albert	26	Frauenfeld	71-0712
STAEBLER, Margaretha Catharina 37	59	Oberdiek	68-0707
STAEDLER, Georg	26	Poppenhausen	69-0968
STAEMME, Charles Therese 26	30	Tennstedt	68-0534
STAERKER, Johann Marie 48, Johann 23, Michael 13, Dorothea 18, Georg 9	49	Salmsdorf	71-0429
STAEVER, Carsten Diedrich 23	16	Suestedt	71-0684
STAFFREGEN, Amalia Adolph 6 months	29	Bueckeburg	68-0707
STAGE, Carl	25	Sachsen	69-0559
STAHL, Caroline	17	Mademuehlen	68-0314
STAHL, Everhard	26	Alfeld	68-1002
STAHL, Joh.	15	Oberselters	68-0314
STAHL, Marie Regina 20	19	Hunteburg	68-0820
STAHLE, Hermann G. 18	20	Winterbach	69-0182
STAHLHUT, Friedr.	22	Lippe	71-0736
STAHLMANN, Johann	23	Oberfranken	68-0786
STAHMANN, Meta	20	Leeste	69-0572
STAHMER, Johann	22	Fleeste	68-0534
STAHR, August Caroline 22	18	Kl. Jena	69-1421
STAHRER, Mich.	15	Hochdorf	68-0610
STAIB, Anna	34	Zell	68-0852
STAIB, Caroline	21	Dettensen	71-0456
STAIB, Pauline	18	Stuttgart	69-0572
STAIFFERT, Johann	26	Strassburg	71-0712
STAIGER, Mary	21	Meihringen	69-1011
STAIZER, Robert	16	Deisslingen	70-0308
STAKELENDER, F.	32	Stettin	70-0223
STALBUSCH, Mathilde August 18	24	Wedow	69-0576
STALERMANN, Dorette		Nordheim	68-1002
STALLJOHANN, Johann	16	Westercappeln	71-0736
STALLMEISTER, Sophia Sophia 11 months	26	Detmold	69-0968
STALMANN, Conrad	30	Trooste	69-1086
STALPH, Adam	17	Troesel	70-0728
STAMER, Henriette	22	Bremerhaven	68-0314
STAMM, Aug.	19	Hildesheim	69-1086
STAMM, Caroline Cath. 22	22	Buedingen	68-0786
STAMM, Margarethe Bernhard 6, Johann 4, Franz 9 months	32	Steinfeld	71-0712
STANARIUS, August	15	Schkenditz	69-0572
STANDERMANN, Jacob	23	Wendelsheim	69-0321
STANG, Anna	26	Niederaula	71-0643
STANGE, Anna	25	Hadamar	69-1319
STANGE, Aug. Johanne 33	29	Elbingerode	70-0178
STANGE, Joh. Friedr. Marie 28, Wilh. Ferdinand 6 months	38	Leitning	69-0576
STANGE, Marie	23	Steinau	71-0363
STANGE, Wilh.	19	Mitterode	68-0610
STAPENHORST, Fr.	15	Lengerich	69-0542
STAPF, Jos. Joh.	21	Muenchberg	68-1002
STAPLEY, Magnard Ellen 23	26	Wadhurst	70-0148
STARCK, Julius Joseph 14	18	Ueberlingen	68-0957
STARCK, Maria Anton 6 months	44	Hofheim	68-0707
STARK, Johannes	16	Emartshausen	68-1027
STARKE,	42	Seidenberg	68-0770
STARKE, Carl	32	Mainz	71-0167
STARKE, Eduard	50	Berlin	69-0968
STARKE, Ottilie Marie 18	26	Berlin	70-1003
STARKLOFF, Carl	17	Bopfingen	71-0429
STARY, Leopold	31	Wien	71-0736
STARZINGER, Joh.	20	Wiesen	68-0982
STASSROSKY, Franz	26	Gr. Rautzig	71-0492
STASY, Johann Catharina 30, Johann 1, Joseph 5 m.	31	Andraz	71-0792
STAUBER, Pauline Theodore 22	17	Grenzhausen	68-0566
STAUBER, Therese	28	Fluenau	69-1011
STAUBER, Theresia	20	Schneiderhof	68-0957
STAUBITZ, Julia	18	Niederweimar	68-0534
STAUBITZ, Ruppert	16	Niederweimar	71-0712
STAUDENBAUER, Sophie	23	Hausenheim	71-0492
STAUDENHAUER, Robert	19	Ellwangen	69-1212
STAUDER, Margaretha	13	Neustadt	68-0661
STAUDERMANN, S. Marie 14, Johann 12	47	Wendelsheim	68-1006
STAUF, Magd.	23	Walduelversheim	70-0443
STAUSBERG, Peter	31	Wingendorf	71-0521
STAWET, Wilhelm	30	Ludwigstadt	69-0784
STECH, Bernh.	24	Lichtenborn	71-0167
STECHER, Georg	30	Dorzbach	71-0226
STECHER, Teo	16	Luebbecke	68-0566
STECK, Anton	16	Kreuznach	69-0841
STECKER, Carl	25	Seibach	70-0728
STECKER, Georg	22	Wolfgruben	71-0479
STECKER, Otto	18	Detmold	71-0521
STECKERT, Helene	19	Muenster	69-0771
STEEB, Barbara	19	Gruenthal	68-0820
STEEB, Dorothea	16	Gruenthal	69-0429
STEEFELD, Friederike	26	Celle	68-0852
STEEGEWALD, Jeanette	22	Deiningheim	69-0771
STEENKEN, Anna	24	Oldenburg	69-0572
STEERS, Gerhard Marie 29, Anna 8, Adelheid 5, Anna 9 months, Johann 35	41	Bawinkel	69-0968
STEFFEN, Catharine Caspar 27, Marie 24, Louise 18, Wilhelm 12	51	Ostkiloer	69-0923
STEFFEN, Conrad	20	Bremervoerde	68-0786

NAME	AGE	RESIDENCE	YR-LIST
STEFFEN, Friedr.	17	Bernsten	68-0647
STEFFEN, Gottfried	26	Coeln	68-1049
STEFFEN, Rudolf	23	Essen	70-0148
STEFFEN, Wilhelm	27	Gersche	70-0308
STEFFENS, Anna	18	Dedesdorf	68-0566
STEFFENS, Anna	16	Bremervoerde	71-0479
STEFFENS, Auguste	9	Solingen	69-0457
STEFFENS, Catharine	21	Gertenroth	70-1003
STEFFENS, Claus	22	Hannover	69-1086
STEFFENS, Daniel	54	Michelshaus	69-0457
Christine 50, Julius 21, Ida 18, Hermann 16			
STEFFENS, Friedrich	30	Schwelm	69-0182
STEFFENS, Gesche	20	Hannover	69-0672
STEFFENS, Heinr.	24	Wohlenbeck	71-0736
STEFFENS, M. Cathar	36	Wremen	70-1161
Anna 10, Eide 9, Wilhelm 7, Diedrich 4, Bertha 11 months, Johann 11 months			
STEFFENS, Theodor	18	Hannover	70-1035
STEFFENS, Trina	18	Nordeeda	68-0314
STEFFER, Johann	37	Ostfriesland	69-0542
Johanne 35, Peterdine 7, Friederika 6, Johanne 5, Gerhard 4, Johann 10 months			
STEGE, Joh. H.	46	Hustedt	68-0610
Anna 42			
STEGEMANN, Fr. Carl	47	Halle	68-1002
STEGER, Friedrich	16	Hannover	68-0865
STEGMANN, Carl	29	Hannover	70-0076
STEGMANN, Diedrich	21	Bremen	69-0429
STEGMANN, Heinrich	22	Bremen	69-1212
STEGMANN, Magdalene	19	Meiningen	70-0452
STEGMEIER, Joseph	26	Beilngries	68-314
Crescencia 37			
STEGMEYER, Auguste	33	Darmstadt	69-1086
STEHLE, Christian	52	Revingen	69-0576
STEHLE, Engelbert	16	Riedlingen	68-0625
STEHLE, Wilh.	25	Ettingheim	69-0100
STEHMANN, Heinrich	23	Westercappeln	71-0736
STEHMEL, Wilhelm	20	Landsberg	69-0542
Julie 27, Emma 2, Minna 4 months			
STEHRMANN, John	20	Wiedenbrueck	68-0957
STEIBER, Fred.	32	Goeppingen	69-1421
STEIDINGER, Jac.	24	Betzweiler	68-0957
STEIDLER, Johannes	20	Wellendinger	70-0378
STEIER, Carl	32	Mecklenburg	69-0067
Elisabeth 26, Friedrich 7, Liebrecht 4			
STEIGER, Barbara	36	Bonn	69-1212
Eugene 7, Carl 6, Francisca 5, Wilhelm 2			
STEIGER, Clementine	32	Lichtenstein	69-0542
STEIGER, Maria	50	Hanau	71-0712
STEIGER, Sophie	30	Neukirch	71-0581
STEIGERWALD, Joh.	30	Weinheim	68-0647
STEIGERWALD, Lorenz	32	Habichsthal	68-0625
STEIGLEIN, Marie	58	Neuhaus	71-0684
STEIL, Arthur	16	Hagen	71-0300
STEIL, Catharina	32	Wannen	68-0625
Georg 9, Heinrich 5			
STEIL, Friedrich	26	Hagen	69-0208
STEILEN, Johann	16	Seedorf	68-0982
STEIN, Anna	22	Stuttgart	69-1086
STEIN, August	18	Germersheim	71-0429
STEIN, Bertha	15	Esslingen	69-1059
STEIN, Bertha	20	Olsenstdt	71-0479
STEIN, Caspar	52	Ermenrod	69-0672
Anna 51, Catharina 29, Caspar 9, Conrad 6, Anna 17			
STEIN, Cath.	19	Feischborn	71-0581
STEIN, Catharina	24	Eiderfeld	68-0661
STEIN, Heinrich	23	Niederaula	68-0314
STEIN, Heinrich	29	Niederaula	68-0939
Christiane 27, Marie 4			
STEIN, Joh.	17	Blankenbach	68-0820
STEIN, Johann	57	Oldenburg	71-0393
STEIN, Lisette	18	Wimpfen	70-1035
Rosine 17			
STEIN, Margarethe	31	Lindenholzhs.	71-0226
STEIN, Max	16	Leipzig	71-0712
Franz 15			
STEIN, S.	44	Pleschen	70-1035
Minna 42, Israel 12, Helena 9, Levy 7, Juliane 3			
STEIN, William	15	Nuernberg	68-0957
STEINACKER, Wilhelm	26	Ladbergen	69-0015
Minna 19			
STEINBACH, Catharine	21	Uttrichshausen	69-0592
STEINBAR, Michael	17	Selchow	68-0770
STEINBECK, John	15	Peugeln	69-0672
STEINBECKER, Herm.	18	Hannover	71-0821
STEINBERG, Adam	23	Niederaula	68-0939
STEINBERG, Bernhardine	12	Niederaula	68-0939
STEINBERG, Elisabeth	22	Wetter	69-0457
STEINBERGER, Helene	17	Stoecken	68-0760
STEINBORN, Heinr.	29	Gehofen	71-0821
Johanne 29, Minna 8, Franz 4			
STEINBORN, Johanne	30	Salzdettfurth	71-0492
Ernst 7, Albert 5			
STEINBRECHER, Benedik	28	Wedel	69-0771
Agnes 19			
STEINBRENNER, Eva	21	Zagenhausen	71-0393
STEINBRENNER, Fritz	17	Gerabronn	68-0982
STEINBRUECK, Julius	45	Schwerin	70-0148
STEINCKE, Adolf	15	Hannover	70-0523
STEINCKE, Gerd	34	Oldenburg	69-0268
Maria 34, Heinrich 17, Georg 4			
STEINDEL, Emilie	25	Burg	70-1142
Franz 5, Anna 4, Maria 1, Eduard 3 m.			
STEINDINGER, Andreas	17	Munich/Bavaria	69-0547
STEINDLE, Barbara	39	Gutenberg	70-0223
Marie 44, Gottl. 9			
STEINDLE, Johann	23	Gichwand	69-0015
STEINECK, Henry	14	Wallhofen	71-0456
STEINER, Cathrine	24	Huetten	70-0355
STEINER, Heinrich	34	Osnabrueck	69-0050
STEINER, Roekle	25	New York	70-1003
STEINERT, Marie	50	Rochester	69-1011
Mary 9			
STEINFELD, Albertine	18	Eschwege	68-0534
Pauline 20			
STEINFELD, Wilhelm	23		68-0852
STEINGRAEBER, Anton	47	Augsburg	71-0712

NAME	AGE	RESIDENCE	YR-LIST
Maria 44, Otto 9, Arnold 5			
STEINHABER, Elise	29	Ostheim	69-0576
STEINHAEUSER, Heinr.	16	Bremerhaven	70-0569
STEINHAGE, Christ.	33	Sabbenhausen	68-0884
Wilhelmine 25			
STEINHAUER, Dorothea	20	Pyrmont	71-0815
STEINHAUER, Hugo	34	Berlin	71-0712
Elise 30, Amande 8, Margarethe 6, Gertrude 3, Johann 9 months			
STEINHAUS, Wilhelmine	45	Rothenfelde	70-1035
Christine 17, Fritz 14, Minna 9			
STEINHAUSER, Mart.	30	Wagenstadt	70-1066
STEINING, Mart.	28	Niederuml	69-0771
STEININGER, Cath.	25	Zail	71-0363
STEINKAMP, Sophie	20	Luebbecke	68-0884
STEINKAMP, Wilh.	25	Sabbenhausen	68-0884
STEINKE, Heinr.	42	Hannover	69-1004
Magd. 43, Heinr. 16, Doris 15, Marie 9 months			
STEINLAGE, Georg	29	Osnabrueck	70-1023
Fritz 28, (Hamilton)			
STEINLER, Simon	20	Ignanitz	71-0479
STEINMANN, Elis.	59	Gronau	70-1142
Marg. 24, Barbara 21			
STEINMANN, Elise	23	Imsbach	70-0384
Friederike 19			
STEINMANN, Samuel	17	Schoppingen	68-0939
STEINMANN, Susanne	26	Imsbach	69-0457
Christine 22			
STEINMEIER, Caroline	21	Bruchhausen	68-0907
STEINMETZ, Albin	14	Gotha	70-0329
STEINMETZ, Caroline	55	Mainz	70-1161
Jean 8			
STEINMETZ, Friedrich	41	Bergen	69-1212
STEINMETZ, Juergen	68	Mursum	68-0770
Catharina 65			
STEINMETZ, Olga	17	Geistungen	71-0821
STEINMETZ, Philipp	17	Derdingen	71-0429
STEINMETZ, Therese	44	Wuerzburg	69-0542
STEINMUELLER, Vincenz	22	Rothelmeyer	71-0821
STEINSCHNEIDER, H.	14	Wien	71-0733
STEINSIEPEN, Aug.	44	Loehdorf	69-0560
STEINSTARDT, Anna	27	Sebbertrodt	69-0490
Johann 20			
STEITZ, Carl	40	Vendershausen	69-0268
STELDER, Henriette		Havianow	69-0547
STELLER, Heinrich	22	Boesse	69-0457
STELLER, Lena	52	Lesum	70-1142
Melina 9			
STELLING, Marie	19	Otterndorf	69-0542
STELLING, Metta	60	Altenbruch	68-0661
STELLJES, Anna	19	Schredlitz	68-0982
STELLJES, Jan	35	Hannover	69-0672
STELLJES, Minna	18	Hannover	69-0672
STELLMACHER, Anton	35	Berlin	69-0321
Caroline 34			
STELLMANN, Andreas	29	Saatholt	68-0939
Johanna 22, Thientje 3, Carl 9, Gretje 21			
STELLMANN, Henry	26	Beckedorf	71-0643

NAME	AGE	RESIDENCE	YR-LIST
STELLOH, Heinr.	26	Nordsulingen	68-0884
STELLOH, MArie	42	Holzhausen	71-0363
Minna 17, Wilh. 8, Sophie 9 months			
STELLWAG, Gustav	20	New York	69-1396
STELLWAGEN, Marie	15	Wendelsheim	71-0643
STELMACH, Catharina	24	Zarmarta/Polen	69-0576
Stanislaus 2, Victoria 6 months			
STELTER, Heinrich	29	Hannover	68-0610
STELTER, Margarethe	33	Bade	69-0798
Margarethe 9, Anna 7, Johann 5, Trina 3			
STELTER, Metta	7	Lesumbrock	68-1027
STELZLE, S.	21	Aufhausen	71-0681
STELZNER, Friedr.	28	Jesnitz	70-0089
STEMINETZ, Heinr.	24	Oestrich	70-0089
STEMM, Moses	16	Luettgemder	70-1003
STEMME, Ferdinand	31	Sonderhausen	69-1396
Ferdinand 13			
STEMMERMANN, Cath.	20	Gustendorf	68-0982
STEMMERMANN, Joh.	14	Bremervoerde	71-0581
STEMMEYER, August	36	Brake	68-0852
STEMMLEI, Jacob	22	Darmstadt	69-0923
STEMMLER, Elise	19	Wichte	68-0566
STEMPE, Elisabeth	26	Sassenberg	70-0452
STEMPEL, Philipp	22	Lambsheim	69-0015
STENCK, Elis.	29	Salzungen	69-1086
STENDEBACH, Johann	19	Harbach	69-0490
STENDECKE, Joseph	27	Obermaisberg	68-1027
STENDER, Henry	60	Charleston	69-1059
Minna 55			
STENEK, Adolf	20	Ambergen	69-1086
STENGEL, Carl	21	Carlsruhe	69-0208
STENGEL, Joh.	37	Gebersdorf	71-0815
STENGER, Barbara	25	Strassbesenbach	68-0566
STENLITZ, Josef	36	Boehmen	70-0728
Theresia 29, Josef 7, Franz 4, Wenzel 11 months			
STENNERMANN, Nicolas	16	Kirchwistedt	69-0429
STEPHAN, Aug.	14	Bischhausen	68-0534
STEPHAN, Carl	22	Meissen	69-0079
STEPHAN, Catharina	26	Romersreck	68-0939
August 9 months			
STEPHAN, Marie	28	Leitmeritz	70-1035
STEPHANI, Marie	33	Minden	68-1002
STEPHANSKI, A.	36	Loegen-Soegen	70-0204
STEPPERT, August	26	Wiesbaden	70-1003
Marie 24, August 2, Josef 6 months			
STERN, Abraham	17	Heppenheim	71-0521
STERN, Bery	30	Hardford	71-1046
STERN, E.	50	Gedern	71-0643
L. 14, Bertha 9			
STERN, Elisabeth	27	Raidwangen	69-1212
Elisabeth 5, Sophie 3, Marie 1			
STERN, Fanny	23	Schachtena	69-0268
STERN, Hedwig	33	Bremen	70-0728
M. 14			
STERN, Heinrich	17	Baglingen	71-0492
STERN, Isaac	22	Londorf	69-1059
STERN, Julius	39	Wiesbaden	69-1059
Jetta 34, Henriette 3, Baby 10 months			

NAME	AGE	RESIDENCE	YR-LIST
STERN, Lazarus	20	Gelnhausen	70-0089
STERN, Max	18	Mittelbach	70-1142
STERN, Meyer	15	Koenigsbach	71-0492
STERN, Moses	13	Darmstadt	70-0508
STERN, Salomon	25	Ziegenhain	68-1002
STERN, Salomon	16	Niederohmen	69-0229
STERN, Salomon	16	Niederklier	71-0167
STERNBECK, Wilhelm	32	Grabow	68-0907
Friedrich 29			
STERNBERG, Isaac	14	Werder	71-0167
STERNBERG, Marie	23	Steinfurt	68-1002
STERNBERGER, H.	20	Neulemingen	69-0208
STERNHEIMER, H.	26	Darmstadt	68-0456
STERNSCHEIN, Simon	20	Ullstadt	68-0957
STESSE, Therese	30	Furland	69-0049
Gustav 7, Clara 5, Anna 7 months			
STETTJES, Gesche	22	Worpswech	71-0681
Metta 19			
STEUBE, Hy.	28	Oldenburg	70-0308
Mary 21			
STEUBER, Catharina	26	Bromskirchen	68-0625
Louise 19, Rosine 13, August 17			
STEUDLE, Adeline	17	Kayna	70-0384
Emma 15			
STEUER, Samuel	29	Grossen	70-100
STEUERWALD, Joh.	30	Weinheim	68-0647
STEUMLER, Catharine	20	Oberstaufenb.	70-0308
Henry 15			
STEUVERS, Arend	59	Holland	70-0384
Johanne 51, Aubert 24, Moritz 17, Johanne 18, Gesine 9			
STEYERWALD, A. F.	21	Meissen	69-1004
STICH, Anna	30	Dabrisch	68-1027
STICHER, Franz	16	Mainz	70-0329
STICHLER, Pauline	38	Lichtensteia	70-0006
Caroline 9, Edward 8, Marie 2			
STICHT, Agnes	20	Hannover	68-0786
STICKEL, Christ.	18	Egenhausen	71-0226
STICKEL, Elisabeth	22	Spielberg	68-1027
STICKFORT, Gerhard	46	Gehrde	69-0798
Maria 36			
STIEB, Christian	27	Simmerfeld	68-0786
Marga. 24			
STIEBEL, Tecla	20	Lengsfeld	69-1076
STIEBELING, Lorenz	50	Darmstadt	69-0672
Ricke 13, Sophie 11, Elise 9			
STIEBER, Bernhard	24	Lauingen-Laning	69-0798
STIEBER, Joseph	36	Goetzingen	68-0314
Caroline 37, Lina 16, Catharina 12, Johann 10, Heinrich 5, Anna 3			
STIEBER, Martin	25	Niedlingen	70-0184
STIECH, Barbara	26	Floss	71-0429
STIEDEMANN, Henrike	32	Colberg	70-0272
Wilhelm 2, Alwine 8, Carl 4, August 2, Minna 7,			
STIEFEL, Babette	19	Gruenstadt	70-1055
STIEFEL, Lea	20	Vockerode	68-1006
STIEFEL, Maier	17	Wuestensachsen	71-0429
STIEGER, John	26	Bonn	69-1004
STIEGLER, Elisab.	25	Reichenbach	70-1055
Baby			
STIEHL, Justus	14	Anzelahn	69-0162
STIELER, Marie	25	Zuerich	69-0576
Lina 4, Carl 9 months			
STIENE, Anna	20	Westfalen	70-0728
STIENICKER, Wilhelm	26	Ladbergen	69-0015
Minna 19			
STIENS, Johann	30	Bensen	68-1002
STIER, Joachim	20	Bubsheim	70-0308
STIERLEN, Catharina	17	Oberdiek	68-0707
STIESFORT, Caroline	49	Hemelingen	71-0521
Dorette 24, Johanne 9			
STIEWE, Joseph	26	Entrup	69-0429
STIGGE, Joh. H.	42	Twelbaeke	68-1006
STILLER, Fredr.	45	Stadthagen	69-0049
Dorette 39, Dorette 18, Sophie 15, Heinrich 13, Lina 7, Ludolph 5, Friedrich 6			
STILLER, Robert	45	Silberberg	69-1309
STILLING, Wilhelmine	15	Dorum	69-1086
STILZENBAUER, Cath.	24	Merxheim	69-0490
STIMPE, Elisabeth	26	Sassenberg	70-0452
STISSKAL, Barbara	67	Boehmen	69-1396
STOBEL, Cath.	18	Rotenburg	68-0753
Elisabeth 16			
STOBER, Carl	18	Rinteln	68-0314
STOCH, Amalie	23	Zepfenhan	71-0643
Sabine 4			
STOCK, Anton	16	Kreuznach	69-0841
STOCK, Elisabeth	29	Oberstrut	70-0452
STOCK, Fritz	21	Coeln	69-0029
STOCK, Gottfried	56	Allstedt	68-0534
Christine 57			
STOCK, Hermann	42	Detmold	68-0852
Wilhelmine 38, Hermann 7, Heinrich 5, Augusta 2			
STOCK, Marg.	59	Sargenzell	68-0647
Barb. 26, Therese 9 months			
STOCKBOND, Therese	19	Tscheinitz	71-0815
STOCKBURGER, Anna	17	Wittendorf	71-0456
STOCKBURGER, Elisa	20	Wittendorf	68-0760
STOCKE, Jacob	36	St. Louis	69-1076
STOCKEMER, Otto	19	Heilsbronn	69-0457
STOCKER, Carl	20	Treunbach	71-0815
STOCKER, Jacob	20	Rothenburg	69-1059
Barbara 23			
STOCKHAUSEN, H.	24	N. Etscheid	69-0208
STOCKHOFF, Hermann	17	Herde	70-0184
STOCKMEYER, Hermann	25	Westphalen	69-1212
Marie 30, Caroline 6, Marie 3, Johann 9 months			
STOCKSECKER, Joh.	31	Hannover	70-0308
STODK, Caroline	20	Burkhardt	71-0479
STODOLA, Gg.	20	Neubidzow	68-0610
Franz 24			
STOECKER, Aug.	26	Trigloff	69-1004
STOECKER, Friedr.	25	Solingen	70-0089
STOECKER, Margarethe	21	Walbenfels	70-100
STOECKLE, Julius	24	Stuttgart	68-1027
STOECKLEIN, Anna		Regensburg	68-0957

NAME	AGE	RESIDENCE	YR-LIST
STOEGER, Ferdinand	22	Muenchen	70-0329
STOEHRER, Hermann	40	Meerane	68-0456
STOELZEL, Anna	20	Coburg	68-1298
STOELZEL, Jacob	15	Willstein	68-0647
STOERE, Barb.	26	Hartzingen	71-0789
Rebula 7			
STOERMER, Wilhelm	17	Osterode	69-0572
STOESS, Lina	18	Asch	68-0610
STOETTER, Anton	32	Plaslingen	68-0770
Anna 36			
STOETZER, Max	17	S. Gotha	69-0572
STOEVER, Anna	30	Nordholz	71-0821
STOEVER, Friedrich	16	Willstedt	71-0521
STOEVER, John	22	Buente	70-1003
Henry 20			
STOFFEL, Cath. Elis.	43	Messel	68-0884
Elis. 12, Anna 8, Elisab. 7			
STOFFELS, Hubert	24	Weisshosen	69-0798
STOHLMANN, Heinr.	31	Merisville	71-0226
Wilhelmine 21			
STOKENIUS, Justus	28	Cassel	69-1396
STOLBEN, Simon	36	Merzheim	71-0393
Anna 34, Helene 7, Eduard 6, CLara 5, Elisabeth 3, Cath. 6 months			
STOLE, Conrad	17	Langegons	68-0647
STOLL, Friedrich	26	Trutenhof	68-0820
STOLL, Johann	33	Unteraichen	69-0268
Christian 22, Georg 3, Regine 2			
STOLL, Johann	35	Langenkandel	71-0684
Ottilie 32, Margareth 8, Da. 5, Johann 10 months			
STOLL, Maria	9	Laupheim	71-0792
STOLL, Moritz	23	Heroldishausen	69-0560
STOLL, Susanne	20	Hall	71-0736
STOLLBINGER, Josef	19	Geisfeld	71-0643
STOLLE, Behrend	24	Oldenburg	69-0268
STOLLE, Robert	17	Warnsdorf	71-0300
Anna 19			
STOLLMANN, Gerhard	31	Miskolitz	68-0625
STOLP, August	23	Pempertin	71-0429
STOLT, M.	26	Bremerhaven	68-1006
STOLTE, Carl	16	Rechtenfleth	71-0479
STOLTE, Friedrich	18	Delenburg	68-0753
Bernhardine 20			
STOLTEFUSS, Heinr.	33	Hermede	68-0982
Caspar 29			
STOLZ, Caroline	20	Neuenstadt	68-0707
STOLZ, Catharina	15	Mergentheim	68-0014
STOLZ, Margarethe	34	Schmidtweiler	68-0314
STOLZ, Maria	27	Ottenheim	71-0712
STOLZE, Johannes	60	Vorwerk	68-0625
Caroline 60			
STOOS, Friederike	22	Offenhausen	70-0223
STOPFER, Marg.	16	Tachau	68-0647
STORCH, Amalia	46	Ruhla	68-1002
Reinhold 18			
STORCH, Johann Wilh.	32	Hessen	69-0559
Eva Maria 30, Caroline Christine 6, Bertha Rebecca 4, Anna Margaretha 2, Adam			
STORCH, Philipp	23	Steinheim	68-0661
STORCK, Bertha	29	Eschborn	68-0566
Catharina 11 months			
STORCK, Josef	23	Tyrol	71-0167
STORF, Christine	20	Neuenstein	69-1319
STORK, Peter	26	Tyrol	70-0170
STORR, Eva	24	Selzen	70-0583
STORTZ, Wm.	26	Hanssen	69-0338
STORZ, Friederike	28	Stassfurt	71-0643
Wilhelm 3, Anna 1			
STOTZER, Valentin	34	Toutogany	69-0067
STOTZKY, Charles	30	Elisabethtown	70-0308
Elisabetha 18, Mary 24, Bertha 3			
STOWELL, Edward	22	New York	70-0135
STOY, Heinr. Aug.	27	Grosselten	69-0182
STRADMANN, Marie	41	Bremerhafen	69-0771
Adele 15, Wilhelm 10			
STRAESSLER, Elise	20	Loyl	68-0820
STRAHL, Abraham	19	Gilsenberg	71-0815
STRAHL, Louis	18	Schwiezhausen	70-0569
Magd. 24			
STRANGMANN, Marie	20	Nienburg	71-0581
STRASS, Samuel	18	Kuekesheim	71-0363
STRASSBURG, Gottfried	30	Wartin	68-0770
Caroline 25, August 11 months			
STRASSBURGER, Eva	58	Altenkirchen	68-0610
Wilhelmine 24			
STRASSBURGER, Fritz	41	Sonnenberg	69-0672
STRASSEMEYER, H.	23	Osnabrueck	68-0865
STRASSER, Catharine	14	Achim	68-0566
STRASSER, Henry	14	Achim	70-0508
STRASSER, Josefa	19	Schreibersgmb.	69-1011
STRASSHEIM, Heinrich	17	Darmstadt	70-0259
STRASSHEIM, Volkert	47	Darmstadt	71-0300
Marie 44, Phil. 16, Anna 20, Elise 14, Wilhelm 10, Caroline 9, Carl 5, Emil 3			
STRASSINGER, Catharine	66	Auerbach	68-0907
Margarethe 42			
STRATHMANN, Clemens	18	Eilstadt	69-0457
STRATHMANN, Henry	25	Rodewald	70-0508
STRATHMANN, Hermann	37	Harpenfeld	71-0429
Marie 31			
STRATHMEYER, Louise	20	Loehne	71-0226
STRATMANN, Clara	20	Hamm	68-0610
STRATTON, Johann	30	Leipzig	69-0100
STRAUB, Chr. Fr.	18	Bole	68-0647
STRAUB, Georg	29	Schwarzach	68-0760
STRAUB, Joh.	25	Hausen	71-0521
STRAUB, Joh. Pap.	50	Brueckenau	63-0244
Antonie 44, Anna 13			
STRAUB, Johann	36	Pliningen	69-0208
STRAUB, Peter	25	Emartshausen	68-1027
STRAUCH, Julie	19	Eichelsachsen	69-0672
STRAUSS, Abraham	18	Doerzbach	68-0760
STRAUSS, Anna	18	Landau	69-1309
STRAUSS, Bertha	41	Barwalde	71-0479
STRAUSS, Cath.	58	Muntermagertier	71-0681
Christine 23, Marg. 16			
STRAUSS, Const.	25	Riga	69-0457
STRAUSS, Ferdinand	30	Auerbach	69-0968

NAME	AGE	RESIDENCE	YR-LIST
STRAUSS, Frieda	28	Leitmar	68-0907
STRAUSS, Friederike	21	Darmstadt	71-0736
STRAUSS, Friedrich	19	Eslingen	68-0770
STRAUSS, Heinrich	6	Kirchschilde	69-1309
Louise 9 months			
STRAUSS, Hobel	48	Langenschwarz	69-0968
Saleine 51, Ester 17, Caroline 15			
STRAUSS, JAc.	16	Dieburg	71-0521
STRAUSS, Johann	31	Wittenberg	68-0456
Christine 29, Johann 9 months			
STRAUSS, Josef	33	Sommershausen	70-0682
Caroline 20			
STRAUSS, Martin	58	Mainz	70-1161
STRAUSS, Max	18	Gruenstadt	70-1055
STRAUSS, N.	32	Nuernberg	70-1142
Lina 19			
STRAUSS, Philip	42	New York	70-1003
Anna 30, Friedrich 6, Albert 5, Rosa 20			
STRAUSS, Regine	20	Sterbfritz	69-0592
STRAUSS, Rosa	26	Kleindimbach	71-0456
Nanette 19			
STRAUSS, Samuel	23	Mainz	70-0443
STRAUTMANN, Anne	15	Laer	71-0429
STRAUTMANN, Wilh.	20	Reichenberg	69-1004
STREBEL, Elise	23	Worms	70-100
Georg 17			
STREBES, Elisab.	53	Worms	70-0308
Wilhelmine 17, Anna 9, Charles 21			
STRECK, Catharine	20	Frankenheim	70-0308
STRECK, Cathr.	28	Muennich	70-0170
Auguste 22			
STRECK, Christian	29	Sachsen Meining	69-0321
STRECK, Louis	36	Ostheim	71-0521
Johanne 32, Johanne 9, Sophie 7, Marie 9 months			
STRECK, Wilhelm	31	Baden	69-0798
STRECKFUSS, Caspar	17	Forchtenberg	68-1006
STRECKTENFINGER, J.	31	Langenau	69-0672
STREEK, Johann	24	Landshut	69-0268
STREHLE, Carl	46	Oberaichen	69-0268
Dorothea 46, Carl 19, Christian 17, Catharine 7, Jacob 6, Caroline 4			
STREHLE, Marie	17	Grumbach	68-0884
STREHLOW, Max	15	Zehlendorf	68-0314
STREIB, Andr.	55	Unterebisheim	68-1006
STREIBICH, S.	19	Fautenbach	71-0226
STREICH, Lorenz	21	Jactorowo	69-0592
STREICHLEDER, M.	25	Krautheim	68-0852
STREIN, Josef	27	Aschhausen	69-0229
Gabriel 25			
STREIT, Carl	23	Zimswein	71-0792
STREITHE, Wilhelmine	23	Lingen	69-0968
STREMEL, Ludwig	16	Briedenhof	68-0707
STREMKE, Johann	25	Unterkrain	68-0707
STREMPEL, Catharine	25	Ostheim	71-0492
STRENTZEL, Emilie	26	Teschendorf	68-0314
STRETY, Lorenz	24	Oberhaid	70-1003
STRETZ, Lorenz	24	Oberhaid	70-1003
STRICKER, Minna	17	Rothenfelde	69-1004

NAME	AGE	RESIDENCE	YR-LIST
STRICKROTH, Johanna	23	Bremen	68-0753
Marie 3, Caroline 9 months			
STRIEBEL, J.	18	Sasbach	71-0789
STRIEDER, Cunrad	20	Berghausen	68-0760
STRIEFFERT, Johann	26	Strassburg	71-0712
STRIEGEL, Friedrich	19	Heilbronn	69-1396
STRIEGEL, Veronica	23	Tiefenbach	69-0457
STRIMMING, Cath.	25	Niederneff	68-0647
STRIPPEL, Heinr.	27	Altenstaedt	68-0884
Elisab. 25			
STRITTMATTER, Pauline	24	Alberl	69-0771
STROB, Heinrich	21	Neuenkirchen	69-0923
STROBEL, Andreas	53	Haicherdorf	69-0429
Marie 53			
STROBEL, Bruno	26	Auerbach	70-0170
STROBEL, Hugo	3	Miltenberg	69-0592
STROBEL, Johann	42	Schlittis	68-0760
Anna 33, Eduard 8, Maria 6, Johann 5			
STROBEL, Johann	31	Bausor	71-0733
STROBEL, Leonhard	20	Heilgersdorf	68-0939
STROBEL, Marie	18	Gotha	69-0429
Nicolaus 31			
STROESSNER, Johann	18	Oberfranken	69-0784
STROH, Franz	19	Homburg	71-0821
STROH, Fried.	17	Markoebel	71-0581
STROH, Philipp	17	Laubach	68-0760
STROHL, Peter	27	Westum	69-0229
STROHLE, Caspar	28	Steinbruch	69-0429
STROHLMANN, Friedr.	54	Huellhorst	68-0566
Marie 57, Caroline 18, Ilsabein 9			
STROHMANN, Anna	18	Bruckhausen	68-0884
STROHMEIER, Friedrich	35	Braunschweig	68-1027
Marie 35, Carl 6, Antoniette 3, Johann 2			
STROHMEIER, Wilhelm	35	Wenzen	68-0625
Johanna 36			
STROHRMANN, Wme.	34	Uchte	71-0363
STROHSACK, Hinrich	17	Ritzebuettel	69-0672
STROMBACH, Aug.	19	Wagenstadt	68-0957
STROMPS, Wilhelm	16	Bonn	71-0736
STROPLE, Anna	21	Riedlingen	69-0771
STROSINSKY, Julius	39	Granow	68-0647
Sophie 36, Emilie 3, Augusta 1			
STROTHMEYER, Johanna	25	Vauensen	68-1002
STROTHOFF, Catharina	15	Oldenburg	71-0492
STROTMANN, Ernst	18	Solingen	71-0492
STRUBE, Aug.	16	Magdeburg	70-0569
STRUBE, Wilh.	31	Eisenach	68-0982
Wilhelmine 39, Ferdinand 8, Augusta 7			
STRUCKHOFF, Heinrich	15	Braunschweig	68-0647
STRUCKMANN, Charlotte	48	Rannenberg	71-0479
Heinr. 20			
STRUCKMEYER, Caroline	20	Rehren	71-0479
STRULLER, Louis	64	New York	70-1003
Bertha 22			
STRUMPF, Johann	51	Tuebingen	69-0672
STRUSS, Adolph	24	Otterndorf	68-0786
STRUSS, Anna	28	Hannover	69-1076
Rebecca 4, Sophie 2, Conrad 10 months			
STRUSS, Friedr.	40	Sabbenhausen	68-1027

NAME	AGE	RESIDENCE	YR-LIST
Helene 36, Charlotte 9, Sophie 6, Anton 63, Charlotte 58			
STRUSS, Wilhelm	16	Hannover	69-1212
STRUVE, Cath.	19	Bunchhoven	71-0581
STRUVE, Fr.	16	Gronau	68-0884
STRUVE, Hans	19	Dresden	69-1076
STRUZEL, Marhias	17	Unterkrain	68-0707
STRYBA, Thomas	45	Lisnau	69-0547
STUB, Conrad	16	Volkenshausen	68-0852
STUBBE, Conrad	32	Lobbach	68-0456
STUBBE, Gottl.	40	Koffenhammer	68-0647
STUBBE, Rebecca	24	Neuenlande	68-0456
STUCKERT, Adam	29	Schweisweiler	69-1059
Catharine 21, Christine 3 months			
STUCKRADT, Heinrich	16	Niederthalhause	69-0592
STUCKS, Ludwig	22	Kerwenheim	69-1319
STUDER, Carl	26	Hahlberg	69-0182
STUDER, Sebastian	34	Stein	68-0939
Juliane 24, Wilhelm 7 months			
STUDTE, Hermine	29	Blankenburg	69-1319
STUEBE, Heinrich	32	Detmold	69-1319
Minna 28, Louise 5			
STUEBER, Emma	24	Klettenberg	70-1055
STUEBING, Marie	60	Uckermark	71-0479
Alma 19			
STUECKER, Carl	24	Solingen	70-0031
STUECKER, Hermann	17	Bielefeld	71-0712
STUEHLDORF, Franz	36	Combahn	69-1086
STUEHREN, D.	20	Hannover	71-0393
STUEMEL, August	23	Reuth	68-0760
STUERENBURG, Seb.	24	Bockhorn	68-0625
STUERER, Meta	23	Ottersburg	68-0939
STUERGEL, Friedrich	7	Engstlath	70-0523
STUERKEN, Johann	20	Nendersum	68-0939
STUERMER, Alfred	28	Koenigsberg	68-0770
STUEVE, Hedwig	20	Widdern	68-0534
STUEWE, Wilhelmine	26	Elverdissen	68-1006
Wilhelmine 3			
STUFT, Carl	20	Freudenstadt	69-0429
STUHMER, Henriette	22	Bremerhaven	68-0314
STUHR, Wilhelm	33	New York	69-1086
Willy 8 months			
STULKEN, Elise	20	Oldenburg	69-1086
STUMMEL, Therese	22	Leisgeniges	69-0049
STUMPE, M. A.	28	St. Louis	70-1035
Adelheid 24, Adolph 11 months			
STUMPF, Gottl.	48	Ostheim	71-0521
STUMPF, John	59	Margrethhausen	69-0338
Anna 41, Anton 8, Theresia 4, Josef 2, John 10 months, Caspar 53			
STUMPF, Maria	24	Argenrod	68-0939
STUMPFF, Sebast.	22	Hessen	70-0178
STUMPFFELD, Helene	25	Wabern	70-0378
STUMPP, Joh.	60	Toledo	71-0815
Christ. 24			
STUNDER, Friedr.	36	Furt-Wangen	69-0050
STUNZE, Wilhelm	53	Cerne	70-0682
STUPPBACH, Gottl.	57	Thun	71-0789

NAME	AGE	RESIDENCE	YR-LIST
Ernst 2			
STURCKE, Barb.	23	Mainz	71-0167
STURM, Caroline	22	Pforzheim	68-0610
STURM, Elisabeth	16	Hermersheim	71-0712
STURM, Fridolin	21	Deisslingen	70-1161
STURM, Marie	22	Mergentheim	68-0852
STURM, Martin	65	Windsbach	71-0736
STUTE, Johannes	24	Wewelsburg	68-1002
STUTH, Magnus	36	Stettin	70-0223
STUTZ, Carl W.	20	Zweibruecken	69-0079
STUVE, Clara	18	Niedorf	69-0923
SUDBRUECKER, Lena	19	Neunkirchen	70-0728
SUDHOFF, Ludwig	28	Herben	68-0939
SUDMANN, Friedr.	25	Wesenstaedt	68-0786
SUDNASINORSKY, M.	24	Markelinsdorf	69-1309
Veronika 4, Jacob 2, Ignatz 10 months			
SUDSCHLAG, Ernestine	52	Klasdorf	68-0770
Louise 22, Ernestine 7, Gustav 1			
SUEDENBURG, John	15	Bremen	71-0581
SUEDERMANN, Doris	24	Langwedel	68-0852
Marie 20			
SUEDHOD, Jacob	23	Hardenstetten	69-1086
SUEDHOF, Louise	22	Hardenstetten	69-1086
SUEHLFLEISCH, Jul.	17	Meiningen	69-0560
SUEHRMANN, Marie	21	Wellingen	71-0363
SUESS, Carl	25	Stadtamhofe	69-0162
SUESS, Joseph	31	Bodenweis	69-0542
SUESSENGUTH, Louise	20	Goettingen	68-1006
SUESSFELD, Fanny	20	Wuerzburg	68-0982
SUFFRIAN, Mina	25	Altenhagen	69-0542
SUHR, Anna	19	Wuesting	68-0625
Meta 16			
SUHR, Heinrich	28	Hardegen	68-0786
SUHR, Hermann	17	Visselhoerde	71-0736
SUHR, Maria	34	Bremen	68-1002
Gesine 9, Johannes 7, Louise 11 months			
SUHRE, Heinrich	20	Halle	69-0457
SUHRHOFF, Alb.	27	Hoya	68-0884
SULING, Anna	18	Schweringen	69-0229
SULING, Wilhelm	16	Schweringen	70-0184
SULLWOLD, John	24	Oldenburg	69-1421
SULTAM, Martha	24	Rotenburg	68-0314
SULTZ, Ernst	43	Camnitz	71-0821
SULZ, Rosine	30	Moessingen	68-0566
SULZBACHER, Moritz	26	Friesen	70-0583
SUMP, Johann M.	44	Ollendorf	70-0006
Christiane 50, Ricke 19, Carl 16, Wilhelm 13, Heinrich 11			
SUNDERLAGE, Helene	20	Hannover	70-1003
SUNDERMANN, Maria	31	Hannover	71-0792
SUNDERMEIER, Carl	25	Rehme	68-1027
SUNDHEIM, Meier	18	Brunskirchen	68-0760
SUNGHERTCHEN, Fried.	16	Debstadt	69-1309
SUNSCHEN, Christian	24	Rodenkirchen	71-0733
SUPPES, Rudolph	19	Bechtolsheim	69-0229
SURG, Carl	14	Carlsruhe	70-0184
SURGES, Lorenz	66	Dreis	69-1011

NAME	AGE	RESIDENCE	YR-LIST
SUSTKE, Friedrich	24	Felstau	69-0457
Wilhelmine 18			
SUTER, Friedrich	19	Soulgau	69-1059
SUTOR, Aloys	30	Graubuenden	68-0957
SUTTER, Magdalene	38	Havre	69-1076
SUTTMEIER, Adam	18	Asbruch	68-0786
SUTTON, Mary	55	Dover	69-1086
SUVRIKAR, Maths.	23	Krain	70-0384
Josef 15			
SUWALKA, Rosalia	26	Margoninsdorf	69-0229
SUX, Heinrich	25	Gailingen	71-0521
SWEIFT, William	42	New Bedford	69-1076
SWOBODA, Josef	48	Wescheherd	71-0429
Marie 44, Josefa 22, Wenzel 17, Marie 14, Anna 9, Johanne 6, Juliane 4			
SWYTER, Krine	60	Emden	68-0419
Akje 53, Krine 25, Garrelt 18, Moeder 25, Entje 9, Akje 7			
SYMENS, Ude	49	Hannover	69-0229
Ida 39, Catharine 18, Petrus 16, Symen 14, Anna 2			
SYNDERHAUF, Johann	23	Rodesgrun	68-0939
SYRBENS, Johannes	22	Koenitz	68-0661
SYROVATHKE, Josef	32	Boehmen	70-1161
Anna 19, Marie 3, Johanne 6 months			
SZEBO, A.	26	Wuerzburg	69-1086
SZPICHAL, Anna	56	Schlupawa	69-0592
SZRAMBOWSKY, Peter	26	Exin	69-0547
Stanislaus 31, Francisca 29			
Schueler, Magdalena	26	Ettingen	68-0760
TAEPKE, Florentine	42	Kielan	69-1011
Caroline 21, Florentine 14, Charles 16, Auguste 8, Martha 4			
TAHLBUSCH, D.	16	Oldenbuettel	71-0521
TAKENBERG, Sophie	26	Jever	68-0957
TAKES, Maria	19	Gelahausen	70-0272
TALBER, Joseph	23	Hirnkirchen	70-0223
Eva 21, Thomas 11 months, Xaver 2 months			
TALGE, Hubert	24	Naschod	68-0982
TALIAN, Elisabeth	40	Mainz	68-0786
TALLDORF, Sophia	32	Blumenthal	69-1076
TALLER, Pauline	22	Zunsweiler	71-0792
TALLER, Sophie	20	Buchholz	69-0542
TAMBKE, Claus	26	Hannover	68-0456
Metta 22, Claus 9 months			
TAMM, Aug.	16	Altenbruch	68-314
TAMMEN, Carl	20	Steger	69-0208
TANNEN, Hugo	30	Wangerooge	69-0923
TANNENBERGER, Emma	20	Stranow	71-0643
TANNER, Eduard	32	Wassingen	71-0456
Elise 33, Auguste 9, Louise 6, August 3, Marie 9 months			
TANNER, Julka	40	Emden	69-0572
Georg 5, Siebold 3, Gerhard 11 months			
TANYOWIAK, Simon	55	Pawoa	69-0547
Christine 60, Joseph 7, Franz 6			
TAPKEN, Anton	26	Oldenburg	69-1421
TAPKEN, Henry	16	Oldenburg	70-1003
TAPPE, Joh. Heinrich	15	Oldenburg	70-0204
TAPPENBECK, Lena	45	Oldenburg	70-0355

NAME	AGE	RESIDENCE	YR-LIST
TAPPER, Heinr.	24	Aurich	69-0490
TAPPER, Louis	25	Estorf	68-0820
TAPPERT, Carl	19	Schlon	68-0456
TARNOW, Johann	28	Ploetz	69-0321
Agnese 26, Minna 4, Agnese 3 months			
TATJEN, Heinrich	37	Hueddingen	68-0566
TAUBENHEIMER, Jacob		Reckendorf	68-0625
TAUBER, Johann	48	New York	69-0457
Ida 42, Christina			
TAUBERT, Herm.	28	Altenburg	71-0736
Agnes 24			
TAUCHER, Anna	7	Nuenberg	71-0521
TAUK, Johann	38	Stuchow	69-0429
Sophie 38, Wilhelmine 9			
TAUPER, Cathr.	4	Oberweitz	70-1035
Joh. 7, Georg 11 months			
TAUPSER, Barb.	28	Oberweitz	70-1035
TAUSCHER, Magdalena	50	Landshut	68-0820
Marie 13, Magdalene 12			
TAUSER, Catharina	19	Stuttgart	69-0457
TAUSSIG, Julie	22	Getsikowitz	68-0770
TAX, Henry	6	New York	70-1003
TEALEY, August	34	Hildesheim	68-0014
Catharina 38			
TEETZ, Franz	30	Neudorf/Prussia	69-0547
Caroline 24, Albert 3, Wilhelm 1			
TEGER, Heinz	52	Claumen	69-0049
A. Elisabeth 42			
TEGGEMANN, Carl	16	Darmstadt	70-1035
TEGTMEYER, Herm.	23	Rodenberg	71-0479
TEGTMEYER, W.	25	Bueckeburg	69-1004
TEGTMEYER, Wilh.	21	Heitbrink	71-0479
TEICH, Maria	27	Bremen	69-0050
TEICHLER, Emilie	26	Liegnitz	68-0456
TEIG, Catharina	24	Volkmannsgruen	69-0542
TEIGEN, Dooks	36	Dhielerhaid	68-0753
Bianka 32, Peter 6, Eike 3			
TEIHLBAUM, Mina	32	Pest	70-0355
Ilka 8, Piroska 4			
TEIMER, Regine	21	Kallin	70-1023
TEIPE, Aleida	40	Lingen	70-0508
TEITZE, Johann	26	Sachsen Meining	69-0798
TELGMANN, Heinr. Wilh.	37	Weetzen	69-0321
TELTMANN, Wilhelm	32	Bielefeld	71-0643
TELTMANN, Wilhelm	32	Bielefeld	71-0643
TEMBANN, Franz	24	Borghorst	69-1086
TEMME, Cath.	21	Wiebnich	70-1035
TEMME, Franz	18	Dissen	68-0957
TEMME, Wilh.	19	Rippen	69-0572
TEMPS, Wilhelmine	21	Oberurtel	70-0031
TENBRUCK, W.	30	Aspel	71-0363
Gesine 28			
TENGLER, Joh.	48	Budweis	71-0581
Josefa 48, Anna 23, Adolf 16, Maria 9			
TENIS, Carl	33	Briesenhorst	69-0771
TENNA, Augusta	18	Zernich	68-0647
TENNER, Emilie	30	Niederbeerbach	68-1002
TENSLAFF, Auguste	21	Stettin	69-0572
TENSPOLDE, Johann	61	Crosewick	68-0884

NAME	AGE	RESIDENCE	YR-LIST
Marie 60, Johann 22, Marie 19, Gertrud 18, Dina 16, Johannes 16			
TEPE, Carl	31	Oldenburg	69-0592
TEPE, Johann	39	Natbergen	68-0852
Elise 39, Gerhard 9, Elise 8, Adam 7, Louise 6, Mathias 3, baby 2 months			
TEPEL, Christian	24	Schwehn	69-0572
TEPP, M.	23	Lippe Detmold	70-0223
TERBACH, Heinrich	28	Legden	69-0771
TESAR, Vincenzia	29	Kuttenburg	71-0736
Anna 6			
TESCH, Wilhelm	46	Pommern	69-0672
Wilhelmine 37, Wilhelmine 16, Maria 14, Louise 4			
TESKE, Johann	18	Lendewerder	69-0457
TESKE, Joseph	28	Erichfier	68-1027
Mathilde 31			
TESSE, Cath.	18	Wersabe	71-0479
TESSMANN, Bernhard	31	Dunkuhlens	71-0456
TESTERS, Christ.	29	Muckenschopf	71-0521
TEUBER, Anton	30	Kaltenbrunn	69-0182
TEUBER, Sebastian	34	Thuelb	71-0821
TEUBERG, Gerhard	18	Mettingen	71-0712
TEUFEL, Georg	33	Nuernberg	68-0957
TEUFEL, Mich.	33	Bug	71-0167
TEUN, Michl.	27	Lohr	71-0300
Anna 26, Mathilde 2, Josefa 9 months			
TEWES, Eide	50	Volkenshausen	68-0852
TEWES, Mary	18	New York	69-0572
TEWES, Trina	25	Rotenburg	71-0479
TEWES, Wilhelm	25	Rhoden	71-0736
Wilhelmine 30, Baby girl 9 months, Johanne 58			
TEWS, Carl	33	Bredow	69-0672
Friederike 27, Wilhelm 2, Wilhelmine 64, Auguste 24			
TEXTOR, Adam	24	Calkobes	68-0534
THADEN, Gerd	33	Neufunnia Siel	69-0429
Amalie 29, Theodor 9, Johanne 7, Gerhard 5, Martin 3, Helene 9 months, (Neusunn			
THAETER, John	15	Schwabach	70-0508
Mary 17			
THALHEIMER, Max	18	Valzechheim	68-0982
THALMANN, Carl	24	Bochlitz	69-0841
THALMANN, Ernst	22	Mannheim	68-0982
THALMANN, Richard	28	Norden	68-0647
Bertha 5, Wilhelmine 3			
THAMMEN, Jac.	16	Thunum	69-1363
THEES, H.H.	38	Barglei	68-0610
Marie 45, Minna 14, Diedrich 13			
THEES, Hinrich	23	Bederkesa	68-0456
THEILE, Alfred	20	Elberfeld	71-1046
THEILIG, Emma	19	Altenburg	69-0542
THEISMEIER, Marie	26	Osnabrueck	71-0581
THEISS, Balthasar	15	Gruesen	71-0429
THEISS, Carl	15	Mutzenbach	70-0384
THEISS, Daniel	16	Matzenbach	68-0820
THEISS, Johann	36	Buedingsheim	69-0592
Cath. 25, Elisab. 4, Marie 2, Cath. 6 months			
THEISS, Valentin	36	Mainz	68-0419
Elisabeth 46			
THELE, Sophie	22	Bremen	69-0457
THEODORSKY, Adam	60	Warschau	69-0321
Marie 34, Oscar 9, Max 8, Marie 6, Gustav 11 months, Alexander 1 months			
THERKORN, Catharine	20	Rodenburg	70-0204
THESING, Helene	24	Clyten	69-0672
THEU, Ignaz	35	Waldbach	70-0508
THEURER, Marie	19	Altensteig	68-0820
THEUSS, Caroline	24	Heilbronn	69-0572
THEVES, Gustav	24	Rheine	70-0089
THEWS, Edward	19	Neudorf Abbau	69-1011
THEYS, Anna	17	Hadamar	69-0771
THIEL, Anna	18	Herford	71-0643
THIEL, Dorette	33	Hameln	68-1298
Charlotte 16, Fritz 14, Henriette 12, Dora 13, Diedrich 11, Andreas 7, Wilhelm			
THIEL, Johann	27	Chemnitz	68-0456
THIEL, Marie	26	Wodnau	70-0329
THIELBER, Wilhelmine	18	Storbeck	69-1059
THIELE, Marie	24	Osterode	68-0939
THIELE, Theodor	18	Hannover	71-0733
THIELEMANN, Sophie	21	Rhaden	71-0479
THIELEN, Anton	28	Herschbroich	69-0457
THIELERT, Wilhelmine	31	Madelwitz	68-0982
Anna 6			
THIELHELM, Anna	18	Bremen	68-0852
THIELMEYER, Diedr.	27	Strohen	68-0456
Marie 24, Friedrich 3, Caroline 6 months			
THIEM, Herm.	23	Heuthen	71-0521
THIEMANN, Heinrich	18	Kirchlengern	68-1027
THIEME, Ferdinand	28	Mittelhausen	71-0821
THIER, Margareth	22	Nesselbach	68-0957
THIERAUF, Babette	22	Helmbrechts	71-0643
THIERER, Josef	20	Treffelhausen	69-0338
THIERGARTEN, Louisa	21	Dachsbach	70-0728
THIEROLF, Balthasar	26	Darmstadt	69-1212
THIES, Anabecka	24	Hannover	70-0443
THIES, Anna	17	Hadamar	69-0771
THIES, Herm.	26	Brammer	68-0566
THIES, Mathilde	5	Bremerhaven	71-0363
THIESMEIER, August	14	Detmold	68-0314
THIESS, Ernst	24	Bremerhafen	69-1212
Martha 4, Mathias 9 months			
THIESSEN, Carl	16	Bremen	68-1027
THOELKE, Joh.	14	Affinghausen	71-0581
THOENE, Marie	19	Beverungen	71-0393
THOENKE, Heinr.	35	Colberg	68-1002
THOENKE,Jacob	28	Doellnik	71-0429
THOIRWANGER, Marx	49	Bruchweiler	68-0770
Elisabeth 44, Franziska 16, Catharina 11 months, Johann Jacob 4			
THOKE, Sophie	22	Bremen	70-1055
THOLEN, August	23	Herzlake	68-0707
THOLEN, Wilhelmine	18	Ockenhausen	68-0939
THOMA, Carl	15	Schrinbein	69-0672
THOMA, Elisabeth	25	Saussen	68-0907
THOMA, Gottfried	20	Dertingen	69-0592

NAME	AGE	RESIDENCE	YR-LIST
THOMA, Johann	19	Neustadt	71-0429
THOMAE, Carl	37	Grochwitz	69-1396
THOMAE, Gottlieb	26	Stuttgart	70-1003
Sophie 26, Emilie 3			
THOMANN, Kunigunde	19	Unterweiler	71-0643
THOMANN, Magdalene	20	Asselheim	69-0798
Friedrich 14			
THOMAS, Clara	25	Glauchau	68-0786
Clara 11 months			
THOMAS, Friedrike	26	S.C.Gotha	70-0728
THOMAS, Johann	24	Dittmannsdorf	68-0456
THOMAS, M.	20	Osnabrueck	69-0050
THOMAS, Margreth	24	Mengshausen	71-0456
John 23			
THOMAS, Siegfried	25	Muehlheim	70-0682
THOMASCHEROSKY, A.	26	Patskau	68-0770
Louise 21			
THOME, Jacob	20	Ulbstadt	69-0798
THOMFORDE, Peter	57	Mulsum	68-0534
Anna 53, Adelheid 23, baby-daughter 11 months			
THOMPSON, John	27	Bradford	70-0355
THOMS, J. (male)	16	Brake	68-0884
THOMSMEYER, Friedrich	28	Echinghausen	68-0907
THON, Carl	17	Keltersbach	68-0610
THON, Georg	41	Kreuzeber	68-0786
Elisabeth 37, Theresia 11, Balthasar 9, Christine 11 months			
THON, Louise	21	Sontra	68-0610
THON, Stephan	33	Kreuzeber	68-0786
Dorothea 29, Augusta 2, Marie 1 months			
THONE, Eduard	26	Ostheim	69-0049
H. Sophie 58, Heinrich 28			
THOR, H. Louise		Lemsbringe	69-0049
THORBECK, Lisette	22	Laer	69-0429
Marie 19			
THORMANN, F.		Vegesack	68-1002
THORN, Julius	24	Oberfranken	69-1363
THORN, M.	24	Lucca	71-0363
Miss 22			
THORNDEKE, Emmy	26	Bislan	70-0178
THORNI, Friedrich	23	Geckhausen	69-0542
THORS, Joh.	23	Haag	71-0815
THORSEL, Henry	32	Leeland	68-0625
Johanna 32			
THREN, John	36	Gomersdorf	70-0170
THRIES, Joh.	41	Essel	68-0610
Marie 40, Marie 12			
THRUNFARL, Carl	40	Semin	68-0770
Carolina 44, Bertha 6, Hulda 5, Alwine 3			
THUEMANN, Amalia	19	Bremen	69-1212
Anna 17, Diedrich 8, Christ. 8, Hermann 6, Heinrich 9 months			
THUERER, Christ.	20	Untergussringen	71-0300
THUERWAECHTER, M.	19	Rechtenbach	69-0672
THUERWANGER, Marx	49	Bruchweiler	68-0770
Elisabeth 44, Franziska 16, Catharina 11 months, Johann Jacob 4			
THULEN, Wilhelm	25	Essen	69-0923
THUMANN, Marg.	27	Prag	70-0569
THUNNBUECHLER, Cath.	46	Grimstadt	70-1055
THURAU, Fredr.	28	Jeetze	69-1212
THURM, Carl Edw.	50	Altenburg	68-0770
THURMANN, C. H.	20	Herringhausen	70-1035
THURMANN, Doris	26	Dettmold	69-0542
THURMANN, W.	25	Harrendorf	69-1004
THURNHEER, Gottlieb	17	Dornbirn	68-0610
Marie 24			
THYNEKE, Marianne	19	Caminchen	69-0321
TIBBE, Lambert	28	Waldseite	68-0566
TICKEN, Marg.	16	Wellen	70-1035
TIEDEMANN, Anna	18	Bederkesa	69-1059
TIEDEMANN, Anna	20	Otterndorf	68-0566
TIEDEMANN, Anna	34	Otterndorf	71-0821
Heinrich 9, Menda 6, Anna 6 months			
TIEDEMANN, August	16	Otterndorf	71-0429
TIEDEMANN, Auguste	1	Colberg	70-0272
TIEDEMANN, C.	39	Burlington	71-1046
Elise 33			
TIEDEMANN, Diedrich	18	Hannover	70-0031
Drewes 19			
TIEDEMANN, Johann	16	Koehlen	69-0784
TIEDEMANN, Th. H.	20	Oberndorf	68-0647
TIEDEMANN, Wilhelm	22	Otterndorf	69-0583
TIEGEL, Joh.	19	Kirchheim	70-0089
TIEGEL, Marie	26	Bochterbeck	69-0429
Agnes 26			
TIEKEN, Diedr.	18	Oldenburg	68-0707
TIELKING, Louis	18	Stadthagen	70-0355
TIELPAPE, Christian	36	Hannover	70-0076
TIEMANN, Francisca	23	Metelen	69-0229
TIENKEN, Anna	19	Hannover	69-1212
TIENKEN, Diedrich	31	Beverstedt	68-0456
TIENSCH, Bertha	27	Hoya	70-1003
TIETJE, Emilie	30	New York	69-1011
Emma 4, Alwine 10 months			
TIETJEN, Anna	22	Meienburg	69-0572
Margaretha 18			
TIETJEN, Dorothea	18	Erlangen	71-0429
TIETJEN, Gretchen	18	Hannover	69-0672
Emmy 9 months			
TIETJEN, Heinr.	17	Bremen	70-1142
Wilh. 17			
TIETJEN, Hermann	24	Jaderbollenhage	69-0429
TIETJEN, Joh.	50	Hoboken	71-1109
Anna 45, Elise 48, Oscar 8, Leop. 6			
TIETJEN, Joh. Andr.	25	Bremen	69-0182
TIETJEN, John	16	Teufelsmoor	71-0456
TIETJEN, Meta	16	Lehnstedt	71-0363
TIETZE, Johann	21	Hannover	70-0031
TIETZEN, Hermann	53	Hannover	69-1059
Georg 16			
TILEE, Julie	60	Baden	68-0566
TILL, Caroline	22	Cassel	69-0457
TILLMANN, Emilie	22	Romberg	68-0610
TILMES, Ba.	20	Freiburg	69-0050
TIMIOTHI, Julia	29	Frankfurt	70-0378
TIMKE, Heinr.	27	Altenratt	71-0479
TIMM, Christoph	32	Grabzonne	71-0581

NAME	AGE	RESIDENCE	YR-LIST
TIMM, Marie	26	Marolschen	68-0707
TIMM, Mary	29	Mittelhagen	68-0760
Emilie 3, Catharina 71			
TIMMERMANN, Alb.	56	Sudweyhe	68-0534
Beka 26			
TIMMERMANN, Anna	18	Altenbruch	68-0625
TIMMERMANN, Carl	28	Oldenburg	68-0566
Helene 22, Friedrich 9 months			
TIMMERMANN, Dorothea	34	Calbe	71-0492
Johanne 8, Oscar 6 months			
TIMMERMANN, Heinrich	17	Lehe	69-0848
TIMPE, Wilhelm	16	B. Lesse	68-1027
TIMPER, Louis	26	Alexanderhad	68-0314
TIMPKE, Wilhelm	24	Strackholt	69-0457
TINATH, George	40	Berkum	70-0135
Adolf 28			
TIRATKA, Josef	37	Boehmen	70-0569
Marie 26, Wenzel 9 months			
TISCH, Moses	23	Walicka	71-0712
TISCHER, Marie	52	Rausbach	71-0581
TISCHLER, Adam	40	Baiern	69-0559
Eva 42, Margarethe 17, Peter 12, Johann 27			
TJARDEN, Tiarde	21	Hannover	70-0384
TJARKS, Herm.	25	Waddewarden	68-0610
TOBELKA, Lorenz	28	Selchow	68-0770
TOBIAS, Friedrich	20	Passau	69-0268
TOBIAS, Regine	47	Arnhausen	69-0784
Bertha 14, Pauline 12, Sahra 9, Tobias 8, Isaak 6, Johanne 4			
TOBIASSEN, Heinrich	60	Marx	71-0492
Sophie 56, Catharina 13, Maria 9			
TOBY, Simon	22	Strassburg	69-0547
Johann 21			
TOCHTERMANN, Babette	19	Hornbach	71-0492
TOCKAN, Wenzel	46	Friedland	68-0852
Eleonore 38			
TODTENHAUPT, Rudolph	29	Berlin	69-0572
TOEBELMANN, Reinhard	16	Bremen	69-0182
TOECKER, Gustav	33	Unterberg	68-0610
TOEL, William	38	New York	70-1161
Adele 30			
TOELKE, Carl	49	Brakelsiek	68-314
Sophie 24, Fiedrich 13, Heinrich 11, Carl 6			
TOELL, Johann	17	Bebra	68-0770
TOELZER, Franz	30	Trepptowitz	71-0521
TOENSING, Heinr.	24	Wimmers	69-0572
Clara 32, Clara 11 months, Marie 23			
TOEPFER, Carl	24	Sievern	68-0566
C. 22			
TOEPLITZ, Lischmann	48	St. Francisco	70-0178
TOEPPE, Carl	30	Gr. Turra	71-0712
TOERL, Gottl.	31	St. Louis	68-0884
Wilhelmine 23			
TOGGENBURGER, C.	38	Zuerich	71-0363
TOGGENBURGER, S.	7	Herzogenweiler	68-0707
TOKE, Friederike	9	Herford	69-1309
TOLL, Johann	23	Beilstein	69-0457
TOLL, Michael	20	Stoehrberg	69-0457
TOLLWERTH, Minna	27	Lippstadt	70-1003
Henry 5			
TOMANN, Bart.	15	Nieder-Ottenhau	68-0610
Caroline 10			
TOMASZEWSKI, Clara	20	Inowroclaw	68-0456
Oswald 2, Selma 8 months			
TOMTKOVIACK, Martin	31	Gibenow	69-0547
Justine 28, Stephan 2, Michael 10 months, Agnes 63			
TONNE, Heini	17	Sodler	68-0534
TONNIESSEN, Tonnies	50	Stummeldorf	68-0610
Ant. Aug. 16			
TONTRUP, Eleonore	19	Eilstadt	71-0429
TOPEL, Auguste	25	Karwenbrach	69-0672
TOPF, Ottomar	38	New York	69-1212
Elisabeth 32, Minna 14			
TOPMANN, Johann	43	Diefnellen	69-0784
TORNAY, Catharine	41	Hoboken	69-0968
Cath. 15, Gesine 9			
TORNEFETT, Wilhelmine	27	Hannover	69-0559
Dorette 14			
TORTIN, Ges.	27	Haarstedt	70-0728
TOSEN, Gesche	18	Sottrum	71-0712
TOSETTE, Alex	30	Cheyenne	70-0355
TOSSINGE, Carl	25	Neusalz	71-0581
TOSSMANN, Johann	43	Diefnellen	69-0784
TOSTMANN, Heinr.	30	Kuependorf	71-0684
TOTTLEBEN, Emanuel	26	Marienburg	71-0792
TOTTLEBER, Carl	28	Herstelle	68-0939
TOURTE, Jean	27	Schwabendorf	68-0770
TOUSTE, Marie	18	Westrup	69-0798
TRAB, Heinr.	14	Lobenstein	71-0681
TRAEDER, Gottlieb	58	Neuenburg	69-0542
Caroline 56, Ferdinand 33, Auguste 28, Julius 21, Bertha 18, Wilhelm 14			
TRAEFFLER, Friederich	35	Albany	70-0184
TRAEGER, Paulus	24	Wuerzburg	69-0923
TRAEUKLER, Carl	40	Stotternheim	71-0479
Emma 35			
TRAGER, Anna	23	Weimar	69-0559
TRAPEN, Philipp	30	Croen	69-0321
TRAPP, Heinrich	32	Feldbruecken	69-0490
TRATZMUELLER, Michael	31	Unterboeckingen	68-0770
TRAUB, Lorenz	19	Gundingen	71-0681
TRAULE, Joh.	18	Rosenfeld	69-1363
TRAUPE, Heinrich	19	Hilwartshausen	68-0707
TRAURIG, Josef	27	Fuerth	71-0429
Caroline 27			
TRAUSTEIN, Marie	24	Preussewize	69-1309
TRAUTMANN, Caroline	27	Theningen	69-0490
TRAUTMANN, Elise	22	Meiningen	71-0456
TRAUTMANN, Georg	17	Darmstadt	69-1212
TRAUTMANN, Maria	22	Regensburg	71-0736
TRAUTMANN, Marie	43	Boston	69-1076
TRAUTMANN, Marie	27	Querfurt	71-0684
TRAUTMETTEN, Elisabeth	28	Weimar	70-0569
TRAUTWEIN, John	55	Berlin	68-0786
TRAWERS, Joseph	24	Germersheim	68-1002
TREBACH, Emilie	21	Berlin	71-0456
TREBBE, Heinrich	19	Wehringsdorf	70-0728
TREFFINGER, Christine	18	Derdingen	71-0429

NAME	AGE	RESIDENCE	YR-LIST
TREFFURT, Christine	49	Langensalza	71-0712
Friederike 24, Julian 19			
TREHER, Ad.	23	Wien	70-0443
Philippine 18, Baby girl 3 months, Henriette 25			
TREICHEL, Henriette	20	Bumonkel	69-1309
TREICHLER, Louise	25	Richterswyl	68-0610
TREISS, Rud.	16	Oberstein	71-0521
TREITZ, Nicolaus	67	Eisen	68-0566
Elisa 60, Marie 18			
TREMBERGER, Helene	27	Fuerth	68-0786
Nanette 5			
TREMKE, Elise	19	Altenbruch	71-0300
TRENSCH, Heinrich	16	Hessen	70-0204
TREPHAHN, Johann	40	Ploetz	69-0321
Friederike 39, Johann 14, Wilhelmine 9, Caroline 7, Marie 6, Wilhelm 4, Bertha			
TREUHLER, Louise	25	Richterswyl	68-0610
TREUKAMP, Mar.(female)	20	Damme	68-1002
TREUTING, Anton	13	Trapstadt	69-0457
TREUTLER, Albertin	43	Altwasser	69-1011
Minna 18			
TRIBOLET, Joh.	16	Ins	71-0479
TRIEB, Adolf	30	Horgin	71-0815
TRILLING, Lewin	24	Stadtbergen	68-0820
Elisabeth 42, Elisabeth 20			
TRIMBORN, Mathilde	24	Coeln	68-0852
TRIMPF, C. H.	20	Otterndorf	69-0583
TRINHOSER, Christine	20	Freudenthal	70-0728
TRINKE, Josef	19	Moosbach	71-0429
TRINKHORST, Magdalene	19	Leipzig	71-0492
TRION, Christ.	25	Carlsruhe	71-0363
TRITJE, Louis	17	Griningen	69-0923
Heinrich 30			
TROBER, Friedrich	30	Obertind	68-0939
Louise 28, Lina 3, Paul 9 months			
TROEGER, Aug.	32	Sachsen	69-1004
TROEGER, Johann	36	Thierstein	69-1076
Margrethe 39, Maria 11 months			
TROELKE, Elisa	20	Remsede	69-1086
TROELKEMEYER, August	15	Hannover	71-0821
TROJE, Louis	26	Verden	70-0184
TROMBGEN, Peter	34	Waldorf	69-0229
TROMMER, Hermann	19	Hersfeld	71-0456
Elise 18			
TROMMER, Jean	19	Hersfeld	68-0534
Catharina 9			
TROMMEYER, Arnold	18	Neuenkirchen	71-0521
TROMP, Mary	25	Gmuenden	68-0534
TROMP, Wilhelm	17	Gemuenden	71-0456
TROSCH, Therese	16	Koenigsheim	70-0378
TROSE, Alexander	36	Wachterbach	70-0006
TROST, Benedict	43	Bruechs	68-0786
Julie 40, Roman 4			
TROST, Catharina	25	Steinbach	70-0204
TROST, Johann	45	Augsburg	68-0939
Elisabeth 45, Rosine 19, Christian 19			
TROST, Marie	53	Villmar	68-0625
Anna 14, Elisabeth 9, Johann 7, Marie 8			
TROTSCHER, Carl	21	Bausa/Saxony	69-0547
TROTTA, Louis	28	Paris	69-1363
TROWER, Louis	25	Hemptendorf	70-0184
Wilhelmine 27			
TRUDE, Therese	25	Altenheerse	69-1059
Josef 8 months			
TRUEMPF, Anna	20	Severn	68-0566
TRUEMPF, Georg	19	Forchtenberg	68-1006
TRUMM, Dorothea	25	Nuernberg	69-1086
TRUNER, Anna	24	Schnellenwelde	68-0707
TRUPP, Carl	29	Altsaalfeld	68-1027
TRUSCH, Christine	20	Knibis	71-0792
TSCHARNOWSKER, T.	33	San Francisco	69-1212
TSCHAU, Auguste	32	Waldkirch	69-0229
TSCHAU, Joseph	18	Waldkirch	69-0229
TSCHUDI, Hermann	16	Wiesbaden	71-0492
TUCHEER, Wilhelm	16	Zappeln	69-0429
TUCHLER, Marie	39	Kralowitz	71-0456
TUEBKE, Metta	19	Hannover	68-0456
TUELL, Diedr.	20	Kissingen	70-0052
TUELS,	25	Rollmannsthal	71-0736
TUENNEMANN, Georg	25	Duderstadt	69-0968
TUERCK, Louise	31	Barmen	68-0566
TUERK, Hermann	21	Chemnitz	68-0707
TUMP, Johann	53	Olpe	71-0712
TUPZ, Tam	18	Zwerkowitz	70-0329
TURGE, Fritz	31	Neustadt	69-0848
TURLIN, Charles	27	Dijon	68-0014
TUSEMEGGER, Caroline	45	Tyrol	70-1035
Carl 19, Felix 18, Betty 16, Marie 14,August 12, Adolph 9, Kunigunde 7, Franz			
TWARDOMS, Gottl.	23	Neuernhagen	69-0321
TWEGER, Ludw.	27	Falkenstein	70-0308
TWEITMANN, Koenke	20	Burgdam	69-1086
TYARKS, Heinrich	13	Tellens	68-0760
TYRIAX, Traugott	33	Frimar	68-0661
UBELHARDT, Victor	23	Kiemberg	69-0338
UBRICH, Friedr.	30	Giessen	68-0982
UEBELEISEN, Christ.	25	Genzenhausen	68-0647
UELKEN, Wilke	30	Zetel	68-0647
Gesche 32, Hilke 2, Baby girl 3 months			
UELZEN, Adolph	25	Bremerhaven	68-0314
UETRECHT, Wilhelmine	24	Twixhausen	68-0907
UFEN, Weert	16	Norden	68-1027
UFER, Friedrich Heinrich	24	Kornheim	69-0559
UGI, Georg	22	Lahr	68-1027
UHDE, Gustav	30	Hamburg	69-0848
UHL, Wilh.	18	Gottheim	71-0300
UHLIN, Jacob	24	Zuerich	68-0014
UHLMANN, Carl	20	Ansbach	69-1076
UHLMANN, Marie	23	Eibenstock	70-0135
UHMEYER, Adeline	21	Luetetsburg	68-0647
UHNSCHNEIDER, Math.	23	Laufen	69-0560
UHRBACH, F.	22	Matanzas	69-1004
UHRBROCK, Ernst	40	Bremen	69-0208
UKENA, Falkea	22	Raudermor	69-0576
UKENS, Wessel	34	Holte	68-0610
UKERMANN, Peter	29	Coeln	68-0707

NAME	AGE	RESIDENCE	YR-LIST
ULBRECHT, Emilie	26	Driesen	68-0820
ULFKES, Johann Gesche 24	30	Holtrup	69-0208
ULLAPERGER, Therese	18	Thein	70-0329
ULLRICH, Dorothea	26	Kirchlein	71-0429
ULLRICH, Louis	23	Hannover	68-1002
ULLSCH, Johanna Johann 13, Peter 9	50	Oberkolzau	68-0852
ULMER, Albert	22	Zuerich	69-0321
ULMER, Georg	26	Altenbach	68-1027
ULRICH, Daniel Eva 39, Catharina 18, Georg 12, Margarethe 3, Adam 10 months	37	Koenig	68-0760
ULRICH, Friedrich	27	Wuergen	70-0148
ULRICH, Friedrich	17	Frebershausen	68-0625
ULRICH, Fritz	32	Hahndorf	69-0162
ULRICH, Heinr. Christine 33, Hermann 11, Marie 9, Emilie 5, Helene 11 months	38	Sangerhausen	68-0786
ULRICH, Herm.	33	Bantzen	68-0957
ULRICH, Jacob	27	Muenchingen	68-1002
ULRICH, Luise	20	Cannstadt	70-0135
ULRICH, Marie	22	Bischofsteinitz	68-0625
ULRICH, Rud.	26	Celle	71-0581
ULRICI, Richard	22	Buer	69-1011
ULTSCH, Friedrich	19	Oberkotzau	69-0338
UMBACH, L.	29	Hansen	71-0681
UMBREIT, Heinrich	76	Muehlberg	68-0852
UMGELTER, Emma	16	Stuttgart	69-1059
UMLAND, Carl	25	Hackemuehle	69-0592
UMSTATTER, Ger.	26	Einsheim	70-0170
UNBEHAUEN, Christian	30	Erlangen	68-0939
UNDIETRICK, John	19	Bremerhaven	70-0355
UNDUETSCH, Helene	26	Wedderwanden	70-0355
UNFRIED, Friedericke	30	Markgroningen	70-0204
UNGAR, Louise	22	Bonn	69-0592
UNGEMACH, Christine	17	Neuweiler	69-0268
UNGENTHUM, Albine	17	Elsterberg	71-0479
UNGER, Anna	23	Riede	69-0968
UNGER, Robert	24	Bruchmachtersse	71-0581
UNGERER, Albrecht	25	Michelbach	71-0681
UNGERER, Christian	40	Ellentown	69-0208
UNHOFER, Wilhelmine Carl 11 months	16	Freudenstadt	71-0792
UNKELBACH, Peter	18	Gundersheim	68-0534
UNKRAUT, A.	26	Bremen	69-1004
UNRUH, Herm.	16	Parlin/Russia	69-0049
UNRUHE, Elias Louise 29, Friedr. 8, Gustav 6, Friederike 4, Margarethe 2	33	Oberkaufungen	68-0647
UNSELA, John	30	Grimmelfinger	71-0456
UNTERKIRCHEN, Chr.	14	Binswangen	68-0014
UNTERLEITER, Margareth	24	Gr. Zimmern	69-0848
UPHEBER, Ernst	17	Wimmers	69-0572
URBAN, Joh. Otto Th.	32	Popelken	68-1002
URBAN, Wenzel	19	Rzebnitz	71-0581
URFF, Joh.	26	Wiehdorf	68-0314
URICH, Heinrich	19	Darmstadt	70-1142

NAME	AGE	RESIDENCE	YR-LIST
URNSTATTER, Ger.	26	Einsheim	70-0170
URTEL, Friedrich Marie 41, Friederike 13, Marie 11, Wilhelmine 7, August 5, Ferdinand 1	45	Potsdam	68-0661
UTHOFF, Louise	25	Westkilver	68-1027
UTHOFF, P.	59	Wiedenbrueck	71-0479
UTT, Johann Lina 22	60	Berlin	71-0643
UTTRECH, Hermann Bertha 20	23	Witzenhausen	69-0572
UTZ, Andreas	18	Unterleifstedt	68-0610
UTZ, Margarethe	22	Hingstfeld	68-0939
Ulrich, Julius	29	Halberstadt	70-0031
VACHOD, Eleonore	22	Prag	68-1002
VAG, Anna M. Eva Catharina 23	25	Ober Finkenbach	68-0661
VAGEN, H.	31	Rothenburg	70-0443
VAGT, Geerd Joh. 24	30	Theringsfehn	68-0314
VAGTS, Wilhelm Margarethe 59, Johann 14	26	Hannover	68-0456
VAHL, Conrad	23	Landenhausen	69-0968
VAHLE, Wilh.	36	Bielefeld	69-0100
VAHRENHORST, Philipp Catharina 29, Catharina 2	30	Osterwez	68-0707
VALENTIN, Wilhelm Charles 15	18	Friedberg	68-0957
VALKE, Ad.	16	Fritzlar	69-1004
VAMBERG, Maria	16	Meiningen	68-0707
VAN DER BERGH, J.	30	Raamsdonk/Holla	69-1086
VANDERFORN, Caroline	42	St. Petersburg	69-0560
VANGEROW, Julius	27	Blackwitt	71-0429
VANNI, Nicolaus	18	Lucca	71-0363
VANOOLSEEN, J. J.	36	Trier	71-0363
VANPEL, Louise	21	Loehlbach	68-0884
VARENHORST, Rudolph	16	Etzel	71-0492
VARRELMANN, —		Lemfoerde	68-1002
VARRELMANN, Heinr.	16	Nordsulingen	68-0884
VASS, Albert	36	Halle	71-0492
VASS, Anna Marie 22, Dorothee 16	24	Eitze	69-1004
VASS, Hamke Friedr. 5 months, Friedrich 58	25	Hannover	69-1004
VATASCHEK, Carl	5	Gaug	71-0581
VATER, Wilhelm Wilhelmine 40, Wilhelm 17, Louise 15,-Otto 13, Wilhelmine 7, Emma 6, Bertha 5,	44	S. Altenburg	70-0329
VAUPEL, Catharine	21	Lobbach	68-0456
VAUPEL, Christine	28	Zella	70-0452
VAUPEL, Josephine Hermann 13, Elise 9, Charles 4	36	Arolsen	70-0308
VAUPEL, Marie	17	St. Katharin	70-0452
VAYHINGER, Hugo	29	Stuttgart	69-0162
VEBATT, Marie	21	Wlasewitz	71-0581
VEER, Widow Ellater Johanne 26, Eildine 24, Nanco 20, Eddo 17, Peter 15, Ernestine 11 months	52	Emden	69-1076
VEERSENMEYER, B.	50	Ulm	68-0566
VEHN, Hermann	25	Stavern	69-0229
VEID, Georg	16	Hamschen	68-0456

NAME	AGE	RESIDENCE	YR-LIST
VEIT, Leonhard	29	Ruppertshofen	68-0939
Margarethe 32, Friedrich 4			
VEIT, Rudolf	25	Neuenstadt	68-0786
VEITH, Anton	75	Roedelheim	69-0841
Susanne 62, Christine 26			
VELTEN, Marg.	17	Darmstadt	71-0521
VENANTE, Louise	31	Havel	69-0771
VENF, Friedke.	34	Niedergruensted	71-0815
Emil 4			
VERACH, Christian	36	Crefeld	69-0457
VERDIER, Henri		Havre	70-0259
VERHOEFF, Ferd.	24	Werden	70-0443
VERTH, Johann	25	Remagen	69-0229
VERWOHLT, Caroline	26	Brunswik	70-0508
VESBACH, Julius	27	Belbuech	68-1002
Caroline 26			
VESPERMANN, Friedrich	34	Gr. Rhieden	69-0208
VETT, Carl		Dorum	71-0581
VETTEL, Sophie	28	Bernsheim	68-0314
VETTELER, Ulrich	19	Wittenberg	68-0872
VETTER, Henry	31	Kositzkau	69-0338
VETTER, Jacob	30	Dirdorf	68-0661
VETTER, Jacobine	23	Boll	68-0566
VETTER, Johann	24	Thueringen	69-0672
VETTER, Tobias	24	Wurmberg	68-1002
VETTERICK, Carl	36	Stralsund	68-1006
Johanna 31, Bertha 1			
VETTERLEIN, Hans	16	Weimar	69-0542
VETTERLIN, Sabina	55	Ricklingen	69-1421
VETZSCH, Georg	24	Watyhenrath	70-0184
VIAGALI, Joseph	24	Bortzheim	69-0429
VICTOR, Georg F.	30	New York	70-0089
Anna 22			
VICTOR, Margaret	14	Neustadt	68-1006
VIDONNE, Philipp	29	Neydant	68-0939
VIEBIG, Mathilde	20	Hildburghausen	69-1059
VIEBRANDS, Wilhelm	17	Calvoerde	68-1027
VIEBROCK, John	16	Balkenwedt	69-0338
VIEHNE, Bernhard	20	Quakenbrueck	69-0923
VIELSTICK, Anna	22	Krotoschin	71-0521
VIERING, Conrad	28	Landau	69-1309
VIERKE, Johanne	48	Schlave	71-0581
Ida 20, Auguste 17			
VIERLE, Mary	19	Romsthal	71-0143
VIERLING, Eva	15	Domdiel	71-0712
VIERLING, Joh.	25	Eisenbach	69-0162
Adam 30, Auguste 31			
VIET, Conrad	30	Schwelentrup	68-0456
VIETZ, Franz	55	Darmstadt	68-0707
Alexander 21, Wilhelmine 57			
VIGER, Franz	30	Horst-Bohemia	70-0006
VIRGIN, Therese	26	Bremen	71-0821
VISCHER, Frd.	32	Stuttgart	68-0820
VISSING, Andrew	17	Coesfeld	70-0076
VLANGALY, Alexander	48	St. Petersburg	70-0682
VLASAK, Josef	25	Boehmen	70-0569
VOCK, Elise	41	New York	69-1396
VOCKEL, Martin	32	Lispenhausen	71-0363
Catharina 28, Christina 6, Elisabeth 3			
VOCKERODT, Wilhelm	36	Muehlhausen	69-0429
Charlotte 29, Marie 8, Ernst 5, Adolph 3, Helene 11 months			
VOCKEROTH, Joh. Conr.	19	Hersfeld	68-1002
Adam 17			
VOCKMUHL, Anton	26	Emsdetten	69-0429
VODDE, Diedr.	70	Bohmte	69-0923
Elisabeth 20, Clara 17			
VOEGELE, Cath.	18	Kleinweiler	70-1142
VOEGTER, Henry	30	Paderborn	69-0798
VOEHLING, E.	18	Bueckeburg	69-1011
VOELCKER, Johann	27	Wuerzburg	68-0456
VOELKEL, Jacob	50	Neustadt	69-0208
Heinrich 13			
VOELKER, Caroline	23	Dodenhausen	70-0355
VOELKER, Friedrich	21	Allendorf	69-0457
VOELKER, Philipp	39	Kirberg	69-0592
Christine 26, Philipp 4, Carl 3, Caroline 9 months			
VOELKERT, Margaret	24	Dittmar	68-0852
VOELKLE, Xaver	19	Unteralphen	68-0456
VOELKNER, Heinrich	16	Richelkirchen	71-0521
VOELLMER, Gg.	31	Herresdorf	70-0443
VOEPEL, Johann	29	Bahlen	68-0566
VOERTMANN, Anna	17	Hoboken	71-0172
VOESSING, Aug.	25	Jacobsberg	68-0982
VOETKIE, Pauline	49	Potsdam	69-0050
Hermann 9			
VOETSCH, Anna	20	Ostdorf	69-1076
VOGE, Charles	25	Arnswalde	69-0798
VOGEL, Anselm	30	Ettlingen	69-0321
Robert 18			
VOGEL, Balth.	24	Elsass	71-0736
VOGEL, Bernhard	14	Doermoschie	71-0733
VOGEL, Carl	34	Fulln	68-0884
VOGEL, Carl	24	Wuerzburg	69-0162
VOGEL, Carl	36	Oldenburg	68-0707
VOGEL, Caspar	26	Stadtlengsfeld	68-0625
VOGEL, Jacob	21	Grafenberg	71-0727
VOGEL, Louise	18	Lengsfeld	71-0456
VOGEL, Marie	38	Trippstadt	69-0015
VOGEL, Mary	23	Hochspeier	70-0170
John 12			
VOGEL, Oscar	36	Lichtenstein	70-1142
VOGEL, Sigmund	27	Suess	68-0534
VOGEL, Theo.	34	Praest	68-0957
VOGEL, Walpurga	19	Augsburg	68-0610
VOGEL, Wilhelm	30	Darmstadt	68-0707
VOGELER, Carl	26	Bremen	71-0456
VOGELSANG, Adele	24	Eslingen	69-1212
VOGELSANG, Henriette	24	Exter	68-1027
VOGELSANG, Johann	24	Boerninghausen	68-0566
Catharina 24, Heinrich 9 months			
VOGELSANG, Max	16	Hagen	68-0625
VOGELSANG, Wilhelm	16	Dettmold	69-0542
VOGLER, Carl Friedr.	39	Stettin	69-0182
Henriette 38			

NAME	AGE	RESIDENCE	YR-LIST
VOGT, Carl	40	Guetersloh	70-0204
VOGT, Christine	21	Minden	68-0786
VOGT, Emma	22	Merkawitz	69-0429
VOGT, Friedrich	27	Lippe-Detmold	71-0727
Wilhelmine 22, Wilhelm 9 months, Friedrich 55, Louise 20			
VOGT, Hermann	63	Bremen	69-0576
Elise F. 50, Charlotte 9, Friederike 5			
VOGT, Otto	30	Blankenhain	68-0786
VOGT, Philipp	55	Heitenfeld	68-0661
Marie 57, Margarethe 23			
VOGT, Theo	20	Neckarsulm	69-0338
VOGT, Wilhelm	16	Eisenberg	71-0429
VOGTS, Kordt	25	Estorf	71-0429
VOIGT, Augusta	51	Norden	68-1027
VOIGT, C.	24	Glauckau	69-1421
VOIGT, Christoph	14	Kullstedt	69-0923
VOIGT, Franz	22	Nonnedorf	68-0753
VOIGT, Hermann H.	47	Hudermoor	69-0321
Sophie 49, Gerhard 14			
VOIGT, Jacob	21	Koenigsberg	71-0681
VOIGT, Julius	28	Ziemeritz	70-0135
VOIGT, Julius	40	Hohburg-Saxonia	70-0006
VOIGT, Ludwig	45	Schwarzb.Rudolp	69-0968
Louis 9			
VOIGT, Michel	18	Breitzbach	69-0560
VOIGT, Regine	25	Steinbach	70-0204
VOIGT, Theod.	28	Rittzitz	68-0610
VOIGT, Valentin	24	Monchl-Monehl	70-0135
VOIGTS, Julius	28	Braunschweig	69-0560
VOLBREATH, Andreas	60	Maseberg	69-1004
Albert 19, Friedrich 9, Sophie 50			
VOLGER, Fritz	33	New York	70-1003
Wilhelmine 30, Anna 9, Henry 7			
VOLHERT, Anna	17	Neuenlande	69-1076
VOLK, Dorothea	25	Eggelstetten	71-0492
VOLK, Ferd.	35	Lobau	71-0393
Pauline 35, Paul 6			
VOLK, Theodor	44	Gotha	69-1011
Friderike 44, Johanne 20, Therese 17, Fred 15, Friederike 6, Arnold 3			
VOLKAMMER, Marg.	21	Gleisauthausen	68-0957
VOLKE, Friedr.	21	Melsungen	68-1002
VOLKEN, Heinrich	17	Hiemsdorf	70-0259
VOLKER, Carl	16	Hannover	69-0771
VOLKER, Peter	20	Edenkoben	71-0643
VOLKERS, Frd.	19	Neuenlande	68-0820
VOLKERS, Johann	33	Oldenburg	69-0229
VOLKERT, Rosine	30	Mergentheim	71-0456
Elise 4			
VOLKMANN, Anna	20	Oldenburg	71-0733
VOLKMANN, Joh.	74	Polzin	70-0728
Henriette 55, Albert 22, Marie 17			
VOLKMANN, Mathilde	26	Duesseldorf	68-0907
VOLKMANN, Nic.	23	Bederkesa	68-0647
VOLKMAR, P.	25	Chemnitz	71-0712
VOLKMER, John	22	Hanau	69-0049
VOLKMUTH, John	26	Roedelmeyer	70-0355
VOLKNER, Ang.	33	Gehra	71-0521

NAME	AGE	RESIDENCE	YR-LIST
Bertha 30, Hermann 5, Bertha 3			
VOLKWEIN, Gottfr.	15	Ehlen	71-0479
VOLLBRECHT, Adolph	5	Muenden	68-1002
Minna 2, Elisa 9 months			
VOLLBRECHT, Wilh.	30	Muenden	68-1002
Charlotte 28, Wilhelm 7			
VOLLMAR, Conrad	55	Heringen	68-0884
VOLLMER, Adolf	24	Stadtberge	70-0355
VOLLMER, Anna	24	Wolf	69-0208
VOLLMER, Emil	29	Lennep	70-0135
VOLLMER, Louise	24	Hannover	71-0736
Anna 1			
VOLLMER, Thomas	38	Olhausen	70-0223
Friederike 35, Lisette 3			
VOLLMEYER, Jacob	39	Karlshafen	66-0413
Johanne 39			
VOLLMUTH, Babette	21	Wohnfort	69-1059
VOLLRAB, Elisab.	18	Alsfeld	71-0581
VOLLROTH, Christian	81	Rudolstadt	68-0760
Jacob 42, Johanna 43, Augusta 18, Hermann 16, Oscar 7, Minna 7, Gustav 9 mo			
VOLMER, Johann	54	Blankenhain	69-1059
Cathrine 53, Wilhelm 15, Johann 12			
VOLMER, Ulrich	18	Boergen	69-0490
VOLTING, Christian	42	Pillenbruch	68-0456
Sophie 37, Heinrich 9, Louise 7, Fritz 6, Lena 3, August 11 months			
VOLTMER, Heinrich	24	Bergen	68-0760
VOLTPLAND, Amalia	52	Friedericke	71-0492
Friedericke 17			
VOLZ, Martin	27	Erbach	69-0208
VON ASEN, Anna Cath.	20	Erichshafen	68-1006
VON BARGEN, Adelheid	8	Ottersberg	69-0560
VON BARGER, Helene	17	Ottersburg	68-0982
VON BINDER, Gustav	28	Marienthal	70-0204
VON BONDA, Fokelina	18	Lingen	69-0229
VON BOOS WALDECK	24	Regensburg	70-0443
VON BORRIES, Otto	18	Peckelsken	69-1086
VON BRAUN, Sophia	24	Oehringen	69-1076
VON BREDHORST, Sixt.		Hannover	66-0577
Peter 28			
VON BUENAU, Rudolph	44	Zehmen	68-0707
VON BUSSE, Ida	28	Berlin	71-0582
VON DAEHLEN, Jacob	30	Charleston	69-1059
VON DAHLE, Wilh.	27	Berlin	68-0753
VON DAHLEN, Eibe	16	Hannover	69-0457
VON DELDEN, Max	41	Melborn	69-1396
VON DER AHE, Marie	14	Hille	70-1035
VON DER BRELIE, Heinr.	42	Harten	68-1002
Doris 30, Fritz 8, Marie 7, Heinr. 5, Wilh. 3, Herm. 11 months			
VON DER DECKEN	23	Wien	68-0647
VON DER ESCHE, Friedr.	16	Damme	68-1002
VON DER HAAR, Jos.	18	Schwagsdorf	68-1002
VON DER HAMM, Johann	30	Brake	68-0907
Wilhelmine 27, Theodor 4, Carl 9 months			
VON DER LIED, Louise	24	Lamstedt	70-1003
VON DER LIETH, Claus	16	Elmlohe	69-0560
VON DER MIESCHEN	16	Steinau	71-0363

NAME	AGE	RESIDENCE	YR-LIST
VON DER NIENBURG	16	Hannover	70-0508
VON DER OSTEN, M.		Osterbruch	71-0363
VON DER SCHAER, Anna	17	Erdwarden	68-0907
VON DETTHEIM, R.	31	Braunschweig	70-1035
VON DOEHLEN, Conrad	16	Drangstedt	69-0429
Juergen 15			
VON DOHLEN, Klaus	16	Hannover	70-1003
VON ENDE, Wilhelm	26	Ruhrort	68-1027
VON FINTELN, Johann	17	Schwalingen	68-0820
VON FREITAG, Kamor	15	Hannover	70-0728
VON GEISMAR, Anna	21	Osnabrueck	71-0712
VON GLAHN, Gottlieb	25	Ostfriesland	70-0378
VON GLAHN, H.	16	Cappeln	71-0363
VON GLAHN, Heinrich	17	Lamstedt	69-0457
VON GLAHN, Marie	20	Hannover	70-0443
VON GLAHN, Wilhelm	17	Lehe	69-0162
VON GOETZ, Hedwig	24	Wien	69-0457
VON GROENING, Albert	21	Richmond	68-0770
VON HARTEN, Heinr.	14	Bremervoerde	71-0581
VON HOORN, Trientje	46	Loquard	68-1027
Jan 12, Tjalde 9, Junna 7			
VON KALTENBORN	24	Marburg	68-0566
VON KAMPE, Kuno	20	Hannover	68-0982
VON KAMPEN, Claus	27	New York	69-0457
VON KAUMEN, Fr.	16	STEINSFURTH	70-0508
VON LEBINSKY, Theodor	39	Gr. Buetzig	69-0321
VON LINGEN, Heike	24	Lintelmarsch	68-0852
VON LOCKNER, A.	32	Pressberg	71-0733
Adele 36			
VON MALACHOWSKY	24	Goersbach	68-0566
VON MUENCHHAUSEN	23	Braunschweig	71-0456
VON MUENSTER, Johann	37	Emmerich	69-0162
VON NES, Johann	27	Rothenfelde	70-0204
Henrich 17			
VON OTTENFELD, W.	25	Berlin	71-0684
VON PLOINES, Carl	35	Darmstadt	71-0684
Katinka 17			
VON RAHDON, Elise	30	Glatz	71-0582
VON RIEDE, Xaver	43	Wien	69-0542
Ernestine 34			
VON SALZEN, Doris	17	Dippersen	68-0770
VON SCHAUER, Carl	16	Creins	68-0610
VON SCHLOTHEIM, Ed.	35	Oeynhausen	70-0728
Emma 30			
VON SCHNEDEN, Agnes	23	Oldenburg	70-1023
VON SCHNEIDER, Carl	48	Karlsruhe	69-0182
VON SPECKELSEN, Marie	18	Oberndorf	68-1006
Mathilde 16			
VON STADEN, Anna	30	Beverstedt	70-0452
VON STADEN, Heinrich	26	Hannover	70-0523
VON STARKENBURG, J.	30	Wageningen	69-0321
VON THEINBURG, W.	26	Wien	68-0456
VON THUN, G. W.	17	Troisdorf	69-0583
VON TWISTERN, Anna	24	Otterndorf	68-0625
VON VETHHEIM, Rud.	29	Hachenberg	68-1006
VON WESSELY, Chevalier	45	Wien	69-0208
VON WILLIEB, Wilhelm	25	Stuttgart	69-0067
VON WOLFFRADT, Carl	28	Stolpemuehle	69-0429

NAME	AGE	RESIDENCE	YR-LIST
VON ZESCHAU, Leop.	27	Dresden	70-0135
VON, RUDGISCH, Elise	25	Brieg	71-0363
VONAH, Franz	26	Unterwald	69-1309
Joseph 23			
VONNS, Franz	50	Argenthal	68-0907
Jacob 21, MAria 17			
VOPERT, Hin.	18	Meinersville	70-0355
VORHAUER, Elise	30	Elgershausen	71-0821
VORHAUS, Julius	17	Fuerth	68-0852
VORHOLZ, Gustav	32	Chemnitz	69-0923
Francisca 32, Emma 9, Gustav 7, Ida 6, Rosa 3, Gustav Adolf 2			
VORNHEBER, Wilhelm	19	Markendorff	69-0490
VORRATH, Georg	21	Bederkesa	71-0792
VORTMANN, Diedr.	26	Wachendorf	69-0572
VORWERK, Henry	14	Geestendorf	71-0456
Marie 16			
VOSHAGEN, Chr.	67	Sabbenhausen	68-0884
Dorette 68, Wilhelmine 31, Louise 16 months			
VOSMOBENNER, Peter	52	Engerte	71-0643
Anna 54, Caspar 19, Auguste 16, Anna 13			
VOSS, Anna	26	Niedorf	69-0208
Heinrich 8, Diedrich 6, Johann 3			
VOSS, Christ.	28	Braunschweig	68-0647
VOSS, Clemens	26	Hagen	69-0229
VOSS, Fanny	19	Loler	71-0712
VOSS, Friedrich	27	Frotheim	69-1076
Louise 24, Wilhelm 9 months			
VOSS, Hamke	25	Hannover	69-1004
Friedr. 5 months, Friedrich 58			
VOSS, Heinrich	28	Diessen	69-0292
VOSS, Peter	26	Oberselters	68-0314
Margarethe 23, Joseph 6 months			
VOSS, Wilhelm	17	Fretheim	69-1076
VOSS, Wilhelmine	29	Lengerich	68-0647
VOSSBERG, H.H.	25	Pensum	68-0820
VOSSELER, Xaver	33	Laufen	69-0560
Pauline 25, John 4 months, Mary 4 months			
VOSSKE, Minna	45	Berlin	70-1055
Anna 9			
VOSSMANN, Joh. Heinr.	36	Dackmar	69-0572
VOSTEEN, Gesine	25	Deichhorst	68-0566
VOTZ, Fried.	46	Groetzingen	71-0681
VOZMELEK, Josef	43	Kallin	70-1023
Cath. 40, Joseph 14, Wenzel 8, Sophie 4, Franz 11 months			
WAASECK, Joh.	50	Lichtenberg	71-0479
Elise 52, Fried. 17, Christ. 11			
WACHAL, Josef	43	Opolschitz	71-0429
Catharine 42, Josef 17, Johann 12			
WACHENFELD, Wilhelm	22	Wolfhagen	69-0429
WACHHOLZ, Carl	25	Crampe	68-1006
WACHSMANN, Maria	17	Steinau	71-0363
Anna 13			
WACHSMUTH, Ludwig	15	Soden	68-1006
WACHTER, Ludwig	30	Schaan	71-0736
WACK, Heinr.	18	Laisa	71-0821
WACKENHUTH, Louise	23	Altenstaig	68-0625
WACKER, Catharine	20	Obersautheim	70-0682

NAME	AGE	RESIDENCE	YR-LIST
WACKER, Gottlieb	42	Degenloh	68-0939
Christine 35, Wilhelm 4			
WACKER, Hermann	21	Wien	68-0456
WACKER, Johann	27	Rodensohl	68-0770
WACKER, Kilian	28	Sulz	68-0982
WACKERMANN, J.	17	Buchshofen	71-0643
WADE, Daniel	29	Hattorf	71-0736
Louise 22, Baby girl 8 months, Andreas 47, Johanne 36			
WAECHTER, Carl	30	Hannover	69-0592
WAECHTER, Marie	23	Ostkilver	68-0786
WAECHTER, Reinh.	26	Auma	71-0479
Otto 16			
WAEPSE, Diedrich	18	Hannover	68-0753
WAERTH, Wilhelm	17	Essenhausen	71-0712
WAESCH, Jette	20	Lichtenberg	70-0443
WAESCH, Sophie	18	Lichtenberg	69-0542
WAESCHLE, Joh.	28	Eberhein	68-0760
WAETHER, Christian	43	Erbsleben	69-0429
WAETJEN, Heinr.	15	Eissel	68-0610
WAETJEN, Hermann	23	Sudweye	68-0456
WAGEMANN, Elisabeth	27	Rammelsbach	69-0572
WAGENBAUER, Georg	19	Dettingen	70-0259
WAGENBRETT, Caroline	29	Bremen	69-0268
WAGENHOF, Henriette	50	Oppenwehe	71-0300
Christ. 9			
WAGENKNECHT, August	21	Preussen	68-0456
WAGENLAENDER, J.	59	Groeningen	69-0490
Barbara 20			
WAGNER, Adam	18	Unterrostleben	71-0821
WAGNER, Alois	59	Regensburg	68-0707
WAGNER, Anna	24	Weilbach	70-0682
WAGNER, Anna	22	Friedewald	71-0736
WAGNER, Anna M.	23	Richmannsdorf	68-0647
WAGNER, Anton	25	Ahrhausen	69-0050
WAGNER, Apollonia	24	Wittlich	68-0610
WAGNER, Carl	24	Muenster	69-0771
WAGNER, Carl	30	Schwarzburg-Rudolstadt	69-0015
WAGNER, Carl	30	Hingsberg/Pruss	69-0547
Anna 30			
WAGNER, Carl	19	Nordheim	69-0490
WAGNER, Cath.	37	Dillenburg	71-0736
Carl 24			
WAGNER, Cathrine	48	Boston	69-0848
Jacob 16, Friedrich 14			
WAGNER, Christina	25	Wien	70-1161
WAGNER, Christine	24	Nordheim	68-0982
WAGNER, Dorothea	26	Kitzingen	71-0581
WAGNER, Dr.W.	40	Chicago	69-0572
WAGNER, Ferdinand	55	Germsheim	69-0067
WAGNER, Franz	16	Klissenrath	69-1319
WAGNER, Franz	19	Mehla	68-0786
WAGNER, Fried.	27	Blochingen	70-0728
WAGNER, Friederike	30	Kleichenbach	68-0957
WAGNER, Gertrud	31	Nettel	68-0884
WAGNER, Gertrude	20	Unterbaske	69-0457
WAGNER, Heinr.	32	Zeittingen	71-0792
Marianne 29, Catharina 3 months			

NAME	AGE	RESIDENCE	YR-LIST
WAGNER, Heinrich	19	Hammertsch	69-1363
WAGNER, Heinrich	18	Bensheim	70-0076
WAGNER, Heinrich	36	Rudolstadt	69-0542
Wilhelmine 39, Raimund 7, Emil 6			
WAGNER, Henriette	29	Duesseldorf	68-0610
WAGNER, Henry	41	Friedrichsthal	63-0244
John 18, Lewis 22, Christian 17			
WAGNER, Joh.	22	Kattenheim	69-1004
WAGNER, Johann	18	Koppern	69-0798
WAGNER, Johann	45	Meysberg	68-0456
Anna 42, Elisabeth 14, Helwig 12, Catharina 8, Conrad 4, August 7 months			
WAGNER, Johann	31	Fuerfeld	68-1027
Eva 28, Anna 3 months			
WAGNER, Johannes	14	Darmstadt	70-0204
WAGNER, Josef	15	Reichenberg	69-1004
Marie 18			
WAGNER, Josef	28	Grossenschwend	70-0355
Cathrine 23			
WAGNER, Julius	19	Wien	70-0089
WAGNER, Karl	25	Gosnitz	71-0393
WAGNER, Katharina	24	Kandel	71-0429
WAGNER, Lisette	25	Asch	68-0610
WAGNER, Louis	25	Corbusen	71-0643
WAGNER, Louise	28	Schoenflies	70-0259
Albert 2, Ernst 9 months			
WAGNER, Ludwig	29	Coblenz	68-0456
WAGNER, Marg.	54	Wiennenberg	71-0789
WAGNER, Margaret	20	Oberkolzau	68-0852
WAGNER, Marianne	25	Sierstahl	68-0014
WAGNER, Marie	28	Trier	68-0610
WAGNER, Math.	25	Kaisereseh	69-1086
Martha 20			
WAGNER, Mathias	32	Brinkum	69-0457
WAGNER, Mathias	17	Heimerath	71-0521
WAGNER, Michel	18	Oberkotzau	69-0338
WAGNER, Michel	60	Strassburg	71-0643
WAGNER, Otto	26	Berlin	69-0162
WAGNER, Peter	31	Kellberg	71-0581
WAGNER, Philipp	17	Frankfurt	70-0272
Wilhelm 17, Jacob 16			
WAGNER, Pr.	24	Mit.Schefflanz	71-0684
WAGNER, Reinfeld	44	Neuschuetz	69-0321
Henriette 37, Robert 12, Agnese 9, Hilda 8, Hugo 6, Emilie 4, Martha 2			
WAGNER, Robert	19	Zeitz	68-0770
WAGNER, Siebert	33	Warzenbach	71-0821
WAGNER, Susanne	58	Rudolphstadt	71-0712
WAGNER, Thekla	15	Trais	69-0542
WAGNER, Wilh.	38	Carlsruhe	68-0786
WAGNER, Wilhelmine	40	Greiz	71-0684
Hermine 21, Rosa 19, Marie 18, Anna 17, Meta 15, Hedwig 12, Egmont 9			
WAGNER, Wolfgang	43	Glachau	69-0542
Emilie 46, Hedwig 7, Elise 6			
WAGNER, Xaver	18	Westernheim	68-0610
WAHE, Georg	22	Floersheim	69-1396
WAHL, Franz	50	Walldorf	71-0393
Kath. 51, Eva 16, Helene 15, Katharina 13, Wilhelmine 17, Wilhelm 6, Jacob			

NAME	AGE	RESIDENCE	YR-LIST
WAHL, Michael	26	Rodenberg	69-0576
Margaretha 22			
WAHL, Robert	46	Berlin	71-0581
WAHL, Therese	22	Geschwind	68-0820
Catharina 8 months			
WAHLERS, Meta	15	Mussendorf	68-0982
WAHLES, Henrich	15	Hannover	69-0771
WAHLFEIL, Johann	33	Ziegahner	69-1212
WAHLMANN, Carl	25	Braunschweig	68-0786
WAHLPART, Peter	19	Trunstadt	71-0821
WAIDMANN, Joh.	58	Loewenstein	70-1142
WALBRACH, Otto	36	Conitz	70-0076
Therese 26			
WALBRUCK, Sibille	16	Westum	69-0229
WALBRUT, Theodor	24	Weimar	69-0542
WALCHER, Georg	59	Huettesheim	69-0672
Catharina 22, Susanne 20, Marie 9			
WALD, Anna	20	Lengsfeld	68-0661
WALD, Friederike	31	Freudenstadt	71-0226
WALD, Martin	16	Mutterscheid	71-0172
WALDAU, Wilhelmine	56	Iwitz	71-0479
Louise 18, Aug. 16, Ottilie 11 m.			
WALDECK, Ernst	28	Linzen	70-1003
WALDMANN, Heinrich	28	Duderstadt	69-0547
WALDMANN, Henry	46	Schiffelbach	71-0456
WALDMANN, Louise	31	Wolfenbuettel	70-0452
WALDSTEIN, Joh.	26	Rabenstein	71-0581
WALFRED, Rud.	23	Hamburg	69-1004
WALKER, Johann	26	Balingen	69-0848
WALKLING, Henry	27	Braunschweig	69-0560
WALKMUELLER, Andr.	18	Schneweissach	69-0542
WALLACK, John	32	New York	70-0135
WALLACK, Wilhelm	19	Bayern	68-0456
WALLAU, Leopold	16	Frankfurt a/M	69-1212
WALLE, Josef	20	Omersheim	71-0429
WALLEIN, Marga.	20	Ober Franken	69-1086
WALLER, Christ.	13	Lorch	69-0542
WALLERSTEIN, Clara	24	Bischoffsheim	69-1059
WALLERSTEIN, Fanny	18	Gochsheim	69-0572
WALLHEINKE, Fr.	34	Celle	71-0581
WALLIN, Carl	20	Wartin	68-0770
WALLIS, B.	30	New York	69-1421
WALLMANN, Bodo	17	Hannover	69-0848
WALLMANN, Maria	55	Dedesdorf	68-0907
Marichen 7			
WALLRATH, Louise	43	Grimmen	71-0521
WALLTRUP, Cathar.	20	Stebin	69-0542
WALSER, Alois	16	Vorarlberg	69-0560
WALSS, Wolfgang	18	Maroldweisbach	69-0968
WALTENBERG, Emma	30	New York	70-1003
Alexander 10, Richard 4			
WALTER, August	24	Lagershausen	68-0852
Caroline 22			
WALTER, Carl	15	Baden	70-0148
WALTER, Catharine	15	Oberfloersheim	71-0429
WALTER, Ernst	17	Bonn	68-0456
WALTER, Georg	43	Altdorf	69-0162
Johann 41, Adam 32, Barbara 27, Johann 3, Georg 11 months, Gottlob 19			
WALTER, Georg	17	Schleitheim	71-0456
Barbara 17			
WALTER, Gesine	26	Brochterbeck	69-0429
WALTER, Helene	30	New York	69-0457
WALTER, Leonhard	25	Waldmichelbach	68-1002
WALTER, Marg.	28	Bairen	71-0429
WALTER, Nannie	25	Wulsdorf	70-0384
WALTER, Pauline	26	Magdeburg	68-0884
Mathilde 3, Ida 9 months			
WALTER, Sophia	57	Duerkheim	69-1059
Christine 19, Carl 4			
WALTER, Wilhelmine	23	Rosenfelde	71-0736
WALTERS, Henry	35	Marysville	70-0355
WALTERSCHEID, Wm.	26	Opladen	69-1011
WALTHER, Carl	30	Oberkamstadt	71-0736
WALTHER, Cath.	7	Gempertshausen	68-0566
WALTHER, Elisabeth	49	Espa	71-0492
WALTHER, Georg	23	Speyer	68-0760
WALTHER, Joseph	13	Neuhausen	69-0672
WALTHER, Maria	19	Neuhausen	71-0521
WALTHER, Otto	17	Weingarten	69-0015
WALTHER, Wilhelmine	24	Grotzingen	71-0226
WALTJEN, Cord	16	Sudweihe	71-0521
WALTJEN, Hermann	16	Bremen	68-0907
WALZ, Anna	69	Ebhausen	69-1363
Henrike 25, Sara 20, Johann 23, Johannes 14			
WALZ, Christine	29	Etmansweiler	68-0534
Eva 8, Christian 6			
WALZ, Ernst	39	Schleiz	70-0076
WALZ, Heinrich	23	Kuppenheim	69-0321
WALZ, Louis	17	Carlsruhe	68-0786
WALZ, Martin	9	Ebhausen	69-1363
WALZ, Sophie	18	Gruenettstetten	68-0957
WAMGERIN, Herm.	36	Burhaw	69-1004
Albertine 34			
WAMMANGER, Jacob	24	Surhessen	68-0456
WAMSGANZ, Marg.	23	Candel	70-1035
Elisabeth 21			
WANCKE, Theo.	26	Schneidemuehl	70-0170
WANDERKE, Wilhelmine	54	Wollin	71-0684
Hermine 16, Emilie 22, Gustav 9			
WANDRE, Wilhlmine	43	Schoken	71-0226
WANGER, Albert	24	Allensbach	68-0014
WANITZECHKA, Franz	14	Wilenz	69-0771
WANKE, Christiane	20	Dorum	69-0429
WANNER, Gottlob	22	Ulm	68-0884
WANNER, Theresia	20	Regensburg	68-0456
Maria 5 months			
WANNSCHAFFER, Bertha	34	Gronau	71-0363
Alfred 14, Hermann 9, Gustav 6, Carl 4, Johanne 9 months			
WANSNEST, Jacob	28	Albershausen	68-0820
WANZELER, Carl	64	Peine	69-0050
Margar. 53			
WAPLER, Heinrich	36	Waldcappel	70-0443
WARAHRENS, Louise	29	Braunschweig	69-0672

NAME	AGE	RESIDENCE	YR-LIST
Johann 11 months			
WAREN, Wilhelm	28	Glashuette	70-0523
Henriette 28, Hermann 8 months			
WARGAST, Christine	15	Saarlouis	71-0727
Marie 7, Peter 7			
WARMUTH, Georg	42	Eierdorf	69-1396
WARNECK, Joh.	26	Hasloch	71-0393
WARNECKE, August	16	Osnabrueck	68-0939
WARNKE, Ferd.	17	Luedingsworth	71-0479
WARNKEN, Beta	31	Bremen	71-0429
Hermann 9 months			
WARNKEN, Carl Chr.	21	Bremen	68-0884
WARNKEN, Diedrich	35	Bremen	69-1396
WARNKEN, Dorothea	35	Bremen	70-0523
Friedrich 7, Helene 5, Anna 6 months			
WARNKEN, Joh.	17	Lohhausen	68-0982
WARNKEN, Johann	16	Obereistedt	68-0852
WARNS, Adelheid	23	Syterdamm	69-0490
WARSA, Pauline	13	Boehmen	70-0728
WARTENBERG, Friederike	57	Berlin	70-0031
WASEM, Philipp	48	Stolzenburg	69-0321
Magdalena 16, Christine 9, Minna 8, Lina 6, Carolina 18			
WASMANN, Emil		Rhade	68-0625
WASMUTH, Sofie	9	Homberg	71-1046
WASSERMANN, Babette	18	Crailsheim	71-0521
WASSERMANN, Bernhard	30	Lauschheim	69-0229
WASSERMANN, Conrad	24	Hersfeld	68-0647
WASSERMANN, Georg	16	Assmannshausen	68-0820
WASSMANN, J.	18	Hille	69-0560
WASSMUND, Wilhelm	21	Mecklenburg	70-1023
WASSMUTH, Fransizka	18	Westfalen	70-0728
WATERMANN, Martha	48	Binde	70-0272
WATERMEYER, H. R.	25	Bremen	68-1006
WATJEN, Becke	23	Dreye	71-0521
WATTENBERG, Aug.	25	Hannover	69-0079
WATTLER, Elisab.	26	Diesbach	71-0363
WATTROTH, Fried.	32	Magdeburg	70-0569
WEBBEL. Margareth B.	18	Ensheim	69-0321
WEBBES, Anna	20	Hastedt	71-0821
WEBEL, Gusta	17	Magdeburg	68-1006
WEBENDOERFER, Rudolf	28	Greitz	68-0566
Louise 26, Mathilde 6			
WEBER, Anna	60	Rosshaupt	70-0308
Mary 31, Therese 5, John 2, Luers 18 months			
WEBER, Anna	30	Hannover	71-0479
WEBER, Apollonia	22	Ettlingen	68-0786
WEBER, Barbara	18	Mainleus	69-0848
WEBER, Carl	28	Soesth	71-0643
WEBER, Catharine	22	Darmstadt	69-0672
WEBER, Catharine	36	Simmern	70-0076
Regina 26			
WEBER, Cathr.	33	Oberpleisertom	70-0170
WEBER, Cathrine	24	Carlsruhe	71-0643
WEBER, Clara	23	Bremen	71-0226
WEBER, Conrad	27	Niederwommen.	69-0784
WEBER, Elisabeth	29	Volkartshain	68-0760
WEBER, Friedr.	29	Hildburghausen	71-0393
WEBER, Friedrich	25	Hermannsstein	71-0643
Siegmund 21			
WEBER, Georg	25	Ottenheim	71-0712
H. 32, Karl 27			
WEBER, Georg	26	Lichtenborn	71-0167
WEBER, Gottlieb	26	Erdmann	70-0204
WEBER, Jacob		Reichenweier	70-1055
WEBER, Jacob	24	Marbach	69-0592
WEBER, Jacob	36	Espa	71-0492
Susanna 49, Heinrich 7			
WEBER, Johann	59	Betsch	69-0672
Justine 41, Johanne 27, Marie 19, Traugott 28, Johanne 6			
WEBER, Johann	27	Niedlingen	70-0184
WEBER, Johann	26	Zell	69-0490
WEBER, Johann	31	Westum	69-0229
Marie 34, Gertrude 22, Christian 17			
WEBER, Johann	18	Friedrichsthal	69-0429
WEBER, Johann	26	Meiningen	69-0583
WEBER, Johann	29	Noeda	71-0733
Louise 28, Louise 25, Therese 6, Carl 3, Auguste 9 months			
WEBER, John	26	Ufhoven	71-0456
WEBER, Josef	39	Forchheim	71-0684
WEBER, Juliane	52	Ruhlkirchen	71-0521
Marie 17, Catharine 15, Dorothea 9			
WEBER, Louis	25	Wunschendorf	69-0968
Johanne 30, Arnst Louis 11 months			
WEBER, Lucie	28	Bremen	69-0841
son 5, son 2			
WEBER, Margarethe	62	Stuttgart	69-0672
Christian 6, Anna 3, Valentin 11 months			
WEBER, Margarethe	24	Werda	70-0378
WEBER, Margarethe	36	Zuerich	71-0363
WEBER, Maria	22	Hofgarten	68-0707
WEBER, Marie	21	Mockmuehle	68-0852
WEBER, Marie	18	Barkhausen	68-0939
WEBER, Peter Joseph	41	Selbach	69-0572
WEBER, Philipp	18	Wetz	71-0581
WEBER, Philipp	32	Richelkirchen	71-0521
Catharine 63, Maria 23, Catharina 16			
WEBER, Renke	34	Ostfriesland	69-1059
Chelina 24, Hauke 9, Gesche 7, Anna 57			
WEBER, Rosine	22	Westercappeln	71-0736
WEBER, Sophie	20	Friedrichsthal	71-0226
WEBER, Valentin	29	Frankin	69-0162
WEBER, Vincenz	18	Gosheim	70-0135
WEBER, Wilhelm	18	Erbenhausen	68-0456
WEBER, Wilhelmine	17	Wusterhausen	69-0338
WEBGOLD, Elise	17	Waldmichitten	71-0681
WEBLER, Agnes	32	Berlin	71-0684
WEBLER, Wilhelm	29	Ensheim	70-0204
Christine 19			
WECHSLER, Carl	19	Sappenheim	71-0821
WECHTER, Aucke	44	Loppersum	69-0560
Bernhard 8, Wilharm 6, Henriette 4			
WECHTUNG, Hermann	37	Sondershausen	69-0672
Johanne 32, Hugo 9, Emilie 5, Albert 3			
WECK, Friedrich F.	34	Auma	68-0661

NAME	AGE	RESIDENCE	YR-LIST
Wilhelmine 34, Franz Emil 7, Ida Mathilde 6, Anna Maria 5, Franz Paul 2, Emma			
WECKESSER, Johann	23	Schrecksbach	68-0852
WECKMANN, Hermann	35	Lueneburg	69-0208
WECKNITZ, Johann	28	Margonin	68-0707
Cacilie 25, Julia 24, Charl. 9 months			
WECKWERTH, Emilie	24	Marienhof	68-1002
WEDDINGFELD, Heinr.	17	Frotheim	71-0479
Fried. 15			
WEDEL, Friedrich	25	Pfreindt	70-0355
WEDELEK, Kasimir	34	Czeslina	71-0429
Katharina 29, Johann 10 months, Valentin 22			
WEDELL, Kunigunde	24	Struttendorf	71-0167
WEDELSTEDT, Wme.	59	Stettin	69-1059
WEDEMEYER, Johann	23	Hannover	69-1076
WEESEBERG, Heinr.	15	Meienburg	70-0052
WEFERLING, Wilharm	45	Vechold	68-0907
Anna 35, Maria 2, Henry 11 months			
WEGE, Christian	22	Wura	69-0547
Margarethe 19			
WEGE, Daniel	52	Wohra	68-0661
Catharina 40, Heinrich 18, Anna 14, Margaretha 7, Marie 6, Elisabeth 2			
WEGENER, Aug.	24	Hermsdorf	69-0592
WEGENER, Caroline	21	Lippe Detmold	70-0223
WEGENER, Christ.	42	Neu Hardenberg	71-0456
Sophie 51, Friedrich 20, Caroline 15			
WEGENER, J. F.	32	Hannover	69-1421
WEGENER, Rudolf	23	Sommrathin	69-1363
WEGENER, Wilhelm	17	Lippe Detmold	70-0223
WEGERLE, Peter	26	Lampertheim	69-0338
WEGHORN, Johann	28	Burgstall	69-0229
WEGHORST, Heinr.	22	Westrup	71-0821
WEGMANN, Elisabeth	19	Lampertheim	68-0957
Adam 22, Elisabeth 41, Wilhelmine 16, Georg 14, Peter 11, Johannes 6			
WEGMANN, Minna	22	Metterzimmer	71-0643
WEGMANN, Theodor	24	Hiltrup	69-1212
WEGNER, Robert	39	Kallies	68-0957
WEGREITER, Florian	19	Hessenthal	69-0560
WEHDEL, Maria	31	Neuenkirchen	68-0661
WEHE, Adeline	23	Williamsburg	69-1363
WEHENBERG, Heinrich	17	Euyter	69-0798
WEHLER, Mary	9	Westernohl	68-0760
Philipp 7			
WEHLHEIM, Carl	19	Kirdorf	71-0821
WEHMANN, Claus	14	Bergdamme	69-0429
WEHMANN, Diedrich	32	Bassum	70-1161
WEHMANN, Heinrich	24	Bererstaedt	69-0592
WEHMANN, Marie	24	Aumund	69-1396
WEHMEIER, Henriette	22	Bielefeld	71-0581
WEHMEYER, Heinrich	32	Hannover	69-0672
Marie 25			
WEHMEYER, Ludwig	19	Holsen	68-1006
WEHMUELLER, Th.	15	Inspel	68-0760
WEHNER, Polykarp	36	Wissels	68-0610
Justine 30, Bab. 11 months, Ottilie 74, Ignatz 27, Antonia 25			
WEHNES, Cath.	17	N.Thalhammer	71-0479
WEHRENBERG, Elise	20	Hoboken	70-1003
WEHRFRITZ, Emilie	25	Creuznach	70-0223
WEHRHEIM, Johannes	34	Kirdorf	71-0821
Maria 26, Caroline 3, Marie 11 months			
WEHRLE, Victoria	18	Ditishausen	68-0982
Anna 20			
WEHRMANN, Herm.	16	Arrenkamp	70-1066
Wilhelm 12			
WEHRSTEIN, Walpora	47	Revingen	69-0576
WEIBLIN, Albert	32	Gmuend	68-1027
WEIBRECHT, Sophie	22	Wasungen	68-0534
WEICHARDT, Wilhelm	28	Berlin	68-0852
WEICHSELBAUM, Th. H.	34	Ogden	68-1006
Fanny 30, Josephine 4, Sam 2			
WEICK, Friedrich	17	Rheinbischoffsh	71-0712
WEIDE, Heinrich	54	Nordhausen	68-0753
Johanna 48, Amalie 24, Wilhelmine 13			
WEIDE, Joh. W.	18	Treisbach	68-0647
WEIDELE, Conr.	26	Schapbach	68-1002
WEIDELICH, Michael	20	Simmerfeld	68-0786
WEIDEMANN, Chr.	25	Wildelem	70-0223
WEIDEMANN, Johann	44	Oberaula	69-0798
Ann 42, Margarethe 8, Elisabeth 6, Johannes 3			
WEIDENROTH, Henry	39	Braunschweig	69-0560
Sophia 45			
WEIDIG, Cathinka	24	Giessen	69-1363
WEIDINGER, Aug.	36	Nuernberg	70-0569
Marie 30			
WEIDMANN, Johann	29	Freudenstadt	71-0226
WEIDMANN, Louise	24	Lofingen	68-0760
WEIDNER, Caroline	26	Gerbertshofen	68-0939
WEIDNER, Regine	26	Herenalb	69-0968
WEIGAND, Adam	42	Thuelb	71-0821
Marie 36, Justine 15, Eva 13, Adalbert 8, Geo. 11 months			
WEIGEL, Philipp	26	Ritthausen	69-0182
WEIHER, Elisabeth	27	Hahn	69-1076
Philipp 18, Barbara 24			
WEIHERICH, Magdalene	31	Gemuenden	68-0907
WEIJE, Georg	36	Paussa	69-0798
WEIK, Christ.	30	Rath	70-0569
Heinrich 23			
WEIKEL, Johann	17	Hesse Darmstadt	70-0329
WEIL, Agnes	30	Bildweis	71-0581
WEIL, Catharina	56	Kwetow	71-0521
WEIL, Jasias	36	Huntsville	69-1004
Isidor 13, Hermann 9			
WEIL, Jo.	30	Budweis	71-0581
WEIL, Lotti	43	Tedien-Techen	68-0770
WEIL, Louise	28	Stuttgart	68-0661
WEIL, Maria	43	Prag	70-0443
WEIL, Nicolas	41	Bodenheim	69-0457
Theela 46			
WEIL, Taubine	25	Meilheim	71-0492
Markus 7, Amalie 4, Deborah 11 months			
WEILAGE, Mary	17	Gehrde	69-0923
WEILAND, Elisabeth	19	Plittersdorf	68-0647
WEILAND, Mathias	27	Zirkwitz	68-0786

NAME	AGE	RESIDENCE	YR-LIST
Anton 32			
WEILAND, Peter	78	Offenbach	68-0753
Christine 36 (Peter died on board)			
WEILER, Bertha	17	Medebach	68-0939
WEILL, A.	17	Muttersholz	71-0643
L. 17			
WEILL, Max	17	Randegg	68-0566
WEIMANN, Marie	26	Aixheim	69-0923
Joseph 2			
WEIMAR, Elisab.	29	Neukirchen	71-0363
WEIMAR, Heinr.	16	Hannover	70-0052
WEIMAR, Mich.	30	Geifingen	69-0560
WEINACHT, Jacob	34	Beichken	71-0712
WEINBERG, Abraham	27	Erdmannsrod	68-0760
WEINBERG, Alex	68	Langenschwarz	68-0939
Henriette 55, Rosa 9			
WEINBERG, Christian	17	Levern	70-1161
WEINBERG, Johann	65	Muenster	68-0786
Anton 28, Johanna 29			
WEINBERG, Philippine	16	Heinifeld	69-0592
WEINBERGER, Alois	44	Javestred	68-1006
WEINDIECK, Gust. H. W.	18	Osnabrueck	70-0089
WEINER, Michel	30	Doningen	68-0957
WEINFELD, Catharine	19	Klein Bor	69-0968
WEINGAERTNER, C.	24	Bretzenheim	70-0308
WEINGARTH, Carl	41	Hueffler	71-0521
Elisabeth 33, Elisabeth 4, Philippine 2			
WEINHEIMER, Caspar	26	Kempten	68-0820
WEINKAUF, C.	33	Berlin	68-0753
WEINKEN, Maria	29	Bremen	70-0523
Heinrich 6, Magdalene 1 months			
WEINMANN, Heinrich	27	Frankfurt/M	68-1027
WEINMANN, Hermann	27	Weilen	69-0429
WEINMANN, Jac.	20	Harthausen	69-0560
Charles 20			
WEINREICH, Therese	20	Struth	68-0314
WEINSHEIMER, Marg.	46	Bamberg	68-0760
WEINSPACH, Andreas	34	Bruchsal	69-0457
WEINSTOCK, Isaac	15	Uffenheim	69-1396
WEIPERT, Anna	26	Wallerfangen	71-0393
Marie 6 months			
WEIS, Heinr.	30	Eisighofen	68-0982
WEIS, Henriette	28	Boehmen	68-0456
WEISBECKER, A.	34	Salmuenster	69-0560
WEISBROD, Chs.	27	Meiningen	70-0170
WEISE, Caroline	24	Ranis	71-0492
WEISE, Catharina	26	Altenkirchen	68-0820
WEISE, Hermann	25	Berlin	71-0712
WEISEL, Simon	35	Hannover	71-0712
WEISENSEE, Therese	22	Ostheim	69-0798
WEISKOPF, J.	25	Rhaude	71-0712
WEISS, Andreas	18	Orschwein	68-0786
WEISS, Anna	22	Meeringen	68-0753
Barbara 23			
WEISS, Brigitta	23	Hechingen	68-0610
WEISS, Catharine	27	Ruedesheim	70-0378
WEISS, Christine	24	Aschersleben	69-1086
Gustav 11 months			
WEISS, Eva	26	Neukirch	71-0643
WEISS, F.	21	Pensygola	69-0968
WEISS, Franz	25	Godramstein	71-0712
WEISS, Franz.	20	Hagenau	71-0736
WEISS, Georg	31	Grossbaerweiler	69-0848
WEISS, Heinr.		Germersheim	71-0581
WEISS, Ignatz	29	Neukirch	70-0378
WEISS, Jacob	21	Wiebelsbach	68-0760
WEISS, Joh.	22	Trossdorf	71-0821
WEISS, Ludwig	27	Rheinprovinz	70-0443
Elisabeth 23, Wilhelm 3, Ludwig 1			
WEISS, Michael	28	Tuschenbach	69-0229
WEISS, Therese	18	Waldkirch	70-0272
WEISSBECK, Wilhelmine	28	Schlitz	69-0968
WEISSE, Friedrich	34	Goettingen	71-0736
WEISSENBERG, Caroline	40	Nuernberg	68-0957
WEISSENBOM, Johann	27	Niederorla	69-0560
WEISSENBORN, Albin	17	Erfurt	69-0542
WEISSENBORN, Christ.	40	Thueringen	70-0443
Mariea 38, Christ. 13, Susanna 7, Louise 4, Jacob 3			
WEISSENBORN, Christine	23	Kreuzburg	70-1011
WEISSENSEE, Christ.	24	Weissensee	71-0167
WEISSER, Sarah	27	Mauchenheim	68-0566
WEISSIG, Gustav	21	Freiburg	68-0661
WEISSKOPF, Michael	25	Perlach	71-0429
WEISSMUELLER, K.	19	Giessen	68-0610
WEISSNER, Mathias	24	Phlingen	68-0625
WEISZ, David	27	Teteny	68-0014
WEIT, Wilh.	42	Leipzig	71-0789
WEITERMUELLER, Franz	41	Pausa	68-0786
Elisabeth 40, Johanna 8, Carl 3, Ottilie 9 months, Mathilde 18, Heinrich 15			
WEITHAS, Paul	25	Dresden	69-0592
WEITLER, Elise	17	Butzbach	68-0661
WEITMANN, Wilhelmine	40	Sandhausen	68-0786
WEITSCHAT, August	45	Graudenz	69-0182
Wilhelmine 46, Louise 14, Marie 4			
WEITZ, Marg.	18	Hannover	70-1066
Carl 15			
WEITZ, Mathilde	32	Sondershausen	68-0707
WEITZ, Matthilde	15	Sandershausen	69-0771
Louis 7			
WEITZEL, Carl	16	Bergheim	70-0452
WEITZEL, Casp.	60	Allendorf	71-0581
WEITZEL, Conrad	24	Cassel	70-0076
WEITZENKORN, Levy	19	Leitmar	68-0907
Bertha 19			
WEIZMANN, Thomas	30	Grossueften	68-0566
WELCHER, Philippine	37	Gladbach	70-0223
WELCHES, Marie	31	Gladbach	70-0223
Jacob 6, Heinrich 4, Wilhelm 2			
WELCKER, Carl	25	Neuwied	69-1004
WELFLICK, Johann	18	Kralowitz	71-0429
WELKE, Emil	15	Smiskanowo	69-0547
WELKE, Emilie	27	Wronke	69-0457
Robert 20			
WELKER, Carl	19	Heilbronn	69-1363
WELKER, Christine	27	Heselsbronn	68-0852

NAME	AGE	RESIDENCE	YR-LIST
Georg 6			
WELKER, Jac.	21	Toledo	71-1046
WELKER, Joh.	26	Mittelfranken	70-1142
WELKY, Katharina	49	Wescheherd	71-0429
Josef 18			
WELLBROCK, Anna Cath.	26	Ballhoefen	68-0770
WELLBROCK, Gebert	30	Worpedahl	71-0456
WELLBROCK, Luder	15	Hannover	69-1059
WELLENWEBER, Caroline	30	Cassel	71-0792
WELLER, Anna	56	Gutenberg	70-1055
Anna 15			
WELLER, Carl	18	Einseltham	69-0968
WELLER, Georg	46	Frieburg	68-0456
Christine 35, Marie 65, Johann 4, Wilhelm 1			
WELLER, Johannes	31	Oppenrod	68-0907
WELLER, Rosine	24	Kaisersbach	69-0429
WELLHOEFER, John	19	Falkendorf	70-0170
WELLNER, Anna	25	Gutenberg	68-0939
WELLNITZ, Gust.	24	Cram	71-0167
WELMANN, Char.	26	Osnabrueck	69-1011
WELPOT, Sophie	19	Trotheim	69-0182
WELSCH, Helene	27	Speyer	68-0534
WELSCH, Marie	21	Bliekweiler	71-0736
Susanne 19			
WELTE, Otto	25	Weingarten	69-0490
WELTENKAMP, Fritz	16	Wesenstedt	68-0884
WELTER, Sophie	34	Pansa	70-0135
Franz 9, Martin 7, Minna 5, Martha 3, baby 9 months			
WELZ, Louise	42	Belliad	69-0049
WEMPE, Elise	22	Cloppenburg	69-0208
WENCKE, Gottfried	31	Grossbuschla	68-0770
WENCKER, Marie	20	Lockhausen	71-0456
WENDE, Adam	19	Affoldern	68-0625
WENDE, Marie	52	Magdeburg	68-0982
WENDEL, Augusta	17	Cassel	68-1002
WENDEL, Christian	58	Anhalt Dessau	71-0712
WENDEL, Clara	31	Pfalz	68-0566
Philipp 5			
WENDEL, Johann	40	Bruesken	71-0736
Louise 37, Carl 9, August 8, Peter 7, Julius 5, Heinrich 11 m.			
WENDEL, Marie	20	Morstadt	68-0625
Jacob 37			
WENDELN, Mary	28	Vries	68-0534
WENDLAND, Emil	17	Seefeld	68-0707
WENDLAND, Wilhelmine	21	Repplin	68-0314
Daniel 18			
WENDLER, A.	33	Schwarzenbach	69-0050
WENDLER, Friedrich	39	Weissdorf	68-1006
Margarethe 41, Margar. Barb. 6			
WENDLER, Johann	26	Lichtenfels	71-0581
WENDLING, Rosina	19	Rheinbischoffsh	71-0712
WENDOLIN, Johann	30	Etzel	71-0492
Maria 27, Tobias 8			
WENDT, Bekka	17	Hemelingen	69-1212
WENDT, Friedr.	47	Berlin	68-1002
Johanna 41, Marie 9, Friedr. 8, Anna 11 months			

NAME	AGE	RESIDENCE	YR-LIST
WENDT, Friedr.	49	Schieda	68-314
Helene 49, Helene 23, Marie 18, Minna 12, Ernst 18			
WENDT, Friedrich	27	Rosenthal	68-0647
WENDT, Gottlieb	44	Rehnitz	69-1309
Louise 44, Justine 20, Wilhelm 7, Emilie 5			
WENDT, Heinrich	16	Elberfeld	69-0162
WENDT, Heinrich	31	Syke	68-0760
WENDT, Johanne	27	Conitz	68-0610
WENDT, Just. Heinr.	18	Friedewaldt	69-0572
WENDT, Marie	23	Brakelsiek	68-314
WENDTKER, Therese	24	Mettingen	69-0583
WENDTLAND, Clara	52	Berlin	68-1002
Otto 16, Ida 13, Conrad 7, Ernst 6, Charlotte 4			
WENIG, Augusta	22	Schweina	68-0314
WENKE, Joh. Heinr.	52	Heckeler Moor	69-0321
Margaretha 50, Anna 17			
WENKE, Louis	17	Buer	69-0542
WENNIGER, Dina	27	Leer	71-0479
WENNING, Adelheid	30	Schuettdorf	69-0572
WENNING, Louis	41	Dachau	69-0923
Maria 44, Louis 9, Hy. 7, Arthur 11 months, Josef 22			
WENNINGHOFF, Rud.	19	Bramsche	68-0534
Georg 15			
WENSGER, Ferd.	42	Koenigser	71-0167
Louise 16			
WENSGER, Ferd.	40	Koenigser	71-0167
WENT, Mathias	46	Fegernbach	71-0736
Susanne 44			
WENTE, Christ.	16	Antendorf	71-0479
WENTZEL, Franziska	23	Dresden	71-0681
WENZ, Christine	21	Cutingen	70-0184
WENZ, Jacob	20	Schoenfeld	69-0771
WENZ, Wilhelm	22	Michelsheim	71-0363
WENZEL, Andreas	22	Rhina	69-0457
WENZEL, Helene	18	Breslau	68-0625
WENZEL, Margarethe	50	Wingershausen	68-0314
Margarethe 17, Anna 13, Carl 9, Herman 7			
WENZEL, Thadaeus	19	Cassel	69-0672
WENZLER, Carl	34	Conitz	68-0610
WENZLER, Ottmar	34	Seitingen	71-0684
WEPEL, Lina	55	Ostfriesland	69-1059
WEPNER, Lina	27	Gr. Freden	68-0625
WEPPER, Maria	54	Muenchen	68-0314
WEPPLER, Ludw.	19	Oberaula	71-0521
Justus 19			
WEPPNER, Hermann	30	Bremen	69-0268
Therese 33, Catharine 6, Hermann 9 months			
WERCHAN, Wilhelm	17	Buecken	71-0456
WERDENHOLT, Friedr.	22	Cassel	68-0982
WERDES, Johann	27	Oberstows	69-0798
WERGNER, Carl	50	Moschuetz	71-0521
Emil 7, Auguste 5			
WERK, Emilie	28	Ratzeburg	70-0170
Baby 11 months			
WERKA, Joseph	31	Boehmen	70-0508
Mary 24, Frantz 11 months			

NAME	AGE	RESIDENCE	YR-LIST
WERKENS, Hermann	34	Ludingworth	68-0534
WERKMEISTER, Johanna	17	Sulingen	68-1027
WERL, Julius	22	Kusel	70-0135
WERLING, Henry	36	Hannover	70-0508
Anna 30			
WERMEIER, Maria	23	Lengsrich	68-0625
Elisabeth 21			
WERMICH, Aug.	30	Bruenn	68-0884
WERNER, Adolph	22	Langen	68-0939
WERNER, Auguste	38	Berlin	69-0841
Wanda 16			
WERNER, Catharine	50	Bensheim	69-1011
WERNER, Cecilie	34	Darmstadt	70-0272
WERNER, Christ.	26	Moenchpfiffel	68-314
WERNER, Christiane	68	Freiburg	68-1002
WERNER, Emma	19	Camberg	69-1319
WERNER, Friederich	29	Hohenstein	70-0184
WERNER, Friedrich	24	Baumbesberg	70-0223
WERNER, Gg.	17	Morbach	71-0581
WERNER, Gottlieb	30	Bromberg	68-0419
Henriette 23, Friedrich 8, Ludwig 6 months			
WERNER, Gottlieb	49	Werdau	68-0625
Hermann 23			
WERNER, Harm	16	Wachdorf	69-0572
WERNER, Minna	22	Apolda	68-0786
Theo 11 months			
WERNER, Simon	48	Lichtenfels	68-1002
Barbara 56, Franz 13, Catharine 12			
WERNER, Solomon	15	Zempelburg	68-0707
Hanna 7			
WERNER, Th. Rud.	34	Naumburg	71-0736
WERNER, Wilhelmine	20	Unterhausen	69-1076
WERNIK, Catharine	30	Bruesken	71-0736
WERNING, Adam	57	Hessen	70-0178
Jeanette 52, Elise 27, Conrad 18, Catharine 15, Julius 12, Anton 9, Wilhelm 7			
WERNSDORFER, Maria	9	Halbersdorfer	71-0643
WERTAU, Herm.	16	Buecken	68-1027
WERTEMUELLER, Chr.	16	Sessenheim	71-0581
WERTERMANN, Meta	22	Hannover	69-0672
WERTH, Elisabeth	19	Spielberg	69-0592
Catharina 17			
WERTH, Henriette	21	Niewinko	68-0707
WERTHEIM, Abraham	16	Carlshafen	68-0939
WERTHEIMER, Josef		Carlsruhe	71-0363
WERTHEIMER, S.	30	Hannover	70-0523
WERTHMUELLER, Ad.	23	Elsbach	68-0753
WERTHMUELLER, Carl	19	Fulda	70-1161
WERWALZ, Helene	57	Giessen	68-0610
Augusta 22, Johanna 16			
WESCHKE, Aug.	20	Cassel	69-1421
WESEL, August	19	Rodelheim	69-0292
WESELY, Bernharde	33	Kuttenberg	69-0560
Anna 8, Anton 6, John 3			
WESEMANN, Friedrich	31	Lippe Detmold	70-0355
WESEMANN, Joh.	14	Harpstede	68-0647
WESEMANN, Johann	22	Harpstadt	68-0852
WESERMANN, Heinrich	31	Lahde	69-1076
Louise 30, Friedrich 2, Louise 6 months			

NAME	AGE	RESIDENCE	YR-LIST
WESHY, Helene	20	Bieberich	69-1319
WESKE, Emilie	34	Zarinkow	69-0672
WESPERMANN, H.	31	Hannover	71-0815
WESSEL, Anna	20	Herben	68-0939
WESSEL, Friedrich	26	Hannover	71-0821
Engela 20			
WESSEL, Heinrich	25	Delmenhorst	70-0384
Anna 14, Carl 1			
WESSEL, Minna	21	Hannover	71-0684
Anna 18			
WESSEL, Reinhard	15	Ostfriesland	69-1059
WESSEL, Sophie	20	Quernheim	68-0610
WESSEL, Wilhelm	27	Nettelstedt	68-0707
WESSLER, Joh. Heinr.	17	Holsen	68-1002
WESSNER, Gustav	28	Haulah	69-0292
WEST, Mathias	46	Fegernbach	71-0736
Susanne 44			
WESTE, Charlotte	24	Hannover	68-0982
WESTERFELD, Wme.	20	Rahden	68-0982
WESTERHOFF, Louise	18	Nettelstedt	68-0957
WESTERKAMP, Justus	30	Osnabrueck	70-0355
WESTERMAIER, Eduard	38	Regensburg	68-1002
Sophie 30, Eduard 9, Robert 8, Alfred 6, Ar-thur 3			
WESTERMANN, Anna	24	Pleiswiller	69-0592
WESTERMANN, Franz	23	Sulzbach	69-0208
WESTERMANN, Hermann	37	Hannover	69-0229
WESTERMANN, Maria	39	Paderborn	68-0456
Martin 15, Johann 13, Clemens 11, Carl 9, Andreas 8, Anna 7, Fritz 3			
WESTERMEYER, Herm.	26	Kuppel/Russia	69-0049
Marie 26			
WESTFEL, Christ.	44	Lichtenberg	71-0479
Elise 39, Babette 15, Lisette 12, Christ. 8, Marie 5			
WESTHEIM, Lina	59	Langenschwarz	69-0968
WESTHOFEN, Chr.	20	Mainz	70-0308
WESTJANN, Catharine	18	Cloppenburg	69-0208
WESTPHAL, Johann	27	Bitow	69-0547
Emilie 26			
WESTPHAL, Josephine	25	Marienfelde	69-0321
WESTPHAL, Wilh.	52	Weidermark	71-0393
Auguste 23, Carl 14			
WESTRUP, Elise	20	Jegger	71-0643
WESTWEBER, Joh.	15	Densberg	69-0592
Anna 14			
WETER, Am.	17	Rust	71-0300
WETGEN, Diedrig	39	San Francisco	69-0572
WETJEN, G. G.	30	Varel	70-0508
WETJEN, Marie	19	Scharmbeck	68-1006
WETTENDORF, William	50	New York	69-1421
WETTENSTEIN, Cornelius	19	Detmold	69-0229
WETTER, A.	27	Crottingen	71-0684
Johann 33			
WETTEROTH, Marie	18	Babenhausen	71-0363
WETTINGFELD, Sophie	18	Isenstaedt	68-0907
WETTLAUFEN, Henriette	19	Waltenbrueck	69-1212
WETTLAUFER, Conrad	15	Breitenbach	69-0672
WETTLIK, Amand	39	Steinstart	69-1363

NAME	AGE	RESIDENCE	YR-LIST
WETZEL, August	46	Langenhagen	68-0625
Eleonore 44, Wilhelmine 23, Friederike 19, Wilhelm 16, Augusta 5			
WETZEL, Friedrich	19	Tuebingen	69-0229
WETZEL, Friedrich	26	Nuertingen	68-0661
WETZEL, Philipp	43	Darmstadt	69-0067
WETZLER, Gotz	24	Langstedt	68-0939
WETZSTEIN, Gustav	37	Greiz	68-0786
Wilhelmine 38, Anna 14, Richard 9, Tilly 6, Adele 2, Max 3 months			
WEYDEMANN, Hulda	18	Redschitz	71-0479
WEYDEMANN, Joseph	26	Bremerhafen	70-0329
WEYGAND, Gustav	16	Ellweiler	71-0429
WEYGOLD, Christine	25	Glatten	70-0329
WEYH, Louise	18	Schmalkalden	70-0329
WEYL, Wilhelm	31	Toledo	71-0643
WEYRAUCH, Michael	17	Darmstadt	69-1212
Sibilla 28			
WEYRICH, Daniel	26	Selchenbach	69-0572
Julie 24, Daniel 3 months			
WHITE, F.	21	Pensygola	69-0968
WICH, Kunigunde	23	Kronach	69-0572
WICH, Ottilie	20	Haltstadt	68-0647
WICHBOLD, Johann	54	Mellenhoff-Pomm	70-0006
Henriette 55			
WICHELHAUS, Emilie	29	Wald	70-0443
Hugo 6			
WICHERT, Olga	22	Elbing	68-0982
Max 9			
WICHMANN, Hinr.	17	Sandstedt	68-0884
WICHMANN, Johann	29	Oldenburg	69-0268
Ulke 23			
WICHMEHLER, Sophie	20	Ibbenbuehren	68-0982
WICHT, Christ.	48	Osterbruch	69-0572
lived in California			
WICHTERICH, Peter	26	R.B. Coeln	68-0610
WICK, Friedrich		Havre	70-0259
WICK, Mathilde	28	Rothenburg	69-0560
WICKE, Friedrich	28	Lagershausen	68-0852
WICKE, Heinr.	25	Imbshausen	68-1002
WICKE, Marie	20	Wustrow	69-0542
WICKE, Sophia Reb.	21	Posthausen	68-0770
Meta 17			
WICKENTRAGER, C.		Melle	68-0610
WICKERT, Martin	17	Haldorf	70-0569
WICKESSER, Barb.	31	Loshausen	71-0363
WICKSELBERGER, Josef	29	Tyrol	71-0167
WIDENER, Elisabeth	30	Bern	71-0736
WIDER, Wilhelmine	22	Dornham	69-0784
WIDMANN, Jacob	20	Zang	68-1298
WIDMANN, Jacob	50	Olpfinger	71-0792
Anna 52, Tilomena 17, Alfon 9, Friedrich 24, Barbara 28			
WIDMER, Johann	55	Hainringen	69-1319
WIEBE, Peter	26	Plantendorf	68-0786
WIEBKING, Wilhelm	34	Schneeren	68-0647
WIEBOLD, Anna	18	Hannover	71-0429
WIEBUSCH, Rebecca	26	Hannover	70-0443
WIECHELAND, Joh.	24	Mit.Schefflanz	71-0684

NAME	AGE	RESIDENCE	YR-LIST
WIECHERS, Heinr.	22	Rodenbeck	70-0508
Henry 20			
WIECHERT, Paul	20	Steglitz	69-1212
WIECK, Charles	34	Bremen	68-0534
WIECKMANN, Joh.	36	Sandstedt	70-1161
Fr. 9			
WIEDEMANN, Gust.	32	Breslau	68-0760
WIEDEMANN, Marie	43	Bahnertshofen	69-0229
Chrecentia 5			
WIEDENBAHN, Christ.	24	Braunschweig	71-0684
WIEDENBRUEKER, Henry	18	Engerte	71-0643
WIEDENHOEFER, Ant.	18	Coeln	69-0079
WIEDER, Julius	24	Berlin	69-0208
WIEDERHOLD, Andr.	23	Eeglis	68-0957
WIEDERING, Jh.	28	Hessen	70-0508
Sophie 20, Sophie 9 months			
WIEDESITZ, Ludwig	23	Neu Ulm	71-0643
WIEDMANN, Johann	26	Winzingen	69-0208
D. 25, Ursula 65			
WIEDMOSER, Susanne	22	Kufstein	68-1002
WIEGAND, Adam	21	Langenschwarz	70-0378
WIEGAND, Anna	21	Eisenach	68-0760
WIEGAND, Eduard	36	Bielefeld	68-0753
WIEGAND, Ernst	19	Roehrda	68-0982
WIEGAND, Franz W.		Soisdorf	68-1002
WIEGAND, Frieda	30	Cassel	71-0736
WIEGAND, Georg	36	New York	70-1003
Amalie 30, John 28			
WIEGAND, Georg	17	Weimar	71-0821
WIEGAND, Henry	25	Erbsen	71-0643
WIEGAND, Johann	29	Gray	69-0457
WIEGAND, Johannes	16	Hessen	70-0178
WIEGAND, Mich.	18	Herda	68-1002
WIEGANDT, Julius	16	Frankenthal	71-0492
WIEGANT, Franz	38	Rudolstadt	71-0789
Kath. 30, Fritz 4, Conr. 6 months			
WIEGELMANN, Albert	25	Berlin	69-0162
WIEGEN, Diedrich	14	Affromkel	71-0492
WIEGERT, Engelb.	22	Voerstetten	71-0167
WIEGMANN, Heinrich	53	Sonnebom	68-0456
Maria 45, Maria 18, Heinrich 16, Friedrich 7, Anna 4, Hermine 9, Caroline 13			
WIEHL, Jos.	28	Fritzlar	70-0728
WIEHMANN, Hinr.	17	Sandstedt	68-0884
WIEKE, E.	45	Bremen	69-1011
Adele 21			
WIEKE, John	27	Jaeglitz	69-0560
WIEKE, Julius	32	Leipzig	69-1086
WIEKER, Johann	30	Oldenburg	68-0625
WIELAND, Aug.	20	Merdrowiz	71-0479
WIELAND, Berend	38	Neermoor	68-0760
Engel 32, Daniel 6, Heinrich 3, Peter 6 months			
WIELAND, Christine	20	Erlach	69-1363
WIELAND, Friedr.	16	Ehringen	71-0821
WIELAND, Georg	20	Grab	68-0820
WIELAND, Gottlieb	25	Mauerhardt	69-0798
WIELAND, Math.	29	Rielasingen	71-0684
Pauline 25, Caroline 3, Maria 9 months			

NAME	AGE	RESIDENCE	YR-LIST
WIELAND, Rosina	12	Schlattstern	70-1142
WIENCKE, Heinrich	29	Forstenhagen	71-0733
Wilhelmine 23, Heinrich 3, Hermann 10 months			
WIENECKE, Anna	36	Bornhold	69-0429
Henrich 9			
WIENEKE, Heinrich	29	Forstenhagen	71-0733
Wilhelmine 23, Heinrich 3, Hermann 10 months			
WIENEKE, Wilhelm	27	Cassick	69-0321
WIENER, Theodor	22	Ulm	69-0208
WIENHOLT, Gesche	28	Oldenburg	70-0031
WIENKEN, Hermann	9	Bremen	71-0429
WIENKEN, Marie	27	Bremen	69-1309
WIENTJE, Charlotte	47	Osnabrueck	71-0429
Fritz 15			
WIERICHS, Elisabeth	25	Hoya	68-0957
WIERZBIENCI, Johann	32	Warchau	69-0542
WIESATZKY, August	23	Gr. Kressin	69-0547
WIESCHAHN, Carsten	27	Hannover	70-0443
WIESE, Albert	31	Woldegk	68-0647
WIESE, Anna	17	Voigtstedt	71-0363
WIESE, Carl	57	Jena	70-0728
Christiane 55, Pauline 18			
WIESE, Christian	50	Minden	68-0939
Christine 44, Louise 19, Christine 7, Wilhelm 9 months			
WIESE, Harm	27	Grossefehn	69-0338
WIESE, Heinrich	31	Minden	68-0939
Caroline 32, Heinrich 6, Caroline 4, Christiane 9 months			
WIESE, Louise	18	Rhein Pfalz	70-0355
WIESE, Wilhelm	44	Werden	69-1396
WIESEL, Wilhelm	40	New York	69-1076
L. Frank 30			
WIESELMANN, Ph.	16	Koenigsbach	69-0229
WIESEMANN, Catharine	23	Waldeck	70-0384
WIESEMANN, Heinrich	25	Wildungen	68-0566
WIESEN, Sophie	17	Goslar	71-0429
WIESKING, Augusta	15	Osnabrueck	68-1006
WIESMANN, Elise	27	Telgte	68-0907
WIESMANN, Hermann	21	Gross Benz	69-0771
Ernestine 21, August 9 months			
WIESMANN, Louise	18	Adolzfurth	68-0786
WIESMANN, Wilhelm	16	Hannover	69-0771
Sophie 20			
WIESNER, Claus	32	Zeven	68-0456
Anna 28			
WIESSNER, Leonh.	17	Else	68-0753
WIESSNER, Mich.	18	Muehlheim	71-0393
WIESTNER, Catharine	18	Baechlingen	69-0572
WIESTRICH, Wilhelm	13	Siemern	68-0707
Marie 18			
WIETENHEK, John	19	ZUELZ	71-0643
WIETER, Catharina	15	Wilmandingen	68-0566
Joh. 13			
WIETZ, Juliana	60	Olpfinger	71-0792
WIGGER, Adolph	57	Louisville	69-1076
WIGMANN, Fr.	23	Leifoerde	68-0820
WIHMANNS, Ernst	25	Lage	71-0736

NAME	AGE	RESIDENCE	YR-LIST
Paul 17			
WILBENHEID, Jacob	43	Ulmen	68-0610
Barbara 45, Catharina 8, Johann 4			
WILBERN, Geo.	40	S. Francisco	69-1421
Margrethe 26, Wilhelmine 9, Georg 6			
WILD, Wilhelm	27	Gr. Lubs	71-0733
WILDE, Fred.	48	Berlin	68-0957
WILDEMANN, Leonhard	29	Loeningen	69-1212
Jenny 27, Alfred 3			
WILDENBURG, Heinrich	53	Coeln	69-0968
Theodor 16, Adele 9			
WILDER, Hans M.	34	Copenhagen	68-0820
WILDFANG, Geesche	20	Groothusen	68-1027
WILDHACK, Elise	17	Blumenthal	71-0479
WILH, Kunigunde	32	Burgebach	68-0939
Carl 10 months			
WILHARM, Carl	19	Hildesheim	71-0792
WILHEARM, Wilh.	32	Bueckeburg	69-0292
WILHELM, Adolph	17	Pirmasens	70-0508
WILHELM, Amandus	37	Rudolstadt	70-1003
Emmeline 30, Marie 9, Katinka 7, Martha 5, Rudolph 3			
WILHELM, Carl	22	Gehren	69-0848
WILHELM, Franz	23	Meerane	68-0907
WILHELM, Jac.	24	Hostenbach	71-0581
WILHELM, Johann	46	Hintersee	69-0672
WILHELM, Jos.	17	Endingen	71-0393
WILHELM, Louis	17	Rudolstadt	68-0760
WILHELM, Louise	42	Braunschweig	68-1298
Minna 14, Clara 8			
WILHELM, Peter	27	Oldenburg	69-0067
WILHELM, Z.	33	Adelaide	70-1035
Catharina 30, Alfred 6, Anna 13			
WILHELMI, Anton	59	Walzenbach	69-1076
Wilhelmine 88, Wilhelm 20, Louise 18			
WILHELMI, Carl	16	Hille	69-1076
WILHELMI, Conrad	23	Bordeaux	68-0707
WILHELMI, Hermann	22	Bremen	70-0378
WILHELMS, H.	33	Oldenburg	70-0308
Anna 31			
WILHELMS, Theo	17	Hannover	70-0384
WILHEM, Geo.	40	S. Francisco	69-1421
Margrethe 26, Wilhelmine 9, Georg 6			
WILK, Johann	56	Braunschweig	69-0592
WILKE, Aug.	20	Traumburg	68-0753
WILKE, Christ.	29	Neundettelsau	70-1055
WILKE, Christine	42	Steinbach	68-0534
Libette 13, Ferdinand 9, Elise 5, Gustavus 3			
WILKE, Ferdinand	38	Kirschhagen	68-0760
Louise 45			
WILKE, Fritz	14	Stettin	69-0672
WILKE, Heinrich	33	Winckelstetten	69-0321
WILKE, Henriette	29	Bremerhaven	70-0523
Louis 2			
WILKE, J.	28	Braunschweig	71-0684
WILKE, Michel	60	Grabau	71-0581
Marie 50, Auguste 20, Emilie 15, Wilhelmine 9, Lorette 6			
WILKE, Reinhard	16	Herstelle	69-1212

NAME	AGE	RESIDENCE	YR-LIST
WILKE, Wilhelm	48	Brauen	69-0798
WILKEN, Alste	26	Burhave	71-0492
WILKEN, Asmus	15	Horsten	68-1006
WILKEN, Thade	21	Neufunnia Siel	69-0429
Widow 47, Wilhelm 6, Gerhard 13, Str. 60 (Neusunnia Siel)			
WILKENING, Christ.	29	Steinhude	68-0534
Wilhelmine 28, Minna 3, baby-daughter 11 months			
WILKENING, Christian	17	Niedernwoehren	68-0456
WILKENS, Adelheid	19	Oetzen	68-0707
WILKENS, Anna	20	Altenbruch	68-0625
WILKENS, August	36	Berlin	69-0968
Auguste 28, Bertha 9 months			
WILKENS, Benedict	27	Embsen	71-0492
Lene 24			
WILKENS, Diedrich	26	Langwedel	69-0576
WILKENS, Heinrich	16	Ottersberg	70-0378
WILKENS, Johann	15	Leeste	71-0521
WILKENS, Marie	19	Brinkum	68-0786
WILKENS, Rebecca	19	Wremen	71-0492
WILKER, Gerhard	24	Osnabrueck	68-0957
WILKER, Joh.	17	Stockum	69-1086
WILKING, Marie	15	Barkhausen	68-0939
Gertrud 29			
WILL, Anna	58	St. Steinach	71-0479
WILL, August	24	Goldlauter	69-0429
WILL, Carl	41	Greiffenberg	68-0884
Julie 40			
WILL, Marg.	41	Gardesheim	68-0647
Anna 16, Magdalene 15, Georg 13, Heinrich 8, Johann 6, Anna 2			
WILL, Maria	18	Unterfranken	69-0798
WILLBROCK, Wilhelm	16	Heissenbuettel	69-1059
WILLE, Diedrich	30	Oldenburg	69-0672
WILLE, Sophie	31	Steinau	69-1309
WILLE, Wilhelm	18	Altenplathow	68-0534
WILLENBUCHER, Emilie	16	Reichelsheim	69-1076
Wilhelm 14, Otto 11			
WILLER, Caroline	18	Detmold	69-0583
WILLERS, Rosa	17	Hildesheim	70-1011
WILLICH, Justus	25	Asbach	68-0852
WILLMANN, Anna	18	Schwenningdorf	69-1011
WILLMANN, Maria	25	Herford	71-0492
WILLMS, Christen	30	Wesel	69-0771
WILLMS, Margarethe	18	Friedeburg	71-0492
WILLWEBER, Carl	41	Leipzig	68-0907
WILLWEBER, Max	16	Schlei	69-0672
WILMES, Joseph	33	Obersorte	68-1027
WILMS, Henry	20	Vogelsang	70-0508
WILMS, Wilhelmine	30	Strohhausen	69-0672
WILMSEN, Dorothee	20	Emden	71-0643
WILP, Catharine	45	Emsdetten	69-1309
Wilhelmine 15, August 13, Anton 9			
WILS, Hermann	16	Heilbronn	69-0208
WILSMANN, Wilhelm	35	Lotte	68-0907
Sophie 35			
WILTHEIS, Dorothea	21	Wiedermuss	71-0492
WILTS, Heike	19	Flachsmeier	71-0643

NAME	AGE	RESIDENCE	YR-LIST
Aglena 30			
WIMBERG, Joh.	17	Sedelsberg	71-0581
WIMMEL, Martha	52	Kurhessen	69-0968
Marie 15, Heinrich 14			
WIMMER, Franz	46	Burglengenfeld	71-0226
Franz 17			
WIMMER, Hubert	35	Esch	68-0982
WIMMER, Johann	20	Bonfeld	68-0661
WIMMER, Wilh.	33	Bueckeburg	70-1023
Caroline 31, Meta 4, Emma 11 months			
WINCKLER, Anna	55	Darmstadt	70-1142
WINCKLER, Heinz	38	Zschageitz	69-0100
WINCKLER, Herm. Th.	24	Burkersdorf	68-1002
WINCKLER, Martin	23	Luebeck	69-0848
WINCKLER, Wilh.	18	Oetisheim	71-0815
WINDELER, Georg	25	Lobendorf	71-0712
WINDELER, Hermann	18	Engler	70-0443
Wilhelm 15			
WINDELKE, Sophie	18	Rotenberg	70-0508
WINDELN, Fr.	17	Rothenburg	71-0736
WINDERKEN, Catharina	19	Hannover	71-0821
WINDFELD, Simon	27	Weimar	71-0821
Georg 37			
WINDHEIM, Sophie	24	Hannover	71-0733
WINDHORST, Albert	20	Osnabrueck	70-0148
WINDHORST, Diedr.	16	Wesenstedt	68-0884
WINDHUSEN, Theodor	21	Bardowieck	69-0321
WINDMUELLER, Aug.	26	Borken	71-0300
WINKEL, Henry	48	San Francisco	69-1011
WINKEL, Johann	36	Debsteckerbuett	70-0076
WINKEL, Martha	31	Heimarshausen	69-1011
Elizabeth 34			
WINKELER, Albertina	56	Entzsch	68-0456
Amalie 17, Gottlieb 53			
WINKELHAKE, Emma	18	New York	69-1086
WINKELMANN, Carl	40	Homfeld	70-0329
WINKELMANN, Christine	22	Vegesack	71-0300
WINKELMANN, Marga	17	Otterndorf	71-0821
WINKELMANN, Minna	18	Dorum	71-0521
WINKLE, Martha	19	Heimarshausen	69-1212
WINKLER, Carl	10	Bremerhaven	68-0707
Fritz 7			
WINKLER, Cath.	16	Schoenfeld	71-0581
WINKLER, Gustav	17	Leipzig	70-0378
WINKLER, Heinr.	26	Grafenhagen	69-0229
WINKLER, Louis	22	Gotha	68-0957
WINKLER, Mathilde	23	Zemmen	69-0576
WINKLER, Matth.	21	Kisenbach	68-0647
WINKLER, Rosine	30	Arndorf	69-1011
WINN, M.	24	Boston	70-1035
WINNE, Pauline	19	Arnstadt	68-0707
Louis 10 months			
WINNIG, Aug.	45	Blankenburg	63-0244
Jeanne 14			
WINTELS, Anna	19	Borghorst	69-0923
WINTER, Abraham	31	Mastville	68-0907
Bertha 18			
WINTER, Andr.	26	Mundingen	68-0884

NAME	AGE	RESIDENCE	YR-LIST
WINTER, Anna	31	Hannover	71-0456
Cathrine 23			
WINTER, Anton		Soisdorf	68-1002
WINTER, Cath.	21	Bremerhafen	70-0508
WINTER, Fritz	35	Bremen	69-1059
Anna 28, Baby 9 months			
WINTER, Heinrich	25	Wien	69-0015
WINTER, Henry	52	Weseritz	71-0456
Peppi 29			
WINTER, Johann	31	Kuttenberg	70-0329
WINTER, Margaret	29	Bughof	69-0229
WINTER, Mathilde	18	Rasdorf	69-0015
WINTER, Meta	16	Schadinbeck	71-0521
WINTER, Mich.	33	Offenbach	68-0753
Agatha 26, Peter Jos. 2			
WINTER, Sophie	24	Hannover	69-0923
WINTER, Wilhelm	26	Pinnow	71-0733
WINTERBERGER, S.	17	Winterberg	68-0907
WINTERHALTER, Gust.	20	Bruchsal	68-1298
WINTERMANN, H.	17	Varel	70-0308
Hermann 19			
WINTERMANTEL, Clara	19	Eichingen	71-0456
WINTERMANTEL, Johann	18	Brauslingen	69-0848
WINTERMEYER, August	27	Herford	71-0492
WINTERNITZ, Rosalie	34	Boehmen	69-1396
Pauline 7, Rudolph 4			
WINTERS, Sophie	16	Balding	70-0508
WINTERSTEIN, Louise	20	Koenigsberg	71-0681
WINTH, Georg	20	Lepten	71-0681
WINTJEN, Catharine	18	Lintig	68-1006
Catharine 16			
WINTSCH, Marie	32	Rieden	71-0712
WINTZ, Reimer	27	Buesdorf	68-1027
WINZENBURG, Dorette	24	Goettingen	69-0572
WIPPEN, Minna	42	Meppen	70-1003
WIPPER, Ed.	26	Berlin	70-0170
WIPPERMANN, Hy.	25	Guetersloh	68-0957
WIRTH, Julius	25	Brueckenau	70-1161
WIRTH, Wilhelm	21	Worms	69-1319
WIRZ, Peter	37	Bremen	69-0208
WISCH, Albert	23	Berkum	70-0135
WISCHHUSEN, Diedr.	13	Ritterhude	68-0534
WISCHHUSEN, Meta	16	Retterhude	69-0321
WISCHMEYER, Elisabeth	59	Hanteburg	70-0378
WISMANN, Charlotte	47	Hannover	71-0821
Louise 19			
WISSENBACH, Jacob	18	Niederweimar	68-0534
WISSERT, Karl	17	Endingen	71-0393
WISSING, Heinrich	26	Maria Lake	70-0583
WISSING, Peter	36	Lahnstein	71-0172
WISSINGER, Aug.	21	Danzig	69-0583
WISSLER, Clothilde	22	Hinchau	70-1066
WISSMANN, Chr. W.	17	Pente	68-0820
WISSMANN, Friedrich	28	Oldenburg	70-0523
WISSMEYER, Kunigunda	39	Ansbach	68-1002
WISSNER, Anna Marg.	25	Dornhain	69-1212
Christina 2			
WITHAUER, Agnes	35	Katzhidde	68-0534
Anna 16			
WITSCH, August	18	Weisenburg/Aust	69-0049
WITSCHINSKY, Benno	22	Wistek	71-0521
WITT, Andreas	33	Pollersreuth	70-1161
WITT, Wilhelm	19	Ritschwol	69-0547
WITTE, Amalie	15	Lippe Detmold	70-0223
WITTE, Emilie	18	Bueckeburg	71-0226
WITTE, Georg	21	Bremen	70-0816
WITTE, Heinrich	32	Woller Wuestig	70-0204
WITTE, Heinrich	14	Siegen	68-0456
WITTE, Sophie	18	Hoysighausen	68-0982
Minna 14			
WITTEFELD, Hermann	29	Osnabrueck	68-0907
WITTEKIND, Elisabeth	18	Kalkobes	69-0923
WITTENBECK, John	17	St. Johannis	69-0560
WITTENBERG, Franz	33	Gr. Markmin	69-0490
WITTENBERG, Joh.	19	Hannover	70-0089
WITTENBERG, Wilhelm	30	Danzig	69-0547
Dorette 27			
WITTENBERG, Wilhelm	17	Westerholz	68-0456
WITTER, Christian	27	Ilmenau	71-0821
WITTER, Eduard	47	Neustadt	71-0712
Ludwig 20			
WITTER, Emil	26	Meiningen	69-0560
WITTGENSTEIN, M.	56	Liebenau	70-0184
WITTHAUER, Georg	26	Neustadt	69-0079
WITTHOEFT, Dorothea	18	Windhorst	71-0581
Marie 16			
WITTHUS, Aug.	19	Hartum	68-0647
WITTICH, Adam	13	Bebra	71-0363
WITTIGSCHLEGER, Mary	20	Hoboken	70-1003
WITTKOP, Vincenz	18	Brakel	68-0566
WITTLIEF, Jacob	44	Rudolstadt	69-0547
Marianne 40, Theodor 6, Helene 4			
WITTLINGEN, Jacob	20	Haingingen	68-0014
WITTMANN, Valentin	14	Gerresheim	68-0786
WITTNER, Mrs.	25	Odessa	71-1046
WITTPENN, Marie	18	Hannover	69-0457
WITTROCK, Minna	22	Bruchhausen	70-0355
WITTSCHEN, August	35	Charleston	69-1059
WITTSCHEN, Sophie	26	Hannover	69-1059
WITTSUNN, Metta	26	Hannover	71-0479
WITZEL, Adam	42	Sinna	68-0534
WITZEL, Ch.	24	Krefeld	70-0728
WITZEL, Fritz	17	Hannover	70-0355
WITZEMANN, Wilhelmine	27	Tuebingen	71-0363
Louise 5, Paul 1, Friedrich 33			
WITZMANN, Karl	17	Rudolstadt	68-0872
WLADI, Joseph	46	Collischow	68-0770
Catharina 50, Maria 25, Veronica 18, Barbara 16, Franz. M. 2 months			
WOBA, Josef	37	Boehmen	70-1035
Anna 6			
WOBBE, Clemens	28	Thuene	68-0760
WOBBERS, Heinrich	16	Steltenfelde	69-0572
WOBERMIN, Wilhelm	26	Hausberg	69-1086
Henriette 29			
WOBRIOFT, Sophie	19	Bremervoerde	68-0939

NAME	AGE	RESIDENCE	YR-LIST
WOCHNER, Rosine	16	Strassburg	68-0566
WODEGEL, H.	18	Hannover	69-0841
William 18			
WOEBBER, Anna	18	Altentruck	71-0429
WOEBKE, Nicolas	45	Bremervoerde	70-0031
WOECKEL, Auguste	22	Bayreuth	69-1086
WOEHRMANN, Anton	22	Lohne	70-0178
WOEHRMANN, John	32	Buente	71-0736
Dorothea 42			
WOEHST, Carl	16	Steinau	69-0457
WOELK, Lucia	25	Lehe	70-0384
Reinhard 3, Anna 9 months			
WOELKEL, Marie	16	Issiglen	71-0479
WOELL, Aloys	26	Kiefersfelden	68-1002
WOELTERN, John B.	38	Neunhoefen	69-1421
Anna Marg. 30			
WOERDEN, Binatum	53	Lehe	68-0625
WOERNER, Augusta	16	Hanau	68-0610
WOERNER, Gustav	19	Rotenburg	71-0521
WOERNER, Joh.	19	Nufringen	70-0170
WOERSCHING, Wilhelm	30	Oldenburg	69-0292
WOERTH, Marie	17	Flonheim	68-1006
WOERTNER, Vincenz	42	Wien	68-1002
Anna 36			
WOEST, Johann	18	Neuenkirchen	71-0429
WOESTMANN, Marie	23	Steinfurt	68-0907
WOHLENHAUS, Diedr.	43	Lohe	68-1027
Marie 43, Louise 5			
WOHLENHAUSEN, S.	17	Lohe	68-0610
WOHLERS, Dorothea	20	Graul	71-0821
WOHLERT, Caroline	31	Braunschweig	70-0683
WOHLERT, Wilhelmine	32	Coslin	68-0939
Hermann 7			
WOHLFAHRT, Balthasar	28	Bramberg	69-0338
WOHLFEIL, Aug.	17	Ciganer	71-0479
WOHLFEIL, Carl	30	Ziegahnen	69-0848
Gottliebe 24			
WOHLFELD, Chr.	76	S. Weimar	69-1309
Ernestine 42			
WOHLFELD, Louise	27	Breszone	68-0820
David 5			
WOHLFROM, Ursula	26	Randersacker	69-0572
Joseph 6 months			
WOHLKE, Doroth.	24	Hannover	70-1066
WOHLLEBEN, Maria	27	Altenburg	71-0792
WOHLTMANN, Fritz	38	Weissenberg	69-0457
WOHN, John	50	New York	69-0321
WOHNSNER, Jacob	17	Sigmaringen	70-0006
Anna 20,			
WOKAC, Thomas	23	Boehmen	69-1309
WOLDERS, Johanne	15	Achim	70-0682
WOLDNER, Franz	20	Schwaben	69-1309
WOLF, Adam	15	Freudenstadt	69-0848
WOLF, Adam	26	Buchen	68-0939
WOLF, Adolf	18	Frankenthal	69-1011
WOLF, Bernh.	19	Sausenheim	70-1055
WOLF, Carl	33	Marienfelde	69-0321
Marie 32, Amalie 9, Minna 8, Wilhelm 6, Friedrich 4, Caroline 3, Carl 9 months			
WOLF, Cath.	27	Sulzheim	71-0479
WOLF, Emma	15	Hochstetten	71-0712
Caroline 13			
WOLF, Franz	23	Borwitz/Austria	69-0547
Anna 20, Joseph 18			
WOLF, Georg	28	Beerfelden	69-0321
WOLF, Gertrud	31	St. Mauritz	71-0684
WOLF, Heinr.	34	Bruchhausen	68-0610
Dorothea 34, Joh. H. 5			
WOLF, Herm.	16	Postheisen	69-0572
WOLF, Hermann	36	Heidenheim	71-0429
WOLF, Jacob	22	Birkenfeld	71-0492
Therese 22			
WOLF, Jette	26	Oberstein	68-0939
WOLF, Johann	26	Forchheim	71-0684
WOLF, Johannes	41	Kreuzeber	68-0786
Anna 35, Dorothea 9, August 7, Christine 5, Bertha 3, Apollonia 11 months			
WOLF, Joseph	18	Boehmen	70-0508
WOLF, Mathilde	18	Mainz	70-0682
WOLF, Philipp	19	Sponnenberg	70-0184
Stronnenberg			
WOLF, Philipp	20	Sausenheim	69-0162
WOLF, Richard	40	Rudolstadt	71-0363
Friedrike 33, Annette 8			
WOLF, Simon	19	Habitzheim	68-0939
WOLFAENGER, Peter A.	48	Oberndorf	69-0321
WOLFF, Amalia	41	Batchi	69-1309
Babine 21, Wolff 8, Rahel 6, Sophie 5, Louis 4, Abel 11 months			
WOLFF, Anna Maria	38	Mainz	69-1076
WOLFF, Elisabeth	20	Riedesheim	70-1055
WOLFF, Emil	32	Preussen	68-0456
WOLFF, George	18	Buffalo	69-0490
WOLFF, Hermann	28	Zeitz	69-1076
WOLFF, Johann	33	Schmalkalden	69-0229
WOLFF, Johann	28	Ulrichswalde	68-0852
Friederike 30, Emil 11 months, Gottlieb 26, Therese 21, Christine 32, Emilie 7			
WOLFF, Leopold	16	Frankfurt a/M	70-1023
WOLFF, Louis	42	Radenberg	68-0982
WOLFF, Louise	33	Liebenberg	68-1298
Mary 14, Ida 9, Richard 2, Carl 9 months			
WOLFF, Mathilde	25	Wuerzburg	68-0982
WOLFF, Michael	51	Hainsbach	69-0015
WOLFF, Otto	28	Berlin	69-0067
WOLFFI, Friederike	18	Sessenheim	71-0581
Julie 20			
WOLFING, Agnes	47	Rudolphstadt	71-0712
Maria 19, Emma 14			
WOLFMUELLER, Ludwig	23	Elsenz	71-0492
WOLFRAM, H. W.	59	Stolp	69-0560
Lina 54, Rosalie 30			
WOLFRAM, Louise	19	Schwarsbg-Rudol	70-1055
Pauline 17			
WOLFRECHT, Babette	24	Ochsenfurt	71-0429
WOLFSTEIN, Andreas	41	Wohlsdorf	68-1002
WOLITZ, Eva	22	Strakonitz	70-0728
WOLKEN, Henry	17	Hasbergen	70-0170
WOLL, Eleonore	30	Immendingen	68-0534

NAME	AGE	RESIDENCE	YR-LIST
WOLL, John	32	Petersberg	71-0456
Anna 32			
WOLLE, August	28	Langensalza	68-0786
Constanze 26, Roeschen 3, Clara 10 months			
WOLLEBEN, Helene	35	Schoetmar	68-1027
WOLLENIE, Wilhelm	15	Schapen	68-0939
WOLLENWEBER, H.	32	Wenzen	68-0625
Marie 29, Wilhelm 2, Heinrich 8 months			
WOLPERS, Henry	33	Hildesheim	68-0939
Stina 36, Christel 3			
WOLPERT, Conrad	27	Steinbrueck	69-0162
Heinrich 31			
WOLSEIFER, Anna 35	35	Duesseldorf	69-0457
Fanny 3, Elly 2, Marie 9 months			
WOLSKY, Albrecht	50	Towolla/Polen	69-0576
Eva 47, Joseph 18, Ignatz 15, Catharina 8, Franz 6, Anton 6 months			
WOLSOWSKY, Josepha	55	Sucheranz	71-0733
Marinka 4, Francisca 9 months			
WOLTER, Albert	24	Thyn	68-0566
WOLTER, Wilhelmine	23	Rosenfelde	71-0736
WOLTERMANN, B.	21	Wehbergen	69-0208
WOLTERS, Heinr.	32	Braunschweig	70-0089
WOLTERS, Lina	25	Hannover	68-0625
WOLTHER, Bruno	35	Berlin	71-0789
WOLTMANN, Gerd	24	Quendorf	68-0566
WOLTMANN, Henry	27	Osterwanna	68-0884
WOLTMANN, Meta	16	Beverstedt	71-0733
WOLTMANN, Wilhelm	16	Johannesroth	70-0378
WOLTSCHE, Ernst	29	Waldeck	68-0907
WOLZER, Louis	43	Hannover	68-0456
WOOTKE, Maria	22	Cuestrin	69-0547
WOPLAKAL, Josef	37	Bachow	70-0329
WORACEK, Catharine	60	Opolschitz	71-0429
Anna 18			
WORACEK, Jacob	29	Opolschitz	71-0429
Anna 30, Adalbert 5			
WORBS, Heinrich	16	Voigtstedt	71-0363
WORDRAN, Ludwine	22	Frankin	69-0162
WOREL, Norbert	19	Boehmen	69-0559
WORM, Julius	31	Colberg	68-0419
WORNER, Christine		Muehlberg	69-0429
WORNHOTZ, Louis	19	Hardenstetten	69-0429
WORPEL, Fried.	23	Dobberfuhl	71-0581
WORTMANN, Eduard	38	Grasehagen	68-0661
Christiane 31, Emma 4, (Eduard died on board)			
WORTMANN, Franz	31	Bennin	71-0521
WORTMANN, Sophie	17	Ethelsen	68-0707
WORTMEIER, Sophie	19	Dielingen	69-0542
WOTAWA, Jacob	39	Tatin	68-0770
Elisabeth 29, Matthias 7, Anna 3			
WOTKA, Ant.	19	Boehmen	69-1363
WOTRUBA, Josef	26	Albrechtitz	70-0329
WOTTINGFELD, Sophie	18	Isenstaedt	68-0907
WOZECKY, Emanuel	36	Kuttenberg	71-0821
Marie 4			
WREDE, Hyronimus	17	Loxstedt	71-0643
WRENGLER, Simon	24	Wehren	68-0610

NAME	AGE	RESIDENCE	YR-LIST
WRIGGE, C. F.	33	Hannover	69-1004
WRITTSCHEN, Nic.	18	Hannover	70-0308
WROCKLAGE, Anna	22	Nortrup	68-0566
Catharina 20			
WRONKER, Amalie	43	Stettin	69-0182
Sophie 22, Pauline 20, Simon 16, Hermann 14, Adolf 9, Max 6, Dorothee 3, WRUCH, Albert	33	Grunau	71-0479
Johann 19, Emilie 16			
WRZEZEZ, Paul	26	Lischkowo	71-0456
WUEBBELING, Wilhelm	17	Buecken	71-0456
WUEBBEN, Ebbert	40	Ostfriesland	69-0559
Hinnertje 36, Ude 11, Jan 7, Engel 10 months			
WUELBERN, Emma	26	Bremen	68-0982
WUELFT, Wolfgang	31	Passau	71-0821
WUEMBKES, Peter	50	Oldersum	68-0647
Marie 48, Wuemke 18, Eilert 15, Weihd. 8, Justus 6			
WUEMSCHEL, Ph.	23	Lesnirsheim	69-1004
WUERSCHMIDT, Maria	23	Kronach	68-0884
WUERTH, Johann	18	Wernsreuth	71-0712
WUERZBURGER, Ludwig	35	Totonto	69-1309
WUESTEFELD, Carl	18	Herstelle	71-0712
WUESTENFELD, Adolph	28	Koeplitz	69-0208
WUETTER, Doris	19	Brilis	71-0300
WUETTIG, Alfed	29	Jena	71-0712
WULF, Heinrich	24	Potsdam	68-0707
Johann 17			
WULF, Louise	26	Berlin	68-1002
Ida 9 months			
WULFEKUHL, Lisette	20	Langwege	69-0208
WULFERS, Friedr.	22	Ritzenbergen	68-0786
WULFF, Johann	54	Neustadt	68-0625
Anton 15, Anna 16			
WUNDER, Helene	20	Straisberg	71-0736
Margarethe 21			
WUNDER, Michel	42	Knitzgau	71-0456
Barbara 38			
WUNDERLICH, Christ.	17	Gutenberg	71-0479
WUNDERLICH, Franz	16	Eulenberg	68-0852
WUNDERLICH, Heinrich	34	Laaspe	68-0625
Christine 30, Carl 9, Baby 9 months			
WUNDERLICH, Henriette	18	Boehmen	69-0848
WUNSCH, Severin	24	Lautenbach	68-314
WURDER, Wilhelm	18	Mannheim	69-0542
WURSTER, Carl	19	Freudenstadt	70-1142
WURSTER, Carl F.	9	Freudenstadt	71-0226
WURSTER, Franz	17	Grafenberg	69-0229
WURSTER, Joh.	40	Bremen	70-0452
Elisabeth 38, Johann 8. Anna 2			
WURSTER, Johann	15	Etmansweiler	68-0852
WURSTER, Johs.	58	Enzkloesterle	68-0610
Jacob 25, Friederike 27			
WURSTER, Marie	27	Schoenbrunn	68-0982
WURTMANN, Meta	18	Arbergen	69-1212
WUSTER, Friedrich	38	Lippe Detmold	69-0268
Anna 25			
WUSTMANN, Auguste	25	Dresden	69-0015
ZABEL, August	21	Wonzow	71-0581

NAME	AGE	RESIDENCE	YR-LIST
ZACH, Anna	56	Boehmen	69-1309
ZACHORONSKY, Noah	32	Zempelburg	69-0968
ZACHOW, Julius	19	Schoenlanke	71-0821
ZAEPAL, Joh.	16	Vina	70-1023
ZAHL, Rud.	16	Beinhagen	71-0581
Ida 22, Franz 14			
ZAHN, Carl	34	Frankfurt	71-0456
Margreth 37, Christine 7			
ZAHN, Emil	17	Eickendorf	71-0479
Ernst 15			
ZAHN, Emilie	19	Bittenfeld	68-0865
ZAHN, Fritz	40	Philadelphia	70-1003
Louise 35			
ZAHN, Heinr.	30	Quernheim	68-0610
W. (f) 30, D. (f) 6, D. (f) 3, Bab. 11 months			
ZAHN, Josef	53	Obergrund	71-0581
Catharina 51, Josefa 18			
ZAHRT, Friedrich	50	Ibitz/Baden	69-0576
Caroline 40, Carl 25, Ernestine 16, Friedrich 7, Henriette 5, Ludwig 4, Michae			
ZAIGER, Gottlieb	18	Oberboichingen	69-0457
ZAIGER, Jacob	19	Knittlingen	69-0182
Johann 21			
ZAJICEK, Joh.	30	Boehmen	70-1142
Barb. 21			
ZAK, Franz	5	Liebenitz/Siebe	70-0329
ZAK, Maria	21	Boehmen	69-1363
Wenzel 2 months			
ZAKOSTELECKY, Joh.	35	Dabruen	68-0770
Catharina 48, Maria 8, Barbara 6, Catharina 1, Catharina 42			
ZANDER, Ludolf	23	Muenchen	69-0848
ZANDER, Wilh.	34	Storken	68-0820
Augusta 30, Carl 8, Anna 6, Marie 5, Friedrich 4, Augusta 3, Louise 2			
ZANDER, Wilhelm	33	Halle	70-0259
Johanna 32, Paul 6			
ZANGENBERG, Erhardt	22	Osnabrueck	70-0184
ZANGG, Friederike	19	Joerdon	68-0625
ZANGL, Michl	29	Kleinsteintoh	69-0542
Cathar. 28, Anna 2			
ZANTER, Heinrich	56	Nienburg	68-0884
Minna 30, Georg 8, Heinr. 4, Bertha 9, Reinhold 2			
ZAPEL, Friedrich	55	Moelln/Mecklenb	69-0547
Friedericke 54, Georg 24, Sophie 24, Theodor 17, Caroline 13, Wilhelm 7			
ZAPF, Herm.	28	Nordlingen	71-0681
ZAPF, Marf.	20	Tschirn	69-1309
ZAPFF, Martin	57	Rossbach	68-0884
ZAPP, Carl	15	Heimkirchen	70-1142
ZARBUREK, Anna	18	Stainslake/Bohe	69-0049
ZARENDAL, Joseph	33	Merdaken/Bohe	69-0576
Maria 27, Catharina 5, Natesta 2			
ZARLIG, Albert	26	Wisba	71-0581
Bertha 26			
ZASKOW, Martin	37	Peutz	69-0049
Anna 29, Friedrich 18, Marie 7, Anna 4			
ZATOR, Cath.	21	Strichlowa	68-0566
ZECH, Oscar	17	Saalfeld	69-0321
ZEDIK, Peter	48	Kralowitz	71-0456
John 20, Josef 17, Marie 9, Emilie 4			

NAME	AGE	RESIDENCE	YR-LIST
ZEESE, Ottilie	23	Frankfurt a/O	68-1298
Bertha 25			
ZEIBIG, Emil	22	Kamenz	69-0292
ZEIDLER, Hermine	22	Wien	68-0566
ZEIDLER, Pauline	23	Gera	68-0456
ZEIGLER, Harm	19	Burg	71-0821
ZEILEIS, Joseph	17	Oberfranken	69-0968
ZEILINGER, Leonhard	23	Dietenhofen	68-0770
ZEIMER, Joachim	18	Mallinetz	68-0456
ZEIS, Maria	19	Dodenhausen	71-0581
ZEISER, Gustav	24	Basel	69-1076
ZEISS, Georg	20	Dodenhausen	70-0355
ZEISSLER, Elisa	17	Leihorst	70-0135
ZEITLER, Louis	34	Harrisburgh	70-1035
ZEITNER, Barbara	29	Lohn	70-0355
John 6			
ZEITUNG, Johann	23	Bruecken	68-0456
ZEITZ, Anton	16	Volkersbier	68-0625
ZELENKA, Anna	26	Boehmen	70-1035
ZELEZINSKA, Therese	27	Radezyk	69-0672
ZELLER, Ernst	29	Muehlheim	68-0610
ZELLER, Louis	19	Ubun	69-1004
ZELLHOEFER, Louis	23	Redwitz	69-1086
ZELLNER, August	29	Bernsten	68-0647
Augusta 30, Louise 2			
ZEMANN, Johann	23	Hoozdan	70-0329
ZERENNA, Auguste	28	Rudolstadt	70-1003
ZERGICHEL, Franz	23	Altenburg	69-0672
ZERKEWITZ, Heinrich	40	Wien	71-0733
ZERMAK, Therese	22	Boehmen	70-1035
ZERMOOK, Gottl.	46	Bethlehem	71-0789
J. 7			
ZERTZ, Peter S.	32	Reichenbach	69-0321
ZESSIN, Heinrich	36	Klein Markmin	69-0490
ZETHNER, Elise	18	Oberfranken	71-0643
ZETSCHE, Helene	21	Altenburg	69-0583
ZETTLER, Ernst	27	Hameln	68-0957
ZEUCH, Wilhelm	31	Oberdinzenbach	69-1363
Doroth. 9			
ZEUSS, Andreas	44	Mangersreuth	69-1059
Christine 32, Johannes 2, Hans 9 months			
ZIBELL, Chls.	23	Coeslin	70-0508
Amalie 17			
ZICK, Martin	25	Lutziow	70-0006
ZICKEL, Ad.	24	New York	70-0135
ZIEBOLD, Emil	25	Grottkau	68-0610
ZIEGENHAGEN, Aug.	30	Mirstirstrup	69-1309
Carl 26			
ZIEGENHAGEN, Gustav	16	Mrasteczko	71-0429
ZIEGENSPECK, Chr.	61	Ranis	71-0733
Emma 17, Emilie 15			
ZIEGLER, Anna	34	Bickelsberg	71-0521
ZIEGLER, Barbara	28	Lengfeld	68-1006
ZIEGLER, Carl	18	Stuttgart	70-0076
ZIEGLER, Carl	18	Wernigerode	71-0479
ZIEGLER, Frd.	18	Worms	68-0820
ZIEGLER, H.	22	Speyer	71-1046
ZIEGLER, Johann	15	Neukirch	70-0329

NAME	AGE	RESIDENCE	YR-LIST
ZIEGLER, Meta	20	Worpswede	71-0429
ZIEGLER, Wilhelmine	16	Eisenach	70-1055
ZIEGMANN, Johann	29	Rosbach	71-0492
Barbara 29, Barbara 3			
ZIEHER, Anton	26	Bieberach	70-0170
ZIEHR, Carl	35	Oerierzeck	68-0707
ZIEMER, Hermann	27	Luebchow	68-0661
Albertine 25			
ZIEROTTS, Michel	26	Zuppeln	69-0429
ZIESCHE, Gottfried	45	Bittenfeld	68-0865
Christiane 34, Wilhelmine 7, Gottfried Karl 12			
ZIESCHE, Margarethe	51	Hamm	71-0429
Emil 9			
ZIKA, Wenzel	44	Chmelna	68-0770
Franziska 42, Mario 8, Joseph 6, Franz 4			
ZIMM, Adam	26	Wehrda	69-0592
Elisabeth 29, Jacob 3, Elisabeth 9 months			
ZIMMER, Adam	37	Espa	71-0492
Catharina 35, Ernst 7			
ZIMMER, Carl	16	Obernhofen	69-1004
ZIMMER, Eva	58	Trier	68-0610
ZIMMER, Heinrich		Espa	71-0492
ZIMMER, Joh.	24	Obergrund	71-0581
ZIMMER, Peter	17	Lahren	71-0300
ZIMMER, Thecla	25	Horbach	69-0457
ZIMMER, Therese	45	Kurhessen	71-0736
Friedrich 13, Johanne 9, Anna 7, Balthasar 6, Richard 4, Gustav 11 m.			
ZIMMER, Wilh.	22	Villingen	68-0884
ZIMMERER, Constantin	19	Wellendingen	68-0786
ZIMMERMANN, Adolph	51	Weener	68-0786
Renkidina 52, Engelina 13, Adolph 9			
ZIMMERMANN, Antonia	30	Neustadt	68-0566
Richard 5, Carl 3, Antonia 6 months			
ZIMMERMANN, Babette	15	Stein	71-0479
ZIMMERMANN, C. M.	48	Joh. Georgensta	69-0182
Carl Th. 14			
ZIMMERMANN, Carl	48	Greiz	70-0569
ZIMMERMANN, Cath.	9	Botnang	68-0982
ZIMMERMANN, Conrad	24	Neustrelitz	68-0707
ZIMMERMANN, Doroth.	21	Bornbach	71-0789
ZIMMERMANN, Elisabeth	48	Schotten	69-0321
Eleonora 18, Friedrich 8			
ZIMMERMANN, Franz	27	Heuthen	71-0521
Cath. 26, Augustin 2, Franz 6 months			
ZIMMERMANN, Friedrich	32	Berlin	71-0429
ZIMMERMANN, Gerhard	33	Bentheim	71-0429
Louise 33			
ZIMMERMANN, Herm.	47	Gaschen	71-0821
ZIMMERMANN, Herm.	35	Bethlehem	71-0789
ZIMMERMANN, J.	18	Strokholt	69-1421
ZIMMERMANN, J.	18	Ewattingen	71-0815
ZIMMERMANN, Joh.	25	Breid	70-0683
ZIMMERMANN, Joh.	26	Dammin	71-0521
ZIMMERMANN, Joh.	46	Potzewo	71-0363
Anna 32, Emilie 9, Ferd. 7, Ottilia 11 months			
ZIMMERMANN, Johann	43	Meissenheim	71-0492
Maria 30, Georg 8, Maria 6, Andreas 4, Friederich 2			
ZIMMERMANN, John	17	Niederweimar	68-0534
ZIMMERMANN, Joseph	15	Romersreck	68-0939
ZIMMERMANN, Karl	29	Bornbach	71-0789
Marie 25, Z. 3, Carl 10 m., Joh. 19			
ZIMMERMANN, Marie	21	Bornbach	71-0789
ZIMMERMANN, Marie	20	Weil	71-0681
ZIMMERMANN, Meldine	24	Leer	69-1059
ZIMMERMANN, Otto	22	Poechgau	68-0770
ZIMMERMANN, Peter	32	Domnitz	71-0581
ZIMMERMANN, Philippine	20	Niederscheld	68-0534
ZIMPEL, Wilhelm	23	Weschine	69-1421
ZINGLER, Carl Fr.	30	Berlin	68-1002
ZINK, Barbara	17	Katschenreuter	68-0707
Christian 13			
ZINK, Ernestine	17	Botnang	68-0982
ZINK, Ernestine	59	Gessken	71-0733
Theodor 16			
ZINK, Jacob	17	Moerlenbach	69-1059
ZINK, Lep.	19	Sachsbachwalden	71-0456
ZINKE, Caroline	21	Polzin	70-0728
ZINKEL, Franz	40	Steiermark	71-0712
ZINN, Barbara	27	Ettinghausen	69-0672
ZINN, Caroline	24	Wuerzburg	69-1059
ZINN, Friedrich	38	Marburg	68-0661
August 7, Elise 6, Heinrich 4, Catharina 3			
ZINN, Marg.	23	Miesebach	68-0753
Margaretha 1			
ZINNE, Friedrich	42	Hannover	69-1212
Charlotte 35, Louise 7, Friedr. 5, Wilhelmine 1			
ZINNER, Michael	21	Zeil	70-1035
ZINSENHOF, Henriette	31	Rolsberg	69-0798
Ida 11 months			
ZINSMEISTER, Margareth	15	Duerkheim	71-0643
ZIPF, Philipp	48	Schluechtern	69-1319
Caspar 13, Cath. 9			
ZIPPENER, Franz	24	Mannheim	71-1046
ZIRCKLER, Carl	33	Eitze	69-1004
ZIRKEL, Caroline	17	Eicheldorf	68-0625
Amalia 15, Eduard 9, Lina 7			
ZIRKEL, Otto	19	Deggingens	70-1035
ZIRKEL, Otto	15	Dresden	71-0492
ZISCHKAU, Heinr.	18	Gerstungen	71-0521
ZITECK, Johann	18	Boehmen	69-1309
ZITZEMANN, Marie	43	Tachau	70-0569
Marg. 19			
ZITZMANN, Alwin	16	Meiningen	71-0736
ZLUTAN, Chr.	52	Urach	68-0884
Beatrix 58, Ang. 17			
ZOBEL, Chr.	21	Marktbreit	71-0393
ZOCH, Gust.	24	Wittenberg	69-0162
ZOCHIEGCHER, Louis	28	Coburg	69-0968
ZOCHMANN, Joseph	26	Weingarten	71-0521
ZOCK, Theodor	27	Fritzlar	71-0815
Catharina 26			
ZOELLER, Frd.	18	Sasbach	71-0789
ZOELLER, Jacob	26	Mannheim	68-0753

NAME	AGE	RESIDENCE	YR-LIST
ZOELLNER, Friedrike	30	Gruenrade	68-0566
Ernestine 30, Hulda 5, Anna 3, Carl 3 months, Julius 12, Johanna 60, Louise 40			
ZOLLER, Philipp	17	Kleinhausen	69-0542
ZOOCH, Anna	26	Hannover	69-0079
ZOSTERLITZ, Simon	18	Gross Strelitz	68-0661
ZUERBACH-ERBACH	25	Cassel	69-1011
ZUCKER, Betti	22	Wildhausen	69-1309
ZUCKER, Theresia	23	Wiesbaden	70-0184
ZUCKERN, Christiane	32	Prokan	68-1006
ZUEHLKE, Paul	25	Stolp	68-1298
ZUERCHER, Alois	35	Mensingen	71-0226
Marie 23			
ZUESP, Veron.	37	Gruesch	69-0771
Jakob 9, Anna 3			
ZULICH, Bernhard	27	Hallingen	69-0229
ZUM HOFE, Heinrich	37	Nordkampen	69-0592
ZUMPF, Amalie	25	Minden	68-0786
ZUNG, Georg	17	Langenheim	69-0429
ZUNKER, Ferd.	35	Virchow	69-0338
ZUR MOEHLEN, Marie	16	Schweringen	70-1003
ZURICH, Friedr.	22	Colditz	69-0542
ZWACK, Margarethe	21	Schlemesitz	68-0456
ZWASCHKEN, Johann	15	Schlemesitz	68-0456
ZWASCHKUS, Wenzel	48	Semoschitz	71-0393
Katharina 38, Jos. 7, Wenz. 14, Franz 7			
ZWICKER, Mathaeus	20	Hainingen	68-0014
Johannes 16			
ZWIRN, Friederike	18	Darmstadt	70-1035

CPSIA information can be obtained at www.ICGtesting.com
261043BV00005B/7/P

9 780806 313689